SOMETHING ABOUT THE AUTHOR®

Something about
the Author *was named
an* **"Outstanding
Reference Source,"**
*the highest honor given
by the American
Library Association
Reference and Adult
Services Division.*

ISSN 0276-816X

SOMETHING ABOUT THE AUTHOR®

**Facts and Pictures about Authors
and Illustrators of Books for Young People**

volume 122

GALE GROUP

THOMSON LEARNING

*Detroit • New York • San Diego • San Francisco
Boston • New Haven, Conn. • Waterville, Maine
London • Munich*

STAFF

Scot Peacock, *Managing Editor, Literature Product*
Mark W. Scott, *Publisher, Literature Product*

Frank Castronova, *Senior Editor;* Katy Balcer, Sara L. Constantakis, Kristen A. Dorsch, Lisa Kumar, Thomas McMahon, Colleen Laine Tavor, *Editors;* Shayla Hawkins, Motoko Fujishiro Huthwaite, Arlene M. Johnson, Michelle Poole, Thomas Wiloch, *Associate Editors;* Alana Joli Foster, Madeline Harris, Jennifer Kilian, Maikue Vang, *Assistant Editors,* Anna Marie Dahn, Judith L. Pyko, *Administrative Support,* Joshua Kondek, Mary Ruby, *Technical Training Specialists*

Alan Hedblad, Joyce Nakamura, *Managing Editors*
Susan M. Trosky, *Literature Content Coordinator*

Victoria B. Cariappa, *Research Manager;* Tracie A. Richardson, *Project Coordinator;* Maureen Emeric, Barbara McNeil, Gary J. Oudersluys, Cheryl L. Warnock, *Research Specialists;* Sarah Genik, Ron Morelli, Tamara C. Nott, *Research Associates;* Nicodemus Ford, *Research Assistant;* Michelle Campbell, *Administrative Assistant*

Maria L. Franklin, *Permissions Manager;* Margaret Chamberlain, *Permissions Associate*

Mary Beth Trimper, *Manager, Composition and Prepress;* Dorothy Maki, *Manufacturing Manager;* Stacy Melson, *Buyer*

Barbara J. Yarrow, *Manager, Imaging and Multimedia Content;* Randy Bassett, *Imaging Supervisor;* Robert Duncan, Dan Newell, *Imaging Specialists;* Pamela A. Reed, *Imaging Coordinator;* Dean Dauphinais, *Senior Editor;* Robyn V. Young, *Project Manager;* Kelly A. Quin, *Editor*

Library of Congress Catalog Card Number 72-27107

ISBN 0-7876-4710-1
ISSN 0276-816X

Printed in the United States of America

10 9 8 7 6 5 4 3 2 1

Contents

Authors in Forthcoming Volumes

Below are some of the authors and illustrators that will be featured in upcoming volumes of *SATA*. These include new entries on the swiftly rising stars of the field, as well as completely revised and updated entries (indicated with *) on some of the most notable and best-loved creators of books for children.

*Nicholas Allan: An author who cites revenge as his primary reason for writing, Allan is also the illustrator of nearly twenty books for children. Allan especially enjoys writing stories about kids who outwit tyrannical adults. One such title, *The Magic Lavatory*, tells of a friendship that develops between an orphan named Jeffrey and the toilet that swallows his neurotic aunt.

*Kathryn Cave: British writer Cave has published over a dozen books, including *Out for the Count*, *The Boy Who Became an Eagle*, and *Andrew Takes the Plunge*, that usually impart a moral lesson alongside a good dose of humor. Her 1991 book *William and the Wolves*, for example, is about a young boy who is tormented by the imaginary wolves he created to devour his baby sister.

Maria Ferrari: Ferrari is a professional photographer who has illustrated a series of books written for preschoolers by Rebecca Kai Dotlich. These books, including *What Is Round?*, *What Is Square?*, and *What Is a Triangle?*, introduce the concepts of shape through a rhyming text that critics praise as perfectly designed for the preschool audience.

*Russell Freedman: The author of more than forty nonfiction books for children, Freedman has been honored with many prestigious writing awards, including the Newbery Medal for *Lincoln: A Photobiography* and the Laura Ingalls Wilder Medal for his entire body of work. Freedman pioneered the form he calls "photobiography," a creative utilization of text and images in a book.

*Virginia Hamilton: One of the most revered writers of the twentieth century, Hamilton has written nearly forty books, most of which, including *The People Could Fly*, *Drylongso*, and *Many Thousand Gone*, explore the history and folklore of African Americans. Hamilton has won virtually every major award for children's literature. Her novel *M. C. Higgins, the Great* was the first work ever to win both the National Book Award and the Newbery Medal. In 1992, Hamilton was awarded the Hans Christian Andersen Award from the International Board on Books for Young People.

David S. Kirshner: Driven by his childhood fascination with animals (particularly reptiles), Kirshner has dedicated his life to studying wild and domestic creatures. A Canadian who lives in Australia, Kirshner has a Ph.D. in zoology and has provided animal illustrations for numerous books, including *Encyclopedia of Reptiles and Amphibians*, *Encyclopedia of Birds*, and *Investigate: Snakes*.

Mark Mathabane: Mathabane earned enormous critical acclaim for his 1986 memoir *Kaffir Boy: The True Story of a Black Youth's Coming of Age in Apartheid South Africa*. An active proponent of human rights, Mathabane is a popular lecturer and has written several other books, including *Kaffir Boy in America* and *Miriam's Song*.

Phyllis Pollema-Cahill: Pollema-Cahill helps bring children's stories to life through her vivid, traditional watercolor paintings. Since 1995, she has been a full-time illustrator and has drawn pictures for a variety of children's books, including *The Day Mama Played*, *Free to Learn*, and *Tell Me the Story of Jesus*.

*James E. Ransome: The work of artist and illustrator Ransome has graced the books of many well-known authors, including Charlotte Zolotow and James Weldon Johnson. Ransome specializes in illustrating the traditional history of African Americans and has worked on numerous children's books, including *Uncle Jed's Barbershop*, *The Creation*, and *Does Your Grandpa Say Galoshes*?

*Judith Viorst: Popular journalist Viorst has earned critical and social praise for her wryly humorous and entertaining books for young people. Among her nearly twenty children's books are *Sad Underwear and Other Complications* and *Alexander and the Terrible, Horrible, No Good, Very Bad Day*, for which Viorst received a "Best Books of the Year" citation from *School Library Journal*.

Introduction

Something about the Author (*SATA*) is an ongoing reference series that examines the lives and works of authors and illustrators of books for children. *SATA* includes not only well-known writers and artists but also less prominent individuals whose works are just coming to be recognized. This series is often the only readily available information source on emerging authors and illustrators. You'll find *SATA* informative and entertaining, whether you are a student, a librarian, an English teacher, a parent, or simply an adult who enjoys children's literature.

What's Inside SATA

SATA provides detailed information about authors and illustrators who span the full time range of children's literature, from early figures like John Newbery and L. Frank Baum to contemporary figures like Judy Blume and Richard Peck. Authors in the series represent primarily English-speaking countries, particularly the United States, Canada, and the United Kingdom. Also included, however, are authors from around the world whose works are available in English translation. The writings represented in *SATA* include those created intentionally for children and young adults as well as those written for a general audience and known to interest younger readers. These writings cover the entire spectrum of children's literature, including picture books, humor, folk and fairy tales, animal stories, mystery and adventure, science fiction and fantasy, historical fiction, poetry and nonsense verse, drama, biography, and nonfiction.

Obituaries are also included in *SATA* and are intended not only as death notices but also as concise overviews of people's lives and work. Additionally, each edition features newly revised and updated entries for a selection of *SATA* listees who remain of interest to today's readers and who have been active enough to require extensive revisions of their earlier biographies.

New Autobiography Feature

Beginning with Volume 103, *SATA* features three or more specially commissioned autobiographical essays in each volume. These unique essays, averaging about ten thousand words in length and illustrated with an abundance of personal photos, present an entertaining and informative first-person perspective on the lives and careers of prominent authors and illustrators profiled in *SATA*.

Two Convenient Indexes

In response to suggestions from librarians, *SATA* indexes no longer appear in every volume but are included in alternate (odd-numbered) volumes of the series, beginning with Volume 57.

SATA continues to include two indexes that cumulate with each alternate volume: the Illustrations Index, arranged by the name of the illustrator, gives the number of the volume and page where the illustrator's work appears in the current volume as well as all preceding volumes in the series; the Author Index gives the number of the volume in which a person's biographical sketch, autobiographical essay, or obituary appears in the current volume as well as all preceding volumes in the series.

These indexes also include references to authors and illustrators who appear in Gale's *Yesterday's Authors of Books for Children, Children's Literature Review,* and *Something about the Author Autobiography Series.*

Easy-to-Use Entry Format

Whether you're already familiar with the *SATA* series or just getting acquainted, you will want to be aware of the kind of information that an entry provides. In every *SATA* entry the editors attempt to give as complete a picture of the person's life and work as possible. A typical entry in *SATA* includes the following clearly labeled information sections:

• *PERSONAL:* date and place of birth and death, parents' names and occupations, name of spouse, date of marriage, names of children, educational institutions attended, degrees received, religious and political affiliations, hobbies and other interests.

• *ADDRESSES:* complete home, office, electronic mail, and agent addresses, whenever available.

• *CAREER:* name of employer, position, and dates for each career post; art exhibitions; military service; memberships and offices held in professional and civic organizations.

• *AWARDS, HONORS:* literary and professional awards received.

• *WRITINGS:* title-by-title chronological bibliography of books written and/or illustrated, listed by genre when known; lists of other notable publications, such as plays, screenplays, and periodical contributions.

• *ADAPTATIONS:* a list of films, television programs, plays, CD-ROMs, recordings, and other media presentations that have been adapted from the author's work.

• *WORK IN PROGRESS:* description of projects in progress.

• *SIDELIGHTS:* a biographical portrait of the author or illustrator's development, either directly from the biographee—and often written specifically for the *SATA* entry—or gathered from diaries, letters, interviews, or other published sources.

• *BIOGRAPHICAL AND CRITICAL SOURCES:* cites sources quoted in "Sidelights" along with references for further reading.

• *EXTENSIVE ILLUSTRATIONS:* photographs, movie stills, book illustrations, and other interesting visual materials supplement the text.

How a SATA Entry Is Compiled

A *SATA* entry progresses through a series of steps. If the biographee is living, the *SATA* editors try to secure information directly from him or her through a questionnaire. From the information that the biographee supplies, the editors prepare an entry, filling in any essential missing details with research and/or telephone interviews. If possible, the author or illustrator is sent a copy of the entry to check for accuracy and completeness.

If the biographee is deceased or cannot be reached by questionnaire, the *SATA* editors examine a wide variety of published sources to gather information for an entry. Biographical and bibliographic sources are consulted, as are book reviews, feature articles, published interviews, and material sometimes obtained from the biographee's family, publishers, agent, or other associates.

Entries that have not been verified by the biographees or their representatives are marked with an asterisk (*).

Contact the Editor

We encourage our readers to examine the entire *SATA* series. Please write and tell us if we can make *SATA* even more helpful to you. Give your comments and suggestions to the editor:

BY MAIL: Editor, *Something about the Author,* The Gale Group, 27500 Drake Rd., Farmington Hills, MI 48331-3535.

BY TELEPHONE: (800) 877-GALE

BY FAX: (248) 699-8054

Something about the Author Product Advisory Board

The editors of *Something about the Author* are dedicated to maintaining a high standard of excellence by publishing comprehensive, accurate, and highly readable entries on a wide array of writers for children and young adults. In addition to the quality of the content, the editors take pride in the graphic design of the series, which is intended to be orderly yet inviting, allowing readers to utilize the pages of *SATA* easily and with efficiency. Despite the longevity of the *SATA* print series, and the success of its format, we are mindful that the vitality of a literary reference product is dependent on its ability to serve its users over time. As literature, and attitudes about literature, constantly evolve, so do the reference needs of students, teachers, scholars, journalists, researchers, and book club members. To be certain that we continue to keep pace with the expectations of our customers, the editors of *SATA* listen carefully to their comments regarding the value, utility, and quality of the series. Librarians, who have firsthand knowledge of the needs of library users, are a valuable resource for us. The *Something about the Author* Product Advisory Board, made up of school, public, and academic librarians, is a forum to promote focused feedback about *SATA* on a regular basis. The five-member advisory board includes the following individuals, whom the editors wish to thank for sharing their expertise:

- **Eva M. Davis,** Teen Services Librarian, Plymouth District Library, Plymouth, Michigan

- **Joan B. Eisenberg,** Lower School Librarian, Milton Academy, Milton, Massachusetts

- **Francisca Goldsmith,** Teen Services Librarian, Berkeley Public Library, Berkeley, California

- **Monica F. Irlbacher,** Young Adult Librarian, Middletown Thrall Library, Middletown, New York

- **Caryn Sipos,** Librarian--Young Adult Services, King County Library System, Washington

Acknowledgments

Grateful acknowledgment is is made to the following publishers, authors, and artists whose works appear in this volume.

ARONSON, VIRGINIA. Aronson, Virginia, photograph. Reproduced by permission.

BAKER, JAMES W. Ayres, Carter M., photographer. From a cover of *Illusions Illustrated,* by James W. Baker. Lerner Publications Company, 1984. Copyright © 1984 by Lerner Publications Company. Reproduced by permission./ Baker, James W., photograph by Carter M. Ayres. From a jacket of *Illusions Illustrated,* by James W. Baker. Lerner Publications Company, 1984. Copyright © 1984 by Lerner Publications Company. Reproduced by permission.

BAT-AMI, MIRIAM. Andreasen, Dan, illustrator. From a cover of *Dear Elija,* by Miriam Bat-Ami. Jewish Publication Society, 1997. Originally published by Farrar Straus Giroux. Cover illustration © 1995 by Dan Andreasen. Reproduced by permission of Farrar, Straus and Giroux./ Mosberg, Hilary, illustrator. From a jacket of *Two Suns in the Sky,* by Miriam Bat-Ami. Front Street/Cricket Books, 1999. Jacket © 1999 by Hilary Mosberg./ Bat-Ami, Miriam, photograph. Reproduced by permission.

BAURYS, FLO(RENCE). Baurys, Flo, photograph. Reproduced by permission.

BEN-EZER, EHUD. Shulevitz, Uri, illustrator. From an illustration in *Hosni the Dreamer: An Arabian Tale,* by Ehud Ben-Ezer. Farrar, Straus & Giroux,Inc., 1997. Text copyright © 1997 by Ehud Ben-Ezer. Illustrations copyright © 1997 by Uri Shulevitz. Reproduced by permission of Farrar, Straus & Giroux, Inc.

BORGMAN, JAMES (MARK). From a cover of *Disturbing the Peace.* Colloquial Books, 1995. Illustrations copyright ©1995 by Jim Borgman. Reproduced by permission./ Borgman, Jim, line drawing. Reproduced by permission.

BUGNI, ALICE. Cartwright, Shannon, illustrator. From a cover of *Moose Racks, Bear Tracks, and Other Alaska Kidsnacks,* by Alice Bugni. Sasquatch Books, 1999. Illustrations copyright © 1999 by Shannon Cartwright. Reproduced by permission.

CHAPMAN, JANE. From an illustration in *The Emperor's Egg,* by Martin Jenkins. Candlewick Press, 1999. Illustrations copyright © 1999 by Jane Chapman. All rights reserved. Reproduced by permission./ From an illustration in *One Duck Stuck,* by Phyllis Root. Candlewick Press, 1998. Illustrations copyright © 1998 by Jane Chapman. Reproduced by permission.

DE VOS, GAIL. De Vos, Gail, photograph. Reproduced by permission.

DELGADO, JAMES P. Manning, S. F., photographer. From a photograph in *Shipwrecks from the Westward Movement,* by James P. Delgado. Watts Library, a division of Grolier Publishing, 2000. © 2000 Franklin Watts, a divisionof Grolier Publishing. All rights reserved. Reproduced by permission./ Delgado, James P., photograph. Reproduced by permission.

DORROS, ARTHUR (M.) From an illustration in *This Is My House,* by Arthur Dorros. Scholastic Inc., 1992. Copyright © 1992 by Arthur Dorros. Reproduced by permission of Scholastic Inc./ Dorros, Arthur, photograph. Reproduced by permission.

DUCHARME, LILIAN FOX. Ducharme, Lilian Fox, photograph. Reproduced by permission.

ELLIOT, DAVID. Elliot, David, photograph. *Otago Daily Times,* Allied Press Ltd. Reproduced by permission.

ENGDAHL, SYLVIA LOUISE. Roberson, Rick, age sixteen, reading advanced copy of *Anywhere, Anywhere,* photograph. Reproduced by permission./ All other photographs reproduced by permission of the author.

FISHER, LEONARD EVERETT. From a design of four U.S. Postal stamps detailing colonial craftsmen performing trades, July 4, 1972, in the collection of the Smithsonian Institution. Reproduced by permission of the U.S. Postal Service./ From an illustration in *The Great Wall of China*. Aladdin Paperbacks, 1995. Copyright © 1986 by Leonard Everett Fisher. Reproduced by permission of Simon & Schuster Macmillan./ From a jacket of *Cyclops.*Holiday House. Reproduced by permission of Leonard Everett Fisher./ From an illustration in *Sky, Sea, the Jetty, and Me.* Marshall Cavendish, 2001. Text and illustrations © 2001 by Leonard Everett Fisher. All rights reserved. Reproduced by permission./ All other photos reproduced by permission of the author.

FRITZ, JEAN. All photographs reproduced by permission of the author.

GARNER, ELEANOR RAMRATH. Garner, Eleanor Ramrath, photograph. Reproduced by permission.

GEASON, SUSAN. Geason, Susan, photograph. Reproduced by permission.

something ABOUT the AUThOR

ADLER, Irene
See STORR, Catherine (Cole)

*   *   *

ARONSON, Virginia 1954-

Personal

Born March 30, 1954, in Boston, MA; daughter of Melvin (an accountant) and Barbara (a homemaker; maiden name, Corrigan) Aronson; married James P. Goss (a writer), February, 1993; children: Mel. *Education:* University of Vermont, B.S. (nutrition), Framingham State College, M.S.

Addresses

E-mail—VAcelstia@aol.com.

Career

Harvard School of Public Health, Boston, MA, educator and writer, 1980-85; freelance writer, 1985—.

Awards, Honors

Received honorable mention in the South Florida Writer's Contest, 1995-96, for *Bad Girls,* a one-act play for teenagers.

Writings

JUVENILE

Venus Williams, Chelsea House (Philadelphia, PA), 1999.
Women in Literature, Chelsea House (Philadelphia, PA), 1999.
How to Say No, Chelsea House (Philadelphia, PA), 2000.
Drew Barrymore, Chelsea House (Philadelphia, PA), 2000.
Jennifer Love Hewitt, Chelsea House (Philadelphia, PA), 2000.
Ann Landers and Abigail Van Buren, Chelsea House (Philadelphia, PA), 2000.
The Spanish Influenza Pandemic of 1918, Chelsea House (Philadelphia, PA), 2000.
Everything You Need to Know about Breast Health, Rosen, 2000.
Everything You Need to Know about Hepatitis, Rosen, 2000.
Ethan Allen, Chelsea House (Philadelphia, PA), 2001.
Venus and Serena Williams, Chelsea House (Philadelphia, PA), 2001.
The History of Motown, Chelsea House (Philadelphia, PA), 2001.

OTHER

Thirty Days to Better Nutrition, Doubleday, 1984.
(With Henry Haller) *The White House Family Cook Book,* Random House, 1988.
(With Steven Jonas) *The I Don't Eat (But I Can't Lose) Weight Loss Program,* Macmillan, 1989.
Guidebook for Nutrition Counselors, second edition, PrenticeHall, 1990.

Virginia Aronson

The Dietetic Technician: Effective Nutrition Counseling, second edition, Van Nostrand Reinhold, 1990.

Different Minds, Different Voices, Paradux & Gossling, 1996.

Celestial Healing: Close Encounters That Cure, Penguin, 1999.

Columnist for *Runners' World* and *SHAPE,* 1985-86. Contributor of poems to literary magazines and author of plays *Double Exposure* (performed, 1994) and *Bad Girls.*

Work in Progress

Shaman Dreams and *A UFO Cured My Cancer! and Other True Tales of Weird Medical Miracles.*

Sidelights

Virginia Aronson came to her writing career as an outgrowth of her other interests: long-distance running and vegetarianism. While in college she earned degrees in nutrition and then worked as a health counselor. "But I found myself focusing on writing about nutrition and exercise," Aronson told *SATA.* "Once I had published around a dozen books on the topic, I decided I was actually a writer rather than a health expert."

Among her first books were textbooks on nutrition and health, which she cowrote with senior authors, and books on weight loss and running cowritten with medical doctor Steven Jonas. Another early work was

The White House Family Cookbook, which she wrote with then White House Chef Henry Haller. "This hefty volume offers an intriguing glimpse of presidential history," commented a *Publishers Weekly* reviewer. Indeed, Haller and Aronson presented the favorite foods and eating habits of such United States presidents as Lyndon Johnson, Richard Nixon, Gerald Ford, Jimmy Carter, and Ronald Reagan. They even included the recipes for presidential favorites.

Aronson had long been interested in biography. "As a young reader, I was most influenced by biographies about women of achievement," she recalled for *SATA.* "I remember the day I decided to read every biography on women in my school library—which I then proceeded to do." Aronson has written a handful of works for Chelsea House's various juvenile biography series, including biographies of athletes Venus and Serena Williams, actresses Drew Barrymore and Jennifer Love Hewitt, and journalists Ann Landers and Abigail Van Buren. Aronson's 1999 biography of tennis phenomenon Venus Williams caught the attention of critics. In *Booklist* Ilene Cooper called the work well written, though a *Horn Book Guide* reviewer likened it unflatteringly to a "fan magazine." Writing in *School Library Journal,* Janice C. Hayes deemed the "smooth-flowing, informative text" a "smashing success."

In 2001 Aronson published a joint biography of sisters Venus and Serena Williams. She had written about two other sisters as well—advice columnists and twins Ann Landers and Abigail Van Buren. In a review for *School Library Journal,* Marilyn Fairbanks asserted that *Ann Landers and Abigail Van Buren* is written in "light, lively prose" and would "serve as good recreational reading."

Aronson has written titles on medical matters other than nutrition, including *Everything You Need to Know about Hepatitis, Everything You Need to Know about Breast Health,* and *How to Say No.* In *How to Say No* the author presents information for middle-school students on the dangers of drug and alcohol abuse in what *Science Books and Films* critic Cathy Brown called a "quite thorough" and balanced treatment of the subject. During the 1990s Aronson became interested in not only medical topics but such areas as "creativity, spirituality, and the healing power of the mind and soul," as she explained to *SATA.* "I try to let my intuition, dreams, or voice of the soul dictate what I will write next. Once, achievement and publishing success were my goals. Now, I am driven by an inner force to allow the spirit to express itself, often by looking for and sharing stories of healing and miracles." Thus, for adult readers she published *Celestial Healing: Close Encounters That Cure,* while for younger readers she worked on the manuscripts of *Shaman Dreams* and *A UFO Cured My Cancer!*

Biographical and Critical Sources

PERIODICALS

Booklist, April 15, 1999, Ilene Cooper, review of *Venus Williams,* p. 1524.

Horn Book Guide, January-June, 1999, review of *Venus Williams,* p. 363.

Publishers Weekly, October 16, 1987, review of *The White House Family Cookbook,* p. 83.

School Library Journal, May, 1999, Janice C. Hayes, review of *Venus Williams,* p. 134; July, 2000, Marilyn Fairbanks, review of *Ann Landers and Abigail Van Buren,* p. 113.

Science Books and Films, January-February, 2000, Cathy Brown, review of *How to Say No,* p. 32.

*   *   *

AUVIL, Peggy A(ppleby) 1954-

Personal

Born February 19, 1954, in Springfield, MO; daughter of Sam, Jr. (a judge) and Anne (a housewife) Appleby; married Tom Auvil (a dentist); children: Mark, Travis, Trent, Laura Dalton. *Education:* Southwest Missouri State University, B.S. (education), 1976, M.A.Ed., 1986. *Politics:* Republican. *Religion:* Christian.

Addresses

Home—500 Bluestem Rd., Ozark, MO 65721. *Office*—Mathews Elementary School, 605 South Gregg, Nixa, MO 65714.

Career

Nixa Schools, Nixa, MO, elementary school teacher, 1976—. Motivational speaker and demonstrator for education classes at Southwest Missouri State University, Springfield, MO, 1994—, and Drury University, Springfield, 1999-2000.

Writings

We Bought a Bird that Said Dirty Words, Dorrance, 1999.

Contributor to *Mailbox* magazine, 1993—.

Work in Progress

Poem "If You Toot Your Horn Too Loud, You Can't Hear the Rest of the Band," and a children's story called *Pigs Get Fat ... Hogs Get Slaughtered.*

Sidelights

Peggy A. Auvil told *SATA:* "As I looked at the questionnaire to be filled out for *Something about the Author,* I knew I'd have trouble with the 'Awards' part. My only claim to fame came in 1972, my senior year in high school, when I won 'Teacher's Headache,' an award given by the faculty and staff. Not an award one would necessarily *want* listed in a publication! Although, as I think about it ... I was 'awarded' with an eighteen-pound ham at a drawing held at the opening of a local grocery store. Other than that, fame has eluded me.

"My family and my youth experiences are the main reasons I turned to writing. In 1954, the year of my birth, my grandmother Lucile Anderson founded our county library (Christian County Library). Having a grandmother as a librarian, I'd watch her read every book (no kidding) before it went on the shelf, I'd know that every holiday she'd present me with my own copy of my 'favorite' book. I would run my hands along the spines of the books lined on the shelves (I think I was supposed to be dusting); I would stop to peruse the picture and later to lie on the floor and read myself into the next adventure. These were the events of my youth.

"It is important to note that I had an older brother and sister, David and Judy, who led me to believe I was an 'adopted princess.' [It was] not a true description, but one a gullible little sister might believe. As time went on it became clear that the 'brain cells' in the family had gone their way. Both received top awards in school and later became successful in their careers. To them I give credit for inspiring my rather creative imagination.

"My only published book, *We Bought a Bird that Said Dirty Words,* was inspired by a few of my elementary students. Teaching dictionary skills was a part of my third-grade curriculum. To begin the unit, I would start by passing out dictionaries and letting the students peruse for a few minutes on all the possible things we could learn from its usage. A few of my 'spunky' students opted to look up 'dirty' words—you know, the four-lettered kind. Eureka!! If dirty words could inspire such interest in a dictionary, I decided to write a book about 'dirty words' to use as an introduction to dictionary usage. The students think it's funny to go home and tell their parents, 'Mrs. Auvil had us look up dirty words in the dictionary!' The parents are relieved to know those 'dirty' words include: squalid, befoul, quagmire, frowzy, etc.

"My teaching career has led me to write, entertain, and inform. My style of writing is *not* one which would land me on the *Rosie* or *Oprah* show ... but in the minds of my students, I am the next Mitchell, Twain, Grisham, and Harper Lee in combination. That is some kind of success ... even better than being awarded with a ham!!"

B

BAKER, James W. 1926-

Personal

Born December 20, 1926, in Emporia, VA; son of Otis Fletcher (a draftsman) and Hazel (a homemaker; maiden name, Webb) Baker; married Elaine Campton (a librarian), December 15, 1951; children: James W., Glenn Campton. *Education:* College of William and Mary, A.B., 1951. *Religion:* Presbyterian.

James W. Baker

Addresses

Home—510 Spring Trace, Williamsburg, VA 23188. *E-mail*—mrmystic@widowmaker.com.

Career

Richmond News Leader, Richmond, VA, reporter and education writer, 1951-63; U.S. Information Agency, Washington, DC, foreign service officer, 1963-83; *Virginia Gazette,* Williamsburg, VA, columnist and writer, 1983—. *Military service:* U.S. Marine Corps, 1945-46, served in Tientsin, China. *Member:* International Brotherhood of Magicians, Order of Merlin, Society of American Magicians.

Awards, Honors

Virginia Press Association, certificates of merit, 1956 and 1969; first place, American Trucking Association safety writing contest, 1958; U.S. Information Agency, director's award for creativity, 1972, meritorious honor awards, 1973 and 1982.

Writings

Illusions Illustrated: A Professional Magic Show for Young Performers, Lerner Publications, 1984.
Valentine Magic, Lerner Publications, 1988.
Halloween Magic, Lerner Publications, 1988.
Christmas Magic, Lerner Publications, 1988.
Birthday Magic, Lerner Publications, 1988.
New Year's Magic, Lerner Publications, 1989.
Presidents' Day Magic, Lerner Publications, 1989.
April Fools' Day Magic, Lerner Publications, 1989.
Thanksgiving Magic, Lerner Publications, 1989.
Columbus Day Magic, Lerner Publications, 1990.
St. Patrick's Day Magic, Lerner Publications, 1990.
Arbor Day Magic, Lerner Publications, 1990.
Independence Day Magic, Lerner Publications, 1990.

Work in Progress

A book containing one hundred fifty columns from the *Virginia Gazette;* a syndicated newspaper column on simple magic tricks for children.

Sidelights

"I feel that I have been extremely fortunate in having three distinct careers, each of which was in its own way exciting, interesting, stimulating," James W. Baker once commented. "From 1951 to 1963 I was a reporter and education writer on the *Richmond News Leader,* covering at various times the county government, the police beat, the Virginia state legislature, courts, and general assignments. In early 1954 I was named education editor of the paper, and within months the U.S. Supreme Court ruled in the *Brown vs. Board of Education* decision, which outlawed racially segregated schools. Education became the hottest news subject in the South, and as a young reporter I was suddenly covering the paper's biggest stories. Because of legal battles, I ended up spending more time covering education from the courthouse than from the schoolhouse. Heady stuff for a reporter still in his twenties.

"During twelve years on the *News Leader* I covered just about every 'beat' the paper had. By the early 1960s I began to get itchy feet and a desire to see the world. Realizing I could never do this as a tourist on a reporter's salary, I began to look for a job that would take me overseas. I applied to the U.S. Information Agency (U.S.I.A.) and in 1963 was offered an appointment as a foreign service officer.

"In July, 1963, my family (my wife and our two sons, then seven and five years old) and I flew to Madras, India, for a three-year assignment. By the time the tour was over we had become committed nomads. I stayed with U.S.I.A. for twenty years, serving in Turkey, Pakistan, the Philippines, Tunisia, and Washington, DC. It was a wonderful, exciting two decades. We took advantage of opportunities most Americans never get. We traveled in more than eighty-five countries, once got hijacked to Cairo, Egypt, and saw most of the world's famous structures and places.

"Throughout my first two careers—on the newspaper and in the foreign service—I had avidly pursued a hobby I discovered at the age of nine: magic tricks and sleight of hand. I gave numerous shows in Richmond. In the foreign service I performed magic shows for schools, orphanages, hospitals, ambassadors and other diplomats, the mentally retarded, and the college educated in a couple of dozen foreign countries. I discovered that magic was an international ice-breaker that cut across language and cultural barriers like an invisible magic wand.

"Entering my third career—'retirement'—I began to combine my two loves, writing and magic, while writing a weekly column and numerous feature stories for the *Virginia Gazette.* This combination of writing and magic

Illusions Illustrated, *Baker's first book, combines his two passions of writing and magic in an instructive text that describes the performance of various tricks. (Photo by Carter M. Ayres.)*

resulted in the publication of my first book, *Illusions Illustrated.* Some months afterward I got a phone call from Elizabeth Petersen, then the editorial director of Lerner Publications. Her words still ring clearly in my ear many years later. 'Children,' she said, 'love magic and they love holidays. Is there any way the two could be combined in a children's book?' It was as if she had turned on a one-hundred-fifty-watt light bulb inside my head. Of course; why hadn't I ever thought of that? The result is history."

The fateful phone call from Lerner led Baker to create a series of magic books for children, with each volume focused on a particular holiday. Baker includes ten tricks per volume, and the series features step by step illustrations to guide kids through the mechanics of each trick. Reviewing *Arbor Day Magic, Columbus Day Magic, Independence Day Magic,* and *St. Patrick's Day Magic* in *School Library Journal,* Trish Ebbatson praised Baker's explanations as "excellent," but felt that the small size of the volumes rendered the illustrations somewhat "uninspired." By contrast, *Booklist* contributor Denise M. Wilms found the drawings in *Christmas Magic* and *Halloween Magic* "both decorative and instructive" and concluded that overall the books "offer a full measure of magical fun for aspiring magicians." Writing in *School Library Journal,* Leslie Chamberlain noted that Baker presents children with "imaginative and doable projects" and commented favorably on his "clear and straightforward" writing style.

Biographical and Critical Sources

PERIODICALS

Booklist, December 15, 1988, Denise M. Wilms, review of *Halloween Magic* and *Christmas Magic,* p. 704.
Bulletin of the Center for Children's Books, January, 1989, Betsy Hearne, review of *Birthday Magic, Christmas Magic, Halloween Magic,* and *Valentine Magic,* p. 116.
Richmond News Leader, April 30, 1984.
Richmond Times-Dispatch, October 31, 1988.
School Library Journal, December, 1989, Leslie Chamberlain, review of *April Fool's Day Magic, New Year's Magic, Presidents' Day Magic,* and *Thanksgiving Magic,* p. 105; March, 1990, Trish Ebbatson, review of *Arbor Day Magic, Columbus Day Magic, Independence Day Magic,* and *St. Patrick's Day Magic,* p. 222.

*   *   *

BAT-AMI, Miriam 1950-

Personal

Surname pronounced "Bott a-me"; born June 26, 1950, in Scranton, PA; daughter of Simon H. (a rabbi) and Huddie (a violinist; maiden name, Weinstein) Shoop; married Ronald Rubens (a builder), April 11, 1976; children: Aaron Rubens, Daniel Rubens. *Education:* Hebrew University, Jerusalem, B.A., 1974; California State University, Los Angeles, M.A., 1980; University of Pittsburgh, Ph.D., 1989. *Religion:* Jewish. *Hobbies and other interests:* Research on multiple perspectives in American historical fiction and nonfiction for children, gardening, caring for the family's many pets, horseback riding, acting, reading.

Addresses

Home—23750 64th Ave., Mattawan, MI 49071. *Office*—Dept. of English, Western Michigan University, Kalamazoo, MI 49008. *Agent*—Barbara Kouts, P.O. Box 558, Bellport, NY 11713.

Career

University of Pittsburgh, Pittsburgh, PA, teaching fellow in English, 1980-84; Southwest Missouri State University, Springfield, instructor in English, 1984-89; Western Michigan University, Kalamazoo, assistant professor, 1989-94, associate professor of English, 1994—. Has also worked as a tutor for Special Services at California State University, taught English as a Second Language at Los Angeles City College, worked as an executive assistant at the Israeli Consulate in Los Angeles, and consulted on college texts and multicultural literature for Harcourt Brace Jovanovich and Simon & Schuster publishers. *Member:* Modern Language Association, Children's Literature Association, National Council of Teachers of English, Society of Children's Book Writers and Illustrators, Michigan Council of Teachers of English.

Awards, Honors

First prize, CELERY Short Story Award, Western Michigan University, 1982, for "Nielah"; John Gilmore Emerging Artists' Grant, 1991, for completion of *When the Frost Is Gone;* Faculty Research and Creative Arts Support Grant (FRACAS), Western Michigan University, 1993, for completion of *Punctuation Porpoises and*

Miriam Bat-Ami

Other Space People; Highlights Awards Foundation Scholarship, 1993; Scott O'Dell Award for Historical Fiction, 2000, for *Two Suns in the Sky.*

Writings

Sea, Salt, and Air, illustrated by Mary O'Keefe Young, Macmillan, 1993.

When the Frost Is Gone, illustrated by Marcy Dunn Ramsey, Macmillan, 1994.

Dear Elijah, Farrar, Straus, 1995, Jewish Publications Society, 1997.

Two Suns in the Sky, Front Street/Cricket Books, 1999.

Contributor of short stories, including "My Beautiful Feet" and "All Because of the Pines," to *Cicada.* Contributor of critical essays to journals, including *Beacham's Guide to Literature for Young Adults, Children's Literature in Education, Children's Literature Association Quarterly,* and *Language Arts Journal of Michigan,* among others. Contributor of short stories and poetry to periodicals, including *Voices: A Magazine for English Poetry in Israel, Response, Davka, Tree, Gargoyle,* and *Statement: California State University Journal.*

Work in Progress

Horse's Right Eye, a young adult novel.

Sidelights

Miriam Bat-Ami is the author of books for children and adolescents that examine topics such as friendship, prejudice, and religion. Her works *When the Frost is Gone, Dear Elijah,* and *Two Suns in the Sky* feature teenage protagonists who struggle to establish their own identities under confusing and often painful circumstances.

Bat-Ami once said: "I have always wanted to move people. I love to hear children laugh. I love to see them laugh when I'm reading to them. I suppose I get this from my father, who would stand on the pulpit and move us all to laughter and tears. I love the tears, too, that come after the laughter when suddenly the world opens, and we see something new, something perhaps that's always been there.

"I think I've always had a gift for voice, for remembering how people say things. Dialogue is very important to me, even when I write picture books. I find that, in speech, I reach down into what my characters are about. I also have a flair for the dramatic, and my years working in the theatre have influenced the way I write."

Bat-Ami continued, "In many respects teaching is very important to me. I don't want to tell people what to think, but I love posing questions and guiding my students into new thoughts.

"As a child, I often felt somehow different. Given my background, I was different, and so I find my characters

In Bat-Ami's novel for middle-school readers, a Jewish girl struggles with her father's illness and her own uncertainties which she expresses in letters to the prophet Elijah. (Cover illustration by Dan Andreasen.)

to be sensitive to difference—slightly outside looking in on many worlds. I've also thought it very important to have an empathetic imagination. I want children to feel worlds that aren't necessarily their own and yet, also, to delight in worlds they have.

"My second book grew out of my experiences on what one might call a 'marginal' block. On that block, though, I found deep community, and so I wanted to tell children how what is outside (poverty) sometimes masks a real richness of people pulling together. This book, *When the Frost Is Gone,* was written because I needed to believe in harmony. I still do. I also want my literature to sometimes address action. Children will read it and feel optimistic about what they can do in the world."

Bat-Ami once remarked, "My first and third books came from personal feelings about my own past. *Sea, Salt, and Air,* my first picture book, deals with the yearly summer trips my family took to the beach: how we packed for the trip, the long ride, our feelings of freedom when we swam in the ocean, and the whole sense of timelessness one feels at the beach. It also deals with my love for my grandparents, who welcomed us into their summer cottage. Mary O'Keefe Young, working in vibrant pastels, wonderfully captured that sense of freedom and love."

Bat-Ami's 1994 book, *When the Frost Is Gone,* marked the start of her venturing into fiction for older children. In this story, twelve-year-old Natalie recounts an eventful, if difficult summer. Natalie lives with her father, and carries with her a certain degree of anger toward her mother, a substance abuser who has left them. She resents entering her teen years without a sympathetic female figure to discuss things, but when her mother returns for a time that summer and tries to build a new relationship, Natalie cannot see past her own anger at her mother's former behavior. Tasha, Natalie's close friend, lives nearby in the rough urban neighborhood, and Natalie recounts her friend's own woes that summer, which culminate in a fire that destroys the house for which Tasha's grandmother has just finished paying.

In an upstate New York town during World War II, a teenage girl falls in love with a boy from the nearby government camp for Jewish refugees. In chapters alternately narrated by the girl and boy, Bat-Ami depicts their deepening relationship and the prejudice of the town's residents. (Cover illustration by Hilary Mosberg.)

Natalie forges an unlikely but positive friendship with her neighbor, a stonemason named Mr. Pettinato, who offers to rebuild Tasha's grandmother's house and "helps Natalie achieve equilibrium," noted a *Publishers Weekly* review, which commended *When the Frost Is Gone* as "a portrait of urban life in all its colors." Connie Tyrrell Burns, writing for the *School Library Journal,* described it as "a deceptively simple, richly written depiction of a young girl's coming of age."

Bat-Ami once described the substance of her next book, *Dear Elijah,* as "a middle grade novel [that] explores a young Jewish girl's feelings about God. Rebecca's father has had a heart attack; Passover is coming; and no one in her house is doing anything to get ready. She writes to the prophet Elijah, and, in the writing, begins to understand herself. She needs to find her own route to prayer: it isn't her father's. She also needs to find her own place in the world. In this sense, she is not only a Jewish girl coming to terms with faith, she is every girl exploring female identity." Bat-Ami also stated, "Her questions are closely tied to ones I had at her age, ones which have no easy answers and which, sometimes, I still ask. In this sense, *Dear Elijah* was a particularly painful book for me to write. Painful, too, was the fact that my own father died of a heart attack. Rebecca's father does not die, though the reader doesn't know what will ultimately happen. I don't think I could have made him die. It would have been too painful."

Dear Elijah earned its author mixed reviews. A *Publishers Weekly* review faulted Bat-Ami's portrayal of the confused Rebecca, asserting that the girl "never becomes a flesh-and-blood character," while her letters to the biblical prophet "sometimes seem like the effort of an ambitious religious school teacher." Sharon Grover, writing for *School Library Journal,* concurred, remarking that "while the premise is interesting, the choice of Elijah as a pen pal for an adolescent girl seems strange." Yet Becky Korman, writing in *Voice of Youth Advocates,* felt the work had a more positive message. "The issue of whether to adopt your parents' faith is one that most young people will face," Korman noted. A *Booklist* critique from Ilene Cooper commended Bat-Ami for delving into some weighty topics about life, Jewish heritage, and general spiritual issues. "There are certainly too few books that deal with that topic," Cooper remarked.

Bat-Ami won rave reviews for another work for adolescent readers, *Two Suns in the Sky,* which appeared in 1999. The story is set in 1944 in Oswego, New York, a time when the United States was in the midst of World War II. A teenage girl, Chris Cook, is bored by life in upstate New York, and duly fascinated when the federal government establishes a refugee shelter for European Jews at nearby historic Fort Ontario. It was the only such shelter in the United States for Jewish refugees, though at the time, the presence of Nazi Germany's concentration camps in Eastern Europe, where Jews were systematically murdered, was not known to the general public.

There are nearly one thousand Jews living at Fort Ontario, and Chris establishes a friendship with Adam, one of the teenagers from the camp who attends her high school. Both she and Adam recount their stories in alternating first-person narrative chapters. Adam was fortunate enough to leave Rome with his mother and sister when that part of Italy was liberated from Nazi occupation by the Allied forces but, as with the others, is dismayed to find himself fenced inside in what he believed was the land of freedom. As *Two Suns in the Sky* progresses, the friendship between the two quickly turns to romance. Chris's xenophobic father vehemently expresses his disapproval, and even her Roman Catholic priest warns her to stay away. Their prejudicial attitudes reflect the conflicts that other residents of Oswego have about the refugee camp in their midst. Bat-Ami includes actual recollections of the camp from surviving residents and refugees as epigraphs that precede each chapter. However, the attitudes of Adam's teachers also reflect how many people in the community came to the aid of the refugees.

Some reviewers compared Bat-Ami's against-all-odds teen romance to Shakespeare's *Romeo and Juliet*. "Bat-Ami captures the startled awareness of young adolescents in love for the first time, the awareness of two individuals who, briefly, exist only in relation to one another," noted a *Bulletin of the Center for Children's Books* review. Though the townspeoples' suspicion toward foreigners and Jews is a strong undercurrent in the work, Martha Walke, writing in *Horn Book,* commended the way the issue was handled: "Never didactic, Bat-Ami uses her story to probe this issue with sensitivity and depth." *Booklist* critic Hazel Rochman offered a similarly positive assessment. "The relationships are complex," she noted, and commended the author's creation of "a docunovel that gives a strong sense of the times." A *Publishers Weekly* review described the epigraphs as "convincing observations," and asserted that readers "will be challenged by the questions Bat-Ami realistically frames about tolerance and its absence."

Bat-Ami recalled her own youth as a Jewish girl growing up in America in the postwar years in an interview with *Authors and Artists for Young Adults* (*AAYA*). "I was both an active kid and a quiet kid. I had a lot of 'block' friends," she said. "Back in the fifties, kids often made these kinds of friends in the neighborhood and activities centered around the block. We had a big back yard and so did our neighbor who had children my age. We played outdoor games, many of them quite imaginative in nature and full of ancient rituals. One was 'pies,' a form of tag wherein the 'devil with the dirty hands and face' had to guess the name of pies. When he did, he chased them, and, if they were caught, they got put in the pickle jar. There was TV tag. You shouted out a TV show before you got tagged. If you repeated a show, you were 'frozen' and we played 'statues,' another tag game wherein we actually role played parts that came to the twirlers' mind by the way we were twirled. We also played 'king of the mountain' on the

hill behind our house and some fairly standard games like 'kick the can,' 'red Rover,' and 'dodge ball.'"

Bat-Ami once stated, "I liked to bike ride to the candy store near our house with friends and I liked to roller skate down hills. I came from Scranton, Pennsylvania, and lived in what was referred to as the hill section, and so we had wonderful skating hills and bumpy slate sidewalks. These were neighborhood things I did. On an organized level, I was in Girl Scouts and took ballet lessons. I also rode a horse (generally once a week) with a friend. Stories were always part of my life. My parents liked to tell stories about their childhood. In our synagogue I belonged to the storytelling group, and we learned Jewish tales that we told during the service.

"I actually had a very difficult first reading experience," Bat-Ami once acknowledged. "I think part of this has to do with my eyes. I had an operation when I was five and wore glasses (or contacts) from then on. At first I didn't read well and was tutored by a wonderful teacher. I loved learning from her. After school, I'd sit on her porch—her name was Mrs. Farber and we'd read together. I liked the shared experience of reading. At school I wasn't a 'blue bird.' Those were the best readers. I think I was in the second group. I always felt compelled to do better. But at school we read aloud in circles and it didn't feel as communal as it did on Mrs. Farber's porch. When I was a pre-teen I caught the reading bug. I guess I'm a lot like my second son: a late reading bloomer who now delights in the whole venture of moving into imaginary worlds. I loved to lie in bed with the covers over me, eat chips or ice cream, and read and read and read. Later I loved reading to my mother, particularly plays. After the initial fear of reading in groups, I loved reading aloud to people. I liked to dramatize events.

"I read just about everything. I wasn't a discriminating reader. My parents got *Reader's Digest Books of Stories.* I'm not quite sure that's the right title, but the *Reader's Digest* people put out books of short stories. I read those. I read any horse book I could get my hands on. I read Golden Books. My favorite was an abridged version of *Heidi.* Summers, I'd join the Reading Clubs and I read "Nancy Drew Mysteries" and "The Bobbsey Twins" series, and I loved Hans Christian Andersen. His sad stories always touched me. I remember sitting in a big stuffed chair in our attic and wishing that the little mermaid would be able to marry the prince. I remember wondering how she could endure suffering so much. I read books about girls who suffered and survived: biographies about people like Helen Keller. I was particularly attracted to Madame Curie. If only I could be an inventor like her. And I imagined myself a 'National Velvet' racing my horse. My parents always encouraged me to read."

Bat-Ami once recalled, "In school I was a good student, not a genius but good. I was persistent and worked hard. I liked algebra and had a good deal of trouble with geometry. I loved English and hated art. I had no faith in my abilities to draw and very little patience. I also asked many questions. Some teachers liked this. Some didn't.

"As a teenager I wanted to be a ballet dancer with some dance company. I had famous dancers on my wall (alongside pictures of running horses), and I always saw myself in movement, but I wasn't cut out to be a dancer. I came to writing slowly. My freshman year, I had a teacher who really encouraged me and put me on the writing staff of our high school newspaper. I began by writing poetry. Poetry cleanses the soul, and I continue to return to it when I want to suck on the seeds of life.

"I went to Boston University my first year of college and then transferred to Hebrew University in Jerusalem," Bat-Ami once stated. "I finished my B.A. in Israel.... I loved college. [At] Hebrew University I got to travel quite a bit. I remember swimming in oases, in the Mediterranean, picking dates, hiking, seeing Greece and Paris. I lived in Jerusalem and felt it to be the most spiritual place on the earth. After graduation, I went back to the States as I always thought of myself as American. Perhaps, though, this sense of myself as Jewish and American influenced a great deal of my writing, for in this duality there was that sense that I was neither fully one thing or another, or rather I was two things. I belonged to a people whose roots were not in the States. My grandparents were immigrants from Poland and Russia. And yet, I have always felt very American. After graduation I held many insignificant jobs, worked part-time and wrote, traveled around the United States until, at the age of 28, I went back to school. I did my master's at California State University, Los Angeles, and my doctorate at the University of Pittsburgh."

Discussing her entry into the world of children's book publishing, Bat-Ami once stated, "I was amazed when my first book was published. I was very fortunate to work with Harold Underdown, children's book editor. In 1989 he was an assistant editor at Macmillan and working his way up. I was new. He was looking for fresh voices. I sent him *Sea, Salt, and Air* and he literally showed me how to make a picture book from it. It is scary to be a picture book writer when you are not the illustrator. You have to trust that the illustrator will carry the vision you had—and even extend that. I still love looking at *Sea, Salt, and Air,* although I was saddened that Macmillan Children's books folded.

"Where do I get my ideas? Listening to kids, and being with my children. My books have tended to follow my children, in that I've written for an older and older audience. My last book was for teens and some of what my older son said was in it. My children keep me in touch with how kids are thinking because one can forget. Just recently my eldest got his permit and I experienced that whole feeling of being behind the wheel, taking your mom's keys and hanging onto them, asking your mom to move over into the passenger's side. An event that occurred to me or my kids will trigger ideas. My youngest grew the biggest sunflower the summer before kindergarten, and he measured his growth through that sunflower. This became the basis of a picture book manuscript, 'The Practicing Sunflower.'

"For historical fiction, I read history books and become intrigued by certain events in history. When I researched *Two Suns in the Sky,* I depended quite a bit on interviews and newspaper articles. The newspaper can give you so much: tell you of fashions, prices, current events (of that time), movies that are popular, hair styles. I use the newspaper like freezer paper. It gives me grounding."

Asked about her writing practices, Bat-Ami told *AAYA,* "When I write, I need quiet. I write in my office on the second floor of our house. I face a window because I need to look out at the trees from time to time. How do I balance my time? I'm fortunate in that I teach at a university and so don't have a 9 to 5 job. I write mornings, teach afternoons and prepare classes/grade papers in the evenings.

"I write children's books because they tell us the truth about ourselves," Bat-Ami continued. "They sustain us. Because when the child in us dies, we die. The unique thing about young readers is that they so willingly enter into a fictional world and are engaged with characters in that world. A friend of mine told me about how her daughter read my book. She took it out to the back yard, sat against a tree trunk and read all afternoon. Fourteen-year-old girls need that escape, and, in escaping, they handle their own worlds so much better. They are refreshed. I think I love adolescent readers because they read like they eat—hungrily. I also am intrigued that young readers possess a willingness to enter into other worlds, to engage with characters inside a fictional context and to be moved by it. I myself want my readers to discover new worlds and see things they hadn't before—consider questions which they hadn't thought about."

"I try to give a reader something which tastes good but isn't pabulum. I want my readers to use their teeth and their tongues and feel the swallowing. Regarding goals, the majority of my work addresses community. 'No man is an island' has become a cliché, but there is truth in this statement. We are all connected, and I ask my reader to consider connections. I ask my reader to think about what we can do for each other, and I want them to have faith in themselves. My characters feel the immensity of life, often they are close to getting lost in the bigness of it all, but they find support. Often support comes from an older person, Mrs. Dubchek in *Two Suns in the Sky,* and Mr. Pettinato in *When the Frost Is Gone.* That older person is close to nature or to God [and] feels comfortable with life. My main characters find best friends who move them to see differently and they are willing to take chances. Living for them is taking a chance and exploring the other.

"I hope that my readers feel good about themselves, that they believe they can do something for others, can work with others to affect some change for the better in this world. Chris says this in *Two Suns in the Sky.* She says, 'Roosevelt had been the president of the United States almost as long as I'd lived on the earth. He said that we were citizens of the world. We couldn't be ostriches or dogs in the manger. We had to be responsible. We had to act responsibly. So I had to figure out what to do for myself.'

"When I think of all my books, I realize that I speak of family and community, of being inside a group and of feeling left out or outside, of wanting to become part of a larger circle. My characters are in the midst of change, sometimes bored with their lives, feeling that they need to connect to something bigger than themselves."

Biographical and Critical Sources

PERIODICALS

Booklist, May 15, 1993, p. 1695; April 1, 1995, Ilene Cooper, review of *Dear Elijah,* p. 1391; April 15, 1999, Hazel Rochman, review of *Two Suns in the Sky.*
Bulletin of the Center for Children's Books, April, 1994, Betsy Hearne, review of *When the Frost Is Gone,* p. 251; July, 1999, review of *Two Suns in the Sky,* pp. 379-380.
Horn Book, July, 1999, Martha Walke, review of *Two Suns in the Sky,* p. 460.
Kirkus Reviews, April 15, 1994, review of *When the Frost Is Gone,* p. 552.
Publishers Weekly, March 7, 1994, review of *When the Frost Is Gone,* p. 72; January 16, 1995, review of *Dear Elijah,* p. 455; May 17, 1999, review of *Two Suns in the Sky,* p. 80.
School Library Journal, June, 1993, p. 70; April, 1994, Connie Tyrrell Burns, review of *When the Frost Is Gone,* p. 124; May, 1995, Sharon Grover, review of *Dear Elijah,* p. 104; July, 1999, Shirley Wilton, review of *Two Suns in the Sky,* p. 92.
Voice of Youth Advocates, August, 1994, Kitty Krahnke, review of *When the Frost Is Gone,* p. 142; August, 1995, Becky Korman, review of *Dear Elijah,* p. 154.

*   *   *

BAURYS, Flo(rence) 1938-

Personal

Surname is pronounced "Baurs;" born September 27, 1938, in Wilkes-Barre, PA; daughter of Sidney (a sheet metal worker) and Florence (a cafeteria server; maiden name, Eroh) Carne; married Thomas Baurys (in U.S. Air Force), April 18, 1959; children: Lori Baurys Shelton, Wendy Baurys Smith, Thomas, Jr., Jeff, Vicky Baurys Colbert. *Education:* Robert Packer Hospital School of Nursing, R.N., 1959. *Religion:* United Methodist. *Hobbies and other interests:* Reading, family activities, travel, "fitness walking."

Addresses

Home—6126 Lark Valley Dr., San Antonio, TX 78242-2010. *E-mail*—fbaurys@aol.com.

Flo Baurys

Career

Freelance writer. Worked as a registered nurse, 1959-84. Public speaker and workshop leader. *Member:* Society of Children's Book Writers and Illustrators.

Writings

A Time for Alzheimer's, Emerald Ink, 1998.
A Spur for Christmas, illustrated by Gerald Holmes, Gulf (Houston, TX), 1999.

Editor and author of a spiritual enrichment column for a Chapel Hill United Methodist Church newsletter, 1995-98. Author of "The Field," published in the anthology *A Fountain of Words,* Alamo Writers Unlimited, 1995. Contributor to magazines, including *Hi-Call* and *Good Reading.*

Work in Progress

The Coyote Calf; Christmas Visitors, the story of a family who tries to adopt a wild javelina as a pet; *Sacagawea: Native American Golden Girl,* a biography; research for *Black Kettle* (tentative title), biographical fiction about a Cheyenne Indian chief; *Minnie-Mocker: Sass and Glory,* a middle-grade reader about the naming of the mockingbird as the Texas state bird; *Chico's*

Song, a picture-book adaptation of a Texas-Mexican folktale; *Sand Dollars,* an adult novel.

Sidelights

Flo Baurys told *SATA:* "When I was in high school, my English teacher encouraged me to be a writer, but I opted for a nursing career instead. In retrospect, I wish I had listened to her. Eventually, I gave up the erratic work schedule of nursing to be a stay-at-home mom to my five children. Enticed by a magazine ad, I enrolled in a correspondence course on writing for children. After completing that, I took an advanced course. I had found my true passion!

"I took a vacation from the juvenile genre to write the true, inspirational story of caring for my mother, an Alzheimer's disease victim. After circulating through publishing houses for two years and being rejected thirty-three times, the manuscript was bought and released in 1998, just weeks before my sixtieth birthday. Perseverance pays!

"The publication of *A Time for Alzheimer's* took me in an unexpected direction when a television host who interviewed me about the book persuaded me to enter the Ms. Texas Senior Pageant. Although I didn't win, my family, [including] seven grandchildren, enjoyed seeing Grammy as a contestant in this gala affair.

"In 1997 the *San Antonio Express-News* held a contest for children's fiction, and I entered it. As one of the winners, my story received full-page coverage, complete with art work, on Christmas Day. This brought me back to working actively on children's literature. Many of my stories have a 'Texana' flavor. As a Yankee transported to Texas during my husband's military career, I found the land and people to be fascinating subjects. Visiting schools to talk about writing is a joy, and the letters I receive from students, teachers, and parents are priceless. One student wrote, 'I learned you can't give up because you didn't when you published your book.' A mother of a third-grader stated, 'My children loved your visit. My son, who's in third grade, now wants to be an author, too.' What a privilege to have that kind of impact on young minds!

"Writing in two genres can be tricky, especially when I'm trying to promote a children's book while researching an adult novel, but I would never give up either one. Both genres offer unique and challenging opportunities. My writing goals fall into two categories: preserving my history for family (including a book on growing up in a Pennsylvania coal-mining town in the 1940s) and entertaining readers with heart-touching stories. Arranging words to portray beautiful images and evoke deep emotions is a desire too strong to abandon even if I never publish another thing."

Biographical and Critical Sources

PERIODICALS

San Antonio Express-News, December 23, 1999, Rene A. Guzman, "Armadillos 'Spur' Writer."

ON-LINE

Flo Baurys Website, http://www.flobaurys.com/ (September 28, 2000).

*   *   *

BEN-EZER, Ehud 1936-

Personal

Born April 3, 1936, in Petah Tikva, Palestine (now Israel); son of Binyamin (an agriculturist) and Devora (Lipsky) Ben-Ezer; married Anat Fienberg, August 31, 1969 (divorced, 1972); married Yehudit Tomer (a nurse), September 24, 1974; children: (second marriage) Binyamin. *Education:* Hebrew University of Jerusalem, B.A., 1963. *Religion:* "Jew, Secular."

Addresses

Home—20 Hakalir, P.O. Box 22135, Tel Aviv, Israel.

Career

Freelance writer, lecturer, and editor. Member of Kibbutz Ein Gedi on shore of Dead Sea, Israel, 1956-58; teacher in night school for adults, near Jerusalem, Israel, 1959-66. *Military service:* Israeli Army, Nahal troops, 1955-56. Israeli Army Reserve, 1959—; served in first aid unit in Six Day War, 1967. *Member:* PEN, Hebrew Writers Association.

Awards, Honors

Israeli Prime Minister Prize for creativity, 1975.

Writings

FOR CHILDREN

Laila Beginat Hayerakot Hanirdamim (title means "Night in the Sleeping Vegetable Garden"), Massada, 1971.
Oferit Blofferit (title means "Offerit the Bluffer"), Yavneh, 1977.
Mi Mesaper Et Hasaparim? (title means "Who Barbers the Barbers?"), Yavneh, 1982.
Otzar Habe'er Harishona (title means "The Treasure of the First Well"), Schocken, 1982.
Be'eikvot Yehudei Hamidbar (title means "In Search of the Jews of the Desert"), Schocken, 1983.
Betset Yisrael Mimitsraim (title means "When Israel Went Out of Egypt"), illustrations by Nachum Gutman, Yavneh, 1987.
(Editor) *Haggadah* (title means "Order of the HomeService on Passover Night"), illustrations by N. Gutman, Yavneh, 1987.
50 Shirei Mitbagrim (title means "50 Puberty Cracks"), illustrations by Dani Kerman, Rachgold-Sagiv, 1987.

A young shepherd boy spends all he has on a verse he is certain will bring him luck in **Hosni the Dreamer,** *Ehud Ben-Ezer's retelling of an Arabian folktale. (Illustrated by Uri Shulevitz.)*

Hosni the Dreamer: An Arabian Tale, illustrated by Uri Shulevitz, Farrar, Straus, Giroux, 1997.

OTHER

Hamahtzeva (novel; also see below; title means "The Quarry"), Am Oved, 1963.

"*Hamahtzeva*" (two-act play; based on his novel of the same title), first produced in Tel Aviv at Zuta Theatre, April, 1964.

Anshei Sdom (novel; title means "The People of Sodom"), Am Oved, 1968.

Lo Lagiborim Hamilhama (novel; title means "Nor the Battle to the Strong"), Levin-Epshtien, 1971.

(Editor) *Unease in Zion* (interviews), Quadrangle, 1974, Hebrew translation published as *Ein Sha'ananim Betsion,* Am Oved, 1986.

Hapri Ha'asur (short stories; title means "The Forbidden Fruit"), Achiasef, 1977.

Efrat (short stories), Tarmil, 1978.

Hasheket Hanafshi (novel; title means "Peace of Mind"), Zmora, Bitan, Modan, 1979.

Bein Holot Vekhol Shamaim (title means "Sand Dunes and Blue Sky"), illustrations by Nachum Gutman, Yavneh, 1980.

(Editor) *Ester Raab: Gan Sheharav* (selected stories and poems of Ester Raab; title means "A Ruined Garden"), Tarmil, 1983.

(Editor) *Nachum Gutman* (album), Massada, 1984.

Hane'ehavim Vehaneimim (novel; title means "Lovely and Pleasant"), Bitan, 1985.

Lashut Beklipat Avatiach (novel; title means "To Sail in a Watermelon Shell"), Rachgold-Sagiv, 1987.

Erga (short stories; title means "Yearning"), Zmora-Bitan, 1987.

(Editor) Ester Raab, *Kol Shirei Ester Raab* (poems; title means "The Verse of Ester Raab"), Zmora-Bitan, 1987.

(Editor) Yehuda Raab, *Hatelem Harishon* (title means "The First Furrow"; contains *To the History of Eliezer Raab and His Son Yehuda Raab* and *To the History of the First Years of Petah Tikva*), Hasifria Hatsionit, 1987.

Contributor of weekly column to *Ha'aretz* (daily newspaper), 1970-78. Also contributor to periodicals.

Adaptations

Ben-Ezer's novel *Hamahtzeva* was adapted and broadcast on the Israel National Broadcasting Service, Kol

Israel, in 1964, and again in six installments on the "Popular Hebrew" radio program in 1969.

Work in Progress

Research on the image of the Arab in Hebrew literature since the 1880s; a book of poems; a saga about the life of a family in Palestine since the 1830s; a lexicon of articles about more than two hundred Hebrew books; biography of Shraga Netser; second volume of *Oferit Blofferit.*

Sidelights

Israeli author Ehud Ben-Ezer commented: "The Ben-Ezer (Raab) family has been living in Palestine since 1875. Yehuda Raab (Ben-Ezer), my grandfather, was one of the first settlers of Petah-Tikva in 1878, when that first Jewish colony in Palestine was founded."

During a writing career spanning some four decades, Ben-Ezer has penned novels, plays, short stories, and a number of works for children. He teamed with celebrated illustrator Uri Shulevitz to produce *Hosni the Dreamer,* a highly regarded picture book based on an Arabian folktale. In the story, Hosni is a young shepherd boy who listens with fascination to the tales of his tribal elders and dreams of adventures in the city. His chance finally comes when he is invited to join a group of shepherds who are traveling to the marketplace to sell camels. Hosni is awed by the bustle and excitement of the city, but chooses to spend his earnings, not on beautiful garments or other wares, but at a shop offering "one verse for one gold dinar." Although subsequently ridiculed by his fellow shepherds, Hosni maintains faith that the simple verse of wisdom that he has purchased is a charm that will reward him.

Hosni the Dreamer was well received by commentators who responded favorably to Ben-Ezer's storytelling and characterization. "Ben-Ezer uses crisp, vivid language throughout," noted *School Library Journal* contributor Ellen D. Warwick, who added: "he includes descriptions and phrases that suggest the tale's setting." Robin Tzannes, writing in the *New York Times Book Review,* called *Hosni* a "charming" work, praising both Shulevitz's illustrations and Ben-Ezer's "accomplished storytelling" while asserting: "Pictures and text work together to create a portrait of a humble and compassionate hero that young readers should love." Also commenting on the book's appeal for young readers, a *Publishers Weekly* reviewer dubbed *Hosni the Dreamer* "a literary magic-carpet ride," while a *Teaching and Learning Literature* critic maintained, "This story will touch any child who has ever been rejected and teased by his peers."

Biographical and Critical Sources

PERIODICALS

Horn Book, September-October, 1997, Cathryn M. Mercier, review of *Hosni the Dreamer,* p. 585.

New York Times Book Review, November 16, 1997, Robin Tzannes, review of *Hosni the Dreamer,* p. 42.
Publishers Weekly, June 30, 1997, review of *Hosni the Dreamer,* p. 75.
School Library Journal, December, 1997, Ellen D. Warwick, review of *Hosni the Dreamer,* p. 81.
Teaching and Learning Literature, May-June, 1998, review of *Hosni the Dreamer,* p. 91.*

*　　*　　*

BORGMAN, James (Mark) 1954-
(Jim Borgman)

Personal

Born February 24, 1954, in Cincinnati, OH; son of James R. (a commercial artist and sign painter) and Marian F. (an office manager; maiden name, Maly) Borgman; married Lynn Goodwin (a publisher), August 20, 1977 (died, 1999); children: Dylan, Chelsea. *Education:* Kenyon College, B.A. (summa cum laude), 1976.

Addresses

Office—c/o Cincinnati Enquirer, 312 Elm Street, Cincinnati, OH 45202.

Career

Cartoonist. *Cincinnati Enquirer,* Cincinnati, OH, editorial cartoonist, 1976—; *Washington Post,* creator of "Wonk City" comic strip, 1994-96; artist and cocreator (with Jerry Scott) of "Zits" (comic strip), 1997—.

James Borgman

Exhibitions: International Salon of Cartoons, Haslem Gallery, Art Pac Shows, and the Framery on Hyde Park Square. *Member:* National Cartoonists Society.

Awards, Honors

Editorial cartooning award, Sigma Delta Chi, 1978; Thomas Nast Prize, 1980; Post-Corbett Award, 1981; Best of Gannett awards in editorial commentary, 1981 and 1984, special citation, 1985; Pulitzer Prize for editorial cartooning, finalist, 1985, awarded, 1991; second prize, Fischetti Competition, 1985; best editorial cartoonist awards, National Cartoonists Society, 1987, 1988, 1989, and 1994; Ohio Governor's award, 1989; National Headliner Award, 1991; Golden Plate, 1992; Reuben Award for outstanding cartoonist of the year, National Cartoonists Society, 1993; Sigma Delta Chi, 1995; honorary degrees from Kenyon College, Xavier University, and University of Cincinnati.

Writings

AS JIM BORGMAN

Smorgasborgman (editorial cartoons), Armadillo (Cincinnati, OH), 1982.

The Great Communicator (editorial cartoons), Colloquial (Cincinnati, OH), 1985.

(With James F. McCarty) *The Mood of America: A Journey toward Liberty,* Cincinnati Enquirer, 1986.

(Contributor of foreword) Richard S. West, *Satire on Stone: The Political Cartoons of Joseph Keppler,* University of Illinois Press, 1988.

Jim Borgman's Cincinnati, Colloquial (Cincinnati, OH), 1992.

Disturbing the Peace, Colloquial (Cincinnati, OH), 1995.

Author of additional foreword to *Drawing a Crowd: An Editorial Cartoonist's Look at Miami University and Beyond,* by Charlie Zimkus.

"ZITS" SERIES; WITH JERRY SCOTT; AS JIM BORGMAN

Zits: Sketchbook 1, Andrews McMeel (Kansas City, MO), 1998.

Growth Spurt: Zits Sketchbook 2, Andrews McMeel (Kansas City, MO), 1999.

The Humongous Zits: A Zits Treasury, Andrews McMeel (Kansas City, MO), 2000.

Don't Roll Your Eyes at Me, Young Man!: Zits Sketchbook 3, Andrews McMeel (Kansas City, MO), 2000.

Are We an "Us"?: Zits Sketchbook 4, Andrews McMeel (Kansas City, MO), 2001.

ILLUSTRATOR; AS JIM BORGMAN

A. Victoria Pohl-Lauch, editor, *Cincinnati for Kids: A Directory of Children's Activities,* ProKids (Cincinnati), 1990.

Damaine Vonada, editor, *The Ohio Almanac, 1992-1993, An Encyclopedia of Indispensable Information about the Buckeye Universe,* Orange Frazer Press, 1992, revised as *Ohio Almanac, 1997-98: An Encyclopedia of Indispensable Information about the Buckeye Universe,* edited by Michael O'Bryant, Orange Frazer Press, 1997.

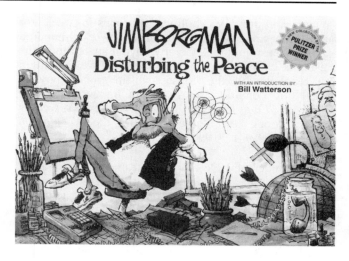

Disturbing the Peace is a collection of Borgman's political cartoons.

The Ohio Sports Almanac: An Encyclopedia of Indispensable Information about the Buckeye Sporting Universe, Orange Frazer Press, 1992.

Richard N. Aft and Daniel J. Ransohoff, *Painful Decisions, Positive Results: United Way and Community Chest, 1915-2000,* Community Chest and Council of the Cincinnati Area, 2000.

Borgman's editorial cartoons have been syndicated to over 200 newspapers, including the *Washington Post, Chicago Tribune, Los Angeles Times, New York Times, Newsweek, New York Daily News, USA Today, Philadelphia Inquirer, Newsday,* and *Atlanta Constitution.*

Sidelights

James Borgman is remembered at his alma mater, Kenyon College, as "the first art major ever to repay a student loan," as noted in an article in *Editor & Publisher.* Illustrating under the first name Jim, Borgman was fortunate enough to be picked up by a major daily, the *Cincinnati Enquirer,* straight out of college in 1976, at the age of twenty-two. He recalled of his early days on the job to *SATA:* "I was laying track as the train was running ... exhilarating but frightening."

Borgman was born on February 24, 1954, in Cincinnati, Ohio, where he has continued to make his home. Over the years Borgman has developed his own style of cartooning and his works now appear in papers countrywide via King Features Syndicate. He has poked fun at and satirized politicians and newsmakers for twenty-five years as the editorial cartoonist for the *Cincinnati Enquirer.* Borgman's talents won him the Pulitzer Prize in 1991 for his cartoons on U.S. President George Bush and Soviet ruler Mikhail S. Gorbachev. He has also repeatedly won the acclaim of his peers through numerous awards conferred on him by the National Cartoonists Society.

While his cartoons seem to appear effortlessly, Borgman contends they are in actuality not so easy to draw.

"When you draw six political cartoons a week for publication and syndication (in about two hundred papers), you simply seek therapy in your spare time," the artist once explained. "Mine involves long walks at night and rehabilitating the houses we invariably buy in apocalyptic condition." Apart from his work for the *Cincinnati Enquirer*, Borgman also drew a weekly political comic strip, *Wonk City*, for the *Washington Post* from 1994 to 1996.

In the summer of 1996 Borgman teamed up with Jerry Scott to create a new comic strip called *Zits*. Launched in July of 1997, *Zits* has gone on to become one of the fastest growing syndicated comic strips of all times. Whereas most successful comic strips rarely get more than one hundred clients in their first year, *Zits* built a list of over 425 newspapers in just six months. By and large the phenomenal success of the comic strip has been attributed to the combined talents of the writer-cartoonist duo. In an article published in *Editor & Publisher*, Borgman noted "There's very much an overlap. It's an organic partnership." David Astor reported in another article for *Editor & Publisher* that comic historian and critic R. C. Harvey felt that, "Jim and Jerry have a track record, and the strip is attractively drawn." In the same article, author Maurice Horn claimed, "It's a funny strip. It has the kind of sarcastic humor that's very current." Many reviewers commented that it is this contemporary flavor, combined with a realistic approach to coming-of-age issues, that has propelled the comic strip to its path of universal popularity. Others praised Scott and Borgman for avoiding a "sanitized" treatment of teens.

In an article for *Editor & Publisher*, Borgman explained that *Zits* "lets me get away from political thoughts, which refreshes that part of my brain." He told *SATA*, "After 20 years of editorial cartooning I was ready to challenge myself with an additional adventure.... The two distinct challenges complement each other and I love both."

Biographical and Critical Sources

PERIODICALS

Editor & Publisher, May 21, 1994, David Astor, "Political Cartoonist Wins Ruben Prize," p. 42; June 15, 1996, David Astor, "Borgman Talks to Fellow Cartoonists," p. 98; February 28, 1998, David Astor, "Why 'Zits' Zoomed up the Sales Charts" and "Cartoonists Discuss Life with 'Zits'," pp. 28-29; May 2, 1998, David Astor, "Will Comic Co-Creators Be Allowed to Share Awards?," p. 37.
New York Times, April 10, 1991, "Winners of 1991 Pulitzer Prizes in Journalism," pp. A10-20.
New York Times Book Review, October 2, 1988, Bill Blackbeard, review of *Satire on Stone*, p. 27.

*   *   *

BORGMAN, Jim
See BORGMAN, James (Mark)

BUGNI, Alice 1951-

Personal

Born 1951, in Juneau, AK; married David Bugni (a speciality contractor), 1983 (divorced); children: Mike, Sarah. *Education:* Kodiak Community College, A.A.; also attended University of Washington. *Politics:* Democrat. *Religion:* Catholic. *Hobbies and other interests:* Genealogy, computer technology, yoga, and swimming.

Addresses

Home—Kodiak, AK.

Career

Author.

Writings

Moose Racks, Bear Tracks, and Other Alaska Kidsnacks: Cooking with Kids Has Never Been So Easy!, illustrated by Shannon Cartwright, Sasquatch Books (Seattle, WA), 1999.
Sourdough for Starters, Alice B. Ventures, 2001.

Sidelights

Alice Bugni told *SATA:* "Both of my grandmothers were of Tlinget descent; one grandfather was English, and the other Irish. My father was born and raised in San Francisco California, and my mother was born and raised in Southeast Alaska, near Juneau. In his spare time my father liked to make/invent gadgets, and I learned from him the endless intrigue and wonder of possibilities. My mother often cooked from scratch during my early childhood years, and showed me how seasonings and spices can turn a good meal into a great one.

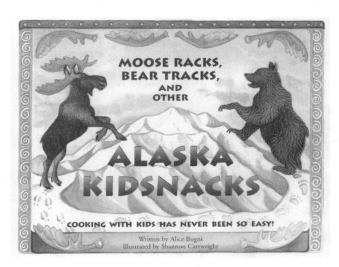

Alice Bugni compiles a tasty selection of recipes for twenty-five intriguing snacks like Denali Peaks and Glacier Ice in her amusing cookbook with an Alaskan theme. (Cover illustration by Shannon Cartwright.)

Born in Juneau, raised in Seattle, I moved to Hawaii after high school and stayed for eight years. I returned to Alaska in 1974 to work on the Trans-Alaska pipeline, after which I stayed in Alaska to work as an airline stewardess for Wein, and then as a long-distance operator for Alascom. I moved to Kodiak in 1981, married a California/Kodiak fisherman, had two kids, and learned how to cook (in that order).

While obtaining an Associate of Arts degree I took a prerequisite expository writing course with Prof. Leslie Fields who taught me the skills I use today as a writer. My first book, *Moose Racks, Bear Tracks, and Other Alaska Kidsnacks,* became a number one seller for my publisher in Seattle; and I currently have a web site devoted to my most recent cookbook, *Sourdough for Starters* which will be my first self-published book.

Living in Alaska has been an adventure and a learning experience which I've attempted to share through my Alaska-themed cookbook with readers, young and old, everywhere."

Biographical and Critical Sources

PERIODICALS

Publishers Weekly, October 25, 1999, review of *Moose Racks,* p. 83.
School Library Journal, December, 1999, Mollie Bynum, review of *Moose Racks,* p. 116.

C

CHANDLER, Karen 1959-

Personal

Born August 25, 1959, in Glen Cove, NY; daughter of Everett and Mary Chandler; married James LePore (a photographer), March 13, 1999. *Education:* Attended Stevenson Academy of Traditional Painting, 1979-83; New York Institute of Technology, 1984, 1993; and School of Visual Arts, 1992.

Addresses

Home and office—5 Serenity Pl., South Salem, NY 10590. *E-mail*—chandlerk@earthlink.net.

Career

Freelance illustrator, 1984-92; National Video Industries, New York City, art director, 1992-93; NakedEye-Images, Inc., South Salem, NY, computer graphics artist and illustrator, 1993—. *Member:* Society of Illustrators, NASA Space Art Program, Air Force Art Program.

Awards, Honors

MicroPublishing News/Encad digital art contest, first prize, 1996; MACWORLD Expo digital contest, 1999.

Illustrator

Les Martin (adaptor), *Edgar Allan Poe's Tales of Terror,* Random House, 1991.
Les Martin, *Return of the Werewolf,* Random House, 1993.
Ann Garrett, *Keeper of the Swamp,* Turtle Books, 1999.

Keeper of the Swamp was published in a Spanish edition as *El guardian delo pantano,* 1999.

Sidelights

Karen Chandler is an accomplished freelance illustrator whose clients number among the largest in the world and whose works have been included in exhibitions in New York City, Washington, D.C., and California. Chandler, who often combines computer-generated images with images in more traditional media, brings a bright palette to her work as a children's book illustrator. In 1999 she illustrated Ann Garrett's *Keeper of the Swamp,* a coming-of-age story about a boy and his grandfather, who has protected and cared for an ancient alligator named Ole Boots. When the aging grandfather realizes he will soon be unable to continue protecting the alligator, he teaches his grandson how to be the new "keeper of the swamp." For this picture book, which was also published in a Spanish version, Chandler used a combination of oil paints and computer-generated images in bright hues, including blues, yellows, and reds that are uncharacteristic of Louisiana swamps, but are strikingly effective. For her part, Chandler told *SATA:* "I hope to achieve a feeling of interest and drama in the stories that I illustrate."

Biographical and Critical Sources

PERIODICALS

Publishers Weekly, March 29, 1999, review of *Keeper of the Swamp,* p. 104.
School Library Journal, July, 1999, Judith Constantinides, review of *Keeper of the Swamp,* p. 70.

*   *   *

CHAPMAN, Jane 1970-
(Jack Tickle)

Personal

Born September 26, 1970, in Plymouth, England; daughter of Chris (a banker) and Marion (a homemaker; maiden name, Lambell) Chapman; married Tim Warnes (an illustrator), April 16, 1994; children: Noah. *Education:* Attended Redruth Comprehensive and Yeovil Art College; Brighton University, B.A. (graphic design II, first class). *Religion:* Christian. *Hobbies and other interests:* Quilting, embroidery, patchwork, cinema.

Addresses

Home—Lily Cottage, 2 West Court, Templecombe, Somerset BA8 0JT, England. *Office*—c/o Candlewick Press, 2067 Massachusetts Ave., 5th Floor, Cambridge, MA 02140.

Career

Illustrator, 1996—. Worked as a portrait painter, 1995-96; soft-toy designer for Russ Berrie, 1995-97.

Awards, Honors

Times Educational Supplement junior information award, 1999, for *The Emperor's Egg.*

Writings

FOR CHILDREN; SELF-ILLUSTRATED

Mary's Baby, Artists & Writers Guild Books (New York, NY), 1995.

ILLUSTRATOR

H. Benjamin, *What If?,* Little Tiger Press (Wauwatosa, WI), 1996.
Susan Akass, *Grizzly Bears,* ABC, 1996.
Julie Sykes, *Dora's Eggs,* Little Tiger Press (Wauwatosa, WI), 1997.
Hye Diddle, Diddle, and Other Nursery Rhymes, Walker/Early Learning Centre, 1997.
The Three Little Pigs, and Other Nursery Tales, Walker/Early Learning Centre, 1997.
Linda Jennings, *Penny and Pup,* Little Tiger Press (Wauwatosa, WI), 1997.
Tony Mitton, *Where's My Egg?,* Candlewick Press (Cambridge, MA), 1998.
Phyllis Root, *One Duck Stuck,* Candlewick Press (Cambridge, MA), 1998.
Caroline Pitcher, *Don't Be Afraid, Little Foal,* Magi, 1998.
Caroline Pitcher, *Run with the Wind,* Little Tiger Press (Wauwatosa, WI), 1998.
Old MacDonald Had a Farm, edited by Gale Pryor, Candlewick Press (Cambridge, MA), 1999.
Vivian French, *The Story of Christmas,* Candlewick Press (Cambridge, MA), 1999.
Julie Sykes, *Smudge,* Little Tiger Press (Waukesha, WI), 1999.
We Went to Visit a Farm One Day, Walker/Early Learning Centre, 1999.
Martin Jenkins, *The Emperor's Egg,* Candlewick Press (Cambridge, MA), 1999.
Diana Hendry, *The Very Noisy Night,* Dutton (New York, NY), 1999.
Laura Godwin, *Happy and Honey,* McElderry Books (New York, NY), 2000.
Laura Godwin, *Honey Helps,* McElderry Books (New York, NY), 2000.
Vivian French, *Noah's Ark, and Other Bible Stories,* Walker/Early Learning Centre, 2000.
(With Linda Cornwell) *Two Hungry Bears,* NP, 2000.
Turtle, Walker, 2000.
Karma Wilson, *Bear Shores On,* Simon & Schuster, 2000.

Phyllis Root's rhyming text and Jane Chapman's colorful illustrations combine in **One Duck Stuck,** *a counting book about an unlucky duck and all the animals who try to pull him out of a muddy marsh.*

ILLUSTRATOR; UNDER PSEUDONYM JACK TICKLE

Isobel Finn, *The Very Lazy Ladybird,* Little Tiger Press (Wauwatosa, WI), 1999.
Sheridan Cain, *The Crunching, Munching Caterpillar,* NP, 2000.

Adaptations

One Duck Stuck was adapted as an animated segment of the BBC television program *Words and Pictures.*

Sidelights

British artist Jane Chapman has shared her talent with young people in her illustrations for several engaging picture books, among them Tony Mitton's *Where's My Egg?,* Linda Jennings' *Penny and Pup,* and Martin Jenkins' award-winning *The Emperor's Egg.* "I've always loved working in acrylic paint," Chapman explained to *SATA.* "Sometimes I whack it on thickly with lots of textured brushstrokes." Chapman's love of acrylic paint is matched by her expertise; her work is characterized by bright colors balanced with realistic detail, the subtle variations in colors complementing and adding to the author's storyline.

Born in Plymouth, England, Chapman is the product of a middle-class English family. She graduated from Brighton University with a first-class bachelor's degree in graphic design, having specialized in illustration. She began her career by painting portraits, but soon realized that she would have to change tracks. As she told *SATA,* "although my work was commercial, I was never going to be anything other than a penniless artist unless I got some royalties coming in!" Chapman decided to follow in her husband's footsteps and pursue a career as a children's book illustrator.

One of Chapman's first illustration projects was *Mary's Baby,* a picture book she authored for young children that tells the tale of Christ's birth. Jane Marino, reviewing the 1995 book for *School Library Journal,* comments: "The controlled vocabulary and short sentences ... round, childlike figures, with button eyes and little black circles for mouths emphasize the simplicity of the story." Chapman's work in *Dora's Eggs* was praised for its bold yet simple form, at once conveying a harmonious impression and sense of "trusting intimacy" by all the farmyard animals. Jane Doonan, writing in *School Librarian,* takes particular note of Chapman's use of colors and "Nuances of textures."

Run with the Wind, although praised by one critic, led Heide Piehler of *School Library Journal* to comment that its "soft, primarily pastel artwork is sweetly sentimental and lacking in spirit." Chapman told *SATA,* "For me, the challenge is to improve the quality of my work all the time." Bright, cheerful illustrations are used to depict the antics of the characters in *Smudge,* and a *Publishers Weekly* reviewer commenting on *One Duck Stuck* notes that "The illustrator revels in juxtaposing strong colors." Chapman herself admitted that she likes to use strong contemporary colors so that her books have a current feel about them, thus making them appealing to her young audience.

And that's how he'll stay for two whole months, until his egg is ready to hatch.

Chapman's acrylic paintings complement Martin Jenkins's picture book about emperor penguins, whose females leave their eggs in the care of the males for two months of incubation. (From *The Emperor's Egg.*)

1999 saw Chapman receiving the *Times Educational Supplement* junior information award for *The Emperor's Egg.* The book has been universally appreciated for artwork that "balances realistic details with the penguin's implicit charm," as noted by a reviewer for *Publishers Weekly.* The same critic credits Chapman with providing "naturalistic acrylics of the frozen environment, against cold violet or warm orange backdrops." The judges found the subtle variations in Chapman's palette of special mention. Diana Hinds, reviewing the book for the *Times Educational Supplement,* praises Chapman's rendition of the penguins as "engaging and characterful without being in the least cute." Chapman uses color to its maximum strength in all her illustrations and experiments with different combinations for creating outstanding textures and visual appeal.

Chapman's work for the book *The Very Noisy Night* adds a new dimension to the story by detailing every aspect of the physical surrounding—all visual details are coordinated with the central characters—mice. Thread spools are used to depict tables and playing cards are used as beds. Postage stamp pictures, matchbox dresser drawers with button handles, and birthday cake candles for bedside lights present a special challenge of discovery for children. Young readers can explore the book, discovering something new each time that they might have missed the first time around.

Chapman, who sometimes uses the pseudonym Jack Tickle, told *SATA,* "In terms of inspiration, I find my husband a great model! He spends so much time on the research and rough stage perfecting every little detail, that I feel shamed into trying to follow suit!" The illustrator added that "although this career wasn't my first choice when I first left college it certainly is now.... Now I'm happy to say that I wouldn't do anything else."

Biographical and Critical Sources

PERIODICALS

Guardian Education, August 31, 1999, Vivian French, review of *The Very Noisy Night,* p. 5.
Publishers Weekly, September 18, 1995, review of *Mary's Baby,* p. 98; May 4, 1998, review of *One Duck Stuck,* p. 211; November 15, 1999, review of *The Emperor's Egg,* p. 65; November 15, 1999, review of *The Very Noisy Night,* p. 64.
School Librarian, August, 1997, Jane Doonan, review of *Dora's Eggs,* p. 134; winter, 1999, Lucinda Jacob, review of *The Very Noisy Night.*
School Library Journal, October, 1995, Jane Marino, review of *Mary's Baby,* p. 36; September, 1998, Heide Piehler, review of *Run with the Wind,* p. 179; November, 1999, Robin L. Gibson, review of *The Very Noisy Night.*
Times Educational Supplement, March 10, 2000, Diana Hinds, review of *The Emperor's Egg.**

COBALT, Martin
See MAYNE, William (James Carter)

*   *   *

CORMIER, Robert (Edmund) 1925-2000
(John Fitch IV)

OBITUARY NOTICE—See index for *SATA* sketch: Born January 17, 1925, in Leominster, MA; died of complications from a blood clot November 2, 2000, in Boston, MA. Writer, journalist. Cormier was widely acclaimed for his powerful and disturbing novels for young adult readers, though his realistic subject matter—including murder, sex, and terminal illness—at times made his work controversial. While he was primarily known as a novelist, Cormier began his writing career in radio and newspaper journalism, and continued to contribute to various periodicals under the pseudonym John Fitch IV until his death. During the years between 1960 and 1965, he published three books of fiction for adults, before shifting his focus to teenage readers beginning in the 1970s. His works for young adults include *I Am the Cheese* (1977) and *The Chocolate War* (1974), the latter of which was inspired by his son's refusal to sell candy for a high school fundraiser. Both novels were named outstanding books of the year by the *New York Times,* and *The Chocolate War* received the Lewis Carroll Shelf Award in 1979. In the years following the publication of *I Am the Cheese,* Cormier wrote numerous critically acclaimed teenage novels, including 1983's *The Bumblebee Flies Away* and *Tenderness,* released in 1997. He also penned several books for younger children, most notably *Other Bells for Us to Ring,* published in 1990, and 1992's *Tunes for Bears to Dance To.* In *Frenchtown Summer,* published in 1999, Cormier experimented with narrative style, resulting in a novel in verse. Throughout his career, Cormier received critical praise for his ability to portray to a teenage audience the realities of life in contemporary culture. His books reflect both a respect for his readers' idealism and a desire to make young adults aware of the difficult, uncompromising situations life sometimes presents.

OBITUARIES AND OTHER SOURCES:

PERIODICALS

Boston Globe, November 3, 2000.
Horn Book Magazine, March, 2001, Patty Campbell, "A Loving Farewell to Robert Cormier," p. 245.
New York Times, November 5, 2000.
Publishers Weekly, November 13, 2000, p. 33.
School Library Journal, December, 2000, Andrea Glick, "Robert Cormier Dead at 75," p. 24.

D

DANTZ, William R.
See PHILBRICK, Rodman

*   *   *

DE VOS, Gail 1949-

Personal

Born May 7, 1949, in Winnipeg, Manitoba, Canada; daughter of Cecil (a jeweler) and Lillian (a sales

Gail de Vos

manager; maiden name, Taback) Shukster; married L. Peter de Vos (a brand manager), May 8, 1976; children: Esther, Taryn. *Education:* University of Alberta, B.Ed., 1971, M.L.S., 1988.

Addresses

Home—9850 91st Ave., Edmonton, Alberta T6E 2T6, Canada. *Office*—SLIS, 3-20 Rutherford South, University of Alberta, Edmonton, Alberta T6G 2J4, Canada.

Career

Storyteller, 1988—. University of Alberta, adjunct associate professor, 1988—.

Awards, Honors

Storytelling World Award, 1995, for "Boiled Eggs" and 2000, for *New Tales for Old;* Storytelling World Award Honor Title, 1997, for *Tales, Rumors, and Gossip.*

Writings

Storytelling for Young Adults: Techniques and Treasury, Libraries Unlimited (Englewood, CO), 1991.
(With Merle Harris) *Telling Tales: Storytelling in the Family,* Dragon Hill, 1995.
Tales, Rumors, and Gossip: Exploring Contemporary Folk Literature in Grades 7-12, Libraries Unlimited (Englewood, CO), 1996.
(With Anna E. Altmann) *New Tales for Old: Folktales as Literary Fictions for Young Adults,* Libraries Unlimited (Englewood, CO), 1999.

Work in Progress

A follow-up volume to *New Tales;* a revised edition of *Storytelling for Young Adults.*

Sidelights

Canadian storyteller Gail de Vos has done much to popularize storytelling, particularly for young adults, an audience that had long been neglected by performers and scholars alike. After conducting research for a master's degree in library science, de Vos, a one-time secondary school teacher, decided that she would like to share her findings with a wider audience. "I consider myself first and foremost a storyteller and my writing has sprung from the desire to communicate the research that I have uncovered about stories, storytelling and particularly, about young adults as audiences for stories," de Vos told *SATA*. With the goal of demonstrating the importance of telling stories, she wrote *Storytelling for Young Adults.* The work contains 250 stories for young adults arranged by genre, as well as a how-to manual of storytelling techniques, strategies for bringing storytelling into the library and classroom, and an explanation of the value of listening to stories.

According to *RQ* reviewer Ellin Green, de Vos "succeeds admirably" in meeting her goal. Evie Wilson-Lingbloom maintained in *Voice of Youth Advocates* that de Vos's arguments and suggestions would dispel misconceptions that contemporary teenagers would not be interested in listening to storytellers. In the opinion of Kristin Ramsdell of *American Reference Books Annual,* *Storytelling for Young Adults* presents "a wealth of useful information, creative ideas, and story suggestions."

Tales, Rumors, and Gossip "came about because of the fascination audiences had with the one chapter [dealing with the topic] in *Storytelling for Young Adults,* de Vos explained to *SATA*. "Workshops and school visits began to focus on the urban legends and so grew that book." In *Tales, Rumors, and Gossip* the author explains the structure and value of legends in society, explores the value of gossip and rumor (including newscasts), and categorizes modern legends and their variants. "A scholarly yet entertaining compendium" is how Nancy Bell described the work in her *School Library Journal* review. Likewise praising *Tales, Rumors, and Gossip* for its high-quality research and readability, Evie Wilson-Lingbloom of *Voice of Youth Advocates* judged the work to be "delightful reading yet scholarly and eminently useful."

With Anna Altmann, de Vos continued to promote storytelling for young adults in *New Tales for Old,* a discussion guide to the plethora of new versions of traditional fairy tales. After a chapter defining the folktale, the authors treat such common tales as "Cinderella," "Little Red Riding Hood," "Snow White," "The Frog Prince," "Rapunzel," "Rumplestiltskin," "Sleeping Beauty," and "Hansel and Gretel." They describe the historical development of each tale, including different versions in a variety of media. They then discuss interpretations ranging from feminist to psychoanalytic. *Booklist* reviewer Hazel Rochman called *New Tales for Old* a "lively guide to stimulate discussion," and Judy Sokoll of *School Library Journal* also concluded that the work is a "feast for fans of folklore," and an "excellent resource."

De Vos told *SATA* about her evolving interests: "I have become increasingly interested in the correlation between oral storytelling and the reading of comic books and am focusing on convincing others that comic books and graphic novels deserve respect and space in school and public libraries."

Biographical and Critical Sources

PERIODICALS

American Reference Books Annual, Vol. 23, 1992, Kristin Ramsdell, review of *Storytelling for Young Adults,* p. 244.
Booklist, October 1, 1999, Hazel Rochman, review of *New Tales for Old,* p. 367.
RQ, spring, 1992, Ellin Green, review of *Storytelling for Young Adults,* pp. 451-52.
School Library Journal, December, 1996, Nancy Bell, "Folk Legends of Today," p. 46; July, 2000, Judy Sokoll, review of *New Tales for Old,* p. 131.
Voice of Youth Advocates, February, 1992, Evie Wilson-Lingbloom, review of *Storytelling for Young Adults,* p. 403; October, 1996, Evie Wilson-Lingbloom, review of *Tales, Rumors, and Gossip,* p. 242.

*   *   *

DELGADO, James P. 1958-

Personal

Born January 11, 1958, in San Jose, CA; son of Robert D. (a fire chief) and Marilyn Pearl (a homemaker; maiden name, White) Delgado; married Mary Jean

James P. Delgado

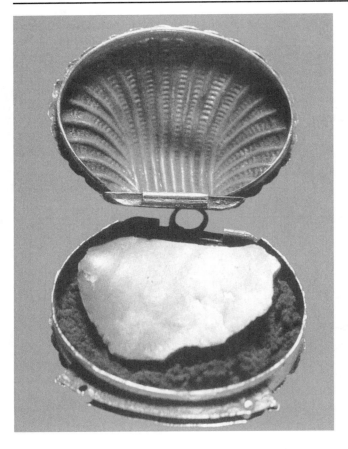

In Delgado's books about underwater archaeology, including **Shipwrecks from the Westward Movement,** *he describes shipwreck excavations and writes about the cultures that the ships came from. (Photo by S. F. Manning.)*

Bremmer (a teacher), October 7, 1978 (divorced); married Ann Goodhart (a librarian), January 14, 1997; children: (first marriage) John Charles, Elizabeth Marie. *Education:* Attended San Jose State University, 1976-78; San Francisco State University, B.A., 1981; East Carolina University, M.A., 1985. *Politics:* Independent. *Religion:* "Agnostic."

Addresses

Office—Vancouver Maritime Museum, 1905 Ogden Ave., Vancouver, British Columbia, Canada V6J 1A3.

Career

U.S. National Park Service, San Francisco, CA, historian at Golden Gate National Recreation Area, 1979-87, Washington, DC, maritime historian and head of National Maritime Initiative, 1987-91; Vancouver Maritime Museum, Vancouver, British Columbia, executive director, 1991—. Co-host, with Clive Cussler, *The Sea Hunters,* a National Geographic weekly television series, 2001—. Underwater archaeologist, and registered professional archaeologist. San Francisco State University, instructor in humanities, 1983-87; Archeo-Tec, consulting historian, 1986-87; National Maritime Alliance,

member of board of directors, 1990-92. San Jose Youth Commission, liaison to Historic Landmarks Commission, 1973-74; member of San Jose Bicentennial Commission, 1974-75, and San Jose Historical Landmarks Commission, 1976-77. International committee on the International Underwater Cultural Heritage, Icomos, Paris, 1993—; Council of American Maritime Museums, trustee, 1996—, president, 1999—; and International Congress of Maritime Museums, director, 1997—. *Member:* Arctic Institute of North America, Canadian Nautical Research Society, Society for Historical Archaeology, U.S. Naval Institute, California Historical Society, fellow of the Explorer's Club (New York), fellow of the Royal Canadian Geographical Society (London), Book Club of California (San Francisco chapter).

Writings

FOR CHILDREN; NONFICTION

Wrecks of American Warships, Franklin Watts (New York, NY), 2000.
Shipwrecks from the Westward Movement, Franklin Watts (New York, NY), 2000.
Native American Shipwrecks, Franklin Watts (New York, NY), 2000.

FOR ADULTS; NONFICTION

Alcatraz Island, KC Publications (Las Vegas, NV), 1985.
(Editor) *The Log of Apollo: Joseph P. Beach's Log of the Voyage of the Ship Apollo from New York to San Francisco, 1849,* Book Club of California, 1986.
"A Symbol of American Ingenuity": Assessing the Significance of the U.S.S. Monitor, National Park Service (Washington, DC), 1988.
(With Stephen A. Haller) *Submerged Cultural Resources Assessment: Golden Gate National Recreation Area, Gulf of the Farallones National Marine Sanctuary, and Point Reyes National Seashore,* Submerged Cultural Resources Unit, U.S. Department of the Interior, National Park Service (Santa Fe, NM), 1989.
(With Haller) *Shipwrecks at the Golden Gate,* Lexicos, 1989.
To California by Sea: A Maritime History of the California Gold Rush, University of South Carolina Press (Columbia), 1990, second edition, 1996.
(Editor, with J. Candace Clifford) *Inventory of Large Preserved Historic Vessels,* National Maritime Initiative, National Park Service, History Division (Washington, DC), 1990.
National Parks of America, Crescent Books, 1991, reprinted, 1993.
(With Clifford) *Great American Ships,* Preservation Press (Washington, DC), 1991, published with new foreword by Edward M. Kennedy, Wiley (New York, NY), 1995.
(With Tom Freeman) *Pearl Harbor Recalled: New Images of the Day of Infamy,* Naval Institute Press (Annapolis, MD), 1991.
(With Daniel J. Lenihan and Larry E. Murphy) *The Archeology of the Atomic Bomb: A Submerged Cultural Resources Assessment of the Sunken Fleet of Operation Crossroads at Bikini and Kwajalein Atoll*

Lagoons, Submerged Cultural Resources Unit, U.S. Department of the Interior, National Park Service, 1991.

Alcatraz: Island of Change, Golden Gate National Park Association (San Francisco, CA), 1991.

Dauntless St. Roch: The Mounties' Arctic Schooner, Horsdahl & Schubart (Victoria, British Columbia), 1991.

The Beaver: The First Steamship on the West Coast, Horsdahl & Schubart (Victoria, British Columbia), 1993.

Ghost Fleet: The Sunken Ships of Bikini Atoll, University of Hawaii Press (Honolulu, HI), 1996.

Made for the Ice: A Report on the Wreck of the Hudson's Bay Company Ship Baymaud, Ex-Polarskibet Maud, 1917-1930, Underwater Archaeological Society of British Columbia, Vancouver Maritime Museum (Vancouver, British Columbia), 1997.

(Editor) *The British Museum Encyclopaedia of Underwater and Maritime Archaeology,* British Museum Press (London), 1997, published as *Encyclopedia of Underwater and Maritime Archaeology,* Yale University Press (New Haven, CT), 1998.

Across the Top of the World: The Quest for the Northwest Passage, Douglas & McIntyre (Vancouver and Toronto), 1999, British Museum Press, 1999, Facts on File (New York, NY), 1999.

Lost Warships: An Archaeological Tour of War at Sea, Facts on File, 2001.

(With Joy Jasper and James Adams) *U.S.S.* Arizona: *Ship and Symbol,* St. Martin's (New York, NY), 2001.

Contributor of numerous articles to history and archaeology journals.

Sidelights

Maritime historian, marine archaeologist, and executive director of the Vancouver Maritime Museum James P. Delgado's *Encyclopedia of Underwater and Maritime Archaeology* is a "lavishly illustrated, scholarly, and comprehensive encyclopedia of nautical archaeology," according to Mary Ellen Quinn in *Booklist.* Editor Delgado, explained Quinn, "was assisted by more than 150 archaeologists, as well as other experts and practitioners from more than 25 countries around the world." The comprehensive encyclopedia covers archaeological sites dating from prehistory to the 20th century.

Critics were largely enthusiastic in their assessment of the *Encyclopedia of Underwater and Maritime Archaeology.* Arguing that the work will appeal to both experts and lay readers, Stanley Itkin in *Library Journal* found that Delgado "has compiled a remarkable encyclopedia of underwater archaeology that includes descriptions of hundreds of shipwrecks, sunken cities, and human-made objects under the sea." Brian E. Coutts and John B. Richard, in a separate *Library Journal* review, called the *Encyclopedia* an "exciting volume that is highly recommended."

In his 1999 offering, *Across the Top of the World: The Quest for the Northwest Passage,* Delgado details the history of exploration in the Arctic, from the sixteenth century to the present. He charts major voyages to the region, and discusses research currently conducted in the area. Characterized by thorough research, and documented with hundreds of images the text is, as one *Publishers Weekly* critic noted "a spectacular reference" for those interested in European encounters in the far north. In her review of the book for *School Library Journal,* Becky Ferrall commented that "young adults will find that the experiences related here are stranger than most fiction and equally satisfying."

Delgado has written several more books with appeal for younger readers. His *Wrecks of American Warships, Shipwrecks from the Westward Movement,* and *Native American Shipwrecks* offer detailed, highly illustrated descriptions of shipwreck excavations and what they teach us about the cultures in which the sailing vessels originated. Reviewing *Native American Shipwrecks* for *Booklist,* critic Hazel Rochman praised Delgado for his ability to write "with authentic detail about particular ancient cultures," and also took note of the book's numerous illustrations and easy to navigate design.

Delgado once commented: "I would like, in my future writing, to demonstrate the pervasive thread of maritime history in the world's culture, and in particular to unlock that past through shipwrecks and the visual and textual exploration of them. I write only about subjects I have experienced firsthand. I have dived on wrecks from the Gold Rush, on the U.S.S. *Arizona* at Pearl Harbor, on the A-bombed fleet at Bikini Atoll, and these experiences inspired me to write about them and to share what I learned and experienced."

Biographical and Critical Sources

PERIODICALS

Booklist, April, 1998, Mary Ellen Quinn, review of *Encyclopedia of Underwater and Maritime Archaeology,* p. 1347; October 15, 2000, Hazel Rochman, review of *Native American Shipwrecks,* p. 458.

Journal of American History, June, 1991.

Library Journal, March 15, 1998, p. 58; April 15, 1999, p. 56; October 15, 1999, p. 82.

Los Angeles Times Book Review, May 20, 1990, p. 6.

Magazine Antiques, September, 1998, p. 252.

Naval History, spring, 1991.

Publishers Weekly, September 27, 1999, review of *Across the Top of the World,* p. 88.

School Library Journal, July, 2000, Becky Ferrall, review of *Across the Top of the World,* p. 128.

*   *   *

DeVRIES, Douglas 1933-

Personal

Born September 4, 1933, in Lansing, IL. *Education:* Calvin College, B.A., 1960; University of Colorado,

M.A. (American history), 1966; University of Iowa, M.A. (elementary education), 1973.

Addresses

Home—3003 Wendy's Way, #9, Anchorage, AK 99517-1466. *E-mail*—jaderam@alaska.net.

Career

Teacher and administrator at Christian schools in Sheldon, IA, 1960-77, Randolph, WS, 1977-84, and Anchorage, AK, 1984-86. *Member:* Society of Children's Book Writers and Illustrators, America Christian Writers Association.

Writings

FOR CHILDREN

Muscles, the Moose Calf, illustrated by Patricia Parker, Jade Ram Publishing (Anchorage, AK), 1989.
Muscles Visits Anchorage, illustrated by Patricia Parker, Jade Ram Publishing (Anchorage, AK), 1990.
Muscles, Bull Moose from Alaska, Jade Ram Publishing (Anchorage, AK), 1995.
Gold Rush Runaway: A Historical Novel of Alaska Exploration and Adventure (young adult historical fiction), Jade Ram Publishing (Anchorage, AK), 1997.
Fevering for Gold: A Historical Novel about the 1900 Rush to Nome, Alaska (young adult historical fiction), Jade Ram Publishing (Anchorage, AK), 1999.
Shepherd of Bethlehem (biblical fiction), Jade Ram Publishing (Anchorage, AK), 2000.
Teen-Age Apostle (biblical fiction), Jade Ram Publishing (Anchorage, AK), 2001.

Also author of short stories and articles published in youth magazines.

Work in Progress

The Gold Rush to Fairbanks, Alaska, due in 2001-2002.

Sidelights

Douglas DeVries told *SATA:* "I believe that the desire to be an author has been in me for a long time. I was the only boy in a creative writing class in high school, and the only boy writing on the high school newspaper staff. Work and the military kept me from pursuing a career as a writer, or perhaps it was the idea that it wasn't something done for 'real' work. I became a teacher. As a teacher I wrote articles for the local newspaper and a few short plays for my students.

"The 'idea' to become an author surfaced in the early 1980s, and I took a correspondence course with the Institute of Children's Literature. But I still did not think of writing as my major occupation. That changed in 1987 when I decided to 'slow down' after quadruple bypass surgery. Since 1987 writing has been my major

interest. I hold a part-time position to have a steady source of income.

"As a youth I enjoyed reading and read books from public, school, and church libraries, anything I could lay my hands on, from the Hardy Boys through Stevenson, Dickens, and Dumas. One of my favorite authors of historical fiction was Joseph Altshellor, and perhaps his influence is why I have turned to that genre for my own writing. My two YA fictions are based on Alaskan history.

"I prefer to write in the morning when my mind is at its full power. To beginning writers I would say this: Find the time for you to do your best writing and try to work at that time every day. Have a good grasp of the mechanics of the English language, or the language you write in. Don't feel that you need to write a book; most of my success as a writer is from the sale of magazine stories and articles."

*   *   *

DORROS, Arthur (M.) 1950-

Personal

Surname is pronounced "doh-*rohs*"; born May 19, 1950, in Washington, DC; son of Sidney (an educator) and

Arthur Dorros

Dorothy Louise (a nurse) Dorros; married Sandra Marulanda (a teacher and translator), May, 1986 (divorced); children: Alex. *Education:* University of Wisconsin, B.A., 1972; Pacific Oaks College, postgraduate studies and teaching certification, 1979. *Hobbies and other interests:* Filmmaking; building; carpentry; horticulture; hiking in Central and South America, Asia; and Spanish language and literature.

Addresses

Office—c/o HarperCollins, 1350 Avenue of the Americas, New York, NY 10019-4703.

Career

Writer and illustrator, 1979—. Worked variously as a builder, carpenter, draftsman, photographer, horticultural worker, and dockhand; teacher in elementary and junior high schools and adult education in Seattle, WA, and New York City for six years; artist in residence for more than a dozen New York City public schools, running programs in creative writing, bookmaking, and video; University of Washington, former teacher of courses on writing in the classroom. Consultant in libraries and schools; director of Children's Writing Workshop, presenting seminars and workshops on writing to students, teachers, and administrators at schools, libraries, and international conferences. *Member:* Authors Guild, Authors League of America, Society of Children's Book Writers and Illustrators.

Awards, Honors

Reading Rainbow Book selection, 1986, for *Alligator Shoes,* 1989, for *Ant Cities,* and 1993, for *Abuela;* Outstanding Science Book, National Science Teachers Association/Children's Book Council (CBC), 1987, for *Ant Cities,* 1989, for *Feel the Wind,* and 1990, for *Rain Forest Secrets; Booklist*'s Best of Year list, 1991, for *Tonight Is Carnaval;* Notable Book citation, American Library Association (ALA), 20 Best selection, *Horn Book,* 25 Best of the Year, *Boston Globe,* Book of Distinction, *Hungry Mind Review,* and Parent's Choice award, all 1991, all for *Abuela;* Notable Book in Field of Social Studies, National Council for the Social Studies (NCSS)/CBC, 1991, for *Tonight Is Carnaval;* American Book Association Pick of Lists citation, 1992, for *This Is My House;* Books for Children List, Children's Literature Center in the Library of Congress, 1992, for *Abuela* and *Tonight Is Carnaval;* Notable Book in Field of Social Studies, NCSS/CBC, 1993, for *Radio Man/Don Radio;* Commended Book, Center for Latin American Studies Programs, and Notable Book in Field of Social Studies, NCSS/CBC, both 1995, both for *Isla;* Book Award Winner, American Horticultural Society, and Orbus Pictus Honor Book, National Council of Teachers of English, both 1998, both for *A Tree Is Growing.*

Writings

JUVENILE

Abuela, illustrated by Elisa Kleven, Dutton, 1991.
Tonight Is Carnaval, Dutton, 1991, translated into Spanish by Sandra Marulanda Dorros, as *Por Fin Es Carnaval,* illustrated by Club de Madres Virgenes del Carmen, Dutton, 1991.
Isla, illustrated by Elisa Kleven, Dutton, 1995.
A Tree Is Growing (nonfiction), illustrated by S. D. A. Schindler, Scholastic, 1997.
The Fungus that Ate My School, illustrated by David Catrow, Scholastic, 2000.
Ten Go Tango, illustrated by Emily Arnold McCully, HarperCollins, 2000.
When the Pigs Took Over, Dutton, 2001.
City Chicken, HarperCollins, 2001.

SELF-ILLUSTRATED; JUVENILE

Pretzels, Greenwillow, 1981.
Alligator Shoes, Dutton, 1982.
Yum Yum (board book), Harper, 1987.
Splash Splash (board book), Harper, 1987.
Ant Cities (nonfiction), Harper, 1987.
Feel the Wind (nonfiction), Harper, 1989.
Rain Forest Secrets (nonfiction), Scholastic, 1990.
Me and My Shadow (nonfiction), Scholastic, 1990.
Follow the Water from Brook to Ocean (nonfiction), HarperCollins, 1991.
This Is My House (nonfiction), Scholastic, 1992.
Animal Tracks (nonfiction), Scholastic, 1992.
Radio Man/Don Radio (Spanish translation by Sandra Marulanda Dorros), HarperCollins, 1993.
Elephant Families (nonfiction), HarperCollins, 1994.

Also illustrator of children's books *Charlie's House, What Makes Day and Night,* and *Magic Secrets.* Scriptwriter and photographer for filmstrips, including "Teaching Reading, a Search for the Right Combination," released by the National School Public Relations Association, and "Sharing a Lifetime of Learning," released by the National Education Association. Author and director of *Portrait of a Neighborhood* and other videos. Contributor of articles and illustrations published in periodicals and purchased by Dodd-Mead Publishers and *USA Today.*

Work in Progress

Julio's Magic, for HarperCollins, expected in 2002.

Sidelights

Arthur Dorros is the author-illustrator of award-winning titles in both fiction and nonfiction. His science books for young readers, such as *Ant Cities, Feel the Wind, Rain Forest Secrets,* and *A Tree Is Growing,* present the processes of nature in a clear and concise form, while his fiction entries, such as the highly praised *Abuela* and *Isla,* plumb the multicultural experience. Others, such as the popular *Alligator Shoes* and *The Fungus that Ate My School,* are humorous pieces that delight children. All of these books, as well as the critical praise and a devoted readership, come as a surprise to Dorros, who never imagined that writing and illustrating would be his ultimate career.

Growing up in Washington, D.C., the young Dorros loved to read and draw and was enthralled with animals. His family and friends fostered his latent talent. "First there was my grandfather, who would occasionally send me letters, all with the same drawing of a bird on them," Dorros once wrote in a profile for Scholastic Books. "Then there was the ninety-year-old neighbor who made sculptures out of tree roots he found, and my mother who kept a set of oil pastels in a drawer and would provide ... art supplies or a bottle of tempera paint at the drop of a hat. And my father was a great storyteller." His own personal imagination and recollections also formed part of the mix. "When I was four years old," he told *SATA*, "I sat on the tail of an alligator—a live alligator, ten feet long. Later (when I was thirty years old), I remembered that experience and wrote a story about an alligator."

Despite this environment, Dorros did not pursue drawing through elementary and junior high school. Dorros remembers that he grew frustrated with his attempts to draw, and he "quit drawing in the fifth grade." He did not begin to draw again until he reached high school and had to draw amoebas and animals in biology class. He has been drawing ever since. Dorros makes a point of encouraging children to persist in their endeavors despite frustration. When he gives bookmaking seminars and workshops in schools internationally, he tells children that they should continue to create even if they make mistakes. Jeff Green of the *Oakland Press* reported that Dorros told a group of children: "I wasn't born an author. I had to learn, just like you guys. You have to keep on trying and don't let anyone make you stop."

Dorros himself began to create picture books at the age of twenty-nine, after exchanging stories with children who wandered close to watch him remodel houses. "I found I really enjoyed swapping stories, and my interest in making pictures had continued," he explained in his Scholastic Books profile. His first book, *Pretzels*, provides a whimsical account of the invention of the pretzel. The silly crew members of the *Bungle* let the anchor chain rust away, and the ship's cook, I. Fryem Fine, replaces it with biscuit dough. When the salt-encrusted dough anchor chain is no longer needed, the cook shapes it into a twisted biscuit. First Mate Pretzel loves the cook's invention so much that it is named after him. Two other tales, "The Jungle" and "A New Land," are also included in this account of the *Bungle* crew's adventures. With Dorros's "knack for writing straight-faced nonsense" and the book's "droll" pictures, concluded a commentator for *Kirkus Reviews, Pretzels* is "mighty companionable." A reviewer for the *Bulletin of the Center for Children's Books* wrote that the "ineptitude of the characters" and "humor in the writing style" will be enjoyed by children, while a reviewer for *School Library Journal* decided that the stories have a "refresh-

ing, slightly off-the-wall feel," concluding that "[k]ids will enjoy the absurdities."

Dorros's next published work, *Alligator Shoes,* was inspired by his earliest childhood memory: sitting on an alligator's tail. In *Alligator Shoes* an alligator fascinated with footwear visits a shoe store. Locked in after closing time, he tries on pair after pair, until he finally falls asleep. When he wakes up in the morning, he hears a woman say that she would like a pair of alligator shoes. Realizing that not having shoes is better than becoming shoes, the alligator flees. *Alligator Shoes* was eventually selected as a book for the *Reading Rainbow* children's television series on PBS.

The publication of *Ant Cities* in 1987 marked Dorros's debut as a writer of children's nonfiction. In *Ant Cities* Dorros uses text and cartoon-like illustrations to explain ants and their various activities, from processing food to caring for eggs. Instructions for building an ant farm are also provided. A reviewer for the *Bulletin of the Center for Children's Books* characterized the illustrations as "inviting and informative." Ellen Loughran, writing for *School Library Journal,* noted that the book would be a "useful addition to the science section." Reviewing the Spanish translation of the same book, a critic for *Booklist* felt that "young Spanish-speaking children will find the information well within their grasp." *Ant Cities* was selected as an Outstanding Science Book of 1987 by the National Science Teachers Association/Children's Book Council. *Feel the Wind,* published in 1989, and *Rain Forest Secrets,* released in 1990, also earned this distinction, and his other picture books about science—*Me and My Shadow, Elephant Families, Follow the Water from Brook to Ocean,* and *Animal Tracks*—have also been well received. *Booklist*'s Carolyn Phelan felt his *Rain Forest Secrets* was "written in a conversational tone," while the "[e]ffective pen-and-wash drawings suggest the lush greenery of the settings." Jack Bennett, writing in *Science Books and Films,* commented that Dorros's *Elephant Families* "is an excellent book for the preschool or primary school child." Bennett further noted, "The story is clear and conveys much of the life and behavior of elephants."

Dorros's 1997 *A Tree Is Growing* continues this same approach to presenting scientific facts to young children. Margaret Bush, reviewing the title in *School Library Journal,* thought that "Dorros's short, informative explanations," along with the illustrator's "skillfully etched views of trees ... offer an exceptionally attractive science lesson." Bush concluded, "The slim volume invites browsing and will encourage observation of the natural world." A writer for *Kirkus Reviews* dubbed the same title a "verdant testimony to the noble plants that shade our lawns and line our streets," and went on to suggest that readers "will be exploring woods, sidewalks, and yards—anyplace there are trees—with new eyes." *Booklist*'s Hazel Rochman found *A Tree Is Growing* to be a "clear, handsome introduction" to the topic of trees and how they grow.

SAUDI ARABIA

In his informative book, Dorros describes twenty-two houses from various locations throughout the world, ranging from stone houses in Bolivia to the car that serves as a residence for an otherwise homeless family in the United States. (From This Is My House, *written and illustrated by Dorros.)*

Dorros, who spent a year living in South America and speaks Spanish, has made a significant contribution to children's literature in the United States with the publication of *Abuela* and *Tonight Is Carnaval* (both translated by his Colombian-born, former wife, Sandra Marulanda Dorros, and released in Spanish as *Abuela* and *Por Fin Es Carnaval*), as well as *Radio Man/Don Radio* and *Isla,* a sequel to *Abuela.* In *Abuela* young Rosalba imagines that she and her Abuela (or grandmother) fly together over New York City. While the text is primarily in English, Spanish words are interspersed throughout the story. Readers may infer meaning from the text or look up these words in the glossary provided. Elisa Kleven's vivid illustrations complement the text, and the resulting book is, according to Molly Ivins, "just joyful." In a review for *New York Times Book Review* Ivins asserted that *Abuela* "is a book to set any young child dreaming." Kate McClelland, writing in *School Library Journal,* concluded that the "innovative fantasy"

will enrich "intellectually curious children who are intrigued by the exploration of another language." In its 1995 sequel, *Isla,* which was also illustrated by Kleven, Rosalba takes a trip to the Caribbean, where her grandmother, mother, and uncle grew up. There she visits all the places dear to the heart of her relations. "Dorros's language is rich and magical," observed Vanessa Elder in a *School Library Journal* review. Again, as with *Abuela,* Dorros peppered his text with Spanish words and expressions and included a glossary at the end of the book. Annie Ayres called *Isla* "a tropical treasure" in a *Booklist* review, while a contributor for *Publishers Weekly* characterized it as a "fanciful flight."

In *Tonight Is Carnaval* a young boy tells of his community's preparation for carnaval. The tapestries, or arpilleras, sewn by Club de Madres Virgenes del Carmen of Lima, Peru, illustrate the beauty and excitement of the cultural event Dorros describes. A reviewer for *Horn Book* described the book as "brilliant, beautiful . . . affirmative and valuable." Dorros also wrote *Radio Man/Don Radio,* and his former wife provided the Spanish translation. The story centers on friends Diego and David, children who are members of migrant farm worker families. Diego, who constantly listens to the radio, has earned the nickname of "Radio Man" from David. The boys lose touch with one another when Diego's family begins a journey to Washington state, where they intend to work in the apple orchards. Diego, however, finds a way to contact David through the radio. Reviewer Janice Del Negro noted in *Booklist* that Dorros's illustrations provide "a solid sense of place and reflect the strong family ties and efforts at community Dorros conveys in his story." A writer for *Publishers Weekly* found that *Radio Man* "is noteworthy in presenting a protagonist who would be just as interesting in another milieu."

The nonfiction book *This Is My House* conveys the respect and admiration for other cultures communicated in *Abuela, Tonight Is Carnaval,* and *Radio Man/Don Radio.* In this book, Dorros describes twenty-two houses around the world and discusses the climate in which they are built, the people whom they shelter, and their construction. These dwellings range from stone houses in Bolivia to the car in which an otherwise homeless family in the United States lives. The phrase, "This is my house" is included on every page in the language of the people who occupy each house. Mary Lou Budd, writing for the *School Library Journal,* praised this "engaging" book by noting that there is "unlimited value in the succinct, interesting text and pictures" and that the watercolors are "bright" and "pleasing."

In a much lighter vein, Dorros has also created bouncy and humorous picture books that hark back to his original antic titles. With the counting book *Ten Go Tango,* Dorros developed "toe-tapping" rhythms, according to a reviewer for *Publishers Weekly.* Connie Fletcher, reviewing the picture book in *Booklist,* called it a "laugh-a-page counting book" that "offers preschoolers lively lessons to help them learn numbers, animals, and even dance steps." In *The Fungus that Ate My School,* another 2000 publication, Dorros creates an "unapologetically silly . . . hyperbolic romp," as a *Publishers Weekly* contributor described the book. In *The Fungus that Ate My School,* a science-class mold takes over the school during spring break, sliming all over the classrooms, the hallways, and out onto the playground. The reviewer concluded that the book would be good for "plenty of yucks." *Booklist* reviewer GraceAnne A. DeCandido called the book "a tale of a science experiment gone psychedelic," and praised both Dorros's text and the illustrations by David Catrow for the "utter silliness of weird eggheaded kids and their equally weird-looking teachers" they portray.

Whether writing clear and concise facts in his science books, imaginative and sensitive fiction from a multicultural perspective, or being just plain silly in humorous picture books for young readers, Dorros always manages to entertain, according to critics. "I think of a good writer or illustrator as a detective with all senses alert," Dorros concluded to *SATA,* "always on the lookout for clues that help to put the whole story together."

Biographical and Critical Sources

PERIODICALS

Booklist, January 15, 1994, Janice Del Negro, review of *Radio Man/Don Radio,* p. 924; June 1, 1995, review of *Ciudades de Hormigas/Ant Cities,* p. 1790; November 1, 1995, Annie Ayres, review of *Isla,* p. 476; July, 1996, p. 1834; February 1, 1997, Hazel Rochman, review of *A Tree Is Growing,* p. 942; December 1, 1997, Carolyn Phelan, review of *Rain Forest Secrets,* p. 628; April 15, 2000, Connie Fletcher, review of *Ten Go Tango,* p. 1550; June 1, 2000, GraceAnne A. DeCandido, review of *The Fungus that Ate My School,* p. 1907.

Bulletin of the Center for Children's Books, January, 1982, review of *Pretzels;* March, 1987, review of *Ant Cities;* January, 1994, p. 151; June, 1997, p. 355.

Children's Book Review Service, November, 1992, p. 27.

Five Owls, September-October, 1995, p. 21.

Horn Book, May-June, 1991, review of *Tonight Is Carnaval,* p. 360; March-April, 1996, pp. 230-231; March-April, 2000, p. 183.

Junior Bookshelf, February, 1990, p. 25.

Kirkus Reviews, November 1, 1981, review of *Pretzels;* August 15, 1990, p. 1167; September 1, 1993, p. 1142; January 15, 1997, review of *A Tree Is Growing,* p. 141.

Los Angeles Times Book Review, December 3, 1995, p. 27; February 25, 1996, p. 11.

New York Times Book Review, December 8, 1991, Molly Ivins, review of *Abuela,* p. 26; November 9, 1997, p. 24.

Oakland Press, April 18, 1991, Jeff Green, "Children's Authors Visit Area Schools."

Publishers Weekly, August 14, 1987, p. 100; November 15, 1991, p. 71; August 3, 1992, p. 70; September 27, 1993, review of *Radio Man/Don Radio,* p. 63; October 9, 1995, review of *Isla,* p. 84; April 5, 1999, p. 243; March 6, 2000, review of *Ten Go Tango,* p. 109; May 15, 2000, review of *The Fungus that Ate My School,* p. 117.

School Library Journal, December, 1981, review of *Pretzels,* p. 74; August, 1987, Ellen Loughran, review of *Ant Cities,* pp. 66-67; May, 1990, p. 96; September, 1991, p. 245; October, 1991, Kate McClelland, review of *Abuela,* pp. 90-94; September, 1992, Mary Lou Budd, review of *This Is My House,* p. 215-216; July, 1994, p. 93; September, 1994, pp. 145-146; August, 1995, p. 166; September, 1995, Vanessa Elder, review of *Isla,* pp. 168-169; November, 1995, p. 136; March, 1997, Margaret Bush, review of *A Tree Is Growing,* p. 173; April, 2000, p. 104; May, 2000, p. 140.

Science Books and Films, January-February, 1995, Jack Bennett, review of *Elephant Family,* p. 21.

OTHER

Arthur Dorros (publicity profile), Scholastic Books, c. 1992.

*   *   *

DUCHARME, Dede Fox
See DUCHARME, Lilian Fox

*   *   *

DUCHARME, Lilian Fox 1950-
(Dede Fox Ducharme)

Personal

Born Lilian Fox, October 8, 1950, in Houston, TX; daughter of Richard (a purchasing agent) and Freda (an elementary school counselor; maiden name, Lewis) Fox; married Charles Edward Ducharme (a systems analyst), May 7, 1972; children: Sara Elizabeth, Amy Elyse. *Education:* Attended University of the Americas, Mexico, D.F., 1968-69; Washington University, St. Louis, MO, A.B. (English and elementary education), 1972; Georgia State University, G.T. endorsement, 1974; Stephen F. Austin State University, M.Ed., 1977. *Hobbies and other interests:* "Travel, walking, reading, playing with my dog, Lucy."

Addresses

Home—19 Brookline Ct., The Woodlands, TX 77381. *Office*—Collins Intermediate Library, 6020 Shadowbend Pl., The Woodlands, TX 77381. *E-mail*—dducharme@ texed.net.

Career

Sanderson Elementary, Houston, TX, Head Start aide, 1967; University City Schools, Missouri, intern, 1971-72; Benteen Elementary, Atlanta, GA, teacher, 1973-74; Crogman Elementary, Atlanta, teacher, 1974-76; West Memorial Junior High, Katy, TX, teacher, 1977-78; Bear Creek Elementary, Katy, teacher, 1977-78; All Elementary, Katy, teacher in gifted education, 1979-81; Wilkerson Intermediate, Conroe, TX, teacher, 1982-84; Salyers Elementary, Spring, TX, teacher, 1984-88; Jenkins Elementary, Spring, teacher, 1988-93; Collins Intermediate, Conroe, teacher, 1993-96, librarian, 1998-2000; Creighton Intermediate, Conroe, librarian, 1996-98. Performs community service for numerous organizations, including the National Charity League, Special Olympics, Toys for Tots, and Race for the Cure. *Member:* International Reading Association, National Charity League, National Education Association, Society for Children's Book Writers and Illustrators, Texas Jewish Historical Society, Texas Library Association, Houston Area Reading Association.

Lilian Fox Ducharme

Awards, Honors

Golden Pen Award for Juvenile/Young Adult Fiction, Southwest Writers Conference, 1988; Honorable Mention for Juvenile Fiction, Golden Triangle Writers Guild Conference, 1989; writing workshop scholarship, Rice University, 1990, for "Fang in the Fridge"; Sydney Taylor Manuscript Competition winner, 1993, and Honor Book, Association of Jewish Libraries, 1998, for *The Treasure in the Tiny Blue Tin.*

Writings

(Under nickname Dede Fox Ducharme) *The Treasure in the Tiny Blue Tin* (young adult), Texas Christian University Press (Fort Worth, TX), 1998.

Contributor to *Texas! Teacher Edition,* Rand McNally, 1997.

Work in Progress

Bomb Scare, historical fiction for middle-grade readers set in the 1950s; research on Israel.

Sidelights

Lilian Fox Ducharme told *SATA:* "I love to write for the same reason that I love to read—it's a great escape. When I'm on overload from my teaching and librarian jobs or from my family roles as wife, mother, sister, daughter, I can write, transporting myself to another time and another place, an immediate mental vacation.

"Another thing that I love about writing is that *sometimes* I can be very bossy. I'm in total control. I can tell the characters what to wear, how to act, what to say, where to go . . . and they have to listen! But then, those very same characters have the nasty habit of coming to life and talking back to me like my daughters, saying things like, 'That's crazy. I'd never say that or do this.'

"When that happens, and the characters talk to me, they begin to tell the stories themselves, and I'm just along for a very adventurous ride. I love it. No roller coaster in the world could match the thrills of watching a story come to life on a printed page. Come along for a great ride!"

E

ELLIOT, David 1952-

Personal

Born November 10, 1952, in Ashburton, New Zealand; son of Robert (an insurance salesman) and Joy (a homemaker; maiden name, Harrison) Elliot; married Gillian Whitehead (a librarian), May 10, 1986; children: Mhairi, Jess. *Education:* Wellington Polytechnic, stage-1 graphics, 1971; University of Canterbury, fine arts diploma (painting), 1976; Christchurch College of Education, teaching diploma, 1986.

Addresses

Home and office—11 Burns St., Port Chalmers, Dunedin, Otago, New Zealand; fax: 64-3-472-8394. *E-mail*—snarkart@southnet.co.nz.

Career

Hutt Valley High School, New Zealand, assistant art teacher, 1987-88; Queens High School, Dunedin, New Zealand, art teacher, 1989-93, head of art department, 1994-97, part-time tutor in painting and drawing for adults, 1998—; freelance illustrator, 1986—. Dunedin Teacher's College, writer-in-residence, 2000. *Member:* New Zealand Illustrators' Guild, New Zealand Society of Authors, Children's Literature Foundation of New Zealand.

Awards, Honors

Russell Clark Illustration Award, 1991, for *Arthur and the Dragon;* Queen Elizabeth II Arts Council/Unilever/Choysa Award, 1991, and Russell Clark Illustration Award finalist, 1995, both for *Dragon Tangle;* International TV Association New Zealand, best interactive illustration title, 1995, for *Mungo: The Only Pirate Left;* Honour Award, *New Zealand Post* Children's Book Awards, 2000, for *Sydney and the Seamonster.*

Writings

FOR CHILDREN

Arthur's Star, Whitcoulls (New Zealand), 1986.
Dragon Tangle, Ashton Scholastic (New Zealand), 1994.
Sydney and the Seamonster, Random House (New Zealand), 1999.
Sydney and the Whalebird, Random House (New Zealand), 2000.

ILLUSTRATOR

Pauline Cartwright, *Arthur and the Dragon,* Nelson Price Milburn (New Zealand), 1989.
Anna Kenna, *A Close Call,* Learning Media, 1998.
Kenna, *The Bad Dad,* Learning Media, 1998.
Janice Marriott, *The Curse of Being Pharaoh,* Learning Media, 1998.
One Hundred New Zealand Poems for Children, Random House (New Zealand), 1999.
Pauline Cartwright, *Annie and Rufus,* Bridgehill (New Zealand), 1999.
30 New Zealand Stories for Children, Random House (New Zealand), 2000.
Tu'akoi Feana, *Cooped Up,* Learning Media, 2001.

David Elliot

Illustrator of book covers for Jack Lasenby's *Dead Man's Head, The Waterfall,* and *The Battle of Pook Island,* and for the CD-ROM *Mungo: The Only Pirate Left.* Contributor of illustrations to juvenile periodicals.

Work in Progress

Pigtails the Pirate.

Sidelights

After studying fine art, New Zealander David Elliot came to illustration gradually—while living in the gatekeeper's cottage at Edinburgh Zoo in Scotland. Elliot told *SATA,* "The Zoo was a wonderful stimulus, especially after the gates were closed and the animals were more relaxed." He started sketching them in pencil and found himself "playing around on the edge of illustration," he later confessed to Charmain Smith of the *Otago Daily Times.* After returning to New Zealand, Elliot taught art at Queens High School for eight years while doing small illustration projects, such as drawings for magazines and book covers. Though Elliot was encouraged and was growing increasingly confident in his work, finding time outside of school to do that work was difficult. "The problem with being a secondary school teacher is you have to unwind from it and wind up to the other," Elliot confided. "It was progressively harder to keep up with my work and I was doing smaller and smaller things, like book covers."

In 1998 Elliot made the leap to full-time illustrating after his younger daughter began school and his partner went back to work full-time. The following year his work appeared in bookstores in the form of both a collection of poetry titled *One Hundred New Zealand Poems for Children* and Elliot's own picture book, *Sydney and the Seamonster. Magpies* reviewer Frances Plumpton found much to like about *One Hundred New Zealand Poems for Children,* which contains works written for and by children. Calling Elliot's black pencil illustrations for this work "a treat," Plumpton noted, "His witty illustrations underpin, but do not overwhelm, the poetry," thus demonstrating the illustrator's "versatility interpreting a variety of moods."

In Elliot's *Sydney and the Seamonster* a penguin named Sydney is an inventor whose experiments wreck havoc on his island home. A reviewer for *Reading Times* praised the picture book highly, describing it as a "great story with superb visual skills" that contains "visual excitement and humour." As is the case with *Sydney and the Seamonster,* Elliot likes to make his illustrations meaty with subtext. "I've always liked fantasy that has an edge and a darkness to it," the illustrator admitted to Smith. "If I have the chance I will try and give an image that quality. It makes the images more important and gives them a strength and gravity that you feel belongs to it."

"I love drawing!," Elliot told *SATA.* "Through it my imagination materialises before me and continues to sprout ideas as I draw. Things grow out of the paper; characters, places, situations take on lives of their own, and it often becomes a race to nail them down, before they wander off, or meander into untieable knots. I have found through experience that the best nail is a good story, something that pins [my ideas], squealing and squirming though they may be, firmly to the plot. It is then just a matter of helping them be what they want to be, to the best of my ability. I hope what I am able to find in the paper reflects the enjoyment I have had in the search."

Elliot, who makes his home in Otago, New Zealand, with his wife, Gillian, and their two daughters, works at a studio behind his home. From there he can easily visit the local school down the hill to try out his illustrations on the students there.

Biographical and Critical Sources

PERIODICALS

Junior Bookshelf, December, 1994, review of *Dragon Tangle,* p. 202.
Magpies, November, 1999, Frances Plumpton, "A Look at *One Hundred New Zealand Poems for Children.*"
Otago Daily Times (New Zealand), April 4, 2000, Charmain Smith, "Fantasy: Elliot Drawn to the Edge," p. B13.
Reading Times, November, 1999, review of *Sydney and the Seamonster,* p. 41.
School Librarian, November, 1994, Peter Andrews, review of *Dragon Tangle,* p. 145.

Autobiography Feature

Sylvia Louise Engdahl

1933-

As far back as I can remember I felt different from people around me. Perhaps that was one reason I chose to write about other worlds. It was not the main one—mainly I write about them because I believe the humanization of space is vitally important to the future of our species. But before talking about my books, I should tell something about my life.

I was born and grew up in Los Angeles, California, which is a place I never have liked and do not recall with nostalgia. My father, born in 1881, came to America from Sweden as a small child, but he had forgotten his Swedish heritage at the time I knew him and had no living relatives except a grown son and granddaughter from a previous marriage. He was a real estate salesman, only occasionally successful. My mother came from New England, and my grandmother, her mother, lived with us during most of my youth. I had no brothers or sisters other than my half brother, whom I seldom saw and thought of as an uncle. A second cousin, ten years older than I, was the one relative outside my immediate family that I knew well.

I never had anything in common with other children and didn't enjoy playing with them. My mother tells me I was a happy child so I must have seemed outwardly content, but I don't remember being happy often. On the other hand, I was rarely especially unhappy, either. I simply waited, in a sort of resigned way, to grow up, assuming that in the adult world life would really begin. It didn't turn out like that, of course, but I have done quite a few interesting things as an adult, whereas not much of interest happened during my school years.

I was bored by school. What I learned, I learned at home from my mother and from reading; school was mainly hours to live through, punctuated by moments of fierce anger at teachers who wanted me to participate in active games not only during Phys Ed periods, which I despised, but during recess. This I considered (and still consider, despite today's faddish idolization of "fitness") an intolerable injustice—I can remember hiding in the girls' room to get out of it. At that time it was thought very important to keep children who were poor readers and yet manually skilled from feeling inferior. The reverse, alas, was not true. I got no recognition for superior reading and writing ability, but all too much for my deficiency of physical coordination (I was the only child in kindergarten who couldn't skip) and my total lack of interest in physical activities, which arose in part from an inborn lack of energy that made all such activities exhausting for me. I did not feel inferior on this account, but I was given the impression that I ought to, and perhaps as a result learned very early to ignore the opinions of so-called authorities in other areas, too. I was never openly rebellious except in refusing to play ball games and to socialize with my peers; certainly I never told teachers or classmates that my views on most subjects didn't match those of society. But my inner convictions were always my own.

Outside school I had little companionship apart from that of my mother, who was, and remains, the chief personal influence on my life. Our tastes were similar, though as I grew up my specific interests became very

Sylvia Louise Engdahl

Sylvia Engdahl at age ten.

different from hers. Mother, who had been an English teacher and a little theater director, fostered my innate enthusiasm for reading, writing, and the world of ideas. Her marriage was an unhappy one, for my father liked none of these things (I cannot remember his ever opening a book or magazine) and she thus turned to me, much as I turned to her because I found no friends of my own age with compatible interests. Neither of us had any domestic inclinations; Mother kept house only because at the time she had no alternative. Had she told me when I was small that she disliked it, I would have helped more with the housework, but she made the mistake of trying to persuade me to learn such skills for my own future good, and I reacted against that right from the beginning. I had no desire to marry, raise children, or be a homemaker, though in those days it was assumed that a girl "naturally" would—and unlike my mother, I didn't believe one should do things merely because they were expected. When I was older I envisioned someday marrying for love, but the sad example of my parents' marriage had put me on guard against falling in love with anyone who did not share my intellectual interests and who had none of his own that I could admire. This, I believe, was fortunate, since I might otherwise have plunged rashly into a conventional life for which I was not at all suited.

The highlights of my younger years were our short summer vacations at Bass Lake, north of Los Angeles in the Sierra Nevada. We went there for the first time when I was ten, and ever since I've dated the beginning of my life from that trip; no earlier memory has any meaning for me. When I saw Bass Lake, I realized what was missing in Southern California, which I'd hitherto taken for granted. At Bass Lake trees cloaked the mountains and shoreline—forest trees, in this case Ponderosa pines, very unlike the cultivated trees found in Los Angeles. There was green forest undergrowth and clear, fresh air. And of course, there was the water. We rented a boat that first year; later on my father bought one, the only thing he ever did that I found enjoyable. I counted the days between our trips to Bass Lake, and during my teen years I was convinced that nothing could make me happier than to live there permanently. I even hoped I might someday get a job teaching the one-room school there.

I planned from earliest childhood to be a teacher. Even when I was so young as to enjoy dolls, I always imagined myself as "teacher" rather than "mother," and by the time I was eleven I was running a Saturday morning "nursery school" for neighborhood children. During my early teens I organized summer arts and craft classes through which I earned some spending money. What I really enjoyed was planning and being in charge, not the actual contact with children; but I was too young to realize that. Anyway, I preferred it to social contact with my agemates, of which I had little because I could not share the interests of other teens.

If I were a teenager today, it would be different. Today many teenagers are interested in computers, and I often think of what a social life I'd have had if I had grown up in such an era. When I phone electronic bulletin boards used largely by teens, I am reminded that had these existed during my own youth I would not have been isolated and lonely. In addition to having a natural bent for programming, I communicate better via a keyboard than in person, and would have done so even in adolescence. At that time it was assumed, even by me, that I could not talk because I was shy; but now I know that it was the other way around. I was shy because I could not talk easily, and I could not do so because I need visual feedback rather than audible feedback when expressing my ideas. I am a natural writer, and today natural writers are coming into their own socially via electronic mail and interactive computer conferencing. But of course, when I was in my teens, no one had heard of computers at all, let alone home computers.

So high school, like the earlier period, was merely a time of waiting for me. I kept busy with my own pursuits but had as little to do with school as possible. I didn't get particularly high grades because the classes didn't seem worth bothering with, and also because teachers often marked down students who didn't talk effectively, however well they did on written work. Still I met the requirements for graduation easily enough, and in fact met them in time to graduate a semester ahead of schedule—but the counselor wouldn't let me do it because I was "too young" and not "socially mature," by which she meant she thought I ought to participate in class activities. As usual, I was silently resentful, and not as assertive in fighting that decision as I now feel I should have been. I was indeed young, barely sixteen, but ironically my few friends happened to be in the class ahead. They graduated, while I was forced to remain without any classes of substance left to take (I hadn't been permitted to enroll in physics because I didn't plan a science major in college). I repeated Library Practice, which I enjoyed, and signed up for the class that produced the yearbook, ending up as Assistant Editor; I suppose this looked good on my record but it did not really involve much editing work.

The one school incident with lasting influence on my life happened when I was twelve, in a ninth-grade science class. It was there that I first heard about space. We were studying astronomy, which for a while captured my imagination; but more significantly, one day the teacher read aloud a short description of what it might be like to travel in space, and for some reason it excited me in a way nothing else ever had. I had not read any science fiction, and had never talked to anyone who knew of it; and of course this was in 1946, before space travel was widely discussed. Yet I went home that day and began drawing pictures of rockets on the way to Mars. A friend happened to be with me; I said to her—on the basis of no information or reading whatsoever—that I was willing to bet a spaceship would reach the moon within twenty-five years. As it turned out, I was just two years off, on the conservative side, in my wild estimate. I will never know what prompted it.

From then on I read whatever I could find about space, though I did not care for much of the science fiction I encountered. I was interested in what space travel and colonization of other planets might actually be like, not in wild adventure tales or stories designed to be as exotic and far-removed from real life as possible—and for this reason, I still don't consider myself a "science fiction fan." I honestly don't know why space fascinated me in those early years. It was before I had developed the convictions about its importance that have been so central to me since, and though it may seem as if, being a social misfit, I might understandably have daydreamed about some better world, that was not what happened. I didn't imagine alien societies. I simply thought about man's coming exploration of nearby planets. It never occurred to me to doubt that space travel would come.

The year I was sixteen, my life changed radically. My parents finally separated, and after I graduated from high school our house was sold; I moved with my mother and grandmother into an apartment while waiting for college to start in the fall. All these events were welcome. I had everything I thought I wanted—I had been accepted by Pomona College in Claremont, California, which I'd long planned to attend, deliberately avoiding the large universities to which other members of my class applied. I hated big cities, and Pomona seemed ideal. When I got there, however, I met exactly the same problems I'd had in high school: classes that were uninspiring and no social life of a kind that appealed to me. Furthermore, I found the company of dorm residents less congenial than that of my mother and the lack of privacy burdensome. I don't know what would have happened if I'd stayed. A further change, however, drove any thought of staying from my mind. My mother decided to get a master's degree in drama at the University of Oregon in Eugene. We went for a preliminary visit there during Christmas vacation, and after one look at Oregon I knew that under no circumstances would I be willing to be left behind in Southern California.

It seems strange to me now that I did not immediately enroll in the University of Oregon myself; but we still felt—probably because Mother was a Wellesley graduate—

that a small private college would have advantages, and though we didn't have much money, my grandmother had planned to pay my tuition. So I transferred to Reed College in Portland for the spring semester of my freshman year. When I didn't fit in there, either, we belatedly realized that for both financial and personal reasons I would be better off in Eugene. My sophomore year, I did attend the U of O. We lived in a small old-fashioned rented house on a tree-lined street near the campus; I still think of it with longing, though we have had many nicer homes since. It was different from anything I'd known in California, and in my eyes much to be preferred. I loved Oregon; I loved the tall firs and the greenness and the change of seasons, and even the steady soft rain. Then too, I was seventeen, and had left childhood and its scenes behind without yet having met any disillusionments of maturity.

This interlude couldn't last. Mother's degree program took only a year and a half, and there was nothing for her to do in Eugene afterwards. I didn't want to live in a dormitory despite my liking for the campus—which had turned out to be the best thing about the U of O from my standpoint. Then too, at that time no elementary teaching certificate was offered there, and I still believed I wanted to teach; so it was necessary to transfer again for my junior and senior years in any case. Mother planned to return to Los Angeles with my grandmother (who remained with us through all our moves until she died in 1965 at the age of 101). I was unwilling to go there, so I chose the nearby University of California at Santa Barbara, in part because it was the only place I could get a B.A. without foreign language courses, and whereas I'd been good at reading and writing languages in high school, my strongly visual mode of expression made me incapable of learning to speak them.

When at the beginning of my junior year we got back from a summer in the East, my father having died in the meantime, Mother decided to come to Santa Barbara too and start a theater group for children. We lived there two

With her parents and cousin at Bass Lake, 1946.

years. But after all my transfers I needed longer than that to get the required credits for a degree and teaching certificate. Mother was offered a directing job at the Portland Civic Theater—which, incidentally, she had directed long before in 1927-29—and I could not escape staying behind to finish up. I roomed off-campus, counting the days till I'd be in Oregon again. Fortunately I was able to visit during the winter to interview for teaching jobs, and managed to obtain one in the Portland area for the following fall.

All this time, I had remained firm in my conviction that teaching was the career I wanted, perhaps because I could think of no other, and also because I wanted the summers free for camp work. Summers had been the high spot of my college years, just as Bass Lake had highlighted the earlier era; I had worked as a camp counselor my first year in Oregon, and later in New York State, California, and best of all at Camp Sweyolakan on Coeur d'Alene Lake in Idaho, where I was a Unit Director during the summers of 1954 and 1955. Aside from its beauty, Sweyolakan was particularly enjoyable because I had opportunity to go on canoe trips—though my lack of physical energy kept me from doing much hiking at any of the camps and I spent my time teaching handcrafts and planning campfire programs, I found that paddling was far less tiring for me than walking. I will always cherish the memory of those trips on the water. Also, I liked organizing camp life, and dreamed of someday directing a camp of my own. The fact that being with children was becoming more and more nerve-wearing somehow escaped my attention.

When I found myself at last a fourth-grade teacher in a Portland suburb, however, my temperamental unfitness for the job became all too apparent. It was a disaster. I could tutor the children effectively on an individual basis, but I could not cope with them as a group, nor could I handle classroom discipline. As a matter of fact, I was asked to resign after the first year; but nothing could have induced me to continue in any case. I discovered that I really didn't like young children, even apart from the fact that I violently disagreed with the theories of education and psychology then in vogue: a fact that had made my college training merely something to be endured for the sake of the required certificate.

So I didn't know what to do. We had acquired a lovely old house on a hilltop in Portland where I was determined to remain, yet I had to earn a living, and I was not qualified for any job outside the field of education. I knew I could never teach at the high school or college level because I could not express ideas effectively aloud, and anyway I didn't want to specialize in a particular subject. I would have liked to be a librarian, but that would have meant two more years of expensive college training outside the state of Oregon, which did not offer a librarianship program. I couldn't do clerical work since my poor physical coordination made it impossible for me to type by the touch system (I still, after many years as a writer, use only two fingers on each hand in typing, which does not bother me but means I can't attain a typist's speed). By default, therefore—after a summer as Resident Camp Director at a Camp Fire Girls camp nearby—I began to work toward a Master of Education degree through night courses available in Portland, thinking this would enable me to become a school counselor.

Strangely, the year I spent on that graduate work proved one of the most fruitful of my life. The courses, which demanded little study, were even less inspiring than undergraduate Education courses; but they left me with a great many free hours at home, and for the first time I devoted deep thought to my ideas about space. Furthermore, I began to write them down. Unlike most authors, I had never written stories during my youth, other than a few unpublishable pieces of children's fiction about such things as Bass Lake and camp life. My creative ideas were abstract intellectual ones, not incidents for stories. It had never occurred to me to become a writer because I knew people didn't want to read philosophical tracts. But that one year, for reasons I still haven't been able to decipher, I did get ideas for stories, albeit stories of a quite offbeat sort that were not then marketable. Partial drafts of those that ultimately became my novels were all written then—and I haven't had an idea for a real story since! I only hope it will someday happen again.

Also during that year, I developed my beliefs about the importance of space to human survival; and that, of course, is something I've had a great many more ideas about since. I am by nature more of an analytical person than a storyteller. I can write endlessly about speculations concerning not only space but other subjects; but to express these in story form requires more than writing skill. It demands ideas not just about truths but about happenings. It demands not merely portrayal of characters, but the ability to visualize action in which those characters are involved—and that type of creativeness is not something that can be learned. Most writers have plenty of it; it's a faculty they start out with and must learn to channel. I, as in so many areas of life, am the opposite of most others; the analytical skills, those taught in writing courses, came naturally to me, but the story-creation faculty has arisen in me rarely.

I did try to put some of my ideas into short-story form that year of 1956-57, but they were not suitable for short stories and were of course rejected by the magazines to which I sent them. I never thought of making novels of them then. At that time such novels would not have been publishable; space was not yet a topic of general interest.

Among these stories was the one that later became *The Far Side of Evil*, based on the concept of the Critical Stage about which I was (and still am) entirely serious. Young people today may believe that worry about nuclear war is new, but it isn't—in 1956 it was a major concern. I thought to myself then, and attempted to say in the story, that planet Earth was indeed in a Critical Stage, that if we didn't turn our attention to space soon we would very likely be wiped out by a nuclear war. I saw no signs, unfortunately, that we were making any attempt to get into space. One of the most encouraging experiences I've ever had was hearing the very next year that Sputnik had been launched into orbit, making it impossible, I believed, for the setting of my story to be Earth. I still believed this when the novel was published in 1971; I assumed after the Apollo moon landing that Earth was fully committed and thus safely past the crisis. Now I am not so sure. Now I am nervous again when I see cutbacks in the space program, since evidently a planet can stay in the Critical Stage much longer than I first thought.

Sylvia with her grandmother Sarah Louise Butler, 1948.

In the spring of 1957, nearing the end of my graduate work and without hope of earning money through writing, I came to another turning point. I did not really want to be a school counselor, but I'd been putting off thinking about that problem. I had to go to summer school in Eugene in order to qualify for the degree. One day in May—the most fateful day of my life—I drove down to Eugene from Portland to make the arrangements. I talked to one of the professors there. And some casual remark I made suddenly opened my eyes to the futility of the whole plan. I was, I saw, a hypocrite! I was pretending to believe the officially-approved theories of Educational Psychology when I privately thought they were rubbish, and sooner or later I would be found out. Even if I went on pretending long enough to receive a degree in the field, I would despise working in it. To continue would be intolerable.

I barely managed to conclude the conversation with the professor, then, without registering for summer school, I numbly drove the 125 miles back to Portland. At home, not knowing what to do next, I picked up the nearest magazine and glanced through it; it was Mother's Wellesley alumnae magazine, something I never read. In it was an article about a young woman who was learning to program computers, which I skimmed with some interest, but did not connect in any way with everyday life—I'd heard of computers, I suppose, in science fiction, but didn't imagine that people not trained as scientists could experiment with them. Next,

I picked up the want-ad section of the newspaper. I'd never looked at that before either, since jobs in the education field aren't listed in classified ads. To my amazement, there was a box ad there for people to join the same computer programming project mentioned in the magazine article.

The project was the SAGE Air Defense System, then a new and unique concept, which was being developed by the Rand Corporation. Its recruiter was touring the country, stopping in Portland just that one day. The ad appeared in the paper that day only; I will never stop marveling at the uncanny series of coincidences that caused me to see it.

The qualifications mentioned in the ad were not too far from mine; more math courses than I'd taken were specified, but I had done well in math and thought it might be possible to catch up on my own. The listing appeared under "Help Wanted—Men" (in those days newspapers separated jobs by sex) but the magazine article had told me women were included. So I called the recruiter. They did hire women, he said, but his interview schedule was filled; I would have to go to see him late that night at his hotel. Dubious as this might otherwise have sounded, having read about the work in the Wellesley magazine convinced me that it was legitimate, and so I went. When I got there, he gave me a written aptitude test, then asked me to return for a second interview the next morning. And that morning I was hired on the spot. He told me he'd have accepted me the night before except that it was so obviously a sudden move on my part that he wanted me to think it over.

I didn't have to think long; I was twenty-three years old with no other prospect of employment, and though I had little idea what computer programming was, it sounded interesting. To be sure, it meant leaving Oregon, but my sorrow over that was overshadowed by the excitement of doing something entirely new. Also the salary offered me was astonishing—$400 a month, which in that era, by my standards, seemed like a fortune; it was far more than I had earned as a teacher. I later learned that many of the people hired for the project were former teachers. Now, computer programmers are trained in college; but there was no such thing as a college Computer Science department then. There were no programmers at all except a few mathematicians doing developmental work. SAGE was a large project and its staff had to be found among men and women with degrees in other fields. Our training was provided on the job.

At the end of June, 1957, I reported for work at Rand's SAGE headquarters in Lexington, Massachusetts. Since this was to be a temporary location and I had no idea where I'd be sent next—we were to be moved around the country to install the system at different Air Force bases—I rented a room in a private home; the most convenient location proved to be in Wellesley Hills, where Mother had lived many years before. The initial phase of training, to my surprise, was a formal course given by IBM on the MIT campus in Cambridge. I was nervous the first day, since I didn't have all the math prerequisites I'd been told would be expected, but it turned out that no math at all was needed. (Most kinds of programming do not involve mathematics; they'd specified math background only because people with math aptitude are likely to also have programming aptitude.) I found programming easy and loved it right from the start. How strange it seemed to be paid a salary for attending a class much more interesting than any I'd had in college! My free time was filled with more activities than in the past, too, since I had a car, a whole new region of the country to explore, and classmates to take trips with on weekends. That summer was one of the happiest of my life.

I'll never forget my first look at the computer. Computers in those days were not at all like what they are today—the one used for SAGE, the IBM ANFS-Q7 (called simply the Q7 for short) filled several rooms. In Lexington we had access only to an experimental prototype located at MIT's Lincoln Laboratory. Since a great many people had to share it besides trainees, our brief computer time during the course was scheduled at three o'clock in the morning. Our government security clearances hadn't come through yet, so we had to wait in a locked classroom while pairs of students were escorted to the computer room to try out short programs. These programs were of course written in assembly language, the only computer language that yet existed for non-mathematical applications (besides binary machine language, which we also learned). The Q7 didn't have a keyboard as personal computers now do; to communicate with it, you had to put a deck of punched cards into the card reader. Then, after the program was assembled, you got a deck of binary cards out of the automatic punch machine and put them into the card reader in turn. In later years these operations became very familiar to me, though later, we used magnetic tape rather than cards for most program assemblies. But that first night it all seemed mysterious and exciting.

To modern computer users it might seem mysterious still, for the Q7 had a room-wide "front panel" of flashing lights. If you knew machine language, you could read the contents of CPU and memory registers in these lights; that's how debugging was done. The computer room was dimly lit so the lights could be easily seen; the adjacent room containing consoles with air defense displays was called the Blue Room because its dim light was blue. There were still more rooms filled with frames of vacuum tubes. Yet despite its immense array of hardware, the Q7 had only an 8K memory! It seemed ample to us, and several years later, when it was expanded to 64K, we thought that was phenomenal. Now [1987] the computer on my own desk, on which I'm writing this article, has a memory ten times that large (though it's not quite a fair comparison because it stores less information per address than the Q7 did). There has been a lot of progress in the past thirty years. Yet I still feel affection for the old Q7 and in some ways I rather miss it. It did its job well; the reason it could handle air defense surveillance with so little memory was that in those days we used programming techniques more efficient, from the machine language standpoint, than those now commonly employed.

When my training was finished, I was sent, somewhat ironically, to Santa Monica, California, a part of greater Los Angeles near where I'd grown up; but since that too was to be temporary, I didn't object. In the summer of 1958 I was transferred to Madison, Wisconsin, and in 1959 to Tacoma, Washington. I had my own apartment in each of these places and enjoyed the variety of moving to different areas, but my life centered on my job.

Most of my work was not with the air defense program itself, but with programs of the type now called systems software. SAGE was a real-time system, the most advanced of its era. At the field locations, I had a lot of time to operate the computer personally, since there were only a few programmers at each Air Force base and the computers (which we weren't allowed to touch except for their front panel switches) needed to be kept busy continuously to break them in. So I became an expert on systems software of the sort—primitive by today's standards—that existed then, and had a chance to develop some of what was used. In 1960 I was transferred back to Santa Monica on a permanent basis; that was the home office of SDC, for which I had worked since it separated from its parent company Rand. It was the place where I would have the most opportunity to do developmental programming, so I wanted to be there; moreover, Mother had left Portland and was living in Santa Barbara again. It did not seem that I would ever have an opportunity to return to Oregon.

I sometimes see it said, even today, that there is prejudice against women in technical fields like computer science. That strikes me as strange, since I never encountered any, and if it is now true, then SDC must have been an exception. There were relatively few women among the SAGE programmers, but I certainly received raises and promotions as fast as the men did, and I never went out of my way to seek them. I was the first female Unit Head in my group, but nobody seemed to think that was any big deal. By 1965 I ranked as a Computer Systems Specialist. I didn't want to get away from programming into a wholly supervisory job, for which I wasn't temperamentally fitted; so in lieu of line promotion I became a Technical Assistant

College senior portrait, 1954.

to the Group Head and was Project Head for design and development of a major experimental change in the program organization of SAGE. Also, I did more and more technical writing—I liked it and was good at it, which is the exception rather than the rule among programmers. Though the normal procedure was to use a secretary, I convinced my boss that I could neither write drafts by hand nor dictate, and was thus entitled to have a typewriter in my own office. How much more I could have produced with a word processor, something then not even dreamed of!

There were problems with this situation, though. In the first place, writing began to take me away from programming. Furthermore, what I wrote was either classified (secret) or proprietary, so that I couldn't show it to anybody outside the company. And I began to feel that if I was going to write most of the time I would like to do it in a form that would appear publicly under my name. I did not have energy to do writing of my own in my off-hours, as many authors do; one full-time job was all I could manage without collapsing from fatigue. In the evenings I could do no more than read. Strangely, I didn't even think much about space during those years, pleased though I was by the manned missions of the early sixties. I suppose underneath I avoided it because I wasn't personally involved in the space effort. Many programmers worked on Gemini and Apollo, but I was neither energetic nor assertive enough to seek a new job and in any case, neither Florida nor Houston was a place we wanted to live.

By this time, Mother and I were sharing a home; for a while we'd had a very pleasant one with a swimming pool in the San Fernando Valley, but after my grandmother's death we moved closer to Santa Monica because we preferred its climate and because commuting in rush hour traffic, which took longer and longer, tired me too much. Despite our new home's high-priced locale and ocean view, I wasn't happy there. I didn't mind my lack of social life, since that of my office acquaintances appeared to revolve around sports and/or drinking, neither of which was my idea of fun; still my days seemed increasingly monotonous. My salary had enabled us to take wonderful vacations, including two to Europe—but these were somewhat shadowed by the fact that I was no better able to stay on my feet in Europe than anywhere else. I wanted freedom to travel at a more leisurely pace. Mother, for her part, was nearing seventy and found she didn't want to be home alone all day while I worked, whereas I didn't want to share our home with a housekeeper as had been necessary during the many years when my grandmother couldn't be left alone.

Above all, I was homesick for Oregon; yet I had too much seniority to switch to the type of programming job then available in Portland. For the first time I seriously considered trying to write professionally. Mother's income, we thought, had become more than ample for us to live on indefinitely (we didn't foresee what inflation would do to it). Although once I'd have been unwilling to give up programming, my job didn't involve much actual programming any more. Among the other difficulties I was being sent on business trips—for example, to talk with some Air Force officers at an underground installation in North Bay, Canada—and I found such assignments physically exhausting; yet I felt that to refuse them would mean the loss of my

program design responsibilities. All in all, it seemed the time for another change was at hand.

I had worked as a programmer for almost exactly ten years when, in May of 1967, I came back to Oregon to stay. We bought another house in Portland—the first of several homes we've since had here—and I began to write novels. I didn't look on writing as a career in the income-production sense, for I knew that very few authors earn a living from their books (and as it turned out, even the most successful of mine never brought in enough money for me to do that). It's important to make this plain, because I wouldn't want aspiring writers to assume that one can quit a job thinking that publication of books like mine will provide support. I had no such illusions; I simply wanted to share some of my ideas. One reason I'd begun to feel I could publish in the young adult field was that Mother had recently begun to write for young people herself. Her second and best-known book, *Twice Queen of France*, was published that same spring (under her maiden name, Mildred Allen Butler). I thought that if she could do it, then, maybe, so could I.

I wrote *Journey Between Worlds* first. I felt it would appeal to readers of romances for girls, and I wanted very much to make teenage girls aware of how important the colonization of space is to mankind's future. I deliberately did *not* direct the book to science fiction fans. One such person wrote to me once, saying rather indignantly that I should have known no science fiction enthusiast could sympathize with a young woman who *did not want* to go to Mars—and of course I did know that! The idea was to reach girls who don't ordinarily like science fiction. Unfortunately, in many places the book never did reach them because librarians put it on the "science fiction" shelf instead of the "romance" shelf. (I'd be happy if any librarians reading this would please go and move it right now.) Where it got into the hands of its intended audience, however, it was well liked. One of my happiest experiences as a writer was having a librarian tell me my book had convinced her that the space program really is worthwhile.

All this was quite a bit later, though. I submitted *Journey Between Worlds* to several publishers, all of which rejected it, and in the meantime I wrote *Enchantress from the Stars*. I didn't feel *Enchantress* would ever be publishable—it wasn't the sort of book that could appear as an adult novel (though I felt some adults would like it) yet it was over the heads of most readers below teenage and seemed far too long and complex to be called a children's book, at least by the standards of the fifties and sixties. But the story took hold of me and I simply couldn't leave it alone. I would forget all the rules, I decided, and amuse myself with something that didn't fit any market while I waited for *Journey Between Worlds* to find a publisher; I couldn't submit a new manuscript while that was unsettled in any case.

When *Enchantress from the Stars* was finished, though, I found I couldn't bear not to have it read by anyone. I put *Journey* away and submitted *Enchantress* instead, after learning that at least a few publishers of junior books would consider manuscripts of its length. I sent it to Atheneum because they had published the longest children's book I could find in the library, and also because the editor's taste appeared compatible with mine. This proved to be a good guess; the book was accepted, after some revision, and went on to be a Junior Literary Guild selection and a Newbery Honor Book. I was fortunate in having written it just at a time when a trend toward issuing more mature fiction as "young adult" was beginning. For of course, *Enchantress* was never intended for preadolescent children, and its Newbery Honor status was therefore somewhat misleading.

I have never written a novel for children—unless one considers teenagers "children," which personally I don't—and it bothers me somewhat to be known as a writer of children's books. This doesn't mean I don't admire the gift of people who are able to work in that field; I'd be much better off professionally if I possessed it. But I, after all, didn't identify with children even while I was a child myself, and have never understood them or their activities well enough to write about them. The characters in my novels are all in late adolescence or older.

The reason I mind being classed with children's authors is that it tends to prevent my books from being found by the majority of readers most apt to like them. Teenagers do not consider *themselves* children, after all. Comparatively few of them visit the children's rooms of libraries. The larger libraries shelve extra copies of my novels in their young adult or adult collections; that's where teenagers are most likely to come across them. There are, to be sure, a few teen library users who know not all books in the children's room are beneath them, and a few advanced readers below teenage for whom my books aren't too mature. By and large, however, the "junior" label limits my audience, especially by keeping my books out of high school libraries, where I feel they'd reach more young people.

This labeling of books by age group does a great deal of damage, I think, except in the case of those meant for preadolescent readers. The reason for it is solely commercial; it arises from the structure of the publishing business. The "children's book" departments of publishers issue young adult novels because of the way books are marketed, not because there's any good reason for fiction directed toward older teens to be branded as different from adult fiction. This is not to say that editors of children's books, such as my own editor, Jean Karl, have not done a fine job with novels appropriate for high school age or that they shouldn't be the ones to edit them—but they should be allowed, I feel, to do so without having such novels categorized as being on the "juvenile" side of a firm dividing line in literature. Even Library of Congress catalog numbering marks this division! Worse yet, because children's libraries are patronized mainly by children, books for younger readers usually sell better than those that demand more maturity; and consequently publishers' sales departments often list a novel as being for a lower age group than the author had in mind. This can backfire. Some of my novels were criticized by reviewers for being "too difficult for ages 10-14," a judgment with which I wholeheartedly agreed.

With *Enchantress from the Stars* this problem was not as serious as with my later novels, since it could indeed be enjoyed by many readers of junior-high age. But *Enchantress* was given by teachers even to fifth and sixth graders; I was often asked to talk to those grades, and got letters from

Mother, Mildred Butler Engdahl, 1965.

children who'd evidently read the book as a school assignment without having the slightest notion of what it was all about. I found this very frustrating. To me, a story's plot incidents are not what matter; they were what I always found hardest to think of, and such action scenes as I managed to put in (usually long after the first draft of the rest) were a real struggle to write. The ideas in the story, plus the thoughts and feelings of the characters, were what inspired me, and in most cases these could be absorbed only by introspective older teens.

Adult readers, on the other hand—having less of a Space Age outlook than teenagers—didn't all grasp what *Enchantress* was about either. To my dismay, some of them didn't realize it dealt literally with relationships between peoples of different worlds. They assumed it was an allegory about our own world not merely in its portrayal of human feelings, but in a specific political sense; they thought that in saying an advanced interstellar civilization shouldn't try to help less advanced ones, I was saying Americans shouldn't give technological aid to undeveloped nations. I never meant that at all; people of different nations on this planet are all members of the same human race, the same species. Whether highly evolved species can help those younger than themselves is another issue entirely. *Enchantress from the Stars* was intended to counter the "Gods from Outer Space" concept, the growing idea, especially prevalent among young people, that UFOs may come here and solve all Earth's problems for us. I simply don't believe that's how advanced interstellar civilizations act; I feel, as my novels explain, that it would be harmful to young species and that they know that. As I recall, I got tired of seeing Captain Kirk violate his Federation's nominal noninterference policy in *Star Trek,* and that was what prompted me to create a Federation that lived up to its own code.

It's tempting, of course, to hope that one will be contacted by people from the stars, especially if one doesn't quite fit into society on this planet—and I suspect that dream is more common among the young than adults suppose. In my own late teens I indulged in it at times, very secretly, because there was no *Star Trek* or *Close Encounters* then and no one I knew was interested in space and I thought the wish for contact must be unique to my special form of imagination. A few years ago I heard a rock singer express the same wish in lyrics about a girl in a bar who longed to be taken aboard the "silvery ship" she was sure must be overhead. Evidently it is a universal longing. But I don't think we should let it shape our view of the universe, because it's a lot more constructive to assume we of Earth are going to have to solve our own world's problems.

Do I really believe interstellar civilizations exist? I've often been asked that, and the answer is that I do, though I don't believe we are going to have any proof of it before we build starships of our own to explore with. But of course I don't think inhabitants of other solar systems are as much like our species as they are shown to be in my fiction. Actually I rarely describe what they look like—partly because I'm not good at physical descriptions, but partly, too, because I want to leave readers free to imagine the characters as being like themselves. (In *Enchantress from the Stars,* for instance, I hoped black readers would picture Elana as black, and I've often wondered if any of them did.) This, I think, is just as accurate as making up weird descriptions for them would be; we haven't the faintest idea what alien races look like, so why not portray them in a way that makes them easy to identify with? To me it's the same form of literary license as writing the dialogue in English when we know that alien beings don't speak English: it's necessary for the sake of the audience. Few science fiction fans agree with me about this, but many people who don't like other science fiction say they like mine, and I feel this is one reason why.

Alien cultures aren't as much like ours as those in my books, either. And in fact, all the cultures in *Enchantress from the Stars* were purposely portrayed in an unrealistic, stylized way. This was something else a lot of adult readers didn't understand. They saw that part of the book was told in fairy-tale style, and though they knew medieval cultures were not just like those in fairy tales, they recognized this as a literary device—which, if they were folklore enthusiasts, they enjoyed. Surprisingly, a lot of the same people said the culture of the invaders in the book was "stereotyped!" Indeed it was, deliberately so; real interstellar invaders would no more behave like comic-book villains with ray guns than real medieval heroes went around looking for dragons to slay. (This might have been clearer if my original Foreword had been printed intact, but that, like a number of other passages in *Enchantress* and a good deal of the punctuation, was altered by Atheneum without my knowledge, and it wasn't possible to fix everything after the book was in galleys—something I've always regretted. Though I'm glad to revise my work repeatedly, I

do not believe any author's wording should be changed without his or her approval.)

Even the very advanced culture in *Enchantress from the Stars,* the Federation, was not shown realistically. How could it have been? I don't know what the day-to-day life of people belonging to interstellar civilizations is like, but I'm fairly sure it's not like Elana's—in particular, a society composed of people possessing spectacular psychic powers would have to be very different and, from our standpoint, incomprehensible. Yet I believe that species more advanced than our own do possess such powers, and perhaps could awaken them in exceptional individuals of younger worlds. That, in fact, was the portion of the story I started with, the part conceived in 1957. Though its premise is classed with "magic" by today's science, the book wasn't meant to be fantasy in the sense that tales of magical worlds are fantasy. Rather, it was based on mythology (which is something quite different from fantasy)—not just traditional mythology, but that of our own age. At the time I wrote it, I didn't fully appreciate the extent to which interstellar travelers with telepathic and psychokinetic powers are a contemporary myth; I was inclined to believe in their literal existence. Now I recognize that our current conceptions of advanced civilizations are much further from reality than fairy tales are from history. Nevertheless, I think the underlying ideas of the book, and of my subsequent ones, are valid.

When I finished writing *Enchantress from the Stars* (and had revised *Journey Between Worlds,* by then also accepted by Atheneum) I went ahead with *The Far Side of Evil.* It fit naturally into the same Federation setting as *Enchantress,* though my original story about the Critical Stage, which involved only Randil's role, was set on Earth. I've sometimes been asked why the book's conclusion didn't reveal the key to the Critical Stage for which the Federation was searching: the reason why some worlds conquer space while others fail to, and blow themselves up in a nuclear war. My reply has always been that if I *knew* the key, I'd tell the President of the United States instead of putting it in a novel! For some reason this seems to surprise people; they don't realize that I believe the Critical Stage is real. More disturbingly, some, again, thought the book was about politics instead of about space; they assumed I used a space story as a vehicle for political statements when in fact, it was the other way around: I used political melodrama as a vehicle for ideas about the importance of space exploration. I would like to think that readers of the book have found these ideas convincing, because they become more and more relevant to our world's situation with each passing year. It frightens me when I hear people say we should solve the problems on Earth before we devote money and effort to leaving it. I do not believe they *can* be solved as long as our species is confined to a single planet. The natural course of evolution is for all successful species to expand to new ecological niches, and space is the one awaiting us. Attempts to postpone that destiny can lead only to disaster, for us and for all other life here on our home world.

My last remaining story draft was the one that became the foundation for *This Star Shall Abide,* which eventually turned into a trilogy. My previous novels had been written mainly from young women's viewpoints, and had been praised for that reason by people who'd noticed the lack of space stories for girls. (Though there are quite a few of these now, *Enchantress from the Stars* was the first science fiction novel with a female protagonist to be issued as young adult.) But I wanted to try something different, and in any case, the society in which the new novel was to be set was not one in which an adolescent girl would act as the plot required. It was a society that had regressed from its former state; the very sexism of its people was typical of their backward attitudes about a lot of other things—a point that somehow escaped feminists who later criticized the book and its sequel for portraying a sexist culture. So my main character was necessarily a boy, and he became very real to me, which was not surprising since Noren, more than any of my other characters, had a personality like mine. He viewed life as I had always viewed it: as a loner and a heretic. In my own case this had never been a very dramatic stance, but our society is not as bad as Noren's, and I had not been forced to choose, as he was, between unjustifiable conformity and persecution. I can't be sure that I would have acted as Noren did if I'd been born into his world, but I know I would have wanted to.

At the time *This Star Shall Abide* was written, the issue of youthful heresy was a major one in America, so I believed teenage readers would sympathize with him. Young people seemed a great deal more serious-minded than they had been during my own youth. To be sure, I felt that many of the causes to which they were devoting themselves were misguided, and that their methods of protest were often neither justified nor effective—I would not have felt at home in the counterculture of the sixties. Still, the young had begun to *care* about the world, and that in itself was progress. It's better to care and make mistakes than not to care; both *The Far Side of Evil* and *This Star Shall Abide* dealt with that theme. In both there was real evil to fight, and in both, a young man's sincere effort to oppose it turned out to be based on false premises: the point being that it's right to defy authority for the sake of one's conscience, yet necessary to take responsibility if one's view of the situation proves inaccurate. But in Noren's case deeper issues were involved. The original theme of the story concerned heresy not in the political but in the religious sense, and this facet of it became more and more central to me as the books developed.

I had never been an overtly religious person; my parents were not churchgoers, and though I'd taught Sunday School for a while during my high school years, I'd given it up because it made me feel hypocritical. I didn't believe the teachings of any church literally, and at that time I knew of no other way to view them. That myth *is* true—that the underlying idea is more significant than the words and imagery through which it's expressed—was something I came to understand slowly over a long period of years. I didn't connect it specifically with religion at first. Even when I based *Enchantress from the Stars* on that theme, I wasn't conscious of the fact that I was saying something about religious symbolism. Then, later, when I read *Enchantress* over after publication, it dawned on me that I had unknowingly written a strong defense of religious views I'd long rejected. To this day I don't know if anybody else interpreted the book that way.

At that time, I had been ill for some months and was very depressed. Though my condition was not medically serious, I was not only too lacking in physical energy to do even what little had previously been possible for me, but had lost all desire and enthusiasm for such things as travel. I could write—and often did write ten hours a day—but leaving the house for more than brief errands brought on nervous exhaustion. Intellectually I was thrilled by the publication of my books, but emotionally I could feel no joy in that or anything else; my optimistic view of the universe did not extend to my private life. In desperation, I began to attend church, looking for some anchor in the dark sea that was engulfing me. For the first time I found the ritual meaningful—not because my beliefs had changed, but because I now recognized it as an expression of what I'd believed all along.

This was the period from which *This Star Shall Abide* and its sequel *Beyond the Tomorrow Mountains* emerged. Originally, I tried to tell the story in just one volume, but its structure was all wrong. When my editor didn't find it convincing, I soon realized why: a lot of important things were still in my mind instead of on paper. So I expanded it to two and received a contract for both before the second was even partially written. Revising the first volume was merely a matter of removing an anticlimactic chapter from the end and adding a lot more detail in the portrayal of the planet's society; that completed the novel as I'd first conceived it, the part I already had a plot for. But it didn't finish Noren's story, not even the love story to which readers would naturally want a conclusion, and my editor felt that it didn't make the reasons for the inescapably bad situation on the planet clear enough. I agreed; moreover, by this time some of Noren's later conflicts had become more crucial to me than his initial rebellion.

Presenting these conflicts in a way meaningful to young readers—or for that matter, to any readers at all—proved tremendously difficult. I didn't yet have a plot, at least not in the sense of the action. I knew how Noren's outlook would change but I hadn't any idea what events would bring this about; thinking of them was a year-long struggle. Furthermore, *Beyond the Tomorrow Mountains* dealt more explicitly with religion than was customary in the young adult field. The old taboos concerning sex and politics had fallen, but judging from the books I saw, I feared religion might still be off-limits, if not to my publisher, then perhaps to reviewers and book-buyers. I thought I might offend some readers by suggesting that a religion unlike any on this planet could be valid to its adherents, and went out of my way in an Author's Note to make plain that the colonists in the story were not descendants of Earth people. To my surprise, I later encountered adults who did not realize that the novel was really about religion! It didn't mention God by name, so they apparently went on thinking of the faith depicted in the way Noren did initially, as no more than a feat of social engineering. But in my eyes, his ultimate commitment to a priest's role was genuine.

This Star Shall Abide was well received, and won a Christopher Award for "affirmation of the highest values of the human spirit." Despite good reviews *Beyond the Tomorrow Mountains* was less successful; the majority of those who evaluated it by young-adult criteria considered it too heavy and slow-moving, and my British publisher refused to accept it. (They had not liked the religious aspect of even the first volume and had insisted on changing its title to remove any suggestion of religious content—not because of a taboo, but because they felt, probably with justification, that religion doesn't appeal to average science fiction fans.) Then too, some reviewers objected to the plot climax, calling it *deus ex machina* as if I'd been unable to think of any better way to save Noren than to drag in an improbable coincidence. There was much irony in this, since though I do indeed have trouble thinking up plot incidents, in this case the unforeseeable nature of Noren's rescue was entirely deliberate. That was the *point*—sometimes one must have faith in an improbable outcome. That was what awakened Noren's faith in the still more improbable salvation of his endangered people. But the book was not an action-adventure story, and those looking for excitement didn't like its departures from action-adventure story rules.

Beyond the Tomorrow Mountains was primarily a psychological story. The younger readers had no comprehension of Noren's emotions, especially during his period of what one reviewer aptly called "existential anxiety"— still I remained firm in my conviction that older adolescents would identify with them. I got confirmation that some did when one day a teenage girl approached me in a library and remarked appreciatively, "Noren really tripped out, didn't he?" So much for the prevalent theory that action-adventure is what science fiction for young people has to focus on.

After publication of the second volume, some people felt the story still wasn't complete; they told me I should write another sequel in which Noren succeeded in saving his people. I resisted this idea, since only in action-adventure fiction is it credible for a hero to single-handedly

With Mother reading galley proofs, 1969.

save the world. The book was about faith in the face of impossible odds, and that theme would be overridden if I altered the odds to the extent of saying that even during Noren's lifetime, they hadn't been so impossible after all. Besides, I'd done such a thorough job of making them impossible that I couldn't think of a way out myself—and knew that even if I could, that would weaken the justification for the planet's social system, which was an evil defensible only on the basis of its offering the sole means of temporary survival.

Years later, however, something happened that changed my mind. I got interested in the new field of genetic engineering, and learned to my dismay that the system on Noren's world really *wasn't* the sole means of survival! I'd honestly believed it was, since I'd been ignorant of genetics, but I was ignorant no longer and had just published a nonfiction book on the subject; what if people thought I'd known all along? I couldn't let them assume I had let Noren endorse a morally objectionable system on false grounds. And so I wrote *The Doors of the Universe,* and once I got into it, I could scarcely believe that I hadn't envisioned Noren's story as a trilogy in the first place.

It was truly uncanny the way things fit together. Details that just happened to have been mentioned in the earlier volumes looked like "plants" for essential premises of the new book. Moreover, in the new volume I had a chance to emphasize the theme, implicit in the earlier ones, of the tragedy that can result if a civilization turns its back on a promising technology—something I feel very strongly about. And I brought in connections with the themes of my books about the Federation. All this came easily (though as usual, I had trouble thinking of events through which Noren actually *could* reach his goal and was stalled in the middle for over a year without any more notion of the solution than he had). So now, the conclusion of *Beyond the Tomorrow Mountains* does indeed seem incomplete to me, which for a middle volume of a trilogy is entirely proper. I hope that young people who grew up during the interval between publication of the second and third volumes have found that the third exists, though in most cases this is unlikely; the story really is much better when read as a whole.

The Doors of the Universe got excellent reviews but was not widely distributed because by then the library market was diminishing, and, dealing as it did with Noren as an adult, it was much too heavy for average readers of young people's fiction. Genetic engineering being a timely topic, I hoped it would go into paperback even if the whole trilogy did not, but Atheneum did not succeed in selling the reprint rights.

My greatest disappointment as a writer has been the lack of mass-market paperback editions of my novels. This is a matter not so much of money (though by now I surely need the money) but of the fact that many teenagers prefer paperbacks. Science fiction readers in particular don't all have access to, or opportunity to use, public libraries; I've talked to some on electronic bulletin boards who'd like to read my books, yet cannot get copies. I would have a far larger audience, particularly for the trilogy—which unlike some of my books, did not appear even in children's paperback form—if it were available on racks where science fiction is sold. Yet according to Atheneum, my novels were repeatedly offered to reprint houses and turned down. It was not because they were originally issued as young adult novels—I think I'm the only author of teenage science fiction whose books had success in hardcover and yet were not picked up for mass-market reprint. I was told it was because they hadn't enough action, that they were considered "too difficult" even for average adults. Possibly so; but I think a larger factor was the restrictive categorization of the paperback field.

Under the current marketing system, a mass-market paperback line must be labeled either "general audience" or "science fiction"—there is no common ground between the two. Books about other worlds are not issued in "general audience" lines. Yet my novels don't appeal to typical SF fans; I don't slant them that way. A science fiction writer once told me that in order to do so I would have to direct them to people who have read at least 500 other science fiction novels previously! Such readers are looking for far-out material that I wouldn't be able to imagine even if I wanted to, and I don't want to. I write for those, adults as well as teens, who care about the real world and its relation to the rest of the universe.

Once *Beyond the Tomorrow Mountains* had gone to the typesetter, I had no other story idea. But I did have something else in mind. I wanted to try nonfiction. Especially, I wanted to write about what people have thought in the past about other worlds: not science fiction authors, but scientists, philosophers, and average citizens. Radio astronomers were then implying, and in some cases saying, that their belief in the existence of other inhabited solar systems was something new; but I was aware that this view of history was a limited one. The philosopher Giordano Bruno was burned at the stake in the year 1600 for holding to such ideas. And if a conviction that we're not alone in the universe goes back that far—if it's not an invention of science fiction at all—then surely that is an important fact. Perhaps it reveals something of what people instinctively sense to be true.

Ordinary history books don't tell the facts about things like views of extrasolar worlds; only a few specialized scholars know them. None of these scholars had written about the subject in detail—the information was to be found only in actual writings of the past. I had never done scholarly research before, but I soon became fascinated with it. I ended up spending an entire year searching the writings of well-known people who lived in the seventeenth, eighteenth and nineteenth centuries, plus a lot of magazines printed in those centuries. Portland's libraries didn't have all I wanted to see, and I thought with regret of the lost years in Southern California, where I'd lived near many great libraries without ever using them for research purposes. I sent for a few crucial books via interlibrary loan, obtaining them from cities in the East as well as California, often finding them so frail from disuse that they fell apart in my hands. And what I learned was that the educated people of those centuries almost *all* believed that other inhabited solar systems exist. Benjamin Franklin and Thomas Jefferson did. The majority of clergymen did. In the nineteenth century, the few writers who argued against the idea were considered dissenters.

These facts are still not generally known. My collection of Xeroxed sources on the subject provided material

Rick Roberson, coauthor and coeditor, with advance copy of Anywhere, Anywhen, *1976.*

not merely for a young people's book, but for a long scholarly one—which I still intend to write when I have opportunity. I have found that both my writing style and my approach to ideas are far better suited to scholarly writing than to anything else, and that that's the type of work I normally find most fulfilling. I've since gathered material for a number of other scholarly books on different subjects, and have enough ideas to last for the rest of my life. Scholarly writing, however, is not usually publishable unless it's the work of a college professor or other recognized authority. It remains to be seen whether any of the projects I'm working on will ever appear in print.

During 1973, I wrote *The Planet-Girded Suns: Man's View of Other Solar Systems,* which was publishable when a scholarly book would not have been. I did my best to make it understandable to young readers; it was revised many times at the request of Atheneum, and was eventually accepted and well reviewed. However, it was actually neither one thing nor the other—not scholarly, though it presented material that popular-level adult books don't include, and yet much too difficult reading for average teens. It was interesting to some because the subject of other worlds is interesting, but on the whole I am unable to explain complicated ideas in a way that appeals to large audiences. I hoped, because adult books about extraterrestrial intelligence were then popular, that *The Planet-Girded Suns* would have a better chance than the novels at paperback publication, but paperback houses showed no interest in it. Perhaps this was because, in the section about modern scientific beliefs, I didn't endorse the existence of UFOs.

There followed a period of years during which I tried desperately to write yet could not produce any fiction. Several times I thought I had the basis for a new novel, but despite interesting themes and settings I proved unable to think of events. Unlike the situation of authors who experience "writer's block," this was not a matter of having trouble putting words on paper, or of producing things that weren't good. I couldn't write narrative at all because I had no incidents or images in mind to describe, but I wrote thousands of words, constantly, about abstract ideas, often in long letters to friends. At the time I felt I *should* write more novels because I'd assumed I would keep on doing so, and Atheneum was waiting for one; it seemed terrible not to take advantage of that opportunity. Apart from liking to publish I was beginning to need income; Mother's no longer went so far because of inflation, yet I couldn't work outside my home because her health was poor and she needed me. So for a long time I kept struggling. But I've since come to realize that the mystery is not why I could no longer write fiction, but why I'd ever been able to do it in the first place. Most people with analytical minds (the kind now called "left-brain dominant") never can.

One of the friends I wrote long letters to was a young man named Rick Roberson, who lived in Tennessee. He'd first written to me when he was sixteen, and just the type of teen reader toward whom I'd directed my books—he grasped what was in them and identified with the characters more than anyone else I knew. Rick and I went on corresponding because we were both seriously interested in space and the future, and neither of us had other friends who were. Also, he had writing talent. The year he entered college and I had no book ready to publish, science fiction anthologies for young people were needed, and it occurred to me that between us we could produce one. I had little background even as a reader in the SF short-story field, but Rick did, and he knew what young people liked. We mailed stories we found back and forth to each other and enjoyed discussing them; then Rick wrote the introductions and I handled the business of obtaining permission to reprint them. This became the anthology *Universe Ahead.* Rick wrote a story for the book, and when we became desperate to fill a remaining "slot" I produced one myself, which I was able to write only because I based it on his ideas and which therefore appeared under both our names.

I found I liked editing. The next year Rick wrote another story and I asked some of my other friends, all published authors, to do so also for a new anthology, *Anywhere, Anywhen,* which contained only fiction that hadn't been printed before. Again, I co-authored a story, this time with my mother. Sadly, Mother's career in writing for young people had come to an abrupt end when book markets changed so that her special interest—history—was no longer an acceptable topic; it was felt that teenagers weren't interested in history. (After four books for Funk & Wagnalls she had had a new one accepted by Harcourt Brace, only to have the new management there decide not to issue it despite their loss of the advance already paid.) Finding it hard to believe young people couldn't see the relevance in history, I adapted one of Mother's historical narratives into a time-travel story that we felt made that relevance plain. I don't know if readers of *Anywhere, Anywhen* agreed or not. In any case the book was not successful, largely because it was usually passed to science fiction specialists for review. Naturally, such specialists didn't like it; everything in it was "old hat" to them, since it had been deliberately designed to appeal to people in the children's literature field who don't care for typical science fiction anthologies. Hardly anyone, though, recognizes the wide gap in taste that exists between genre-oriented SF fans

and other readers, or that efforts to bridge that gap are not welcomed by the specialists.

In the summer of 1976 Rick Roberson came to Portland and stayed with us while attending summer school at Portland State University. His college major was physics, and I felt that there would be interest in a children's book about the exciting new discoveries being made in high-energy physics. I wouldn't have ventured to write nonfiction on such a subject alone, since I knew nothing whatsoever about it; but together we produced *The Subnuclear Zoo.* Then the next year, Rick started to write a similar book about genetic engineering, a subject in which he was also knowledgeable—but as it turned out, he didn't have time to finish it, so we co-authored that one also: *Tool for Tomorrow.* Atheneum wanted these books to be for younger readers than my previous ones, and I tried very hard to comply. Nevertheless, I wasn't able to achieve a style appropriate for sixth graders. That being where the major market was, neither book did well, though they both got some good reviews.

I tried a picture book. While working as a science consultant for a textbook literature series, I discovered that there weren't any picture books about space, and I felt that even very young children were aware of space from television and movies. So I wrote *Our World Is Earth.* Ironically, that book was assumed by reviewers to be for *older* readers than I intended! (Some of them said it was too elementary to appeal to the first and second grades, which of course it was; I'd meant it to be read aloud to preschoolers.) I tried other nonfiction that I never submitted; though my major interest had come to be in the promise of orbiting colonies, which I now feel are the solution to Earth's long-term problems, I was unable to express my thoughts about them in words concrete enough for children. This is an insurmountable problem for me— once I wrote a controlled-vocabulary piece about Skylab for a reading series, and was told that the editor had to rewrite it because despite my accurate vocabulary/sentence structure calculations, my approach was "too abstract" for the intended audience. This is the underlying difference between my view and other people's, and it bars me not only from writing children's nonfiction, but from the popular-level adult science field.

But working on *The Subnuclear Zoo* and *Tool for Tomorrow* had opened new doors for me. Though originally, I had assumed Rick would provide all the technical information, I found myself inwardly compelled to absorb it myself before I could express any ideas on paper. Furthermore, I found it wasn't as obscure as I'd been expecting. One day, coming back from a summer school class to find me reading a technical article about physics in *Scientific American,* Rick said, "Oh, Sylvia, you can't understand that!" And I reacted indignantly—I felt challenged, and became aware that there really was no subject I couldn't comprehend if I made the effort. To be sure, I couldn't understand the mathematical equations, not having nearly as much math background as Rick did; but contrary to what's often asserted, math is not necessary to the understanding of concepts, indispensable though it is for practical or experimental work. My lack of college training in science did not limit the subjects I could deal with as a writer.

So while I was working on the genetic engineering book, I got very deeply involved in the source material. That was when I saw its application to Noren's situation, and started *The Doors of the Universe* (an exception to my inability to think of stories because it was a continuation of the original story). But besides that, I wanted to learn more about the relation of genetics to human evolution. I visited Rick's home in Tennessee to put the finishing touches on *Tool for Tomorrow;* he was then making plans to enter graduate school. I realized that soon he would have a master's degree, while I had none. My mother and most of my friends had master's degrees in one subject or another, though they knew far less about scholarly research than I. Also I felt that perhaps a master's degree would enable me to publish adult nonfiction about other worlds without its getting classed with the sensational variety—I'd gotten tired of hearing "Oh, you mean like *Chariots of the Gods?*" when trying to tell people about my research for *The Planet-Girded Suns.*

In 1978 I had a contract with Atheneum for a book about future human evolution. I knew little about past evolution, but instead of learning from books alone I decided to try taking a class. I had never been fond of the Academic Establishment or in agreement with its accepted theories, but the appeal of a master's degree was at that time motivating me; I found out that it would be possible for me to get one in anthropology at Portland State University. The professor for the evolution class in which I enrolled turned out to be excellent, and, by coincidence, interested both in genetics and in philosophy of science— both fields in which I'd developed background. He encouraged me to apply for admission to the graduate program, and I was accepted. For the next two years I attended part-time and met all the M.A. requirements, receiving almost straight A's because I found researching and writing term papers easy. The book for young people on future evolution, however, was never written. My views on that subject proved to be at odds with those of anthropologists, and I could scarcely express them in print while a candidate for a degree; moreover, to do so wouldn't have been fair to Atheneum. Nonfiction published for young people (as opposed to fiction) is supposed to reflect the current views of authorities, not the heretical ones of its author. I transferred the contract to *The Doors of the Universe* and abandoned children's nonfiction with little regret.

I never did get the master's degree. I had to stop work on my thesis temporarily for personal reasons, and then wasn't able to go back; it had become too expensive to have someone stay with Mother during my hours on campus. I wasn't too disappointed, for by then, I realized that the degree would not really enable me to publish nonfiction for adults. The scholarly book field was in a depressed state and it was unlikely that I could get the thesis accepted by a university press, as I'd first hoped. Without that prospect, I didn't want to write it under Academic Establishment guidance—term papers are one thing, but an original book-length manuscript containing controversial ideas is something else! I would rather use my material for something wholly my own, far longer than a master's thesis is allowed to be. I do plan to finish that

book whether or not it proves publishable; it's about the significance of space colonization to human evolution.

Going to graduate school was largely a matter of pride with me, and though I gained confidence from it, with hindsight it appears to have been the most expensive mistake I ever made. Those two years were when personal computers first came on the market. I avoided looking at the ads because I longed to program again and yet saw no way I could ever afford such an expensive luxury; but if I had put the money I spent on graduate courses into a computer, I undoubtedly could have sold software profitably. Although my programming experience was by then too outdated to be applicable to large business computers, I had just the kind of systems software knowledge that was needed for programming early microcomputers in assembly language. But I didn't realize people were selling programs by mail from their homes. I assumed one would have to work in an office, which I wasn't free to do.

When in 1981 my electric typewriter gave out, and I'd developed a vision problem that made it difficult for me to use a typewriter anyway, I did get a computer for word processing. I couldn't afford to buy software but I enjoyed writing my own. By that time I'd become aware of what was going on and tried to market what I wrote, but it was already too late. Advertising rates were by then geared to the price of products for business customers rather than home users. Though my software was bugfree and my few customers were pleased with it, there wasn't any way to

With Mother, 1981.

publicize it—and furthermore, my computer soon became too obsolete to use for commercial software development. It was a cassette-based TRS-80, which like the old Q7 did its job well, but was scorned by people interested in having the latest and most efficient equipment. Personally, I liked it, and did all sorts of things with it that are supposedly impractical with cassette text storage.

The attempt to market my software, like so many other things I've done, had serendipitous results. That was what got me into telecommunications and computer conferencing, a fascinating new field in which I'm now active. I hope that ultimately it, or the contacts I make through it, will offer me ways to earn money at home, for I no longer foresee any writing income; my talents don't fit present markets. I will write in the future as I did at the first, for the satisfaction it brings to me and to prospective readers. But even if I were to get an idea for a novel like my others, it's unlikely that it would be published. Libraries are low on funds these days and books for advanced readers, long and costly to print yet without appeal for typical younger teens, are no longer salable. The seventies were really the only time during which they were; I was very lucky to go through my story-creation period in the right decade.

Mother is over ninety now. Though her mind is sharp and she does a lot of reading, she's very weak physically due to medical problems; I can't leave her alone at any time. During my grandmother's lifetime we could get someone to live with us for little more than room and board, but that's no longer possible, so except for taking her to the doctor I'm virtually homebound. We live very quietly with two beloved cats, Hesper and Phoebus (called Sunny), who are the center of our household. Recently we sold the house we'd owned for thirteen years—far longer than either of us had lived in one place before—and moved into a mobile home west of Portland. It's in a beautiful park surrounded by tall firs, with a view of tree-rimmed fields and a red barn from my bedroom window.

I don't mind this lifestyle, except for its financial drawbacks—after all, I stayed home by choice before it became necessary. I have always been an observer of this planet more than a participant in its affairs. All writers are good observers; the difference between me and most others is that I tend to observe in terms of long-range things, like the evolution of space-faring species, rather than nearby specific ones.

It has been ten years since I've traveled anywhere and I see few people, yet I am not isolated. My computer is my link to the world, not only because I write with it, but because of computer conferencing. At present I am on the staff of Connected Education, an organization headed by Dr. Paul Levinson that offers graduate courses for credit from the New School for Social Research in New York City. Every night I connect my computer by phone to a central computer in New Jersey, where Connect Ed's "electronic campus" is located. Though I haven't met Dr. Levinson in person and I have never seen the New School itself, I've team-taught a class there, and will be teaching more courses as the program grows. Connect Ed has students and faculty all over the world—Japan, South America and England, among other places. These people are as easy to "talk" to as they would be if they lived in my own city. In my case, because writing's easier for me than speaking, it's far better than attending face-to-face confer-

ences. Long ago I assumed that because I couldn't lecture I would never be able to teach in college, yet now technology has found a way to break down barriers not only of distance, but of individual differences in skills. In computer conferencing, people's minds and personalities are all that matter. Irrelevant things like foreign accents or physical handicaps aren't even visible; we all meet on equal ground. This is truly the medium of the future, I believe.

Of course computer conferencing isn't just for people who can't meet otherwise; most Connect Ed students live ordinary lives and choose online courses for scheduling convenience. Because it's an expensive medium at present, the majority of them are business people, though other adults such as teachers are certainly welcome. But I foresee a day when young people will be involved, as they now are with free electronic conferencing on local BBS systems. National recreational computer conferencing has great appeal for teens. In 1985 I was a helper and volunteer writer for the Participate conferencing system on The Source, which I learned about while participating in Paul Levinson's public "electure" conference about Space Humanization there. We had enthusiastic teen users as well as adults, though there too, the expense barred all but those from affluent families. I'm hoping for a time when all young people will have access to such systems. There may even be a time when young readers can exchange ideas with their favorite authors via a computer conference.

In any case, computer conferencing is an exciting field to pioneer in. It's something I'll be doing for many years to come. I have a brand new computer now (this article is the first thing I've written with it) and many hundreds of thousands of words will scroll across its screen. Some won't ever be printed on paper; I send words to readers nowadays merely by pressing a few keys. But there's still an important place for books—unlike some of my fellow electronic text enthusiasts, I don't believe books will ever become obsolete. I hope to write more of them someday.

Postscript (Spring of 2001)

What a difference a few more years made in computer technology! The desktop PC that was new in 1987 when I wrote my original essay, primitive by today's standards, is long gone; I've just acquired my third successive improved model. I said then that online communication was expensive (which it was, in the days when we paid by the minute for connections to host conferencing systems) but that I hoped someday all teenagers would have access to it. Now they can contact people all over the world, from schools and libraries if they lack computers at home, via the Internet—a development I then hadn't imagined.

There might even be a time, I said, when readers could exchange ideas with authors online; but I pictured that as a quite futuristic possibility. Only ten years later I opened my own Web site and began corresponding by e-mail with fans of my books in many regions of the United States, as well in other nations. As a direct result of this, I've at last been able to get most of my novels back into print.

But before that, there were other major changes in my life.

In the fall of 1987, shortly after my autobiographical essay went to press, my mother died. This loss was crushing for a while, although it was scarcely unexpected, since she was ninety years old and had serious medical problems. We had lived together all my life, except for a few years during the 1950s, and for most of that time she'd been more like a sister to me than a parent. I will never stop missing her company.

And there was another problem. I had chosen to share a home with my mother not only because of our closeness, but because she wanted a full-time companion and, ultimately, caregiver. Had I not been present she would have hired someone; thus I didn't object to the arrangement whereby her modest income—inherited from my grandmother, for whom she had cared in turn—supported both of us. After all, I had never craved a high-powered career or upscale lifestyle. Our assumption was that after she was gone I could live comfortably on my own inheritance. We didn't anticipate the extent to which it would be depleted by inflation.

It's just as well that we didn't, I suppose, because there was nothing different I could have done. After I stopped publishing I tried—and have since tried—to earn money at home; but the amounts have been small, and though I would have been free to take a job in the years immediately following Mother's death, there was no position for which I was qualified. My programming knowledge was by that time far too outdated to have value in the marketplace, and because of my lifelong typing-speed limitation I could not do office work. Moreover, I didn't have the physical stamina for a regular job; I'd always found commuting exhausting, and by this time there were often days when I hadn't the energy to go out—though I am always able to work at home at my desk.

So the immediate question was where I was going to spend the rest of my life. I owned the mobile home we'd been living in, but it was sited in a park where there was rent to pay; I knew that I must own my land, too, in order to make ends meet in the future. I couldn't afford property in the Portland area—and found that I didn't want to stay there in any case. For years I'd been virtually homebound, and had few local contacts; now I discovered that the distances I had to drive through traffic in order to get anywhere, even the main public library, were too great to make the effort seem worthwhile. Portland had changed. It wasn't the same place I'd so eagerly moved to, twenty years before. I felt I must make a new beginning.

At this point came another of the astonishing coincidences that have shaped my life, and which, along with several other instances of fortunate timing, have made me wonder whether such synchronicities may be more than mere chance. Strangely, a trip from Portland to Eugene triggered both of them. Since the spring day in 1957 when I went to Eugene and made a sudden decision resulting in my coincidental entry into the computer programming field, I had been there only three times. But in April of 1988, I decided to drive down to Eugene again. I wasn't really sure it was where I wanted to live, although I had loved it during my brief stay in the early 1950s—and when I arrived, mobile home lots proved scarce and costly. I was about to give up the search. Then, through a casual inquiry, I discovered a subdivision of such lots involved in a bank foreclosure, the prices of which had been drastically reduced the day before. Realizing I must act fast, I bought one of them. By the next weekend they were all gone; if I

had not picked that particular time to visit, I would never have found land within my means.

So all my early contacts with Eugene proved fateful—not to mention the fact that I've settled permanently here, and thus may, in due course, come to the end of my life in the hospital less than a block from where I lived that magical year when I was seventeen. How surprised I'd have been then to know that Eugene was where I'd grow old! Going through boxes of papers not long ago, I came across a houseplan I drew in a high school homemaking class. We were required to design our dream homes. I labeled mine "Engdahl Home, Eugene, Oregon" although at that time I had never been to Oregon and had no reason to expect that I'd ever have occasion to see this particular city. I just picked it from a map. Prescience? Who can say?

Having my mobile home moved from Portland to Eugene proved to be quite an adventure. Actually it was easier (for me, anyway) than a regular move, since all the furniture moved with the house; I didn't have to pack anything that wasn't fragile. The double-wide home was split in two; though I moved the books from shelves to the floor, I have such a lot of them that their weight caused one half's hitch to break, and it got stuck overnight on the highway. I was already in Eugene by that time, wondering why only the bedroom side of my house had arrived. Eventually it was all put together, the only other snag being the requirement of Eugene's building inspectors that my sloping carport be built with strong enough timbers to support four feet of snow, although it rarely snows more than a few inches here and some years get none at all. The expense of this proved so great that I'd have been better off building a garage, which, if I'd realized I would be keeping my 1978 Chevrolet—now approaching "classic" status—for the rest of my life, I would have done. There were a few other lot-development choices I now regret, but on the whole, the move was a big success.

My cats, Hesper and Sunny, moved with me, of course. Hesper lived to be nearly nineteen, which for a cat is very old indeed. Sunny died much earlier, and I got Marigold, an orange tabby who now rules the house. Cats have always been important to me; I could never be happy without feline companionship.

I love this place, although the site isn't as pleasant as when I first came. Then, wild geese flew low overhead, and over the back fence I saw trees between here and the river; I often sat in my screen porch and watched the sunset. Now those trees are gone and they have built a rock quarry bordered by huge berms of dirt that block the western view, and fill the porch with dust every time the wind blows. They are planning to widen the highway in back, which I don't welcome since it's only a short distance from my bedroom and is bound to create more dust and noise. But the trees in my yard have grown tall, and I can still see forested hills from my living room windows.

Eugene is just the right size city for me. It has everything, including a major university, yet it takes me only ten minutes to get downtown from the outskirts where I live—even less time to reach the main shopping mall. It has retained the natural beauty of its setting. And I'm active in community organizations in which, in a large metropolitan area, I could never have become involved. I've been on the board of the Friends of the Eugene Public Library since a few months after I arrived, and as a volunteer, I desktop-

Sylvia Engdahl at Children's Literature Association conference, San Diego, 1990, after accepting the Phoenix Award, with Alethea Helbig.

publish the library's newsletter at home on my computer. I also produce a newsletter for the Alzheimer's Association, and I'm on the advisory council of the local RSVP (Retired Senior Volunteer Program), for which I've done various computer tasks.

Nevertheless, I live quietly, and am home most of the time, usually with the computer on (my latest enthusiasm is for selling things I no longer need on *eBay* and *Half.com*). It's the way of life that best suits me. I no longer drive to the nearby mountains or coast as I sometimes used to, partly because of my car's aging condition and partly because of my own. I have no specific medical problems, just ongoing depletion of my already-low energy level and, in recent years, chronic muscle pain. I lack both the funds and the stamina for travel, and were I to be miraculously provided with one, I would still be held back by the absence of the other. It's been nearly a decade since I even visited Portland.

Yet sitting at my computer, I come alive! I will never tire of the various pursuits it makes possible for me.

In 1989, to my great surprise, I was informed that I would receive the 1990 Phoenix Award for *Enchantress from the Stars*. This award is given annually by the Children's Literature Association, a national organization of scholars in the field, "from the perspective of time" to a book published twenty years prior to the award date. I received an expense-paid trip to San Diego to accept the award and speak at the organization's 1990 conference. Also in 1989, rack-size trade paperback editions of *Enchantress* and *The Far Side of Evil* were issued, which stayed in print for a while; but their covers didn't attract the right audience and they weren't widely distributed where teens would find them. It seemed that although my novels were still valued by critics, they were destined to remain inaccessible outside of children's rooms of public libraries.

In the late eighties and early nineties I was still doing the part-time online work for Connected Education that I described in my original essay; but the cost of that program—the same as on-campus tuition at New York's New School for Social Research—put it out of the reach of all but the most affluent students, and enrollment was never large. I did teach an online graduate course titled "Science Fiction and Space Age Mythology" in 1989, 1994, and 1995, which I greatly enjoyed; I wish there had been enough students for it to run every year that it was offered. The course dealt with popular culture science fiction, not the literary kind, and was focused largely on films. (An idea of its content is given in my Phoenix Award acceptance speech, "The Mythic Role of Space Fiction," a slightly revised version of which is now at my Web site.) In my opinion this new mythology is an extremely significant reflection of our culture's outlook on the universe. I have worked, off and on, on a nonfiction book on the subject, the scope of which keeps growing; but because it's not suitable for publication in today's commercial market, and I would not have the academic credentials to publish scholarly books even if there were a bigger demand for them, I have not given it high priority.

Connected Education was conducted via private text-based online conferencing systems rather than on the Internet, which in those days was just getting started. In 1996, when the public was becoming aware of the Web, I was asked to develop a site publicizing Connect Ed's offerings, and was provided with access to the Net. This was all new to me. I had been online for more than a decade but had never seen a Web page; I didn't even have Windows on my computer, and didn't have memory enough to run it—they also paid for me to install more memory and get a faster modem. But when I started to learn HTML, I found it fascinating. This is a wonderful new career! I thought. It's something I'm naturally fitted for!

Alas, it has not turned out that way. Web design is a highly competitive field in which a freelancer cannot find work without contacts or money for advertising. I haven't been able to get much, though I did create, and continue to maintain, one site for another author. By now, of course, there are thousands of Web designers looking for freelance jobs and plenty of high school and college students with as much capability as I have—and besides, today's software enables people to produce their own Web pages.

So as in the case of all my ventures, the financial return was not large. But the rewards of developing my personal Web site were another matter.

Early in 1997, Connect Ed's program came to an end, and I was faced with having to pay for my own Internet account, an ongoing expense I could not justify unless it brought me income. I had some extra copies of my novels left, and since I saw that a few people had been searching for them through Usenet groups, it occurred to me that it might be possible to sell them. I didn't think many Internet users would have heard of them; still, I placed a notice saying they were available, and also opened a Web site where they were offered. As their original prices were out of line with current ones, I thought it would be legitimate to charge what a new book of equivalent format would cost—

even a few dollars more, in the case of those that were scarce and had never been issued in paperback.

The response was overwhelming. It seemed I was better known than I thought, although often viewed as a bygone author (comments appeared in a couple of places expressing surprise that I was not dead!) I sold all the hardcovers—of which I had only a few—within a week or so, and the paperbacks in about three months. I could have charged much more; I later found that used book dealers were getting well over $100 apiece for some of the hardcover titles. If only I had bought more while they were still in print! I hadn't dreamed then, of course, that there might someday be a way to contact potential buyers.

My Internet presence was paying off, but more than that, I began to wonder if it might not lead to new hope of attracting reprint publishers. For much more gratifying than the sale of copies was the e-mail I received. I'd had no idea that my novels were so widely remembered.

Nothing in my experience, at any time in my life, has pleased (or astonished) me more than the discovery of how many adults had read my books during their childhood or teen years and felt that they had been influenced by them. Not only did people send e-mail, but in searching the Web for ways to publicize my site I came across comments made previously in public forums. In former years, I had received praise from reviewers and librarians, and had sometimes gotten letters from children assigned to write to authors in school, but only on rare occasions had I heard from readers who reacted personally to the novels. I was, and still am, deeply touched to know they've had lasting impact.

After I suggested at my site that Guest Book comments might help to get the books back in print, many were made. Then in 1998, Meisha Merlin—at that time a brand new press—stated at their own Web site that they would welcome e-mail about books people would like to see reprinted. I asked the people who had written to me to respond, and a lot of them did. Subsequently Meisha Merlin offered me a contract, and in 2000 my trilogy—*This Star Shall Abide, Beyond the Tomorrow Mountains,* and *The Doors of the Universe*—was published, with minor updating and a new Afterword, in an omnibus edition under the title *Children of the Star.* It was issued as adult science fiction. The Web has created a whole new way of reaching people who like books of a kind not interesting to large mass-market audiences.

All that I said in 1987 about publishing categories is still true, and furthermore, large publishers have become increasingly oriented toward commercial success. Meisha Merlin specializes in reprinting science fiction and fantasy with good reviews and an established following, but not enough mass appeal to be wanted by those publishers. It has issued the work of many authors whose books had gone out of print. Without the Web and its new outlets, such as online bookseller, publisher and author sites, the marketing of such novels would not be possible; small presses cannot get books into many local stores, and there would be no way to publicize them sufficiently for conventional distribution. The wide reach of the Web is now changing the rules of the game.

Unlike some traditional publishers, small presses don't object to authors selling copies of their own books, and—since I get a bookseller's share of the cover price—I have earned far more per copy from offering *Children of the Star* at my Web site than I earn in royalties. The book, which has stunning cover art by noted fantasy artist Tom Kidd, had a limited print-to-order hardcover edition for which both the publisher and I took advance orders, followed by a high-quality trade softcover edition that's available through normal book trade channels. The only problem is that few people discover it unless they're already familiar either with my books or with Meisha Merlin's. Catch-22: science fiction media didn't review the original editions because they were YA books, and now that it has been issued as adult, they won't review it because it's a reprint. There have been some enthusiastic reader reviews at *Amazon.com,* though (which unfortunately are seen only by people who search for me there). And I do what I can to publicize it myself via the Internet, something many authors are now doing; the days of expecting even a major publisher to handle all publicity are past. I hope that in time it will reach new readers, both older teens and adults besides those who've read it previously.

An even more exciting development is the publication of a new hardcover edition of *Enchantress from the Stars* this spring by Walker and Company, with an introduction by Lois Lowry and a striking new jacket plus interior vignettes by artists Leo and Diane Dillon, who have won top awards in both the children's and the science fiction fields. Walker, which has a large and successful children's book department, contacted me last year about obtaining the rights to it for their Newbery Honor Roll series. Whether this resulted from the revival of interest in my work brought about by my Web presence, I don't know. But I'm delighted that *Enchantress* is available to a new generation, and furthermore, I am glad it's been issued by a different publisher than the trilogy. They will both benefit from separate marketing; having my books side by side in the same catalog often misled people as to their intended readership.

This limited not only the trilogy's original audience, but that of *The Far Side of Evil,* which I regret having made a sequel to *Enchantress from the Stars.* I should have used a different protagonist, for the two books, despite being set in the same SF "universe," are quite different from each other and generally don't appeal to the same people. Some do like both, but the younger fans of *Enchantress* are often disappointed or even depressed by *Far Side,* which is a darker story demanding greater maturity on the part of both heroine and reader. Of course, when I wrote *Far Side,* I had no idea that *Enchantress* would become a Newbery Honor Book and be given to as many pre-teen readers as it was, so I didn't foresee that problem. Nor did I realize that few of the older teen readers for whom *Far Side* was intended would discover a sequel to a children's book. If it is reprinted in the future, it will be treated as independent, and it won't be issued as a book for children.

Yet I still feel strongly about the theme of *Far Side,* and I would like to see it back in print, as would quite a few readers who've written to me. I still believe that expansion into space is essential to our species' survival, and have a page at my Web site discussing my ideas about this in detail (which, I'm happy to see, gets even more visitors than my home page; there are links to it from many other space sites). The difficulty is that *Far Side* is somewhat dated: not by the political situation it portrays, as some people assume—the setting was never current, since the planet in the story resembles Earth of the fifties rather than the seventies—but by the fact that it's now obvious that merely developing space travel capability does not necessarily cause a world to use that capability. And it's also obvious that nuclear war is not the only peril that exists during the Critical Stage. Thus in addition to the oversimplification of the book due to its having been written as young adult, some of its statements turned out to be oversimplified in terms of what we now know after thirty years of neglecting the space program. All it says about the need to explore space is, in my opinion, true. But there is a good deal more that should be said about why a species able to expand beyond its home world fails to do so, and what its fate is likely to be if it continues to cling solely to that world. I suspect that an advanced interstellar civilization would know these things, and that Elana too would know them later in her life.

Unfortunately, I myself do not know the solution to such a species' apathy. I would like to write a sequel, to appear in an omnibus with *The Far Side of Evil,* in which Elana visits a world where it's almost too late; but I haven't yet come up with an idea of how her people could save its inhabitants—any more than I know what will ultimately save our own world. Will Mars be a sufficient impetus for us? I thought so when I wrote *Journey Between Worlds,* and I hope that book, which I've revised to fix portions that today seem sexist, will eventually be reprinted in a teen paperback line. It has new relevance now that there's public interest in Mars missions and active Mars enthusiasts are on the Web. For a while in the eighties I believed orbiting colonies would come sooner than the colonization of Mars; but despite their practicality, the concept has failed to win wide support. Mars inspires more emotion if traces of life were found there, might that not prove the crucial factor in getting us back on track? I pray that it will, and that it will happen soon.

Space is not the only topic of interest to me. More and more, in recent years, I've turned to ideas about human potential, especially in the area of "paranormal" capacities such as those portrayed in *Enchantress from the Stars.* Unlike most people as strongly science-oriented as I am, I have always believed that ESP is real, and that it's been a much larger factor in human history than is recognized. I have never had psychic experiences myself; I'm much too "left-brained" for that—but I don't doubt that other people do, and that in the future we'll learn to control such powers. (Some of what I "made up" about them for *Enchantress* has been validated by recent nonfiction.) And we'll also learn more about the relationship between mind and body. Human beings are far more than biological machines.

In this connection, and in accord with my usual tendency toward heretical views, I deplore the attitude fostered by our society's medical philosophy, which I believe is based on false premises. I've devoted a good deal of thought and research to this issue; I once taught a Connect Ed media studies course on "Technology and 21st Century Medicine," dealing with assumptions I feel will be abandoned. Not that I favor "natural" or "alternative" healing methods, with which I don't agree either—unlike some today, I have no doubts about the benefits of high technology. Twice since moving to Eugene I have had major surgery for life-threatening conditions (which were

quickly and completely cured) and I am thankful that this was available; modern medicine is very good at essential surgical repairs. But in most other respects, it's apt to cause more problems than it solves, and worse, its conception of health has become a virtual religion to many, overshadowing all other scales of value. Some years ago I began an adult novel about a planet where the Medical Establishment had acquired dictatorial political power, which I still believe is a valid theme; but it lacked the key incidents needed to make a story.

It was the same old stumbling block—I'm no more action-oriented in my imagination than in real life. I can write about thoughts and feelings of characters, but I don't visualize scenes in my mind as do most authors. Though I may know a desired plot outcome, I can't think of events to bring it about. And I can no more *force* such material into consciousness than I could when I stopped producing fiction for Atheneum, despite my longing to do so and my enjoyment of the actual writing process. This is my greatest regret, and it is intensified by the frequent e-mails I receive that urge me to write another novel. People naturally believe that if I wanted to, I could. As if all I needed was encouragement! As if I hadn't been frustrated for the past twenty years and more, wishing that it would again become possible for me!

To be sure, novels like mine, with the possible exception of a sequel to *The Far Side of Evil* that could appear in the same volume, would not be publishable today even if I could write them. Meisha Merlin publishes reprints and continuations of series; traditional publishers of adult fiction want books with bestseller potential, a situation affecting many authors with far greater past success than I. And "young adult" nowadays means books suitable for average middle school kids, not advanced readers or older teens. But if I had an idea for a *story* rather than a mere philosophical treatise—for readers of any age—I would not let lack of a publisher for it hold me back. I might even investigate electronic publishing, as I

Engdahl in 1992 with her cat Marigold.

may in time for nonfiction; that's a growing technology that may transform the way writers' work is disseminated.

It's not my lack of energy that has kept me from writing more books. And it certainly isn't lack of motivation. In the past, I resigned myself to the fact that except during one mysteriously atypical long-ago period, the creation of fiction was just not among my talents. But now, I feel I'm letting down the fans I've so recently discovered I have—and there's no way to explain in a short e-mail reply that it isn't by choice. People assume that proven writing ability is all it takes to produce a novel. If only that were true!

Lately, I've begun to be aware that I have less time ahead than I used to have. Since I never had much youthful vigor at any age—at least not in the physical sense—growing older hasn't changed my lifestyle; so it's a bit startling to realize that now, I really am well along in years. Perhaps this will produce the urgency needed to bring my nonfiction projects to fruition. But it can't change anything as far as new fiction is concerned. For that, I can only hope that someday the door to imaginative realms may once more open for me. It surprised me (and everyone who knew me) when it happened before. Might I not, without warning, be surprised again?

Meanwhile, my best-known novels are back in print, in beautiful new editions. I know from the many e-mails I treasure that they've affected readers' lives. And that's much more enduring success than I ever anticipated.

Writings

FOR YOUNG ADULTS; FICTION

Enchantress from the Stars, illustrated by Rodney Shackell, Atheneum (New York, NY), 1970, revised edition (jacket and vignettes by Leo and Diane Dillon), Walker (New York, NY), 2001.

Journey Between Worlds, illustrated by James and Ruth McCrea, Atheneum (New York, NY), 1970.

The Far Side of Evil, illustrated by Richard Cuffari, Atheneum (New York, NY), 1971.

This Star Shall Abide, illustrated by Richard Cuffari, Atheneum (New York, NY), 1972, published in Great Britain as *Heritage of the Star,* Gollancz (London, England), 1973.

Beyond the Tomorrow Mountains, illustrated by Richard Cuffari, Atheneum (New York, NY), 1973.

(Editor; with Rick Roberson), *Universe Ahead: Stories of the Future,* illustrated by Richard Cuffari, Atheneum (New York, NY), 1975.

(Editor) *Anywhere, Anywhen: Stories of Tomorrow,* Atheneum (New York, NY), 1976.

The Doors of the Universe, Atheneum (New York, NY), 1981.

Children of the Star (omnibus containing this *This Star Shall Abide, Beyond the Tomorrow Mountains,* and *The Doors of the Universe,* issued as adult fiction), Meisha Merlin (Atlanta, GA), 2000.

FOR YOUNG ADULTS; NONFICTION

The Planet-Girded Suns: Man's View of Other Solar Systems, illustrated by Richard Cuffari, Atheneum (New York, NY), 1974.

FOR CHILDREN; NONFICTION

(With Rick Roberson) *The Subnuclear Zoo: New Discoveries in High Energy Physics,* Atheneum (New York, NY), 1977.

(With Rick Roberson) *Tool for Tomorrow: New Knowledge about Genes,* Atheneum (New York, NY), 1979.

Our World Is Earth, (picture book), illustrated by Don Sibley, Atheneum (New York, NY), 1979.

F

Leonard Everett Fisher

1924-

It was 1926. I was two years old. Claude Monet had just died in France. The Impressionists were all gone, not that I was aware they had ever existed. I did not know that a more innocent age had slipped beyond my reach.

A Buster Brown hairstyle would mark me for the next few years. It hid gaping wounds behind each ear. Later, the job of giving me a proper haircut to ease my way into first grade went to a dapper barber with a pair of snapping scissors. He, too, had been scarred by mastoiditis and played the heavy as he whispered into each ear how he had been carved up without ether. All the while his scissors kept snapping. I shuddered in that barber's chair every month, listening to his malevolent whispers. I wished he would evaporate. I thought him only too willing to extend my surgery with those snapping scissors. My mother would only smile, discounting the obvious menace.

As I look back through the haze of recollection, that barber represented a hostile world. Snatched by a mastoid operation from death's door while still an infant, I had become the object of family attention and concern. The barber was lucky to get near me. My parents, close relatives, and a Bronx, New York apartment were my shield against the likes of strangers with snapping scissors. And it was in that apartment, made safe and secure by parental enthusiasm for my well-being, that at age two I performed a single compulsive act that led to all that I am and ever will be. Perhaps it was not compulsion at all, but a predestined beginning. Whatever it was, I would begin to be an artist.

My father kept a small drafting table in the front bedroom of the apartment. The room overlooked a sloping parkland, Mosholu Parkway and DeWitt Clinton High School beyond. Here, Dad pursued his constant, tantalizing dream of becoming an artist. It would never happen. But here he struggled with stiff drawings, fussy watercolors, and frustration. An idle ship designer in a world of closing shipyards, he now worked as a draftsman for New York City's Department of Plant and Structures creating working drawings of jail cells, among other things. Later, he would elevate himself to the Board of Transportation as a civil engineer designing subway stations for the yet unborn Eighth Avenue subway. Eventually, he would find his way back to ships. But not until the Great Depression would lower him into the abyss of unemployment and menial work. At the moment he was planning his great escape through art.

I was much too young to know or even remember his desperation. I saw only pictures, color and the minutiae within them—the expressions of too linear and logical a mind. Dad was a marvelous draftsman and letterer, however. He delighted in the precise turn of a letter and in the measured curve of an arc. And on that bedroom drafting table he tried to free himself of those restraints.

Still, I had an itch to do what Dad was trying to do—make pictures. The moment came. He turned his back on an unfinished work and I was into a bottle of India ink with a sable brush. It was all over in a flash. The picture was permanently altered. Years later, Dad would always insist that I had a "strong and direct approach," whatever it was I scribbled. He never allowed for abstraction—surely not a man of his mental precision—in 1926. His heroes were well defined: Julius Caesar, Michelangelo, Howard Pyle, Admiral Dewey, Theodore Roosevelt, and Benny Leonard, the Lightweight Champion of the World—a play on both our names. Dad's given name was Benjamin.

My early deftness produced immediate results. Instead of being strangled for overpainting my father's picture, I was rewarded. A front hall closet was cleared out. A small dropleaf table and two small chairs were installed inside. I was supplied with paper, pencils, and crayons to challenge my muse—out of harm's way. Liquids were barred. I was not given a bottle of India ink; ergo, no brush either. Paints

Leonard Everett Fisher

were a few years down the road. Nevertheless, I was cozily in business, ensconced in my first studio, lit from the ceiling by a naked bulb and about six steps from the kitchen. My father continued his struggles in the bedroom, safely.

Over the next several years I graduated from scribbles to violent scenes of the Civil War, World War I, and Jack Dempsey the heavyweight boxing champion. Once in a while I broke the pattern with linear profiles of my parents or assorted relatives. The choice of subject matter was dictated by impressive events. Jack Dempsey was everyone's hero in the 1920s. My drawings of soldiers and war were seeded by the various parades we always attended, my father's uncompromising patriotism, and the rotogravure section of the Sunday papers which continued to publish gruesome photographs of death and destruction in France, 1914-1918. These crude drawings amused my father's younger brother, Harvey. He had been there.

Uncle Harvey was a bona fide decorated hero. He served in France with Company L, 30th Infantry, 3rd Division—the "Rock of the Marne." I think Uncle Harvey was the rock. The 30th Infantry, comprising a few thousand men, defended Paris with a six-and-a-half-mile line along the Marne River east of Château-Thierry. A German offensive of 24,000 men—three divisions—fell on them one July morning, 1918, in an attempt to capture Paris. The 30th Infantry, outnumbered about eight-to-one, held. The Germans never got to Paris. Not that time, anyway. At the center of this historic battle was Company L. Uncle Harvey was one of a handful of survivors of that brutal combat. He went on to fight elsewhere and was wounded at the Meuse-Argonne. It was all in the papers. He told me everything. I was mesmerized by these accounts and I tried to draw them all. Another uncle was in the Meuse-Argonne, too. The experience left him uncommunicative his entire life. My turn would come, although not quite in the same way. I would serve with the 30th Engineers instead of the 30th Infantry.

Every so often, Dad would look in on me in my closet studio. Mostly, he checked to see if I was using a "how to draw this and that" loose-leaf book he had made for me, containing exercises in basic perspective, simple anatomy, and boats from every angle. He tried to teach me to play chess in there, too. He always won.

My mother would keep an eye on me from the kitchen. Occasionally, she would sit in one of the little studio chairs and read to me from *Mother Goose* or *A Child's Garden of Verses* while I drew battlefield ambulances filled with bleeding heroes. Shortly before I entered first grade my parents purchased *Compton's Picture Encyclopedia.* Each of those twenty-six leather-bound volumes was part of the "read to" repertoire. My father loved all that incidental encyclopedic information without which no one could succeed in this world. So he thought.

My mother must have considered her own introduction to first grade. She could not even speak English. A native of Czarist Russia, six-year-old Mera Shapiro—my mother—arrived in Brooklyn via Ellis Island in October 1906. I related much of that early history in *A Russian Farewell.*

The day after the immigrant Shapiros were settled in their new home on Moore Street in Brooklyn, Mom was taken by an American relative to the local public school for registration. Her account of her Americanization was quick and blunt when she was asked to describe how it felt to be an alien kid in a Brooklyn elementary school: "When I was registered my name was changed to Ray. That was on a Monday. By the end of the week, Friday, I spoke English."

The impulse that gained a studio for me at the age of two—albeit a spare closet—sprang from my father's psyche. Art had been a part of him since his birth on a desolate Brooklyn farm. His own father, Simon, dreamed the same dreams. He made his living in the waterfront cafes of Riga, Latvia, drawing caricatures of the patrons. Riga was something of an artistic city during the 19th century. It was called the "Paris of the Baltic." The proceeds from these sketching efforts were used to take his wife, my grandmother, Lena Eve, and a couple of small children to America in 1890. Nothing ever came of grandfather Simon's artistic activity beyond one son's artistic yearning and another son who was a minor actor. There were other siblings—sons and daughters. None of them showed any artistic interests.

My father was perceptive enough to know that he was chasing a fantasy. He knew enough about art, artists, and skills to realize his delusion. There was something missing in his chemistry and he searched for it in vain. Somehow, he saw himself in me, making a fresh start, and was encouraged. The same thing seemed to be true for my younger brother, Richard. He would, in effect, become one side of my father's brain, a civil engineer and an architect. I would become the other side, an artist. My later interest in writing, a maternal trait, would grow out of my desire to communicate in words those ideas and events that could not be expressed with pictorial imagery.

My career direction was confirmed in second grade—at P.S. 80, 1931. I drew a picture of a pilgrim shooting a turkey. The drawing won a prize in the Wanamaker Art Competition for New York City School Children. I had no idea what it was all about, but the applause and the attention from an important department store—Wanamaker's—made me feel good. Eight years later, in 1939, another drawing of mine won another department store prize. This time it was the R. H. Macy Thanksgiving Day Parade Float Design Competition for New York City School Children. I cannot remember what the drawing was. No matter. By that time I was studying life drawing with Moses Soyer in his Fourteenth Street studio and we were no longer living in the Bronx. Moreover, I was exhibiting for the first time. My pencil drawing of backyards was being shown with other works by high school students at the Brooklyn Museum.

In between all of this, I attended art classes at the Heckscher Foundation (1932) on Saturday mornings. My mother waited the three hours for me, in a nearby hallway, I assume. I spent months there trying to paint watercolors of horses. I have no idea why. I recall a well-traveled bridle path near or around Van Cortlandt Park, plenty of mounted police, and the Cavalry on parade. Buried in there is a youthful reason. Those classes were painful. I struggled against my peers whose talents were larger. My indifference today to watercolor and horses is perhaps attributable to that first professional school experience. Many years later, while attending a function at Mount Holyoke College—my wife's alma mater—I met August Heckscher, a trustee of the college. He was amazed to find someone who had attended his grandfather's school pursuing art as a life work.

Saturday afternoons following the art classes were also programmed by my mother. We prowled the American Museum of Natural History, or stalked the galleries of the Metropolitan Museum of Art. Sometimes we attended performances of the Civic Repertory Theater. Visions of Eva LeGallienne as Peter Pan still dance around in my head. My cultural horizons were being broadened. All too often I would have preferred a football or baseball game.

I had a library card, too, well stamped and a year old in 1932. The steady stream of books was always more vital to me than what went on in school. They transported me to places and events far beyond the unimaginative basic school readers. These library books were continuously supplemented by dozens of secondhand books my father would buy in Manhattan for pennies. I could read comfortably beyond my school grade. I seemed to respond to words easily. Paintings were a more mysterious matter. I seemed to know what I was reading in a book. Robert Louis Stevenson's *Treasure Island* with N. C. Wyeth's illustrations haunted me, as did much of what Rudyard Kipling wrote about India. But I was never sure of what I was seeing in a painting. The differences between El Greco and Rubens or Titian and Gainsborough were too abstract

and confusing for my youthful, uneducated vision. I did not respond to French impressionism, Italian medieval painting, or any of the more recent movements—cubism, fauvism, dadaism, and more. I was struck by the drama of Rembrandt, the faultless technique of Ingres, the romance of Delacroix and Géricault. I had never been face-to-face with a Michelangelo painting, yet I knew from what I could see in reproductions that the power was persuasive. By the time I was ten years old I knew what was out there. But that was all. I had no real knowledge of painters or paintings, or of illustrators, for that matter. I read a great deal, but my visual responses were all primitive and subjective. Underneath it all there was a surging desire never to be a spectator.

All that transpired in the Bronx during those early years, 1924-1934, might not have happened if my mother had not decided to change the place of my arrival at near-zero hour. Following their marriage in New York in 1922 and a brief honeymoon up the Hudson River on the New York-Albany Nightliner, my parents settled first in Cleveland, Ohio, then in Detroit, Michigan. Dad bounced back and forth between the American Shipbuilding Company and the Ford River Rouge plant, designing lake and river workboats. Apparently Mom had second thoughts about where to give birth. Fourteen days before my appearance, she grabbed a train and headed for the Bronx, for Charlotte Street where her parents, Benjamin and Anna Shapiro, lived. Dad followed a week later. He would not see the inside of another shipyard for ten years; nor would he ever

Parents, Ray Mera and Benjamin M. Fisher, 1922.

leave New York again to work. I was born there June 24, 1924, my parents' second wedding anniversary.

By 1935, my parents were beginning to climb out of the Depression. My brother was two years old. Dad found work in the Brooklyn Navy Yard's Hull Design Division. And we had moved to the water's edge, Sea Gate.

Sea Gate is a square-mile landsend in Brooklyn. Once the home of the New York Yacht Club and a long gone turn-of-the-century playground for millionaires, it juts into Lower New York Bay east of Staten Island, west of Coney Island. The community's presence by the sea is distinguished by the red beacon of the landlocked Norton's Point Lighthouse. The Point itself, the very spot on which our house sat, and its jetty, separated the tidal flow of the North Atlantic from the quiet waters of Gravesend Bay. Powerful currents swept that rolling sea only to be deflected by the jetty. That jetty, our house, Sea Gate, and the general area served both as background and subject in several of my published works—*The Death of Evening Star, Noonan,* and *Storm at the Jetty,* a picture book, which was culled from an unpublished novel about the jetty.

Sea Gate was not a new experience. We had spent every summer there since I was a baby, except for a couple of Depression years. And even then, I was sent there to visit relatives for a few weeks. My mother's family had been vacationing in the "Gate" for fifteen summers. I had friends there. I could hardly wait to become a year-round resident. What adventure!

In those early days, Sea Gate was a sleepy place at the end of the world, let alone Brooklyn. And we lived at the very tip of that end, with our back to the community and our face to the sea. Not unlike Brigadoon, Sea Gate seemed

Fisher at Little Falls, Bronx Park, New York, 1931.

to hibernate in the wintry months and wake up every summer. It was an extraordinary ghetto where a well-defined boundary—an iron fence and the sea—kept out the unacceptable instead of ostracizing the inhabitants. It was an association of homeowners who had a unique deal with the City of New York. Its privacy was assured long ago by a ninety-nine year lease. One needed a pass to enter. No business was permitted to be conducted inside the Gate. There was no movie house. There was no school. We all had to attend school outside the Gate. The practice of medicine, dentistry, law, and the like was forbidden. Those services abounded outside. Doctors did make house calls, however.

There were exceptions. The Sea Gate Garage was one. Another was Johnny Gudice's Fruit and Produce truck. There were a couple of ice cream parlors, too. One was at the rambling Whittier Inn, a hotel—hotels and rooming houses were allowed. The other was at the Riviera, a beachside snack bar by day; an alfresco night club after dark. That was it.

Sea Gate winters were lonely and damp. In the dreary chill of those months, the evenings were long, if not depressing. Movie-going was infrequent and there was no television. Only radio. Besides the usual chores of homework and housework, everyone had something to do—my father tinkered around in his basement workshop, a place I had absolutely no interest in; my mother tinkered around in her kitchen; I tinkered around with clay, pad, and pencil but not much of anything else. I was floundering in that isolation until there arrived on radio an Art Appreciation program sponsored by New York University. The home listener was provided with a substantial portfolio of masterpiece paintings. These reproductions were large and clear. The radio commentator provided the discussion dealing with one of the prints each week. My art interests began to quicken, not so much for drawing but for art history and analysis. Finally, someone began to lift the veil of mystery about the craft and the background of paintings. Some of these paintings were very familiar. I had seen them at the Metropolitan. Most of the works were less familiar. I had never seen them in the flesh, only in books. Of course, there were those I had never seen in my young life. My thirst was unquenchable now. I wanted to make masterpieces. The sooner, the better.

Toward that end I seemed to race through the New York City Public School System. I was restless and wanted to be done with each day, each week, each month, each year. I had skipped a grade in the Bronx. By 1938, in Brooklyn, I was completing the David A. Boody Junior High School Rapid Advance Program.

As graduation neared, the school staff suggested that I attend the new High School of Music and Art. But my parents objected. They felt such a curriculum would be too weighted in favor of art and that everyone, even an artist, needed a well-balanced education. I registered at Abraham Lincoln High School, a "regular" school that was much closer to home. What neither my parents nor I knew was that Lincoln offered the most intensive art program of any high school in New York City, including the High School of Music and Art. The guiding light of the Lincoln art program was Leon Friend, who also had an influential impact on all art instruction in New York City public education. At Lincoln, he did all he could to whip his art majors, including me, into some kind of shape as graphic designers. Leon Friend was a disciple of the Bauhaus.

Friend had some difficulty with me. I wanted to be a painter. And I wanted to go to college. He discouraged both goals among his potential graphic designers. In fact he once growled at me, "Bauhaus, not Poorhouse." The man was sincerely trying to save me. I did not want to be saved that way. We fought. I refused to take his Graphic Design course. He refused to let me illustrate *Cargoes,* the school literary magazine. Still, I became a member of the elite Art Squad and graduated with a gold medal. Friend was a wonder. Without him I never would have had such early contact with a number of the nation's leading artists who were brought to our classes. Among these were Moses and Raphael Soyer with whom I studied for almost a full year.

In 1938, having just entered Lincoln High, another kindred spirit and I discovered that for fifty cents we could draw from nude models. We knew we needed the experience. We were both fourteen. The class was being offered at a distant school on Saturday mornings. We found the place and a sign: UNDER 17 NOT ADMITTED. A receptionist asked our ages. "Seventeen," we replied casually. I ran my hand over my face so that she would not notice that I had not yet begun to shave. My companion coughed violently as an excuse to turn his head for the same reason.

"That's what you say," she shot back. She knew. "You got fifty cents?"

"Yup."

"OK. You can go in."

The nude lady took one look at us and quickly put her robe on, complaining that this was no place for "kids." I was glad she did. It gave me a chance to catch my breath and get organized. The instructor, whose name escapes me, convinced her it would be all right. Fifty cents was fifty cents. And we represented a whole dollar. We had to prove ourselves, however, or be tossed out as a couple of fourteen-year-old voyeurs. We did. I attended that class for some weeks and continued to attend other life drawing and life painting classes intermittently over the next ten years: with Moses and Raphael Soyer; with Reginald Marsh at the Art Students' League; Olindo Ricci at Brooklyn College; in a brief night class in Sacramento, California, while I waited to be discharged from the army; and with Professor Deane Keller at Yale. The entire figure study experience came to a climax during my third year at Yale, when I was privileged to dissect cadavers at the Yale Medical School.

Leon Friend did not summarily pass out of my life when I graduated from Lincoln in January 1941. Grudgingly, he saw to it that I would major in art as a freshman at Brooklyn College. No one majored in anything there until junior year. Friend was going to save me in spite of myself.

Brooklyn College was not an easy passage. I was too young to be in any college, if for no other reason than my social isolation. I had entered in January, age sixteen and a half. That alone was awkward enough on any academic calendar. Also, Europe was at war. By December 1941, Pearl Harbor had come and gone; and so had drawing

Sergeant L. E. Fisher (seated at left) with the 30th Engineers, October 1944, traveling from Affreville to Oran, Algeria.

and painting at Brooklyn College. Enter, Serge Chermayeff, an English architect who helped to introduce a new order to American college art departments: the Bauhaus tradition and Graphic Design. I was disappointed. I felt betrayed. I thought the classes were vacant and humorless. Instead of trying to discover how to probe the human presence and project it with paint, I was now learning how to be a servant of industry in a program designed to produce disposable images for disposable products—learning to create appearances for corporate ideas. That was my perception of the program at the time. Even then, as young as I was, and however much I could not clearly state my own beliefs, I did subscribe to the singularity and independence of art and artists, and to the superiority of content over appearances. To me, painting was, and still is, a spiritual extension of the human presence. In my mind, art was not to be a marketing tool. I could never be a creative adjunct to commerce. I was interested in humanizing not civilizing.

However, I went along with the new curriculum. I had little choice. The war was coming for me soon enough, anyway. Still, I plotted my escape. On December 1, 1942, I became a U.S. Army Enlisted Reservist and soon thereafter requested active duty. Assigned to the 30th Engineer Topographic Battalion, I joined the war as a would-be mapmaker. A work scholarship obtained that summer at the Art Students' League would have to wait. It still waits. Another scholarship to the Jamesine Franklin School of Art would have to wait. It, too, still waits.

Between the end of January and the beginning of March 1943, I languished first in Camp Upton, Yaphank, New York, while the army ran a security check; then in the

In Fisher's studio, 1964. On the easel: **American Lament,** *1964.*

Fort Hamilton Post Hospital, Brooklyn. I had come down with the measles. Finally, I reported to Fort Belvoir, Virginia, and the 30th Topographic Engineers. The work that I would eventually do would be so highly classified that all of my training was conducted solely by the 30th Engineers out of view of the rest of the army. It was my art background, coupled with nearly two successful years of collegiate study in geology, that brought me to the 30th.

The war became a celluloid fantasy on a Norfolk, Virginia, pier in November. While bands played and flags flew and 5,000 of us boarded the *General A. E. Anderson,* including the first contingent of women GIs—WACS—to go overseas, I imagined I was seeing a double-feature movie. It was an unreal scenario. The troops slowly moving ahead of me were, in my imagination, Pathé News segments. It was happening to someone else, not to me. Reels of *Dawn Patrol* and *What Price Glory* ran off on my mental screen.

We sailed Thanksgiving Day. According to Admiral Samuel Eliot Morison, the Navy's historian, it was a memorable voyage. Not only were we the first American troopship to go it alone—without escort— through the worst period of enemy submarine activity in the North

Atlantic, it was the *Anderson*'s maiden voyage. "We were the first that ever burst into that not so silent sea," to paraphrase Samuel Taylor Coleridge's line in his *Rime of the Ancient Mariner.* Terrific! We zigged and zagged for ten days—and made it.

But in the dark morning hours before landing at Casablanca, French Morocco, while the ship's murky interior glowed eerily red in its blackout lights, and we were locked deep in a hold without a quick exit, the cacophonic din of a general quarters alarm jarred us from every sweet dream. "This is no drill! Bong. Bong. Bong." For a few minutes dull hammering sounds echoed around and above us. I never knew what happened. But in the ruby glow of that hold, shoeless and wearing a useless life jacket, I clung to my bunk paralyzed. The movie was over.

Later, on deck I saw the French battleship *Jean Bart* on its side in the harbor, awash like a monstrous dead whale. She had been scuttled months before. Despite that first eye-popping scene, my soul was permanently invaded right then and there by wanderlust, as the minarets and rooftops of exotic Casablanca shimmering in the morning sun caught my eye.

Traveling in box cars—"40 & 8s" (forty men and eight horses)—through Rabat, Meknes, Fez, Oujda, Tlemcen, Sidi-bel-Abbès, and Oran—shades of *Beau Geste*—we arrived in Affreville, Algeria, ninety miles south of Algiers, high in the Atlas Mountains. I spent some nine months in this place with Battalion Operations. Here, two- and three-dimensional invasion, tactical, and field maps, and other topographic necessities were produced for United States forces and other military clients. Our group was responsible for the Italian Campaign north of Naples, part of the Normandy invasion, the invasion of Southern France and beyond into Germany. This was my first experience with meeting professional deadlines. And these deadlines were truly deadly. We were mapping predictable battles and battlegrounds that had not yet occurred. I have been a stickler for meeting deadlines ever since.

Before the year was out—in November 1944—I came back to the United States in an emotional homecoming. To all intents and purposes I was out of the war. Three weeks after arriving I was on the *Matsonia* sailing for Hawaii. I remained in the Islands, on Oahu, until the end of the war. There I participated in the mapping of the assault on Iwo Jima, the invasion of Okinawa, and in what turned out to be the cancelled invasion of Japan.

I was not artistically lazy, either in Africa or Hawaii. There was a mural in Affreville destroyed by local Arabs as we departed. It contained offensive material—a harem. I painted another decoration for a military hospital in Hawaii. The building has been gone for years. The whereabouts of the painting, which was commissioned by the American Red Cross of Hawaii, is unknown. Another painting of mine received a first prize in an army art exhibition during the summer of 1945. I filched the canvas from Boris Karloff's USO show while he was on stage performing. In addition, I was ordered to do a pastel portrait of the Deputy Commander of the Tenth Army, a marine general named Smith. Working on maps midnight to noon, for the most part, I had little time to deal competently with art. The mural was painted in my spare time in our underground complex. I struggled with another canvas above ground on a gun rack in a latrine. An account of some of these shenanigans can be found in an article in *Design* written by Stanley Witmeyer (November 1945 issue).

When the war ended I wrote to Yale seeking admission to the university's art school. I was accepted the following April. Meanwhile, I vacationed on the "Big Island"—Hawaii—and awaited my release from the army.

In February 1946, a month following my service discharge, Abraham Lincoln High School mounted a one-man show of drawings and watercolors I had done during the war, chiefly in Africa. The exhibition, my first solo show, was hung in connection with the awarding of the Lincoln Medal to Mrs. Eleanor Roosevelt. Over the next seven months, I painted two or three dark and heavy-handed canvases; spent more time rediscovering the hometown girls than worrying about painting; and became reacquainted with my brother. Nine years separated us in age. We hardly had a boyhood together.

In July, the Norfolk Art School of Yale University, Norfolk, Connecticut, opened its studios for the first time. I was there painting meaningless pictures with Lewis York, chairman of Yale's painting department; Herbert Gute; and Dean Everett Meeks. I had no idea what I wanted to paint. I had nothing to say. I was lost in that idyllic introduction to the Yale tradition. Those Berkshire foothills seemed more menacing than the formidable Atlas Mountains of North Africa. I could hardly believe the peace, the quiet, the freedom, independence, and solitude.

I spent the next four years in New Haven. In an address before the fiftieth anniversary convention of the Catholic Library Association of America in Cincinnati, Ohio, April 13, 1971, I described the Yale Art School education as I had perceived it:

> Here I was taught a discipline like never before; its history, mechanics and philosophy. Here I learned about optical physics, the chemistry of application, the scheme of drawing, the intent of painting. Here I was exposed to technical and esthetic possibilities I never knew existed. Now I knew what an innocent I really was.... Whatever Yale art had been before the war (a school of classic revival) it certainly was different now ...

I may have some trouble with that today. My perspective has since softened. Times change. We change or perhaps grow differently. Art schools at best represent the composite direction and fallibility of faculty ego. Too many artists use academia to justify their own creative presence, and by institutional association give respectability to what otherwise could be insignificant esthetic adventures. Impressionable students are expected to comply. Art faculties, and thus, art schools, have no right to represent finite, uncompromising esthetic values. From the French academic Beaux Arts to the German new order Bauhaus, art schools have traditionally sought to impose their artistic definitions upon unsuspecting students and laypersons alike. The Yale Art School I attended did everything it could to explore the nature of our craft in every direction and to every depth without dragging the student around in an arena of conforming esthetics. Yale may have been out-of-touch with the realities of the new movements that would reshape the entire artistic world, but

Colonial Craftsmen, United States Postal Service Bicentennial postage stamp issue, July 4, 1972. In the collection of the Smithsonian Institution.

that was not professionally fatal. It is the student who must recognize or sense or consider how to use the information and skills being offered. Schools do not make artists. Artists make themselves.

Although in hindsight I may take issue with parts of the Yale curriculum to which I was subjected, my art has evolved from that matrix, underwritten by pre-war and other influences, never radicalized by fast-moving trends or by an esthetic imposed by Yale. Lewis Edwin York, who stood at the center of the painting program of my time, had a deep influence on us all. He was a compelling teacher, the most informed person I ever knew in my life, the pure intellectual. The gifted faculty and student body were a supreme challenge to one's esthetic raison d'être. And all of us, faculty and students alike, in our great desire to achieve something artistic, were wedged in a cultural limbo between the end of the old era and the coming of the new; the art world was on hold in that twilight zone between the war's end and the arrival of the abstract expressionists. It would take me years to shake it all loose. Nevertheless, the Yale experience was memorable. It prepared me for every artistic eventuality. It was up to me to discover those eventualities.

I did manage to keep a quiet professional life going in New York while struggling with the practice of egg tempera painting at Yale. I was a member of "Twenty-Five and Under," a group sponsored by Jacques Seligmann Galleries. Not only were my paintings being seen in Manhattan, but elsewhere in America, arranged by Seligmann. In April 1950, while working on a graduate degree and teaching Design Theory at the art school, I was invited by Lincoln Kirstein to participate in a show, *Symbolic Realism,* at the Edwin C. Hewitt Gallery in Manhattan. I was included with a large allegorical egg tempera, *Coney Island.* Suddenly I was in the company of Andrew Wyeth, Paul Cadmus, Isabel Bishop, and others, who comprised the exhibition. Kirstein wrote, "Art is a cosa mentale, a thing of the mind." Perhaps. In May I received the Pulitzer painting award. By September 1950, my Sea Gate sojourn was ending. My life would take me elsewhere.

Glutted with funds from the William Wirt Winchester Traveling Fellowship (Yale University School of Fine Arts, 1949) and the Joseph Pulitzer Painting Fellowship (Columbia University and the National Academy of Design, 1950), I sailed for Europe aboard the British liner *Mauretania* to finally see all the art I had only known through book and magazine reproductions. As the ship came abreast of Hoffman and Swinburne Islands on the starboard, I could see clearly the lighthouse and "4810" at the seawall on the port-side. It was late in the afternoon. The sun setting over Staten Island illuminated the Sea Gate shore. Standing on the seawall were waving relatives and friends. They were holding aloft a white bedsheet and a large American flag both of which fluttered wildly in the breeze.

My first stop was London where I was spellbound by Carlo Crivelli's *Annunciation* at the National Gallery. There were other spellbinders I never dreamed I would ever see—and all these in one room. There were Mantegnas, Bellinis, Verrocchios, DaVincis, Turas, and Sassettas, and more. But it was the Crivelli *Annunciation* that held my interest. A year before, I painted *Coney Island.* There was a direct influential link between what Crivelli had done with egg tempera and one-point perspective and what I did. At the Victoria and Albert Museum I met Jonathan Main, Curator of Painting. I spent the afternoon with him looking at Raphael's tapestry cartoons. I could not have had a better guide.

In Paris at the Louvre, I was struck dumb by two works: Géricault's *Raft of Medusa* and David's *Napoleon Crowning Himself.* It was the scale of them, the size of them that astonished me. In Paris, too, I met Nadia Boulanger, the legendary piano teacher. I was reminded of my own piano teacher, Ruth Benach, an organist in a Brooklyn church. I gave Miss Benach a hard time for three or four years. How I dreaded her student recitals. Neither the piano nor I had much of a future with each other.

I spent a few weeks in Switzerland visiting with friends from home who were studying medicine in Lausanne. My adrenalin overflowed in Italy, everywhere from Milan to Venice to Florence, Pisa, Pistoia, Arezzo, Siena, Perugia, Orvieto, Rome, and on to the tip of the peninsula, across to Sicily and back again. I spent some time at the American Academy in Rome. I saw every painting I came to see and more. The works that made the most enduring impact on me were Michelangelo's *Sistine Ceiling* and *The Last Judgment.* They claimed my soul. And in a less persistent manner so did all the Botticellis.

I returned home in January 1951 aboard the *Queen Mary,* eager to paint pictures. I painted a few egg temperas and began to realize that this ancient eggyolk-and-water medium on a smooth gessoed surface, which I prepared myself, belonged to a frame of artistic reference from which I had been drifting. While I questioned its validity for me, I continued to comfortably use the medium for nine years, leaving it finally in 1960. Shortly after my return I found myself working for Auriel Bessemer, a commercial muralist. I needed some money. I lasted a week. My trees were not his trees. My rocks, clouds, grass, and pilgrims were not his either. We were working on panels for railroad dining cars. On Friday, as I was being fired, the phone rang. The caller, Lewis Edwin York, invited me to become dean of the Whitney School of Art, a small independent professional school in New Haven. I accepted. York, no longer at Yale, was now a member of my faculty.

That October I met Margery Meskin. Margery knew exactly where I was coming from—art. She knew more about Donatello than I thought I knew about Botticelli. Moreover, Margery knew exactly what the world was coming to—the computer. Margery was a systems service representative for IBM and lived on the top floor of a house in Manhattan where Chester A. Arthur took the oath of office as twenty-first President of the United States. Margery reminded me of no one I had ever known, so rare was her outlook, manner, and appearance. Suddenly, nothing seemed as important as spending the rest of my life with her.

In February 1952, I opened in Manhattan with my first New York exhibition. The Edwin C. Hewitt Gallery showed a few drawings and some recent egg temperas. The reviews were encouraging. The *New York Times* approved of my craftsmanship. No one bought a thing but the future looked promising. I convinced Margery of that promise.

The Fisher children: Julie, Susan, and James, 1984.

We were married that December in Rockville Centre, New York.

Margery had first to ease her father's fears. He was not sure of the reliability of artists, especially, as he put it, those who paint "gremlins." Margery had to cope with me, too. I was a full menu of unshakeable truths. Margery's mother, Ruth, and her sister Betty were my only allies. Considering the vicissitudes of married life in our time, Margery and I continue to illuminate each other and to be illuminated by our three children.

Following a trip to Bermuda, we settled in a New Haven apartment. Margery represented systems for IBM while I juggled two roles: painting and being an art school dean. The pressure put upon me by the school was enormous. The pressure I put upon myself with regard to painting commitments was also enormous. I was driven to achieve in both areas. The only person who understood what kind of an effort that took in time, concentration, and dedication was Margery. The only person who realized the scope of the effort besides Margery, but who knew the spectre of failure, was my father.

As it turned out, the school began to drown in financial problems. In tandem with that slow demise, my paintings began to look tired and hollow. The art world was beginning to spin too many revolutions per minute. Something was happening on the cultural landscape and to me. A new, aggressive, entrepreneurish esthetic was emerging in New York. I had recurring dreams that all my paintings were under water—Lower New York Bay—held there by Ottoman Turkish rug salesmen with great scimitars. Enough! I needed a new perspective and time.

Conversations with Alex Ross, an illustrator friend, led to Oscar Ogg, designer for the Book-of-the-Month Club. He turned me toward children's books. I went to see Warren Chappell. His advice was so discouraging it hardened my determination to illustrate books.

I left the Whitney Art School in September 1953. Shortly thereafter, Oscar Ogg introduced me to Louise Bonino, children's book editor of Random House. She was nonplussed by my portfolio: some photographs of paintings too large to carry around, and a handful of drawings from the nude. She asked me if I could handle Bourges color separation. "Of course," I replied. I had no idea what she was talking about. I figured I could find out later. I did. Meanwhile, I came away with my first book to illustrate, Geoffrey Household's *The Exploits of Xenophon,* a Random House World Landmark edition.

I asked everyone at Yale about "Bourges color separation." No one knew. I asked Mr. Michaels, the owner of the art supply shop on Chapel Street. He knew. "Mike" had never gotten past the eighth grade but he sold the stuff. I spent several sessions with him in the gloomy basement of his shop. There he taught me how to use this acetate material to separate flat colors for printing.

I set three goals with regard to *Xenophon.* The first was researching ancient Greek and Persian military life and matériels, including uniforms. The second goal was to use a graphic technique that had reproduction clarity. The third, to create a series of illustrations in two colors, black and brown, that could evoke a sense of solid form in a spatial setting.

Researching was easy. I knew my way around libraries and museums where books, manuscripts, prime source writings, paintings, statues, and ceramic decorations held the information I needed. Drawing clearly was no problem either. The big problem was creating the illusion of form in the final printing by overlapping two different materials in the artistic process. I knew a great deal about "form drawings"—those black-and-white drawings on toned papers of various colors. Albrecht Dürer's famous *Praying Hands* is a form drawing. I made hundreds of these drawings myself. And I studied hundreds more in the basement of the British Museum. I thought I could bring such drawing to life in this book even though I had to work with a separate color overlay. The outcome fell short of my desire. A true form drawing cannot be effected by some mechanical process aimed at printed reproduction. I should have known that. Nevertheless, it was my way of making a transition from what I knew I wanted to see as a painter to what I did not know how to produce as an illustrator. The effort in all this was monumentally time-consuming: researching, sketching, submitting the sketches for approval or disapproval, creating the finishes, and then nervously awaiting the outcome.

Xenophon finally appeared in September 1955. It was not perfect. I quickly knew I was in a new craft and needed some polishing. A month later, our daughter, Julie, appeared during a violent hurricane. But unlike the imperfections of *Xenophon,* Julie was perfect in every way. I had to give up my studio room to make way for a nursery. I ended up in the building's basement, where my kindly landlord had remodeled a studio room for me linked to our apartment by a surplus army field telephone. It was like being in a wartime bunker. I did not get much painting done down there. I spent every spare minute running upstairs to admire our new daughter. After *Xenophon* was published, I became extremely busy illustrating a six-volume reading anthology, *Our Reading Heritage,* for Henry Holt and Company.

Margery and Leonard Fisher on the Li River, China, 1984.

My mentor at Holt was Marjorie Wescott Barrows, who kept me and several others frantic in creating the great variety of illustrated material for the anthology. Marjorie was the boss. She had a great deal to say about every design, composition, technique and molecule of artistry. But Marjorie Barrows was being pressured by higher authorities, including state textbook adoption boards who also had a great deal to say about what the art should look like right down to the last buttonhole. I fought every inch of the way for my self-respect, my art and professionalism, not to mention my independence. It went on like that for a number of years, over hundreds of illustrations. I expected to be replaced every time the phone rang. The product of an artist is the result of long hours of concentration followed by long hours of working with one's hands. It is a product that cannot be duplicated. It is a singular item containing its own unique energies. To have these works rejected—after sixteen-hour days of lonely labor without a paycheck in sight, until the works are revised in ways that demean one's abilities—can be heartbreaking. And it happened. But I persisted. So did Marjorie. She refused to dismiss me even when I once jokingly begged her to do just that.

Instead, she sent me to the New York offices of Science Research Associates (SRA), a Chicago-based company. Lee Deighton, executive vice-president, was looking for artists to work on a new educational concept, the *Multilevel Reading Laboratory* originated by educator Don B. Parker. The first "laboratory," a box, would

contain, among other things, 150 reading selections requiring 150 two-color illustrations. Deighton's idea was to commission ten artists to illustrate fifteen selections each. My idea was to do all 150. I convinced Deighton that he would be better off dealing only with me rather than with a group of ten. The depth of my experience at Holt in creating two-color pre-separations, my educational background, literary knowledge, reading skills, and art abilities became the deciding factors. Between 1956 and 1962, I illustrated seven pioneering "Reading Laboratories" involving about 1,000 two-color pre-separated illustrations and countless rough sketches submitted to Chicago for approval—possibly more than 3,000 items in all. About 1,000 of these sketches are, today, in the DeGrummond Collection of the University of Southern Mississippi. Lee Deighton left SRA to become board chairman at Macmillan. The project was continued under the direction of Lee Brown, who later founded Learning Materials, Inc. I was busy here, too.

I cannot say that these illustrations were my "finest hour." It was art by committee. I was not always free to follow my instincts, which in too many cases would have proven better than what we ended up with. Still, for me, it was a challenge to see how often I could break through. The SRA "Reading Laboratories" were not only a foundation course in editorial textbook illustration, they were also a learning experience in how to deal—or how not to deal—with others.

SRA was not the only project that absorbed me in the cellar studio at 20 Lake Place, New Haven. I had obtained my first Holiday House book from Helen Gentry and Vernon Ives—Manley Wade Wellman's *To Unknown Lands.* It was the second "trade" book (non-textbook) of my blossoming career. It was the beginning of a thirty-year relationship between Holiday House and myself that would continue under the egis of Kate and John Briggs. I showed a portfolio of tear sheets to Alice Dickinson at Franklin Watts. I was immediately commissioned to illustrate Richard B. Morris's *First Book of the American Revolution.* That was the start of a twenty-year association that put me on the road illustrating and writing American history for young readers.

American history had a strong presence during my growing years. To my parents, one an immigrant, the other the son of immigrants, the United States was heaven-sent. To all of us it was important to understand American institutions and their origins in order to remain free. Knowledge of American history took precedence over other kinds of information, including art and the Bible. "We are the living miracle," my father would intone. Nothing else mattered with respect to continuity. We had not a single European connection. This was indeed the New World.

My interests were wider, nevertheless. I illustrated "Vision" and "Covenant" series for Farrar, Straus and Cudahy—books dealing with Catholic and Jewish histories in America. G. P. Putnam's Sons hired me to illustrate Peter Freuchen's *Whaling Boy.* I met Anico Surany at Alfred Knopf when I illustrated Robert Payne's *The Splendor of Persia.* She and I became good friends and later collaborated on a number of picture books dealing with Latin America, including *The Golden Frog,* a Putnam book. All of these found their way to audiovisual filmstrips.

Soon, other publishers became clients—Little, Brown; Abelard-Schuman; Crown; Vanguard; Appleton, Century and Crofts. It was time to crawl out of the basement.

We moved to Westport in June 1957. Julie cried the entire summer, preferring the cement and din of New Haven to the softer flora and fauna of Westport. I did not sleep the whole summer either. Every snapping twig and chirp in the woods behind us was a lion roaring in my ears. Screaming sirens never kept me awake in New Haven. Crashing tides never kept me awake in Sea Gate. But here, in Westport, silent and green, removed from the commotion of civilization, I heard every marching ant. Margery slept. This is where she belonged.

At last I had an aboveground studio, one of our three bedrooms. Swamped by book illustrating projects, I could now keep a painting in the works as well. But by 1959 I had to give up the bedroom. It was a move in the right direction. We had become five. Susan was born in 1958, James a year later. I was removed to a newly completed studio added on to the house with a library/den. We could never live without books, whether or not I created them. In time we would push out all the walls and remake our home where it stood.

Margery's dad, Hy, who would rather have worked a farm than travel back and forth on slow boats to Australia as he did in his youth, had our blessings, horticulturally speaking. His was the greenest thumb of all. An artist of the soil, a planter with an eye and a heart, he created at the base of the large northern window of my studio a bank of lush ferns, a mass some twenty-five-feet long and three-feet deep. He specially transplanted these ferns from Camp Fernwood, Maine, where his two daughters enjoyed many summers. A book collector as well, he taught me a thing or two about rare editions.

As Marge's dad toiled everywhere with his spade, planting annuals, perennials, trees and shrubs, Marge and I began to think there must be a world beyond children, relatives, friends, Cape Cod retreats, and volunteer work— not to mention just plain work. In October 1962, and without children, who we thought needed a rest from us, I dragged Margery all over Italy for three weeks, taking the identical routes I had traveled twelve years before. In two instances time seemed to stand still. A waiter I knew in a tiny Chocolateria in the Piazza della Signoria, Florence, was still there flicking his worn whisk broom over the backs of everyone who tipped him properly. Again, two clay pots brimming with geraniums huddled in a corner of an open window that could only be seen from the roof of the Clock Tower in Venice's Piazza San Marco. They were still there. For one fleeting moment I thought I saw the same scene, with its clay pots and geraniums, huddled in the same corner of a windowsill of a look-alike house on a recent visit we made to Suzhou in the People's Republic of China. Why not? Marco Polo, the Venetian, had been there.

From **The Great Wall of China,** *written and illustrated by Leonard Everett Fisher, 1986.*

The late 1950s and early 1960s were experimental years both artistically and parentally. For one thing I was a daddy who worked at home. I was around all the time. I am sure the children were put upon from time to time. But I loved every minute of it. The studio door was always open. They wandered in and out, observing what went on or did not go on. They had free access to every bit of material and equipment in the place. They created their own pictures and never felt compelled to alter any of mine with the quick swish of a sable brush loaded with India ink. Frequently I would look up from whatever it was I was doing and see the three of them with friends outside, pressing their noses against the window watching me. Their friends were always curious about this species of father who did not take a train to work. My children obliged all young disbelievers with on-the-spot guided tours.

These incidents provided the inspiration for one of two books that Margery wrote and I illustrated: *But Not Our Daddy* (1962). The other was *One and One* (1963), a number book. Both were published by the Dial Press. These two works were very unsophisticated. They were aimed at our own children.

These were the years I began to do scratchboard drawings for books; and I began to paint some transitional works that would slowly lead me out of the vacuum I had been locked in since the early 1950s. The paintings were gelatine temperas which spun off egg temperas and dealt with theo-philosophical concepts, for the most part—prophets and their symbols, etc.

In 1959, Connie Epstein at William Morrow asked me to consider doing one-color illustrations for a distinguished set of books by Gerald W. Johnson, Managing Editor of the *Baltimore Sun.* The books comprised a trilogy: *America Is Born, America Grows Up, America Moves Forward.* I suggested scratchboard. I liked the drama of scratchboard when the rendering of sharp light picked off the form. It was linear, strong, and direct. I could relate to it through all those form drawings I did, and which I had learned to do at Yale. I could see it in my mind as being appropriate in conveying a strong sense of history without being historically imitative. Connie agreed. I just had to take care to make them less precise and methodical than metal engravings. It was my beginning of twenty-five years of soft engraving.

During this same period Dial published my first—and their first—written and illustrated picture book, *Pumpers, Boilers, Hooks and Ladders.* I was not prepared to write a book for young readers. But I did it. I wrote and wrote and wrote. I revised and revised again. It seemed to take forever. By the time the book was published in 1961, the itch to write was firmly in place.

In the year of *But Not Our Daddy*, Franklin Watts asked me to write and illustrate something of my choice. The conversation took place during a seventeen-minute cab ride to a Children's Book Council luncheon. I suggested art—paintings. Watts did not absorb that notion until 1973 when he published my book *The Art Experience: Oil Painting 15th-19th Century.* Instead he countered with a series on colonial American crafts—nineteen titles in all and fourteen years in the publishing process. I spent the first two years, 1962-1964, researching the material. These books became a staple item in virtually every American school. They finally went out of print in the late 1970s and early 1980s. Some of the titles will reappear in the near future, courtesy of David Godine, Publishers.

From Cyclops, *written and illustrated by Leonard Everett Fisher, 1991.*

I enjoyed doing these books. They had more meaning for me than just conveying some colonial American history. More than that I tried to communicate a strong sense of pride in craftsmanship, in working hard to achieve excellence in one-of-a-kind objects. It was something I felt our children knew little about and it was time that they did.

My yen to write some adult material related to art came to fruition in 1984 when Thomas G. Aylesworth, formerly my editor at Doubleday, but now at Bison Books, asked me to write a tome on American painting. That book, *Masterpieces of American Painting,* along with a newer one, *Remington and Russell,* a lesser tome on two painters of the Old West, have become published entities.

Wandering in the realm of my interests had been the look of letters and alphabetic history. The story of written communication surely belonged within my arena of activity. I never locked onto a strong image around which I could pictorialize this theme until Margery, my wife, now an experienced Westport school librarian, proposed an alphabet book with exotic letters large enough for youngsters to use for social studies projects. Judith Whipple, then editor at Four Winds Press, responded to the concept. In its final form, *Alphabet Art* developed into a series of various alphabets with large scale letters accompanied by an historical account and fully illustrated, both calligraphically and pictorially. *Alphabet Art,* published in 1979, was followed by *Number Art* and the very recent *Symbol Art.*

Some of these works, no doubt, had been seeded in part by my return to teaching. It is difficult to know what generates creative impulses beyond suggestion in so many subject areas, and what generates the compulsion to communicate it all. I returned to teaching part-time in 1966 at the Paier School of Art in Hamden, Connecticut. I gave it up in 1978 to become the school's academic dean, in order to participate in the institution's quest for a State Charter to grant a Bachelor of Fine Art degree. We succeeded in 1982 and I went back to part-time teaching. The school is now the Paier College of Art. My association with the newly chartered college began in 1948 while I was a student at Yale. I was its first contract faculty member, lecturing in Art History.

My need to be connected with the educational process is woven into the tapestry of my creative being. Communication is part of personal expression and creation. Sometimes the creative process is enough. There is no further need to communicate what has been wrought. Then again, there are times when creation requires communication. Moreover, I like to be around young professional students. I think there is an obligation to see to it that professional generations are not disconnected.

I believe that the information books I write and illustrate are part of that rationale. Books like "Nineteenth-Century America," the seven-volume miniseries (Holiday House, 1979-1983) which describes areas of life in a growing United States, deal with my determination not to disconnect. In a culture like ours, wherein today's material gratification seems to deny any historical link, knowledge of the past is often and mistakenly brushed aside as irrelevant to our present and future values, much less the course of our nation. I try to say otherwise.

The Fishers with their grandchildren, (front row, from left) Gregory, Michael, Jordan, Lauren; back row: Sam and Danielle between Leonard and Margery Fisher, 2000.

In any case, creative disconnections were hardly a problem for me in the 1970s. After the death of my father in 1968, I was irrationally victimized by my lawnmower which took its revenge on my right hand. I recovered from that trauma. But in the process I came to realize my own mortality and the mortality of those around me whose lives mean more to me than my right hand. Life and art took on new meaning.

The grayness and low-key quality of the paintings I created during the 1960s disappeared. Gone, too, was the heavy philosophy. Brighter, more colorful, and higher-keyed paintings took their place. The medium was all acrylic. It was as if a veil had been lifted. While the paintings of the 1960s seemed overly concerned with cries in the wilderness and the loneliness of the human presence in an inhospitable world—much of this reflecting events, from the murder of John F. Kennedy through Vietnam and my own isolation from the hyped world of painting—the newer works were an attempt to define endless, boundless, infinite space. The paintings were of tapestries and boxes, conveying a less introspective view with more optimistic overtones than previous works. In addition, I began to write books with more lengthy texts: *The Death of Evening Star* and *Noonan* for Doubleday; *Across the Sea from Galway, Letters from Italy,* and *A Russian Farewell* for Four Winds.

Early in that decade I painted the *Stations of the Cross* for St. Patrick's Church, Armonk, New York. These fourteen acrylic panels were the closest I had been to wall decoration since the National Park Service used some of my art for a mural in the Washington Monument in 1964. Between 1972 and 1978, along with everything else I was doing, I designed a number of United States postage stamps depicting American history and crafts. Eight of these were Bicentennial issues of July 4, 1972, and July 4, 1977. One issue was the 1974 commemorative *The Legend of Sleepy Hollow,* a stamp close to my literary heart.

There were exhibitions and more exhibitions. The largest and most significant of these was the retrospective mounted by the New Britain Museum of American Art in 1973. The exhibition covered twenty-four years of my art.

As the 1970s tumbled along, Julie, Susan, and James began their successful collegiate careers—Julie at Mount Holyoke College, Susan at Brown University, James at Union College. Margery and I spent nine wonderful years enjoying the whole experience with them, including their army of friends. It was an energetic time in our lives. Beyond children, family, publishing commitments, painting projects, and professional school duties, there were serious community activities. I was connected to numerous organizations either as board member, minor officer, president, or all three. These included the Westport-Weston Arts Council, the Westport Council on Continuing Education, the Westport Bicentennial Committee, the Silvermine Guild of Artists, The New Haven Paint and Clay Club, and the Yale Art School Alumni Association. There was considerable traveling during this period as well: countless book fairs, lectures, and workshops everywhere in America, trips to Europe, Mexico, and the Caribbean. It all seemed to reach a soaring climax in a five-day stretch in Washington, D.C., when I functioned as a delegate-at-large to the 1979 White House Conference on Library and Information Services. It was a singular honor. But I felt so ineffectual among the 2,000 delegates that I fled the conference a half-day early with the wrong raincoat. I do not know what we accomplished. I do not know why libraries had to be justified to the nation in the first place. In a great and free democracy such as ours, libraries should have unquestioned priorities. They form the backbone of our educational systems. Our freedom is inextricably tied to those educational systems and the free access to information. That information resides in our libraries. And libraries are the repositories of our will to be free, as much as our elected and appointed branches of government.

It is not possible to describe the "free-lance" professional effort that reaches out to a larger world, dividing and subdividing like a living organism, creating with each growing part new interests, new obligations, new responsibilities, more anguish, excitement, and pleasantries, one on top of the other. The invisible thinking and physical activity that ends up in the marketplace—as words, pictures, lectures, speeches, books, paintings, posters, stamps, coins, and whatnot—is staggering. I could not have it any other way. The true witnesses to this are Margery and our children. As no other people can, they bring their bright perceptions and keen understanding to the whole process and the chores upon which that process leans. They make it easier, endurable, and enjoyable. Impacting on all of this, obviously, are our private, personal lives.

Not surprisingly, I reached the 1980s with a different resolve. It felt like a new beginning. I began to shed civic and professional involvements that impinged upon my creativity. There are some exceptions: my seat on the Board of Trustees of the Westport Public Library, for one. I turned

away from professional school administration. Now I work my wiles a few hours a week on unsuspecting tyros and have them improve my expressive posture at the same time. Once in a while I try it at Fairfield University. Also, I have become more comfortable at the easel and at the typewriter. The paintings are more fluid. The illustrations, chiefly in the picture book area, are similar to my easel paintings. They are done with a broader, more relaxed brush, reflecting a larger view. The writing seems easier and is at many levels. Margery, patient and trusting, knew all along what had to emerge. After thirty years my wife finally got through to me.

Margery Cuyler, my Holiday House editor, must have tuned in. She made a courageous decision to let me do *The Seven Days of Creation* (1981) with an abstract full-color sweep. On the basis of the *Creation,* a fitting piece to signal one's "new beginning," she effected a collaboration between poet Myra Cohn Livingston and me. The happy result was *A Circle of Seasons, Sky Songs, Celebrations,* and *Sea Songs.* These books have a vastly different approach and appearance than all that came before, including those I write as well. They are still not in the expected mold of fairy tales, talking giraffes, teen problems, or what the public at large assumes to be appropriate children's literature or children's pictures. I offer alternatives. I make young people stretch for experience, much as I had to reach and struggle for whatever it was I wanted in my life. I do not reflect, either in my art or my writing, experiences already experienced. And this I do, I trust, without resorting to the occult or worlds of fantasy. My purpose is never entirely factual or the rendering of the obvious, although it may appear to be.

From Sky, Sea, the Jetty and Me, *written and illustrated by Leonard Everett Fisher, 2001.*

I think Deborah Brodie at Viking sensed these things when she and designer Barbara Hennessy visited me and responded to the sharp dimensional realism of the "box" paintings I had done during the 1970s. I had already illustrated and written the fiercely bleak, monochromatic *Storm at the Jetty.* Now we took a great color leap forward and landed with *Boxes! Boxes!* (1984).

The Great Wall, a Macmillan project, is still another work in another dimension, as will be books about the Statue of Liberty and Ellis Island.

The creative essence that consumes me forms the pattern of my artistic leanings—expressions of form, space, form in space, space and movement, survival and continuity. Those are the things that I am all about.

What happens next? More of the same. The looks of these creations—what I have to say pictorially or verbally—might even be a surprise to me. There are ideas and feelings that knocked around inside of me for countless years before they finally emerged. And there are things inside of me hammering to get out that I cannot identify. What seems to have been fundamental to me all of my life is a hunger to express the inexpressible, to make visible the invisible.

Postscript Fall 2000

The past fifteen years have come and gone in less time than it takes to blink, or so it seems. In personal terms, the years 1985-2000 were a bittersweet mixture. The sweetest part of all was the arrival of six grandchildren. They have grown into a most interesting and winning bunch of kids. Obviously! They are ours! How they are loved—probably spoiled forever. Their coming and their presence—not to exclude their parents who are also much loved by us all—have softened and just about obliterated the sorrows that invaded our lives during this period. The death of my young brother, Richard, ravaged by cancer in 1985—age fifty-two—was a terrible blow. How he struggled and fought! It laid me low for quite a while. I still find some disbelief in that moment. An architect and civil engineer, known for his professional contributions to the Yankee Stadium modernization of the 1960s, the Brown University Athletic complex, the Washington, D.C., subway system, and other projects, he was in the midst of a noteworthy life with his greatest promise before him. My mother, and my one and only favorite mother-in-law, both lived to see ninety—my mother ninety-six—before leaving this world to us. Now, Margery and I are no longer sandwiched between young and old. We are the top piece of bread.

Margery and I continued our travels during these past fifteen years: France, Spain, Portugal (the source for *Prince Henry the Navigator*), Italy (where Galileo first crossed my mind), the Low Countries (and the Kinderdike legend), Switzerland (*William Tell,* another legend that became a book), Greece and the Islands (*The Olympians, Theseus and the Minotaur, Jason and the Golden Fleece, Cyclops,* all grew out of these wanderings), Russia, Scandinavia, Austria, the Czech Republic, Hungary, Mexico, Guatemala, Costa Rica, transited the Panama Canal west to east, visited the San Blas Islands (the setting for *The Golden Frog*), and revisited the Island of Jamaica (once the inspiration for *Sweeney's Ghost*), an old haunt of ours—when our children were young. We took winter breaks almost every year, walking the beach at La Jolla Shores, California, and spring breaks driving through New Mexico, Arizona, Colorado, and Utah with decompressions in Las Vegas—where we would catch a flight home.

A planned trip to Tucson, Arizona, in April 1998, proved to be just right. It turned out that I was able to recover there from the successful removal of an encapsulated malignant tumor from my chest the month before. I had no idea it was there—not even when a routine X-ray exposed its presence. I recall asking the anesthetist who hailed from Madras, India, if he would like an autographed copy of my book *Gandhi.*

"Absolutely," he said.

"Only on one condition," I said. "That I wake up!"

Needless to say, the good doctor got the book. All's well that ends well. Whew!

Unmentioned in all of this traveling are the uncounted trips to everywhere in America in the service of my publishers, publishing, and my art. I have not missed a beat in that regard.

Flowing seamlessly through all of this have been my creative juices: more books, more paintings, and some civic activity. During the late 1980s I became involved in the Westport Public Library, becoming president of its board of trustees for three years in a brand new building which has since been rebuilt. My work with the library is not quite over. I have spent the past several years co-curating the art exhibitions the library sponsors on its main floor. As if that is not enough, I became a member of the Sanford Low Committee of the New Britain Museum of American Art. This group oversees the wonderful Low Illustration collection that is an important part of the museum's holdings. Recently, I accepted an invitation to join the advisory committee for the master of arts degree program in painting and illustration of Western Connecticut State University.

One of the watershed moments in our lives was when in 1995 Margery retired after serving the Westport School system as a middle school librarian for twenty-five years. When Marge decided to pack it in—which she still has not done, for she is very active on the Bank Street College (New York) Book Committee, among other book related commitments—she told me that I had to get out of my home studio at least once a week and give her some space. I not only agreed to this, I gave her five days of space and moved into a downtown Westport Art Center studio. When the Center, once an elementary school, was returned to its academic tradition several years ago, I moved to another studio in nearby downtown Norwalk. Now I have two studios to fuss in—the one in Norwalk and my original one at home in Westport. These workplaces are conveniently only ten minutes apart.

With respect to my books and paintings I have at once much to say and again nothing to say. The books keep coming in spite of myself. The easel paintings I produced between 1990-2000 are very different from those that came earlier. In fact the easel paintings I created between 1980-1990 are different from the previous decade. In response to a query from the Stamford Museum, which was showing nine of my paintings during the late summer of 2000, I stated: "Since 1990, I have tried to define a moment in time...that communicates...a simple inner vision. At times, these...paintings appear enigmatic to me."

When I consider the fifty books that I have created during the past fifteen years—forty-eight for young readers—two for adults: mythology, biography, history, legend, memoir, fiction, nonfiction, picture book, non-picture-book—not to mention the thirty miscellaneous writing and/or illustrating projects, exhibitions like the Fifty Year Retrospective at the Museum of American Illustration (Society of Illustrators, New York), and professional whatnots, my mind cannot process the effort. All I can say about the productivity is my enthusiasm and energy runs high for people, places, and things that interest me—fiction or nonfiction. And there are a lot of things that interest me! It never seems to end. It is overwhelming when I stop to think about it. I am especially appreciative of my editors, Regina Griffin (Holiday House), Beverly Reingold (Macmillan and Farrar, Straus and Giroux), and Judith Whipple (Marshall Cavendish), who continue to suffer me. Kate and John Briggs of Holiday House continue to be in my corner for more years than I can count. My relationship to Holiday House stretches over some forty-five years!

Coming along soon enough are two picture books in the works at this writing: *The Gods and Goddesses of the Ancient Norse* and *The Gods and Goddesses of Ancient China*. A third book, a memoir of World War II, *Once a Soldier* (formerly called *Soldier Boy, Soldier Boy*) continues to be a work in progress. One day it will see the light of day. Another work in progress is a diary of recollections of my sojourn in Europe a half century ago when I was afforded an extravagant travel opportunity as a Winchester Fellow and Pulitzer Scholar.

My most recent book, *Sky, Sea, the Jetty and Me*, I might add, is a happy reprise recently brought out by Judy Whipple. This book is a drastically different redo of *Storm at the Jetty* published by Viking twenty years ago. It has a much larger format. It is in full color rather than the former monochrome, and the text has been altered to come from the first person—me—rather than a third person—someone else. Judy also published the only book I ever created without illustrations, *The Jetty Chronicles*. This manuscript languished unpublished for twenty years. It was from part of its text that *Storm at the Jetty* was originally culled. I am happy to report, too, that Judy Whipple is responsible for reissuing my "Colonial American Craftsmen" series—all nineteen volumes, slightly redesigned—originally published by Franklin Watts in the 1960s and 1970s.

But when it comes right down to it, the highlight of these past fifteen years is without question my two granddaughters and four grandsons. Nothing in my long career—none of the recognition that has come my way—not the awards—not the museum acquisitions—not the public reviews—nothing can compare to the meltdown that happens when our little ones give us a hug. For "Dips" — that's what they call me—and "Duma"—that's what they call Marge—I have no idea how that came about—I tried to get them all to say "Sarge" and "Marge"—it is the real magic in our lives. They are the ultimate prize. It is the end of a never ending, delicious fairytale. And we live happily forever after.

Writings

FOR CHILDREN; SELF-ILLUSTRATED

Pumpers, Boilers, Hooks and Ladders, Dial, 1961.
Pushers, Spads, Jennies and Jets, Dial, 1961.
A Head Full of Hats, Dial, 1962.
Two If by Sea, Random House, 1970.
Picture Book of Revolutionary War Heroes, Stockpole, 1970.
The Death of Evening Star: The Diary of a Young New England Whaler, Doubleday, 1972.
The Art Experience: Oil Painting 15-19th Century, F. Watts, 1973.
The Warlock of Westfall, Doubleday, 1974.
Across the Sea from Galway, Four Winds, 1975.
Sweeney's Ghost, Doubleday, 1975.
Leonard Everett Fisher's Liberty Book, Doubleday, 1976.
Letters from Italy, Four Winds, 1977.
Noonan, Doubleday, 1978, Avon, 1981.
Alphabet Art: Thirteen ABCs from Around the World, Four Winds, 1979.
A Russian Farewell, Four Winds, 1980.
Storm at the Jetty, Viking, 1980.
The Seven Days of Creation, Holiday House, 1981.
Number Art: Thirteen 1, 2, 3's from Around the World, Four Winds, 1982.
Star Signs, Holiday House, 1983.
Symbol Art: Thirteen Squares, Circles and Triangles from Around the World, Four Winds, 1984.
Boxes! Boxes!, Viking, 1984.
The Olympians: Great Gods and Goddesses of Ancient Greece, Holiday House, 1984.
The Statue of Liberty, Holiday House, 1985.
The Great Wall of China, Macmillan, 1986.
Ellis Island, Holiday House, 1986.
Calendar Art: Thirteen Days, Weeks, Months and Years from Around the World, Four Winds, 1987.
The Tower of London, Macmillan, 1987.
The Alamo, Holiday House, 1987.
Look Around: A Book about Shapes, Viking, 1987.
Monticello, Holiday House, 1988.
Pyramid of the Sun, Pyramid of the Moon, Macmillan, 1988.
Theseus and the Minotaur, Holiday House, 1988.
The Wailing Wall, Macmillan, 1989.
The White House, Holiday House, 1989.
Prince Henry the Navigator, Macmillan, 1990.
Jason and the Golden Fleece, Holiday House, 1990.
The Oregon Trail, Holiday House, 1990.
The ABC Exhibit, Macmillan, 1991.
Sailboat Lost, Macmillan, 1991.
Cyclops, Holiday House, 1991.
Galileo, Macmillan, 1992.
Tracks Across America: The Story of the American Railroad, 1825-1900, Holiday House, 1992.
Gutenberg, Macmillan, 1993.
David and Goliath, Holiday House, 1993.
Stars and Stripes: Our National Flag, Holiday House, 1993.

Marie Curie, Macmillan, 1994.
Kinderdike, Macmillan, 1994.
Gandhi, Atheneum, 1995.
Moses, Holiday House, 1995.
William Tell, Farrar, Straus, and Giroux, 1996.
Niagara Falls: Nature's Wonder, Holiday House, 1996.
The Gods and Goddesses of Ancient Egypt, Holiday House, 1997.
The Jetty Chronicles, Marshall Cavendish, 1997.
Anasazi, Atheneum, 1997.
To Bigotry No Sanction: The Story of the Oldest Synagogue in America, Holiday House, 1998.
Alexander Graham Bell, Simon and Schuster, 1999.
Gods and Goddesses of the Ancient Maya, Holiday House, 1999.
Sky, Sea, the Jetty and Me, Marshall Cavendish, 2001.
The Gods and Goddesses of the Ancient Norse, Holiday House, 2001.

"COLONIAL AMERICAN CRAFTSMAN" SERIES; FOR CHILDREN; SELF-ILLUSTRATED

The Glassmakers, F. Watts, 1964.
The Silversmiths, F. Watts, 1964.
The Papermakers, F. Watts, 1965.
The Printers, F. Watts, 1965.
The Wigmakers, F. Watts, 1965.
The Hatters, F. Watts, 1965.
The Weavers, F. Watts, 1966.
The Cabinet Makers, F. Watts, 1966.
The Tanners, F. Watts, 1966.
The Shoemakers, F. Watts, 1967.
The Schoolmasters, F. Watts, 1967.
The Peddlers, F. Watts, 1968.
The Doctors, F. Watts, 1968.
The Potters, F. Watts, 1969.
The Limners, F. Watts, 1969.
The Architects, F. Watts, 1970.
The Shipbuilders, F. Watts, 1971.
The Homemakers, F. Watts, 1973.
The Blacksmiths, F. Watts, 1976.

"NINETEENTH-CENTURY AMERICA" SERIES; FOR CHILDREN; SELF-ILLUSTRATED

The Factories, Holiday House, 1979.
The Railroads, Holiday House, 1979.
The Hospitals, Holiday House, 1980.
The Sports, Holiday House, 1980.
The Newspapers, Holiday House, 1981.
The Unions, Holiday House, 1982.
The Schools, Holiday House, 1983.

FOR ADULTS

Masterpieces of American Painting, Bison/Exeter, 1985.
Remington and Russell, W. H. Smith, 1986.

ILLUSTRATOR

Geoffrey Household, *The Exploits of Xenophon,* Random House, 1955, revised edition, Shoestring Press, 1989.
Florence Walton Taylor, *Carrier Boy,* Abelard, 1956.
Manley Wade Wellman, *To Unknown Lands,* Holiday House, 1956.

Roger P. Buliard, *My Eskimos: A Priest in the Arctic,* Farrar, Straus, 1956.
Richard B. Morris, *The First Book of the American Revolution,* F. Watts, 1956, revised edition published as *The American Revolution,* Lerner Publications, 1985.
L. D. Rich, *The First Book of New England,* F. Watts, 1957.
Kenneth S. Giniger, *America, America, America,* F. Watts, 1957.
Henry Steele Commager, *The First Book of American History,* F. Watts, 1957.
James C. Bowman, *Mike Fink,* Little, Brown, 1957.
Robert Payne, *The Splendor of Persia,* Knopf, 1957.
Peter Freuchen, *Whaling Boy,* Putnam, 1958.
Richard B. Morris, *The First Book of the Constitution,* F. Watts, 1958, revised edition published as *The Constitution,* Lerner Publications, 1985.
Jeanette Eaton, *America's Own Mark Twain,* Morrow, 1958.
Harry B. Ellis, *The Arabs,* World, 1958.
Robert Irving, *Energy and Power,* Knopf, 1958.
Estelle Friedman, *Digging into Yesterday,* Putnam, 1958.
E. B. Meyer, *Dynamite and Peace,* Little, Brown, 1958.
E. M. Brown, *Kateri Tekakwitha,* Farrar, Straus, 1958.
C. Edell, *Here Come the Clowns,* Putnam, 1958.
L. H. Kuhn, *The World of Jo Davidson,* Farrar, Straus, 1958.
Catharine Wooley, *David's Campaign Buttons,* Morrow, 1959.
Maurice Dolbier, *Paul Bunyan,* Random House, 1959.
Edith L. Boyd, *Boy Joe Goes to Sea,* Rand McNally, 1959.
Gerald W. Johnson, *America Is Born,* Morrow, 1959.
Richard B. Morris, *The First Book of Indian Wars,* F. Watts, 1959, revised edition published as *The Indian Wars,* Lerner Publications, 1985.
Elizabeth Abell, editor, *Westward, Westward, Westward,* F. Watts, 1959.
Phillip H. Ault, *This Is the Desert,* Dodd, 1959.
Robert Irving, *Sound and Ultrasonics,* Knopf, 1959.
Gerald W. Johnson, *America Moves Forward,* Morrow, 1960.
Gerald W. Johnson, *America Grows Up,* Morrow, 1960.
Robert Irving, *Electromagnetic Waves,* Knopf, 1960.
Declaration of Independence, F. Watts, 1960.
Trevor N. Dupuy, *Military History of Civil War Naval Actions,* F. Watts, 1960.
Trevor N. Dupuy, *Military History of Civil War Land Battles,* F. Watts, 1960.
Edward E. Hale, *The Man Without a Country,* F. Watts, 1960.
Anico Surnay, *Ride the Cold Wind,* Putnam, 1960.
Natalia M. Belting, *Indy and Mrs. Lincoln,* Holt, 1960.
Natalia M. Belting, *Verity Mullens and the Indian,* Holt, 1960.
Richard B. Morris, *The First Book of the War of 1812,* F. Watts, 1961, revised edition published as *The War of 1812,* Lerner Publications, 1985.
Emma G. Sterne, *Vasco Nuñez De Balboa,* Knopf, 1961.
James Playsted Wood, *The Queen's Most Honorable Pirate,* Harper, 1961.

Harold W. Felton, *A Horse Named Justin Morgan*, Dodd, 1962.

Charles M. Daugherty, *Great Archaeologists*, Crowell, 1962.

Margery M. Fisher, *But Not Our Daddy*, Dial, 1962.

Robert C. Suggs, *Modern Discoveries in Archaeology*, Crowell, 1962.

Paul Engle, *Golden Child*, Dutton, 1962.

Jean L. Latham, *Man of the Monitor*, Harper, 1962.

Gerald W. Johnson, *The Supreme Court*, Morrow, 1962.

Harold W. Felton, *Sergeant O'Keefe and His Mule, Balaam*, Dodd, 1962.

Gerald W. Johnson, *The Presidency*, Morrow, 1962.

Jack London, *Before Adam*, Macmillan, 1962.

Eric B. Smith and Robert Meredith, *Pilgrim Courage*, Little, Brown, 1962.

E. Hubbard, *Message of Garcia*, F. Watts, 1962.

Charles Ferguson, *Getting to Know the U.S.A.*, Coward, 1963.

A. Surany, *The Golden Frog*, Putnam, 1963.

Gerald W. Johnson, *The Congress*, Morrow, 1963.

Margery M. Fisher, *One and One*, Dial, 1963.

Andre Maurois, *The Weigher of Souls*, Macmillan, 1963.

Jack London, *Star Rover*, Macmillan, 1963.

Helen Hoke, editor, *Patriotism, Patriotism, Patriotism*, F. Watts, 1963.

Gettysburg Address, F. Watts, 1963.

Gerald W. Johnson, *Communism: An American's View*, Morrow, 1964.

Eric B. Smith and Robert Meredith, *Coming of the Pilgrims*, Little, Brown, 1964.

Richard Armour, *Our Presidents*, Norton, 1964.

Eric B. Smith and Robert Meredith, *Riding with Coronado*, Little, Brown, 1964.

Robert C. Suggs, *Alexander the Great, Scientist-King*, Macmillan, 1964.

John F. Kennedy's Inaugural Address, F. Watts, 1964.

Robert C. Suggs, *Archaeology of San Francisco*, Crowell, 1965.

Martin Gardner, *Archimedes*, Macmillan, 1965.

Florence Stevenson, *The Story of Aida* (based on the opera by Giuseppe Verdi), Putnam, 1965.

Lois P. Jones, *The First Book of the White House*, F. Watts, 1965.

Ernest L. Thayer, *Casey at the Bat*, F. Watts, 1965.

John Foster, *Rebel Sea Raider*, Morrow, 1965.

A. Surany, *The Burning Mountain*, Holiday House, 1965.

Martha Shapp and Charles Shapp, *Let's Find Out about John Fitzgerald Kennedy*, F. Watts, 1965.

Robert C. Suggs, *Archaeology of New York*, Crowell, 1966.

Clifford L. Alderman, *The Story of the Thirteen Colonies*, Random House, 1966.

John Foster, *Guadalcanal General*, Morrow, 1966.

Robert Silverberg, *Forgotten by Time*, Crowell, 1966.

Gerald W. Johnson, *The Cabinet*, Morrow, 1966.

Washington Irving, *The Legend of Sleepy Hollow*, F. Watts, 1966.

A. Surany, *Kati and Kormos*, Holiday House, 1966.

A. Surany, *A Jungle Jumble*, Putnam, 1966.

Eric B. Smith and Robert Meredith, *Quest of Columbus*, Little, Brown, 1966.

Madeleine L'Engle, *Journey with Jonah*, Farrar, Straus, 1967.

L. Sprague and Catherine C. De Camp, *The Story of Science in America*, Scribner, 1967.

Nathaniel Hawthorne, *Great Stone Face and Two Other Stories*, F. Watts, 1967.

Gerald W. Johnson, *Franklin D. Roosevelt*, Morrow, 1967.

George B. Shaw, *The Devil's Disciple*, F. Watts, 1967.

A. Surany, *Covered Bridge*, Holiday House, 1967.

A. Surany, *Monsieur Jolicoeur's Umbrella*, Putnam, 1967.

Washington Irving, *Rip Van Winkle*, F. Watts, 1967.

Richard B. Morris, *The First Book of the Founding of the Republic*, F. Watts, 1968.

A. Surany, *Malachy's Gold*, Holiday House, 1968.

Bret Harte, *The Luck of Roaring Camp*, F. Watts, 1968.

(With Cynthia Basil) J. Foster, *Napoleon's Marshall*, Morrow, 1968.

Gerald W. Foster, *The British Empire*, Morris, 1969.

Eric B. Smith and Robert Meredith, *Exploring the Great River*, Little, Brown, 1969.

A. Surany, *Lora Lorita*, Putnam, 1969.

Julian May, *Why the Earth Quakes*, Holiday House, 1969.

Victor B. Scheffer, *The Year of the Whale*, Scribner, 1969.

Victor B. Scheffer, *The Year of the Seal*, Scribner, 1970.

Berenice R. Morris, *American Popular Music*, F. Watts, 1970.

Victor B. Scheffer, *Little Calf*, Scribner, 1970.

Loren Eisely, *The Night Country*, Scribner, 1971.

Julian May, *The Land Beneath the Sea*, Holiday House, 1971.

Isaac B. Singer, *The Wicked City*, Farrar, Straus, 1972.

Jan Wahl, *Juan Diego and the Lady*, Putnam, 1973.

Gladys Conklin, *The Journey of the Gray Whales*, Holiday House, 1974.

James E. Gunn, *Some Dreams Are Nightmares*, Scribner, 1974.

E. Thompson, *The White Falcon*, Doubleday, 1976.

Milton Meltzer, *All Times, All Peoples: A World History of Slavery*, Harper, 1980.

Myra Cohn Livingston, *A Circle of Seasons*, Holiday House, 1982.

Richard Armour, *Our Presidents*, revised edition, Woodbridge Press, 1983.

Myra Cohn Livingston, *Sky Songs*, Holiday House, 1984.

Myra Cohn Livingston, *Celebrations*, Holiday House, 1985.

Myra Cohn Livingston, *Sea Songs*, Holiday House, 1986.

Myra Cohn Livingston, *Earth Songs*, Holiday House, 1986.

Myra Cohn Livingston, *Space Songs*, Holiday House, 1988.

Myra Cohn Livingston, *Up in the Air*, Holiday House, 1989.

Alice Schertle, *Little Frog's Song*, Harper, 1992.

Myra Cohn Livingston, *If You Ever Meet a Whale*, Holiday House, 1992.

Eric A. Kimmel, editor, *The Spotted Pony: A Collection of Hanukkah Stories*, Holiday House, 1992.

David and Goliath: Retold from the Bible, Holiday House, 1993.

Eric A. Kimmel, reteller, *The Three Princes: A Tale from the Middle East*, Holiday House, 1994.

Moses: Retold from the Bible, Holiday House, 1995.

Myra Cohn Livingston, *Festivals,* Holiday House, 1996.

Eric A. Kimmel, reteller, *The Two Mountains: An Aztec Legend,* Holiday House, 1999.

TEXT BOOKS AND LEARNING MATERIALS; ILLUSTRATOR

Our Reading Heritage (six volumes), Holt, 1956-58.

Marjorie Wescott Barrows, *Good English through Practice,* Holt, 1956.

Don Parker, editor, *The Reading Laboratories* (eight volumes), Science Research Associates, 1957-62.

Marjorie Wescott Barrows and E. N. Woods, *Reading Skills,* Holt, 1958.

Dolores Betler, editor, *The Literature Sampler* (two volumes), Learning Materials, Inc., 1962, 1964.

How Things Change, Field Enterprise, 1964.

AUDIO-VISUAL FILMSTRIPS; ILLUSTRATOR

Edgar Allan Poe, *Murders in the Rue Morgue,* Encyclopaedia Britannica, 1978.

Robert Louis Stevenson, *Dr. Jekyll and Mr. Hyde,* Encyclopaedia Britannica, 1978.

Bram Stoker, *The Judge's House,* Encyclopaedia Britannica, 1978.

A. B. Edwards, *Snow* (from *The Phantom Coach*), Encyclopaedia Britannica, 1978.

Edgar Allan Poe, *The Tell-Tale Heart,* Encyclopaedia Britannica, 1980.

OTHER

Also illustrator for *Cricket* and *Lady Bug* magazines. Many of Fisher's manuscripts, illustrations, drawings, and correspondence are housed at the Leonard Everett Fisher Archive, University of Connecticut, Storrs, the Kerlan Collection, University of Minnesota, Minneapolis, the de Grummond Collection, University of Southern Mississippi, Hattiesburg, the library of the University of Oregon, Eugene, and at the Postal History Collection, Smithsonian Institution, Washington, DC.

ADAPTATIONS

Filmstrips, all by Anico Surany and all produced by Random House: *The Golden Frog, The Burning Mountain, A Jungle Jumble, Monsieur Jolicouer's Umbrella, Ride the Cold Wind,* and *Lora Lorita.*

FITCH, John IV
See CORMIER, Robert (Edmund)

Autobiography Feature

Jean Fritz

1915-

It was raining in Hankow, China, on the night of November 16, 1915, which complicated matters. For it was then I decided to make my appearance in the world and my mother, sick with dysentery, had to be carried to the hospital on a stretcher. The servants carried the stretcher; my father, walking beside my mother, held an umbrella over her. Had I heard this story as a child, I would not have been impressed that it was either unusual or picturesque. This was China, the only world I knew. A stretcher, if needed, was no more unlikely than any other mode of travel: rickshas mostly, horse-and-buggy on special occasions, sedan chairs, sampans, and always in summer donkeyback when we were in Peitaiho. Until the last few years of our stay in China, an automobile ride ranked among the high treats of life, along with ice cream,

Jean at Peitaiho, China, 1920s.

snowfalls, and rare visits to the movies (Jackie Coogan, Douglas Fairbanks, Rin Tin Tin).

I have chronicled my childhood years in China in *Homesick: My Own Story,* but in deference to the shape of the book, I had to omit (except for a brief reference) all my wonderful summers in Peitaiho, a resort for foreigners on the ocean north of Peking. When I was there, I didn't waste time being homesick for America. Indeed this was such a magical spot that later my children came to use it as a yardstick for measuring the relative merit of all ocean resorts. "Is this as good as Peitaiho, Mom?" they would ask.

Young Jean on the veranda, Hankow, China, 1918.

And I would have to answer, No. In my eyes no place has ever been able to compete with Peitaiho. The ocean lay down a small slope at the end of a narrow goat path from our house. Our beach was bounded on one side by a peninsula which my father and I referred to as the "three-cornered island" and where at low tide we would chip oysters from the rocks. On the other side was Eagle Rock on top of which sat a house occupied by friends who every Sunday evening invited the American community to gather on their porch for a brief worship service. As we watched the sun sink into the sea, we sang "Day Is Dying in the West," a hymn of praise that I supposed had been written with that place specifically in mind.

The highlight of every summer was the day my parents and I and a few friends went for a picnic to Shanhaikuan where the Great Wall comes down to the sea. We started at five in the morning on donkeyback, following the shore, crossing miles of mountainous dunes, carefully avoiding the areas of quicksand. We ate our breakfast on the dunes and our lunch on top of the Wall itself where I could look down at Mongolia on the other side. I loved being on the edge of Mongolia. It had a faraway, wild sound as if it were a place in a story and automatically that put me in the story too.

Compared to Hankow—a dull, gray industrial city—Peitaiho did indeed have a storybook quality. Hankow in the 1920s was for a while the seat of the new Communist party, the headquarters of Russian advisors, and a hotbed of antiforeign demonstrations. Several times I was in real danger. My mother and I were once stoned by angry peasants on a country road; we had a gang of union workers break into our living room and riot. Time and again, along with other foreign women and children, we had to evacuate Hankow on a moment's notice. Of course I was scared but it was nothing compared to the terror I felt one night in Peitaiho. My mother woke me in the middle of that night as I slept on my bed on the veranda. She hurried me into her bedroom, pushed me behind an upstanding wardrobe trunk, and told me to sit on the floor and not move. At the side of the house I could hear gunshots. The police, she told me, were shooting it out with a pirate who had landed on our beach.

A pirate! I suppose if I'd seen him, he would have looked like an ordinary Chinese fisherman but the word "pirate" flung me into the heart of a story and struck more terror in me than any mob of angry Chinese. After all, I was used to Chinese mobs. But a pirate!

Stories played a great part in my childhood. They existed on the other side of what was for the most part a lonely time, but the boundaries were not clear—not then and not now. Whenever my emotions run deep, whenever I am overtaken by surprise or confounded with wonder, I feel that I have slipped into Story. Certainly I felt like the central character when I stood at the prow of the ship which finally returned me to America and in keeping with the moment, I recited the lines which begin "Breathes there the man with soul so dead . . . " Is this me, I asked, sailing through the Golden Gate?

Sometimes I wonder if I would have been a writer if I'd not had so many stories to lean on, so many backdrops to my life, such a variety of characters weaving themselves through my days. I was surrounded by different cultures—

Picnic on the Great Wall, Jean on the tree, about 1925, father, Rev. Arthur Minton, lower right in white hat; mother Myrtle Minton, upper right, in riding pants and necktie.

With grandparents and mother in the United States.

not only the Chinese, but in the international settlement in which we lived, I had friends of all nationalities. I celebrated Christmas the German way with German children, the English way with English friends, played with the daughters of the Italian consul, lived for a while with a Russian family who had crossed Siberia to escape their revolution. My parents entertained American sailors, visiting evangelists, and once a Chinese warlord, but when it came to Bertrand Russell, my father drew the line. He didn't want a proponent of "free love" at his dinner table. So with such a cast of characters at hand, I began early wondering about people, recognizing more and more as time went on that everyone is a story waiting to be pieced together. I was alert to the conversation of adults which, I had discovered, might at any moment drop a clue to the mysteries of life, the incomprehensibility of adulthood. I kept up the habit of listening to everything within earshot and so over the years I have developed a talent for eavesdropping. My record in a restaurant is a conversation eight tables away.

We came to America in 1928 and I spent the first year in Washington, Pennsylvania, becoming acquainted with my relatives, discovering such marvels as the five-and-ten, summer circuses, vegetables that could be eaten raw, drinking water that came straight from the tap. The list of discoveries stretched on and on, for America seemed not only a different country but a different world—newer, cleaner, more homogenous, luckier. It was an additional, a second world, however, in no way replacing my first one. Most China-born Americans feel this double-love, double-loyalty; it is a kind of tie of mutual memory that binds us together in a unique way.

After a year in Pennsylvania, my father went to work for the YMCA in Hartford, Connecticut, and we moved into the first American house of our own. My mother hung yellow silk curtains at our dining room windows, put down our Chinese rugs (which are on our floors now in Dobbs Ferry), and for my room she bought a white bedroom set which included a vanity table with a long mirror in the center, drawers on either side, and a bench in front of it. I

was old enough to know now that (at least in the 1930s) "sophistication" was the ultimate in feminine achievement but I was also smart enough to know that I could never acquire the assurance, the coolness, the chic bound up in the word. Yet when I sat at my vanity table and brushed my hair languorously before the long mirror, I experienced a glow of sophistication, so fleeting that I attributed it to a magical quality in the table itself.

During these high school years I had my first contact with teachers who were interested in stimulating their students rather than simply drilling them. Largely on my own, however, I discovered Amy Lowell, Walt Whitman, boys, Emerson's Journal, lipstick, Edna St. Vincent Millay, boys, Greta Garbo, and other vintage teenage enthusiasms. And thanks to my parents I became better acquainted with North America. Every year we vacationed in a new area— Maine, Nova Scotia, West Virginia, Cape Cod, Vermont. Generally when the local people heard of my father's background, they invited him to preach which, as far as I was concerned, cast a shadow over any holiday. Once he was in the pulpit, my father lost all sense of time and although my mother and I had secret signals we could give him from our pew, he never looked in our direction. His record was two hours at a vesper service in South New Fane, Vermont. I still suffer when I think of it.

After high school and in spite of a miserable record in mathematics, I was accepted at the college of my choice— Wheaton College in Norton, Massachusetts. A small women's college, it was just right for me. On the one hand,

Fritz, about 1938, "enjoying a beach."

Fritz with husband Michael and son David in New York after the Second World War.

there was a close relation between faculty and students and on the other hand, sophistication was not as important a criterion for success as it had been in high school. I had always known I wanted to write, so of course I majored in English and never throughout my entire career have I felt more elated than when my first freshman composition was read aloud to the class. I acted in plays, wrote for the college newspaper, and headed up the Wheaton chapter of the Veterans of Future Wars, a satirical antiwar movement started at Princeton. I loved my college years—so much so that at times they assumed that old storybook quality. Is this really me, I would ask, walking across a college campus in the United States of America? Even so, I knew I was still experiencing life in the lower case. I wouldn't really live Life with a capital L until I was out in the world on my own. Preferably in Greenwich Village.

Graduating from college in 1937, however, I soon discovered that I wasn't prepared to do much of anything "on my own." My parents had moved to New York my senior year, so though I had to abandon dreams of Greenwich Village, I did have a view of the Manhattan skyline from my bedroom window on Morningside Drive.

The Depression may have been winding down but not enough for inexperienced college graduates to notice. I had no luck landing a newspaper or magazine job and when I tried writing advertising copy for coming movie attractions, I was told my adjectives were not sensational enough. So I went the way of most women college graduates of that day: I took a crash secretarial course. Before I was quite finished, I was interviewed for a job with a dramatic coach at Carnegie Hall. The woman had no interest in my educational background; all she wanted to know was the date of my birth. Then after lengthy mathematical calculations, she announced that our stars coincided; I could begin work the next day. Ah, this must be Life, I decided. Bohemian style.

Within two weeks, however, I was disillusioned. The woman was fearsome and tyrannical. Our stars, far from coinciding, clashed so irrevocably that I quit. Back to the Help Wanted pages, I found an advertisement for a secretary to fly to China with a man who was selling munitions to Chiang Kai-shek in Chungking. Better than Bohemia, this was Adventure and one which would take me back to China. I had never been up in a plane and if "flying over the front" sounded dangerous, it also sounded story-like. At the interview, I informed the munitions man that I could speak Chinese which I thought would surely clinch the matter, but the munitions man shook his head. No, he said, I wouldn't do.

"Why not?" I asked.

"You're too innocent."

Shattering as this was to a twenty-one-year-old ego, I had to admit later that whatever he had in mind, he was probably right.

I ended up working for a textbook company on Union Square, which didn't say much for my stars. Yet having had consistently unhappy school experiences as a child, I had developed strong ideas about education and looked forward to watching an organization experimenting with methods, working for improvement. I was, as the munitions man had pointed out, innocent. For as well-intentioned as textbook publishers may be, their primary thrust must be not toward innovation but toward sales. Textbook editors cannot be leaders; they must be followers and please as many segments of the public as they can. This insight into

"Our house in Dobbs Ferry, New York."

Daughter Andrea and son David.

the textbook world would serve me well later when in my own way, and through a different route, I entered the field of education. At this time I also took a course in children's literature at Teachers College, Columbia University. I was, of course, delighted when my term paper, "Style in Children's Literature," was printed in a professional journal, but I still had no idea that this was the direction my own work would eventually take.

L ife with a capital L suddenly took over and made all plans irrelevant and the future itself problematic. I was married to Michael Fritz on November 1, 1941, and six weeks later the Japanese bombed Pearl Harbor. It seemed like the end of the world to me and yet, as it turned out, I was, as a war wife, lucky. Although Michael went into the army in early 1942 and served until December 1945, he was an officer in a radio intelligence unit, stationed first at the Presidio in San Francisco and then at Fort Lewis, Washington, and I was able to be with him all the time. Our son, David, was born in San Francisco and though being a mother without any of the amenities of washing machine, disposable diapers, or car was a time-consuming business, I felt I had somehow to keep my hand in the working world. I wrote stories for children as well as for adults and was disappointed but not surprised when all were rejected. I also talked the *San Francisco Chronicle* into letting me review new educational books and later in Tacoma, Washington, I managed to persuade the feature editor (a soft-hearted man) to abandon William Lyon Phelps and his syndicated column in favor of a weekly (and much cheaper) column by me.

After the war, we returned to New York. Our daughter, Andrea, was born in 1947, and I was able to make a fairly

steady business of free-lance editing and ghostwriting for textbook houses. At the same time I continued to write; and I continued to be rejected.

It was after 1951 when we had moved to Dobbs Ferry, New York (where Michael took an administrative job with a Columbia University laboratory), that I began to channel my work more and more into writing trade books for children. When I found that the Dobbs Ferry Library had no children's room, no children's programs, and few children's books, I volunteered to conduct a weekly story hour. This proved so popular that I was asked to become the children's librarian, plan a separate room for children, and order books. For two years I immersed myself in children's books, reading ten to twenty books a week so that I would know not only how to order books but how to match books to children. This wide, continuous reading, along with reading aloud, gave me a strong feeling for plot, pacing, and for subject matter that appealed both to children and to me. In short, without being consciously aware of what I was doing, I developed a sense of story and in the process found my own voice. That children should be my audience is not surprising, for I held tight to the memories of my own childhood, always afraid that second world of mine would fade away.

I began sending out manuscripts again. A true account of a trip when my four-year-old son warmed up his baby sister's bottle on the engine of a train became a story in which the magazine *Humpty Dumpty* showed interest but, the editor said, I should "loosen up" my style. I was not averse to loosening, was grateful for the advice, and as a result, found myself at last in print. I graduated to Wonder

Jean and her father in the 1960s "sitting on the one remaining original bench from the church Ann Hamilton and her family attended in the late 1700s."

Fritz in Ireland on a research trip for **Brendan the Navigator.**

Books and in 1954 sent out my first full-length picture book manuscript, *Fish Head,* about a "raggedy, scraggledy, patched-up, scratched-up cat" who quite by accident found himself at sea in a fishing boat. It seems logical to me that I settled on such a story for these were crowded years with a young family and a job, so of course there were times when I longed to find myself at sea just as Fish Head did.

Coward McCann accepted the book; Marc Simont illustrated it; and best of all I was now in the hands of Alice Torrey, a sensitive and demanding editor who made me feel excited about my potential and at the same time pushed me to try more difficult forms. My first full-length novel for children was a fanciful story of the children on our street in Dobbs Ferry which I renamed Pudding Street and which, in truth, had such an American, small-town look, it seemed ready-made for a story. The plot had the ups and downs that I knew now that plots must have but it was essentially a wish-fulfilling plot. By moving a retired sea captain into the neighborhood, I turned the street into a kind of dream street in which parents did not interfere and the children, with the help of this imaginative captain, had the time of their lives. I gave myself, however, a technical problem that would be difficult for experienced writers and was far beyond me at the time. The story revolved not around a central character but around multiple characters, a street full of children with equal story importance. Alice Torrey kept telling me to get further *inside* my characters, so I

rewrote and rewrote. In the end I think readers did respond to the fun the characters had in *121 Pudding Street,* but it was, as Alice and I both agreed, a "learning" book, one which made me face technical problems, see alternatives, and most of all, one which convinced me that I could indeed sustain a long book with chapters.

My next book was much easier to write. I told the story through the voice of a single character, a girl with whom I identified so closely I had no trouble getting "inside" her. For years I had wanted to extend a story that had come down in our family into a book, but I had not been able to do it. The story was of my grandmother's grandmother, Ann Hamilton, a pioneer girl in western Pennsylvania in the 1790s, whose family one night entertained George Washington as he was traveling west to inspect land that he owned. It was a true story, but by itself, it was simply an anecdote. I would have to invent a plot to go with it. When I began looking inside Ann, I discovered that she was lonely, resentful of living in an out-of-the-way place where, she felt, nothing happened. I would use the George Washington episode as the climax. The book was *The Cabin Faced West.* It was not until after the book was in print that I realized I had in a roundabout way told my own story except that the location and circumstances were different. In a way I was carrying on a dialogue with myself. The adult me was asking why I couldn't have appreciated my own faraway experience while I was still a child. The child in me was answering: "But it was lonely."

It was while I was working on this book that I discovered the excitement of historical research—reading old newspapers, letters, church records, county histories filled with colorful bits and pieces of the past that never make it into textbook history. I had not thought of writing about America's past but, after this experience, I was hooked. Just as I had been eavesdropping all my life in search of clues, so now I extended my arena to a new circle of people, those who had both lived and died and whose stories were complete.

I wrote three more historical novels *(Brady; I, Adam; Early Thunder)* but I became increasingly frustrated with the fictional framework into which I was fitting the history. I realized not only that life truly is stranger than fiction, but that I wanted to gather all that strangeness together and put it down as it actually is and was. I rushed into writing biographies; indeed I felt as if I must have been preparing for this all along, for I knew this was where I belonged. I started with the Otis family of Massachusetts whom I had met while working on *Early Thunder*. I wanted to know more about them but this, I realized, would be a book for adults, not children.

I identified easily with Mercy Otis Warren, my central character, for she was a writer and unsure of herself, and she was a mother who lay awake at night, worrying about her growing boys. My own children were teenagers now

and I, too, was a worrier. And like many writers, I, too, needed reassurance. Yet there were others in Mercy's life whose stories I wanted to include: her brother, James Otis, one of the first revolutionaries who later became so divided in his loyalties that he lost his mind; Mercy's father; her sons; Abigail and John Adams, her best friends who became embittered as their politics differed. So my cast was large and, although Mercy was at the center, I shifted voices. After I spent five years in research and writing, Houghton-Mifflin published *Cast for a Revolution*. Although it did not sell well, I have never been sorry that I wrote it. My attachment to Mercy was so strong, I felt compelled to bring her back to life, even if in a limited way.

The research for this book made me feel so much at home in Colonial and Revolutionary Massachusetts that when I went through the Granary Burying Ground in Boston, I kept running into familiar names, not of people who had played a big part in history, but of those who had been on the sidelines and whom I had come across by chance. Again and again I would hear myself exclaim, "Why, there you are!" as if I'd suddenly met up with an old friend. Two Massachusetts figures made their way into short biographies I wrote for children—Paul Revere and Sam Adams. I wanted to tell their stories without any fictional embroidery, with humor, gusto, and with concrete bits of out-of-the-way information which, I thought, would help bring them to life. I had such fun writing these two

"Finding my childhood home in China."

books *(And Then What Happened, Paul Revere?* and *Why Don't You Get a Horse, Sam Adams?)* that I went on to do more "question" books: *Where Was Patrick Henry on the 29th of May?; Will You Sign Here, John Hancock?; Can't You Make Them Behave, King George?; What's the Big Idea, Ben Franklin?; Who's That Stepping on Plymouth Rock?; Where Do You Think You're Going, Christopher Columbus?*

People often ask me if I am a "disciplined" writer. I tell them, No, I am a compulsive writer. The discipline comes when I have to go to the store, cook supper, vacuum, and perform other housekeeping chores. But I don't write all the time; I do other things too. For six years I conducted a writing workshop which was a happy experience for me in every way. Although some members dropped out, the core of the group remained the same. With a chance to write, rewrite, resubmit, rewrite again, most of the members had a long, ongoing experience that turned them into professional writers. Not only did I learn from the shared criticism of this group, but, more important, the people in the workshop became and have remained my best friends.

When asked by children if I have a "hobby" (a word I dislike), I usually say, No, because I don't collect stamps or play golf or garden, which are acceptable avocations. I am not sure that children would admit that reading and traveling are legitimate hobbies, and I certainly would not care to trivialize them by using the word. Yet that is how I use my spare time. When our children were young, we used our vacations to explore new areas, just as I had done as a child with my parents. Our longest and most memorable trip was a five-week drive across the continent and back, cooking on a camp stove, staying at motels within a fixed price range.

When the children were older, Michael and I were able to take occasional trips to Europe. By this time I had done enough traveling as part of research projects to realize that simply being a tourist was no longer enough for me. I wanted to travel with a *purpose.* I have always liked islands and I have, of course, liked far-away places with an end-of-the-world feeling, such as Mongolia had once been for me. When Mollie Hunter told me about the Orkney Islands, I knew that this was a place I had to go. In the North Sea between Scotland and Scandinavia, the Orkney Islands were historically the last stop explorers made when they were looking for the Northwest Passage. The *New York Times* expressed interest in a travel article on the Orkneys, so off we went.

Once there, I was carried away by the old sense of Story. Was this me at the top of the world with the sun setting at midnight and rising at three in the morning? I lay down on the summer-warm ground in the center of a prehistoric ring of monolithic stones and dreamed myself into the beginnings of time. Yet time itself, like space, seemed undefined in this watercolor world where sea, land, and sky ran in and out of each other so that they seemed all of a piece, distinguishable only to the oyster-catchers, the cormorants, the guillemots with their summit view. The people went with the place: the man who could imitate the cry of seals and call them to the shore; the woman who went out on the rocks every night to talk with the homing gulls; the farm-woman who gave me a bottle of grottie-

Fritz visiting a school in Wuhan, China, 1983.

buckies (tiny Arctic seashells) to place on my kitchen windowsill in the same way all native Orkney islanders keep their grottiebuckies close at hand. On our last day we were on a dock talking with a Scotswoman when a spectacular double rainbow suddenly arched over us. "Oh, I think John Knox must have sent us that rainbow," I said. "Because it's our last day here."

"Not John Knox," she replied tartly. "He wouldn't do anything for a foreigner."

I laughed both at John Knox and myself, for however far away I am from home, I never feel like a foreigner. Perhaps because I was a foreigner for so much of my childhood, the term has little meaning for me now.

There have been other memorable trips. Once to the Isle of Man for a travel piece and once to Ireland in preparation for my book, *Brendan the Navigator.* Sometimes people ask me if I need help with my research and I am always surprised. Help? The research is the most fun; I would stop writing before I would farm out any of the research.

Although from time to time I have written short books, retelling legends—*The Good Giants and the Bad Pukwudgies,* for example, and *The Man Who Loved Books*—I have also been interested in exploring characters at more depth than I was able to do in the "question" books. These books have been longer and designed for the upper elementary or junior high level: *Stonewall; Traitor: The Case of Benedict Arnold; The Double Life of Pocahontas;* and most recently *Make Way for Sam Houston.*

But throughout my writing career, I have wanted to capture the China-part of me and somehow shape it into a book. I did write several adult magazine stories (for the *New Yorker, Seventeen, McCall's*) based on China material, but every time I tried to encompass my childhood in a book-length story for children, I felt at a loss. I didn't like the sound of my adult voice remembering nor did I feel comfortable putting myself directly into an invented plot set in China. Yet as time went on, I felt increasingly the need to shorten my distance from this childhood by getting it into words. When my father died in 1981 at the age of ninety-six, I lost my last direct tie to the China years and the China memories, and then it seemed urgent to transcend the problems and repossess those years.

In the meantime China had opened up and Americans were going back. I longed to go too, but part of me was afraid. Would the strong, immediate experience of China today dull or confuse the memories? I concentrated again on trying to write the book I had so often attempted and so often abandoned. Somehow this time I did find my own voice as a child and by letting go of the real sequence of events, I was able to find a story shape where my China experience seemed to be at home. I called it fiction since I

make such a point in my nonfiction of being able to document facts and dates, but emotionally the story, *Homesick,* was as true as I could tell it.

And when I had finished, I was really ready to go back, not just to validate memory but to make China part of my present life. The trip, which resulted in the book *China Homecoming,* was one of the most exhilarating experiences of my life. China is not just another country; it is another world and to rediscover and discover it at the same time stirred up emotions that kept me at fever pitch. Moreover, it was an additional joy not only to share China with Michael (who had been subjected to so much China talk throughout our marriage) but to see him take the experience and make it also his own.

Sometimes I feel like Columbus who went with such joy from place to place, planting his flag, taking possession. Perhaps because as a child I was made to feel that I was not "home," I have the habit now of claiming places as my own, once I have dug into the history, once I have made friends with the people both past and present. China is, of

Fritz, 1985, "entertaining sugar birds on a Caribbean island."

The author leaning over her typewriter.

course, especially close to my heart, and, if luck is with us, we hope to go back. But as I have worked on my biographies, I have planted my private flag on many scattered bits of territory. And I have added islands to my personal map. For a number of winters now Michael and I have taken a few weeks vacation and gone to the island of Tortola in the Caribbean. During these vacations I have at last acquired a "hobby"; at least it serves as an answer when I am asked the question.

"Do you have a hobby, Mrs. Fritz?"

"Yes," I say, "I do. I snorkel."

"And how old are your children?" This is another common question, and it indicates how defensive I have become when I hesitate to reveal to school audiences the age of my children. But now I have an answer to that too.

"I have a grandchild now," I say. "My first. Michael Scott Fritz. Born in April 1985."

"Will you keep on writing?"

"Of course. I don't expect to run out of ideas."

Postscript (Spring of 2001)

No matter how carefully one makes plans, life has a way of stepping in and taking over. We were due to leave again for China when the riots at Tienanmen kept us home. So that extra trip to China has never taken place. Instead I turned back to American history and began research on the Lost Colony. But when I began having physical problems, that plan too fell by the wayside. A persistent pain in my left leg took me to orthopedists, rehabilitation, an acupuncturist, and finally to a neurological surgeon who said I would have to have a disc removed from my spine. No big deal, he said—five days in the hospital. The surgeon made a mistake during the operation, damaging some nerves, killing others. I have been in a wheelchair or walker ever since (five years).

Friends wondered why I didn't write while in the hospital. How could I? There were too many real stories being worked out around me. I was on the spinal floor and of course I worried about the boy who was brought in one night with gunshot wounds. Two young boys who had dived into too-shallow water were in much the same condition as Christopher Reeves. And there were amputees, an angry man suffering from Lou Gehrig's disease. My roommate was a girl who had been thrown from a car when her boyfriend fell asleep at the wheel. I learned a lot while in the hospital. I don't suppose any specific characters will find their way into my writing, but I'll never forget the people and how they dealt with their personal crises.

I wasn't quite through with my own problems, however. I broke a hip soon after coming home and had to return to that same spinal floor. Then in July 1995, my husband died of heart complications. I decided to go on living in the same house but had a bedroom and bath added to the first floor.

Finally, I was ready to think about the Lost Colony again. I had been afraid that my physical limitations would keep me from having the adventures I so often had when engaged in research. One of my first steps was to talk on the phone to the Park Ranger at the Lost Colony. In the course of the conversation he mentioned that there was at that very moment an archaeological team on a dig at Cape Hatteras where Indians once friendly to the Lost Colonists had lived. Well, I wanted to go on that dig and was lucky enough to find a friend who was willing to go with me.

I didn't expect to dig but I was allowed to sieve, and although I didn't personally find anything, I arrived on the scene just after a sixteenth-century gold ring had been unearthed. After it was sent to the College of Heraldry in England, it was identified as having belonged to a man in a previous expedition or possibly to his brother, a captain in Sir Francis Drake's fleet. Well, this is not a solution to the puzzle, not even a clue, but it was part of an adventure

But that book has been postponed again. About this time I became acquainted with the replica of Leonardo's famous twenty-four-foot horse which Leonardo had been working on when the French invaded and destroyed the horse. Leonardo was inconsolable. Coming upon the story over five hundred years later, Charlie Dent, a pilot in Pennsylvania, was determined to make up for the loss. He had done much of the work when he died of Lou Gehrig's disease. His family, however, had become so involved with the project, they commissioned a well-known Japanese sculptress, Nina Akuma, to take over.

I first saw the finished horse on display at the foundry, just before it was shipped to Milan. I had not expected to be captivated, but there was that majestic horse, a creature out of mythology, ready to take off into the sky. He belonged in a picture book and that's where I have put him. My daughter and I went to Milan to see him unveiled. And now I am back to the Lost Colony. There won't be solutions or many clues. But adventures? I'm hoping.

Fritz wearing sunglasses, sitting outdoors with walker nearby, 2000.

Writings

FOR CHILDREN

Bunny Hopwell's First Spring, illustrated by Rachel Dixon, Wonder, 1954.

Help Mr. Willy Nilly, illustrated by Jean Tamburine, Treasure, 1954.

Fish Head, illustrated by Marc Simont, Coward, 1954.

Hurrah for Jonathan!, illustrated by Violet La Mont, A. Whitman, 1955.

121 Pudding Street, illustrated by Sofia, Coward, 1955.

Growing Up, illustrated by Elizabeth Webbe, Rand McNally, 1956.

The Late Spring, illustrated by Erik Blegvad, Coward, 1957.

The Cabin Faced West, illustrated by Feodor Rojankovsky, Coward, 1958.

(With Tom Clute) *Champion Dog, Prince Tom,* illustrated by Ernest Hart, Coward, 1958.

The Animals of Doctor Schweitzer, illustrated by Douglas Howland, Coward, 1958.

How to Read a Rabbit, illustrated by Leonard Shortall, Coward, 1959.

Brady, illustrated by Lynd Ward, Coward, 1960.

Tap, Tap Lion, 1, 2, 3, illustrated by Leonard Shortall, Coward, 1962.

San Francisco, illustrated by Emil Weiss, Rand McNally, 1962.

I, Adam, illustrated by Peter Burchard, Coward, 1963.

Magic to Burn, illustrated by Beth Krush and Joe Krush, Coward, 1964.

Surprise Party (reader), illustrated by George Wiggins, Initial Teaching Alphabet Publications, 1965.

The Train (reader), illustrated by Jean Simpson, Grosset, 1965.

Early Thunder, illustrated by Lynd Ward, Coward, 1967.

George Washington's Breakfast, illustrated by Paul Galdone, Coward, 1969.

And Then What Happened, Paul Revere?, illustrated by Margot Tomes, Coward, 1973.

Why Don't You Get a Horse, Sam Adams?, illustrated by Trina Schart Hyman, Coward, 1974.

Where Was Patrick Henry on the 29th of May?, illustrated by Margot Tomes, Coward, 1975.

Who's That Stepping on Plymouth Rock?, illustrated by J. B. Handelsman, Coward, 1975.

Will You Sign Here, John Hancock?, illustrated by Trina Schart Hyman, Coward, 1976.

What's the Big Idea, Ben Franklin?, illustrated by Margot Tomes, Coward, 1976.

The Secret Diary of Jeb and Abigail: Growing Up in America, 1776-1783, illustrated by Kenneth Bald and Neil Boyle, Reader's Digest Association, 1976.

Can't You Make Them Behave, King George?, illustrated by Tomie de Paola, Coward, 1977.

Brendan the Navigator, illustrated by Enrico Arno, Coward, 1979.

Stonewall, illustrated by Stephen Gammell, Putnam, 1979.

Where Do You Think You're Going, Christopher Columbus?, illustrated by Margot Tomes, Putnam, 1980.

The Man Who Loved Books, illustrated by Trina Schart Hyman, Putnam, 1981.

Traitor: The Case of Benedict Arnold, illustrated with engravings and prints, Putnam, 1981.

Back to Early Cape Cod, Acorn, 1981.

The Good Giants and the Bad Pukwudgies (folktale), illustrated by Tomie de Paola, Putnam, 1982.

Homesick: My Own Story, illustrated by Margot Tomes, Putnam, 1982.

The Double Life of Pocahontas, illustrated by Ed Young, Putnam, 1983.

China Homecoming, illustrated with photographs by Mike Fritz, Putnam, 1985.

Make Way for Sam Houston!, illustrated by Elise Primavera, Putnam, 1986.

Shh! We're Writing the Constitution, illustrated by Tomie de Paola, Putnam, 1987.

China's Long March: 6000 Miles of Danger, illustrated by Yang Zhr Cheng, Putnam, 1988.

The Great Little Madison, illustrated with engravings and prints, Putnam, 1989.

Bully for You, Teddy Roosevelt!, illustrated by Mike Wimmer, Putnam, 1991.

George Washington's Mother, illustrated by DyAnne DiSalvo-Ryan, Putnam, 1992.

(With Katherine Paterson, Fredrick and Patricia McKissack, Margaret Mahy, and Jamake Highwater) *The World in 1492*, illustrated by Stefano Vitale, Holt, 1992.

Surprising Myself, photographs by Andrea Fritz Pfleger, Owen (Katonah, NY), 1992.

The Great Adventure of Christopher Columbus: A Pop-up Book, illustrated by Tomie de Paola, Putnam & Grosset, 1992.

Just a Few Words, Mr. Lincoln: The Story of the Gettysburg Address, illustrated by Charles Robinson, Grosset & Dunlap, 1993.

Around the World in a Hundred Years: From Henry the Navigator to Magellan, illustrated by Anthony Bacon Venti, Putnam, 1994.

Harriet Beecher Stowe and the Beecher Preachers, illustrated with engravings and prints, Putnam, 1994.

You Want Women to Vote, Lizzie Stanton?, illustrated by DyAnne DiSalvo-Ryan, Putnam, 1995.

Why Not, Lafayette?, illustrated by Ronald Himler, Putnam, 1999.

Leonardo's Horse, illustrated by Hudson Talbott, Putnam, 2001.

OTHER

Cast for a Revolution: Some American Friends and Enemies, 1728-1814 (adult biography), Houghton-Mifflin, 1972.

(Contributor) William Zinsser, editor, *Worlds of Childhood: The Art and Craft of Writing for Children*, Houghton-Mifflin, 1990.

Book reviewer, *San Francisco Chronicle*, 1941-43, and the *New York Times*, 1970—. Contributor of short stories to periodicals, including *McCall's, Seventeen, Redbook*, and the *New Yorker*.

Fritz's papers are housed in a permanent collection in the Children's Literature Collection at the University of Oregon, Eugene, and included in the Kerlan Collection at the University of Minnesota, and in a collection at the University of Southern Mississippi.

ADAPTATIONS

Fritz's writings have been recorded on audio cassette.

G

GARNER, Eleanor Ramrath 1930-

Personal

Born May 25, 1930, in Philadelphia, PA; daughter of Josef (an engineer) and Mathilde (a homemaker; maiden name, Rump) Ramrath; married Louis J. Garner (an accounting executive), September 22, 1951; children: James, Thomas. *Education:* Attended Boston University. *Religion:* Catholic. *Hobbies and other interests:* Painting in oils, gardening, hiking, "student of C. G. Jung."

Addresses

Home—6439 Lake Apopka Pl., San Diego, CA 92119.

Career

Episcopal Community Services, grant writer and social worker, 1975-80; Harcourt, Brace & Co., copyright and permissions editor for college textbooks, 1980-93; freelance permissions editor and copyright consultant for textbook publishers, 1993-99. *Member:* Friends of Jung of San Diego (founding member), Foothills Art Association, National League of American Pen Women, Art Alliance.

Awards, Honors

San Diego Book Award for Children's Nonfiction, and *Voice of Youth Advocates* Honor List, both 1999, Children's Book Award, International Reading Association, Best Book for Young Adults designation, American Library Association, Notable Children's Trade Book in the Field of Social Studies, National Council for the Social Studies/Children's Book Council, and Teachers' Choice Project, all 2000, all for *Eleanor's Story*.

Writings

Eleanor's Story: An American Girl in Hitler's Germany (memoir), Peachtree (Atlanta, GA), 1999.

Contributor of articles on psychology and religion to periodicals.

Sidelights

After a decade spent working in the publishing field as a permissions editor, Eleanor Ramrath Garner took the suggestion of a colleague and wrote a book of her own:

Eleanor Ramrath Garner

Eleanor's Story: An American Girl in Hitler's Germany. The American-born daughter of German immigrants to the United States, eight-year-old Garner suddenly found herself an outsider in Germany after her parents returned there in 1939 after her father accepted a two-year long engineering position in Berlin. Then war broke out, and the intended two years turned into a seven-year ordeal. Garner continued her childhood habit of keeping diaries and creating poetry albums as an outlet for her feelings. It would be to this material, as well as family photographs and letters, that Garner returned to many years later when she set out to write her memoir, a process that proved to be both painful and cathartic.

In *Eleanor's Story* Garner describes her efforts to avoid trouble while at the same time abhorring the Nazi culture of cruelty and prejudice. Like others, her family suffered hunger, experienced bombings by Allied forces, mourned the death of friends, survived the battle of Berlin, and withstood occupation by Soviet forces. These experiences comprised much of Garner's childhood, as she had reached her teen years by the time she returned to the United States.

For Garner, writing *Eleanor's Story* proved to be a healing experience. She revealed to *SATA:* "After completing my memoirs, I felt a forgiveness of the past. The child buried beneath the rubble of painful memories was restored to her rightful place in my personality. It has left me with a sense of wholeness. The split between the young girl and the older woman has been healed."

For its truthfulness and evocative qualities, *Eleanor's Story* garnered positive reviews. Heidi Borton, writing in *Voice of Youth Advocates,* praised the "immediacy and power in her recollections," judging the work to be "outstanding." Borton also found Eleanor's relationship with her father to be of "particular interest." Garner's "story is rich in detail and insight," praised Sandra Morton in *Book Report.* So too, *Booklist* reviewer Anne O'Malley called the memoir "stunning," explaining, "This powerful coming-of-age tale is told with intensity and also the freshness of teenage years remembered."

For Garner, *Eleanor's Story* is more than simply her own family's story. "I see *Eleanor's Story* not so much as a looking back at the past, but more as a collective remembrance, a common experience true on many different levels, one that not only reflects my personal history, but the larger one as well," she explained to *SATA.* "It's an historical document, written from the unusual perspective of an American teen whose eyewitness account describes daily life under the Nazi regime and the struggle of civilians for survival. The book seeks to pull the reader into the heart of war and how the young girl coped with the tragedies that unfolded around her, what sustained her, what gave her hope and strength to endure in the face of great odds. In essence, it's a story about growing up too fast against the backdrop of monumental events in world history.

"Wartime historical nonfiction tells the personal side of conflicts. These stories are of real people, how they lived, how they coped with the tragedy and horror of war. They speak for the masses and for the kind of society they lived under. These stories tell a truth that needs to be told."

Biographical and Critical Sources

PERIODICALS

Booklist, October 1, 1999, Anne O'Malley, review of *Eleanor's Story,* p. 354; March 15, 2000, review of *Eleanor's Story,* p. 1339; July, 2000, Hazel Rochman, review of *Eleanor's Story,* p. 2026.

Book Report, February, 2000, Sandra Morton, review of *Eleanor's Story.*

La Jolla Light, November 11, 1999, review of *Eleanor's Story,* p. 11

Publishers Weekly, May 1, 1999, Bob Summer, "From Peachtree a Historic Memoir," p. 12.

Voice of Youth Advocates, December, 1999, Heidi Borton, review of *Eleanor's Story;* July, 2000, "Best of the Year—Holocaust Literature for Youth," p. 2026.

*   *   *

GEASON, Susan 1946-

Personal

Born August 23, 1946, in Australia; daughter of Urban (an academic) and Joan (a homemaker; maiden name, Oakford) Geason. *Education:* University of Queensland, Australia, B.A. (history and politics), 1968; University of Toronto, M.A. (political philosophy), 1974. *Hobbies and other interests:* Reading, films, yoga, politics.

Addresses

Home—P.O. Box 496, Bondi Junction, New South Wales 1355, Australia. *E-mail*—susan@susangeason.com.

Career

National Times (newspaper), education editor, 1978-81; Parliamentary Research Service, legislative researcher, 1979-80; New South Wales Premier's Department, cabinet advisor, 1981-85; New South Wales State Pollution Control Commission, head of information and publications, 1985-87; *Sun Herald,* literary editor, 1991-97; University of New South Wales, National Center in HIV Social Research, editor, 1999-2000. Freelance writer, 1987—. *Member:* Sisters in Crime (New South Wales branch), Jessie Street Women's Library, Australian Journalists Association.

Awards, Honors

Cowinner, Cleminger/*Billy Blue Magazine* short story award, 1985; Australian Writers and Art Directors Award, 1986; shortlist, Steele Rudd short story award, 1991, for *Shaved Fish;* shortlist, Ned Kelly Australian Crime Novel Award, 1996, for *Wildfire;* Children's

Susan Geason

Section shortlist, NSW Premier's History Awards, 2000, for *Great Australian Girls.*

Writings

Shaved Fish (stories), Allen & Unwin (Sydney, Australia), 1990.
Dogfish (novel), Allen & Unwin (Sydney, Australia), 1991.
Shark Bait (novel), Allen & Unwin (Sydney, Australia), 1993.
Wildfire (novel), Random House (Sydney, Australia), 1995.
(Editor) *Regarding Jane Eyre* (stories and essays), Random House (Sydney, Australia), 1997.

JUVENILE; NON-FICTION

Great Australian Girls, ABC Publishing, 1999.
Australian Heroines: Tales of Adventure and Survival, ABC Publishing, 2001.

WITH PAUL WILSON

Crime Prevention: Theory and Practice, Australian Institute of Criminology (Canberra, Australia), 1988.
Designing out Crime: Crime Prevention through Environmental Design, Australian Institute of Criminology (Canberra, Australia), 1989.
Preventing Car Theft and Crime in Car Parks, Australian Institute of Criminology (Canberra, Australia), 1990.

Preventing Graffiti and Vandalism, Australian Institute of Criminology (Canberra, Australia), 1990.
Preventing Retail Crime, Australian Institute of Criminology (Canberra, Australia), 1992.

OTHER

Contributor of short stories to anthologies and magazines. Geason's fiction has been translated into French, German, Norwegian, and Swedish.

Sidelights

Australian author Susan Geason is a writer of many talents, with a long list of varied works to her credit, including novels, short stories, and nonfiction. "I always wanted to be a writer," Geason told *SATA.* "I began writing little poems as a child and had my first short story published at nineteen. University sidetracked me from literature into politics and history, and I didn't really begin writing seriously again until I was in my thirties. I've been able to combine my interest in writing and politics in my career, working as a journalist and researcher."

In 1987 Geason decided to give up full-time work, opting for a freelance writing career, and turned her hand to fiction. In 1990 she published a collection of short stories, *Shaved Fish,* about a detective named Syd Fish. Geason followed up the collection with a sequel, *Dogfish,* a "slim novel fat with laughs," to quote Pat Dowell of the *Washington Post Book World.* Syd Fish, who is a wisecracking, hard-boiled detective in the American mold, finds himself involved in solving the murder of a transvestite in an old neighborhood in Sydney. "If you take him more for fun than for real, Fish has a certain rude charm," conceded Marilyn Stasio in the *New York Times Book Review.* Although Stasio pointed out the stereotypical qualities of the main character, she found it "worth indulging Fish his tough-guy affectations for the pleasure of making the rounds with him." About *Shaved Fish* and *Dogfish,* Dowell commented, "Both volumes whet the appetite for more Aussie adventures."

Geason continued her Fish stories with the 1993 publication *Shark Bait,* before creating her first detective novel featuring a female crime-stopper, *Wildfire,* in 1995. "By some form of synchronicity, I started writing my detective novels when many other women began writing feminist mystery novels and became part of a literary movement," Geason told *SATA.*

In 1997 Geason edited a collection of short stories and essays, *Regarding Jane Eyre,* about the heroine of Charlotte Brontë's classic novel. *Regarding Jane Eyre,* Geason told *SATA,* "made me realise how few role models exist for girls apart from actresses, singers, and sportswomen." Geared toward girls aged ten through sixteen, Geason's *Great Australian Girls* tells the stories of twenty-three notable Australian women who lived during the last two hundred years of that country's history. Among them are tennis champion Evonne Goolagong, businesswoman Mary Reibey, Aboriginal lawyer Pat O'Shane, jockey Beverley Buckingham, and heart transplant recipient Fiona Coote. Geason thoroughly researched her subjects, conducting numerous interviews in the process. For greater appeal to her young audience, she purposefully chose women who had begun pursuing their lifelong goals while still girls. As Geason revealed in her home page: "Girls have been seen and not heard for too long. I felt their voices needed to be heard.... That's why I wrote this book. I wanted girls to be able to read about other girls who decided what they wanted and went out and got it."

"This is a better collective biography of Australian women than many on the market," noted a *Magpies* reviewer of *Great Australian Girls,* citing the book's "well-written" text "based on sound historical research" and an "interesting mix of subjects." Noting her degrees in history and politics, *Australian Financial Review* contributor Julie McCrossin suggested that Geason's educational background is evident in her "great research." McCrossin further claimed that "If there's a girl in your life that you'd like to inspire, Susan Geason's *Great Australian Girls ...* offers plenty of ideas about how to live a life bravely."

Biographical and Critical Sources

PERIODICALS

Australian Financial Review, September 24, 1999, Julie McCrossin, "Thank Heavens for Great Aussie Girls," p. 12.
Magpies, November, 1999, review of *Great Australian Girls,* pp. 44-45.
New York Times Book Review, January 17, 1993, Marilyn Stasio, review of *Dogfish,* p. 25.
Washington Post Book World, June 20, 1993, Pat Dowell, "Mysteries down Under," p. 6.

ON-LINE

Susan Geason Home Page, http://www.susangeason.com (May 5, 2000).

*   *   *

GIBLIN, James Cross 1933-

Personal

Surname is pronounced with a hard "g"; born July 8, 1933, in Cleveland, OH; son of Edward Kelley (a lawyer) and Anna (a teacher; maiden name, Cross) Giblin. *Education:* Attended Northwestern University, 1951; Western Reserve University (now Case Western Reserve University), B.A., 1954; Columbia University, M.F.A., 1955.

Addresses

Home—200 East 24th St., Apt. 1606, New York, NY 10010. *Office*—Clarion Books, 215 Park Ave. S., New York, NY 10003.

Career

Freelance writer, 1955—. Worked as a temporary typist and at the British Book Centre, 1955-59; Criterion Books, Inc., New York City, assistant editor, 1959-62; Lothrop, Lee & Shepard Co., New York City, associate editor, 1962-65, editor, 1965-67; Seabury Press, Inc., New York City, editor-in-chief of Clarion Books (for children), 1967-79, vice-president, 1975-79; Houghton Mifflin Company, New York City, editor and publisher of Clarion Books, 1979-89, contributing editor, 1989—. Adjunct professor at Graduate Center of the City University of New York, 1979-83. *Member:* Society of Children's Book Writers and Illustrators (member of board of directors), Authors Guild, Children's Book Council (president, 1976).

Awards, Honors

American Library Association notable children's book citations, 1980, for *The Scarecrow Book,* 1981, for *The Skyscraper Book,* 1982, for *Chimney Sweeps: Yesterday and Today,* 1985, for *The Truth about Santa Claus,* 1986, for *Milk: The Fight for Purity,* 1987, for *From Hand to Mouth,* 1988, for *Let There Be Light: A Book about Windows,* 1990, for *The Riddle of the Rosetta Stone: Key to Ancient Egypt,* 1991, for *The Truth about Unicorns,* 1993, for *Be Seated: A Book about Chairs,* 1995, for *When Plague Strikes: The Black Death, Smallpox, and AIDS,* 1997, for *Charles A. Lindbergh: A Human Hero,* and 2000, for *The Amazing Life of Benjamin Franklin;* Golden Kite Award for nonfiction,

James Cross Giblin

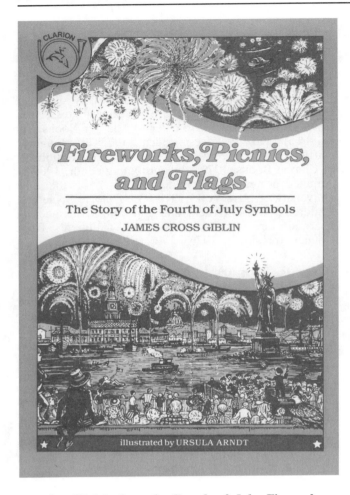

A **fun-filled** *look at the Fourth of July,* **Fireworks, Picnics, and Flags** *explains the symbols associated with the holiday and offers enjoyable activities for young readers. (Cover illustration by Ursula Arndt.)*

Society of Children's Book Writers and Illustrators (SCBWI), 1982, and American Book Award for children's nonfiction, 1983, both for *Chimney Sweeps: Yesterday and Today;* Golden Kite Award for nonfiction, SCBWI, 1984, for *Walls: Defenses throughout History,* and 1989, for *Let There Be Light: A Book about Windows; Boston Globe-Horn Book* Nonfiction Honor Book, 1986, for *The Truth about Santa Claus; Washington Post*-Children's Book Guild Award for Nonfiction, 1996, for body of work; Honor Book, National Council of Teachers of English Orbis Pictus Award for nonfiction, 1998, for *Charles A. Lindbergh: A Human Hero,* and 2001, for *The Amazing Life of Benjamin Franklin;* several of Giblin's books have been Junior Literary Guild selections.

Writings

NONFICTION; FOR CHILDREN

(With Dale Ferguson) *The Scarecrow Book,* Crown, 1980.
The Skyscraper Book, illustrated by Anthony Kramer, photographs by David Anderson, Crowell, 1981.

Chimney Sweeps: Yesterday and Today, illustrated by Margot Tomes, Crowell, 1981.
Fireworks, Picnics, and Flags: The Story of the Fourth of July Symbols, illustrated by Ursula Arndt, Clarion Books, 1983.
Walls: Defenses throughout History, Little, Brown, 1984.
The Truth about Santa Claus, Crowell, 1985.
Milk: The Fight for Purity, Crowell, 1986.
From Hand to Mouth; or, How We Invented Knives, Forks, Spoons, and Chopsticks & the Table Manners to Go with Them, Crowell, 1987.
Let There Be Light: A Book about Windows, Crowell, 1988.
The Riddle of the Rosetta Stone: Key to Ancient Egypt, Crowell, 1990.
The Truth about Unicorns, illustrated by Michael McDermott, Harper, 1991.
Edith Wilson: The Woman Who Ran the United States, illustrated by Michele Laporte, Viking, 1992.
George Washington: A Picture Book Biography, illustrated by Michael Dooling, Scholastic, 1992.
Be Seated: A Book about Chairs, HarperCollins, 1993.
Thomas Jefferson: A Picture Book Biography, illustrated by Michael Dooling, 1994.
When Plague Strikes: The Black Death, Smallpox, and AIDS, illustrated by David Frampton, HarperCollins, 1995.
Charles A. Lindbergh: A Human Hero, Clarion, 1997.
The Mystery of the Mammoth Bones: And How It Was Solved, HarperCollins, 1999.
The Amazing Life of Benjamin Franklin, illustrated by Michael Dooling, Scholastic, 2000.
(Editor and author of introduction) *The Century That Was: Reflections on the Last One Hundred Years,* Atheneum, 2000.
Adolf Hitler: An Extraordinary Villain, Clarion, in press.

FICTION; FOR CHILDREN

(Reteller) *The Dwarf, the Giant, and the Unicorn: A Tale of King Arthur,* illustrated by Claire Ewart, Clarion, 1996.

OTHER

My Bus Is Always Late (one-act play; first produced in Cleveland, OH, at Western Reserve University, 1953), Dramatic Publishing, 1954.
Writing Books for Young People (adult nonfiction), The Writer, Inc., 1990.

Also author of a play based on William Styron's novel *Lie Down in Darkness.* Contributor of original short stories to anthologies: "Three Mondays in July" in *Am I Blue? Coming out of the Silence,* edited by Marion Dane Bauer, HarperCollins, 1994; "Night of the Plague" in *Tomorrowland: Stories about the Future,* edited by Michael Cart, Scholastic, 1999.

Contributor of articles and stories for children to *Cobblestone, Cricket,* and *Highlights for Children,* and of articles for adults to *Children's Literature in Education, Horn Book, Publishers Weekly, School Library Journal, Washington Post, Writer,* and *Writer's Digest.*

Sidelights

James Cross Giblin has been a major figure in the field of children's book publishing since the 1970s. Not only has he edited the work of many important authors during his years at Clarion Books, but Giblin himself has written many nonfiction books for young readers. He has won awards and critical acclaim for his children's books, including *Chimney Sweeps: Yesterday and Today, The Truth about Santa Claus, Let There Be Light: A Book about Windows,* and *Charles A. Lindbergh: A Human Hero.* As Giblin once explained, "Nonfiction books for children aged eight to twelve [give] me the opportunity to pursue my research interests, meet interesting and stimulating experts in various fields, and share my enthusiasms with a young audience. I try to write books that I would have enjoyed reading when I was the age of my readers."

Giblin was born July 8, 1933, in Cleveland, Ohio. A shy, bookish child, he grew up in nearby Painesville. As a boy, he enjoyed the comic strip "Blondie," and, with his mother's help, he began drawing his own strips. Giblin once recalled, "I filled sketchbook after sketchbook with action-filled pictures drawn in boxes like those of the comics. Mother helped me to print the words I wanted to put in the balloons, and later I learned how to print them myself." Giblin also enjoyed going to the movies as a youngster; he once noted "My favorites weren't films made for children but spy movies set in Germany and Nazi-occupied areas such as *Casablanca.* I also liked melodramas starring emotional actresses like Bette Davis and Greer Garson, especially if they took place in exotic settings ... or had to do with World War II."

In junior high, Giblin worked on the school paper, which helped him overcome some of his shyness. He reminisced in his autobiographical essay in *Sixth Book of Junior Authors,* "Robert K. Payne, my ninth-grade English teacher, did more than anyone to draw me out of my isolation. Mr. Payne encouraged his classes to try new things, including a mimeographed class newspaper. And he was determined that I should not only contribute pieces to the paper but also edit it." Giblin continued, "I backed away from the responsibility at first, as I backed away from so many things then. But Mr. Payne was persistent, and at last I allowed myself to become involved. Once I did, I discovered that I loved working with my classmates on the paper and thinking up ideas for each new issue."

Giblin discovered a new interest when he got to high school. He answered a notice in the local paper about auditions for a community theater production of the play *Outward Bound,* and, as he once recalled, "My parents drove me to the barn theatre on the outskirts of town, and I nervously entered the rustic auditorium. When I arrived home three hours later—one of the actors had given me a ride—I couldn't restrain my excitement. 'I got a part! I got a part!' I shouted as I raced through the darkened house to the back porch, where my parents were sitting. The director had cast me as the idealistic young Reverend Duke in the play, which tells the story

of a group of English people traveling on an ocean liner who gradually realize that they have died and are on their way to Heaven ... or to Hell." Giblin added, "As a shy youth of sixteen I might be reluctant to reveal my feelings, but I found I had no trouble expressing them through the character of the Reverend Duke. When the play was over and I walked to the center of the stage to take my bow, the applause seemed like an endorsement not just of my acting but of me personally. I felt a surge of confidence that I had never known before.... After *Outward Bound* I was hooked on the theatre. I tried out for and got parts in all of the Le Masque Club productions ... at Harvey High School, and the following summer I was cast in the small but funny role of the Lost Private in a professional production of the comedy *At War with the Army* at Rabbit Run Theatre in nearby North Madison."

After graduating from high school, Giblin studied drama at Northwestern University. However, he was unhappy there, and after one semester he transferred to Western Reserve University (now Case Western Reserve University) near his parents' home. He did well; in addition to starring in many stage productions at Western Reserve, he won a contest to costar in a radio drama in New York City with actress Nina Foch. As Giblin gained experi-

A suffragette pickets in front of the White House. (From The Century That Was: Reflections on the Last One Hundred Years, *edited by James Cross Giblin.*

ence on the stage, his ambitions changed. He once noted, "The actor has very little control over his situation, and I now knew that I wanted control. So I turned my attention to directing and playwriting." An experience with an old woman on a bus inspired him to write his first play, *My Bus Is Always Late,* which was produced locally and published by the Dramatic Publishing Company in 1954.

Soon after, Giblin began studying for a Master of Fine Arts degree in playwriting at Columbia University in New York. Upon earning it, he remained in New York City to write, supporting himself by working as a temporary office employee. He became involved in efforts to adapt William Styron's novel *Lie Down in Darkness* for the stage, but the project fell through for various reasons. This failure deeply affected Giblin. He once explained, "I'd put almost a year of hard work and anticipation into *Lie Down in Darkness.* I'd drawn on my deepest feelings in order to write it, and in the process it had become my personal statement as much as Styron's. I tried to start a new play in that late spring of 1957, but I discovered, painfully, that I'd already expressed most of what I had to say in *Lie Down in Darkness.*"

After a recuperative visit home to Painesville, Giblin returned to New York in hopes of finding a more dependable career. He started out as a special-order clerk at the British Book Centre, then joined the staff of Criterion Books in 1959, first as a publicity director, and later as an editor. He enjoyed the work, especially when given the opportunity to edit books for young readers. Deciding to concentrate solely on works for children, he moved on to Lothrop, Lee and Shepard in 1962.

While working at Lothrop, Giblin started to think about writing his own books. He once recalled, "In 1964, after editing J. J. McCoy's career book, *The World of the Veterinarian,* I decided to try writing a similar book about publishing, and drafted an outline for it and several sample chapters." Though a publisher expressed initial interest in the book, in the end, it was rejected since the potential market was felt to be too small. Giblin had ambivalent feelings, as he noted in his autobiographical essay in *Sixth Book of Junior Authors:* "I really wasn't sorry. While part of me wanted to resume my writing career, another part—remembering the *Lie Down in Darkness* experience—hung back from making the necessary commitment to it."

In the late 1960s, Giblin went to work for Seabury Press, where he was instrumental in developing the company's children's division, Clarion Books. In the 1970s, a trip to China inspired him to try another book project of his own—"an anthology of Chinese writings about the doings of Chinese young people in the years since the Communist Revolution of 1949," as he once described it. But this time the project did not go through because it was considered "too political." However, by this time Giblin was writing again, contributing articles about children's books to periodicals and lecturing at conferences of children's book writers and librarians.

In 1980, Giblin collaborated with Dale Ferguson on his first children's book, *The Scarecrow Book.* Since then, he has written nineteen more children's nonfiction titles on a wide range of subjects, among them *The Skyscraper Book* (1981), *Walls: Defenses throughout History* (1984), and *Let There Be Light: A Book about Windows* (1988). In 1989, Giblin decided he was tired of juggling his role as editor-in-chief of Clarion Books with his expanding career as a writer, so he retired to contributing editor status.

The author's children's books have continued to range far afield. Giblin has explored such topics as milk pasteurization, Fourth of July celebrations, eating utensils, chairs, plagues, and mammoth bones, among many others. Many reviewers have praised Giblin's ability to tell complex stories in a way that is simple, understandable, and entertaining. Elizabeth S. Watson, writing in a *Horn Book* review of *The Riddle of the Rosetta Stone: Key to Ancient Egypt,* stated that "the author has done a masterful job of distilling information, citing the highlights, and fitting it all together." *New York Times Book Review* contributor Philip M. Isaacson lauded Giblin's writing skills in *Let There Be Light,* noting that the author "has condensed a daunting body of material to provide young readers with a great deal of information about the evolution and technology of windows."

Some critics have also pointed out that Giblin's accounts, while easy to understand, are loaded with valuable detail. "[His] relaxed, affable manner belies the amount of information he offers," wrote Amy L. Cohn in a *School Library Journal* review of *Chimney Sweeps: Yesterday and Today.* Other critics have observed that this wealth of information is derived from the author's painstaking research. "Giblin has such a flair for historic detail and research that he translates hordes of tales into a singular creation of Santa Claus," proclaimed a *School Library Journal* reviewer about *The Truth about Santa Claus.* An evaluation of the same book in *Bulletin of the Center for Children's Books* lauded Giblin's command of his subject, stating that the author had done "his usual good job of research and well-organized presentation." Reviewing Giblin's 1999 book, *The Mystery of the Mammoth Bones,* a *Publishers Weekly* critic praised the author for having "the pacing of an ace detective [as he] unveils the painstaking steps in artist and naturalist Charles Willson Peale's 1801 discovery of mammoth bones."

In addition to his books about interesting subjects and events, Giblin has written biographies of such historical figures as founding fathers George Washington, Thomas Jefferson, Benjamin Franklin, and aviator Charles Lindbergh, and he has even started to write fiction. Like his earlier works, Giblin's nonfiction books continue to find favor with reviewers and young readers alike. For example, assessing Giblin's 2000 book *The Amazing Life of Benjamin Franklin,* Ilene Cooper of *Booklist* wrote, "[His] writing is lively, and he wisely uses the story of Franklin's estrangement from his only living son, a Royalist, to heighten dramatic tension." *Horn Book* reviewer Mary M. Burns wrote of the same biography, "Giblin demonstrates his mastery of the historical-biographical genre—he knows how to define a theme, develop a narrative, and maintain his focus to the last sentence." Giblin's initial foray into fiction, *The Dwarf, the Giant, and the Unicorn,* met with mixed reviews. Carolyn Phelan of *Booklist* praised it as a "good read-aloud," while a *Publishers Weekly* reviewer stated that Giblin's efforts were "without memorable results."

Giblin's more recent book, *The Century That Was: Reflections on the Last One Hundred Years* is something of a departure for him, although it is a natural extension of his former work as an editor. He compiled and edited a collection of thematic essays by eleven noted children's writers, each one looking at a different aspect of life in America in the twentieth century. Hazel Rochman of *Booklist* pointed out that while editor Giblin made no effort to produce a "comprehensive" history, "The individual approaches, both personal and historical, will stimulate young people to look back and also forward to where we're going next." A *Horn Book* reviewer voiced a similar opinion, stating, "One of the older formulas of outstanding nonfiction ... is the essay. It's back, and in fine fettle for a new generation of readers."

James Giblin has commented on the enjoyment that he derives from investigating the factual details of his subjects and how important this task is to his work. "I love research," the author told *Publishers Weekly* interviewer Wendy Smith. "I love going down to Washington on a vacation week and using the Library of Congress. I enjoy making things clear for readers—maybe 'clear' is a unifying word in my work as an author and editor."

Biographical and Critical Sources

BOOKS

Children's Literature Review, Volume 29, Gale, 1993.
Sixth Book of Junior Authors and Illustrator, Wilson (Bronx, NY), 1989.
Something about the Author Autobiography Series, Volume 12, Gale, 1991.

PERIODICALS

Booklist, December 1, 1996, Carolyn Phelan, review of *The Dwarf, The Giant, and the Unicorn: A Tale of King Arthur,* pp. 666-667; February 15, 2000, Ilene Cooper, review of *The Amazing Life of Benjamin Franklin,* p. 1105; March 1, 2000, Hazel Rochman, review of *The Century That Was: Reflections on the Last One Hundred Years,* p. 1235.
Bulletin of the Center for Children's Books, October, 1983; February, 1985; September, 1985, review of *The Truth about Santa Claus;* November, 1986; December, 1987.
Chicago Tribune Book World, April 11, 1982.
Horn Book, February, 1983, pp. 62-63; January-February, 1989, pp. 33-34; November-December, 1990, Elizabeth S. Watson, review of *The Riddle of the Rosetta Stone: Key to Ancient Egypt,* p. 758; March, 2000, review of *The Century That Was: Reflections on the Last One Hundred Years,* p. 211, May-June, 2000,

Mary M. Burns, review of *The Amazing Life of Benjamin Franklin.*
New York Times Book Review, November 21, 1982, p. 43; March 12, 1989, Philip M. Isaacson, review of *Let There Be Light: A Book about Windows;* January 16, 1994, p. 20; March 15, 1998, p. 24.
Publishers Weekly, July 26, 1985, Wendy Smith, "PW Interviews James Giblin," p. 169; November 15, 1985, p. 56; November 11, 1996, review of *The Dwarf, the Giant, and the Unicorn: A Tale of King Arthur,* p. 75; January 25, 1999, review of *The Mystery of the Mammoth Bones,* p. 97; February 28, 2000, p. 81; May 8, 2000, p. 222.
School Library Journal, January, 1983, Amy L. Cohn, review of *Chimney Sweeps: Yesterday and Today,* p. 75; October, 1985, review of *The Truth about Santa Claus,* p. 192; March, 1987, pp. 113-115; October, 1988, pp. 27-31.
Voice of Youth Advocates, October, 2000, Leah J. Sparks, review of *The Century That Was,* p. 285.
Washington Post Book World, November 10, 1991.

*   *   *

GISE, Joanne
See MATTERN, Joanne

*   *   *

GRACE, Theresa
See MATTERN, Joanne

*   *   *

GREGORY, Philippa 1954-
(Kate Wedd)

Personal

Born January 9, 1954, in Nairobi, Kenya; daughter of A. P. (a radio operator and navigator) and Elaine (Wedd) Gregory; children: Victoria Chislett. *Education:* University of Sussex, B.A. (with honors), 1978; University of Edinburgh, M.Litt., 1980, Ph.D., 1984. *Politics:* "Radical."

Addresses

Home—Northeast England. *Agent*—Rodgers, Coleridge & White, 20 Powis Mews, London, England.

Career

Provincial journalist for newspapers in England, 1971-75; BBC-Radio, Southampton, England, radio journalist, 1978-80 and 1984—. Writer. Founding member and vice president of Hartlepool People, a community center for the unemployed and low-paid.

Writings

FOR CHILDREN

Princess Florizella, Kestrel-Kite, 1988.

Florizella and the Wolves, illustrated by Patrice Aggs, Walker Books (London), 1991, Candlewick Press (Cambridge, MA), 1993.

The Little Pet Dragon, illustrated by David Wyatt, Hippo, 1994.

Diggory and the Boa Conductor, illustrated by Jacqueline East, Hippo, 1996.

FOR ADULTS

Wideacre (first novel in "Wideacre" trilogy), Viking, 1987, Simon & Schuster (New York, NY), 1988.

The Favoured Child (second novel in "Wideacre" trilogy), Viking, 1989, Pocket Books (New York, NY), 1990.

Meridon (third novel in "Wideacre" trilogy), Viking, 1990, Pocket Books (New York, NY), 1990.

Mrs. Hartley and the Growth Centre, Penguin, 1992.

The Wise Woman, Pocket Books (New York, NY), 1993.

A Respectable Trade, HarperCollins (New York, NY), 1995.

Fallen Skies, HarperCollins (New York, NY), 1995.

The Little House: A Novel, HarperCollins (New York, NY), 1996.

Perfectly Correct, Acacia Press, 1997.

Earthly Joys, St. Martin's (New York, NY), 1998.

Midlife Mischief, Severn House (New York, NY), 1998.

Virgin Earth, St. Martin's (New York, NY), 1999.

Zelda's Cut, St. Martin's (New York, NY), 2000.

Bread and Chocolate, HarperCollins (London, England), 2000.

Columnist for *Guardian* under pseudonym Kate Wedd. Contributor of articles and reviews to women's magazines and newspapers. Also the author of *Draco, Mi Pequeno Dragon*, Serres Ediciones.

Sidelights

Philippa Gregory has achieved success as an academic, journalist, children's writer, and novelist. Her historical novels have earned her critical as well as popular success. She is perhaps best known for the books in the "Wideacre" trilogy. In the novels *Wideacre, The Favoured Child*, and *Meridon*, readers follow the dramatic tribulations of the Laceys, a family of wealthy eighteenth-century English landowners. Plagued by greed, incest, violence, and a constant struggle for power, the Laceys fight to retain control over their land holdings in this historical family saga. In her review of *The Favoured Child, Library Journal* contributor Ellen R. Cohen commented that "Gregory's precise images and skillful descriptions make this eighteenth-century microcosm vivid." In the series, Gregory shows a keen concern for issues of class, specifically the disparity between the riches of those who own land and the poverty of those forced to farm it.

Gregory turned from historical romance to children's fiction with the publication of *Princess Florizella* and its sequel, *Florizella and the Wolves*. In these fairytales, she offers a contemporary spin on traditional gender roles: her protagonist Florizella is a high-spirited princess with no interest in marriage who schemes to help the homeless and abolish the monarchy. In the first book, Florizella rejects the notion of romance with a local prince, and demonstrates her independence by rescuing her would-be suitor from a dragon. A *Junior Bookshelf* reviewer praised the book as "a worthwhile fairytale," notable for its "sparkle of originality and humour." In *Florizella and the Wolves*, the Princess befriends a wolf family, adopting the cubs after the parents are killed by hunters. Although Florizella releases the cubs in the forest once they mature, one wolf, Samson, keeps returning. Together with her friend Prince Bennett, Florizella conspires to keep Samson as a pet. A *Kirkus Reviews* critic found the tale "refreshingly offbeat," and praised Gregory's style as "warm, lighthearted, and spiced with humor and suspense." *Booklist* reviewer Jim Jeske welcomed the return of the "plucky heroine" Florizella.

Gregory's other books for children include *Diggory and the Boa Conductor* and *The Little Pet Dragon*. In the former story, Diggory stands up to a bully with the help of a magical boa conductor. In the latter, James adopts a pet dragon named Lassie in lieu of the greyhound he always wanted. Although he eventually encounters the pitfalls of owning a magical pet, James discovers the silver lining of his situation when Lassie is able to help his family prosper financially. Reviewing the book in *School Librarian*, Gillian Cross writes "the story is told neatly and skillfully," and characterizes James' relationship with Lassie as "both funny and moving."

The author tried her hand at a contemporary tale for adults with *The Little House*, the story of an upper-middle-class couple and their failing marriage. A *Publishers Weekly* writer notes that the story "treats familiar, . . . domestic ground with a horrific tilt," but warns that while "Gregory writes smoothly enough, . . . her insights into the dysfunctional family are only pedestrian, laying fallow ground for a surprise ending that neither horrifies nor enlightens." Better-received was her 1998 offering, *Earthly Joys*. This story concerns John Tradescant, a renowned botanical collector and gardener, who is planning a series of elaborate gardens for Sir Robert Cecil, an advisor to Queen Elizabeth I, King James I, and the duke of Buckingham. In that position, he has access to a great deal of privileged information, and is eventually commissioned as a spy to safeguard the security of the kingdom. *Booklist* critic Margaret Flanagan calls it "a cleverly conceived and executed historical narrative spanning one of the most intriguing and turbulent eras in British history," and Kathy Piehl promises in *Library Journal* that the "strong plotting, intriguing characters, and rich evocation of a time and place will leave readers eager for the promised sequel."

Kate Thompson, commenting on the "Wideacre" trilogy in *Twentieth-Century Romance and Historical Writers*, declares that it is "rightly the focus of any appraisal of Gregory's work," but adds that the author's other books also "demonstrate Gregory's power, talent and above all, the sheer readability of her novels." Gregory once commented: "The novels in the 'Wideacre;' trilogy have all been set in the eighteenth century—a period I am familiar with from my doctoral research and one of those crucial periods in which decisions determined the whole future of the country. In the case of England's agricultural revolution the decision was made to starve the poor for the greater profit of the landlords. The legacy of that decision in terms of class snobbery and hardship for low-paid working people is still with us today.

"Since I completed *Meridon* I have found myself writing short stories and increasing my work in children's fiction. I love writing for children because I enjoy their sense of humor—I always test out my stories on my daughter and her friends."

Biographical and Critical Sources

BOOKS

Twentieth-Century Romance and Historical Writers, 3rd edition, St. James Press (Detroit), 1994.

PERIODICALS

Booklist, May 1, 1993, Jim Jeske, review of *Florizella and the Wolves,* p. 1588; October 1, 1993, Denise Perry Donovin, review of *The Wise Woman,* p. 195; October 15, 1996, p. 404; September 15, 1998, Margaret Flanagan, review of *Earthly Joys,* p. 199; January 1, 2001, Bonnie Johnston, review of *Zelda's Cut,* p. 915.
Books for Keeps, July, 1999, George Hunt, review of *Diggory and the Boa Conductor,* p. 11.
Books Magazine, July, 1992, Tim Manderson, review of *The Wise Woman,* p. 7; February, 1996, review of *Respectable Trade,* p. 6.
Canadian Materials, October, 1993, Katheryn Broughton, review of *Fallen Skies,* p. 181.
Junior Bookshelf, February, 1989, review of *Princess Florizella,* p. 21.
Kirkus Reviews, May 1, 1989, review of *The Favoured Child,* p. 647; March 15, 1993, review of *Florizella and the Wolves,* p. 371; September 1, 1996, review of *The Little House,* p. 1256.
Library Journal, July, 1989, Ellen R. Cohen, review of *The Favoured Child,* p. 108; October 15, 1993, p. 87; October 1, 1996, p. 404; September 1, 1998, Kathy Piehl, review of *Earthly Joys,* p. 213.
New Statesman, April 8, 1988, p. 27.
New Statesman & Society, June 19, 1992, Kay Parris, review of *Mrs. Hartley and the Growth Centre,* p. 24; August 6, 1993, Boyd Tonkin, review of *Fallen Skies,* p. 41.
New York Times Book Review, November 1, 1998, Betsy Groban, review of *Earthly Joys,* p. 23.
Publishers Weekly, December 26, 1986, p.48; May 12, 1989, p. 284; June 8, 1990, p. 47; October 4, 1993, p. 64; September 9, 1996, p. 66; July 6, 1998, p. 50.
School Librarian, November, 1991, Alasdair Campbell, review of *Florizella and the Wolves,* p. 145; November, 1994, Gillian Cross, review of *The Little Pet Dragon,* p. 153.
School Library Journal, May, 1993, p. 105.

Times Literary Supplement, July 5, 1996, Trev Broughton, review of *Perfectly Correct,* p. 23; May 28, 1999, Emma Tristram, review of *Virgin Earth,* p. 24*

*   *   *

GROVE, Vicki

Personal

Born in Illinois.

Addresses

Home—P.O. Box 36, Ionia, MO 65335-9327.

Career

Writer.

Awards, Honors

Silver Angel Award, for *He Gave Her Roses.*

Writings

Goodbye, My Wishing Star, Putnam, 1988.
Junglerama, Putnam, 1989.
The Fastest Friend in the West, Putnam, 1990.
Rimwalkers, Putnam, 1993.
The Crystal Garden, Putnam, 1995.
Reaching Dustin, Putnam, 1998.
The Starplace, Putnam, 1999.
Destiny, Putnam, 2000.

Also author of *Circles of Love,* published by Thomas Bouregy in 1988, and *He Gave Her Roses* and *A Time to Belong,* both issued by Group Publishing in 1990.

Sidelights

Vicki Grove has written a number of novels for young readers that revolve around life in the American Midwest, often inside rural farming communities, but the themes and conflicts her protagonists encounter strike a resonant note with adolescent readers everywhere. Grove's teens struggle with sibling rivalry, peer pressure and, most often, economic hardship. As their stories progress, they realize that family, school, and the larger community have provided them with a good moral framework to help them through their particular crises. As Grove once mentioned to *Authors and Artists for Young Adults* (*AAYA*), "I picture my reader as being a young person with an open heart, trying to find the way to live as a decent and compassionate human being in a complicated yet beautiful world."

Grove is a product of the same Midwestern communities in which her novels are set. "My childhood was idyllic," she once said. "I grew up on the Illinois prairie, in a little one-room schoolhouse near the big white houses of my grandparents and great-grandparents. They were all storytellers from the word go, and I heard all about

Vicki Grove

ancestors who took the Oregon Trail, who fought in the Civil War or went to the front to nurse their fallen sons there, uncles who had jumped off the roof with umbrellas, lightning that hit horses in the corral and left four hoof-prints branded in the ground, ghosts in the attics, etc., etc. I imagine they had more respect for the inner truth of a story than for the absolute facts, as I think all first-class storytellers do.

"My family has farmed until our present generation, and from them I also learned a deep respect for the land and the weather. I probably have the most fun writing when I'm using a farm setting. I have a younger sister and a much younger brother. Kathy and I were Peter Pan and Tinkerbell, or Dorothy and the Scarecrow. She's the pretty one, so I was always the boy in our games. Reed was always our baby. We nursed him with nightgowns over our heads to look like "nurses' hats" or we forced him into one of our doll buggies and wheeled him around until he yelled bloody murder. (I think he may still hold that against us a teeny bit—ha!) My mother read to us, usually from the Bible, but also from big, fat books. She never 'read down' to us, always expected us to pick up the meaning of challenging stories. I especially remember Ralph Moody's *Little Britches.*

"I had wonderful elementary teachers," Grove continued, "and from them I learned the excitement of reading. Last summer I saw my second grade teacher again— after over 40 years, she remembered me! 'You were my best reader,' she said. I still glow when I think of that. As a child, once in a while I would think of how wonderful it would be to be a writer, so that your

teachers would be proud of you. So seeing Mrs. Peters, having a chance to send her copies of my books, was literally one of my longest-held and deepest-held dreams, come true.

"I have always been self-conscious," Grove once stated. "Not exactly quiet, but very easily flustered and not very sure of myself. I get embarrassed easily, and always have. For instance, I knew I couldn't catch balls as a child, so I couldn't. It doesn't take long for that kind of thinking to translate into being chosen last every time for the team. I often write characters who are self-conscious, and whose self-consciousness turns out to be a self-fulfilling prophecy. I can relate to that. Confidence breeds confidence. I see that, but can't really emulate it, and never have been able to. As you can probably guess, I loved school, but hated physical-education class. I think my most impressive achievement, maybe ever, is to have started going regularly to a gym four years ago. In middle age, I've become something of a weight lifter! Finally, I'm a jock (kind of). I can do push-ups now, but couldn't in school, and hated not being able to. Also, I often spent time crying in the rest room because of some real or, more usually, imagined slight from one of the other kids. I was far too easily bruised. Probably I still am. Yikes!

"When I was twelve we moved from Illinois to Oklahoma, and I lived there until I was 18, going through both junior high and high school there. Teens in Oklahoma do the car thing, drag Main, build bonfires on the beaches of the lakes, live a frontier life that is very fun and outdoorsy and cool. I set one of my books, *The Starplace,* in Oklahoma and used a lot of those teen memories. Unfortunately, I also remember blatant small-town racism from those years, and that book concerns those not-so-great memories, too. I would never have said I wanted to be a writer when I was a teen, or even in college. I've never had the self-confidence to make that kind of pronouncement. But from about third grade on I always journaled my feelings, and wrote, wrote, wrote to try and understand the world. I wanted to be an English teacher, and went through graduate school thinking I'd eventually do that.

"I fell into writing in my early thirties, much by accident. I sent a few magazine pieces out, and when they began to be accepted I was totally shocked, but I kept with it, and it grew into a career that I love with all my heart. When I'd been writing for magazines for about eight years, I wrote a short book about a farm foreclosure, told from the viewpoint of a twelve-year-old girl. I entered that book in a contest G.P. Putnam's Sons was having for a first novel for young people, and to my vast surprise, it won and was published."

That novel was *Goodbye, My Wishing Star,* published in 1988. The premise was a timely one, for during the 1980s many American farmers had fallen into financial quagmires and were forced to give up their land. The story is told from the point of view of twelve-year-old Jens Tucker, whose mother's family has farmed their property for generations. Jens knows the end is near, however; other farms in the area have been sold off, and her parents discuss following suit and moving to the city to find work instead. The title of the book comes from a knothole in the barn where Jens milks cows before sun-up. Through it, she can see a special star, and wishes upon it that her family's finances might improve. Her father works hard to keep the farm viable, but Jens's mother believes that life in the city will be far easier for Jens and her little brother, Roger.

Jens's story is recounted in diary form, and when it appears that their farm will indeed be sold, she is angry at having to give up the acreage, the animals, and the sense of heritage that the farm gives her. Feeling powerless at first, she plans to hide her journal in the barn, so the new owners might find it and learn how her family agonized over their decision to leave their land, and how heartbroken a twelve-year-old was that she would never be part of its future. But Jens also becomes aware that injustice and hardship are not her own to claim. The father of one of her friends has also lost their farm and then dies of a heart attack. The mother of another classmate drinks and forces the younger brother to beg to support them. In contrast, Jens's best friend, Marla, has had a relatively easy life, but helps Jens come to terms with the change with some astute observations.

Jens must say goodbye to her beloved animals before a public auction in which the Tuckers' farm tools and livestock are sold. When she meets Jack Shire, an eccentric who collects old cars and stores them in an old bank building in town, he reminds her that even if the Tucker farm is sold, it will always remain in her heart. As the diary comes to a close, Jens realizes she is looking forward to the adventure of starting over anew—that after so many farewells "something inside me is about ready for some hellos," she admits. *Goodbye, My Wishing Star* earned enthusiastic reviews for Grove. "The country setting is very appealing as are Jens' family relationships and her friendship with Marla," declared Eleanor Klopp in a *Voice of Youth Advocates* review. "Though the story is sad, there is also a strength as Jens recognizes that she must get on with her life," observed *Booklist*'s Denise M. Wilms.

Grove's next novel for middle-school readers, *Junglerama,* appeared in 1989. In it, a trio of twelve-year-old boys in a small town find an abandoned carnival trailer one summer and creates a traveling exhibition of animals. The boys' particular hardships are the real focus of the story, however. The work is narrated by T. J., whose parents quarrel constantly, and whose mother neglects them. Jack, an orphan, must care for his alcoholic uncle. Mike's father has lost the family farm and now works as a stablehand. Over the course of the summer, a series of incidents incites gossip and then panic through the town, and some come to believe that their community has fallen under a witch's spell. Blame falls upon an eccentric woman, Cora Beeson, and the boys help rescue her from a dangerous situation in a gripping finale. Again, the work won positive reviews for Grove. T. J's narrative, noted *School Library Journal* reviewer Gerry Larson, "conveys both innocence and

discovery .... Plot twists, well-paced action, and T. J.'s gradual maturing make this summer unforgettable."

In her next novel, *The Fastest Friend in the West,* Grove again presents an adolescent heroine who must deal with personal trauma. When Lori's best friend finds a new crowd and rejects her, she suffers as any twelve-year-old might; her situation is made all the more difficult by her weight problem. In response, she becomes obsessed with all things marine, painting her bedroom dark blue and decorating it with shells. She even renames herself Lorelei, after the legendary mermaid. At school, a girl who is somewhat of an outcast strikes up a friendship with her. Other kids shun Vern Hittlinger because of her odd clothes and disheveled appearance, but Lori worries when Vern stops coming to school. A teacher tells her that the Hittlingers live in their car on the outskirts of town.

In the second half of the book, Lori goes to see Vern, and learns about the hardships the Hittlingers have encountered over the past few years. Vern's strategy, when finding herself in a new school, has been to make one friend as quickly as possible. They depart again, and Lori later receives a postcard from Vern, saying that her family has found a real home. Toward the novel's close, Lori comes to terms with her weight problem, and resolves to make some changes in her life. "The specter of homelessness," remarked *Horn Book* writer Nancy Vasilakis, "the strain it puts on a proud family with little in the way of resources and more than its share of bad luck—will be a revelation to young readers."

Grove also won laudatory reviews for her 1993 book, *Rimwalkers.* Told in flashback form from twenty years ahead, the work revolves around the summer that fourteen-year-old Victoria, or "Tory," spent on her grandparents' Illinois farm. Both she and her younger sister, Sara, have been relegated here because their parents have decided to take a second honeymoon overseas. Tory is quiet and studious, and looks forward to the science and nature experiments she will be able to carry out in the country. The more vivacious Sara, however, is resentful at being removed from her familiar world of friends, cheerleading, and the usual summer exploits. Also visiting the grandparents that summer are the girls' cousins, Elijah and Rennie. Elijah, the product of a farm family himself, is there to help the grandfather with the chores and summer crop. Rennie, at sixteen, is the oldest of them all and is a high-school dropout from California. At first, the others are put off by his free-spirited, rebellious attitude and daring pranks.

Tory, Elijah, and Rennie soon begin to bond, however, when they believe they see the ghost of a small child at the boarded-up old homestead that sits at the edge of the family property. It had been built by their great-great-grandparents, and when Tory asks her grandmother about the family history, she learns that a four-year-old boy died one summer in the 1840s when four cousins were visiting. Meanwhile, Sara begins to feel left out, especially when Rennie shows Tory and Elijah how to "rimwalk," or traverse a narrow ledge or attic beam.

They try it successfully over a river bridge; jealous, Sara tries it as well, but falls and is badly hurt. "The true magic" in Grove's tale, noted Margaret Cole in a *School Library Journal* review, revolves around the alliance between the other three, by which "the teens teach one another to believe in themselves and in life's delicate balance between risk and security." Writing for *Booklist*, Jeanne Triner also offered words of praise for *Rimwalkers*. "The setting is richly drawn, making the farm and its magic real to even the most urban reader," she noted.

A death in the family brings changes to her heroine's life in Grove's 1995 novel, *The Crystal Garden*. Eliza's father has been killed in an accident, and she and her mother struggle to make ends meet. In time, they decide to move to a small Missouri town with Burl, her mother's friend, who is also a country-music hopeful. There, Eliza tries to fit in at school, and keeps her distance from a neighbor girl around her own age, Dierdre, whose difficult home life has made her somewhat of an outcast at school. A science-fair project brings them together, and Eliza discovers that one of Dierdre's parents has an alcohol problem, and their household is very nearly destitute. Yet Dierdre manages her situation so well that Eliza realizes that her peer is far more balanced than she is. Other revelations help Eliza come to terms with the loss of her father. "A satisfying ending and epilogue leave room for hope, thought, and discussion," observed *School Library Journal* reviewer Susan Oliver.

Grove won unstinting praise for her 1998 book, *Reaching Dustin*. The tale involves Carly, a sixth-grade aspiring writer who comes from a pleasant, supportive family. But Carly is dismayed by a new school assignment to interview a classmate when she is paired with her grade's most reviled member. Dustin is sullen and withdrawn, and rumors abound around Carly's Missouri farm community involving his family, their isolated compound, and their possible ties to white supremacist militia groups. As Carly recounts, Dustin's behavioral problems began in the third grade, not long after his mother committed suicide, and she and her friends have snubbed him ever since.

Dustin's family is suspected of harboring a cache of weapons and running an illegal drug enterprise as well. As Carly begins to learn more about Dustin's situation, she is surprised by some of the revelations. He loves animals, for example, and carries a pet frog with him; he also "plays the recorder allotted to each sixth grader with a grace that belies his dirty and hard exterior," wrote *Horn Book*'s Susan P. Bloom. When the frog creates an incident and the situation escalates into a town uproar, Dustin is removed from school. Carly, worried and feeling guilty about her own role in one incident back in the third grade, tries to help him. "Carly's inner development is convincingly painful as she realizes the part she played in creating Dustin's problems," noted Steven Engelfried in a *School Library Journal* review. The "heartfelt story," noted a *Publishers Weekly* review, "unmasks the vulnerabilities of two preadolescents from very different walks of life." Bloom's *Horn Book* review

found that "the emotional tone rings true," and *Kirkus Reviews* also praised Grove's talents. "Among a cast of memorable characters, Dustin is obviously pitiable but also noble," its assessment noted, and described *Reaching Dustin* as "written with grace" and "brimming with compassion."

As she noted, Grove drew upon some of her own experiences growing up in Oklahoma for her 1999 novel *The Starplace*. Its story is told through the voice of Frannie, who is thirteen years old in 1961 when an African American family moves into their small town of Quiver. Frannie makes friends with the daughter, Celeste, but soon learns that others in the town, and even at her school, are far less accepting. Celeste is greeted with taunts, and racist incidents occur, but she maintains her poise amidst the ugliness. Her father is a historian writing a book about white-supremacist groups in this part of Oklahoma, and her grandfather was the victim of a lynching in the area. Celeste shows Frannie some old Ku Klux Klan books she found in the attic of their home, which others believe may be haunted, and "Quiver's sunny image is gradually shattered for Frannie," noted a *Publishers Weekly* assessment.

At school, Celeste finds her niche in the school choir because of her talents, but is ejected from the group just before a competition. In a *Kirkus Reviews* critique, the newcomer is described as "beautiful, mature, worldly, and a great singer ... close to being a type," but asserted that the other adolescents presented in the novel offered a more balanced portrait. Writing in *School Library Journal*, Connie Tyrell Burns commended *The Starplace* as a "powerful coming-of-age tale, written with grace and poignancy," and found Grove's "characterizations, particularly of Frannie and Celeste, ... strong and memorable."

The title character of Grove's eighth novel for Putnam, *Destiny*, is another young woman who emerges from hardship to find her own strength. As the work begins, Destiny recounts a home life in which her unskilled mother is addicted to playing the lottery in the hopes of becoming rich. Jack, her mother's deceitful boyfriend, forces Destiny to help him at his job—selling shoddy fruits and vegetables door-to-door in their town, which humiliates her. When a sympathetic adult helps Destiny find better work as a reader to a homebound elderly woman, Mrs. Peck, Destiny starts to see some parallels in her life with the travails of the beleaguered heroes of the Greek myths she reads aloud. When Jack auctions a beloved pet rabbit belonging to Destiny's younger brother, she saves it in her own act of heroism. Mrs. Peck reveals to her some enlightening truths about Destiny's family, and after Jack winds up in jail, Destiny's mother decides to go back to school. The critic Burns, writing for *School Library Journal*, praised "Grove's lyrical writing style" and the "narration, which rings true with Destiny's memorable and poignant voice."

Though some of Grove's characters come from supportive family environments, others are forced to find other role models in their immediate community, as Destiny, Dierdre, Vern, and the boys from *Junglerama* must do. Recognizing that her own encouraging home life was not a universal one spurred Grove to write for adolescents. "My parents always gave me the most amazing encouragement and support of all kinds, and still do," she once stated. "They are my models for compassionate thinking, and I hope I do them honor in my characterizations of people trying to be compassionate in complicated situations. They are always my models for the striving, sacrificing parents in my books—I've been told by readers and teachers that I use a lot of those. They have always put other people before themselves, especially their children."

"I'm very disciplined in my work," Grove once said. "My father built me a wonderful, tiny office in the hayfield behind our house, and I spend most of every day out there (out here!), writing. Writing is really rewriting, and it takes me most of a year to do a book—slow! I begin a book with a character that intrigues me. Sometimes he or she will be from memory, sometimes from observation, or even, occasionally, purely imaginary. This person could be a girl whose father has just died, or a boy in a white supremacist compound, or someone experiencing prejudice at school. At the moment I'm writing about a girl in a family that experiences tragedy and, as a way of escaping from themselves (ultimately impossible, as they will find out), goes on the migrant circuit. I've done lots of research into the lifestyles and challenges of migrant farmworker families, have talked to kids involved in that life, etc.

"Still, it's a huge responsibility trying to put someone else's life on paper, especially a life so much unlike your own, and probably much harder. I take that responsibility very, very seriously. And, as I mentioned, I'm always thankful my parents taught me to view other people with compassion, first and foremost. I hope I learned that lesson well. I hope I learned how to empathize well enough to actually slip into other hearts. I have to have lots of quiet around me when I work, and lots of peace in my life when I'm in the middle of a book. It's a weird sensation, living your own life and also the life of your main character, simultaneously! My family says I zombie out when I'm immersed in a book, and that's true. I burn dinner, have car wrecks (seriously), the whole ball of wax.

"I didn't decide to write for young adults—I wrote for 'regular old adults' like myself when I started magazine writing. But when I wrote the book I entered in the Putnam contest, *Goodbye, My Wishing Star,* I felt like I'd died and gone to heaven. Once I tried it, I realized I absolutely love to write in the voice of a 13- or 14- or 16-year-old. Maybe because I honestly believe young teens are the most interesting and important of people, balanced with one foot in childhood and a heavier foot in adulthood, making the most important decisions they'll ever make, forming the most intense of friendships, having the most bitter of feuds and misunderstandings. I tapped into something deep inside myself when I first wrote in a teen voice, and I've become

addicted to going back to that well of memory, sensation . . . whatever it is."

Grove hopes her readers will take away a lesson from her books through the difficulties that her characters rise above. She realizes that all teens face their own personal challenges. "I want to tell that person that I admire the quest they're on, and think it's worthy of their immense effort," she once commented. "As for the goals and concerns I bring to my work, I guess one more time I'll have to use that word 'compassion.' As the world gets more various and challenging, I think it's got to be a big goal for everyone, to truly empathize with other people. My characters are flawed and vulnerable, but you've got to say for them that in their stumbling ways, they all attain compassion for others. Two of my recent books, *Reaching Dustin* and *The Starplace,* deal with white supremacy and the KKK. These are things that make me livid, so angry I can hardly breathe. For that reason, those books weren't easy to write, but I almost had to write them.

"It still staggers me to think that my books might possibly have some effect—what an idea, and what an obligation. It's thrilling to get a letter from a young reader telling me that one of my books influenced how they thought about someone at their school, or how they acted toward someone, or how they felt about themselves. Mind-boggling, and humbling. I just want my readers to realize what good hearts they have, what amazing creatures they are, how small and intricate the world is, how much love matters. If I had to describe my work to someone, I'd say I hope it's about people who are learning those things."

Biographical and Critical Sources

BOOKS

Authors and Artists for Young Adults, Volume 38, Gale, 2001.

PERIODICALS

ALAN Review, fall, 2000, Anne Sherill, review of *Destiny,* p. 35.
Booklist, April 15, 1988, Denise M. Wilms, review of *Goodbye, My Wishing Star,* p. 1431; July, 1990, Deborah Abbott, review of *The Fastest Friend in the West,* p. 2089; October 15, 1993, Jeanne Triner, review of *Rimwalkers,* pp. 430-431; May 1, 1998, Michael Cart, review of *Reaching Dustin,* p. 1518; June 1, 1999, Hazel Rochman, review of *The Starplace,* p. 1813.
Horn Book, July-August, 1990, Nancy Vasilakis, review of *The Fastest Friend in the West,* p. 455; March-April, 1998, Susan P. Bloom, review of *Reaching Dustin,* p. 220.
Kirkus Reviews, May 1, 1988, review of *Goodbye, My Wishing Star,* p. 692; March 1, 1998, review of *Reaching Dustin,* p. 339; May 15, 1999, review of *The Starplace,* p. 800.
Kliatt, January, 1997, Dean E. Lyons, review of *Rimwalkers,* p. 8.

Publishers Weekly, September 29, 1993, review of *Rim-walkers,* p. 64; May 11, 1998, review of *Reaching Dustin,* p. 68; July 5, 1999, review of *The Starplace,* p. 72; July 31, 2000, review of *Destiny,* p. 96.

School Library Journal, July, 1989, Gerry Larson, review of *Junglerama,* p. 82; October, 1993, Margaret Cole, review of *Rimwalkers,* p. 151; May, 1995, Susan Oliver, review of *The Crystal Garden,* p. 106; May, 1998, Stephen Engelfried, review of *Reaching Dustin,* p. 142; June, 1999, Connie Tyrell Burns, review of *The Starplace,* p. 129; April, 2000, Connie Tyrell Burns, review of *Destiny,* p. 134.

Voice of Youth Advocates, October, 1988, Eleanor Klopp, review of *Goodbye, My Wishing Star,* p. 181; December, 1993, Deborah A. Feulner, review of *Rimwalkers,* p. 291; June, 2000, Roxy Ekstrom, review of *Destiny,* p. 114.

—*Sketch by Carol Brennan*

* * *

GUY, Rosa 1925-

Personal

Surname rhymes with "me"; born September 1, 1925 (some sources say 1928), in Diego Martin, Trinidad, West Indies; came to the United States in 1932; daughter of Henry and Audrey (Gonzales) Cuthbert; married Warner Guy (deceased); children: Warner. *Education:* Attended New York University; studied with the American Negro Theater.

Addresses

Home—New York, NY.

Career

Writer, 1950—. Lecturer. *Member:* Harlem Writer's Guild (co-founder; president, 1967-78).

Awards, Honors

Best Book for Young Adults citations, American Library Association, 1973, for *The Friends,* 1976, for *Ruby,* 1978, for *Edith Jackson,* 1979, for *The Disappearance,* and 1981, for *Mirror of Her Own;* Children's Book of the Year citations, Child Study Association, 1973, for *The Friends,* and 1986, for *Paris, Pee Wee, and Big Dog;* Outstanding Book of the Year citations, *New York Times,* 1973, for *The Friends,* and 1979, for *The Disappearance; The Friends* was selected one of *School Library Journal*'s Best of the Best Books, 1979; *The Disappearance* and *Edith Jackson* were selected among the New York Public Library's Books for the Teen Age, 1980, 1981, and 1982; Coretta Scott King Award, 1982, for *Mother Crocodile;* Parents' Choice Award for Literature from the Parents' Choice Foundation, 1983, for *New Guys around the Block;* Other Award (England), 1987, for *My Love, My Love; or, The Peasant Girl.*

Writings

YOUNG ADULT FICTION

The Friends, Holt, 1973.
Ruby: A Novel, Viking, 1976.
Edith Jackson, Viking, 1978.
The Disappearance, Delacorte, 1979.
Mirror of Her Own, Delacorte, 1981.
New Guys around the Block, Delacorte, 1983.
Paris, Pee Wee, and Big Dog, illustrated by Caroline Binch, Gollancz, 1984, Delacorte, 1985.
And I Heard a Bird Sing, Delacorte, 1986.
The Ups and Downs of Carl Davis III, Delacorte, 1989.
Billy the Great, illustrated by Caroline Bench, Doubleday, 1992.
The Music of Summer, Delacorte, 1992.

OTHER

Venetian Blinds (one-act play), first produced at Topical Theatre, New York, 1954.
Bird at My Window (adult novel), Lippincott, 1966.
(Editor) *Children of Longing* (anthology), Holt, 1970.
(Translator and adapter) Birago Diop, *Mother Crocodile: An Uncle Amadou Tale from Senegal,* illustrated by John Steptoe, Delacorte, 1981.
A Measure of Time (adult novel), Holt, 1983.
My Love, My Love; or, The Peasant Girl (adult novel), Holt, 1985.
The Sun, the Sea, a Touch of the Wind (adult novel), Dutton, 1995.

Also contributor to *Ten Times Black,* edited by Julian Mayfield, Bantam, 1972, and *Sixteen: Short Stories by Outstanding Writers for Young Adults,* edited by Donald R. Gallo, Delacorte, 1984.

Guy's novels have been translated into many languages, including Japanese, German, Danish, French, and Italian. Contributor to periodicals, including *Cosmopolitan, New York Times Magazine, Redbook,* and *Freedomways.*

Adaptations

Documentary of *The Friends,* Thames Television, 1984; *My Love, My Love; or, The Peasant Girl* was adapted in 1990 for the Broadway musical *Once on This Island,* premiering at the Booth Theater, New York, and revived in 1999 for the Cab Calloway School of the Arts.

Sidelights

"In a voice full of probing and anguished sensitivity, Rosa Guy examines the intersection of race and class in twentieth-century urban America," according to Laurie Ann Eno writing in *St. James Guide to Young Adult Writers.* Eno further commented, "The lives of the forgotten ones haunt her world, taking and shaping for themselves identities which society would deny and destroy." R. Baines, writing in *Junior Bookshelf,* put Guy's work into perspective: "Rosa Guy is a black author writing with power, authority and insight about an underprivileged and inward looking world which is strange to most of us. Her themes are distressing, disturbing and unappealing ones which she deals with honestly and sympathetically." In her eleven novels for teens and four adult novels, Guy traces the fault lines of race in America, the disparities and inequalities between blacks and whites as well as between African Americans and African West Indians. Guy has experienced both, a black growing up in New York City, and an immigrant from Trinidad among Harlem blacks who were born in America.

A writer for *Books for Keeps* described Guy as "the creator of some of the most memorable adolescent characters in modern literature" and further remarked that her "stories are hard-hitting and compellingly realistic, with a powerful message for young people," and that Guy herself "demonstrates a deep understanding and sympathy for young people and the many difficulties they face growing up or purely surviving today." If the stories she tells in such award-winning novels as *The Friends, Ruby, Edith Jackson, The Disappearance, New Guys around the Block, And I Heard a Bird Sing,* and *The Music of Summer* are grippingly realistic as well as controversial—she was the first to deal with lesbianism in a teen novel—Guy's ultimate message is one of hope. Her urban background "is unsparingly painted in her novels," commented Beverly Anderson in the *Times Educational Supplement.* "There is no attempt to glamorize the characters or setting, but her message to the young is an optimistic one. Many of her main characters come to feel that they can take control of their lives and climb out of the destructive environment in which they are placed."

"I am a storyteller," Guy wrote in an essay for *Horn Book.* "I write about people. I want my readers to know people, to laugh with them, to be glad with them, to be angry with, to despair with people. And I want them to have hope with people. I want a reader of my work to work a bit more and to care.... A novel to me is an emotional history of a people in time and place. If I have proven to be popular with young people, it is because when they have finished one of my books, they not only have a satisfying experience—they have also had an education."

Guy was born on September 1, 1925 (though some sources note 1928 as her year of birth), the second daughter of Henry and Audrey Cuthbert. Her first seven years were spent in Trinidad, West Indies, at the time of her birth still a British colony. "How proud we were to be a part of that great empire on which the sun never set," she recalled for Jerrie Norris in *Presenting Rosa Guy.* "We learned from British books and rejected as nonsense our folklore—clinging rather to the books that made for great dreams, accepting everyone's myth as our reality." But Trinidad's deep cultural traditions did not go unnoticed. "My life in the West Indies, of course, had a profound influence on me," Guy told Norris. "It made me into the type of person I imagine I am today. The calypso, the carnival, the religion that permeated our life—the Catholic religion—superstitions, voodoo, the zombies, the djuins, all of these frightening aspects of life that combine the lack of reality with the myth

Rosa Guy

coming over from Africa, had a genuine effect on me." In addition, the rich tradition of storytelling "evidenced in the rhythm of everyday Trinidadian speech," according to Norris, developed in the young Guy a feeling for the imaginative use of language.

Such effects ended, however, when, at age seven, Guy and her family came to the United States, settling in Harlem. Theirs was part of a long-held custom of blacks from the West Indies to go north for the promise of a better future. Marcus Garvey, founder of the Universal Negro Improvement Association and a pivotal figure in black resurgence in America, himself came from Jamaica. Rosa's parents went first to America, joined later by Rosa and her older sister, Ameze. Life was hard for the family in the United States, settling into their new surroundings in the midst of the Great Depression. Shortly after the arrival of the daughters, Mrs. Cuthbert fell ill and the children were sent to cousins in the Bronx, who were strong Garveyites. This was a seminal experience for young Rosa, and Guy later attributed much of her love for language and her activism in the cause of human rights to the influence of Garvey and his teachings.

Guy's mother ultimately died of her illness, and the sisters returned to their father for a time, and he remarried a rather flamboyant woman from the South. The father struggled in vain to do well in business, and by the time Rosa was a teenager, he too had died and the two girls were on their own in New York. Years of institutions and foster homes followed. "The whole [experience] of always being on the outside looking in, in a way formed me," she told Norris. Ameze, her older sister, looked out for younger Rosa, until Ameze too, fell ill. Guy quit school at age fourteen and took a job in a brassiere factory to support them. These were hard years, and not only because of economic adversity. Guy also suffered for her race and religion. Victimized for being 'colored' in a largely white society, she was also ostracized by other blacks for her West Indian origins and Catholicism.

By age sixteen, Guy had already married, and in 1942 had a son. Her husband, meanwhile, was among the hundreds of thousands of other Americans to serve in the military during the Second World War. Guy soon became involved with the American Negro Theater, introduced to the group by a young actor with a day job at the garment factory. She studied acting with the troupe, among whom were such future stars as Sidney Poitier and Harry Belafonte. With the end of the war, however, Guy's husband moved the family to Connecticut. But when the marriage fell apart in 1950, Guy and her son moved back to New York and helped found the Harlem Writers Guild. Again working in the brassiere factory by day, Guy honed her writing skills at night, as did others in the collective, including the poet Maya Angelou. "All of us were workers, doing some other type of work," Guy recalled to Norris. "And every evening I had to come home to write. Mornings, I had a son to get dressed and off to school, and then I'd go to work. I did this for a period of years." Her first breakthrough was a one-act play, *Venetian Blinds,* she wrote with a part in it especially suited to her. The play was staged off-Broadway and gave Guy her first taste of public exposure, both as a writer and actor. It would, however, take another dozen years for her first novel to be published.

In her writings, Guy traces the disparities and inequalities between blacks and whites as well as between African Americans and African West Indians. Several of her novels are set in Harlem, where she grew up after immigrating from Trinidad at the age of seven. (Photo by Corbis Corporation.)

"The 1960s, for all its traumas, was one of the most beautiful periods in American history," Guy wrote in *Top of the News.* "Only yesterday? So it seems to those of us who lived through it. Television sets were in the homes but had not yet taken over the responsibility of parents. Drugs on the streets had not yet changed youth gangs, fighting over turf, into addicts, robbing everybody's turf." These were years of promise for American blacks with the civil rights movement and sit-ins and segregation laws being struck down North and South. But these were also dark years, with the killings of Malcolm X and Martin Luther King, Jr. Guy was not personally immune from such turbulence: her ex-husband was murdered in 1962 and Guy decided to leave the U.S. for a time, settling in Haiti, where she began her first novel, *Bird at My Window.* She had earlier turned her hand to short stories, but finally focused on the longer form to tell the story of Wade Williams, a thirty-eight-year-old African American whose life has been one long spiral downward.

The reader meets him first in the prison ward of a New York hospital, secured in a straight jacket after having tried to kill his beloved sister. Through flashbacks, the reader is taken down the painful journey of Wade's life, experiencing racism and violence at almost every turn. Published in 1966, the novel won mostly positive reviews. Thomas L. Vince, reviewing *Bird at My Window* in *Best Sellers,* called it "the most significant novel about the Harlem Negro since James Baldwin's *Go Tell It on the Mountain.*" Vince further noted, "This is Rosa Guy's first novel, but considering the intensity and power it evokes, we can expect more from such a promising talent." Writing in *Dictionary of Literary Biography,* Leota S. Lawrence called this adult novel "ambitious and courageous." Lawrence went on to explain, "Guy attempts not only to explore the racial forces that help to cripple the black man, but she also looks within the black family and shows how racism can destroy familial relationships with disastrous results." Brooks Johnson, writing in the *Negro Digest,* praised the book for its depiction of Harlem and the forces that lead to the "gradual amoralization of a black man in Harlem," but Johnson also criticized what he felt was "false-sounding" dialogue coming out of "very unlikely mouths."

With the assassination of Dr. King in 1968, Guy went on a voyage of discovery in America to record the voices of young black Americans and find out what they were thinking. As she noted in the preface to *Children of Longing,* the resulting nonfiction book published in 1970, "I especially wanted to know how these painful events affected their lives and their ambitions. I traveled throughout the United States from coast to coast, going into black high schools and colleges in urban and rural areas, into writers' workshops, the cotton fields and ghettos, seeking answers from young black people between the ages of thirteen and twenty-three." Guy presented the responses of these young people without corrections of spelling, grammar, or syntax, providing the actual voices of young blacks coming of age in the turbulent Sixties. The one overwhelming opinion voiced,

In the first novel of her trilogy, Guy explores the antagonism often found between African Americans and African West Indians by focusing on two teenagers who struggle to build a trusting friendship despite hostility from their families. (Cover illustration by Neil Waldman.)

according to Lawrence in *Dictionary of Literary Biography,* was that these youths "all want to stand up and be counted." Lawrence further noted, "*Children of Longing* can easily serve as a companion piece to Guy's later fiction, and if there were any doubt as to the authenticity of her themes and characters, a reading of *Children of Longing* would quickly dispel them." Indeed, as Norris pointed out, many of the incidents first recorded by her teenage interviewees in *Children of Longing* later found their way into both characters and incidents of her later novels. Norris concluded, "In *Children,* Guy brought her readers face to face with the devastating realities with which so many young people must struggle. But she demonstrated through their words a new perspective that spoke of pride and hope, and of a belief in cooperative efforts for social change."

Guy spent much of the early 1970s out of the United States, traveling in the Caribbean and living for a time in both Haiti and Trinidad. Living in the West Indies, she decided to build her second novel around her own experiences as a transplanted West Indian. The result was *The Friends,* Guy's first novel for young adults and the first of what became a popular and best-selling trilogy, including *Ruby* (1976) and *Edith Jackson* (1978). These novels explore the relationships between two black families, the Cathys, originally from the West Indies, and the Jacksons, African Americans living in Harlem. Throughout these tales, Guy tackles the difficult and sensitive issues of racism in America and hostility between African Americans and African West Indians. She also focuses on themes such as the difficulties of communication between parents and children, the struggle for acceptance, and homosexuality, once a taboo topic in teen literature. The characters that people these

In Guy's first book in a trilogy featuring Imamu Jones, the teenage dropout is arrested for robbery and befriended by a social worker. When her daughter disappears and suspicion falls on Imamu, he vows to find the missing girl.

novels, Phylissia, Edith, and Ruby, were all youngsters Guy had known when she and her sister had lived in an orphans' home in New York.

The Friends "is Guy's most critically praised work," according to Norris. Phylissia Cathy and Edith Jackson are the friends of the title, two teenagers who come to trust and understand one another after a stormy beginning. Edith is Harlem born and raised, street smart, poor, and growing up almost on her own. Phylissia, on the other hand, is educated and proud, a recent immigrant from the West Indies who is struggling with her outsider status and her oppressive father. Both girls need a friend, but culture and family play against such a relationship. Edith takes Phylissia under her protective wing at school, and the girls form an unlikely bond for a time, but a visit to the Cathys' home proves disastrous for the friendship. Shortly thereafter Phylissia's mother dies and the young girl's relationship with her father becomes even more strained. Phylissia is left to develop a sense of herself on her own.

Guy's second novel and first YA effort was lauded by critics and quickly found a home in the canon of young adult literature. Reviewing the novel in the *New York Times Book Review,* Alice Walker called *The Friends* a "heart-slammer," noting that the book is labeled for juveniles. "So be a juvenile while you read it," Walker advised. "Rosa Guy will give you back a large part of the memory of those years that you've been missing." *Horn Book*'s Ethel L. Heins called it "a penetrating story of considerable emotional depth," and one that was "often tragic but ultimately hopeful—of complex, fully-realized characters and of the ambivalence and conflicts in human nature." A reviewer for the *Times Literary Supplement* felt that Guy's evocations of New York in particular "make this a vigorous and unusual book." The book did especially well in England, where it, as well as the third novel in the trilogy, became required reading in secondary schools.

Phylissia's older sister is featured in the second novel in the series, *Ruby,* in which this pretty but rather vapid girl is desperately unhappy, being dubbed an 'Uncle Tom' at her school because of her West Indian background. She finds little consolation at home with Phylissia forever reading and her father withdrawn and distant, and is slowly attracted to a strong black girl, Daphne, with whom she ultimately forges a lesbian relationship. A reviewer for *Publishers Weekly* called *Ruby* "an intensely sensitive novel talking directly to teenagers," while Walker, writing in *The Black Scholar,* remarked that the novel is at heart "a love story, and like most love stories it is about the search for someone who cares."

Guy completed her trilogy with *Edith Jackson,* in which she focuses on the life of the scruffy teenager who once befriended Phylissia. Edith, now living in a foster home, tries to take care of her three orphaned sisters, vowing to be the mother for them as soon as she reaches adulthood at age eighteen. Edith tries valiantly to create a family for her three sisters, but becomes pregnant instead herself. Finally she decides not to have the baby, but to prepare herself to make something of her life instead. By the end of the novel, she realizes that she must come to terms with herself before she can be responsible for others. As Lawrence noted, "*Edith Jackson* completes Guy's statement about the failure of the American society—the home, the school, the church, and the state—to meet the complex needs of its young people." Writing in *Horn Book*, Paul Heins noted that this final novel in the trilogy "is powerful in its depiction of character and creates scenes memorable for their psychological truth." Zena Sutherland remarked in *Bulletin of the Center for Children's Books* that Guy's "characterization is excellent, the writing style smooth, and the depiction of an adolescent ... strong and perceptive." Reviewing the English paperback publication of *Edith Jackson*, Audrey Laski, writing in the *Times Educational Supplement,* called this concluding volume "an almost unbearably powerful and somehow entirely unmelodramatic account of the horrors that can assail an orphaned ghetto family in care."

Guy has also written a second trilogy of books set largely in Harlem and Brooklyn, featuring young Imamu Jones, a teenager who has dropped out of school after his father was killed in Vietnam and his mother began drinking. The first novel, *The Disappearance,* opens with Imamu arrested for supposedly taking part in the armed robbery of a grocery store. He is found innocent at the trial when it is learned he did not know that one of his friends had a gun with him. A volunteer social worker, Ann Aimsley, persuades the judge to make her Imamu's legal guardian and the boy goes to live with them in Brooklyn. However, when the Aimsley's daughter disappears and suspicion falls on him for a time, Imamu vows to find the missing girl.

"This is a story about fear and its tragic consequences," noted Katherine Paterson in the *Washington Post Book World.* "This is a harsh book, but not a hopeless one," Paterson further commented. "For Rosa Guy, the writer, is not primarily a black or a woman, but one of that rare and wonderful breed, a storyteller." Jean Fritz, reviewing the novel in the *New York Times Book Review,* dubbed the book "both a cliff-hanger and a shrewd commentary on human nature." *Times Educational Supplement* reviewer Geoff Fox found the novel to be a "harsh, relentless and exciting tale of the streets," as did David Rees, writing in the *Times Literary Supplement,* though Rees found that the book was "marred by absurdly improbable twists in the plot."

In the second novel of the Imamu Jones trilogy, *New Guys around the Block,* Imamu, with Olivette and Pierre Larouche, investigates burglaries in a nearby white neighborhood. Again, suspicion falls for a time on Imamu as the burglar, and he vows to track down the criminal to clear his own name. Suspicion thereafter falls on a recently released convict whom the police corner but who dies to avoid capture. Yet Imamu is unconvinced. In the end he discovers the real perpetrator is the one nobody has suspected. In this second Imamu Jones tale, "Guy demonstrates ... that she is a skillful creator of the mystery/suspense tale," according to Lawrence.

"But more important is her relentless effort to focus on the realities of the urban ghettos in which black youths are trapped." Most reviewers conceded the bleakness of this background, and searched for the tiny rays of hope Guy provided in the plot. "The reader cannot resist rooting for Imamu, with his intelligence and growing self-awareness," commented Selma G. Lanes in the *New York Times Book Review.* "One hopes this novel will be read by countless other Imamus in need of encouragement."

In the third book in the series, *And I Heard a Bird Sing,* Imamu is reunited with his widowed mother, helps her to overcome her drinking habit, and finds a job that he likes, delivering food to white customers in Brooklyn. But racism rears its head when he takes a special interest in a young disabled girl and in the girl's aunt. When the young girl, Margaret, is found murdered, Imamu is on the scene to bring the perpetrator to justice. "Guy again proves her skill at creating stirring stories about real people," wrote a reviewer for *Publishers Weekly.*

Departures for Guy from her usually gritty novels, are several books written for a younger age group, picture books, and a novel featuring a non-black protagonist. In the 1981 *Mirror of Her Own,* Guy presents a far different picture than the streets of a ghetto. Set in an affluent, white suburban neighborhood, the book tells the story of shy, plain, and stuttering Mary who tries to win acceptance with the in-crowd at school. Most reviewers felt the novel was a pale comparison beside Guy's other work. Lawrence, for example, called it "anticlimactic" when placed beside her trilogies. With the 1984 *Paris, Pee Wee, and Big Dog,* Guy wrote for much younger readers for the first time, revealing an adventure-filled day in the life of three New York boys. Bruce Brooks, reviewing the title in the *New York Times Book Review,* noted, "Miss Guy gives us no heavy social lessons about our urban horrors and keeps the boys free of 'turning-point experiences.' Instead, they have a play day that is both tough and fun, and so do we." *Booklist*'s Hazel Rochman called the book "an upbeat inner city story" with "usually cheerful, action-packed adventures." In *The Ups and Downs of Carl Davis III,* Guy presents the trials and tribulations of young Carl when he is sent from the dangerous inner city to live with his grandmother in South Carolina. In letters home, the reader learns of his attempts to teach the kids at his new school—and his history teacher—about black history and of their resistance to listen to him. "Carl is sincere and funny," commented a reviewer for *Publishers Weekly,* "a character readers won't soon forget." *Horn Book*'s Lois F. Anderson felt that "Guy has created a unique role model for young adolescents searching for answers."

With her 1992 novel, *The Music of Summer,* Guy moved even farther afield from Harlem, to a vacation house on Cape Cod where Sarah, a dark-skinned African American, does not fit in with the light-skinned, frivolous crowd gathered around her old friend, Cathy. Sarah, an aspiring concert pianist, is about to return to New York when a new houseguest arrives. Jean Pierre is a development worker headed for Africa, and Sarah soon falls for this committed young man and must choose between her dreams of a career and his idealism. Libby K. White, writing in *School Library Journal,* found the novel to be an "engrossing and uplifting title for readers of all backgrounds," while *Booklist*'s Candace Smith felt that "Guy vividly captures the pain of peer pressure as well as the excitement of first love," and that "Sarah's search for self rings true."

Guy is also the author of two picture books, the African tale, *Mother Crocodile,* which she adapted and translated, and *Billy the Great,* which tells of Billy's growing friendship with the boy next door, Rod. Race figures in—Billy's family is black and Rod's white—but class is even stronger: Billy's is middle class, Rod's working class. Yet in the end, the boys find common ground in a story that demonstrates, as *Booklist*'s Janice Del Negro wrote, "while parents may think they know best, kids sometimes know better." A reviewer for *Publishers Weekly* was less laudatory: "A ponderous lesson in overcoming prejudice overwhelms this insubstantial story about friendship and parental short-sightedness."

Guy has also written three further novels for adults, in addition to her debut *Bird at My Window.* These include *A Measure of Time, My Love, My Love; or, The Peasant Girl,* and *The Sun, the Sea, a Touch of the Wind.* In *Measure,* Guy tells the story of a self-made millionaire, Dorine Davis, who grew up poor and black in Alabama, and succeeds in Harlem through the years of the Harlem Renaissance, the Great Depression, and into the beginnings of the civil rights movement of the 1950s. Lawrence noted that there was enough material in the novel for two books, but when telling the story of Dorine, "it succeeds." *My Love* is basically a reworking of the Hans Christian Andersen tale, "The Little Mermaid," a "strange fairy tale," according to Angeline Goreau writing in the *New York Times Book Review,* that "is a moving evocation of the political realities of the Caribbean." *My Love* was adapted for a musical that opened off-Broadway in 1990. And Guy's 1995 novel, *The Sun, the Sea, a Touch of the Wind,* "tells a story of resurrection and renewal," according to a reviewer for *Publishers Weekly.* The novel relates the tale of an African American artist who flees to the supposed solitude of Haiti as a palliative to a near nervous breakdown, only to find that her emotional and mental anguish are compounded by the island's extremes: wealth juxtaposed against poverty. *Booklist*'s Donna Seaman felt that "Guy lives up to her reputation as a lyrical interpreter of human relationships, both personal and political, in her new novel," dubbing the tale "psychologically harrowing and culturally acute."

"I write for people—all people, young and old, black, white, or any others whom my book might fall into the hands of," Guy once noted in *School Library Journal.* "I write about ordinary people who do ordinary things, who want the ordinary—love, warmth, understanding, happiness. These things are universal. But no life is ordinary." It is Guy's gift to make the quotidian full of detail and uniqueness, and to find hope in the darkest corners of life. "There are no good guys," Guy wrote in her *School Library Journal* essay. "There are no bad guys. We are all good guys. We are all bad guys. And we are all responsible for each other." Lawrence concluded in *Dictionary of Literary Biography,* "Guy's reputation as a writer has long been established. Her contribution to the literature of young adults, especially that of young blacks, has been inspiring."

Biographical and Critical Sources

BOOKS

Afro-American Fiction Writers after 1955, Gale, 1984, pp. 101-6.

Black Authors and Illustrators of Children's Books, 2nd edition, Garland, 1992.

Children's Literature Review, Volume 13, Gale, 1987.

Contemporary Literary Criticism, Volume 26, Gale, 1983.

Dictionary of Literary Biography, Volume 33: *Afro-American Writers after 1955,* Gale, 1984.

Guy, Rosa, "Preface," *Children of Longing,* Holt, 1970.

Norris, Jerrie, *Presenting Rosa Guy,* Twayne, 1988.

St. James Guide to Young Adult Writers, 2nd edition, edited by Tom Pendergast and Sara Pendergast, St. James Press, 1999.

Tate, Claudia, editor, *Black Women Writers at Work,* Continuum, 1983.

PERIODICALS

Best Sellers, January 15, 1966, Thomas L. Vince, review of *Bird at My Window,* p. 403.

Black Scholar, December, 1976, Alice Walker, review of *Ruby,* pp. 51-52.

Booklist, December 1, 1985, Hazel Rochman, review of *Paris, Pee Wee, and Big Dog,* p. 572; April 15, 1992, Candace Smith, review of *The Music of Summer,* pp. 1521-22; September 1, 1992, Janice Del Negro, review of *Billy the Great,* p. 66; October 15, 1994, p. 413; August, 1995, Donna Seaman, review of *The Sun, the Sea, a Touch of the Wind,* p. 1929.

Books for Keeps, January, 1985, "Authorgraph No. 30: Rosa Guy," pp. 12-13.

Bulletin of the Center for Children's Books, March, 1979, Zena Sutherland, review of *Edith Jackson,* pp. 116-17; November, 1985, p. 47; March, 1992, p. 180; January, 1993, p. 146.

English Journal, November, 1988, p. 90.

Horn Book, March-April, 1974, Ethel L. Heins, review of *The Friends,* p. 152; September-October, 1978, Paul Heins, review of *Edith Jackson,* p. 524; March-April, 1985, Rosa Guy, "Young Adult Books: I Am a Storyteller," pp. 220-21; September-October, 1989, Lois F. Anderson, review of *The Ups and Downs of Carl Davis III,* p. 629; March-April, 1993, pp. 195-96.

Junior Bookshelf, April, 1982, R. Baines, review of *Ruby,* p. 76.

Kirkus Reviews, June 15, 1995, p. 802.

Kliatt, May, 1997, p. 6.

Negro Digest, March 1, 1966, Brooks Johnson, "Books Noted," p. 33.

New York Times Book Review, November 4, 1973, Alice Walker, review of *The Friends,* p. 26; December 2, 1979, Jean Fritz, review of *The Disappearance,* p. 40;

August 28, 1983, Selma G. Lanes, review of *New Guys around the Block,* p. 22; November 10, 1985, Bruce Brooks, "The Concrete Canyon Raiders," p. 36; December 1, 1985, Angeline Goreau, review of *My Love, My Love; or, The Peasant Girl,* p. 24; June 7, 1992, p. 22.

New York Times Magazine, April 16, 1972.

Publishers Weekly, April 19, 1976, review of *Ruby,* pp. 80-81; June 12, 1987, review of *And I Heard a Bird Sing,* p. 86; May 19, 1989, review of *The Ups and Downs of Carl Davis III,* p. 85; October 5, 1992, review of *Billy the Great,* p. 71; July 3, 1995, review of *The Sun, the Sea, a Touch of the Wind,* p. 49.

School Library Journal, November, 1985, Rosa Guy, "Innocence, Betrayal, and History;" January, 1986, p. 84; June, 1989, p. 124; December 20, 1991, p. 83; February, 1992, Libby K. White, review of *The Music of Summer,* p. 108.

Times Educational Supplement, June 6, 1980, Geoff Fox, "Songs of Innocence and Experience," p. 27; June 3, 1983, Beverly Anderson, "The Orphan Factor," p. 42; March 1, 1985, Audrey Laski, review of *Edith Jackson,* p. 29; July 11, 1986, p. 25.

Times Literary Supplement, September 20, 1974, "Lives against the Odds," p. 1006; December 14, 1979; July 18, 1980, David Rees, "Approaching Adulthood," p. 807; August 3, 1984; February 14, 1992, p. 27.

Top of the News, winter, 1983, Rosa Guy, "All about Caring."

Voice of Youth Advocates, June, 1992, pp. 95, 142; December, 1992, p. 268.

Washington Post Book World, January 9, 1966; November 11, 1979, Katherine Paterson, "A Family of Strangers," p. 21; December 17, 1985.

Wilson Library Bulletin, November, 1989, p. 15.*

—Sketch by J. Sydney Jones

H

HODGE, Deborah 1954-

Personal

Born November 6, 1954, in Moose Jaw, Saskatchewan, Canada; daughter of John Lyndon (a writer, editor, and broadcaster) and Marion Joyce (a nursing instructor; maiden name, Baker) Grove; married David Ian Hodge (a businessman), April 24, 1977; children: Emily, Michael, Helen. *Education:* Simon Fraser University, B.A. (psychology), 1977; graduated from the Professional Development Program, Simon Fraser University, 1978.

Addresses

Office—c/o Kids Can Press, 29 Birch Ave., Toronto, Ontario, Canada M4V 1E2. *E-mail*—dhodge@istar.ca.

Career

Elementary school teacher in Armstrong and Golden school districts, British Columbia, Canada, 1978-91; British Columbia Ministry of Education, writer, editor, and instructional designer of elementary school curriculum, 1991-99; children's author, 1994—. *Member:* Canadian Children's Book Center, Association of Children's Writers and Illustrators (British Columbia), Children's Literature Roundtable, Writer's Union of Canada, Canadian Society of Children's Authors, Illustrators, and Performers (CANSCAIP).

Awards, Honors

Parents' Choice Approval, Parents Choice Foundation, and Pick of the Lists, fall selection, *American Bookseller,* both 1997, both for *Bears, Wild Cats, Wild Dogs,* and *Whales;* Parents' Choice Approval, Parents' Choice Foundation, 1997, and Parents' Guide to Children's Media award, 1997 and 1999, both for *Starting with Science: Simple Machines;* Best Books for Children designation, *Science Books and Films,* 1998, for *Bears,* and 1999, for *Deer, Moose, Elk and Caribou;* shortlist,

Red Cedar Book Award, 2000, for *Beavers;* shortlist, Silver Birch Award, 2000, *The Kids Book of Canada's Railway and How the CPR Was Built.*

Writings

NONFICTION FOR CHILDREN

Bears: Polar Bears, Black Bears, and Grizzly Bears, illustrated by Pat Stephens, Kids Can Press (New York, NY), 1996.

Deborah Hodge

Wild Cats: Cougars, Bobcats, and Lynx, illustrated by Nancy Gray Ogle, Kids Can Press (New York, NY), 1996.

Wild Dogs: Foxes, Wolves, and Coyotes, illustrated by Pat Stephens, Kids Can Press (New York, NY), 1996.

Whales: Killer Whales, Blue Whales, and More, illustrated by Pat Stephens, Kids Can Press (New York, NY), 1996.

Starting with Science: Simple Machines ("Starting with Science" series), photographs by Ray Bourdeau, Kids Can Press (New York, NY), 1996.

Deer, Moose, Elk, and Caribou, illustrated by Pat Stephens, Kids Can Press, 1998.

Beavers, illustrated by Pat Stephens, Kids Can Press (New York, NY), 1998.

The Kids Book of Canada's Railway and How the CPR Was Built, illustrated by John Mantha, Kids Can Press (Toronto, Canada), 2000.

Eagles, illustrated by Nancy Gray Ogle, Kids Can Press (New York, NY), 2000.

Work in Progress

Salmon, for Kids Can Press, publication expected in 2002.

Sidelights

"A child's thinking level is usually above his or her reading level, so the children's nonfiction writer must operate on two different planes—providing interesting, thought-provoking information that is accessible through words the child won't stumble over," Hodge told *SATA.* According to Hodge, books have fascinated her ever since she was a young child, "I loved the bedtime stories my parents read to me. Some, like the Brothers Grimm fairy tales, I have never forgotten."

Hodge was born in Moose Jaw, Saskatchewan, and grew up in Burnaby, British Columbia, Canada. She studied psychology at Simon Fraser University (SFU), intending to become a psychologist, but instead ended up as an elementary school teacher in British Columbia after completing a professional development program at SFU in 1978. Her teaching career spanned more than twelve years before she took a temporary leave of absence to work on the curriculum for the British Columbia Ministry of Education. While working on the assignment, Hodge happened to mention to a coworker the lack of stimulating books available to young readers. As a teacher she had often observed young children looking for books that were easy enough to read, yet still contained useful information.

This chance remark to Linda Bailey, creator of the popular "Stevie Diamond" mystery series, paved the way to a new and exciting career for Hodge. On Bailey's suggestion Hodge submitted a proposal for a children's book to Kids Can Press and then immediately followed it up with a completed manuscript. The book was published as *Bears: Polar Bears, Black Bears, and Grizzly Bears* in 1996.

Hodge examines the habits and habitats of the Bald Eagle and the Golden Eagle, in her informational book for early elementary readers. (Cover illustration by Nancy Gray Ogle.)

The choice of subject was not very difficult for Hodge as her years as an elementary school teacher had given her an insight into the mind of young readers. She explained to *SATA,* "They're fascinated by very big, very fast, or very fierce animals. They want answers to such questions as how long are a grizzly bear's claws, or how much does a Blue Whale eat?" Hodge has since published seven different titles dealing with various animals. All the books in her series are about animals that children are drawn to. Both *Bears* and its follow-up, *Wild Cats: Cougars, Bobcats, and Lynx,* were praised by Carolyn Phelan of *Booklist* for not crowding the pages with pictures and sundry facts as most books with a two-page layout do. Each set of pages covers a different topic, such as food, habitat, or birth, and "maintains a sense of visual calm and verbal continuity from one spread to the next." Jonathan Webb claimed in *Quill & Quire* that Hodge's books "fulfill, reliably and attractively, the modest objective they set themselves."

Other titles in Hodge's wildlife series include *Wild Dogs: Foxes, Wolves, and Coyotes* and *Whales: Killer Whales, Blue Whales, and More,* both which were published in 1996, and *Eagles,* published in 2000. These volumes follow the same basic, easy-to-read format of Hodge's earlier books, featuring large print, naturalistic drawings, and cut-away diagrams. They also contain interesting trivia boxes on each page. Fred Boer, reviewing both *Wild Dogs* and *Whales* for *Quill & Quire,* commented, "Both books are well organized, with a glossary and an index." Judy Diamond, reviewing the books for *Science Books and Film,* deemed them effective for an early elementary school readership and praised the material as clearly presented. Diamond concluded that, "Overall the information presented is accurate and complete. The volume will serve as a useful tool for school reports on its topics."

Other books in the series are *Deer, Moose, Elk, and Caribou* and *Beavers,* both of which were published in 1998. *Beavers* was praised by a contributor to *Kirkus Reviews* as having "concise, clearly organized facts corralled into brief, dual-page chapters." Dave Jenkinson, a contributor to *CM: Canadian Materials,* described *Beavers* as "a superb example of a well-written information book for pre-readers which will also appeal to students in the early elementary grades." *Deer, Moose, Elk, and Caribou* was reviewed by Robert G. Hoehn of *Science Activities,* who wrote, "The potpourri of information in this beautifully illustrated book is guaranteed to pique the interest of readers . . . . Adult readers will also enjoy the tidbits they learn about members of the deer family."

Hodge explores the world of science in the "Starting with Science" series published by Kids Can Press. Her book *Starting with Science: Simple Machines* contains a presentation of thirteen attractive and interactive experiments, accompanied by clear and detailed directions in an easy-to-follow format which encourages children's participation. According to critics, the book has much visual appeal and lists all the materials needed along with their methodology and an explanation of the principles engaged. Safety precautions are also addressed in the text or illustrated in sidebars, and further details about each activity are listed in the appendix. Maureen Garvie, reviewing *Starting with Science: Simple Machines* for *Quill & Quire,* noted that "The book reflects energy, esthetics, community, and curiosity . . . . With the aid of kitchen equipment and minimal supervision, science is no longer a fusty world of stained test-tubes, wire coils, and rotten-egg smells."

In 2000, the author turned her hand to the story of the Canadian Pacific Railway (CPR), Canada's first transcontinental railway, in *The Kids Book of Canada's Railway and How the CPR Was Built.* The granddaughter of CPR employees, Hodge details the quest to stretch a single track of rail across Canada and includes information about William van Horne's planning of the railway, the laborers who blasted through mountains and tackled difficult terrain, the types of trains eventually used on the railway, and the impact the CPR had on aboriginal peoples. Writing in *Quill & Quire,* reviewer Gweneth Evans suggested that "The building of the Canadian Pacific Railway is an incredible story, and this informative new book . . . does quite a good job of presenting it."

Although Hodge has not returned to teaching, she admits that the feedback she receives from children motivates her to continue writing and shapes her work as an instructional designer of elementary school curricula. She explained to *SATA:* "Every day when I wake up I have more ideas for books I want to write."

Biographical and Critical Sources

PERIODICALS

Booklist, September 15, 1997, Carolyn Phelan, review of *Bears* and *Wild Cats,* p. 238; April 15, 1998, Carolyn Phelan, review of *Starting with Science: Simple Machines,* p. 448; January 1, 1999, April Judge, review of *Deer, Moose, Elk, and Caribou* and *Beavers,* p. 865; November 1, 2000, Gillian Endberg, review of *Eagles.*

CM: Canadian Materials, August 11, 2000, Dave Jenkinson, review of *Beavers.*

Kirkus Reviews, October 1, 1998, review of *Beavers,* p. 1459.

Quill & Quire, March, 1996, Jonathan Webb, "Charismatic Cats and Winsome Bears," p. 73; December, 1996, Maureen Garvie, review of *Starting with Science: Simple Machines,* p. 39; January, 1997, Fred Boer, review of *Wild Dogs, Whales,* and *Living Things,* p. 38; September 1, 2000, Gwyneth Evans, review of *The Kids Book of Canada's Railway and How the CPR Was Built.*

School Library Journal, November, 1997, Lisa Wu Stowe, review of *Wild Dogs* and *Whales,* pp. 108-109; July, 1998, Kathryn Kosiorek, review of *Starting with Science: Simple Machines,* p. 88.

Science Activities, spring, 1999, Robert G. Hoehn, review of *Deer, Moose, Elk, and Caribou,* p. 39.

Science Books and Films, December, 1997, Judy Diamond, review of *Wild Dogs* and *Whales,* p. 275.

*   *   *

HOLT, Kimberly Willis 1960-

Personal

Born September 9, 1960, in Pensacola, FL; daughter of Julian Ray (a data processing manager) and Brenda (a teacher; maiden name, Mitchell) Willis; married Jerry William Holt (director of Amarillo CVC), February 23, 1985; children: Shannon. *Education:* Attended University of New Orleans, 1978-79, and Louisiana State University, 1979-81.

Addresses

Home—Amarillo, TX. *Office*—P.O. Box 20135, Amarillo, TX 79114. *Agent*—Flannery Literary Agency, 114 Wickfield Ct., Naperville, IL 60563.

Career

Radio news director, 1980-82; worked in advertising and marketing, 1982-87; interior decorator, 1987-93; writer, 1994—.

Awards, Honors

Boston Globe/Horn Book Award for Fiction, 1998, Notable Book selection, American Library Association (ALA), 1999, and Top Ten Best Books for Young Adults selection, ALA, 1999, all for *My Louisiana Sky;* National Book Award for Young People's Literature, 1999, for *When Zachary Beaver Came to Town.*

Writings

My Louisiana Sky, Holt, 1998.
Mister and Me, Putnam, 1998.
When Zachary Beaver Came to Town, Holt, 1999.
Dancing in Cadillac Light, Putnam, 2001.

Sidelights

Kimberly Willis Holt writes poignant coming-of-age fiction for young readers, books that hum with the sleepy rhythms of small-town life in her native South and the cadences of its vernacular. Since her 1998 debut novel, *My Louisiana Sky,* Holt has won a number of awards, including two American Library Association citations for that particular work, and a prestigious National Book Award for Young People's Literature for her third, 1999's *When Zachary Beaver Came to Town.* But all of her titles have garnered enthusiastic praise from critics of young adult fiction for their realistic portrayals of life in the rural South, and for the iconoclastic, but sympathetic characters she creates to lead her stories.

Holt was born in 1960, in Pensacola, Florida, the site of a large U.S. Navy base. Her father worked for many years as a chef for the U.S. Navy, and her mother was a teacher. Julian Willis's job took the family to several far-flung places during Holt's young life, including France and the Pacific Ocean territory of Guam. They also lived in a number of American states, but always made Forest Hill, Louisiana, their spiritual home. Holt's grandmother lived there, and the future author loved spending time in a place where her roots ran so deep. She began to consider writing as a career at the age of twelve, when she read Carson McCullers's *The Heart Is a Lonely Hunter.* This 1940 work, like others by the Georgia native, explored human isolation and life in the South through the vantage point of an eloquent outsider, and the style of fiction moved the young Holt. "It was just life-changing because of the characters," she told *School Library Journal* writer Kathleen T. Horning. "That was the first time I read a book where the characters seemed like real people to me."

Holt studied broadcast journalism at the University of New Orleans in the late 1970s and Louisiana State University until 1981, but left school to work as a news director for a radio station. The work was far from challenging, however, and so she took another job at the station selling advertising time. She also worked as an interior decorator for six years before thinking about writing for publication. As a teen and young adult, she had always envisioned a life as an author, but never pursued it in earnest. Part of the reason she abandoned her calling was due to a tough writing teacher she once had, who refused to provide her with any encouraging feedback. "In all fairness to her, she was a great teacher, but she would praise other people's writing but not mine," Holt told Horning in the *School Library Journal* interview. "I was very shy and insecure and I took it as though I really wasn't meant to be a writer."

Around 1994, Holt—by then married and with a young child—moved to Amarillo, Texas, for her husband's job. She was bereft, as she recalled, but recognized the sudden isolation as a surprise opportunity to begin writing for children. "I didn't know a soul there and I thought, 'If I'm ever going to do it, this is the time,'" she told Horning. The result was *My Louisiana Sky,* published by Holt in 1998. Set in a small town in central Louisiana, the story was inspired by a memorable incident that occurred when Holt was just nine. She had been traveling through rural Louisiana with her parents, and saw a woman carrying groceries walking on the side of the road. "This lady looked strange to me," Holt recalled in the interview with Horning. "She just had a different look about her on her face and I mentioned her to my mom and my mom said, 'That lady's mentally retarded and her husband is mentally retarded and they have a lot of kids.' It haunted me for the rest of my life."

Tiger Ann Parker is the unlikely heroine of *My Louisiana Sky,* which takes place in a town called Saitter in 1957. Tiger is twelve years old. She does well in both school and athletics, but she feels a certain degree of

Kimberly Willis Holt

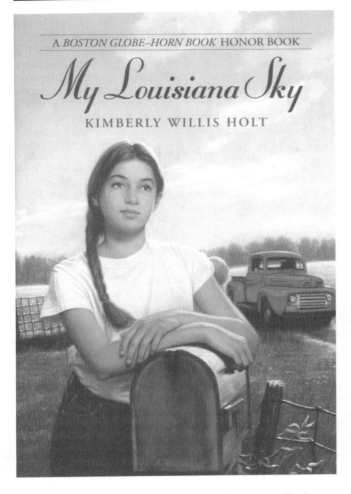

Holt spins the tale of twelve-year-old Tiger Ann Parker, living in Louisiana in 1957, who finds that her budding adolescence makes her sensitive to the scorn of the townspeople and ashamed of her developmentally challenged parents. (Cover illustration by Matt Archambault.)

social ostracism because of her parents. Her father, who works in a local plant nursery, cannot even do simple math, but Tiger's mother is even more developmentally challenged. As a young child, it used to delight Tiger that her mother played games with her so enthusiastically, but entering adolescence and yearning for a more "normal" life, Tiger begins to feel embarrassed by her parents' limitations. She knows that some townspeople view the family as odd and are of the opinion that the Parkers should have never been allowed to marry and start a family.

Fortunately, Tiger also lives with her astute, practical grandmother, who helps her face the teasing of others. Her beloved grandmother points out that "people are afraid of what's different. That don't mean different is bad. Just means different is different," she says in *My Louisiana Sky.* But things begin to change in sleepy Saitter: Tiger's baseball-playing pal surprises her with a kiss one day, and then her grandmother dies suddenly. Tiger's sophisticated aunt comes to Saitter in the midst

of the crisis, and offers to take Tiger home with her to the big city of Baton Rouge. Tiger is torn between her parents, who love her dearly, and the glamorous Dorie Kay and a world of new opportunities far from the small-mindedness of Saitter.

When a natural disaster nearly wrecks her father's workplace and another crisis arises, Tiger begins to realize the more positive aspects of life in Saitter. "With the help of Hurricane Audrey, Tiger learns how strong she is and where she truly belongs," remarked Lynn Evarts in a *Voice of Youth Advocates* critique of *My Louisiana Sky.* The debut work won a slew of awards for Holt, and sincere words of praise from reviewers. Betsy Hearne, writing in the *Bulletin of the Center for Children's Books,* found that in Tiger, the writer had created a character "with a distinctive voice" as well as "a credible resolution showing Tiger's values to be as strong as her family ties." *School Library Journal* writer Cindy Darling Codell asserted that "Holt has nicely portrayed the rhythms, relationships, and sometimes harsh realities of small-town life." Marilyn Bousquin, writing in *Horn Book,* found that Holt "eases the action along with a low-key, unpretentious plot, never resorting to over-dramatization or sentimentality in developing her uncannily credible characters." *Booklist*'s Hazel Rochman opined that "all the characters, including Tiger's parents, are drawn with warmth but no patronizing reverence," while a *Publishers Weekly* assessment asserted that Holt "presents and handles a sticky dilemma with remarkable grace."

Holt followed the success of her debut with another work published that same year, *Mister and Me.* Just eighty pages in length, the work is aimed at younger readers, aged seven to eleven, but still won praise for its depiction of a time and place that had long passed. Young Jolene Johnson, however, knows no other world except the sometimes tough realm of life in the segregated South as an African American child in the 1940s. Jolene lives in a logging town in Louisiana—two of Holt's great-grandfathers had worked in the industry—and is the daughter of a widowed seamstress mother, and also lives with her grandfather. Life begins to change a bit too quickly for Jolene when a Mister Leroy Redfield, a logger new to the town, begins wooing her mother. The presence of this rival for her mother's affection makes Jolene miss her deceased father, whom she never knew, even more.

During the course of *Mister and Me,* Jolene tries in vain to rid "Mister," as she calls him, from their lives, but her strategies only backfire. On one occasion, Leroy buys her mother some expensive fabric, and Jolene cuts it to small, unusable pieces. Then her mother and grandfather must suddenly travel to New Orleans for a brief time, and Jolene is left with Leroy for caretaking. They come to a truce, and then a new beginning. Lynda Short, writing in *School Library Journal,* called it a "touching short novel" that depicts Jolene's coming to terms with the presence of a "man whose love and patience allow her to expand her notion of family." A *Publishers Weekly* review declared that "the warmth and love in the

Johnson household envelops the novel," and Kay Weisman, critiquing it for *Booklist,* noted that "this heartfelt story is filled with richly developed characters who deal with all-too-real problems."

Holt's third novel, *When Zachary Beaver Came to Town,* won the National Book Award for Young People's Literature after its 1999 publication, and it made her a sought-after speaker in schools. On her visits and in her interviews, Holt makes it a point to remind aspiring writers—and all other aspirants—not to become discouraged by perceived negativity from a teacher, as she had once done.

The plot of *Zachary Beaver* originated with another memorable event in Holt's life; when she was thirteen, she went to the Louisiana state fair and paid two dollars to see a youth billed as "the fattest boy in the world." He sat in a small trailer and, in a manner somewhat out of character for the shy Holt, she asked him several questions about himself. He answered them, but he was understandably a bit surly about it.

Later in life, Holt met someone who had met the boy as well when the trailer made a stop near an office. The woman in question paid two dollars every day to see him, but ate her lunch with him. "And I just remember thinking, 'I didn't do that. I didn't come across in a kind way,'" she told Horning in the *School Library Journal* interview. Holt sets her story in Antler, Texas—a composite of two towns she knows in the Texas Panhandle—in the summer of 1971. This time, her protagonist is a boy, Toby Wilson, who is thirteen that summer. Antler is so small that the arrival of a trailer bearing "the world's fattest teenaged boy" is an interesting event, and Toby and his best friend Cal are fascinated by the tragic figure of Zachary.

Toby's life is somewhat difficult for him that summer. His mother has left the family in order to pursue a career in the music industry in Nashville. His father, Otto, is Antler's postmaster, but also runs a worm business for bait-supply shops on the side. Toby and Cal dream of life and its possibilities outside of Antler and, like others, have made Cal's popular older brother, Wayne, a role model. Toby is also suffering from a crush on a girl named Scarlett. When Zachary Beaver arrives in his trailer, Toby and Cal visit the 643-pound boy and ask him innumerable questions. Zachary seems to possess an oddly encyclopedic knowledge of the world, but relies on his legal guardian—who disappears shortly after Zachary's trailer arrives in the parking lot of the local Dairy Maid. Toby and Cal do a bit of sleuthing and wonder why Zachary, who says he's been baptized, possesses a Bible that doesn't register that date in it, as was customary in the rural United States. Zachary finally confesses the truth, and the boys help him fulfill this dream of his. "This rebirth twists the small-town perspective in a way that serves the novel well," noted Bousquin in a *Horn Book* review. "To Zachary, Antler becomes the place on the map that has opened his heart and his life to barely-hoped-for possibilities."

Meanwhile, military officials arrive at Cal's house to tell the family that his brother Wayne has been killed in Vietnam. Toby realizes that his parents' marriage is irreparably damaged, but his quiet, kind father helps him through these difficult times. "Holt tenderly captures small-town life and deftly fills it with decent characters who ring true," wrote Linnea Lannon in the *New York Times Book Review.* Other reviewers gave it equally solid praise. "Picturesque images ... drive home the point that everyday life is studded with memorable moments," stated *Publishers Weekly.*

Holt lives with her husband and daughter in Amarillo still, and published her fourth book, *Dancing in Cadillac Light,* in 2001. Set in Texas, the novel follows the story of Jaynell, an eleven-year-old girl who must change her perception of poverty after her grandfather's death. When Horning asked Holt, in the *School Library Journal* interview, about the eccentricity of her characters and whether she would concur with this assessment, the author agreed wholeheartedly. "I think I am too," she laughed. "I'm attracted to people like that. I like the flaws in people .... And I also love the people that seem normal on the surface and then they're really not. I find that a high compliment when people say that they think my characters are eccentric or quirky, because I guess that's what I love about life."

Biographical and Critical Sources

PERIODICALS

Booklist, April 15, 1998, Hazel Rochman, review of *My Louisiana Sky,* p. 1438; November 15, 1998, Kay Weisman, review of *Mister and Me,* p. 590; January 1, 2000, review of *When Zachary Beaver Came to Town,* p. 820.

Bulletin of the Center for Children's Books, June, 1998, Betsy Hearne, review of *My Louisiana Sky,* p. 364.

Horn Book, July-August, 1998, Marilyn Bousquin, review of *My Louisiana Sky,* p. 489; November, 1999, Marilyn Bousquin, review of *When Zachary Beaver Came to Town,* p. 741.

New York Times Book Review, December 19, 1999, Linnea Lannon, review of *When Zachary Beaver Came to Town.*

Publishers Weekly, May 4, 1998, review of *My Louisiana Sky,* p. 213; August 31, 1998, review of *Mister and Me,* p. 76; November 1, 1999, review of *When Zachary Beaver Came to Town,* p. 85.

School Library Journal, July, 1998, Cindy Darling Codell, review of *My Louisiana Sky,* pp. 95-96; November, 1998, Lynda Short, review of *Mister and Me,* p. 122; February, 2000, Kathleen T. Horning, "Small Town Girl," pp. 43-45; March, 2001, William McLoughlin, review of *Dancing in the Cadillac Light,* p. 250.

Texas Monthly, December, 1999, Mike Shea, review of *When Zachary Beaver Came to Town,* p. 34.

Voice of Youth Advocates, August, 1998, Lynn Evarts, review of *My Louisiana Sky,* p. 202; February, 1999, review of *My Louisiana Sky,* p. 411; April, 2001, Diane Tuccillo, review of *Dancing in the Cadillac Light,* p. 42.*

HOWIE, Diana (Melson) 1945-

Personal

Born June 1, 1945, in Miami, FL; married. *Education:* Attended University of Wales at Cardiff, 1965-66; Tulane University, B.A. (English literature), 1967; Columbia University, M.S. (library science), 1972; University of Houston, M.A. (theater arts), 1992.

Addresses

Office—c/o Contemporary Drama Service, 885 Elkton Dr., Colorado Springs, CO 80907.

Career

Playwright. Librarian, 1972-85; writer 1985—. Country Playhouse, Houston, TX, coordinator of annual "New Play Reading Series," 1993—, and playwright-in-residence, 1996—; teaching artist in elementary schools for Texas Institute for the Arts in Education. *Member:* Dramatists Guild of America, PEN.

Writings

PLAYS

Susanna of Stratford, produced at Edinburgh International Fringe Festival, 1990.
Judy's Friend (one-act), produced at University of Houston, 1992.
(With Jeanette Wiggins) *You Can't Wear It Out,* produced in Houston as *Burette,* 1993.
Marilyn's Boy (one-act), produced in Houston, 1993.
Madame Delicieuse, produced in Houston, 1997.
Top Dogs, produced in Houston, 1997.
The Brightest Light, produced in Houston, 1998.
No Cash Value, produced in Houston, 1999.
At Liberty, produced in Houston, 2000.
Jackson Square, produced in Houston, 2001.

Also author of several short plays, including *Carmen,* produced 1992; and (with Gerald LaBita) *Perryboy,* produced 1993. Has also created other works for the stage, including *I Do Trills Now* (scripted interludes for a piano concert) and *Hansel and Gretel* (for children), produced in Houston, 1999.

OTHER

Tight Spots: True-to-Life Monolog Characterizations for Student Actors, Contemporary Drama Service, 1999.

Contributing editor, *New Jersey Monthly* (magazine).

Work in Progress

Madame Delicieuse, a television adaptation of Howie's play; *Jury,* a musical; *Susanna + Will,* "a two-character version of *Susanna of Stratford.*"

Sidelights

Diana Howie was a reference librarian for nearly thirteen years before she discovered a new vocation: writing. She accidentally stumbled upon this new career when she approached editors at the *New Jersey Monthly* about a magazine article on funding cuts at libraries. Howie ended up writing the piece herself and the article was published as a feature story. She also became a regular contributing editor to the magazine at this point. But it was not until later, when she moved from New Jersey to Houston, Texas, that Howie seriously considered pursuing writing as a career. The fact that her husband was employed and did not mind being "a patron of the arts," as Howie told *SATA,* made the switch easier financially.

Howie was born in Miami, Florida, on June 1, 1945. After obtaining her bachelors' degree in English literature from Tulane University in 1967, she went on to earn a master's degree in library science from Columbia University in 1972. In 1992 she completed a second graduate degree, this time in theater arts from the University of Houston. The turning point in Howie's life came one day as she was taking a driving tour of the Hudson River's west bank. She stopped to read the historical marker at the site where United States Vice President Aaron Burr fought his famous duel with the former secretary of the United States Treasury, Alexan-

Diana Howie

der Hamilton, in July 1804. Howie found the story fascinating and, while researching its details, began to envision it as a play. She completed the first draft in 1985, yet it was another thirteen years before the play, *The Brightest Light,* was actually produced.

In the intervening years Howie completed her studies and wrote six other plays. No one was probably more surprised at this change of career than Howie herself. She told *SATA* that although she had always been an enthusiastic audience member, she had never considered writing for the stage, making her choice of taking up playwriting as a full-time occupation surprising even to her. Her first play, *Susanna of Stratford,* was produced at Edinburgh, Scotland's famous Fringe Festival in 1990. It is a monologue in which William Shakespeare's daughter finally comes to terms with the discrepancies between what society at large thinks of her father and what she herself believes. The play has two forty-five minutes acts, with act one able to be staged on its own. Set in the seventeenth century, the play combines the sensibilities of Elizabethan England and the Puritan Revolution and brings them to life for twenty-first-century audiences.

In 1992 came *Judy's Friend,* a play about an aging midget who lives in a bookstore now marked for demolition. In an effort to stop the demolition, he puts on a display of Judy Garland memorabilia. Insights about the film industry and Judy Garland's death are conveyed through the play. Howie wrote a follow-up to *Judy's Friend* in 1993, titling it *Marilyn's Boy.* In this work, actress Marilyn Monroe's illegitimate son copes with losing his good looks. In addition to being appropriate vehicles for a one-person performance, both plays can be performed separately or as a combined whole. Critics praised the plays for portraying an authentic picture of the destruction of society while offering a ray of hope at the end from an unlikely source.

In 1993 Howie coauthored *You Can't Wear It Out* with Jeanette Wiggins. Produced as *Burette* at Houston's Country Playhouse, the play was also considered as a possible Hollywood script for actor James Garner in 1997. It is a comedy in which the central character, Burette Furder, at age eighty-one gets married for the fifth time. Burette has never lost his zest for life and the play's action is derived from the perseverance and regeneration of his ever-present desire for romance.

You Can't Wear It Out was followed by *Madame Delicieuse* in 1997, a warm-hearted drama about a mother and her two children and their efforts to cope with the absence of the children's father in their lives. *Top Dogs,* which also premiered in 1997, was described by Howie in the *Houston Chronicle* as a "sort of Brechtian Everyman's tale." Michael Harrison, the play's protagonist, is a young, up-and-coming teacher who encounters various levels of power-play at every step of his career. Different character types make their debut through the span of the play to undermine Michael's attempts to establish a life "without having to compete every minute of the day." Reviewers found the

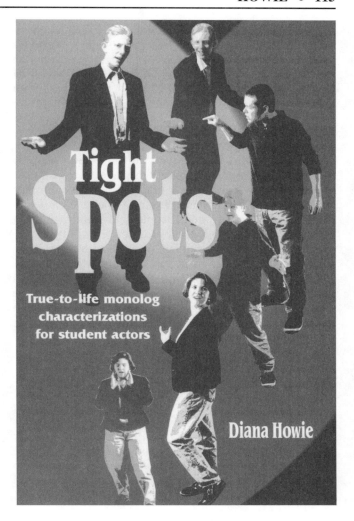

In **Tight Spots,** *Howie offers high-school students fifty monologs ideal for use in contests or in the classroom. (Cover illustration by Janice Melvin.)*

play both funny and sadly true, an unfortunate reflection on modern society where human interaction becomes a competition of sorts.

1998 saw the production of *The Brightest Light,* the play that started it all for Howie. At the core of the play is the duel between Burr and Hamilton, an actual occurrence during which Hamilton was shot and killed by the vice president. Although the shooting occurred in 1804, Howie saw parallels with events occurring within the United States presidency in 1998—similarities between Hamilton's and President Bill Clinton's misfortunes. In her interview for the *Houston Chronicle* she explained: "It dovetails with Clinton's problems," comparing the Democratic president's sex scandal with Hamilton's many romantic affairs, affairs that became public and ultimately led to his demise. Critics acknowledged the play as being powerful and noted that it put contemporary events in a whole new perspective.

Howie told *SATA* that she usually starts with a story that is rooted in detail; the progress of that story eventually reveals a theme to her. Her *No Cash Value,* which explores the twin themes of adolescents taking responsibility for themselves and becoming aware of others needs and the increasing needs of an older man down on his luck, was a departure from her usual method of writing. Here, as the author told *SATA,* she started out with "a character with an attitude" and developed a story around him.

Drawing on her former career, Howie's 2000 play, *At Liberty,* is set inside a public library and focuses on the chaos that develops when a librarian has a determined attitude to avoid problems. Susan, a young librarian, is more than willing to help people find information but refuses to maintain any kind of order. Unwillingness to handle the increasing number of rowdy library patrons gives rise to a situation of farcical proportions. Howie noted in the *Houston Chronicle:* "The library is really a metaphor for democracy. It's like Central Park. It's a big, public space where no one is really in charge, but everyone has to take responsibility for their actions or the system won't work."

Howie noted that the most important elements she considers when writing her plays are structure, dramatic action, conflict, syntax, and metaphor. Though she is not actively involved in the production process, she attends auditions and rehearsals for the first productions of her plays, and retains approval on casting choices. After the first production closes, Howie often makes revisions to her script, basing her changes on audience reactions and critical feedback.

In an effort to promote new talent, Howie also organizes the Houston, Texas-based Country Playhouse's "New Play Reading Series," a program designed to present new plays by local authors. She also edits the theater's newsletter. She commented in her *Houston Chronicle* interview that it remains her dream to have high school theater students perform her plays "over and over again, until the teachers get sick of them."

Biographical and Critical Sources

PERIODICALS

Houston Chronicle, April 18, 1997, Melissa Fletcher Stoeltje, "Playing out a Midlife Fantasy," pp. 1D, 10D; February 21, 1998, Annette Baird, "Play Explores Scandal of U.S. Founding Father," pp. 1, 5, and "'Light' Took More than a Decade to Reach the Stage," pp. 1, 6.

HUBBARD, Michelle Calabro 1953-

Personal

Born January 25, 1953, in Glendale, CA; daughter of Ben (in ceramic mold business) and Jean (a homemaker; maiden name, Collino) Hubbard; married Tony Calabro (an attorney), December 22, 1989. *Education:* Glendale University College of Law, B.S.L. and J.D. *Hobbies and other interests:* Gardening, reading.

Addresses

Home—269 Ilikaa Pl., Kailua, HI 96734. *E-mail*—MBCHubbard@aol.com.

Career

Writer. Kaplan Education, law school admissions consultant, 1997—. *Member:* Society of Children's Book Writers and Illustrators, Mystery Writers of America, Romance Writers of America.

Writings

Sour Notes (novel), Bess Press (Honolulu, HI), 1999. *Heart Sight,* Starlight Writer Publications, in press.

Work in Progress

A romance novel, *Bride, Baby, Two Grooms;* a mystery novel, *Flashback;* several short stories.

Sidelights

Michelle Calabro Hubbard told *SATA:* "I began a writing career because I've always loved to write and thought I could tell a good story. Fortunately I had no idea how hard writing is, or I probably would have quit a long time ago. After six years, two Internal Revenue Service audits, and at least 200 rejections, my first book *Sour Notes,* a Hawaiian-style 'Sweet Valley High,' was published.

"I'm still getting as many rejections as acceptances, but I know my writing keeps getting better and, thanks to a new writing routine, my enthusiasm is riding high. I'm working on several different projects and have ideas for a lot more.

"Writing can be a brutal business, and I've had to take breaks from it to lick my wounds. I have a fabulous husband, a spoiled rotten parrot named Flash, and a garden that can't get enough of my attention. Writing has to be one more good thing, or there just isn't room for it. No matter how long my breaks are, writing always calls me back. It's a call I love to answer."

I–J

IVERSON, Diane 1950-

Personal

Born February 20, 1950, in Fresno, CA; daughter of Raymond Marion Crouch (a farmer and truck driver) and Elizabeth Sue Wall-Arnold (a bookkeeper); married Ronald Olen McDaniel, June 22, 1968 (divorced, 1984); married Douglas Alton Iverson (a high school English teacher), August 2, 1987; children: (first marriage) Carla Michele, Kristin Mae. *Education:* Attended Shasta College. *Politics:* Democrat. *Religion:* Seventh-Day Methodist. *Hobbies and other interests:* Antiques, backpacking, cooking, native plant gardening, bird watching, sustainable building, "reading books related to the Christian faith, the arts, the environment, or children."

Addresses

Home—2243 Mountain Oak Rd., Prescott, AZ 86305. *E-mail*—diverson@cableone.net.

Career

Freelance graphic artist; North Cal Printing, Redding, CA, graphic artist, 1980-82. *A New Communion* magazine, coeditor, 1992—.

Awards, Honors

Notable Children's Trade Book in the Field of Social Studies, National Council for the Social Studies/Children's Book Council, 1994, for *I Celebrate Nature;* Outstanding Book, Parent Council, Ltd., 1999, for *My Favorite Tree: Terrific Trees of North America.*

Writings

SELF-ILLUSTRATED

I Celebrate the World, Mustard Seed, 1989.
I Celebrate Nature, Dawn (Nevada City, CA), 1993.
Discover the Seasons, Dawn (Nevada City, CA), 1996.

My Favorite Tree: Terrific Trees of North America ("Sharing Nature with Children" series), Dawn (Nevada City, CA), 1999.

ILLUSTRATOR

Teddi Grover, *Buttons the Foster Bunny,* Mustard Seed, 1992.

Discover the Seasons has been translated into Chinese.

Diane Iverson

Work in Progress

The Perfect Gift, a picture book about the story of Jesus Christ's birth; research on birds and mammals of the United States.

Sidelights

Children's author and illustrator Diane Iverson grew up on a cotton, dairy, and alfalfa farm outside of Fresno, California. It was in this environment that she was allowed to explore the outdoors and develop a great love for the wilderness, a love that she now shares in her books about nature. In her award-winning book *I Celebrate Nature,* Iverson shows three children learning more about the world around them by visiting a meadow, climbing trees, and watching for wildlife. Throughout the story, Iverson illustrates with words and pictures the joy that can be had in spending a carefree day outdoors. Writing in *Science Books and Films,* reviewer Sister Edna L. Demanche suggested that *I Celebrate Nature* gives children living in an urban setting the opportunity to learn more about nature as well as provides a window "to the existence of outdoor realities ... where the real world can make multidimensional impressions and embed memories that the author so ardently wishes young people to have."

Iverson continues her discussion about the natural world with her 1999 work, *My Favorite Tree: Terrific Trees of North America.* Here the author discusses the characteristics of twenty-seven trees native to the North American continent. Alongside the illustrations for each tree are "detailed fact boxes" as described by a reviewer for *Publishers Weekly.* While noting a few flaws in this "handsome book about trees," Jane H. Bock nevertheless boldly stated in *Science Books and Films:* "I would encourage the author to write more books about trees."

Iverson told *SATA:* "One of the most wonderful memories of raising my two daughters is our story time. Sometimes they would keep begging me to read until my voice was literally gone. So I suppose I think of a book as an excuse to put a child on my lap. I have been pleased to discover it works with grandchildren too.

"A wonderful extension of that sort of connection is the opportunity to visit thousands of children at schools every year. I am always aware just who my readers are, and I love to spend time with them.

"I live in a passive-solar, rammed-earth house that my husband and I helped build. Sometimes classes visit my house to see my studio and earth house construction. They seem to appreciate the natural connection between writing about the wonders of nature and being a good steward of the earth. I try to live those values, so I insist on recycled paper for my books, hang most of my laundry on a line, and eat a vegetarian diet. My life is pretty simple.

"When I am not out on a trail, speaking to kids, or doing research, I keep myself busy doing a wide range of things. I may be planning a party, growing two hundred plants in my greenhouse for an Earth Day benefit, piecing together a quilt, writing a letter to the editor of the local paper, or exploring Native American ruins. I am curious about a lot of things. I enjoy learning and I enjoy telling children about what I have learned.

"It is simply an extra blessing for me that I get to do the illustrations for my books. I love to draw, and that means I get the thrill and anticipation of the stark white page on the drawing table as well as the computer."

Biographical and Critical Sources

PERIODICALS

Publishers Weekly, May 3, 1999, review of *My Favorite Tree: Terrific Trees of North America,* p. 78.
Science Books and Films, January-February, 1994, Sister Edna L. Demanche, review of *I Celebrate Nature,* p. 17; November-December, 1999, Jane H. Bock, review of *My Favorite Tree: Terrific Trees of North America,* p. 280.

* * *

JAMES, Dynely
See MAYNE, William (James Carter)

* * *

JONES, Charlotte Foltz 1945-

Personal

Born November 1, 1945, in Boulder, CO; daughter of Forrest C. (an aeronautical technician) and Mildred E. (an office manager; maiden name, Deibert) Foltz; married William C. R. Jones (a carpet installer and builder), April 17, 1971; children: John Paul. *Education:* Central Business College, advanced secretarial degree, 1964; attended University of Colorado. *Religion:* Roman Catholic. *Hobbies and other interests:* Reading, walking, papier-mâché sculpture, spiritual enlightenment.

Addresses

Home—1620 Quince Avenue, Boulder, CO 80304.

Career

Author, 1976—. Boulder Valley Public Schools, Boulder, CO, secretary, 1966-75; writing instructor, Boulder Valley Schools Lifelong Learning, 1990-2000. *Member:* Society of Children's Book Writers and Illustrators (Rocky Mountain division president, 1989-90), Colorado Authors League, Colorado Center for the Book.

Awards, Honors

Distinguished Achievement Award, Educational Press Association of America, 1984, for an article published in

Charlotte Foltz Jones

Growing Parent/Growing Child; first place essay, *Mentor Magazine* writing contest, 1990; finalist, Colorado Authors League/Colorado Center for the Book Contest, 1991, and Children's Choice Book designation, International Reading Association/Children's Book Council, 1992, both for *Mistakes That Worked;* Top Hand Award for children's nonfiction, Colorado Authors League, 1992, for *Mistakes That Worked,* 1998, for *Fingerprints and Talking Bones,* and 2000, for *Eat Your Words;* Notable Books for Children designation, *Smithsonian,* 1996, for *Accidents May Happen;* New York Public Library's Recommended Books for the Teen-Age, 1998, for *Fingerprints and Talking Bones,* and 2000, for *Eat Your Words;* Notable Children's Trade Book in the Field of Social Studies, National Council for the Social Studies, and Colorado Book Award, Colorado Center for the Book, both 2000, both for *Yukon Gold.*

Writings

Only Child: Clues for Coping, Westminster (Philadelphia, PA), 1984.

Mistakes That Worked: Forty Familiar Inventions and How They Came to Be, illustrated by John O'Brien, Doubleday (New York, NY), 1991.

Colorado Wildflowers: A Beginner's Field Guide to the State's Most Common Flowers, illustrated by D. D. Dowden, Falcon Press (Billings, MT), 1994.

Accidents May Happen: Fifty Inventions Discovered by Mistake, illustrated by O'Brien, Delacorte Press (New York, NY), 1996.

Fingerprints and Talking Bones: How Real-Life Crimes Are Solved, illustrated by David G. Klein, Delacorte Press (New York, NY), 1997.

Eat Your Words: A Fascinating Look at the Language of Food, illustrated by O'Brien, Delacorte Press (New York, NY), 1999.

Yukon Gold: The Story of the Klondike Gold Rush, Holiday House (New York, NY), 1999.

Contributor to periodicals.

Work in Progress

Explorers of the West, scheduled for publication in 2002.

Sidelights

"There must be no greater accomplishment than to touch a child's life in a positive way," Charlotte Foltz Jones once told *SATA.* "And the greatest reward is to have a child say, 'I read *all* of your book and I liked it. I really did!'" Jones' first book for children, *Only Child: Clues for Coping,* was the product of her experiences as an only child and as the mother of an only child. The book offers advice to children with no brothers and sisters and is intended to help them deal with the expectations of those from larger families. In a *School Library Journal* review Phyllis K. Kennemer found that the book offered sound advice regarding "making and keeping friends, coming to terms with feelings, and avoiding boredom." Anne Raymer, reviewing the book in *Voice of Youth Advocates* praised the work for the way it "disputes the old myths characterizing only children as lonely, spoiled, or maladjusted."

Jones' second book, *Mistakes That Worked: Forty Familiar Inventions and How They Came to Be,* published in 1991, is a compilation of anecdotes about inventions and discoveries that were made unintentionally. Brief entries are grouped together under easy-to-read and interesting titles. While it can be disputed whether some of the entries were mistakes or intentional experiments (such as Levi Strauss having pants made from tent canvas), most are recorded as accidents. Zena Sutherland, reviewing the book for *Bulletin of the Center for Children's Books,* opined that, "The writing style is brisk, often humorous, and both the theme and the brevity of the entries should appeal to readers."

Accidents May Happen: Fifty Inventions Discovered by Mistake is similar to *Mistakes That Worked.* While not all events included in this work would be categorized as inventions without some debate, most are interesting and Jones includes informative facts about the origins of a variety of household items, foodstuffs, and medicines. The book addresses the successes as well as the failures on mankind's journey of discovery. Pamela K. Bomboy commented in the *School Library Journal* that *Accidents May Happen* "is a well-conceived introduction to science that will pique the interest of young readers." Elizabeth Bush added in her *Bulletin of the Center for Children's Books* review that it "scores high points for browsability, entertaining trivia enthusiasts with legendary successes ... and even more stunning flops."

Jones' *Fingerprints and Talking Bones: How Real-Life Crimes Are Solved* addresses another contemporary topic of interest to young and old alike: forensic science and its applications in the field of criminology. The book is written in a clear, uncomplicated manner and does not shy away from addressing all aspects of the subject. Jones includes examples of forensic techniques that have been used in real cases, and readers are introduced to the jargon used in the forensic field. Links between everyday life and the application of forensic science are explored throughout the book. A *Kirkus Reviews* critic considered *Fingerprints and Talking Bones* to be "a volume that makes plain the importance of critical thinking and careful research for all types of problemsolving.... Amateur sleuths and aspiring scientists will get a kick out of this police-work primer." Stephanie Zvirin, reviewing Jones' work in *Booklist,* added that it was "A book for the career minded as well as the curious."

Eat Your Words: A Fascinating Look at the Language of Food explores the interesting world of food-related language and the birth of food-inspired idioms. Their history and origin are traced in this entertaining and informative "collection of tongue-in-cheek, entertaining anecdotes for gastronomists and trivia buffs alike" according to a contributor to *Kirkus Reviews.* One section deals with dishes, foodstuffs, and vegetables named after people, places, and animals, another explores the association between food and fun, and a third examines the relationship between popular phrases and food. *School Library Journal* contributor Linda Wadleigh commented that "The layout and accessible writing style make this book easy to understand and interesting to read. It is filled with anecdotes and amusing illustrations."

Jones' *Yukon Gold: The Story of the Klondike Gold Rush* recounts the nineteenth-century search for Alaskan gold, the failures and accomplishment of the people it drew, their discoveries, friendships, and rivalries. A reviewer for *Horn Book* remarked that the work presents "an intriguing picture of a remote event, its place in history, the hardships and successes it encompassed, and the people who are remembered for their part in making it happen." Jones draws on both Canadian and American publications for her material and her writing is complemented by a remarkable collection of vintage photographs. The book does not follow a chronological time line, instead addressing the issues topically. Although this was perceived as a flaw by reviewer Bush in *Bulletin of the Center for Children's Books,* the critic found the pictures accompanying the text to be striking and praiseworthy, and was moved to comment, "An impressive gallery of period photos speaks powerfully of the stampeders' travails and the miners' backbreaking labor—more powerfully, all too often, than the choppy awkward text." A reviewer for *Publishers Weekly* noted that Jones' text serves as "a solid resource for information about the period."

The reason for Jones' choice of unusual subjects for many of her books, including *Mistakes That Worked, Accidents May Happen,* and *Eat Your Words,* was included in her comments to *SATA:* "When I was nine years old, my parents bought me a rocking chair. I loved that chair. I would sit and rock ... and dream ... and stare ... and think ... and write in my notebook.... I was collecting words ... and thoughts ... and images. As I sat rocking, I sorted them. As I dreamed, I arranged them into fascinating stories (fascinating, at least, to a nine-year-old). As I wrote in my notebook, I recorded my favorites.

"Now, as I write for the children who read my books, I try to bring to my young audience some of the wonder and curiosity I captured in my notebook many years ago."

Biographical and Critical Sources

PERIODICALS

Booklist, June 1, 1996, Stephanie Zvirin, review of *Accidents May Happen,* p. 1710; June 1, 1997, Stephanie Zvirin, review of *Fingerprints and Talking Bones,* p. 1692.

Bulletin of the Center for Children's Books, October, 1991, Zena Sutherland, review of *Mistakes That Worked,* p. 41; September, 1996, Elizabeth Bush, review of *Accidents May Happen,* pp. 17-18; June, 1999, Bush, review of *Yukon Gold,* p. 355.

Horn Book, July, 1999, review of *Yukon Gold,* p. 483.

Kirkus Reviews, May 15, 1997, review of *Fingerprints and Talking Bones,* p. 801; May 1, 1999, review of *Eat Your Words,* p. 723.

Publishers Weekly, April 12, 1999, review of *Yukon Gold,* p. 77.

Jones's **Mistakes That Worked** *is a compilation of anecdotes about forty inventions and discoveries that were made unintentionally. (Illustrated by John O'Brien.)*

School Library Journal, February, 1985, Phyllis K. Kennemer, review of *Only Child,* p. 76; October, 1991, Cathryn A. Campher, review of *Mistakes That Worked,* p. 139; June, 1996, Pamela K. Bomboy, review of *Accidents May Happen,* p. 142; July, 1999, Linda Wadleigh, review of *Eat Your Words,* p. 108.

Voice of Youth Advocates, June, 1985, Anne Raymer, review of *Only Child,* p. 146.

* * *

JORDAN, Sherryl 1949-

Personal

Born June 8, 1949, in Hawera, New Zealand; daughter of Alan Vivian and Patricia (Eta) Brogden; married Lee Jordan, 1970; children: Kym. *Education:* Attended Tauranga Girls' College, 1962-64; two years of nursing training, 1967-68. *Religion:* Christian. *Hobbies and other interests:* "Music, friends, conversation, and solitude to write."

Addresses

Home—165 Kings Ave., Matua, Tauranga, New Zealand. *Agent*—Tracy Adams, McIntosh and Otis, Inc., 310 Madison Ave., New York, NY 10017.

Career

Illustrator, 1980-85; full-time writer, 1988—. Part-time teacher's aide in primary schools, working with profoundly deaf children, 1979-87. Writer-in-residence, University of Iowa, 1993. Frequent speaker at schools and conferences in New Zealand, Australia, Denmark, and the United States. *Member:* Children's Literature Association (Bay of Plenty branch, committee member), Society of Children's Book Writers and Illustrators, New Zealand Children's Book Foundation, New Zealand Society of Authors.

Awards, Honors

National illustrating competition winner, 1980; Choysa Bursary, 1988, for *Rocco;* AIM Story Book of the Year Award, New Zealand, 1991, for *Rocco;* AIM Story book of the year award runner-up, and Esther Glen Award shortlist, New Zealand Library Association, both 1992, both for *The Juniper Game;* Esther Glen Award shortlist, New Zealand Library Association, and AIM Junior Story Book of the Year Award, both 1992, both for *The Wednesday Wizard;* AIM Story Book of the Year Award shortlist, 1993, for *Denzil's Dilemma;* selected by *American Bookseller* magazine as a "Pick of the List," 1993, American Library Association (ALA) Best Book for Young Adults, ALA Recommended Book for the Reluctant Young Adult Reader, Children's Book of the Year, Bank Street School of Education, New Zealand AIM Book of the Year Award shortlist, all 1994, and listed in Whitcoull's New Zealand Top 100 books, 1997, all for *Winter of Fire;* short-listed for the New Zealand AIM Book of the Year Awards, short-

Sherryl Jordan

listed for the New Zealand Library Association Esther Glen Award, and ALA Best Book for Young Adults, all 1995, all for *Tanith (Wolf-Woman); New Zealand Post* Children's Book Awards shortlist (formerly the New Zealand AIM Awards), 1997, for *Secret Sacrament;* best book in translation award (Belgium), 1999, and Junior Library Guild selection, 2000, both for *Secret Sacrament;* Junior Library Guild selection, Best Children's Book of the Year, Bank Street College of Education, Best Book, *School Library Journal,* all 1999, Ten Best Books for Young Adults, ALA, Books for the Teen Age, New York Public Library, NASEN Special Needs Award, and Notable New Zealand Children's and Young Adult Books citation, New Zealand Children's Book Foundation, all 2000, all for *The Raging Quiet;* Margaret Mahy Medal and Lecture Award, Children's Literature Foundation of New Zealand, 2001, for contributions to children's literature, publishing, and literacy.

Writings

FICTION

(Self-illustrated) *The Firewind and the Song* (picture book), Kagyusha Publishers, 1984.

Matthew's Monsters (picture book), illustrated by Dierdre Gardiner, Ashton Scholastic, 1986.

No Problem Pomperoy (picture book), illustrated by Jan van der Voo, Century Hutchinson, 1988.

Kittens (school reader), Shortlands, 1989.

The Wobbly Tooth (for children), Shortlands, 1989.

Babysitter Bear (for children), illustrated by Trevor Pye, Century Hutchinson, 1990.

Rocco (young adult fantasy), Ashton Scholastic, 1990, published as *A Time of Darkness,* Scholastic, 1990.

The Juniper Game (young adult), Scholastic, 1991.

The Wednesday Wizard (for children), Scholastic, 1991.

Denzil's Dilemma (for children; sequel to *The Wednesday Wizard*), Scholastic, 1992.

Winter of Fire (young adult), Scholastic, 1993.

The Other Side of Midnight, illustrated by Brian Pollard, Scholastic, 1993.

Tanith (young adult), Omnibus, 1994, published as *Wolf-Woman,* Houghton, 1994.

Sign of the Lion, Penguin, 1995.

Secret Sacrament (young adult), Penguin, 1996, Harper-Collins, 2001.

Denzil's Great Bear Burglary (sequel to *Denzil's Dilemma*), Mallinson Rendel, 1997.

The Raging Quiet (young adult), Simon & Schuster, 1999.

ILLUSTRATOR; WRITTEN BY JOY COWLEY

Mouse, Shortland, 1983.

Tell-tale, Shortland, 1983.

The Silent One, Whitcoull's, 1984.

Mouse Monster, Shortland, 1985.

OTHER

Also contributor to journals, including *New Zealand Author, Southern Scribe,* and *Signal.*

Sidelights

Award-winning New Zealand author Sherryl Jordan began her writing career with picture books, but soon moved on to novels for older readers. Her breakthrough came with *Rocco,* published in the United States as *A Time of Darkness,* and since that time she has gone on to pen many more titles for young adult and juvenile readers which have been published both in her native New Zealand and throughout the world. The recipient of a 1993 fellowship to the prestigious Writing Program at the University of Iowa, Jordan used her time in the United States to speak widely at schools and conferences about her books, which blend fantasy with bits of science fiction and romantic realism. "All my young adult novels have been gifts," she noted in the *St. James Guide to Children's Writers.* "I don't think them up. They hit me over the head when I least expect them; overwhelm me with impressions, sights, and sounds of their new worlds; enchant me with their characters; and dare me to write them."

The road to success, however, was a long one for Jordan. Born in Hawera, New Zealand, in 1949, she started writing stories and even novels when she was only ten years old, works which her hopeful teachers sent out to publishers, but none of them sold. Though she attended a nurse's training school, Jordan was always headed for a career in writing or illustration. "From my earliest days I was also good at art," Jordan once told *Something about the Author* (*SATA*). "I began to seriously work on children's books in 1980, when I won a national competition for illustrations for my work on Joy

In her gripping novel, Jordan portrays a young woman named Tanith who has been raised by wolves. When she is adopted by a barbaric clan who delight in slaughtering the wolves, she must choose between life with the tribe or with the wolf pack. (Cover illustration by Will Hillenbrand.)

Crowley's book *The Silent One.*" Jordan continued illustrating for several more years, but she finally decided writing was the one thing she loved more than anything else.

Throughout her long apprenticeship, Jordan wrote twenty-seven picture books for children as well as twelve novels. Three of her picture books were published and none of the novels. With novel number thirteen, however, she decided she would make or break her career: if the book was rejected, she would give up writing. Fortunately for readers, she hit it big with number thirteen, *Rocco,* which was published in the United States as *A Time of Darkness.* A fantasy for young adults, the book explores themes ranging from the nature of time to parallel worlds through the journey of a contemporary teenager in search of himself. Rocco, the teenager in question, has recurring dreams of a wolf leaping toward him. Each time, he awakes from these dreams scared and smelling of wood smoke. Finally, he awakes to find that he has slipped in time; he is in a valley called Anshur where the people dress in animal skins and live in caves; Rocco quickly adapts to their lifestyle. At first, Rocco believes he is living in the past, but slowly, as the clues accumulate, he realizes he is actually in a post-holocaust future. Suddenly returned to his own time, Rocco feels he must stop the chain of events that will lead to his dreams of Anshur.

Submitted for the 1988 Choysa Bursary prize in New Zealand, *Rocco* won and publication of the novel was assured. Critics around the world were impressed with this debut novel. Writing in *Magpies,* Jo Goodman called the book "an impressive first novel," while a reviewer for *Junior Bookshelf* noted, "So coherently, continuous and convincing is the narration that the reader will be forgiven for taking it as reality." This same reviewer went on to note that the story "plucks cleverly at the hidden hopes and fears of humanity." Reviewing the United States edition of the novel under the title *A Time of Darkness,* Gene Lafaille commented in *Wilson Library Bulletin* that the book "is a strong, dramatic adventure novel that explores interesting fami-

In Jordan's historical romance set in the Middle Ages, sixteen-year-old Marnie is accused of witchcraft when she uses hand gestures to communicate with a deaf boy. (Cover illustration by Paul Zakris.)

ly relationships with their inevitable tensions and moments of humor." Lafaille further noted that *A Time of Darkness* is "suspenseful" and "rapid-paced . . . with a wide range of emotions." Writing in *Voice of Youth Advocates,* Catherine M. Dwyer observed that *A Time of Darkness* has all the right elements: "characters that the reader cares about, a story line that captures the imagination, and an ending that does not disappoint."

With her next novel, *The Juniper Game,* Jordan further explored the world of telepathy, a sub-theme in her first novel. Juniper is a contemporary girl fascinated by the medieval world and by the possibilities of telepathy. She persuades her classmate Dylan to help her with an experiment in sending each other messages. They soon become quite successful at the game, but when Juniper sends him pictures of medieval England, they are transported to a far-distant time and become involved with a young woman, Joanna, who is accused of witchcraft and burned at the stake. "With vividly depicted, believable characters, this is superior fantasy," declared a writer for *Kirkus Reviews. Booklist* contributor Chris Sherman observed, "Fantasy lovers will enjoy Jordan's story," while Dwyer asserted in *Voice of Youth Advocates,* "Jordan has again demonstrated her skill as a storyteller."

Next up for Jordan was a novel for younger readers, *The Wednesday Wizard,* about a medieval sorcerer's apprentice, Denzil, who discovers a spell to send him through time. Reversing the time slip of *The Juniper Game,* Jordan sends this young apprentice catapulting forward through time to 1990s New Zealand, where he takes up lodgings with the MacAllister family with humorous results. "Whoever it is that suffers the most displacement, plenty of humour arises from the inevitable confusions that occur," noted Ann Darnton in a *School Librarian* review. Two more Denzil novels followed: *Denzil's Dilemma,* in which a friend from the future comes back to Denzil's world to visit him, and *Denzil's Great Bear Burglary.* In the latter title, the young apprentice gets into trouble for stealing a dancing bear from a passing circus and rushes forward in time to escape the problems this has created for him in his own time. The MacAllister household is once again his refuge, but this time the future holds as much chaos as the past. In the end, however, all turns out well, as in all the "Denzil" books. But the three books of this trilogy are more than just lighthearted reading, as Frances Hoffman pointed out in a *Magpies* review of the third book in the series. "Some serious issues, in particular the ethics of animal experimentation, are also touched on in the book," observed Hoffman, "giving depth to this well-written and thoroughly recommended novel." Another book for younger readers is the picture book *The Other Side of Midnight,* which is also set in a medieval age. In this story, a young girl who has been orphaned by the plague goes in search of her brother and ends up finding out some hard truths about herself.

Following the writing of the first "Denzil" book, Jordan was diagnosed with Repetition Strain Injury, a result of her many years of typing manuscripts. Her physician told her she might never be able to type again, but she has managed to continue writing, though she concentrates only on novels. In a way, as she told *SATA,* the writing of the young adult novel *Winter of Fire* was something of a salvation for her. This novel about a young slave woman called Elsha helped Jordan work through her own affliction. "Elsha ... was unstoppable, charismatic, and a warrior at soul," Jordan told *SATA.* "It was only because of her that I refused to accept that my writing days were over—only because of her that I picked myself up out of despair and wrote another book. We were warriors together in our battles against the impossible."

In Elsha's future world, the sun has been blocked by a meteorite shower which has caused the natural equivalent of a nuclear winter. Society has been divided into the haves, the Chosen, and the have-nots, the Quelled, who work the coal mines. One of the Quelled, Elsha, longs for freedom for herself and her people. "*Winter of Fire* chronicles Elsha's quest to achieve her desires," noted *Magpies* reviewer Stephanie Owen Reeder, "and does it brilliantly." Reeder further commented, "This is strong, compelling and moving reading of the fantasy/ quest genre," with "strongly delineated" characters and a "carefully crafted" plot. Cathi Dunn MacRae, writing in *Wilson Library Bulletin,* felt that young adult fantasy fans "will certainly appreciate Elsha's courageous pursuit of her revolutionary vision amid persecution and disbelief." MacRae called special attention to the "atmosphere of spirituality" that "pervades the whole tale." A writer for *Publishers Weekly* also observed that "as a whole, the stalwart heroine's visionary struggles are nothing short of inspiring."

In *Tanith,* published in the United States as *Wolf-Woman,* a young girl from the distant past is raised by wolves until the age of three. Then, removed from her den, she lives for many years as the daughter of the chief of a warrior-like clan who delight in slaughtering other tribes as well as the wolves who were once Tanith's protectors. She becomes a companion to the chief's wife, but Tanith never feels really accepted in her human society, and finally she must choose between wolves and men. Reviewing the title in *Booklist,* Candace Smith commented on the "prehistoric imagery and legend" in which Jordan's tale is steeped, and called the story "a compelling search for identity and self-worth within a richly drawn setting." Roger Sutton, writing in *Bulletin of the Center for Children's Books,* concluded, "Tanith's ultimate rejection of human society ... closes the novel on a note of splendid defiance, and most readers will hope for a sequel."

In *Secret Sacrament* Jordan once again employs an imaginary world, Navora, where young Gabriel must come to terms with individual choices. Instead of following in his father's footsteps as a merchant, he opts to become a Healer in the Citadel. Falling afoul of palace intrigues, however, he flees to the Shinali people, who are subjugated by the Navoran Empire, and there falls in love and begins to fight for the rights of the dispossessed. A writer for the *St. James Guide to*

Children's Writers called the novel Jordan's "most ambitious tale to date." Originally published in New Zealand in 1995, a revised edition appeared in the United States in 2001.

Jordan returned to her familiar grounds of the Middle Ages for her 1999 novel, *The Raging Quiet.* In this book the author creates a historical romance rather than a fantasy. Marnie is a young widow who is trying to make the best of her life in a small village by the sea. She befriends a local wild boy whom the villagers think is mad and possessed by the devil, but whom Marnie discovers is simply deaf. When she begins communicating with him with hand gestures, the villagers are sure she is a witch, but the resourceful Marnie refuses to become a victim of ignorance. "This well-written novel is an irresistible historical romance that also offers important messages about love, acceptance, respect, and the tragic repercussions of closed minds," wrote Shelle Rosenfeld in a *Booklist* review. A reviewer for *Publishers Weekly* noted that "Jordan blends a zealous supporting cast with the flavor of Hawthorne with the societal forces of Hardy as she plays out Marnie's tortuous fate." A writer for *Kirkus Reviews* called the book "a passionate and sensuous tale," and concluded, "Fire and sweetness, the pulse of daily existence, how to cope with differences, and the several kinds of love are all present, wrapped in a page-turner to keep readers enthralled." Claire Rosser declared in *Kliatt,* "This novel is quite an achievement, and one that will surely appear on best books lists as more and more people discover it."

Jordan combines a compelling narrative line with rich imagination. According to critics, her fantasy and historical worlds are well thought out and filled with the details of the quotidian, whether actual or fantastical. And lightly sprinkled throughout are lessons to be learned, insights to be gained. "In all of my books there is that lesson that life itself has taught me," Jordan concluded to *SATA.* "I hope all my books will inspire readers to explore these astounding fields themselves— to realize that all is not what it seems and that there are no boundaries between fact and fiction, the tangible and the mystical, the real and the truth we imagine."

Biographical and Critical Sources

BOOKS

St. James Guide to Children's Writers, 5th edition, St. James, 1999.

PERIODICALS

Booklist, November 15, 1991, Chris Sherman, review of *The Juniper Game,* p. 617; November 15, 1994, Candace Smith, review of *Wolf-Woman,* p. 590; August, 1997, p. 1892; May 1, 1999, Shelle Rosenfeld, review of *The Raging Quiet,* p. 1587.

Bulletin of the Center for Children's Books, March, 1993, p. 214; December, 1994, Roger Sutton, review of *Wolf-Woman,* pp. 131-132; June, 1999, p. 356.

Junior Bookshelf, August, 1992, review of *Rocco,* pp. 153-154.

Kirkus Reviews, August 1, 1991, review of *The Juniper Game,* p. 1011; March 15, 1999, review of *The Raging Quiet,* p. 451.

Kliatt, November, 1992, p. 16; September, 1995, p. 22; September, 1996, p. 11; March, 1999, Claire Rosser, review of *The Raging Quiet,* p. 8.

Magpies, November, 1991, Jo Goodman, review of *Rocco,* p. 32; November, 1993, Stephanie Owen Reeder, review of *Winter of Fire,* p. 34; March, 1997, p. 1; March, 1998, Frances Hoffman, review of *Denzil's Great Bear Burglary,* p. 7.

Publishers Weekly, January 4, 1993, review of *Winter of Fire,* p. 73; March 22, 1999, review of *The Raging Quiet,* p. 93.

School Librarian, February 4, 1994, Ann Darnton, review of *The Wednesday Wizard,* p. 21.

School Library Journal, January, 1991, p. 110; October, 1991, p. 145; March, 1993, p. 221; August, 1995, p. 38; May, 1999, p. 125; December, 1999, p. 42.

Voice of Youth Advocates, December, 1990, Catherine M. Dwyer, review of *A Time of Darkness,* p. 298; December, 1991, Catherine M. Dwyer, review of *The Juniper Game,* p. 313; December, 1994, p. 275; August, 1999, p. 184.

Wilson Library Bulletin, April, 1991, Gene Lafaille, review of *A Time of Darkness,* p. 107; April, 1993, Cathi Dunn MacRae, review of *Winter of Fire,* p. 100.

—Sketch by J. Sydney Jones

K

KARL, Jean E(dna) 1927-2000

Personal

Born July 29, 1927, in Chicago, IL; died March 30, 2000, in Lancaster, PA; daughter of William (a salesman) and Ruth (Anderson) Karl. *Education:* Attended Thornton Junior College; Mount Union College, B.A., 1949.

Career

Author and editor. Scott, Foresman & Co., Chicago, IL, junior editorial assistant and assistant editor, 1949-56; Abingdon Press, New York City, children's book editor, 1956-61; Atheneum Publishers, New York City, director of children's book department, 1961-2000, and vice president, 1964-2000. Chair, American Library Association/Children's Book Council joint committee, 1963-65; president, Children's Book Council, 1965; codirector of seminar on children's publications, School of Library Science, Case Western Reserve University, 1969; trustee, Mount Union College, 1974-77. *Member:* American Association of Publishers (member of Freedom to Read committee, 1974-79; member of executive board, General Trade Division, 1975-77).

Awards, Honors

D. Litt., Mount Union College, 1969; Junior Literary Guild Selection, 1976, for *The Turning Place: Stories of a Future Past,* and 1981, for *But We Are Not of Earth.* Many of Karl's editorial efforts won awards, including five Newbery Medals, six Newbery Honors, two Caldecott Medals, eight Edgar Allan Poe Awards, and one National Book Award.

Writings

From Childhood to Childhood: Children's Books and Their Creators, John Day (New York, NY), 1970.

(Compiler and editor, with Harold Tanyzer) *Reading, Children's Books, and Our Pluralistic Society,* International Reading Association (Newark, NJ), 1972.

The Turning Place: Stories of a Future Past, Dutton (New York, NY), 1976.

Beloved Benjamin Is Waiting, Dutton (New York, NY), 1978.

But We Are Not of Earth, Dutton (New York, NY), 1981.

Strange Tomorrow, Dutton (New York, NY), 1985.

Jean E. Karl

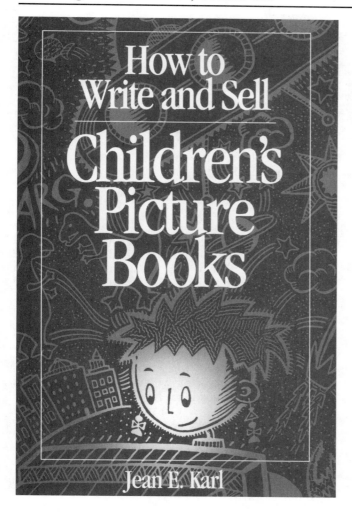

Karl offers advice and tips to beginning writers who have serious aspirations to get their work published. (Cover illustration by Ursula Roma.)

The Search for the Ten-winged Dragon, illustrated by Steve Cieslawski, Doubleday (New York, NY), 1990.
America Alive: A History, illustrated by Ian Schoenherr, Philomel (New York, NY), 1994.
How to Write and Sell Children's Picture Books, Writer's Digest Books (Cincinnati, OH), 1994.

Contributor of articles to periodicals, including *Publishers Weekly, Wilson Library Bulletin,* and *Writer.*

Sidelights

A highly respected editor of children's books, Jean E. Karl was also a successful writer in her own right. "The books I write are a part of me," she once explained in an interview for *SATA.* "They live inside of me. They grow there until they demand to come out. They are part of my life, but not a part of the events around me. They are what I know of life at its core and my dreams of what life might be." Considered a notable force in children's publishing, Karl was the creator of the Atheneum Books for Young Readers division as well as the Aladdin paperback line.

Karl was born on July 29, 1927, in Chicago, Illinois, and developed a love of books at a very early age. In an interview for *Publishers Weekly* she once revealed, "Two Aunts were teachers; one was in charge of a first grade class which had no books. She used to collect piles of them from the library, and I got a chance at them as they were coming and going.... My whole life revolved around stories.... I made my own books too—wrote, illustrated and bound them."

Karl's love and appreciation of books and interest in writing continued in high school where she actively contributed to the school newspaper. During her years attending college, she worked in her school's publicity office writing news reports for the student newspaper. She also wrote for the college alumni bulletin and became involved with proofing, layouts, arranging photographs, and other aspects of publishing.

Although Karl became an accredited high school teacher, she preferred to combine her knowledge of journalism and her literary talent, embarking on a career in publishing. After obtaining her bachelor's degree from Mount Union College in 1949, she got a job as a junior editorial assistant with Scott Foresman & Co. in Chicago, where one of her primary duties was research: looking for material in libraries and other magazines. Her extensive reading also gave her a good perspective on what was lacking in children's books and paved the path for her future career. Karl moved to New York City in 1956 to fill the post of children's books editor at Abingdon Press, from where she made the move to Atheneum Publishers to set up their children's book department in 1961. She was also a regular contributor of articles to *Publishers Weekly, Wilson Library Bulletin, Writer,* and other professional and educational periodicals. Karl's editorial efforts in conjunction with writers such as Beatrice Schenk de Regniers (*May I Bring a Friend?*) and Gail E. Haley (*A Story, a Story*) resulted in awards, among them five Newbery Medals, six Newbery honors, two Caldecott Medals, eight Edgar Allan Poe awards, and one National Book Award. During her long career Karl worked with authors such as Elaine Konisburg, Zilpha Snyder, Robert C. O'Brien, Barbara Corcoran, Ursula Le Guin, and Anna McCaffery.

Karl's move to Atheneum also marked a change in the direction her career would take. As she once revealed to *SATA,* "I would be starting out cold with a promise of no interference, no strings, putting my own ideas into operation." In 1984 Atheneum created the Jean Karl Books imprint, under which she served as editor for a considerable time. She also wrote for a variety of genres, publishing not only fiction, but also nonfiction and science fiction for both children and adults. "I [had] assumed that most of my writing would continue to be in the area of literary commentary and criticism but I found that in speeches and articles I was including more and more elaborate plot outlines as examples of the ideas I was presenting. Finally these became full-blown short stories."

One of these stories, a science-fiction adventure, was so popular with Karl's audience that she decided to set it down on paper. It soon grew into eight stories that were eventually published as *The Turning Place.* "Many of my interest and ideas ... crept into [this book] in surprising ways," Karl added. "The writing was an adventure into new and unexplored territory. Reading what I did is another kind of adventure. Both adventures are worth having."

Addressing the topics she wrote about, Karl once noted: "Many people believe that all fictional writing is autobiographical, and in some ways they are right. The best writing comes out of experience. What matters, I think, for me and for all writers is not what we do and what happens to us but how we react to the circumstances of our lives, what we become as people. It is our inner lives, our true selves, that project our books, not the surface events. And some of what we use to write we do not even recognize ourselves."

Karl's *But We Are Not of Earth,* published in 1981, is a science-fiction story about four teens from the school/home for discoverer's children—children of the men and women possessing the advanced mental ability to power spaceships who left Earth in order to explore the galaxy and were not allowed to return. These children live in underground bases on other planets studying to become explorers. Out on a mission to test their resources and survival skills, the children land on an outpost that is seemingly uninhabited. They soon discover this to be a ruse designed to populate the outpost with selected people. Ultimately, the children rebel against their enforced isolation. Zena Sutherland, in a review for the *Bulletin of the Center for Children's Books,* commented that "There's a great deal of vitality and humor in the dialogue, an unexpected element of danger as well as the expected adventure, and the added appeals of space flight and of a mission accomplished." Conversely Barbara Elleman, reviewing the book for *Booklist,* opined that Karl's "studied style inhibits the free movement the story demands, and the action, though suspenseful, is at times held in reserve." Elleman went on, however, to credit Karl with developing highly individualized characters and raising thoughtful implications.

Commenting on her choice to write science fiction, Karl once explained to *SATA* that "there was a time in my life ... when I was fascinated by particle physics, quantum mechanics, quarks, and the absence of matter at the bottom of any physical object, and at the same time I could not get enough about galaxies and beyond—the scale of the universe. My head and my bookshelves were well stocked with information in this area. Since I have a more than full-time job, I have almost no time to research backgrounds for books. But I have at hand lots of material that lends itself to science fiction, and I like to imagine what could be, someday or somewhere. So when I began to write, I wrote science fiction."

1985's *Strange Tomorrow* is also a science-fiction story in which Earth is attacked by an alien force that destroys carbon and most of the planet's population. Janie Johnson, one out of a handful of people that survive the attack, becomes the "founding mother" of a new world order that is locked into a rigid pattern of behavior. Dorothy M. Broderick, writing in the *Voice of Youth Advocates,* called the book "readable" but "annoying" since it does not explain the enormous change in Johnson's character that leads to all her inflexibility. Broderick concluded that "The abrupt end to the first part of the book requires too big a jump on the readers part to thoroughly enjoy the second part. Not vintage Karl; certainly not in the same league with *But We Are Not of Earth.*"

1994 saw the release of *America Alive: A History,* a work that covers major historical events and social movements from the pre-historic crossing of the Bering Strait to the election of U.S. President Bill Clinton in 1992. The book, in dealing with topical issues, inspired differing reviews. Roger Sutton, reviewing the work in *Bulletin of the Center for Children's Books,* noted, "The writing is clear and informal gracefully segueing between topics ... and occasionally displaying a dry wit." Praising the author's perspective as "generally objective, with gentle reminders of what the blacks and the women and the Indians were doing while the white men waged wars," Sutton concluded that Karl's "sense of historical continuity gives the book a narrative chain that makes it read like a story." A reviewer for *Publishers Weekly* commented that Karl "instills pride in the nation's accomplishments, but she does not gloss over injustices, scandals and controversies."

Reviewing *America Alive* for the *Washington Post Book World,* Michael Kazin presented an entirely opposing view. While commending Karl for taking on a subject of such enormous proportions, he expressed difficulty in accepting her method of treatment of the subject. "[T]he way she condenses the nation's saga into an offensive, mildly flippant stew is unforgivable," Kazin exclaimed. Martha Saxton of the *New York Times Book Review* concurred, noting that "The necessary condensation of the book is so great ... that it forces occasional oversimplifications. Even young children, in my experience, are able and eager to confront moral complexity."

"Books were as important to me in [my childhood] as they are now," Karl once noted of her career as an editor, writer, and publisher. Her childhood love of books certainly transcended time, giving birth to a prolific career in publishing. Karl died on March 30, 2000, at the age of seventy-two in Lancaster, Pennsylvania.

Biographical and Critical Sources

PERIODICALS

Bulletin of the Center for Children's Books, September, 1981, Zena Sutherland, review of *But We Are Not of Earth,* p. 12; December, 1994, Roger Sutton, review of *America Alive,* p. 132.

Booklist, June 1, 1981, Barbara Elleman, review of *But We Are Not of Earth,* p. 1299.

New York Times Book Review, April 26, 1981, review of *But We Are Not of Earth,* p. 60; November 13, 1994, Martha Saxton, review of *America Alive,* p. 32.

Publishers Weekly, February 22, 1971, "Bringing Chicken Licken up to Date"; July 18, 1977, Jean F. Mercier, *Jean Karl;* October 17, 1994, review of *America Alive,* p. 83.

Voice of Youth Advocates, December, 1985, Dorothy M. Broderick, review of *Strange Tomorrow,* p. 324.

Washington Post Book World, December 4, 1994, Michael Kazin, "Presenting America's Past," p. 20.

Obituaries

PERIODICALS

Publishers Weekly, April 10, 2000, "Karl Dies at 72," p. 20.
Detroit Free Press, April 4, 2000, p. 5B.

*   *   *

KAVANAGH, P(atrick) J(oseph Gregory) 1931-

Personal

Born January 6, 1931, in Worthing, Sussex, England; son of Ted (a radio comedy writer) and Agnes (O'Keefe) Kavanagh; married Sally Philipps, 1956 (died, 1958); married Catherine Ward, 1965; children: (second marriage) Cornelius, Bruno. *Education:* Merton College, Oxford, M.A., 1954. *Religion:* Roman Catholic. *Hobbies and other interests:* Walking.

Addresses

Home—Sparrowthorn, Elkstone, Cheltenham, Gloucestershire GL53 9PX, England. *Agent*—Peters, Fraser & Dunlop, The Chambers, Chelsea Harbour, London SW10 0XF, England.

Career

Author and poet. Lecturer at the University of Indonesia, 1957-58. Actor on stage and television, and in films; radio broadcaster and television presenter; literary columnist.

Awards, Honors

Richard Hillary Memorial Prize, 1966, for *The Perfect Stranger;* fiction prize, *Guardian,* 1969, for *A Song and Dance;* Cholmondeley Award, Society of Authors, 1993, for *Collected Poems.*

Writings

POETRY

One and One, Heinemann (London, England), 1959.
On the Way to the Depot, Chatto & Windus (London, England), 1967.
About Time, Chatto & Windus (London, England), 1970.

P. J. Kavanagh

(Contributor) Philip Larkin, editor, *The Oxford Book of Twentieth Century Verse,* Oxford University Press, 1973.
Edward Thomas in Heaven, Chatto & Windus (London, England), 1974.
Life before Death, Chatto & Windus (London, England), 1979.
Selected Poems, Chatto & Windus (London, England), 1982.
Presences: New and Selected Poems, Chatto & Windus (London, England), 1987.
An Enchantment, Carcanet (Manchester, England), 1991.
Collected Poems, Carcanet (Manchester, England), 1992.

NOVELS

A Song and Dance, Chatto & Windus (London, England), 1968.
A Happy Man, Chatto & Windus (London, England), 1972.
Scarf Jack (juvenile), Bodley Head (London, England), 1978, published as *The Irish Captain,* Doubleday (New York, NY), 1979.
People and Weather, Calder & Boyars (London, England), 1979.
Rebel for Good (juvenile), Bodley Head (London, England), 1980.
Only by Mistake, Riverrun Press (New York, NY), 1986.

NONFICTION

The Perfect Stranger (autobiography), Chatto & Windus (London, England), 1966, Greywolf (United States), 1988, Carcanet (Manchester, England), 1995.

People and Places (essays), Carcanet (Manchester, England), 1988.

Finding Connections (travel/autobiography), Hutchinson (London, England), 1990.

Voices in Ireland: A Traveller's Literary Companion, J. Murray (London, England), 1994.

Contributor of regular column to *Spectator,* 1982-94, and *Times Literary Supplement,* 1994—. Also contributor of feature articles to various publications, including *London Daily Telegraph Color Supplement, New Yorker, Grand Street, Transatlantic Review, Encounter,* and *New Statesman.*

EDITOR

(And author of introduction) *Collected Poems of Ivor Gurney,* Oxford University Press, 1982.

(With James Michie) *The Oxford Book of Short Poems,* Oxford University Press, 1985.

(And author of introduction) *The Bodley Head G. K. Chesterton,* Bodley Head (London, England), 1985, published as *The Essential G. K. Chesterton,* 1987.

(And author of introduction) *Selected Poems of Ivor Gurney,* Oxford University Press, 1990, Carcanet (Manchester, England), 1998.

(And author of introduction) *A Book of Consolations* (anthology), HarperCollins (London, England), 1992.

PLAYS

Author of the television features *William Cowper Lived Here,* 1971, and *Journey through Summer,* 1973.

Sidelights

P. J. Kavanagh is a man of many talents, having written poetry, fiction, broadcasts, and travelogues as well as edited books on a number of subjects. His travels, the natural world, and his close associates are a constant refrain through all his writings. Some of his novels are set in Ireland, and he talks of many Irish and English poets in his poems and articles on travel. Much of Kavanagh's poetry also reflects the anguish and questioning that resulted from his first wife's sudden and unexpected death from polio in 1958. However, many critics note that despite frequent references to death and spiritual doubts, his poems are surprisingly optimistic.

Kavanagh's poetry has many autobiographical elements, and he often draws upon family, friends, neighbors, and associates for his subjects. He has also written about life with his children at various stages of their development and a poem addressed to his father. Simon Rae of *Times Literary Supplement* comments that "Kavanagh clearly believes passionately in the private life and it lies at the root of all his poetry." Kavanagh's poetry has also addressed a host of modern poets like William Butler Yeats, Dylan Thomas, Robert Lowell, John Berryman, Ivor Gurney, and Edward Thomas. Other subjects that figure prominently in his poetry are his experiences of war in Korea, life abroad in Indonesia, religion, life in rural England, entrance into middle age, loss, grief, and the periodic moments of epiphany occasioned in the wonder of the natural world.

Kavanagh's poetry is written in a style similar to such nature poets as William Wordsworth and Edward Thomas suggest critics. Some of his earlier poems oppose rural and urban perceptions, but his later, and especially his longer poems, commonly employ observations of nature to illuminate moods and themes. *Spectator* contributor John Bayley commented that "like all the best conversational poems, like Edward Thomas's in particular, Kavanagh's gradually extend a perspective of inner meaning behind the subject of each poem." Other critics note the emotions of grief for the loss of his first wife that are often reflected in his poetry, and its religious or mystical meaning. Writing in *New Statesman,* Julian Symons said of Kavanagh's *Selected Poems* that "the language is sharp, original, moving in its abruptness and clarity," adding that the poet "observes, notes and reflects but doesn't moralise, and the reflections are always worth having." Reviewing the same work in *Times Literary Supplement,* Bernard O'Donoghue noted that "the later poems are characterized by an expert tightening and loosening of tension, as the poet moves between the mystical and the everyday, often blurring the edges."

Kavanagh is a novelist as well as a poet and this, notes David Lloyd in *World Literature Today,* is reflected in the conversational tone he employs while writing in traditional poetic forms, thus allowing him greater independence within these forms regarding line-length and meter. Lloyd goes on to say that Kavanagh's narrative structure often aims at developing a comfortable and informal relationship with his readers, as exhibited in 1992's *Collected Poems,* a work covering seven collections published over thirty-two years. Conversely, Kavanagh's attempt to establish a dialogue with the reader shows certain weaknesses too; Lloyd remarks that "in striving to attain correct rhyme and rhythm ... he too often strains his language, ending with formally correct but rhythmically awkward lines."

Kavanagh's first novel for young adults, *Scarf Jack* (published in the United States as *The Irish Captain*), tells the story of a sudden and half-secret outbreak of an Irish blood feud in a Gloucestershire village in 1798. The story is told through the eyes of a fifteen-year old boy, Francis Place, who is set apart from the common life of the village and the local gentry by virtue of his poverty and social status. When Francis saves the life of a condemned man, he also uncovers the secret of his paternity. According to Charles Causley in the *Times Literary Supplement,* the style and tone of the narrative are swift and "have precisely the same spareness, wit, resonance and searching honesty that distinguishes the best of [Kavanagh's] verse." *Scarf Jack* evokes a realistic sense of the past and place, according to several critics. As a reviewer for *Growing Point* concludes: "A strong political slant makes this well-paced, richly detailed novel relevant today."

Rebel for Good, published in 1980 as a sequel to *Scarf Jack,* addresses the American frontier conflict between the natives and the invading white settlers. Francis Place, the narrator of *Scarf Jack,* is now an assistant surgeon in the Royal Navy. In an effort to find his father he boards an American ship and, after many mishaps, hardships, and delays, finally finds him fighting alongside the Shawanon Indians. The book, which was praised for its grace, clarity, and finely etched characters, also includes a love interest for young Francis. The historical detail includes a dramatic account of the Indian council where Tecumseh tried to persuade the various chiefs to form a confederacy for their survival. Gale Eaton comments in her review of *Rebel for Good* in *School Library Journal* that, "The narrative voice is sophisticated and, in spite of the rapid pace and occasional violence of the plot, rather reflective."

1988 saw the release of *People and Places,* a collection of sixty articles published by Kavanagh in various newspapers and magazines between 1975 and 1987. Many articles are about places: geysers of Iceland, walks through the New England countryside, the wild mountains of Corsica; others are literary essays about G. K. Chesterton and Argentinean nature writer W. H. Hudson, among many others. The book also includes such personal pieces as an account of the author's father and a description of a holiday taken with family. In his review for the *Spectator,* Christopher Booker notes that, "All these things are observed by P. J. in his quietly humorous, reflective way, always sharp-eyed for the telling detail, fundamentally rooted in a religious view of the world."

Kavanagh's first prose book, *The Perfect Stranger,* was published in 1966 and is probably still the most widely read of his books. An autobiography written when he was thirty-three as a memoir to his first wife and the transformation of his own life leading into their marriage, the book described, often with humor, his childhood in wartime England, his army service as a conscript and in battle during the Korean War, and life in the 1950s London and in the newly independent Indonesia. In 1990, the author returned to an autobiographical narrative with *Finding Connections.* Part family history and part travelogue, the volume traces the author's wanderings through Ireland, Australia, Tasmania, and New Zealand in search of his ancestors. The book is also, as he told *SATA,* "part of that continuing attempt ... a wish to make sense of the world."

In 1994's *Voices in Ireland: A Traveller's Literary Companion* Kavanagh emphasizes the fact that Ireland, despite many similarities, is "not a quaint variant of England," reports Mary C. Kalfatovic in *Library Journal.* The book is detailed in its subject matter, quoting from Irish writers of all periods, and includes footnotes and a bibliography. Kalfatovic notes, "Though intended as a traveler's 'companion', Kavanagh's book may be better enjoyed by armchair travelers." The author described the book to *SATA* as "a voyage round the English imagination."

Biographical and Critical Sources

BOOKS

Dictionary of Literary Biography, Volume 40: *Poets of Great Britain and Ireland since 1960,* Gale, 1985.

PERIODICALS

Booklist, April 15, 1985, Hazel Rochman, review of *Rebel for Good,* pp. 1178-1179.
Growing Point, July, 1978, review of *Scarf Jack,* p. 3367.
Irish Times, June 20, 1987, Derek Mahon, "The Other Kavanagh."
Junior Bookshelf, June, 1981, review of *Rebel for Good,* p. 124.
Kirkus Reviews, March 1, 1979, review of *The Irish Captain,* p. 284.
Library Journal, November 15, 1995, Mary C. Kalfatovic, review of *Voices in Ireland: A Traveller's Literary Companion,* p. 92.
London Review of Books, September 18, 1986, Paul Edwards, "Dialectical Satire," pp. 21-23.
New Statesman, 1982, Julian Symons, review of *Selected Poems.*
Publishers Weekly, February 19, 1979, review of *The Irish Captain,* p. 102.
School Librarian, March, 1981, Dorothy Nimmo, review of *Rebel for Good,* p. 51.
School Library Journal, October, 1985, Gale Eaton, review of *Rebel for Good,* p. 182.
Spectator, March 14, 1987, John Bayley, review of *Presences: New and Selected Poems;* October 15, 1988, Christopher Booker, "Celebratory, Tidy Columnist," p. 37; August 8, 1994, Robert Kee, "Sounds and Sweet Airs," p. 30.
Times Literary Supplement, July 7, 1978, Charles Causley, "Solitary Search," p. 766; November 21, 1980, Dominic Hibberd, "Right Is Might," p. 1324; July 16, 1982, Edna Longley, "The Pattern History Weaves," p. 770; December 25, 1987, Simon Rae, "Open Secrets," p. 1435; April 6, 1990, Peter Parker, "On a Different Path," p. 366; March 27, 1992, Marc Wormald, "Natural Intensity," p. 12; November 14, 1992, Frank Kermode, "How Do I Miss You? Let Me Count the Ways"; January 1, 1993, Bernard O'Donoghue, review of *Collected Poems.*
World Literature Today, winter, 1994, David Lloyd, review of *Collected Poems,* pp. 131-132.

*　　*　　*

KELLEHER, Annette 1950-

Personal

Born June 13, 1950, in Kenmare, County Kerry, Ireland; daughter of Albert Fredrick Greenfield (a watchmaker) and Hanorah Frances Simcox (a homemaker); married Anthony Noel Kelleher (a fitter), June 13, 1970; children: David, Tracey, Alison, Anthony. *Education:* Graduated from Holy Cross College (Kenmare, Ireland), 1968. *Religion:* Catholic. *Hobbies and other interests:* Music, reading, "having cups of tea with [my husband] Tony, walking on the beach, and more writing."

Addresses

Home—134 Springfield Ave., Coolum Beach, Queensland 4573, Australia.

Career

Worked variously for National Westminister Bank, N.C.R., and Avis, London, England, 1968-73; Papaw & Mango Orchard, co-owner with husband, 1984—. Part-time teacher's aide, 1990, 1994-95. *Member:* Queensland Writers.

Awards, Honors

Second place, "Writers on the Wharf" short-story competition, 1998.

Writings

Noodles on Our Ceiling, Margaret Hamilton, 1994.
Seaweed in Our Soup, Margaret Hamilton, 1996.
Pet for Elvin, Margaret Hamilton, 1998.
Harriet's Revenge, Scholastic, 1998.
Pumpkin Head Is Dead!, Margaret Hamilton, 1999.
Biddy Blatherskate's Blunder, Margaret Hamilton, 2000.

Work in Progress

Geek Girl versus the Cyber Chick, a young adult novel about "a fifteen-year-old girl having to deal with a virtual rival, family complications, and a growing companionship with a dead poet."

Sidelights

Annette Kelleher told *SATA:* "I am very passionate about writing. Friends of mine have said that when the word 'writing' enters a conversation, my face lights up and I never run out of enthusiasm for the subject. I can't imagine what my life would be like without this burning passion for words.

"I was a writer even before I knew I was a writer. It was just something I always dabbled in. I was about thirty before it even occurred to me that I might be able to write a book. Real writers were people with names like Charles Dickens, Shakespeare, or Leon Uris. It seemed very presumptuous to even consider myself capable of achieving this amazing feat, but once I had decided to do it, I pursued my goal in a very single-minded and determined fashion.

"Writing for children was something I had always been interested in, and when I worked as a teacher's aide, I found that the reluctant readers and the children with learning difficulties got bored really easily with slow or unnecessarily descriptive passages. I was writing *Noodles on Our Ceiling* at the time and those reluctant readers became my target. I wanted to write a book that would capture their attention and hold it to the end. I wanted to write books that children would enjoy rather than books which adults would consider 'suitable

Annette Kelleher

reading.' I wanted to pass on my love of words and the enjoyment of reading to children. I hope I've done this."

"I like my books to deal with everyday issues, but I like positive results, and I always like to end with a note of hope. At one stage during the writing of *Pumpkin Head Is Dead!,* I was concerned because the story was sad and depressing and I didn't really like the way it was going. Then 'hope' popped up in the form of Richard and I could suddenly see my way to a more positive ending.

"I don't plan my books at all. Usually I start with an interesting opening sentence and plough on from there. *Pumpkin Head* was the exception to that method. I had a dream one night about a car crash, a girl who was upset and her father breaking the bad news to her. I got up and wrote the dream in a notebook. It was about four thirty in the morning, so I decided to get up and have a cup of tea and do some writing. Then I felt I had to write an Irish fable, so I wrote the story of "The Children of Lir." I was a bit puzzled as I'd expected to write about the dream. Months later that fable ended up in *Pumpkin Head,* so it's the first book which I didn't start at the beginning."

Kelleher's *Pumpkin Head Is Dead!* features the story of Fingula O'Shea, a teenage girl desperately trying to grow up in a troubled family. Faced with an abusive stepfather who drinks too much, Fingula withdraws from her family and bickers constantly with her would-be boyfriend. Throughout the novel, Kelleher shows how the young teenager must overcome the bitterness she still has about her father's death as well as the tragic loss of her would-be boyfriend. By the end of the summer, Fingula's outlook on life matures. She eventually comes to the realization that not everything in life is easy and no one is entirely good or entirely bad. Claiming the book "deserves to be widely read," *Magpies* reviewer Neville Barnard praised *Pumpkin Head Is Dead!,* saying the "characters are real and believable, the events credible and the storytelling smooth."

Kelleher also deals with teenage angst in her books about Stacey Culver, *Noodles on Our Ceiling* and its sequel, *Seaweed in Our Soup.* In the first novel, the Culver family decides to abandon city life and take up residence in the country. In this new environment, Stacey not only has to deal with the perceived indignities of using a make-shift toilet, but she must also learn how to adjust to the residents of her new community. It is not until the end of the novel, when Stacey finally understands that other people have legitimate needs and wants, does she finally begin to feel at home in her new life. Writing in *Magpies,* contributor Alan Horsfield described *Noodles on Our Ceiling* as "well balanced" and noted that the "resolution of the problems raised is more than plausible."

In the second installment of the series, *Seaweed in Our Soup,* the Culver family begins to feel the pinch of living in the country on a limited income. As a way to make the Christmas holiday more festive and meaningful, Mr. Culver decides the family should make all of their gifts for each other. Not enthused with the idea, Stacey decides to purchase gifts while in Brisbane visiting an old friend. While away, she realizes that despite its hardships, she misses the excitement that life in the country brings. Returning home, Stacey feels disappointed in herself and decides to join the family in celebrating a homespun Christmas. Reviewing the book in *Magpies,* John Murray suggested that the brevity of the chapters "would encourage reluctant readers to persevere to the end, and also make the story an enjoyable one to read aloud."

Kelleher concluded, "My books always have some underlying moral theme. Even though I don't actually set out to write on a moral issue, one always manages to work itself in. I feel that this is quite important when writing for children. A book can be fun to read and still teach an important lesson."

Biographical and Critical Sources

PERIODICALS

Magpies, March, 1995, Alan Horsfield, review of *Noodles on Our Ceiling,* p. 29; March, 1997, John Murray, review of *Seaweed in Our Soup,* p. 38; September, 1999, Neville Barnard, review of *Pumpkin Head Is Dead!,* p. 39.

KENNEDY, Doug(las) 1963-

Personal

Born November 28, 1963, in West Monroe, LA; son of I. G. (a physician) and Carole (an artist) Kennedy. *Education:* Attended Louisiana Tech University. *Religion:* Methodist.

Career

Illustrator.

Illustrator

Kim Kennedy, *Napoleon,* Viking (New York, NY), 1995.
K. Kennedy, *Mr. Bumble,* Hyperion (New York, NY), 1997.
The Big Picture, Hyperion (New York, NY), 1997.
K. Kennedy, *Mr. Bumble Buzzes through the Year,* Hyperion (New York, NY), 1998.
The Job, Disney Press, 1998.
K. Kennedy, *Frankenfrog,* Hyperion (New York, NY), 1999.
Robert D. San Souci, *Six Foolish Fishermen,* Hyperion (New York, NY), 1999.

Sidelights

Doug Kennedy is an illustrator who has collaborated on several titles with his sister, author Kim Kennedy. Together, the Kennedy siblings have released *Napoleon, Mr. Bumble, Mr. Bumble Buzzes through the Year,* and *Frankenfrog. Mr. Bumble* concerns the adventures of its title character, a bee who is transformed from clumsy to graceful during a series of encounters with monsters and benevolent fairies. A *Horn Book Guide* reviewer commented on illustrator Kennedy's "droll figures of bees and fairies," but ultimately found that "the story and illustrations lack vigor." A critic for the *New York Times Book Review,* however, praised the book for its "very pretty illustrations."

In *Frankenfrog,* the Kennedys' 1999 offering, the mad scientist Dr. Franken concocts a potion designed to "hyper-size" lollipops. Unfortunately, the tonic also spawns a multitude of over-sized flies, which the doctor zaps with Frankenfrog, his gigantic amphibious creation. While the *School Library Journal*'s Christine A. Moesch complained that "the writing is forced and self-consciously adolescent," a critic for the *Children's Book Review Service* praised the story for its "lively text and humorous illustrations." A *Horn Book Guide* reviewer noted that writer Kennedy's "puns feel forced," but commented that the book's "illustrations add amusing details."

Kennedy also provided illustrations for *Six Foolish Fisherman,* written by Robert D. San Souci. In this book, San Souci retells a variety of international tales in a Cajun style, with several Louisiana fishermen as protagonists. A *Kirkus Reviews* critic felt that "the droll goings-on will put readers and listeners in stitches," and

Susan Dove Lempke, writing in *Booklist,* found that San Souci adds "enough Cajun Seasoning to enliven the retelling."

Biographical and Critical Sources

PERIODICALS

Booklist, May 15, 2000, Susan Dove Lempke, review of *Six Foolish Fisherman,* p. 1759.

Bulletin of the Center for Children's Books, October, 1999, Janice M. Del Negro, review of *Frankenfrog,* p. 57.

Children's Book Review Service, August, 1999, review of *Frankenfrog,* p. 160.

Horn Book Guide, July-December, 1997, review of *Mr. Bumble,* p. 35; July-December, 1999, review of *Frankenfrog,* p. 43.

Kirkus Reviews, May 1, 2000, review of *Six Foolish Fisherman,* p. 639.

New York Times Book Review, March 15, 1998, review of *Mr. Bumble,* p. 23.

Publishers Weekly, October 2, 1995, review of *Napoleon,* p. 73; August 11, 1997, review of *Mr. Bumble,* p. 401; August 2, 1999, review of *Frankenfrog,* p. 83.

School Library Journal, February, 1996, Virginia Opocensky, review of *Napoleon,* p. 86; September, 1997, Dawn Amsberry, review of *Mr. Bumble,* p. 184; August, 1999, Christine A. Moesch, review of *Frankenfrog,* p. 138.*

L

LANGLEY, Jonathan 1952-

Personal

Born October 31, 1952, in Lancaster, Lancashire, England; son of Raymond (a civil engineer) and Margaret (a homemaker; maiden name, Bickerstaff) Langley; married Karen Arnold (a teacher), February 10, 1978; children: Toby, Holly, Rosita. *Education:* Attended Lancaster College of Art, 1970-71; Liverpool Polytechnic College of Art and Design, B.A. (with honors; graphic design/illustration), 1974; Central School of Art and Design, postgraduate studies; Camberwell School of Art, postgraduate studies in bookbinding, M.A. (with honors; graphic design), 1978. *Politics:* Socialist. *Religion:* "Non-specific." *Hobbies and other interests:* Cinema, music (particularly modern jazz), walking, travel, photography, food and drink.

Addresses

Office—c/o Collins, 77-85 Fulham Palace Rd., Hammersmith, London W6 8JB, England. *Agent*—John Hodgson, 38 Westminster Palace Gardens, Artillery Row, London SW1P 1RR, England. *E-mail*—j@zzer.globalnet.co.uk.

Career

Author and freelance illustrator/designer. Worked in the fields of publishing, editorial, design, advertising, film, gift marketing, and packaging, 1974—.

Awards, Honors

Best Illustrated Book Award, *Parents* magazine, and Play and Learn Awards, both 1998, both for *SNORE!;* Highly Commended Award in picture book category, Sheffield Children's Book Award, 2000, for *The Biggest Bed in the World.*

Jonathan Langley

Writings

SELF-ILLUSTRATED

(Reteller) *The Three Bears and Goldilocks,* Collins (London, England), 1991, HarperCollins (New York, NY), 1993.

(Reteller) *The Story of Rumpelstiltskin,* Collins (London, England), 1991, HarperCollins (New York, NY), 1993.

(Reteller) *The Three Billy Goats Gruff,* Collins (London, England), 1992, HarperCollins (New York, NY), 1998.

(Reteller) *Little Red Riding Hood,* Collins (London, England), 1992, HarperCollins (New York, NY), 1994.

(Reteller) *The Princess and the Frog,* Collins (London, England), 1993, HarperCollins (New York, NY), 1995.

(Reteller) *The Ugly Duckling,* Collins (London, England), 1993, HarperCollins (New York, NY), 1995.

The Collins Book of Nursery Tales, Collins (London, England), 1993.

Nursery Pop-up Book: Goldilocks and the Three Bears, HarperCollins (New York, NY), 1993.

Nursery Pop-up Book: Little Red Riding Hood, Collins (London, England), 1995, Barron's Educational (Hauppauge, NY), 1996.

Nursery Pop-up Book: Three Little Pigs, Collin (London, England), 1995, Barron's Educational (Hauppauge, NY), 1996.

Collins Bedtime Treasury of Nursery Rhymes and Tales, Collins (London, England), 1997.

Nursery Pop-up Book: Hansel and Gretel, Collins (London, England), 1996, Barron's Educational (Hauppauge, NY), 1997.

Babies Bedtime Lullabies and Verse, Collins (London, England), 1997.

Favourite Nursery Rhymes, Collins (London, England), 1999.

MISSING!, Francis Lincoln (London, England), 2000, Marshall Cavendish (New York, NY), 2000.

ILLUSTRATOR

Fay Maschler, *Cooking is a Way round the World,* Penguin Books (London, England), 1978.

Kenneth Grahame, *The Wind in the Willows,* Octopus, 1984.

L. Frank Baum, *The Wizard of Oz,* Octopus, 1985.

Carolyn Sloan, *The Friendly Robot,* Derrydale Books (New York, NY), 1987.

Anne Civardi, *Potty Time,* Simon & Schuster (New York, NY), 1988.

Lizzy Pearl, *What Have I Lost?,* Dial (New York, NY), 1988.

Lizzy Pearl, *What Time Is It?,* Dial (New York, NY), 1988.

Martin Waddell, *Alice the Artist,* Dutton (New York, NY), 1988.

Rudyard Kipling, *How the Whale Got His Throat,* Philomel (New York, NY) 1988.

Rudyard Kipling, *How the Camel Got His Hump,* Philomel (New York, NY) 1988.

Rudyard Kipling, *How the Rhinoceros Got His Skin,* Philomel (New York, NY), 1988.

Martin Waddell, *Daisy's Christmas,* Ideals (Nashville, TN), 1990.

Martin Waddell, *Daisy the Dreamer,* Methuen (London, England), 1990.

The Collins Book of Nursery Rhymes, Collins (London, England), 1990.

Lisa Taylor, *A Pig Called Shrimp,* Collins (London, England), 1990.

Rain, Rain, Go Away!: A Book of Nursery Rhymes, Dial (New York, NY), 1991.

Langley has retold the familiar Little Red Riding Hood story with several new surprises. (From Little Red Riding Hood, *retold and illustrated by Langley.)*

Miss Read, *The Little Red Bus and Other Rhyming Stories,* Penguin Books (London, England), 1991.

Betty Root, *My First Dictionary,* Dorling Kindersley (New York, NY), 1993.

Nursery Pop-up Book: Animal Rhymes, Collins (London, England), 1994.

Nursery Pop-up Book: Favourite Rhymes, Collins (London, England), 1994.

The Giant Sandwich, Ginn (London, England), 1994.

Hilary Aaron, *Three Little Kittens in the Enchanted Forest: A Pop-up Adventure,* Collins (London, England), 1995.

Collins Nursery Treasury, Collins (London, England), 1996.

Michael Rosen, *SNORE!* Collins (London, England), 1998.

Hiawyn Oram, *Where Are You Hiding Little Lamb?,* Collins (London, England), 1999.

Lindsay Camp, *The Biggest Bed in the Whole World,* Collins (London, England), 1999, HarperCollins (New York, NY), 2000.

OTHER

Author of *Doris and the Mice from Mars,* illustrated by Hilary Hayton, 1981.

Work in Progress

Children's picture books for HarperCollins and Frances Lincoln.

Sidelights

Jonathan Langley has been a freelance writer and illustrator of children's books for more than twenty-five years. During these years he has worked in various associated areas such as publishing, editing, design, advertising, film, gift marketing, and packaging. He has also written several books of his own, as well as illustrating them. Many of these are original stories whereas others are refreshing retellings of classic tales for children.

Langley was born on October 31, 1952, in Lancaster, Lancashire. His father was a civil engineer and his mother was a homemaker. Langley attended the Lancaster College of Art and completed his foundation studies in 1971. He went on to attend Liverpool College of Art and Design, where he earned his bachelor's degree in graphic design in the area of illustration in 1974. He followed that up with a master's degree in graphic design from the Camberwell School of Art located at the Central School of Art and Design (London), in 1978. While at Camberwell, he also studied bookbinding as part of his postgraduate course. Langley has a variety of interests like cinema, music (particularly modern jazz), walking, travel, photography, food, and drink which give him breadth of focus and help him in his work.

Rain, Rain, Go Away!: A Book of Nursery Rhymes is a combination of popular nursery rhymes interspersed with less familiar verses, sayings, and poems. Dorothy F. Houlihan notes in *School Library Journal* that Langley's text is accompanied by lively illustrations that are pleasing in their rhythm and imagery. She further states that Langley maintains the tempo throughout the book, loosely grouping his rhymes according to subject. According to Houlihan, Langley's black-pen outline and bright watercolor illustrations are extremely attractive, lending personality and charm to the book. In a tribute to his dexterity in handling the subject, the critic comments that, "Multiracial characters are depicted with disarming ease, ignoring stereotypical assumptions about the nature of traditional nursery rhymes."

The same lively spirit permeates Langley's retelling of the classic *The Story of Rumpelstiltskin*. "Iconoclastic additions [are] freely incorporated into the spritely retelling," according to a *Kirkus Reviews* contributor. The critic further notes that the illustrations are executed with the same vivacious energy, the characters are drawn like cheerful children and even Rumpelstiltskin is less than menacing with hardly an unkind gleam in his eye. Langley's treatment is contemporary and quite naturally leads to a "'fractured' ending that has the king falling victim to (and *into*) his own Crocodile Pool," according to Linda Boyles in *School Library Journal*.

The Three Bears and Goldilocks is subject to the same contemporary treatment, with an extension of traditional gender roles. The father bear helps in cleaning the house by vacuuming it and takes his turn making breakfast while the mother bear uses an electric drill to fix the baby bear's chair. According to reviewers, Langley's lively text is full of good humor and the artwork and the illustrations are detailed with numerous bear motifs for young readers to discover along their journey.

The Princess and the Frog and *The Ugly Duckling* were both praised by critics for their invitingly large format and attractive presentation. Langley's attention to detail in the illustrations, ranging from two-page spreads to depictions of minute insects in the margins, was appreciated. Critic Trevor Dickinson of *School Librarian* similarly admired *The Collins Book of Nursery Tales* for its "briskly energetic" language and its "lively, joyful brashness." Though Langley's *Nursery Pop-up Book: Little Red Riding Hood* follows the traditional pattern of the tale, it nevertheless contains numerous details that give it a modern feel. As with *The Story of Rumpelstiltskin*, Langley adds his unique touch to the end of the classic tale.

In her review of several of Langley's books for *School Librarian*, Cathy Sutton notes that the author/illustrator "rounds off and enhances the tales by attaching a humorous conclusion which tells of later events." It is perhaps such refreshing viewpoints and novel postscripts that make Langley's books widely appreciated and make them stand out from the numerous already available on the subjects.

Biographical and Critical Sources

PERIODICALS

Booklist, May 15, 1991, Carolyn Phelan, review of *Rain, Rain, Go Away!*, p. 1801; February 1, 1992, review of *The Story of Rumpelstiltskin*, p. 1034; May 1, 2000, Carolyn Phelan, review of *The Biggest Bed in the World*, p. 1675.

Books for Keeps, November, 1994, Jill Bennett, review of *The Princess and the Frog*, p. 11.

Junior Bookshelf, February, 1994, review of *The Ugly Duckling*, p. 16.

Kirkus Reviews, December 15, 1991, review of *The Story of Rumpelstiltskin*, p. 1593; February 15, 1993, review of *The Three Bears and Goldilocks*, p. 229.

Magpies, July, 1992, Jo Goodman, review of *The Story of Rumpelstiltskin* and *The Three Bears and Goldilocks*, p. 25.

Publishers Weekly, September 4, 1995, review of *Three Little Kittens in the Enchanted Forest*, p. 68; January 24, 2000, review of *The Biggest Bed in the World*, p. 310.

School Librarian, February, 1993, Cathy Sutton, review of *The Three Billy Goats Gruff, Nursery Pop-up Book: Little Red Riding Hood*, and *The Story of Rumpelstiltskin*, p. 16; May, 1994, Trevor Dickinson, review of *The Collins Book of Nursery Tales*, p. 56.

School Library Journal, August, 1991, Dorothy F. Houlihan, review of *Rain, Rain, Go Away!*, p. 162; February, 1992, Linda Boyles, review of *The Story of Rumpelstiltskin*, p. 82; March, 1993, Kate McClelland, review of *The Three Bears and Goldilocks*, pp. 191-192; January, 1994, Dorcas Hand, review of *My First Dictionary*, p. 110.

LANGREUTER, Jutta 1944-

Personal

Born August 2, 1944, in Copenhagen, Denmark; daughter of Rolf (a diplomat) and Lieselotte (a homemaker); married Friedrich Langreuter (an editor), May 11, 1981; children: Jonas, Jeremy. *Education:* Graduated from Munich University with a degree in psychology, 1968. *Hobbies and other interests:* "Engaged in helping women over forty years who feel disoriented in life."

Addresses

Home—Bischof-Adalbertstrasse 14, 80809 Munich, Germany. *Office*—c/o Millbrook Press, 2 Old New Milford Rd., PO Box 335, Brookfield, CT 06804-0335. *Agent*—Friedrich Langreuter, Bischof-Adalbertstrasse 14, 80809 Munich, Germany.

Career

Author. Worked as a psychologist for Max-Planck Institute and Deutsches Jugend Institute, both institutes for science; also worked as a therapist. Munich Children's bookshop, owner.

Writings

Little Bear Brushes His Teeth, illustrated by Vera Sobat, Millbrook (Brookfield, CT), 1997.
Little Bear Goes to Kindergarten, illustrated by Vera Sobat, Millbrook (Brookfield, CT), 1997.
Little Bear and the Big Fight, illustrated by Vera Sobat, Millbrook (Brookfield, CT), 1998.
Little Bear Is a Big Brother, illustrated by Vera Sobat, Millbrook (Brookfield, CT), 1998.
Belly Buttons, illustrated by Andrea Hebrock, Barron's Educational (Hauppauge, NY), 1999.
Little Bear Won't Go to Bed, illustrated by Vera Sobat, Millbrook (Brookfield, CT), 2000.

Langreuter has also written five books about a bunny, Rötte-Häschen, which have become very popular in Germany; two books about a dinosaur named Julie; and a book about a little wolf titled *Kleiner Wolf Momme.*

Work in Progress

The sixth book in the "Little Bear" series; a follow-up book to *Belly Buttons;* a book about a pig titled *Gunter; Kleiner Bär wartet auf Weihnachten* (title means "Little Bear Is Waiting for Christmas").

Sidelights

Jutta Langreuter is the creator of the "Little Bear" series of books for children. Initially written in German, the books have been translated into English to cater to a wider audience. "Very important for me has been that in my childhood I moved a lot to other countries, because my father was a diplomat," Langreuter explained to

Jutta Langreuter

SATA. "Since then I had this strong feeling of being a *World*-inhabitant."

Langreuter was born on August 2, 1944, in Copenhagen, Denmark. Her father was a diplomat and this gave her a chance to travel around the world early on in life. She studied at Munich University and earned her diploma in psychology, eventually working as a therapist and a researcher for a number of years. In addition to assisting women of middle age refocus their lives, the author also owns a children's bookshop in Munich. Explaining her decision to write for young readers, Langreuter told *SATA:* "[As an] adult I [have] always [dealt] with children—I worked in an institute doing research on children, I led youth-forums, I own the Munich Children's Bookshop, and (the most important thing) I have two children, Jonas and Jeremy! Now they are nineteen and seventeen years old, but I still have their behaviours, their sweet sentences, their views of life ... carved in my heart. I remember a lot, and these amusing and lovable things I write in my books. [My list] seems to be endless."

In the "Little Bear" series Langreuter has created a character with whom toddlers can easily identify, according to critics. Each book in the series deals with a different trial or tribulation in the life of a young preschooler. The young bear behaves with the typical stubbornness, imagination, and logic that is peculiar to a human his age. The "typical toddler rites of passage" notes a reviewer for *Publishers Weekly,* are dealt with humor and affection. A reviewer for *Children's Book*

Review Service notes that while approaching predicaments from the child's point of view, Langreuter's books "make you realize how difficult the maturing process can be."

The first book in the series, *Little Bear Brushes His Teeth* deals with the universal problem of teaching a child the habit of brushing his teeth. When Mama Bear's best efforts and Papa Bear's strict commands fail, Mama comes up with an ingenious way of making her toddler understand the importance of brushing one's teeth: she uses Little Bear's fondness for pretending to enlist her son as a "soldier" in the "battle" against bacteria who are the "enemy." Many children and their parents will find this a familiar scenario. Hazel Rochman comments in *Booklist* that, "Toddlers will enjoy all the messy and loving particulars of their daily world."

The second book in the series, *Little Bear Goes to Kindergarten*, deals with the issue of separation anxiety faced by a small child going to school for the first time. The book opens with Mother Bear preparing Little Bear for school by recalling a previous preparatory visit to the school. The motif of remembering is reinforced throughout the book as the events unfold. In her review of the book for *School Library Journal*, Judith Constantinides notes that "The text is just right—succinct and with the oft-repeated phrase, 'I remember' to give it unity."

Little Bear and the Big Fight examines in detail the confused emotions of the preschooler when he has his first fight with his best friend in school. The account captures the preschooler's intense feelings and fears and how he learns to deal with them. Writing in *Booklist*, Rochman claims that children will particularly empathize with this story and "recognize how quickly friends can become enemies and how it hurts." Similarly, *School Library Journal* contributor Christine A. Moesch suggested that "More emphasis seems to be placed on how bad it feels to be angry at someone, rather than ... that beating someone up isn't necessarily the first course of action." *Little Bear Is a Big Brother* explores Little Bear's changing emotions at the prospect of a new sibling—at first he is excited and then apprehensive when friends at school warn him of the impending problems the new baby will bring.

Biographical and Critical Sources

PERIODICALS

Booklist, February 1, 1997, Hazel Rochman, review of *Little Bear Brushes His Teeth* and *Little Bear Goes to Kindergarten*, pp. 946-948; April, 1998, Hazel Rochman, review of *Little Bear and the Big Fight* and *Little Bear Is a Big Brother*, p. 1331.

Children's Book Review Service, June, 1997, Peggy Munte, review of *Little Bear Brushes His Teeth* and *Little Bear Goes to Kindergarten*, p. 122.

Kirkus Reviews, February 1, review of *Little Bear Brushes His Teeth*, p. 230.

Publishers Weekly, January 27, 1997, review of *Little Bear Brushes His Teeth* and *Little Bear Goes to Kindergarten*, p. 105.

School Library Journal, April, 1997, Judith Constantinides, review of *Little Bear Goes to Kindergarten*, p. 112; July, 1997, Jane Marino, review of *Little Bear Brushes His Teeth*, p. 70; August, 1998, Christine A. Moesch, review of *Little Bear and the Big Fight*, p. 142; April, 2001, Carolyn Jenks, review of *Little Bear Won't Go to Bed*, p. 115.

*   *   *

LITTLESUGAR, Amy 1953-

Personal

Born March 8, 1953, in Bermuda; daughter of Kevin (in sales) and Rosalind (a homemaker) Alme; married David Zuccarini (an artist), 1974; children: Christie, Ethan, Will. *Education:* University of Maryland, B.A. *Politics:* Democrat.

Addresses

Home—7402 Mellenbrook Rd., Columbia, MD 21045. *Office*—c/o Putnam Berkley Group, 200 Madison Ave., New York, NY 10016. *Agent*—Pesha Rubinstein Literary Agency, Inc., 1392 Rugby Rd., Teaneck, NJ 01666. *E-mail*—Littlesugar@mindspring.com.

Career

Author, 1990—. Howard Community College, Columbia, MD, writing instructor. *Member:* Society of Children's Book Writers and Illustrators.

Writings

The Spinner's Daughter, illustrated by Robert Quackenbush, Pippin Press (New York, NY), 1994.
Josiah True and the Art Maker, illustrated by Barbara Garrison, Simon & Schuster (New York, NY), 1995.
Marie in Fourth Position: The Story of Degas's "The Little Dancer," illustrated by Ian Schoenherr, Philomel (New York, NY), 1996.
Jonkonnu: A Story from the Sketchbook of Winslow Homer, illustrated by Ian Schoenherr, Penguin (New York, NY), 1997.
A Portrait of Spotted Deer's Grandfather, illustrated by Marlowe DeChristopher, Albert Whitman, 1997.
Shake Rag: From the Life of Elvis Presley, illustrated by Floyd Cooper, Philomel (New York, NY), 1998.
Tree of Hope, illustrated by Floyd Cooper, Philomel (New York, NY), 1999.
The Rag Baby, Simon & Schuster (New York, NY), 2000.
Lisette's Angel, illustrated by Max Ginsburg, Dial (New York, NY), 2001.
Freedom School, Yes!, illustrated by Floyd Cooper, Philomel (New York, NY), 2001.

Also author of *Clown Child*, Penguin (New York, NY).

Sidelights

Children's book author Amy Littlesugar told _SATA:_ "When I write, the idea for a story usually comes first. But it is the main character in the story who must make you care about that idea." All of Littlesugar's books feature strong, captivating characters. _Marie in Fourth Position: The Story of Degas's "The Little Dancer"_ is an imaginative and realistic story about a chorus girl immortalized by artist Edgar Degas in his sculpture _The Little Dancer._ Littlesugar's book is a fictionalized account of the tale and depicts a shy chorus girl's transformation whose dancing improves dramatically through her modeling work for Degas. Not much is known about the girl and the author clarifies the fact through a footnote at the end of the book. In a tribute to Littlesugar's expert handling of the story, Melissa Hudak comments in a review for _School Library Journal_ that "This gives an added drama to a beautifully written story that focuses not only on Degas's work, but also the suffering Marie endured for both the sculptor and her ballet."

Jonkonnu: A Story from the Sketchbook of Winslow Homer "provides backgrounds for multi-cultural history, stories in paintings and American history," notes Annette C. Blank in _Children's Book Review Service._ Littlesugar's book reconstructs an event from the late 1800s, when painter Winslow Homer visited Petersburg, Virginia, to sketch freed slaves who were celebrating "Jonkonnu," an old slave holiday. Elizabeth Bush, reviewing the book for _Bulletin of the Center for Children's Books,_ finds Littlesugar's treatment of an incident involving Homer and a staring match with a town bigot of particular mention. _Jonkonnu_ is a fictionalized portrayal of a part of Homer's career; the book is based at times on history, even though the War between the States had been over for more than a decade, and former slaves had still not been accepted into the mainstream of southern life. Shirley Wilton of _School Library Journal_ describes Littlesugar's narrative as evocative of "the heat and lush green growth of Southern summer, and with vocabulary and pronunciation suggestive of soft Southern speech."

A Portrait of Spotted Deer's Grandfather draws its inspiration from a journey made in 1836 by the U.S. artist George Catlin. It is a fictionalized account of an old Native American's realization that an artist's impressions are an essential method of preservation and a means to communicate one's culture to future generations. The book, which contains an outline of Catlin's life, is recommended by Karen Hunt in _Booklist_ as "Useful for introducing Catlin's life or a unit on American Indians."

Shake Rag: From the Life of Elvis Presley is a picture-book presentation of Presley's childhood and his introduction to music by gospel singers of the South. It records the influences of people, both black and white, on Elvis and their contribution in shaping his music. Ronald Jobe of _School Library Journal_ comments, "The quality of storytelling is remarkable," and Barbara Baker

agrees in _Children's Book Review Service,_ commenting that _Shake Rag_ is "helpful in the study of American racial history." _Tree of Hope_ explores the rebirth of African-American theatre in Harlem during the Great Depression. A _Publishers Weekly_ review notes that "Littlesugar unobtrusively uses history to anchor the experiences of a particular fictional family."

Littlesugar's next book, _Freedom School, Yes!,_ focuses on the civil rights movement of the 1960s. Explaining the motivation behind the book, Littlesugar told _SATA,_ "In _Freedom School,_ inspiration came out of a photograph of three African-American children and their eighteen-year-old white schoolteacher smiling for the camera in the window of a one-room schoolhouse back in the tense and dangerous Civil Rights summer of 1963. The hand-lettered sign above said _FREEDOM SCHOOL,_ and I soon learned that Freedom Schools were makeshift classrooms built and taught by black and white college students from the North. They mushroomed all across the South, where black children were still denied the opportunity of education. It took courage then, not only to teach, but to experience learning, so I knew I'd need to create the voices of two very brave characters. However, only after tracking down and interviewing some of the teacher volunteers and listening to their experiences, would Annie, an eighteen-year-old, first-time teacher, and Jolie, the Mississippi girl who comes to love learning in spite of her fears, be born."

"For me, the writing of _Freedom School_ was an exciting challenge, yet I knew it would happen, thanks to the support of the real people who participated in it, an agent and editor who believed in it, and characters I felt young readers would care about." The book resulting from Littlesugar's research succeeds, in the opinion of a _Publishers Weekly_ critic, in "personaliz[ing] the events of an era by colorfully detailing one girl's experience." _School Library Journal's_ Barbara Buckley concurs, noting that "Littlesugar has created a slice-of-life story with a potent message." While the _Publishers Weekly_ reviewer feels that at points "the story stumbles a bit," Buckley praises Floyd Cooper's illustrations as "masterful and lush," and summarizes the narrative as "a unique and poignant look at a moment in history."

Biographical and Critical Sources

PERIODICALS

Booklist, January 1, 1998, Karen Hunt, review of _A Portrait of Spotted Deer's Grandfather,_ p. 813; December 15, 1999, Hazel Rochman, review of _Tree of Hope,_ p. 790; February 15, 2000, review of _Tree of Hope,_ pp. 1, 109; February 15, 2001, Hazel Rochman, review of _Freedom School, Yes!,_ p. 1155.
Bulletin of the Center for Children's Books, January, 1998, Elizabeth Bush, review of _Jonkonnu,_ p. 165.
Children's Book Review Service, April, 1998, Annette C. Blank, review of _Jonkonnu,_ p. 102; December, 1998, Barbara Baker, review of _Shake Rag,_ p. 43.
Kirkus Reviews, September 1, 1996, review of _Marie in Fourth Position,_ p. 324; August 15, 1997, review of _A Portrait of Spotted Deer's Grandfather,_ p. 308;

December 15, 1997, review of *Jonkonnu*, p. 836; October 15, 1998, review of *Shake Rag*, p. 533; October 15, 1999, review of review of *Tree of Hope*, p. 1646.

New York Times Book Review, February 14, 1999, Peter Keepnews, review of *Shake Rag*, p. 27.

Publishers Weekly, May 31, 1999, review of *Marie in Fourth Position*, p. 86; November 29, 1999, review of review of *Tree of Hope*, p. 70; January 8, 2001, review of *Freedom School, Yes!*, p. 65.

School Library Journal, October, 1996, Melissa Hudak, review of *Marie in Fourth Position*, p. 101; September, 1997, Pam Grosner, review of *A Portrait of Spotted Deer's Grandfather*, p. 186; February, 1998, Shirley Wilton, review of *Jonkonnu*, p. 86; October, 1998, Ronald Jobe, review of *Shake Rag*, p. 106; November, 1999, Miriam Lang Budin, review of *Tree of Hope*, p. 123; January, 2001, Barbara Buckley, review of *Freedom School, Yes!*, p. 104.*

*   *   *

LOURIE, Helen
See STORR, Catherine (Cole)

*   *   *

LUTZ, Norma Jean 1943-

Personal

Born January 31, 1943, in Bay City, TX; daughter of Norman Hilbert and Helen Louise Sherry-Bronson; stepdaughter of Tom Wayne Sherry; married Clifford N. Lutz (divorced, 1986); children: Kerry Lee, Rhonda Jean Huber. *Education:* Attended college. *Religion:* Christian.

Addresses

Office—4308 South Peoria, Suite 701, Tulsa, OK 74105.

Career

Writer and professional speaker. Notations un-Limited (writing business), Tulsa, OK, founder and owner, 1986—. Founder of Professionalism in Writing School (annual Christian writer's conference), 1983-96; worked for the Institute of Children's Literature, 1988-97. Speaker at seminars, writers conferences, and schools throughout the United States, c. 1983—. *Member:* Toastmasters International, Tulsa Christian Writers Club (founder and former president).

Awards, Honors

First place awards, Tulsa City-County Library Writing Contest, 1989, 1991, 1993; first place awards, *Tulsa Woman News* Fiction Contest, 1997, 1998.

Writings

FICTION; FOR CHILDREN

Blossom into Love, Silhouette, 1985.
Good-bye Beedee, Chariot (Elgin, IL), 1986.
Once over Lightly, Chariot (Elgin, IL), 1986.
Oklahoma Summer, Chariot (Elgin, IL), 1987.
Rock & Romance, Weekly Reader Book Club, 1988.

Contributor to anthology *God Is Everywhere*, Standard Publishing, 1986.

"THE AMERICAN ADVENTURE" SERIES; FOR CHILDREN; ILLUSTRATED BY ADAM WALLENTAJ

Smallpox Strikes! Cotton Mather's Bold Experiment, Barbour (Ulrichsville, OH), 1997.
Maggie's Choice: Jonathan Edwards and the Great Awakening, Barbour (Ulrichsville, OH), 1997.
Trouble on the Ohio River: Drought Shuts Down a City, Barbour (Ulrichsville, OH), 1997.
Escape from Slavery: A Family's Fight for Freedom, Barbour (Ulrichsville, OH), 1997.
Enemy or Friend, Barbour (Ulrichsville, OH), 1997.
Fight for Freedom, Barbour (Ulrichsville, OH), 1997.
The Rebel Spy, Barbour (Ulrichsville, OH), 1998.
The War's End, Barbour (Ulrichsville, OH), 1998.
A Better Bicycle, Barbour (Ulrichsville, OH), 1998.
Marching with Sousa, Barbour (Ulrichsville, OH), 1998.
Clash with the Newsboys, Barbour (Ulrichsville, OH), 1998.
Prelude to War, Barbour (Ulrichsville, OH), 1998.

Norma Jean Lutz

The Great War, Barbour (Ulrichsville, OH), 1998.
Battling the Clan, Barbour (Ulrichsville, OH), 1998.
Rumblings of War, Barbour (Ulrichsville, OH), 1998.
War Strikes, Barbour (Ulrichsville, OH), 1998.

NONFICTION; FOR CHILDREN

Females First in Their Field: Business and Industry, Chelsea House (Philadelphia), 1999.
(Editor) Jean Holmes, *Do Dogs Go to Heaven? Eternal Answers for Animal Lovers,* JoiPax, 1999.
Cotton Mather ("Colonial Leaders" series), Chelsea House (Philadelphia), 2000.
William Penn: Founder of Democracy ("Colonial Leaders" series), Chelsea House (Philadelphia), 2000.
Increase Mather ("Colonial Leaders" series), Chelsea House (Philadelphia), 2000.
Jonathan Edwards ("Colonial Leaders" series), Chelsea House (Philadelphia), 2000.
John Paul Jones: Father of the U.S. Navy ("Revolutionary War Leaders" series), Chelsea House (Philadelphia), 2000.
Benedict Arnold: Traitor to the Cause ("Revolutionary War Leaders" series), Chelsea House (Philadelphia), 2000.
J. C. Watts, Chelsea House (Philadelphia), 2000.
Britney Spears, Chelsea House (Philadelphia), 2000.
Celine Dion, Chelsea House (Philadelphia), 2000.
History of the Republican Party ("Your Government: How It Works" series), Chelsea House (Philadelphia), 2000.
History of Third Parties ("Your Government: How It Works" series), Chelsea House (Philadelphia), 2000.
History of the Black Church ("Black Achievement" series), Chelsea House (Philadelphia), 2000.
Frederick Douglass ("Civil War Leaders" series), Chelsea House (Philadelphia), 2001.
Harriet Tubman ("Civil War Leaders" series), Chelsea House (Philadelphia), 2001.
Sojourner Truth ("Civil War Leaders" series), Chelsea House (Philadelphia), 2001.
Nunavut ("Canada" series), Chelsea House (Philadelphia), 2001.
Jane Austen ("Bloom's BioCritiques" series), Chelsea House (Philadelphia), 2001.
The Brontë Sisters ("Bloom's BioCritiques" series), Chelsea House (Philadelphia), 2001.
F. Scott Fitzgerald ("Bloom's BioCritiques" series), Chelsea House (Philadelphia), 2001.
Tennessee Williams ("Bloom's BioCritiques" series), Chelsea House (Philadelphia), 2001.

"HEARTSONG" FICTION SERIES; FOR ADULTS

Fields of Sweet Content, Barbour (Ulrichsville, OH), 1993.
Love's Silken Melody, Barbour (Ulrichsville, OH), 1993.
Cater to a Whim, Barbour (Ulrichsville, OH), 1994.
The Winning Heart, Barbour (Ulrichsville, OH), 1995.
Tulsa Tempest, Barbour (Ulrichsville, OH), 1995.
Tulsa Turning, Barbour (Ulrichsville, OH), 1996.
Tulsa Trespass, Barbour (Ulrichsville, OH), 1997.
Return to Tulsa, Barbour (Ulrichsville, OH), 1997.

OTHER

(With P. Harold Purvis) *A Matter of Conscience: Court Martialed for His Faith* (nonfiction), Review & Herald Publishing, 1998.

Contributor to *Inspirational Romance Readers,* Barbour (Ulrichsville, OH), 1999. Contributor of articles and short stories to periodicals, including *Christian Herald, Home Life, Sunday Digest, Power for Living, Sunday Visitor, Living with Teenagers, Young Ambassador, Teen Talk, Venture, Ohio Writer, Canadian Writer, Writers Connection, Design for Profit, Single Life, Single Parent, Mahoning Valley Parent, Atlanta Single, Atlanta Parent, South Florida Parenting, Christian Single, Tulsa Woman News, Christian Retailing, Merly's Pen, Mature Lifestyles, Grit,* and *Rotarian.*

Sidelights

Norma Jean Lutz is a professional writer and lecturer who has built a career writing series fiction and nonfiction for young readers. Contributing many installments to Chelsea House publishers' "Colonial Leaders," "Revolutionary War Leaders," and "Civil War Leaders" series, Lutz has also written many tales of historical fiction involving young protagonists through her work for "The American Adventure," a book series published in the late 1990s.

Born in 1943 in Bay City, Texas, Lutz and her family relocated to Kansas when she was still young. "As a young girl growing up in a small Kansas town, we had few books in our home," the author recalled for *SATA.* "There was no public library in the town, only small libraries at both the grade school and the high school. Fortunately for me, at the grade school where I attended each of my elementary teachers read to us every morning before we began our studies. From first grade through sixth, I was introduced to exciting worlds through such stories as *Boxcar Children, Little House in the Big Woods, Betsy-Tacy, Mary Poppins, The Secret Garden,* and scores of others. I believe it was through these precious teachers that I acquired the 'love of story' that I possess today."

Within such a small school system, Lutz's interest in writing was given little in the way of encouragement. "Nevertheless, I constantly dreamed of writing and becoming a writer. In my mind, I pretended to be Laura Ingalls Wilder (she had actually lived in Kansas like I did, which seemed to mean a great deal to me at the time). I kept journals during my junior and senior years, both of which I still have in my possession." Finally, a high school English teacher boosted her confidence when he suggested "that I might have a measure of talent in this area. He even went so far as to say he would help me submit my work," Lutz added. But his encouragement went no further. "When nothing else was said or done, I assumed he had changed his mind and decided I wasn't so talented after all."

After graduating from high school, Lutz attended college for a brief time, but left to marry and raise a family. While "writing remained on the back burner," the author added, "the flame never went out. When my children were in grade school, I enrolled in a correspondence course with the Christian Writers Institute. When I completed that, I enrolled with the Institute of Children's

In **Britney Spears,** *a biographical portrait of the popular singer, Lutz follows Spears from her early childhood to her stardom as a teenager. (Photo by Kevin Frayer.)*

Literature and graduated from there. But before finishing, I was selling magazine articles and short stories, plunking them out on my old black manual Royal typewriter. The check from my very first sale was dated on my birthday—January 31, 1979—a momentous day in my life!" Lutz still has a copy of that check hanging on a wall in her office.

From magazine publications Lutz moved gradually into writing book-length manuscripts and had several teen romance novels published between 1985 and 1988. Among these is *Oklahoma Summer,* which combines a budding summer romance with a thirteen-year-old girl's love of horses in a story that *Booklist* critic Barbara Elleman praised as "perceptive," featuring "warm, likeable characters."

Around 1990 Lutz changed her focus and worked for a few years writing adult romance novels, among them *Love's Silken Melody, The Winning Heart,* and *Return to Tulsa.* In the mid-1990s she began a professional relationship with Barbour Publishing, and her first novel in the "American Adventures" series arrived on bookstore shelves in 1997. *Smallpox Strikes!: Cotton Mather's Bold Experiment* is a fictional tale about an eleven-year-old boy named Robert Allerton who lived in Boston in the early 1720s, the height of a smallpox epidemic in that city. When both his stepfather and his younger stepbrother are stricken by the illness, Rob must take on an adult's responsibility in caring for his family. While *School Library Journal* contributor Connie Tyrrell Burns bemoaned Lutz's use of exclamation points and a "predictable" outcome, she noted the novel's inclusion of "life lessons" as well as its "Christian emphasis." *Smallpox Strikes!* would be followed by such novels as *The Rebel Spy, Clash with the Newsboys,* and *Trouble on the Ohio River.*

In addition to fiction, Lutz has penned several nonfiction titles, among them biographies of such diverse figures as Cotton Mather, John Paul Jones, Harriet Tubman, and Britney Spears. She also contributed one installment to the "Female Firsts in Their Fields" series: *Business and Industry.* In this sixty-five-page book, she profiles six figures, among them media star Oprah Winfrey, reigning home decorating queen Martha Stewart, cosmetics company founder Mary Kay, and Madam C. J. Walker, the country's first black millionaire. *Voice of Youth Advocates* critic Beth E. Anderson praised the series as "the perfect tool for introducing students to a broad field of noteworthy champions," while *School Library Journal* contributor Rebecca O'Connell commented that the somewhat brief treatment given to each woman will still "spark students' interest in seeking out" more detailed biographical information.

From the sale of her first article through the publication of her first book, a romance novel about a young man ready to abort a promising college career to care for his retarded sister titled *Blossom into Love,* Lutz has devoted herself to her writing. "I have nearly fifty books to my credit," she proudly boasted to *SATA,* "and hundreds of magazine articles and short stories. I have ghosted scores of books for clients, as well as assisting many writers through my professional critique service." In 1988 she joined the staff of the Institute of Children's Literature and remained there until 1997, when she left to devote more time to her own work.

"Being a Christian, I give credit to God for my talents and abilities," Lutz added. "I'm thankful to be in a business that allows me to do what I love each and every day. While some may look at what I have accomplished and measure it as a tidy little sum, I feel I've barely begun. I plan to be busy writing books right up until the very moment when God calls me Home. And if He has a computer waiting for me in heaven, I won't miss a beat!"

Biographical and Critical Sources

PERIODICALS

Booklist, June 15, 1987, Barbara Elleman, review of *Oklahoma Summer,* p. 1608.

School Library Journal, January, 1986, Kathy Fritts, review of *Blossom into Love,* p. 81; September, 1987, Patricia G. Harrington, review of *Oklahoma Summer,* pp. 197-198; January, 1999, Connie Tyrrell Burns, review of *Smallpox Strikes!,* p. 128; September, 1999, Rebecca O'Connell, review of *Female Firsts in Their Field,* p. 232.

Voice of Youth Advocates, August, 1999, Beth E. Anderson, review of *Female Firsts in Their Field,* p. 201.*

* * *

LYNCH, P(atrick) J(ames) 1962-

Personal

Born March 2, 1962, in Belfast, Northern Ireland; son of Liam (a builder's laborer) and Anna (McKillen) Lynch. *Education:* Attended Jordanstown Polytechnic, 1980-81; Brighton Art College, B.A. (with honors), 1984. *Politics:* "My own particular brand." *Hobbies and other interests:* Making bronze sculptures, reading, traveling.

Addresses

Home—Top Flat, 86 Upper Leeson St., Dublin 4, Ireland.

Career

Illustrator, 1984—.

Awards, Honors

Mother Goose Award, British Book Trust, 1987, for *A Bag of Moonshine;* Bistro Award (Ireland), for *Fairy Tales of Ireland;* Kate Greenaway Medal, British Library Association, 1995, for *The Christmas Miracle of Jonathan Toomey,* and 1997, for *When Jessie Came across the Sea.*

Illustrator

Alan Garner, *A Bag of Moonshine,* Collins (London, England), 1986.

Joyce Dunbar, *Raggy Taggy Toys,* Orchard (London, England), 1987.

E. Nesbit, *Melisande,* Harcourt (New York, NY), 1989.

William Butler Yeats, *Fairy Tales of Ireland,* Delacorte (New York, NY), 1990.

Oscar Wilde, *Stories for Children,* Macmillan, 1990.

George W. Dasent, translator, *East o' the Sun and West o' the Moon,* Candlewick Press, 1991.

Hans Christian Anderson, *The Steadfast Tin Soldier,* Harcourt (New York, NY), 1991.

Sarah Hayes, *The Candlewick Book of Fairy Tales,* Candlewick Press, 1993.

Hans Christian Anderson, *The Snow Queen,* Anderson Press, 1993.

Antonia Barber, *Catkin,* Candlewick Press, 1994.

Susan Wojciechowski, *The Christmas Miracle of Jonathan Toomey,* Candlewick Press, 1995.

Brendan Behan, *The King of Ireland's Son,* Orchard (London, England), 1997.

Amy Hest, *When Jessie Came across the Sea,* Candlewick Press, 1997.

Douglas Wood, *Grandad's Prayers of the Earth,* Candlewick Press, 1999.

Marie Heaney, *The Names upon the Harp: Irish Myth and Legend,* Arthur A. Levine, 2000.

Sidelights

Irish-born children's illustrator P. J. Lynch has been praised by critics for his ability to capture writer's words and emotions in his art. He is noted as well for paintings reminiscent of the famous children's illustrator Arthur Rackham, an influence he admitted in an interview with *Achuka,* a Web site devoted to the work of children's authors and illustrators in the United Kingdom. Lynch said that he is "very aware of a tradition in children's book illustration," noting that his work is also shaped by illustrators working in the early part of the twentieth century, such as Edmund Dulac, N. C. Wyeth, and Maxfield Parrish.

Such influences were noted by reviewers of Lynch's illustrations for the 1993 retelling of Hans Christian Anderson's classic tale *The Snow Queen.* In the story, a young boy named Kay is kidnaped by the evil Snow Queen. His only hope of rescue is through Gerda, a brave young girl who must endure a terrifying journey to save Kay from the icy grip of the Snow Queen. In *Publishers Weekly,* a critic claimed that Lynch "brings exquisite grace and elegance to his illustrations of Anderson's classic story," while Hazel Rochman, writing in *Booklist,* described Lynch's work as "handsomely illustrated in full-blown romantic style." Calling his paintings "elegant and splendid," *School Library Journal* reviewer Patricia Lothrop Green suggested that "Lynch's artwork evokes illustration's 19th-century Golden Age without being slavishly imitative."

Two years later, Lynch published the first of his two Kate Greenaway Medal-winning books, *The Christmas Miracle of Jonathan Toomey.* When master woodcarver Jonathan Toomey's wife and child die, he becomes known in the valley as "Mr. Gloomy." One day, however, after widow McDowell and her son ask Toomey to carve them a new Nativity set, the reclusive craftsman slowly recovers from his grief and begins to enjoy life again. *Booklist* reviewer Rochman described Lynch's illustrations as "both realistic and gloriously romantic," going on to add that the "striking, oil-on-linen illustrations also convey a complexity of viewpoint." In a *School Library Journal* review of the work, contributor Jane Marino praised Lynch's ability to capture the characters' emotions, noting that the illustrator "sets the mood through an effective use of palette, beginning with dark, somber browns and adding more light as Toomey begins to accept the McDowells' overtures of friendship."

In his interview with *Achuka,* Lynch remarked, "I hadn't realized when I was living in England just how important being Irish was to me in relation to my work. I had chosen to illustrate texts by people like Oscar Wilde and W. B. Yeats, but now that I'm living in Dublin, it's much easier for me to immerse myself in the very strong culture and folk heritage that exists here." Glimpses of this Irish inspiration can be seen in Lynch's work in 1997's *The King of Ireland's Son.* A tale from Brendan Behan, *The King of Ireland's Son* tells how the king's three sons embark on a quest to discover the source of

P. J. Lynch attributes his visit to northern Minnesota with author Douglas Wood as inspiration for his striking watercolor illustrations that grace **Grandad's Prayers of Earth.** *The touching picture book is Wood's tribute to the lessons on praying taught to him by his grandfather.*

the heavenly music heard throughout the country. After a dangerous journey, the youngest son finally discovers where the music is coming from and must outwit a giant into releasing a beautiful princess strumming her harp. "Lynch's ... deft hand has produced a spectrum of unusual characters and watercolor scenes ranging in mood from sinister to romantic to pastoral," claimed a reviewer for *Publishers Weekly.* Added *School Library Journal* contributor Connie C. Rockman: "The exuberance of Lynch's watercolors, from lush gardens to humorous facial expressions, perfectly matches the rollicking rhythm of the text to create a wholly satisfying read-aloud."

With the publication of *When Jessie Came across the Sea* in 1997, Lynch earned his second Kate Greenaway Medal. In this picture book for older readers, thirteen-year-old Jessie finds herself on the way to America after being given a ticket by the village rabbi. Knowing it is for the best, Jessie is nonetheless disappointed to leave her beloved grandmother behind. Once in New York City, Jessie takes up the lacemaking skills she learned at her grandmother's hand and saves enough money for the

older woman's passage to the United States. *Booklist* reviewer Ilene Cooper observed how the "full-page and paneled art, especially the scenes of Jessie at sea, have a panoramic quality." "Lynch's luminous watercolor and gouache illustrations capture the character's feelings," agreed Martha Rosen in a *School Library Journal* review, "at the same time recording the storms at sea and teeming streets of the Lower East Side."

Lynch also demonstrates his skill at capturing the beauty of the natural world in *Grandad's Prayers of the Earth,* as a grandfather teaches his young grandson to be thankful and appreciative of the world around them. Through long walks in the wilderness, the older man teaches his grandson that everyone and everything prays in their own special way. After his grandfather dies, the boy initially feels resentment and anger that his prayers to bring Grandad back to life are not answered. However, the grandfather's lessons still remain with the boy who eventually returns to the forest and hears nature's prayers. Describing the double-page watercolors as "beautiful, meditative, [and] realistic," Patricia Pearl Dole noted in *School Library Journal* that author Douglas Wood's text "is perfectly complimented by the moving, expressive illustrations." In a *Booklist* review, Shelley Townsend-Hudson suggested that "Lynch's realistic watercolors suit the emotions perfectly."

Biographical and Critical Sources

PERIODICALS

Booklist, September 15, 1994, Hazel Rochman, review of *The Snow Queen,* p. 135; September 15, 1995, Hazel Rochman, review of *The Christmas Miracle of Jonathan Toomey,* p. 173; February 1, 1998, Ilene Cooper, review of *When Jessie Came across the Sea,* p. 918; December 1, 1999, Shelley Townsend-Hudson, review of *Grandad's Prayers of the Earth,* p. 715.
Publishers Weekly, November 7, 1994, review of *The Snow Queen,* p. 79; March 17, 1997, review of *The King of Ireland's Son,* p. 84; November 27, 2000, review of *The Names upon the Harp,* p. 75.
School Library Journal, November, 1994, Patricia Lothrop Green, review of *The Snow Queen,* p. 102; October, 1995, Jane Marino, review of *The Christmas Miracle of Jonathan Toomey,* p. 43; June, 1997, Connie C. Rockman, review of *The King of Ireland's Son,* p. 105; November, 1997, Martha Rosen, review of *When Jessie Came across the Sea,* p. 83; January, 2000, Patricia Pearl Dole, review of *Grandad's Prayers of the Earth,* p. 114; January, 2001, Grace Oliff, review of *The Names upon the Harp,* p. 146.

ON-LINE

Achuka, http://www.achuka.co.uk (December, 1997).*

M

MABIE, Grace
See MATTERN, Joanne

*   *   *

MACHT, Norman L(ee) 1929-

Personal

Born August 4, 1929, in Brooklyn, NY; married Lois P. Nicholson (a writer). *Education:* University of Chicago, Ph.B., 1947; University of California (Sonoma), M.A., 1978.

Addresses

Home—266 South Washington St., Easton, MD 21601.

Career

Writer. *Military service:* U.S. Air Force, 1952-55. *Member:* Society for American Baseball Research (director, 1999—).

Writings

NONFICTION; FOR YOUNG ADULTS

Jim Abbott: Major League Pitcher ("Great Achievers: Lives of the Physically Challenged" series), Chelsea House (Philadelphia, PA), 1994.

Julius Erving ("Basketball Legends" series), Chelsea House (Philadelphia, PA), 1995.

Clarence Thomas ("Black Americans of Achievement" series), Chelsea House (Philadelphia, PA), 1995.

Roy Campanella: Baseball Star ("Great Achievers: Lives of the Physically Challenged" series), Chelsea House (Philadelphia, PA), 1996.

(With Mary Hull) *The History of Slavery* ("World History" series), Lucent, 1997.

The Composite Guide to Baseball, Chelsea House (Philadelphia, PA), 1997.

Supreme Court Justice Clarence Thomas meets with his eighth-grade teacher during his confirmation hearing in a photo from Norman L. Macht's **Clarence Thomas,** *a biography that traces Thomas's rise from a childhood of poverty in segregated Georgia of the 1950s to a seat on the highest court of the United States. (Photo by AP/ Wide World Photos.)*

The Composite Guide to Track and Field, Chelsea House (Philadelphia, PA), 1999.

Roberto Alomar: An Authorized Biography ("Latinos in Baseball" series), Mitchell Lane (Childs, MD), 1999.

"JUNIOR WORLD BIOGRAPHIES" SERIES; FOR YOUNG ADULTS

Sojourner Truth, Chelsea House (Philadelphia, PA), 1992.

Christopher Columbus, Chelsea House (Philadelphia, PA), 1992.

Sandra Day O'Connor, Chelsea House (Philadelphia, PA), 1992.

Roberto Clemente, Chelsea House (Philadelphia, PA), 1994.
Muhammad Ali, Chelsea House (Philadelphia, PA), 1994.

"BASEBALL LEGENDS" SERIES; FOR YOUNG ADULTS

Christy Mathewson, Chelsea House (Philadelphia, PA), 1991.
Babe Ruth, Chelsea House (Philadelphia, PA), 1991.
Jimmie Foxx, Chelsea House (Philadelphia, PA), 1991.
Frank Robinson, Chelsea House (Philadelphia, PA), 1991.
Satchel Paige, Chelsea House (Philadelphia, PA), 1991.
Cy Young, Chelsea House (Philadelphia, PA), 1992.
Lou Gehrig, Chelsea House (Philadelphia, PA), 1993.
Ty Cobb, Chelsea House (Philadelphia, PA), 1993.
Tom Seaver, Chelsea House (Philadelphia, PA), 1994.
Reggie Jackson, Chelsea House (Philadelphia, PA), 1994.
Greg Maddux, Chelsea House (Philadelphia, PA), 1997.
Roger Clemens, Chelsea House (Philadelphia, PA), 1999.

OTHER

(With Dick Bartell) *Rowdy Richard: A Firsthand Account of the National League Baseball Wars of the 1930s and the Men Who Fought Them,* North Atlantic (Ukiah, CA), 1987.
(With Rex Barney) *Rex Barney's Thank Youuuu for Fifty Years in Baseball from Brooklyn to Baltimore,* Tidewater (Centreville, MD), 1993.
(With Vince Bagli) *Sundays at 2:00 with the Baltimore Colts,* Tidewater (Centreville, MD), 1995.
(With Jack Kavanagh) *Uncle Robbie,* Society for American Baseball Research (Cleveland, OH), 1999.

Sidelights

In his many biographies of famous people for young adults, Norman L. Macht covers a broad spectrum of influential figures, ranging from professional baseball players to U.S. Supreme Court justices. Part of a series about remarkable individuals overcoming physical challenges, Macht's 1994 work *Jim Abbott: Major League Pitcher* chronicles the life of athlete Abbott as he worked his way to Major League Baseball despite being born without a right hand. In addition to detailing the pitcher's baseball career, Macht also provides young readers with interesting bits of information about Abbott's personal life, such as his favorite topping for french fries. Reviewing the book in *School Library Journal,* contributor Blair Christolon wrote that "Librarians wanting more details on Abbott's career will want to add Macht's book to their collections."

Another of Macht's works about the lives of remarkable Americans, *Clarence Thomas,* details the story of Clarence Thomas, nominated to the United States Supreme Court in 1991. Macht shares with young readers the trials and hardships Justice Thomas endured while growing up as a poor black child in Georgia at a time when segregation and Jim Crow laws still persisted. While noticing the limited amount of information about Justice Thomas's legal career, Carrol McCarthy commented in a review for *School Library Journal* that Macht's "writing style is clear and easy to read." Recommended as a "strong addition to ... biography

collections" by *Booklist* reviewer Anne O'Malley, *Clarence Thomas* is "a very well written biography of a contemporary figure who is not easy to cover."

Macht has also written other books about sports, publishing *The Composite Guide to Track and Field* in 1999. Filled with information about the world of track and field, including portraits of famous athletes, the book includes a brief history about the early origins of the sport as well as its prominent role in the Olympics. In a *Voice of Youth Advocates* review of *The Composite Guide to Track and Field,* critic Chris Crowe noted a few problems with a "disjointed" chronology in the book, though he did go on to say that Macht "should be complimented for including a chapter on notable women in the sport and for acknowledging some of the problems that have dogged modern track and field in the final chapter, 'Money and Drugs.'"

Biographical and Critical Sources

PERIODICALS

Booklist, August, 1995, Anne O'Malley, review of *Clarence Thomas,* p. 1937.
School Library Journal, September, 1994, Blair Christolon, review of *Jim Abbott: Major League Pitcher,* p. 251; September, 1995, Carrol McCarthy, review of *Clarence Thomas,* p. 226.
Voice of Youth Advocates, June, 1999, Chris Crowe, review of *The Composite Guide to Track and Field,* p. 135.

* * *

MANTHORPE, Helen 1958-

Personal

Born January 9, 1958, in Adelaide, South Australia; daughter of John Ross and Doreen June (Valentin) Manthorpe; married William Gregory Duddy (a lawyer), May 25, 1991; children: William, Nicholas, Alice. *Education:* University of South Australia, BAPPSC (occupational therapy), 1980. *Hobbies and other interests:* Animal care, horticulture, silk painting, and music (singing).

Addresses

Home—244 Longwood Rd., Heathfield, South Australia 5153, Australia. *Office*—P.O. Box 616, Stirling, South Australia 5152, Australia. *Agent*—Carole Carroll, 2 Second Ave., Glenelg East, South Australia 5045, Australia. *E-mail*—helen@iweb.net.au.

Career

University of South Australia, Adelaide, tutor in occupational therapy, beginning 1985—. Koala handler, Cleland Wildlife Park. Also serves as speaker. *Member:* Fauna Care and Release.

Awards, Honors

Rotary Foundation (Pittsburgh, PA) scholar, 1982-83.

Writings

"SOLO BUSH BABIES" SERIES

Possum, illustrated by Yvonne Ashby, Omnibus (Norwood, South Australia), 2000.

Kangaroo, illustrated by Yvonne Ashby, Omnibus (Norwood, South Australia), 2000.

Work in Progress

Koala ("Solo Bush Babies" series) for Omnibus.

Sidelights

A trained occupational therapist, author Helen Manthorpe also shares a lifelong love of animals and nature. Her interest in fauna care has led to work as a koala handler at Australia's Cleland Wildlife Park and the adoption of two orphaned kangaroos, now fourteen years old. In 2000 Manthorpe turned her experience and knowledge about animals into the books *Solo Bush Babies: Possum* and *Solo Bush Babies: Kangaroo.*

To help educate her young audiences about animals during author visits to Australian schools, Manthorpe often brings a baby kangaroo or possum with her as she conducts her presentations. In addition to writing and working with animals, Manthorpe teaches at the University of Southern Australia.*

* * *

MARK, Joan (T.) 1937-

Personal

Born June 13, 1937, in Le Mars, IA; daughter of Henry John (a lawyer) and Forest (a teacher; maiden name, Mosier) TePaske; married Edward L. Mark (a clergyman), August 15, 1959; children: Jonathan, Jessica. *Education:* University of Iowa, B.A. (with high distinction), 1959; Radcliffe College, M.A., 1961; Harvard University, Ph.D., 1968. *Politics:* Democrat. *Religion:* Protestant (Dutch Reformed and Methodist). *Hobbies and other interests:* Piano, painting, swimming.

Addresses

Home and office—7 Clinton St., Cambridge, MA 02139. *Agent*—Gina Maccoby Literary Agency, P.O. Box 60, Chappaqua, NY 10514-0060.

Career

University of Massachusetts at Boston, 1966-71, began as instructor, became assistant professor of history; Harvard University, Cambridge, MA, research associate at Peabody Museum of Archaeology and Ethnology, 1973—; lecturer in history of anthropology for extension

Joan Mark

courses, 1976-79. Visiting lecturer in history of anthropology, Tufts University, 1981. Fellow of Bunting Institute, Radcliffe College, 1971-73, of Charles Warren Center, Harvard University, 1979-80, and of Bellagio Study Center, Rockefeller Foundation, 1986 and 1996. Editor for the behavioral sciences, Harvard University Press, 1982-84. *Member:* History of Science Society, PEN American Center.

Writings

Four Anthropologists: An American Science in Its Early Years, Science History Publications (New York, NY), 1980.

(Editor, with Frederick E. Hoxie) E. Jane Gay, *With the Nez Perces: Alice Fletcher in the Field, 1889-1892,* University of Nebraska Press (Lincoln, NE), 1981.

A Stranger in Her Native Land: Alice Fletcher and the American Indians, University of Nebraska Press (Lincoln, NE), 1989.

The King of the World in the Land of the Pygmies, University of Nebraska Press (Lincoln, NE), 1995.

Margaret Mead: Coming of Age in America, Oxford University Press (New York, NY), 1999.

The Silver Gringo: William Spratling and Taxco, University of New Mexico Press (Albuquerque, NM), 2000.

Contributor to periodicals, including *Isis, Science,* and *Perspectives in American History.*

Sidelights

A biographer who specializes in the life histories of prominent scientists, Joan Mark has written about Alice Fletcher, an early anthropologist who studied Native American tribal peoples, Patrick Putnam, an African explorer who became an expert on the Pygmies, and Margaret Mead, an anthropologist known for her controversial claims about Polynesian life.

In *A Stranger in Her Native Land: Alice Fletcher and the American Indians,* Mark details the life of Fletcher, a nineteenth-century American anthropologist. Mark reveals Fletcher as an energetic, informally trained scientist who tried to help the people she was studying. In the 1880s and 1890s, Fletcher successfully lobbied the American government to break up large tribal reservations in favor of giving deeds for small amounts of land to individual Indian families. Unfortunately, this policy, which she thought would enable Indians to stay on their land, led to the loss of much Indian land and the weakening of tribal traditions. Despite this failure, Fletcher was instrumental in shaping the course of American anthropological study in the twentieth century, Mark writes, because of her pioneering methods of field work, including her collaboration with an Omaha Indian, Francis LaFlesche, whom she informally adopted as her son. Critics praised Mark for her balanced, compassionate treatment of her subject.

In *The King of the World in the Land of the Pygmies* Mark tells the story of Patrick Putnam, a wealthy would-be anthropologist from New England whose adventures and travels throughout Africa led him to found his own village in the Congo where he lived with the Pygmies. Mark's account of Putnam's life, according to Alice Joyce in *Booklist,* "shows a truly unconventional man." A critic for *Publishers Weekly* notes that *The King of the World in the Land of the Pygmies* "tells the engrossing story of a true eccentric who fled his family of prominent Bostonians to set up a little kingdom in colonial Africa."

Aimed at a high-school audience, Mark's *Margaret Mead: Coming of Age in America* tells of the influential anthropologist who is best remembered for her early study of Polynesian culture. In this study, Mead made claims about open sexuality and free-form marriage common in Samoa which have since been challenged, but not effectively discredited, and her role as a popularizer of anthropology continues. "Mark does a fine job," writes Shelle Rosenfeld in *Booklist,* "of abstracting Mead's research and published works and showing why they were both critically acclaimed and criticized."

Mark's 2000 offering, *The Silver Gringo: William Spratling and Taxco,* focuses on the life of an American expatriate who managed, between the years 1929 and 1967, to transform the Mexican mining town of Taxco into a hub of silver manufacturing. As Mark details, Spratling's work as a silversmith is notable for its fine design and relation to the Mexican artifacts he collected.

In his review of the biography for *Library Journal,* Rex Klett notes Mark's "exhaustive research, interviews, and photographic study" and praised her work as "both scholarly and accessible."

Mark told *SATA:* "I write for children as I write for adults—a jargon-free narrative based on extensive research in primary sources. I write biographies—mostly of anthropologists. I try to make an honest, fair, in-depth evaluation of a person's life and work—while telling a good story with a lot of fascinating detail."

Biographical and Critical Sources

PERIODICALS

American Historical Review, June, 1996, p. 885.
Booklist, March 1, 1995, Alice Joyce, review of *The King of the World in the Land of the Pygmies,* p. 1164; April 1, 1999, Shelle Rosenfeld, review of *Margaret Mead: Coming of Age in America,* p. 1397.
Kirkus Reviews, December 1, 1998.
Library Journal, February 15, 1989, p. 164; February 1, 2000, Rex Klett, review of *The Silver Gringo,* p. 81.
Los Angeles Times, March 8, 1989.
New York Times Book Review, May 7, 1989, p. 20; April 9, 1995, p. 28.
Publishers Weekly, January 6, 1989, p. 95; February 13, 1995, review of *The King of the World in the Land of the Pygmies,* p. 72.
School Library Journal, March, 1999, p. 224.
Science, February 10, 1989, p. 823.

*　　*　　*

MATTERN, Joanne 1963-
(Joanne Gise, Theresa Grace, Grace Mabie, M. L. Roberts, Mary Scott)

Personal

Born March 5, 1963, in Nyack, NY; daughter of Robert F. (a banker) and Genevieve (a homemaker; maiden name, Porri) Gise; married James J. Mattern (a chef), June 16, 1990; children: Christina Xinwei. *Education:* Hartwick College, B.A. (English), 1985. *Religion:* Roman Catholic. *Hobbies and other interests:* Music, animal welfare, international adoption, baseball, needlework.

Career

Morrow Junior Books, New York City, assistant editor; Troll Publications, Mahwah, NJ, editor of children's books until 1995; freelance writer of children's books, 1990—; Institute of Children's Literature, West Redding, CT, instructor, 1997—. *Member:* Society of Children's Book Writers and Illustrators.

Writings

Young Martin Luther King Jr.: I Have a Dream, illustrated by Allan Eitzen, Troll, 1992.

Joanne Mattern

Brer Rabbit in the Briar Patch, Macmillan/McGraw-Hill, 1997.

I Can't Believe My Eyes! Extraordinary Photos of Ordinary Things, Macmillan/McGraw-Hill, 1997.

Telling Time with Goofy, Advance Publisher, 1997.

Smart Thinking! Clever Ways Animals Make Their Lives Easier, Macmillan/McGraw-Hill, 1997.

Tiger Woods: Young Champion, illustrated by Robert F. Goetzl, Troll, 1998.

(Contributor) *Encyclopedia of American Immigration,* 10 volumes, Grolier, 1998.

The Bighorn Sheep (part of "Wildlife of North America" series), Capstone (Mankato, MN), 1998.

The Coyote (part of "Wildlife of North America" series), Capstone (Mankato, MN), 1998.

Structures of Life, Delta Education, 1999.

Solar Energy, Delta Education, 1999.

Variables, Delta Education, 1999.

The Story of Molly Pitcher, McGraw-Hill, 1999.

The Trojan Horse, McGraw-Hill, 1999.

Big and Small, Homes for All: The Story of Bird Nests, Scott Foresman-Addison Wesley, 2000.

A Visit to the Past, Scott Foresman-Addison Wesley, 2000.

From Flowers to Honey: The Story of Beekeeping, Scott Foresman-Addison Wesley, 2000.

Mountain Climb, Scott Foresman-Addison Wesley, 2000.

Tower of Stone: The Story of a Castle, Scott Foresman-Addison Wesley, 2000.

Claws and Wings and Other Neat Things, McGraw-Hill, 2000.

Recycling with Mickey and Friends, Landoll, 2000.

Mickey's Home and Neighborhood Safety, Landoll, 2000.

Curse of Gold, Lyrick, 2000.

The Shoshone People, Capstone (Mankato, MN), 2001.

The Shawnee Indians, Capstone (Mankato, MN), 2001.

Coming to America: The Story of Immigration, Perfection Learning, 2001.

The Outrageous Animal Record Book, Perfection Learning, 2001.

Crazy Creatures of the World, Perfection Learning, 2001.

Crazy Creatures of Australia, Perfection Learning, 2001.

Going, Going ... Gone? Saving Endangered Animals, Perfection Learning, 2001.

Tom Cruise, Lucent (San Diego, CA), 2001.

Hi-Tech Communications, Enslow, 2001.

Telephones, Enslow, 2001.

100 American Heroes, Kids Books, 2001.

Lizards, Marshall Cavendish, 2001.

Sharks, Marshall Cavendish, 2001.

"ILLUSTRATED CLASSICS" SERIES; ADAPTOR

Mark Twain, *Adventures of Tom Sawyer,* illustrated by Ray Burns, Troll, 1990.

Twain, *Adventures of Huckleberry Finn,* illustrated by Ray Burns, Troll, 1990.

Robert Louis Stevenson, *Kidnapped,* illustrated by Steven Parton, Troll, 1992.

L. M. Montgomery, *Anne of Green Gables,* illustrated by Renee Graef, Troll, 1992.

The Merry Adventures of Robin Hood, illustrated by Susi Kilgore, Troll, 1992.

L. Frank Baum, *The Wonderful Wizard of Oz,* illustrated by Tom Newsom, Troll, 1993.

"A PICTURE BOOK OF" SERIES

A Picture Book of Birds, Troll, 1990.

A Picture Book of Dogs, Troll, 1990.

A Picture Book of Forest Animals, Troll, 1990.

A Picture Book of Underwater Life, Troll, 1990.

A Picture Book of Wild Animals, Troll, 1990.

A Picture Book of Cats, illustrated by Roseanna Pistolesi, Troll, 1991.

A Picture Book of Desert Animals, Troll, 1991.

A Picture Book of Farm Animals, Troll, 1991.

A Picture Book of Horses, Troll, 1991.

A Picture Book of Insects, illustrated by Janice Kinnealy, Troll, 1991.

A Picture Book of Animal Opposites, Troll, 1992.

A Picture Book of Night-Time Animals, Troll, 1992.

A Picture Book of Swamp and Marsh Animals, Troll, 1992.

A Picture Book of Water Birds, Troll, 1992.

A Picture Book of Wild Cats, Troll, 1992.

A Picture Book of Baby Animals (also see below), Troll, 1993.

A Picture Book of Flowers (also see below), Troll, 1993.

A Picture Book of Reptiles and Amphibians (also see below), illustrated by Janice Kinnealy, Troll, 1993.

A Picture Book of Butterflies and Moths (also see below), illustrated by Roseanna Pistolesi, Troll, 1993.

A Picture Book of Baby Animals, A Picture Book of Butterflies and Moths, A Picture Book of Flowers, and *A Picture Book of Reptiles and Amphibians* have also been published, each with audiocassette, in the "A Picture Book of ... Read Alongs" series by Troll in 1993.

ACTIVITY BOOKS

Home Alone 2 Activity Book, Troll, 1992.
Last Action Hero Activity Book, Troll, 1993.
Inspector Gadget Coloring/Activity Book, Troll, 1993.
Thanksgiving Coloring and Activity Book, Troll, 1994.
Summer Fun Fill-in Book, Troll, 1996.
School Days Memory Book, Troll, 1997.
Back to School Puzzle Fun, Troll, 1998.
Teletubbies Giant Coloring Activity Book, Modern, 2000.

"ANIMAL MINI-BOOKS" SERIES

Reptiles and Amphibians, illustrated by Lynn M. Stone, Troll, 1993.
Bears, illustrated by Tom Leeson and Pat Leeson, Troll, 1993.
Lions and Tigers, illustrated by Lynn M. Stone, Troll, 1993.
Monkeys and Apes, Troll, 1993.
Australian Animals, Troll, 1993.
Baby Animals, illustrated by Lynn M. Stone, Troll, 1993.

"WORLD'S WEIRDEST ANIMALS" SERIES

World's Weirdest Reptiles, Troll, 1995.
World's Weirdest Sea Creatures, Troll, 1995.
World's Weirdest Bugs, Troll, 1995.
World's Weirdest Birds, Troll, 1995.
World's Weirdest Dinosaurs, Troll, 1996.
World's Weirdest Bats, Troll, 1996.

"GREAT BEGINNINGS FIRST LEARNING BOOKS" SERIES

Alphabet Party, Troll, 1995.
Amazing Animals, Troll, 1995.
Happy Surprises, Troll, 1995.
Holiday Fun, Troll, 1995.
Rainy Day Fun, Troll, 1995.

"WISHBONE CLASSICS" SERIES; ADAPTOR

Homer, *The Odyssey,* HarperCollins (New York, NY), 1996.
Howard Pyle, *The Merry Adventures of Robin Hood,* HarperCollins (New York, NY), 1996.
Charles Dickins, *Oliver Twist,* illustrated by Ed Parker and Kathryn Yingling, HarperCollins (New York, NY), 1996.
Robert Louis Stevenson, *The Strange Case of Dr. Jekyll and Mr. Hyde,* HarperCollins (New York, NY), 1996.
Sir Walter Scott, *Ivanhoe,* illustrated by Ed Parker and Kathryn Yingling, HarperCollins (New York, NY), 1997.

"FIRST START EASY READERS" SERIES

Good Night, Bear!, illustrated by Susan T. Hall, Troll, 1998.
Candytown, Troll, 1998.
A Special Letter, Troll, 1998.
Halloween Parade, Troll, 1999.
Inchworm Helps Out, Troll, 1999.
Come Back, Class Pet!, Troll, 2000.
Head, Shoulders, Knees, and Toes, Troll, 2000.

"COMPETE LIKE A CHAMPION" SERIES

Gymnastics: The Vault, Rourke, 1999.

Gymnastics: The Balance Beam and Floor Exercises, Rourke, 1999.
Gymnastics: The Pommel Horse and Rings, Rourke, 1999.
Gymnastics: The Uneven Parallel Bars, Rourke, 1999.
Gymnastics: The Parallel Bars and Horizontal Bar, Rourke, 1999.
Gymnastics: Training and Fitness, Rourke, 1999.

"BARBIE FIRST-GRADE WORKBOOKS" SERIES

Hands-on English, Modern, 1999.
Hands-on Math, Modern, 1999.
Hands-on Phonics, Modern, 1999.
Hands-on Reading and Writing, Modern, 1999.

"SAFETY FIRST" SERIES

Safety on the Go, Abdo & Daughters, 2000.
Safety in Public Places, Abdo & Daughters, 2000.
Safety at School, Abdo & Daughters, 2000.
Safety in the Water, Abdo & Daughters, 2000.
Safety on Your Bicycle, Abdo & Daughters, 2000.

"ANIMAL GEOGRAPHY" SERIES

Africa, Perfection Learning, 2000.
Asia, Perfection Learning, 2000.
Australia, Perfection Learning, 2001.
Europe, Perfection Learning, 2001.
North America, Perfection Learning, 2001.
South America, Perfection Learning, 2001.

"LEARNING ABOUT CATS" SERIES

The Abyssinian Cat, Capstone, 2000.
The Main Coon Cat, Capstone, 2000.
The Persian Cat, Capstone, 2000.
The Siamese Cat, Capstone, 2000.
The Birman, Capstone, 2001.
The Exotic, Capstone, 2001.
The Ragdoll, Capstone, 2001.
The Sphinx, Capstone, 2001.

Safety at School *is part of a series of informational books for young readers in which Mattern offers instructions and advice about staying safe in everyday situations. (Photo by Peter Arnold, Inc.)*

Mattern has written a biography of golf pro Tiger Woods for the 'History Makers' series, books that focus on the formative early experiences of famous people. (From Tiger Woods: Young Champion, *illustrated by Robert F. Goetzl.*)

FISHER-PRICE LITTLE PEOPLE STICKER WORKBOOKS

Fisher-Price Little People Sticker Workbooks: Alphabet Zoo, Modern, 2000.
Fisher-Price Little People Sticker Workbooks: Numbers Train, Modern, 2000.
Fisher-Price Little People Sticker Workbooks: Opposite Park, Modern, 2000.

"EXPLORERS" SERIES

John and Sebastian Cabot, Raintree/Steck-Vaughn, 2000.
Samuel De Champlain, Raintree/Steck-Vaughn, 2000.
Vasco Da Gama, Raintree/Steck-Vaughn, 2000.
Henry Hudson, Raintree/Steck-Vaughn, 2000.
Ferdinand Magellan, Raintree/Steck-Vaughn, 2000.

"BEATING THE ODDS" SERIES

Breaking Barriers: Athletes Who Led the Way, Perfection Learning, 2001.
Courageous Comebacks: Athletes Who Defied the Odds, Perfection Learning, 2001.
Record Breakers: Incredible Sports Achievements, Perfection Learning, 2001.
Teamwork: Working Together to Win, Perfection Learning, 2001.

OTHER

Author of books under various pseudonyms, including Joanne Gise, Theresa Grace, Grace Mabie, M. L. Roberts, and Mary Scott.

Sidelights

Joanne Mattern told *SATA:* "I always knew my future lay in books. As a child I wrote stories about anything I could think of, while becoming a voracious reader. During high school and college I worked in the local library and planned to pursue a career in library science. But fate stepped in during my senior year of college when I was offered an internship at Morrow Junior Books. After just a few days in the office, I knew the world of children's books was for me. I was lucky enough to land a job at Morrow after I graduated. Working under the guidance of other editors and editing books by such authors as Beverly Cleary and Norma Fox Mazer taught me invaluable lessons about working with authors to make their books the best they could be.

"But it wasn't until I moved on to an editorial position at Troll that my writing career took shape. Troll was a very hands-on publishing house, and editors were expected and encouraged to be writers as well. When my boss found out I love animals, I was immediately assigned the 'Picture Book of' series. Things just took off from there!

"I left Troll in 1995 to pursue a career as a freelance writer and editor. Working for myself has allowed me to pursue many different projects. Being a full-time writer isn't easy, but the rewards are terrific. You're touching the lives of children and helping them learn about the world. If I can get a child excited about science, about reading, I feel like I've made a difference in the world."

Biographical and Critical Sources

PERIODICALS

Appraisal, autumn, 1991, review of *A Picture Book of Cats* and *A Picture Books of Insects,* p. 95; spring, 1993, review of *A Picture Book of Butterflies and Moths,* p. 106.
Horn Book, fall, 1991, review of *A Picture Book of Cats* and *A Picture Books of Insects,* pp. 305, 302.
Library Talk, May, 1993, review of *A Picture Book of Butterflies and Moths,* p. 42.
School Library Journal, January, 1994, Fay L. Matsunaga, review of *A Picture Book of . . . Read Alongs,* p. 74; January, 2000, Susan Knell, review of *Safety at School* and *Safety in Public Places,* p. 124, and Lucinda Snyder Whitehurst, review of *Safety in the Water, Safety on the Go,* and *Safety on Your Bicycle,* p. 124.

MATTHEWS, Caitlín 1952-

Personal

Given name pronounced "*katch*-leen"; born January 2, 1952, in Portsmouth, Hampshire, England; daughter of Frederick (a recorder) and Olive (Woodward) Stillwell; married John K. B. Matthews (a writer), February, 1976; children: Emrys T. *Education:* Attended the Webber-Douglas Academy of Dramatic Art, 1969-71. *Religion:* Animist. *Hobbies and other interests:* Vocal music; performing Celtic and medieval harps, sruti, and psaltery.

Addresses

Office—BCM Hallowquest, London WC1N 3XX, England. *Agent*—Regula Noetzli, 4096 County Rte. 83, Pine Plains, NY 12567.

Career

Writer and mystic. Ordained priestess, Fellowship of Isis; minister in Circle of the Sacred Earth. Conductor of shamanic and ritual practice in Oxford, England; presenter of seminars and shamanic workshops at schools and other gatherings throughout Great Britain, Australia, Italy, the United States, and elsewhere, on topics related to the Western spiritual tradition; has appeared as an expert on documentaries, including *The New Age,* 1991, *Desperately Seeking Something,* 1996, and *The Quest for the Holy Grail,* Discovery Channel, 1998. Co-presider, with John Matthews, of Order of Bards, Ovates, and Druids, 1989-92; cofounder, with John Matthews and Felicity Wombwell, Foundation for Inspirational and Oracular Studies, *BCM Hallowquest. Member:* Society of Authors.

Writings

FOR CHILDREN

My Very First Book of Princesses, Barefoot (Brooklyn, NY), 1997.
The Barefoot Book of Princesses, illustrated by Olwyn Whelan, Barefoot (Brooklyn, NY), 1998.
The Blessing Seed: A Creation Myth for the New Millennium, illustrated by Alison Dexter, Barefoot (Brooklyn, NY), 1998.
(Compiler, with husband, John Matthews) *The Wizard King and Other Spellbinding Tales,* illustrated by Jenny Press, Barefoot (Brooklyn, NY), 1998.
(Compiler) *While the Bear Sleeps: Winter Tales and Traditions,* illustrated by Judith Christine Mills, Barefoot (Brooklyn, NY), 1999.

FOR ADULTS; WITH HUSBAND, JOHN MATTHEWS

The Western Way: A Practical Guide to the Western Mystery Tradition, Routledge (Boston, MA), 1985-86.
The Aquarian Guide to British and Irish Mythology, illustrated by Chesca Potter, Aquarian (Northamptonshire, England), 1988.

The Arthurian Book of Days: The Greatest Legend in the World Retold throughout the Year, Macmillan (New York, NY), 1990.
Taliesin: Shamanism and the Bardic Mysteries in Britain and Ireland, Aquarian (London, England), 1991.
Ladies of the Lake, Aquarian (London, England), 1992.
The Faery-Tale Reader, Aquarian (London, England), 1993.
The Little Book of Celtic Wisdom, Element (Boston, MA), 1993.
The Arthurian Tarot (with cards), Aquarian (London, England), 1993.
Encyclopedia of Celtic Wisdom: The Celtic Shaman's Sourcebook, Element (Boston, MA), 1994.
British and Irish Mythology: An Encyclopedia of Myth and Legend, illustrated by Chesca Potter, Diamond (London, England), 1995.
(Compiler) *The Little Book of Celtic Lore,* Element (Boston, MA), 1998.
The Winter Solstice: The Sacred Traditions of Christmas, Quest (Wheaton, IL), 1998.

OTHER

The Search for Rhiannon (poetry), Bran's Head, 1981.
Mabon and the Mysteries of Britain: An Exploration of the Mabinogian, illustrated by Chesca Potter, Arkana (New York, NY), 1987.

Caitlín Matthews

Arthur and the Sovereignty of Britain: King and Goddess in the Mabinogian, illustrated by Chesca Potter, Arkana, 1989.

(With Rachel Pollack) *Tarot Tales,* Hutchinson (London, England), 1989.

The Elements of the Celtic Tradition, Element (Longmead, Shaftesbury, Dorset), 1989, Element (Rockport, MA), 1992.

The Elements of the Goddess, Element (Rockport, MA), 1989.

(With Prudence Jones) *Voices from the Circle: The Heritage of Western Paganism,* Aquarian (London, England), 1990.

Voices of the Goddesses: A Chorus of Sibyls, Aquarian (London, England), 1990.

Sophia—Goddess of Wisdom: The Divine Feminine from Black Goddess to World-Soul, Mandala (London, England), 1991.

The Celtic Book of the Dead: A Guide for Your Voyage to the Celtic Otherworld (with cards), illustrated by Danuta Mayer, St. Martin's (New York, NY), 1992.

The Arthurian Tarot Course: A Quest for All Seasons, Harper (New York, NY), 1993.

(Compiler and translator) *The Little Book of Celtic Blessings,* Element (Rockport, MA), 1994.

Singing the Soul Back Home: Shamanism in Daily Life, Element (Rockport, MA), 1995.

The Celtic Book of Days: A Celebration of Celtic Wisdom, illustrated by Stuart Littlejohn and Gill Potter, Macmillan (Dublin), 1995, published as *The Celtic Book of Days: A Daily Guide to Celtic Spirituality and Wisdom,* Destiny (Rochester, VT), 1995.

Celtic Devotional: Daily Prayers and Blessings, Harmony (New York, NY), 1996.

In Search of Woman's Passionate Soul: Revealing the Daimon Lover Within, Element (Rockport, MA), 1997.

(Compiler and translator) *The Little Book of Celtic Lore,* Element (Rockport, MA), 1998.

The Celtic Spirit: Daily Meditations for the Turning Year, HarperSanFrancisco, 1999.

The Celtic Wisdom Tarot, illustrated by Olivia Rayner, Destiny, 1999.

Celtic Love: Ten Enchanted Tales, HarperSanFrancisco, 2000.

Author of poetry, including contributions in *Poetry London,* edited by Tambimuttu. Contributor to periodicals, including *Temenos, Orion,* and *Beltane Papers,* and to anthologies.

Matthews' books have been translated into Danish, German, French, Italian, Czech, Polish, Greek, Hebrew, Spanish, Dutch, and Japanese.

Work in Progress

Celtic Wisdom Sticks: An Ogam Oracle, a divination set; *Remembering the Ancestors: The Art of Generational Healing; Troytown Dances,* a novel.

Sidelights

The Reverend Caitlín Matthews brings her expertise in Western spiritual traditions to her writing for children. In such books as *The Blessing Seed: A Creation Myth for the New Millennium* and *While the Bear Sleeps: Winter Tales and Traditions,* she relates tales based on myths drawn from a variety of religious traditions and cultures, all using what *Booklist* contributor Shelley Townsend-Hudson praised as a "relaxed conversational narrative [style], which flows with the ease of oral storytelling." Other works for young readers include *The Wizard King and Other Spellbinding Tales* and *The Barefoot Book of Princesses,* both of which feature short stories drawn from a variety of cultures. Compiled with her husband, John Matthews, *The Wizard King* contains nine tales that have roots in many storytelling traditions, but all of which feature a powerful enchanter at their core. Commenting on the thought-provoking short stories collected in *The Barefoot Book of Princesses, Booklist* contributor Shelle Rosenfeld asserted that "these well-written, fresh stories feature a diverse group of women who prove money and status don't preclude them from flaws and fateful situations."

In *The Blessing Seed* Matthews reinterprets the story of the creation of all things. Drawing from both Christian and Jewish traditions, she shows God's reaction to man and woman's eating from the Tree of Life in a positive, rather than damning light. As God says to the frightened couple in Matthews' story, "I made human beings for their longing to know—it is time for you to explore the four paths": wonder, emptiness, making, and coming home. After they are clothed, expelled from Paradise, forced to work for survival, and sent to find the blessing seed that God has promised will be revealed once sufficient understanding has been attained, the first humans gain strength from their new experiences in a "rewarding" book that a *Kirkus Reviews* critic maintained "has a place on many shelves." However, Lee Bock noted in *School Library Journal* that the story's unconventional approach—Matthews' self-described intent to replace "the notion of original sin with one of 'original blessing'"—might be "questioned by some, particularly those whose Biblical interpretations are strict."

The winter months have traditionally spawned a host of tales, as people of many cultures have come together to share warmth, food, and camaraderie during the long, dark season. In *While the Bear Sleeps,* Matthews collects stories from Ireland, Africa, Russia, Canada, and other lands, connecting them through the framing story of a young girl who befriends a hibernating brown bear after climbing into its cave to escape the cold. Through the pair's connected dreams while asleep, the bear and the girl travel around the world to learn of many cultures and their traditions surrounding the end of the year, the birth of Christ, and other wintertime events. In her review for the *Times Educational Supplement,* critic Adele Geras praised the work as a "wonderfully inclusive book, ... one which gives us a fascinating glimpse into different celebrations."

A student of Western spiritual traditions, Matthews has authored a number of books with her husband that explore various aspects of shamanism, Celtic spirituality, the Tarot, and Goddess cults. A trained actress, she lectures and performs programs that relate time-honored, historical traditions to contemporary society with an eye to their practical application in the modern world.

Biographical and Critical Sources

PERIODICALS

Booklist, November 15, 1998, Shelle Rosenfeld, review of *The Barefoot Book of Princesses,* pp. 583-584; November 15, 1999, Shelley Townsend-Hudson, review of *While the Bear Sleeps,* p. 627.
Books for Keeps, May, 1998, Elaine Moss, review of *The Blessing Seed,* p. 6.
Kirkus Reviews, August 1, 1998, review of *The Blessing Seed,* p. 1122.
Publishers Weekly, August 10, 1998, review of *The Barefoot Book of Princesses,* p. 387.
School Librarian, winter, 1999, Chris Brown, review of *While the Bear Sleeps,* p. 222.
School Library Journal, September, 1998, Lee Bock, review of *The Blessing Seed,* p. 176; November, 1998, Yapha Nussbaum Mason, review of *The Barefoot Book of Princesses,* p. 108; December, 1998, Sally Margolis, review of *The Wizard King and Other Spellbinding Tales,* p. 110; October, 1999, Lisa Falk, review of *While the Bear Sleeps,* p. 69.
Times Educational Supplement, December 24, 1999, Adele Geras, review of *While the Bear Sleeps,* p. 26.

ON-LINE

Hallowquest Web site, http://www.hallowquest.org.uk/ (July 6, 2000).

*   *   *

MAYNE, William (James Carter) 1928- (Martin Cobalt, Dynely James, Charles Molin)

Personal

Born March 16, 1928, in Kingston upon Hull, Yorkshire, England; son of William (a doctor) and Dorothy (a homemaker; maiden name, Fea) Mayne. *Education:* Cathedral Choir School, Canterbury, England, 1937-42; three years of additional education in Yorkshire. *Religion:* Church of England. *Hobbies and other interests:* Vintage cars, composing music, building additions to his home.

Addresses

Home and office—Parson Hill, Thornton Rust, Leyburn, Yorkshire, England. *Agent*—David Higham Associates Ltd., 5-8 Lower John St., Golden Square, London W1R 4HA, England.

Career

Writer for children and young adults, educator, and composer. Deakin University, Geelong, Victoria, Australia, lecturer, 1976; Rolle College, Exmouth, Devon, England, fellow in creative writing, 1979-80. Representative, Rural District Council, for his village, Thornton Rust.

Awards, Honors

Carnegie Medal commendation, British Library Association (BLA), 1955, for *A Swarm in May,* and for *The Member for the Marsh* and *Choristers' Cake,* both 1956; Carnegie Medal, BLA, 1957, for *A Grass Rope;* Lewis Carroll Shelf Award, 1968, for *Earthfasts;* Carnegie Medal honor book designation, 1970, for *Ravensgill;* honor listing, International Board on Books for Young People (IBBY), 1978, for *A Year and a Day;* Kurt Maschler Award runner-up, 1983, for *The Mouldy;* writing award for Great Britain, IBBY, 1984, for *All the King's Men; Boston Globe/Horn Book* Award, 1989, for *Gideon Ahoy!;* Phoenix Award honor book designation, Children's Literature Association, 1990, for *Ravensgill,* and 1991, for *A Game of Dark;* Guardian Award, 1993, for *Low Tide;* Kurt Maschler Award, 1997, for *Lady Muck;* Children's Books of the Century nomination, 2000, for *A Swarm in May.*

William Mayne

Writings

"CATHEDRAL CHOIR SCHOOL" SERIES; MIDDLE-GRADE FICTION

A Swarm in May, illustrated by C. Walter Hodges, Oxford University Press (London, England), 1955, Bobbs-Merrill (Indianapolis, IN), 1957.

Choristers' Cake, illustrated by C. Walter Hodges, Oxford University Press, 1956, Bobbs-Merrill (Indianapolis, IN), 1958.

Cathedral Wednesday, illustrated by C. Walter Hodges, Oxford University Press (London, England), 1960.

Words and Music, illustrated by Lynton Lamb, Hamish Hamilton (London, England), 1963.

"EARTHFASTS" SERIES; YOUNG ADULT FANTASIES

Earthfasts, Hamish Hamilton, 1966, Dutton (New York, NY), 1967.

Cradlefasts, Hodder (London, England), 1995.

Candlefasts, Hodder (London, England), 2000.

"DORMOUSE TALES" SERIES; AS CHARLES MOLIN; PICTURE BOOKS; ILLUSTRATED BY LESLIE WOOD

The Lost Thimble, Hamish Hamilton (London, England), 1966.

The Steam Roller, Hamish Hamilton (London, England), 1966.

The Picnic, Hamish Hamilton (London, England), 1966.

The Football, Hamish Hamilton (London, England), 1966.

The Tea Party, Hamish Hamilton (London, England), 1966.

"HOB STORIES"; PRIMARY-GRADE FANTASIES

The Yellow Book of Hob Stories (also see below), illustrated by Patrick Benson, Philomel (New York, NY), 1984.

The Blue Book of Hob Stories (also see below), illustrated by Patrick Benson, Putnam (New York, NY), 1984.

The Green Book of Hob Stories (also see below), illustrated by Patrick Benson, Putnam (New York, NY), 1984.

The Red Book of Hob Stories (also see below), illustrated by Patrick Benson, Putnam (New York, NY), 1984.

The Book of Hob Stories (omnibus; contains *The Yellow Book of Hob Stories, The Blue Book of Hob Stories, The Green Book of Hob Stories, The Red Book of Hob Stories*), illustrated by Patrick Benson, Walker, 1991, Candlewick (Cambridge, MA), 1997.

Hob and the Goblins, illustrated by Norman Messenger, Dorling Kindersley (London, England and New York, NY), 1994.

Hob and the Pedlar, Dorling Kindersley (London, England), 1997, published in the United States as *Hob and the Peddler,* Dorling Kindersley (New York, NY), 1997.

"ANIMAL LIBRARY" SERIES; PRIMARY-GRADE FANTASIES

Come, Come to My Corner, illustrated by Kenneth Lily, Prentice-Hall (New York, NY), 1986.

Corbie, illustrated by Peter Visscher, Prentice-Hall (New York, NY), 1986.

Tibber, illustrated by Jonathan Heale, Prentice-Hall (New York, NY), 1986.

Barnabas Walks, illustrated by Barbara Firth, Prentice-Hall (New York, NY), 1986.

Lamb Shenkin, illustrated by Jonathan Heale, Prentice-Hall (New York, NY), 1987.

A House in Town, Prentice-Hall (New York, NY), 1987.

Leapfrog, illustrated by Barbara Firth, Prentice-Hall (New York, NY), 1987.

Mousewing, illustrated by Martin Baynton, Prentice-Hall (New York, NY), 1987.

OTHER FICTION AND PICTURE BOOKS

Follow the Footprints, illustrated by Shirley Hughes, Oxford University Press (London, England), 1953.

The World Upside Down, illustrated by Shirley Hughes, Oxford University Press (London, England), 1954.

The Member for the Marsh, illustrated by Lynton Lamb, Oxford University Press (London, England), 1956.

The Blue Boat, illustrated by Geraldine Spence, Oxford University Press (London, England), 1957, Dutton, 1960.

A Grass Rope, illustrated by Lynton Lamb, Oxford University Press (London, England), 1957, Dutton, 1962.

The Long Night, illustrated by D. J. Watkins-Pitchford, Basil Blackwell (Oxford, England), 1957.

Underground Alley, illustrated by Marcia Lane Foster, Oxford University Press (London, England), 1958, Dutton, 1961.

(With R. D. Caesar, under joint pseudonym Dynely James) *The Gobbling Billy,* Dutton, 1959, Gollancz (London, England), 1959; reissued under authorship William Mayne and Dick Caesar, Brockhampton Press (Leicester, England), 1969.

The Thumbstick, illustrated by Tessa Theobald, Oxford University Press (London, England), 1959.

Thirteen O'Clock, illustrated by D. J. Watkins-Pitchford, Basil Blackwell (Oxford, England), 1959.

The Rolling Season, illustrated by Christopher Brooker, Oxford University Press (London, England), 1960.

The Fishing Party, illustrated by Christopher Brooker, Hamish Hamilton, 1960.

Summer Visitors, illustrated by William Stobbs, Oxford University Press (London, England), 1961.

The Glass Ball, illustrated by Janet Duchesne, Hamish Hamilton (London, England), 1961, Dutton, 1962.

The Changeling, illustrated by Victor Adams, Oxford University Press (London, England), 1961, Dutton, 1963.

The Last Bus, illustrated by Margery Gill, Hamish Hamilton (London, England), 1962.

The Twelve Dancers, illustrated by Lynton Lamb, Hamish Hamilton (London, England), 1962.

The Man from the North Pole, illustrated by Prudence Seward, Hamish Hamilton (London, England), 1963.

On the Stepping Stones, illustrated by Prudence Seward, Hamish Hamilton (London, England), 1963.

A Parcel of Trees, illustrated by Margery Gill, Penguin (London, England), 1963.

Plot Night, illustrated by Janet Duchesne, Hamish Hamilton (London, England), 1963, Dutton, 1968.

Water Boatman, illustrated by Anne Linton, Hamish Hamilton (London, England), 1964.

Sand, illustrated by Margery Gill, Hamish Hamilton (London, England), 1964.

A Day without Wind, illustrated by Margery Gill, Dutton, 1964.

Whistling Rufus, illustrated by Raymond Briggs, Hamish Hamilton (London, England), 1964, Dutton, 1965.

The Big Wheel and the Little Wheel, illustrated by Janet Duchesne, Hamish Hamilton (London, England), 1965.

No More School, illustrated by Peter Warner, Hamish Hamilton (London, England), 1965.

Pig in the Middle, illustrated by Mary Russon, Hamish Hamilton (London, England), 1965, Dutton, 1966.

Rooftops, illustrated by Mary Russon, Hamish Hamilton (London, England), 1966.

The Old Zion, illustrated by Margery Gill, Hamish Hamilton (London, England), 1966, Dutton, 1967.

The Battlefield, illustrated by Margery Russon, Dutton, 1967, Hamish Hamilton (London, England), 1967.

The Big Egg, illustrated by Margery Gill, Hamish Hamilton (London, England), 1967.

The Toffee Join, illustrated by Shirley Hughes, Hamish Hamilton (London, England), 1968.

The Yellow Aeroplane, illustrated by Trevor Stubley, Hamish Hamilton (London, England), 1968, Nelson (Nashville, TN), 1974.

The House on Fairmont, illustrated by Fritz Wegner, Dutton, 1968, Hamish Hamilton (London, England), 1968.

Over the Hills and Far Away, Hamish Hamilton (London, England), 1968, published in the United States as *The Hill Road,* Dutton, 1969.

Ravensgill, Dutton, 1970, Hamish Hamilton (London, England), 1970.

A Game of Dark, Dutton, 1971.

Royal Harry, Hamish Hamilton (London, England), 1971, Dutton, 1972.

The Incline, illustrated by Trevor Stubley, Dutton, 1972.

Skiffy, illustrated by Nicholas Fisk, Hamish Hamilton (London, England), 1972.

Robin's Real Engine, illustrated by Mary Dinsdale, Hamish Hamilton (London, England), 1972.

(Under pseudonym Martin Cobalt) *The Swallows,* Heinemann, 1972, published in the United States as *Pool of Swallows,* Nelson (Nashville, TN), 1974.

The Jersey Shore, Dutton, 1973.

A Year and a Day, illustrated by Krystyna Turska, Dutton, 1976, illustrated by John Lawrence, Candlewick, 2000.

Party Pants, illustrated by Joanna Stubbs, Hodder and Stoughton (London, England), 1977.

IT, Hamish Hamilton (London, England), 1977.

Max's Dream, illustrated by Laszlo Acs, Hamish Hamilton (London, England), 1977, Greenwillow (New York, NY), 1978.

While the Bells Ring, illustrated by Janet Rawlins, Hamish Hamilton (London, England), 1979.

Salt River Times, illustrated by Elizabeth Honey, Greenwillow (New York, NY), 1980.

The Mouse and the Egg, illustrated by Krystyna Turska, Julia MacRae (London, England), 1980, Greenwillow (New York, NY), 1981.

The Patchwork Cat, illustrated by Nicola Bayley, Knopf (New York, NY), 1981.

Winter Quarters, J. Cape, 1982.

Skiffy and the Twin Planets (sequel to *Skiffy*), Hamish Hamilton (London, England), 1982.

All the King's Men, J. Cape, 1982, Delacorte, 1988.

The Mouldy, illustrated by Nicola Bayley, Knopf, 1983.

Underground Creatures, Hamish Hamilton (London, England), 1983.

A Small Pudding for Wee Gowrie, illustrated by Martin Cottam, Macmillan (London, England), 1983.

Drift, J. Cape, 1985, Delacorte, 1986.

Kelpie, J. Cape, 1987.

A House in Town, illustrated by Sarah Fox-Davies, Walker, 1987.

Tiger's Railway, illustrated by Juan Wijngaard, Walker, 1987.

The Blemyahs, illustrated by Juan Wijngaard, Walker, 1987.

Gideon Ahoy!, Viking Kestrel (Harmondsworth, England), 1987, Delacorte, 1989.

The Farm that Ran Out of Names, J. Cape, 1989.

Netta, Hamish Hamilton (London, England), 1989.

Antar and the Eagles, Walker, 1989, Doubleday, 1990.

Netta Next (sequel to *Netta*), Hamish Hamilton (London, England), 1990.

The Second-Hand Horse and Other Stories, Heinemann, 1990.

Rings on Her Fingers, Hamish Hamilton (London, England), 1991.

Low Tide, J. Cape, 1992, Delacorte, 1993.

And Never Again, illustrated by Kate Aldous, Hamish Hamilton (London, England), 1992.

The Egg Timer, illustrated by Anthony Lewis, Heinemann, 1993.

Cuddy, J. Cape, 1994.

Bells on Her Toes, illustrated by Maureen Bradley, Hamish Hamilton (London, England), 1994.

Pandora, illustrated by Dietlind Blech, Knopf, 1996.

The Fox Gate and Other Stories, illustrated by William Geldart, Hodder, 1996.

The Fairy Tales of London Town, Volume 1: *See-Saw Sacredown,* Volume 2: *Upon Paul's Steeple,* illustrated by Peter Melnyczuk, Hodder, 1996.

Midnight Fair, Hodder, 1997.

Lady Muck, illustrated by Jonathan Heale, Houghton (Boston, MA), 1997.

In Natalie's Garden, illustrated by Peter Dale, Walker, 1998.

Captain Ming and the Mermaid, Hodder, 1999.

EDITOR

(With Eleanor Farjeon) *The Hamish Hamilton Book of Kings,* illustrated by Victor Ambrus, Hamish Hamilton (London, England), 1964, published as *A Cavalcade of Kings,* Walck, 1965.

(With Farjeon) *A Cavalcade of Queens,* illustrated by Victor Ambrus, Walck, 1965, published in England as *The Hamish Hamilton Book of Queens,* Hamish Hamilton (London, England), 1965.

(As Charles Molin) *Spooks, Spectres,* Hamish Hamilton (London, England), 1967, David White (New York, NY), 1968.

The Hamish Hamilton Book of Heroes, illustrated by Krystyna Turska, Hamish Hamilton (London, England), 1967, published as *William Mayne's Book of Heroes,* Dutton, 1968.

The Hamish Hamilton Book of Giants, illustrated by Raymond Briggs, Hamish Hamilton (London, England), 1968, published as *William Mayne's Book of Giants,* Dutton, 1969.

Ghosts: An Anthology, Nelson (Nashville, TN), 1971, Hamish Hamilton (London, England), 1971.

Supernatural Stories, illustrated by Martin Salisbury, Kingfisher (London, England and New York, NY), 1996.

OTHER

Contributor to *Over the Horizon; or, Around the World in Fifteen Stories,* Duell, Sloan and Pearce, 1960, and to periodicals. Composer of incidental music for *Holly from the Bongs,* a play by Alan Garner, 1965. Some of Mayne's books have been translated into Spanish. His works are housed in a permanent collection at the Children's Literature Research Collection, State Library of South Australia, Adelaide.

Adaptations

Earthfasts was released on audio cassette by Chivers.

Sidelights

A prolific author of fiction and picture books and an editor, William Mayne is considered one of the major, if not the major, English contributors to the fields of children's and young adult literature. He has been praised as a phenomenon, a genius with a totally original voice and vision. For nearly fifty years, Mayne has produced works in a variety of genres—fantasies, historical fiction, contemporary realistic fiction, school stories, adventure stories, ghost stories, detective stories, folktales, and allegories, among others—that are recognized for reflecting both the brilliance and the enigmatic character of their creator. Mayne often writes extremely ambitious books that deal with serious problems and with sophisticated subjects and ideas; however, he also writes more lighthearted works, especially picture books and stories for young children. Several of his books are considered classics and tour de forces and are often commended as outstanding contributions to their respective genres. Although some of Mayne's works are very accessible, others are thought to be difficult for less skilled readers due to their density, subtlety, absence of strong narrative flow, and idiosyncratic writing style. However, Mayne has been celebrated for broadening the limits of juvenile literature and for contributing to its artistry. He is also respected for preparing his young readers for the style, content, and complexity of adult literature and for influencing other writers for children to forego straight narratives, simplistic language, and superficial themes for deeper, more creative approaches. In addition, Mayne has edited several well-received anthologies, some in collaboration with respected English author Eleanor Farjeon, that focus on royalty, legendary heroes, and supernatural figures such as ghosts and giants.

In his works, Mayne describes the interplay of the past, the present, people, and place in a poetic manner that stresses cosmic awareness through locale and the perceptions of his young male and female protagonists. His books are steeped in English history, tradition, and legend, a characteristic that is credited with giving a mythic quality to many of them. Considered a master of the evocation of landscape and atmosphere, the author generally sets his books in Yorkshire, his birthplace and current residence, although some are also set in Wiltshire, Somerset, Scotland, Wales, New Zealand, and the United States, among other places. Often acknowledged for his ability to tell his stories from the authentic perspective of a child, Mayne is praised for his sensitivity to and understanding of children as well as for his keen observations of human nature in general. He is also commended for his creation of a wide range of characters, all of whom are considered individual and distinctive; several of the author's works portray the alliance between the very old and the very young. Thematically, Mayne addresses such subjects as human relationships, the nature of time, the connection between reality and the supernatural, and the impact of the past on the present. In addition, he combines old tales and the belief in the supernatural with present-day situations; the result of this is that, in Mayne's books, the usual often becomes the unusual. The children in his works are often involved in mysteries, treasure hunts, and quests and deal with supernatural events. Through their experiences, these characters show bravery and resourcefulness and are able to come to terms with their own personal realities. Considering Mayne's themes as a whole, a reviewer in the *Times Literary Supplement* commented that his works present "an extraordinarily hopeful picture of the way people can live together, and how much this state of affairs depends on respect, tolerance, and affection."

Mayne is often celebrated for his gifts as a literary stylist; writing in *Signal,* Charles Sarland called him "the most assured stylist of all modern children's authors." Characteristically, Mayne writes in a poetic, oblique, and concise style that stresses dialogue and uses such techniques as inversion, wordplay, and grammatical shifts. Despite the often serious nature of his stories, the author invests them with a playful, whimsical humor that he reflects in his wordplay and use of puns; he also uses allusions, private jokes, dialect, invented language, and deliberate misspellings. Mayne is often considered a master of writing dialogue and of writing about everyday things as if he were seeing them for the first time. Though he has been praised lavishly for his books, Mayne has also been criticized as the creator of eccentric, overly demanding works that have little appeal to the young. Due to the sophistication of his prose and the darkness of his subjects and themes, he is sometimes perceived as an adult author masquerading as a writer of children's books. Some reviewers have contended that his works are emotionally detached, self-indulgent, and repetitive, and that his overall output is uneven. However, most observers contend that Mayne's books present a wise and profound world view while coming from an extremely personal perspective. In addition, reviewers have noted that young people who are introduced to his works will meet a writer who will provide them with powerful, memorable literary experiences.

Since the beginning of his career, critics have lauded Mayne's talents as extraordinary. Writing in her *Intent upon Reading,* Margery Fisher stated, "Unique among writers for children is William Mayne . . . . [The] child who plunges into his stories has found a companion for life, no less," while Margaret Meek of the *School Librarian* said that Mayne "is in a class by himself." Writing in *In Review,* Helen Stubbs commented that Mayne "has given to the world of children's literature a contribution that vibrates with intimations of immortality." Frank Eyre, writing in his *British Children's Books in the Twentieth Century,* called Mayne "the one living writer of real stature who has already established a secure reputation. Whatever else he may write from now on, he has written sufficient to demonstrate an instinctive understanding of the real nature of children, an infallible, sure ear for the truth of children's conversations, and a subtle, complex way of looking at life, people, and things which makes him unique among contemporary writers." Eyre concluded, "I think him the truest and most creative of those few major authors who are genuinely writing *for* children."

At the same time, reviewers noted the difficulty that Mayne presents in the field of juvenile literature. John Rowe Townsend stated in his *A Sense of Story,* "Next to Enid Blyton, the name of William Mayne is probably the one most likely to start an argument about children's books," while *Signal* contributor Sarland commented that Mayne is "the great 'problem' amongst modern children's writers." However, recent critics appear to have come to an understanding of Mayne. Michele Landsberg, writing in her *Reading for the Love of It,* noted that he "is particularly unclassifiable; there is no more assured and skillful writer in the whole field of children's literature." Peter Hunt of *Twentieth-Century Children's Writers* added that, for all of his virtues, Mayne's status "remain[s]," for many, "ambiguous," yet his "influence has been pervasive . . . in his mild and ironic way, [he has] expanded the capacities of children's books." In a later edition of the same source, Hunt added, "As more critics turn to children's literature, Mayne's genius is being analysed more and appreciated more and more, and his reputation seems likely to grow."

Born in Kingston upon Hull, Yorkshire, Mayne is the son of a doctor and a homemaker and is one of five children, three girls and two boys. From an early age, Mayne was attracted to writing. He wrote in his essay for *Third Book of Junior Authors,* "I began to want to write when I was eight or nine. I knew nothing about it, but it seemed to be the proper thing to do . . . . I think I knew it would be a good excuse for hiding among my own thoughts, away from the rest of the family . . . . I think it is important for everybody to be able to get away from others. It is certainly important for me to be able to, but since I like being with other people too, and want them to know it, what I do when I am alone is to think about other times and places, and write books about

them. It shows me that when I am in my own withdrawn world, I am still in the real one." As a boy, Mayne read such books as *Robinson Crusoe, The Water Babies, Gulliver's Travels,* and, as he wrote in his essay for *Something about the Author Autobiography Series (SAAS),* "a certain book about ants that I had borrowed from a library several times." After reading these books, he decided that he "would write down the things that I thought, and have them printed . . . ."

Mayne demonstrated talent in music as well as in literature. At nine, he won a scholarship to the prestigious choir school at Canterbury Cathedral. During World War II, the school moved to Cornwall to escape German air raids, and Mayne sang services in various churches there. He decided to resist formal examinations and, as he wrote in *SAAS,* "to give the rest of the world the go-by. It was a timid stubbornness, but all I had." Mayne stayed at the choir school until his voice broke at thirteen. He used his experiences there as the basis for his "Cathedral Choir School" series, a quartet of realistic stories for primary graders; later, he wrote the incidental music for *Holly from the Bongs,* a play by Alan Garner, an author to whom Mayne has been compared. After leaving the choir school, he attended Yorkshire schools for another three years, spending this time and an additional four years teaching himself to write. Mayne set his deadline for becoming a published writer as his twenty-first birthday; he agreed to become a doctor like his father if he did not reach his goal. "Without knowing what I was doing, without consulting the experts in travel, without a word to anyone, I bought a ticket to writing for a living," Mayne commented in *SAAS.* He wrote poetry, but then decided to write stories; "in books," he noted, "people are alive." Before Mayne turned twenty-one, Oxford University Press expressed interest in one of his books; although they sent it back, he had written another by that time, "which was better organised; or they had become used to me," he commented in *SAAS.* This book, *Follow the Footprints,* became his first published work.

Released in 1953, *Follow the Footprints* is a mystery story that Mayne used as the blueprint for several of his subsequent works. Two siblings, Caroline and Andrew Blake, become involved in a hunt for hidden treasure after they move to an old tollhouse in the Cumberland countryside. After they hear local legends about a treasure hidden in an abbey, the children set out to find it and encounter danger before things are set right in the end. A reviewer in *Junior Bookshelf* predicted, "Children will greatly enjoy this story . . . . It moves swiftly and is really mysterious and exciting." The critic added that Mayne has a "delightful touch of wit and his children . . . are thoroughly tolerable." Writing in another issue of the same magazine, Hamish Fotheringham stated that *Follow the Footprints* introduced a motif "which William Mayne has developed with freshness and originality." Fotheringham noted that Mayne portrays Caroline and Andrew as being "staunchly independent, clever, but never too clever, thank goodness, and neither precocious nor prigs"; the critic concluded, "This framework of well described country setting, local

Using alliteration, dialect, diminutives, rhyming couplets, and invented words to create a unique pig-language, Mayne tells the story of a couple of pigs whose greed prevents them from selling their truffles to buy a grand coach. (From Lady Muck, *illustrated by Jonathan Heale.)*

legends, excellently drawn pen portraits, sparkling dialogue, and a plot rich in incidents is used by the author in his other 'treasure hunt' stories." Writing in his *A Sense of Story,* John Rowe Townsend said that *Follow the Footprints* is "in many ways characteristic, and could not be mistaken for the work of anyone else."

In 1955, Mayne produced *A Swarm in May,* the first of his quartet of "Cathedral Choir School" stories. Based on the author's experiences as a boarder at the choir school at Canterbury Cathedral, the series, which also includes *Choristers' Cake, Cathedral Wednesday,* and *Words and Music,* is praised for its fresh approach to the often hackneyed genre of the school story. In addition, Mayne is highly regarded for his characterizations and evocation of place; several reviewers have commented that the cathedral is itself as much a character as any of the boys or teachers in the stories. In *A Swarm in May,* John Owen, the youngest Singing Boy, discovers that he must take on the major role in the school's traditional Beekeeping ceremony. John—called by his surname—must sing a solo before the bishop on a Sunday in May; in addition, he must recite the ritual that assures the bishop that the organist will supply good beeswax candles for the cathedral during the coming year. Owen also becomes involved in a mystery and finds the haunts of the earliest beekeeper to the cathedral. At the end of the story, Owen collects bees with the aid of an odd-smelling globe that is attached to a large key by a chain that he has found, and he performs successfully in the

ritual ceremony. Marcus Crouch, writing in his *Treasure Seekers and Borrowers: Children's Books in Britain 1900-1960,* stated that, with *A Swarm in May,* "it became apparent that a major novelist had arrived. *A Swarm in May* was, of all outmoded things, a boarding-school story, but there had never been a school-story quite like this . . . . Mayne's book, like all his subsequent books, was whole and indivisible . . . but the writing was the catalyst. Mayne's prose was a delicate, sensitive instrument, exactly suited to its purpose." In his *A Sense of Story,* John Rowe Townsend stated that, at the time of its publication, *A Swarm in May* "seemed then, and seems now, an outstanding piece of work . . . . Within its limits—and in this case I believe the limits were a source of strength—it is as near to perfection as any children's book of its decade." Townsend concluded that *A Swarm in May* "gives the impression that it might have been written by a marvellously talented schoolboy, a literary Mozart." Writing in his *The Promise of Happiness: Value and Meaning in Children's Fiction,* Fred Inglis predicted that Mayne "is unlikely to write a better book . . . . It has all the Mayne qualities: fine dialogue (the way in which the characters of the different masters are brought out in discussion is remarkable) and a lovingly observed *mise-en-scene* superbly served by one of his best plots." *A Swarm in May* was the first of Mayne's books to receive a major prize, receiving a Carnegie Medal commendation in 1955. It was also nominated as one of the Children's Books of the Century in 2000.

Subsequent volumes of the "Cathedral Choir School" series introduce social and moral issues as well as new characters. For example, in *Choristers' Cake,* Peter Sandwell (nicknamed Sandy) is an older boy who is having difficulty fitting in with the cooperative society of the school. Sandy tries to resist being upgraded to the rank of chorister, an action that leads him to be ostracized by the other boys. Finally, he realizes that he has been behaving inappropriately and changes. In *Cathedral Wednesday,* an epidemic hits the school and depletes much of the student body. Consequently, day student Andrew Young is promoted to Acting Head Boy, a situation that causes problems with the two choristers below him in seniority. Andrew realizes that he must accept his responsibility fully, and he ends up putting these boys on the prefect's list. The "Cathedral Choir School" series is generally considered one of Mayne's most outstanding achievements. Margaret Sherwood Libby of the *New York Herald Tribune Book Review* stated, "The simplicity and potency of William Mayne's writing is extraordinary. Every since we read of the choir school in *A Swarm in May* and *Choristers' Cake,* the boys and their teachers . . . have been as surely a part of our life as the girls of Orchard House or Thumb, Thimble, and Nod." Writing in *The Use of English,* Edward Blishen stated, "The little group of books he wrote about life in a choir school . . . stand slightly apart from the rest. They form a loving tribute to a special way of life. The stories embody characteristic themes— the impact on the present of complex mysteries with their roots in the past, the conflict of attitudes to tradition, the relationships of the young and their elders—but, to my mind, exist as an achievement separate from the rest. They include some of William Mayne's best inventions...." Hamish Fotheringham of the *Junior Bookshelf* noted, "Thanks to William Mayne's art-aided perhaps by having actively shared the milieu—there is nothing 'pye' about the choristers. They remain boys throughout, with whom the reader can identify himself, not surpliced and ruffled little angels." In a review of *Words and Music* in the *School Librarian and School Library Review,* John Ashlin concluded that Mayne "understands the workings of a prep schoolboy's mind as perhaps no one else does."

In 1957, Mayne produced *A Grass Rope,* a story that is often considered the first of his works to explore time and space and the impact of the past on the present. This book, which revolves around a Yorkshire legend about a unicorn and a pack of hounds, features Mary, a young girl who believes in fairies, and her friend Adam, the Head Boy of the grammar school, who believes in the legend but has a more scientific approach. The children, along with Mary's older sister and a cousin, track the source of the legend and search for the silver collars of the hounds, who are thought to have disappeared at the time of the Crusades. Only Mary sees the magical possibilities of the quest: she believes that the hounds have been summoned underground by fairies and that a unicorn was among them. Since she knows that unicorns can only be captured by a grass rope woven by a maiden, Mary weaves a rope in readiness. After she throws her rope down an old mine shaft, Mary succeeds in locating the collars. A critic in the *Junior Bookshelf* wrote of Mayne, "No one could be more traditional in his material; no one could touch the dead material of the adventure story into vivid life with each sure, individual and wonderful magic." The critic concluded, "*A Grass Rope* is an original and enchanting book. No one else could have written it." In her *Intent upon Reading,* Margery Fisher said, "It is certainly not inappropriate to use the word 'magic' of a story where the author makes you aware of the irrational all the time, the poetic below the events of ordinary life, and does this while keeping his characters absolutely real, not eccentric or peculiar, but people with character and drive and personal idiom." Helen Stubbs of *In Review* added that Mayne "makes everything which goes into the conception of a unicorn ... count. He is able to capture for us the essential truth of the basic idea. With Mary, whose faith can move mountains, and who can unerringly follow her own imaginative direction to the end, we find ourselves following with our own grass rope." Writing in *The Use of English,* Edward Blishen noted that, in Mayne's stories, "[f]antasy and realism are beautifully enmeshed," a quality that "is at its best, in my opinion, in *A Grass Rope, ...* in which the various possible interpretations of the near-magical events has its convincing advocate among the characters: a child who believes in magic, a clever boy who brings scientific reasoning to the quest, the children's parents who are simply sensible about it all. The conclusion is perfectly poised: the reader may believe any of the explanations, and perhaps that reader is most worthy of the author who manages to believe all of them. This is a very serious achievement of

William Mayne's, I think: to preserve such an active and enchanting neutrality as between all the levels of our experience. Beside this achievement, much writing for children ... falls awfully short." *A Grass Rope* received the Carnegie Medal in 1957.

With *Earthfasts,* Mayne wrote a fantasy for young adults that is often considered his signature work. Based on an eighteenth-century Yorkshire legend about a drummer boy who went into a hole in the rock of Richmond Castle in search of King Arthur's treasure and was never seen again, the book features two contemporary boys, David Wix and Keith Heseltine, who encounter the drummer boy Nellie Jack John after he emerges from the cave, still beating his drum. Nellie Jack is carrying a candle that burns with an inextinguishable cold flame and possesses unusual powers; David becomes drawn to the candle, which is the Candle of Time, and begins to experiment with it. The worlds of the everyday and the supernatural start to mesh: magical creatures that have been asleep spring to life, including "The Sleepers," King Arthur and his Knights of the Round Table, who have become stone figures frozen in time. David finds himself pulled into the subterranean world of the legend, where time is different. It is up to Keith to return the candle, which has been taken from King Arthur's table, in order to restore the natural order. At the end of the novel, Keith enters the cave and replaces the Candle of Time in its stone socket on the Round Table. Arthur and his knights change back to stone, and time is brought back into balance. Underscoring the story is Nellie Jack John's reaction to the twentieth century and his difficulty in adjusting to it; although he longs to go back to his own time, Nellie Jack John decides to try to live in the strange new world in which he has found himself.

Reviewers generally applauded *Earthfasts,* which takes its name from the stones that rise from the earth during dry seasons and soil that moves in plowed land. Writing in *Twentieth-Century Children's Writers,* Pamela Cleaver called the novel "a brilliant use of fantasy, intricately plotted, exciting and perceptive.... [T]he delicate way that David sees the drummer boy's problems when he meets the 20th century head on is masterly." A reviewer in the *Junior Bookshelf* called *Earthfasts* "a book in a thousand; William Mayne at his very considerable best, and quite impossible to put down from start to finish." Writing in her *The Green and Burning Tree: On the Writing and Enjoyment of Children's Books,* Eleanor Cameron said that *Earthfasts* puts Mayne "triumphantly among that small group who have shown such an audacious and original grasp of the possibilities of time fantasy [and lures us into] another kind of magic." John Rowe Townsend stated in *A Sense of Story* that, with *Earthfasts,* Mayne "at last surpassed his early work." Townsend continued, "The sheer sweep of *Earthfasts,* swift and wide and totally under control, has never been matched by Mayne.... It marks a breakthrough...." Writing in her *The Hills of Faraway: A Guide to Fantasy,* Diana Waggoner claimed that *Earthfasts* is "one of the best of all fantasies, a classic of speculative literature."

Nearly thirty years after the publication of *Earthfasts,* Mayne created a sequel, *Cradlefasts.* Five years later, he produced another sequel, *Candlefasts.* These books again feature David, Keith, and Nellie Jack John. In *Cradlefasts,* which takes place a year after the ending of *Earthfasts,* the drummer boy is still looking for a way to get back to his own time. The novel has as its theme the emotionality of life and death. David meets a seven-year-old girl, Donna Clare, at a bowling alley and becomes convinced that she may be his sister, whom he thought died years ago with their mother. The boy is further convinced by the fact that Donna Clare possesses a toy that he had left at the hospital for his mother to give to his baby sister when she was born. The novel explores the mystery of Donna Clare's identity while examining David's feelings of grief and loss. In his review in *Junior Bookshelf,* Marcus Crouch called *Cradlefasts* "beautifully written, with characters three-dimensional in their consistency and waywardness"; he concluded by dubbing *Cradlefasts* its author's "finest book." In *Candlefasts,* Keith, David, and Nellie Jack John discover an opening to the past and encounter the Attercop, a giant spider. A reviewer in *Reading Matters* called *Candlefasts* "[b]rilliantly atmospheric" and added, "I really enjoyed this book."

During the 1970s and 1980s, Mayne created works that continued to cement his reputation as one of the most gifted—and unusual—writers of literature for the young. Three of his books published during this period—the young adult novels *Ravensgill, A Game of Dark,* and *The Jersey Shore*—are considered particularly representative examples of Mayne's qualities. *Ravensgill* describes how teenage cousins Bob and Judith reconcile a family quarrel that was prompted by an apparent murder committed by a member of one family against another. Ever since the murder took place forty-six years before, the respective families of the protagonists have been at odds. The cousins set out to solve the crime and end the bitterness that exists between their families. Unexpectedly, Bob finds a secret tunnel, an underground watercourse that provides a clue to the solution, and both he and Judith research the situation extensively. At the end of the novel, the teens clear the name of the main suspect in the crime, the late husband of Bob's grandmother, and bring about reconciliation. Bob's grandmother, both lovable and feisty, is considered one of Mayne's most fully realized characters. Writing in *New Statesman,* Leon Garfield said that *Ravensgill* is "his most considerable book for some time. In addition to the usual brilliance of his writing, there is a chilling depth that lends this story a rare excitement." A writer in the *Times Literary Supplement* stated, "No one now writes with more knowledge of and compassion for people in all their roles. And no one contributes more through sheer sensitivity and virtuosity of style and treatment to our increasing realization of children's fiction as an art in its own right."

A Game of Dark is often recognized as Mayne's most controversial book, a highly personal and introspective work that combines reality, fantasy, and psychology. The story features fourteen-year-old Donald Jackson, a boy who comes to terms with his dead sister, dying father, and aloof mother by entering into an alternate life as a squire in a vaguely medieval time. After killing the horrid worm that is terrorizing a feudal village, Donald is able to accept himself and deal with the death of his father and with his life in general. While it has been criticized for its bleakness, coldness, and grimness and is questioned as suitable for adolescent readers for what is interpreted as an Oedipal theme, *A Game of Dark* is also praised as an effective, moving, and daring work that reflects its author's ample talents. Robert Bell of the *School Librarian* commented, "It is becoming almost a *cliché* with reviewers to say that William Mayne's latest book is 'his most powerful to date,' but one cannot avoid saying it of this one."

The Jersey Shore is a novel set in the United States during the 1930s. When protagonist Arthur comes with his mother to stay with Aunt Deborah in a coastal village in New Jersey, he learns about his family's past from his grandfather, who had emigrated from England and now lives in a wooden house in the sand. Arthur hears the tales of his ancestors, who lived in the village of Osney in the East Anglian fens. The tales include one about a stranger who comes from the sea, a dark man hung with chains. The only survivor of a shipwreck, this man settled in the village and married a village girl. The grandfather also tells a story about his true love, whom he was never able to marry. Ten years after his visit to New Jersey, Arthur, who is now a tail gunner in the United States Air Force during World War II, is sent to East Anglia on assignment, and finds the village just as his grandfather described it. In the British edition of the book, Mayne clearly states that the stranger from the sea is an African slave and that Arthur, being his descendant, is black. Mayne also notes that Arthur's grandfather married Florence, who was born a slave, after coming to America. However, the American edition does not include these facts, which explain why Arthur's grandfather never married his true love. Writing in *Horn Book* about the United States edition of *The Jersey Shore,* Paul Heins stated, "The conclusion of the American edition ignores the fact that Arthur is black; but black he must be if Mayne's hints throughout the story are to have any meaning. In the American ending, Arthur's visits to Osney, his grandfather's original home, become a mere act of filial piety and destroys whatever emotional impact the book may have." Peter Hunt of *Twentieth-Century Children's Writers* concluded that the omissions do "violence to the clues laid earlier and to the spirit of the book."

Mayne continued to create well-received books in the 1980s and 1990s. Among the most popular are the "Hob Stories," picture books and fantasies for primary graders about a helpful English household spirit, and *Lady Muck,* a picture book that features a husband-and-wife team of comical pigs. In the stories that bear his name, Hob is a short, plump sprite who lives in a cutch, or cupboard, under the stairs of the homes in which he lives. At night, he does good deeds around the house and tries to banish discordant elements. The first four titles about Hob are "color" books—red, yellow, blue, and green, later collected in one volume as *The Book of Hob Stories*—in which Mayne tells short stories about Hob and the family he services, who are referred to generically. Hob can be seen only by Boy and Girl, not by Mr. or Mrs.; the family also contains Baby and the bird, Budgie. Hob deals with household nuisances, to which Mayne refers descriptively by function—Eggy Palmer, Hotfoot, Temper, Sootkin, Clockstop, etc.—as well as with a boggart. Through ingenuity, perceptiveness, and cunning, Hob puts things right and restores order. At night, Hob finds a gift left for him by the children. However, he cannot accept clothes: by receiving them, he must leave his home. Writing in *School Librarian*, Marcus Crouch said, "By telling use of many authentic details, William Mayne keeps his fantasy well within the bounds of belief and, and always, he enriches the simplest of stories with words tenderly selected and lovingly applied." John Stephens of *Children's Literature in Education* noted, "By introducing into this world a small, almost familiar element of the supernatural, he has been able to use narrative to represent, with remarkable clarity, some major philosophical issues in epistemology, ontology, language, and the imagination . . . . [C]hildren do begin speculating at an early age about such related questions as the nature of being, the existence of supernature, the problem of temporal decay, and the sources of fear, and Mayne's achievement here has been to find subtly indirect ways to express these questions."

Hob and the Goblins is Mayne's first longer story featuring the character. In this work, Hob has a new home, a house in the country called Fairy Cottage, and, since he has accepted a gift of clothes from a grateful human, a new family to serve. Hob must rescue the family he protects from evil forces, goblins who are intent on destroying the world. The spirit must also deal with a witch who is intent on undermining him. At the end of the story, Hob frees his family from the goblins and saves the world. A critic in *Kirkus Reviews* called *Hob and the Goblins* "[b]oth comical and suspenseful, a tour de force from one of Britain's greats," while a reviewer in *School Library Journal* called the story a "spellbinding fantasy with sparkling language that makes the existence of fairies and witches seem perfectly natural." In *Hob and the Pedlar* (published in the United States as *Hob and the Peddler*), Hob is invited into a peddler's traveling wagonhouse while searching for a new home. At their first stop, the peddler sells him to a family in order to help them discover the source of the strange things happening on their farm. In the pond beyond the farm, Hob finds a sea serpent's egg—stolen by the peddler, who has wrapped it in pieces of night sky. After rescuing the sea serpent's child and smoothing out the sky, Hob is rewarded with a well-deserved cup of tea. Virginia Golodetz of *School Library Journal* stated, "Mayne's rich, innovative use of language provides nourishment for serious readers of any age. This book can work as a solitary read or a read-aloud in families or classrooms. Don't miss it." Writing in the *Observer*, Kit Spring said, "Beautifully written, with well-created characters . . . , this is a book that deserves to be called a classic. . . ." Moira Robinson of *Magpies*

Mayne tells the warm story of Adam, the fairy child, and his year-and-a-day with the people who adopt him. (*From* A Year and a Day, *illustrated by John Lawrence.*)

concluded, "[T]his is a story that could have essentially been written during the last five hundred years and which, one hopes, will still be read and loved halfway through the next millennium."

Lady Muck, a picture book published in 1997, is a comic tale that is often acknowledged for the richness and inventiveness of its language. In this work, Sowk and Boark are old married pigs who put on airs but are affectionate with each other. When Boark discovers truffles while rooting for his wife, he decides to keep them for himself. However, Sowk discovers Boark's deception through a veneer of marital courtesy. Sowk convinces her husband to sell the truffles, so they go to market. Sowk comes up with several excuses to eat truffles secretly; finally, there is only one left. Boark uses the profit from it to buy a wheelbarrow in which to push his wife home. When the barrow splits in two, the pigs are muddy once more. However, Sowk doesn't care: she feels that her status has been elevated because now the neighbors call her Lady Muck. Mayne uses alliteration, dialect, diminutives, rhyming couplets, and invented words to create a unique language. Writing in *Bulletin of the Center for Children's Books,* Deborah Stevenson called *Lady Muck* a "luscious story of greed, rationalization, and pork" before concluding that what "makes this more than a tidily amusing tale is Mayne's language: both narration and dialogue are in a rich country pigalect that depends on rhythm and -y suffixes and flows like James Joyce; it's original enough to require a preperformance readthrough, but it makes the book sing." Stevenson advises prospective readers to "dump the inhibitions and be prepared to go the whole hog." Trevor Dickinson of the *School Librarian* predicted that *Lady Muck* may receive a mixed reception from readers, who may find that Jonathan Heale's woodcut illustrations "alone will make possession of it worthwhile. Others will find them more irritating than William Mayne's text. That text, however, will delight others with the willful, piggy liberties it takes with Standard English in these austere National Curriculum times." Writing in *Washington Post Book World,* Michael Dirda concluded, "With such peaty, nut-brown language, the story ... is almost tangential to the savoring of each sentence. As too few readers know, Mayne is one of the greatest children's authors of our time."

Mayne wrote in *Third Books of Junior Authors,* "I like writing books because it's private and comfortable." He added, "The difference between ordinary day-dreaming and what I do is quite small. I write the dreams down, dreamers dream. I don't know why I should be different from others in this way, though I am happy to be as I am." He added that when he is alone, he thinks about other times and places, "and writes books about them. It shows me that when I am in my own withdrawn world, I am still in the real one. And, of course, it doesn't feel like work." In an interview in *Children's Literature in Education,* Mayne commented, "I write for myself, but myself of long ago." He added in a postscript, "My public expression is what I write, and I don't see that 'I' am relevant. I am an observer who makes small temporary classifications, not an interpreter of anything." In his essay in *SAAS,* Mayne stated, "I still want to write everything I SEE: the fields lying patched with different colours across the haytime of the years; the trees and scraps of woodland stitched in relief on the background; in these details river lying blue or slate or white with cloud, a strange narrow pasture for other flocks; and behind them all the hillside rising beyond to its clifflike crest.... In under these hills are the cathedrals of nature herself, great caverns not yet trodden by man in his pilgrimage to read all the tablets and tombs of existence and leave his Latin jokes in the names of creatures and plants. Nature has built all that is needed, inventing the arch, the crypt, the spiral stair, the window; even the organ music of the wind. Somewhere, wandering through it all, am I, still trying to understand it, still impelled to try to sing, for no reason known to me. I wish to celebrate all the past times possible, and bring them closer to hand, out of the Latin of invisibility into the English of my understanding."

Mayne concluded, "Everything that can be remembered is history. History is the only thing that can be remembered, too. What is to happen cannot yet be known. After all, the existence of a ticket to it does not mean that the station is still standing, or was ever built.... But the ticket, whoever writes it, does not take us into the secret parts of our being: there we have to go alone.... We must travel to those places within us, to where in mystery is found one sandal of 1296 ..., to where there gleams once more the hidden wall-painting of an abandoned chapel—in a vast building such things can be.... I, if not you, wish to recall the strange taste of the king and queen sleeping their death away through a later war than any they knew. And now and then there comes to mind something of those maters, their strangeness, their distance, and their nearness come together, and I try to stretch out a hand either side and draw the differences together. And when I have thought of something I write it down; and that is all I set out to do, and I still know no better."

Biographical and Critical Sources

BOOKS

Authors & Artists for Young Adults, Volume 20, Gale, 1997.

Barker, Keith, *Outstanding Books for Children and Young People: The Library Association Guide to Carnegie/ Greenaway Winners, 1937-1997,* Bernan Associates/ Library Association Publishing, 1998.

Blishen, Edward, *The Thorny Paradise: Writers on Writing for Children,* Kestrel, 1975, pp. 65-76.

Blishen, *Good Writers for Young Readers,* Hart-Davis, 1977, pp. 79-85.

Cameron, Eleanor, "Fantasy," *The Green and Burning Tree: On the Writing and Enjoyment of Children's Books,* Little, Brown, 1969, pp. 3-136.

Children's Literature Review, Volume 25, Gale, 1991.

Contemporary Literary Criticism, Volume 12, Gale, 1979.

Crouch, Marcus, "Widening Horizons," *Treasure Seekers and Borrowers: Children's Books in Britain 1900-1960,* The Library Association, 1962, pp. 112-138.

Eyre, Frank, "Fiction for Children," *British Children's Books in the Twentieth Century,* revised edition, Longman Books, pp. 139-142.

Fisher, Margery, "Little Birds in Their Nests Agree: Family Stories," *Intent upon Reading: A Critical Appraisal of Modern Fiction for Children,* Brockhampton Press, 1961, pp. 280-281.

Fisher, *The Bright Face of Danger,* Horn Book, 1986, pp. 318-344.

Inglis, Fred, "History Absolves Nobody—Ritual and Romance," *The Promise of Happiness: Value and Meaning in Children's Fiction,* Cambridge University Press, 1961, pp. 213-231.

Landsberg, Michele, "Taking the Plunge," *Reading for the Love of It: Best Books for Young Readers,* Prentice-Hall, 1987, pp. 32-33.

Otten, Charlotte F. and Gary D. Schmidt, editors, *The Voice of the Narrator in Children's Literature: Insights from Writers and Critics,* Greenwood Press, 1989.

Something about the Author Autobiography Series, Volume 11, Gale, 1991.

Third Book of Junior Authors, edited by Doris De Montreville and Donna Hill, Wilson, 1972.

Townsend, John Rowe, "William Mayne," *A Sense of Story: Essays on Contemporary Writers for Children,* Lippincott, 1971, pp. 130-142.

Townsend, *A Sounding of Storytellers,* Lippincott, 1979, pp. 139-152.

Twentieth-Century Children's Writers, 3rd edition, edited by Tracy Chevalier, St. James, 1989.

Viguers, Ruth Hill, *A Critical History of Children's Literature,* Macmillan, 1969, pp. 567-600.

Waggoner, Diana, "A Bibliographic Guide to Fantasy," *The Hills of Faraway: A Guide to Fantasy,* Atheneum, 1978, p. 240.

PERIODICALS

Booklist, March 1, 1997, review of *Lady Muck,* p. 1167; November 1, 1997, review of *The Book of Hob Stories,* p. 473; January 1, 1998, reviews of *Lady Muck,* p. 736 and *Hob the Peddler,* p. 814.

Books for Keeps, May, 1998, Adrian Jackson, reviews of *Cuddy* and *Midnight Fair,* p. 30.

Bulletin of the Center for Children's Books, August, 1997, Deborah Stevenson, review of *Lady Muck,* p. 290.

Children's Literature, Volume 21, 1993, p. 101.

Children's Literature in Education, July, 1970, William Mayne, "A Discussion with William Mayne," pp. 48-55; March, 1989, John Stephens, "'I Am Where I Think I Am': Imagination and Everyday Wonders in William Mayne's Hob Stories," pp. 37-50; April, 1990, pp. 31-42.

Horn Book, December, 1973, Paul Heins, review of *The Jersey Shore,* p. 581; January-February, 1998, Martha V. Parravano, review of *Hob the Peddler,* p. 77.

In Review, winter, 1972, Helen Stubbs, "William Mayne's Country of the Mind," pp. 5-14.

Junior Bookshelf, July, 1953, review of *Follow the Footprints,* p. 121; December, 1957, review of *A Grass Rope,* pp. 318-319; October, 1959, Hamish Fotheringham, "The Art of William Mayne," pp. 185-189; December, 1966, review of *Earthfasts,* p. 386; August, 1993, p. 154; February, 1996, Marcus Crouch, review of *Cradlefasts,* pp. 38-39.

Kirkus Reviews, July 15, 1994, review of *Hob and the Goblins,* p. 990; March 3, 1997, review of *Lady Muck,* p. 386.

Magpies, March, 1998, Moira Robinson, review of *Hob and the Pedlar,* pp. 33-34.

New Statesman, November 6, 1970, Leon Garfield, review of *Ravensgill,* p. 608.

New York Herald Tribune Book Review, April 3, 1960, Margaret Sherwood Libby, review of *The Blue Boat,* p. 9.

New York Times Book Review, October 26, 1997, review of *Lady Muck,* p. 47.

Observer (London), April 12, 1998, Kit Spring, review of *Hob and the Pedlar,* p. 17.

Publishers Weekly, January 27, 1997, review of *Lady Muck,* p. 106; January 17, 2000, review of *A Year and a Day,* p. 58.

School Librarian, March, 1972, Robert Bell, review of *A Game of Dark,* pp. 63-64; September, 1972, Margaret Meek, review of *The Incline,* pp. 259-260; December,

1983, pp. 319-327; June, 1985, Marcus Crouch, review of *The Blue Book of Hob Stories* and *The Yellow Book of Hob Stories,* p. 131; February, 1997, Cherrie Warwick, review of *The Fairy Tales of London Town, Volume 2,* p. 33; August, 1997, Trevor Dickinson, review of *Lady Muck,* p. 147; spring, 1998, Janet Sumner, review of *Hob the Peddler,* p. 35; summer, 1998, Gillian Cross, review of *Midnight Fair,* p. 102; spring, 2000, Janet Fisher, review of *In Natalie's Garden.*

School Librarian and School Library Review, July, 1964, John Ashlin, review of *Words and Music,* pp. 206-207.

School Library Journal, April, 1997, Elaine E. Knight, review of *Lady Muck,* p. 138; May, 1997, Virginia Golodetz, review of *Lady Muck,* pp. 106-108; November, 1997, Wendy D. Caldiero, review of *The Book of Hob Stories,* p. 94; December, 1997, Virginia Golodetz, review of *Hob and the Peddler,* p. 126; November, 1998, review of *Hob and the Goblins,* p. 89.

Signal, September, 1976, Charles Sarland, "Chorister Quartet," pp. 107-113.

Times Literary Supplement, November 24, 1966, "William Mayne: Writer Disordinary," p. 1080; July 2, 1970, "Yorkshire Family Quarrel," p. 713.

The Use of English, autumn, 1978, Edward Blishen, "Writers for Children 2: William Mayne," pp. 99-103.

Washington Post Book World, October 5, 1997, Michael Dirda, review of *Lady Muck,* p. 11.

ON-LINE

Reading Matters, http://www.readingmatters.co.uk (January 31, 2000).

Taliesin's Successors: Interviews with Authors of Modern Arthurian Literature, http://www.lib.rochester.edu. (December 31, 2000), Raymond H. Thompson, "Interview with William Mayne."

—Sketch by Gerard J. Senick

* * *

McLEAN-CARR, Carol 1948-

Personal

Born April 10, 1948; daughter of Harold Albert Foster (a solicitor) and Winnifred Hopkins Holland; married Peter Fleming Aitken (a mammalogist), March, 1972 (died, 1982); married Donald McLean-Carr (an accountant), 1984; children: (first marriage) Zoe, Rachel, Ingrid. *Education:* University of South Australia, B.A. (illustration), 1984, graduate diploma in adult education, 1994, post-graduate studies, 1997—; Flinders University, post-graduate studies, 1990. *Hobbies and other interests:* Celtia, ancient history, archaeology, mammalogy, cooking, gardening, walking, "people, life, the world, the universe, and all that."

Addresses

Home—88 Albert St., Prospect, South Australia 5082, Australia. *E-mail*—mclean-carr@adelaide.on.net.

Career

Freelance illustrator. Department of Technical and Further Education, advanced skills lecturer in advertising and design, 1986-94. South Australian Museum of Natural History, Education Department, scientific illustrator. *Member:* Illustrators Association of South Australia (founding president, 1986-88), Australian Society of Authors, Illustrators Association of Australia.

Writings

SELF-ILLUSTRATED

Fairy Dreams, Omnibus (Norwood, South Australia), 1999, Scholastic (New York, NY), 2000.

ILLUSTRATOR

Rocky Marshall, *This Was My Valley,* Waratah Enterprises, 1983.

Australian First Aid, St. John's Ambulance Brigade, 1984.

Josephine Croser, *Nanna's Magic,* Childerset (Adelaide, South Australia), 1985.

Josephine Croser, *Crunch the Crocodile,* Ashton Scholastic, 1986, Scholastic (New York, NY), 1987.

Christobel Mattingley, *McGruer and the Goat,* Angus & Robertson, 1987.

Raggylug in Trouble, Longman Cheshire, 1987.

Janeen Brian, *Mr. Taddle's Hats,* Era (Flinders Park, South Australia), 1987.

Betty Zed, *The Cockatoo,* Era (Flinders Park, South Australia), 1987.

Yvonne Winer, *Never Snap at a Bubble,* Educational Insights, 1987.

Josephine Croser, *Clackymucky and the Bulldog,* Keystone (Flinders Park, South Australia), 1988.

Mysterious Monsters of the Past, Longman (London, England), 1988.

Anna Leditschke, *Tiny Timothy Turtle,* Collins Australia, 1989, Gareth Stevens, 1991.

Christobel Mattingley, *The Butcher, the Beagle, and the Dog Catcher,* Hodder & Stoughton, 1990.

Eleanor Nilsson, *A Lamb like Alice,* Angus & Robertson, 1990.

Jackie French, *The Roo That Won the Melbourne Cup,* Angus & Robertson, 1991.

Wendy Orr, *Bad Martha,* Angus & Robertson, 1991.

Sharon Dalgleish, *Boris the Magical Cat,* Keystone (Flinders Park, South Australia), 1992.

Kath Lock and Frances Kelly, *Freya,* Era (Flinders Park, South Australia), 1995.

Work in Progress

Two books for the Omnibus "Magic Lands" series; "downloadable e-books"; Web-based interactive children's books and activities "tied to learning as well as entertainment."

Sidelights

A native of London, Carol McLean-Carr immigrated with her parents to Australia in 1959. Though her early aspiration to be a commercial artist was hindered because, as she writes on her Web site, "for girls it was [teaching], nursing, or office work," the aspiring artist did not give up. "It took me till I was thirty to become the story book illustrator I had always wanted to be. By then I had a wealth of experience and life accidents to bring to it. I think it was worth the wait."

Interested mainly in "drawing as a discipline itself, printmaking, water colour, airbrushing, and coloured pencil work," McLean-Carr explained that she is also fascinated with using the computer as an art tool. "My recent obsession with computers comes from a determination that the drawing, rendering, pre-press and design skills learned in the pre-computer years are the very skills required in the future for the digital graphic artist. Computer art should not look like 'computer art'—the computer is just another painting tool. Where once entrance into a lucrative career in Web or games building meant anybody with a few software skills was king pin, now graphics people in the industry need to have both design training and experience and high level computing skills.

"With broadband technology for the Internet becoming a reality, publishing children's books on the World Wide Web is the exciting possibility for tomorrow. Although today it is very 'in' to talk of the demise of print based publishing and books, I believe books will stay with us, perhaps transformed into the digital book of MIT's design research, but with us nevertheless. Keep reading."

Biographical and Critical Sources

ON-LINE

Carol McLean-Carr Web site, http://www.bigblue.com.au (November 28, 2000).*

* * *

MEDINA, Jane 1953-

Personal

Born June 13, 1953, in Alhambra, CA; daughter of Harry R. (a civil engineer) and Anna M. (a secretary) Peirce; married Pablo Medina (a carpenter), June 14, 1980; children: Annie, Joey. *Education:* Azusa Pacific University, B.A., 1975; California State University, Fullerton, M.S., 1999. *Religion:* Christian. *Hobbies and other interests:* "Walking by the ocean, in the mountains, or just down the street—especially with my family."

Addresses

Home—773 South Breezy Way, Orange, CA 92869. *Office*—California Elementary School, 1080 North California St., Orange, CA 92869. *E-mail*—Demedina@ cs.com.

In **My Name Is Jorge on both Sides of the River,** *a book of poems in Spanish and English, Jane Medina describes the feelings of Jorge, who is trying to adjust to life as an immigrant after his family crosses the river from Mexico to the United States. (Illustrated by Fabricio Vanden Broeck.)*

Career

Orange Unified School District, Orange, CA, elementary music teacher, 1977-82, bilingual education teacher, 1982-96, parent educator, 1995-97, English-as-a-second-language skills center teacher, 1996-97, elementary education teacher, 1997-99, reading specialist, 1999—. California State University, Fullerton, CA, guest instructor, 1997, model lesson teacher, 1998, instructor, 1999—. *The Reading Teacher,* member of review team, 1999, member of executive review board, 1999—. Presenter at elementary schools. *Member:* International Reading Association, California Reading Association, Orange County Reading Association, National Council

of Teachers of English, National Association of Bilingual Educators, Teachers of English to Speakers of Other Languages, California Teachers of English to Speakers of Other Languages, National Education Association, Orange Unified Education Association, Society of Children's Book Writers and Illustrators, Southern California Council on Literature for Children and Young People.

Awards, Honors

Edwin Carr Fellowship, California State University, Fullerton, 1999; finalist, Tomas Rivera Mexican-American Children's Book of the Year, and Notable Book Award, National Council of Teachers of English, both 2000, both for *My Name Is Jorge on Both Sides of the River.*

Writings

My Name Is Jorge on Both Sides of the River, illustrated by Fabricio Vanden Broeck, Boyds Mills Press (Honesdale, PA), 1999.

Contributor of articles to educational journals, including *Language Arts* and *NEA Today,* and books, including *Portfolios in the Classrooms.*

Work in Progress

The Dream on Blanca's Wall, a poetry anthology in English and Spanish; *A Box of Squiggles,* a poetry anthology for young children.

Sidelights

Growing up in Garden Grove, California, poet Jane Medina recalled in a Boyds Mills Press release that she began writing letters and poems while still a teenager. Being sensitive to criticism from others, the budding poet refused to share her work with anyone but her closest friends. However, when writing a letter to thank the "editor of a book for teachers ... for the instruction and inspiration," Medina decided to enclose a short poem as well. "To my surprise," Medina explained, "the editor wrote back—not to thank me for the letter, but to ask if I had any more poetry." Soon after, Medina realized that she had a talent for capturing the emotions of children through her poetry and began work on a collection of children's poems, *My Name Is Jorge on Both Sides of the River.*

In *My Name Is Jorge on Both Sides of the River,* a book of poems written in both Spanish and English, Medina describes the thoughts and feelings of Jorge, a young boy trying to adjust to life in the United States. After his family crosses the river from Mexico, Jorge finds himself in a different world. While his parents keep their Mexican traditions and ways of life alive in the new country, Jorge is torn between fitting in with U.S. society and preserving his Mexican heritage. Throughout the collection of poems, Medina illustrates the challenges Jorge faces as he learns the language and customs of America. Describing the poems as "insightful," *School Library Journal* reviewer Ann Welton claimed the book "depicts the sometimes painful experience of adjusting to a new language and a new culture." A reviewer for *Horn Book Guide* praised the seriousness of Medina's collection, concluding: "Finally—bilingual poems that aren't overflowing with happy colors and tortilla chips."

Biographical and Critical Sources

PERIODICALS

Horn Book Guide, July-December, 1999, review of *My Name Is Jorge on Both Sides of the River,* p. 153.
School Library Journal, February, 2000, Ann Welton, review of *My Name Is Jorge on Both Sides of the River,* p. 136.

OTHER

Press release from Boyds Mills Press, 1999.

* * *

MOLIN, Charles
See MAYNE, William (James Carter)

* * *

MOONEY, Bill 1936(?)-

Personal

Born c. 1936 in Missouri.

Addresses

Office—P.O. Box 17493, Boulder, CO 80303. *E-mail*—BMooney303@aol.com.

Career

Storyteller and actor. Participant in storytelling festivals, including National Storytelling Festival, New Jersey Folk Festival, Jackson Storyfest, Alabama Tale-tellin' Festival, and Cave Run Festival. Storytelling performer for Holland America cruise line. Played role of Paul Martin on the American Broadcasting Company (ABC) soap opera *All My Children.* Guest on television shows, including the *Today Show, As the World Turns, One Life to Live, Loving,* and *The Guiding Light.* Appeared on and off-Broadway, including *A Man for All Seasons, Lolita, We,* and *The Brownsville Raid.* Appeared in motion pictures, including *Network, Beer,* and *A Flash of Green.*

Awards, Honors

Two-time Emmy nominee for role of Paul Martin on the ABC soap opera *All My Children;* Grammy nominee, 1995, Gold Award, Parents Choice, and Notable Chil-

dren's Recording, American Library Association, all for *Why the Dog Chases the Cat;* Grammy nominee, 1998, for *Spiders in the Hairdo: Modern Urban Legends.*

Writings

(With Donald J. Noone) *ASAP: The Fastest Way to Create a Memorable Speech,* Barron's (Hauppauge, NJ), 1992.
(Editor with David Holt) *Ready-to-Tell Tales: Surefire Stories from America's Favorite Storytellers,* August House (Little Rock, AK), 1994.
(And editor with David Holt) *The Storyteller's Guide: Storytellers Share Advice for the Classroom, Boardroom, Showroom, Podium, Pulpit, and Center Stage,* August House (Little Rock, AK), 1996.
(Reteller with David Holt) *Spiders in the Hairdo: Modern Urban Legends* (also see below), August House (Little Rock, AK), 1999.
(Editor with David Holt) *More Ready-to-Tell Tales from around the World,* August House (Little Rock, AK), 2000.

Coauthor, with David Holt, of produced play *Banjo Reb and the Blue Ghost.* Recorded storytelling performances with Holt include *Why the Dog Chases the Cat,* High Windy Audio, 1995; *Half Horse, Half Alligator,* August House Audio, 1997; and *Spiders in the Hairdo: Modern Urban Legends,* High Windy Audio, 1999.

Biographical and Critical Sources

ON-LINE

Bill Mooney, Storyteller, http://www.billmooney.com (April 23, 2001).

* * *

MORGAN, Pierr 1952-

Personal

First name is pronounced "peer"; born May 2, 1952, in Seattle, WA; daughter of Arthur (an interior designer) and Ruth (Orbison) Morgan (a homemaker); married Steve Leitz, 1974 (divorced, 1979); children: Aaron. *Education:* Attended University of Washington, 1970-73; Art Center College of Design, B.F.A. (painting; with distinction), 1987. *Hobbies and other interests:* Sketch-journaling, dancing, bookbinding, collage, sewing, bird watching, traveling, roller coasters, and chocolate.

Addresses

Home and office—421 West Roy St., #406, Seattle, WA 98119. *E-mail*—pierrless@juno.com.

Career

Freelance illustrator, 1973—. Guest lecturer at public schools, libraries, colleges, museums, and conferences across the country, 1989—. Children's Museum, Seattle, WA, artist-in-residence, 1999; Academy of Realist Art,

Seattle, instructor, "Making Children's Picture Books," 1999-2000. *Exhibitions:* Work exhibited at Mazza Collection, Art from Children's Books, Findlay, OH, 1993—; Children's Museum, 1999; and Bellevue Art Museum, Bellevue, WA. *Member:* Society of Children's Book Writers and Illustrators.

Awards, Honors

American Booksellers Association "Pick of the Lists" citation, Junior Library Guild Selection, *Book Links* Top Ten Picture Book, *Bank Street* Notable Book, American Library Association Notable Book, New York Public Library "100 Titles to Be Read and Shared" list, and *Booklist* Editors' Choice, all 1996, all for *The Squiggle.*

Writings

SELF-ILLUSTRATED; FOR CHILDREN

(Adapter) *The Turnip: An Old Russian Folktale,* Philomel Books (New York, NY), 1990.

(Reteller) *Supper for Crow: A Northwest Coast Indian Tale,* Crown (New York, NY), 1995.

ILLUSTRATOR; FOR CHILDREN

Nellie Edge, *Kids in the Kitchen,* Peninsula Publishing, 1975.

Geoffrey Williams, *Treasures of the Barrier Reef,* Price, Stern (Los Angeles, CA), 1988.

Geoffrey Williams, *Adventures beyond the Solar System,* Price, Stern (Los Angeles, CA), 1988.

Gus Cazzola, *The Bells of Santa Lucia,* Philomel Books (New York, NY), 1991.

Marilyn Hollinshead, *The Nine Days Wonder,* Philomel Books (New York, NY), 1994.

Janine Scott, *When Critters Get the Jitters,* Shortland Publications, 1996.

Carole Lexa Schaefer, *The Squiggle,* Crown, 1996.

Nancy Luenn, *The Miser on the Mountain: A Nisqually Legend of Mount Rainier,* Sasquatch Books (Seattle, WA), 1997.

Carole Lexa Schaefer, *Sometimes Moon,* Crown, 1999.

Carole Lexa Schaefer, *Snow Pumpkin,* Crown, 2000.

Christine Widman, *Cornfield Hide and Seek,* DK Ink, in press.

Also contributor of illustrations to *Ladybug, Spider,* and *Cricket* magazines. Also illustrator of *My Personal Tutor 1st and 2nd Grade,* by Microsoft Corporation, a three-set CD-ROM production.

Work in Progress

Illustrations for Carole Lexa Schaefer's *One Wheel Wobbles,* for Candlewick Press. Several short stories, several picture books, and a show of still lifes in oils on canvas.

Sidelights

Pierr Morgan is primarily an illustrator of picture books for children who has also adapted folktales and Native American legends for her own self-illustrated titles.

Unlike some authors and illustrators who stumble upon a career in children's books quite by accident, Morgan made an early commitment to the craft. She once commented to *SATA:* "Writing and illustrating children's books has been my focus since I was eleven years old. At seven I wrote in my diary, 'I want to be a famous poet when I grow up.' So I wrote poetry. At nine I knew I would be an artist as well, and so I illustrated my poetry. My sixth grade teacher read Newbery Award books to us, such as *The Bronze Bow* and *Island of the Blue Dolphins.* It was at that point that I knew I wanted to write books that well and illustrate them. Maurice Sendak's *Where the Wild Things Are* and his Caldecott Award for the work were my inspiration."

Born in 1952, Morgan grew up in Seattle, Washington, "with five larger-than-life brothers and sisters, an award-winning, self-employed, interior-designer, garden-keeping father, and a world-class homemaker, play-the-piano-by-ear, singing, crossword puzzle-loving, read-aloud mother," as the author-illustrator told *SATA.* "I fell in love with books and the magic to be found in them early on."

However, it was the artwork in the books she read that really reached Morgan. "Real drawing was reserved for school," Morgan told *SATA.* "And even then I dabbled around. Things I did in kindergarten were more profound, perhaps, in terms of 'talent.' I was told I was talented, but I never wanted to be singled out for it. Somehow I knew it takes more than talent to be able to really do what you want in life. Children are not idiots. They are very perceptive. And I knew simply from observation that people are ridiculed and beaten and cast out for being 'different,' talented, smarter than the rest. I went underground. Subconsciously, of course. I knew it was better to gather information and teach myself than to blossom and die on the bush too quickly. There would be a time for me later."

Morgan started her writing and illustration while still in school. "For years my goal was to have a children's book that I had written and illustrated published by Harper & Row in New York. So I paid attention to the market, wrote stories and sent them out—bad ones, I admit. But rejection didn't stop me. I tried other publishers and kept tabs on editors and names of favorite authors and illustrators. I had quite a collection of new and old first edition children's books in college. My major, through general studies at the University of Washington, was 'writing and illustrating children's books.' I had an instructor as my sponsor and took every related class I could think of: children's dramatics, children's literature, storytelling, short story writing."

For one drama class assignment, Morgan created a six-page, wordless book on movement that her teacher liked so much that she wanted to make copies for all the students in class. Morgan, however, savvy to the ways of publishing, felt there was something special about these drawings and put the book away for many years. Meanwhile, she got on with her studies only to encounter difficulties with her major. "I met with a snag in the art department," Morgan recalled for *SATA,* "and was told I'd have to become a graphic design major to take the classes I wanted, and that was a five-year program. So I dropped out. I would teach myself, I decided."

Morgan spent the next two years reading children's books and creating note cards and coloring books to sell in shops and street fairs. Determined never to have a nine-to-five job, she decided she would support herself with her art. That is, however, much easier said than done. She married in 1974, had a child, and then divorced in 1979. A single mom for several years, she finally returned to school—art school this time—and earned a bachelor of fine arts degree in painting in 1987.

Though her first publication credit came in 1975, it was not until 1988 that she was regularly illustrating children's books. She provided the artwork for a pair of education books by Geoffrey Williams; then came, in 1991, the illustrations for Gus Cazzola's *The Bells of Santa Lucia.* These were later shown in an original art show, along with the illustrations from her first self-illustrated book, *The Turnip.*

Morgan's second self-illustrated title, *Supper for Crow,* is a retelling of a Northwest Coast Indian tale. Raven, up to his old tricks, tells Mama Crow that he is going to help her get some seal meat for her children, only to substitute a rock for the food. Then he proceeds to trick these young birds into believing that he is preparing the meat for them while instead eating the meat himself. As Patricia Lothrop Green noted in *School Library Journal,* the tale is a morality lesson "on greed and on trust." Green went to observe, "The illustrations effectively pair black ink outlining with soft gouache bodycolor: the style is bold and dynamic." Susan Dove Lempke, reviewing the book in *Bulletin of the Center for Children's Books,* felt that Morgan "tells the story with a sprightly lilt and creates a cast of jaunty birds." Lempke found especially notable Morgan's "skill in painting landscapes with the sea, sand, and pine trees of the Pacific Northwest."

Since that title, Morgan has concentrated primarily on illustrating other writers' texts. Her artwork for Marilyn Hollinshead's *The Nine Days Wonder* complemented this tale of Elizabethan England in which a Shakespearean performer boasts that he can dance from London to Norwich in less than ten days. Morgan's accompanying illustrations were praised by Kay Weisman in *Booklist:* "Morgan's colorful gouache and India ink illustrations bring the text to life." Leda Schubert, reviewing the same title in *School Library Journal,* commented on Morgan's "[l]ively illustrations" and her "backgrounds [which] feature rural England and village scenes." A reviewer for *Publishers Weekly* felt that Morgan's artwork for *The Nine Days Wonder* was "colorful and dynamic," noting in particular a "joyous, whimsical" spread of two playful hares.

Finally, in 1996, the work of over two decades was published. The wordless picture book on movement that

Morgan had created for a drama class while at the University of Washington had grown over the years. A trip to China further inspired Morgan to work on this project; she showed it to publishers, who all felt that she needed a storyline to make the illustrations work. "I knew it was a concept book and put it away again," Morgan explained to *SATA.* Then in 1991 she met the writer Carole Lexa Schaefer. "She saw the pictures," Morgan noted, "and one day, in 1993, she stepped from her shower with *The Squiggle*—exactly what I'd been trying to say, with just pictures, for twenty-two years!"

The Squiggle is a book, according to Stephanie Zvirin in a starred *Booklist* review, that "captures the glories of childhood imagining." A little Chinese girl sees a piece of red string while on an outing with her school class. She stops and picks up the string and in an imaginative flash transforms the inanimate red twine variously into the tail of a dragon, a tightrope for a circus acrobat, and fireworks. Zvirin noted that "the unaffected gouache-and-felt-tipped-marker illustrations evoke the sweep and quiet dazzle of the child's creative spirit as well as the flavor of Chinese culture." Carol Ann Wilson, writing in *School Library Journal,* felt this "paean to flights of fancy is, at once, a simple picture book and a study in subtle contrasts." A reviewer for *Publishers Weekly* noted that this "call to creativity shows that rope need not serve a purely functional purpose." Writing about the paperback reprint of this same title, another reviewer for *Publishers Weekly* called the book a "playful story, winningly illustrated in fluid, calligraphic strokes." *The Squiggle* went on to win numerous awards and citations.

Working with Nancy Luenn, Morgan next provided artwork for *The Miser on the Mountain: A Nisqually Legend of Mount Rainier.* As with her own *Supper for Crow,* Morgan once again found herself at home depicting scenes from her native Pacific Northwest. This Native American legend about the pitfalls of greed is set against the backdrop of Washington's Mount Rainier. A reviewer for *Publishers Weekly,* while noting Luenn's interweaving of Nisqually words into the text, emphasized "Morgan's sweeping brushstrokes that command the pages, summoning all the grandeur of the Northwest in the lush evergreens of the forest and deep blues of sky and water in her gouache-and-ink illustrations."

Teaming up again with Schaefer, Morgan has created further titles. *Sometimes Moon* tells the magical story of a little girl and her grandfather, who are waiting for the full moon to rise to have a picnic. The little girl, named Selene after the moon, hides behind a curtain just as the moon appears from behind a cloud; sometimes she glows like the moon, too. With such images, Schaefer explains metaphorically the waxing and waning of the moon. *Booklist* contributor GraceAnne A. DeCandido commented in a review of the book, "The line is vibrant and lively, and the figures are placed in space in engaging ways, occasionally breaking out of the picture frame." Marian Drabkin, writing in *School Library Journal,* felt that the "illustrations fit perfectly with the text, showing a very real little girl." Drabkin also called Morgan's artwork "warm and solid," concluding that "this is a good science book as well as an enjoyable story."

Morgan and Schaefer have also collaborated on their 2000 title, *Snow Pumpkin.* In this story, Lily and her friend Jesse want to build a snowman in the park after a surprise October snowfall. When they cannot find enough snow for the head, Lily improvises with a pumpkin from her grandmother's plot in the community garden. Even after the snowman melts, the children take the pumpkin home and decorate it for Halloween. In her *School Library Journal* review, Wendy S. Carroll remarked on the "colorful illustrations" Morgan lends to Schaefer's tale. Assessing the title in *Booklist,* Ilene Cooper echoed these sentiments, noting that Schaefer creates a "pleasant" story, with "special touches in text and art that make this book such a standout." In particular, Cooper praised Morgan's "expertly executed watercolor art," and summarized *Snow Pumpkin* as "a pleasure to read [and] a joy to look at."

"With each new project," Morgan concluded to *SATA,* "I am reminded of the activities I loved as a child and still use today to make a picture book—working puzzles, creating new languages, designing paper dolls, coloring in coloring books, and riding my 1958 cobalt blue Schwinn two-wheeler down new streets.... I feel blessed to still be doing the things I loved doing when I was six years old."

Biographical and Critical Sources

PERIODICALS

Booklist, April, 1990; June 1, 1994, Kay Weisman, review of *The Nine Days Wonder,* p. 1839; December 1, 1996, Stephanie Zvirin, review of *The Squiggle,* p. 653; September 15, 1997, p. 232; August, 1999, GraceAnne A. DeCandido, review of *Sometimes Moon,* p. 2066; September 15, 2000, Ilene Cooper, review of *Snow Pumpkin,* p. 237.
Bulletin of the Center for Children's Books, June, 1995, Susan Dove Lempke, review of *Supper for Crow,* p. 354.
Entertainment Weekly, July 13, 1990, p. 70.
Horn Book Guide, fall, 1995, p. 333.
Kirkus Reviews, May 15, 1991.
New York Times Book Review, October 21, 1990.
Publishers Weekly, April 27, 1990, p. 59; November 8, 1991, p. 63; May 2, 1994, review of *The Nine Days Wonder,* p. 307; December 2, 1996, review of *The Squiggle,* p. 59; September 1, 1997, review of *The Miser on the Mountain,* p. 104; July 5, 1999, review of *The Squiggle,* p. 73.
School Library Journal, January 2, 1992, p. 89; July, 1994, Leda Schubert, review of *The Nine Days Wonder,* p. 78; August, 1995, Patricia Lothrop Green, review of *Supper for Crow,* p. 137; December, 1996, Carol Ann Wilson, review of *The Squiggle,* pp. 104-105; September, 1999, Marian Drabkin, review of *Sometimes Moon,* pp. 204-205; September, 2000, Wendy S. Carroll, review of *Snow Pumpkin,* p. 208.*

—Sketch by J. Sydney Jones

MORI, Kyoko 1957-

Personal

Born March 9, 1957, in Kobe, Japan; immigrated to the United States, 1977; naturalized U.S. citizen, 1984; daughter of Hiroshi (an engineer) and Takako (a homemaker; maiden name, Nagai) Mori; married Charles Brock (an elementary school teacher, March 17, 1984 (divorced). *Education:* Rockford College, B.A., 1979; University of Wisconsin—Milwaukee, M.A. 1981, Ph.D., 1984. *Politics:* Democrat, feminist. *Hobbies and other interests:* Fiber arts (knitting, spinning, weaving), running, birdwatching.

Addresses

Agent—Ann Rittenberg, 14 Montgomery Pl., Brooklyn, NY 11215.

Career

Saint Norbert College, De Pere, WI, associate professor of English and writer-in-residence, 1984—; writer. *Member:* Modern Language Association of America, Associated Writing Programs.

Awards, Honors

Editors' Prize, *Missouri Review,* 1992, for poem "Fallout"; American Library Association Best Book for

Kyoko Mori

Young Adults, *New York Times* Notable Book, *Publishers Weekly* Editors' Choice, Council of Wisconsin Writers Best Novel, and Elizabeth Burr Award for best children's book of the year, Wisconsin Library Association, all 1993, all for *Shizuko's Daughter;* Paterson Poetry Center Best Books for Young Adults, Council of Wisconsin Writers Best Novel, American Library Association Best Book for Young Adults, and Children's Books of Distinction Award, *Hungry Mind Review,* 1996, all for *One Bird.*

Writings

Shizuko's Daughter, Holt (New York, NY), 1993.
Fallout (poems), Ti Chucha Press, 1994.
The Dream of Water: A Memoir, Holt (New York, NY), 1995.
One Bird, Holt (New York, NY), 1995.
Polite Lies: On Being a Woman Caught between Cultures (essays), Holt (New York, NY), 1998.
Stone Field, True Arrow, Holt (New York, NY), 2000.

Contributor of short stories to *Apalachee Quarterly, Beloit Poetry Journal, Crosscurrents, Kenyon Review— New Series, Prairie Schooner, South-East Review,* and to the young adult short story collection *When I Was Your Age: Original Stories about Growing Up,* edited by Amy Erlich and published in 1999 by Candlewick Press. Contributor of poems to periodicals, including *Missouri Review, Paterson Review, American Scholar,* and *Denver Quarterly.*

Work in Progress

A novel; poems.

Sidelights

In several of her prose works, award-winning novelist and poet Kyoko Mori describes the devastating pain that haunts a young person who must deal with the death of a beloved parent. After coping with the suicide of her mother when Mori was still a preteen, she was then forced to watch her once secure way of life become drastically altered through the tirades of a selfish, patriarchal, and unfeeling father and an insensitive and equally selfish stepmother. This abiding sense of loss, which deprived Mori of both family and community and which has imbued much of her written work, would eventually prompt her to voluntarily give up yet another tie with her youth: her country. Attending an American high school through an exchange program, she felt more in sync with the relaxed, less emotionally inhibited culture of the United States than she did with the strictures in place in Japanese society. Since her college days, Mori has made her home in the United States, where she has written and published several critically acclaimed novels for young adults, the memoir *The Dream of Water,* and *Polite Lies: On Being a Woman Caught between Cultures,* a book of essays.

Mori was born on the main island of Honshu, in the city of Kobe, Japan, in 1957. Located near both mountains and water, "Kobe is a very beautiful, sophisticated city," she once noted, "but it is also close to nature." The daughter of an engineer and his wife, she was born with both hips displaced and spent her first year in leg harnesses to correct her gait. Fortunately, that condition was corrected and Mori was soon able to accompany her mother on walks in the mountains and enjoy the visits to the country home of her grandparents that the family made before she began school. She was inspired with an early love of reading and a love of beauty by her mother. A sensitive and creative woman, Takako Mori made a cultured home for her children, reading to both Kyoko and her younger brother, Jumpei, from the time both children were small. Tragically, Takako would commit suicide when Mori was twelve, a victim of depression and, perhaps, the repressive Japanese society that relegated women to a subservient status in relation to their husbands.

While, like most Japanese children, Mori had an early exposure to a few English words and phrases, she began a serious study of the language and its literature when

Mori left Japan as a teenager to escape her abusive father and the memories of her mother's suicide. **The Dream of Water** *chronicles her return in 1990 to visit the places she treasured as a child. (Cover illustration by Darlene Barbaria.)*

she was twelve. She was immediately struck with the emotional content of much Western writing in comparison with the restraint of its Japanese counterpart; English would be her major in college and she now writes exclusively in her adopted language. "In my teenage years I read a lot of English books in English," she explained in an interview for *Authors and Artists for Young Adults.* "Before then I don't remember that much what I read, because I don't think that in Japan they really have books written for teenagers. You have to read 'literature'—some 'Great Book' by some guy who died fifty years ago or something. And that was fine; I liked some of that. But to be thirteen and to be a girl and to read that is not necessarily a good experience because [much of Japanese literature] was so male and with such different aesthetics than my everyday life." While she was drawn to the beauty of the language she was exposed to in the books she read in school, Western books such as *Jane Eyre* and *Anne of Green Gables* captured her imagination.

In her junior year of high school, Mori was given the opportunity to study at a school in Mesa, Arizona, for a year as an exchange student. "It was a revelation for me," she once commented. "For the first time in my life I was away from the social constrictions of my society. In Japan there is so much pressure from family. You can't do . . . [certain things] because it will bring shame to your family." After returning to her home, Mori decided to intensify her studies in English; during her first two years of college in Japan she majored in the subject. "After my year in the United States, I began to think of English as my writing language. So much of Japanese aesthetics is involved in not saying what you want to. To talk about yourself in Japanese is considered rude. So English became a much better language for me as a writer." Her focus on writing in English became so intensive that Mori decided to finish her college education in the United States. She earned a scholarship to Rockford College in 1977 and graduated from that school two years later. Since then she has completed her master's degree and Ph.D. and established a career as a writer and educator.

Shizuko's Daughter, Mori's first published book, was released in 1993. Based on a group of short stories that she wrote for her doctoral dissertation, the book tells the story of Yuki, a young girl who returns from a music lesson one day to discover her mother dead by her own hand. "People will tell you that I've done this because I did not love you," reads the suicide note Shizuko leaves for her daughter. "Don't listen to them. When you grow up to be a strong woman, you will know that this is for the best." During the six years that follow, Yuki must learn to deal with the changes in her life that follow her mother's death: the remarriage of her father, the gradual estrangement of grandparents, and her deep feelings of responsibility and guilt over her mother's unhappiness. Calling the book a "jewel," *New York Times Book Review* contributor Liz Rosenberg felt *Shizuko's Daughter* to be "one of those rarities that shine out only a few times in a generation. It begins and ends with a dream, with a death, yet it is not dreamy or tragic."

Shizuko's Daughter wasn't intended to be a young adult novel to begin with. But as Mori began to revise and edit her initial manuscript with the advice of her editor, she realized that conforming it to certain conventions of the genre ultimately made it a better novel: "Because the way I had it before, I time-skipped around a lot. Straightening that out made it a more straightforward book, which is what it needed to be."

One Bird, which Mori published in 1995, was even more concise than Mori's first book. In the novel, fifteen-year-old Megumi watches as her mother packs her suitcase and leaves the house of her husband, Megumi's father. Unable to go with her mother because to do so would be neither "appropriate" in Japanese society nor financially possible, Megumi is forced to deal with the vacuum left by her mother's abrupt departure, a vacuum that her distant father avoids filling by staying with an out-of-town mistress for long periods of time. During the course of the novel, her emotions and reactions shift from those of a little girl to those of a young woman through the support of a woman veterinarian whom she meets while attempting to care for a small bird.

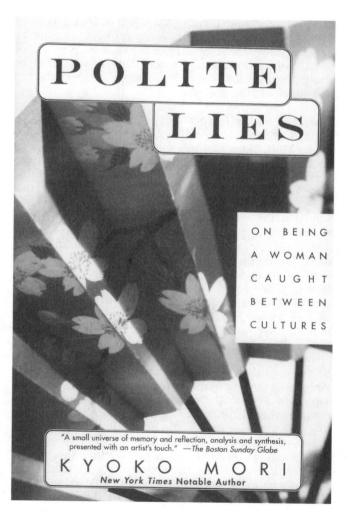

Mori penned a series of twelve essays in which she contrasts living in the Midwestern United States with living in Japan. (Cover illustration by Simon Metz.)

Ultimately, Megumi is able to creatively find a solution to her problem, a solution whereby she and her mother can spend at least part of the year together. "Kyoko Mori's second novel ... is so lively and affecting that one imagines its readers will be too engaged by its heroine's situation to notice how much—and how painlessly—they are learning about another culture," according to *New York Times Book Review* critic Francine Prose. Noting that the book is filled with "small, radiant schemes and glints of observation," Prose added that *One Bird* shows that teen feelings and attitudes toward life are universal.

As Mori once noted, writing for teens requires that authors rely more on character and plot than on imagery and style. "Both [*Shizuko's Daughter* and *One Bird*] had to be more straightforward, and in a way I think that this made them better books, because sometimes it is so easy to rely on your ability to write and, when you get to some crucial moment in the narrative, try to get through it through fine writing and strong imagery. And I see this as something that I am tempted to do because I am also a poet.

"But I think what you do well is also your downfall," Mori added. "And I think that when you're a poet as well as a fiction writer, there is always the temptation to do something poetic at a crucial moment. Writing for teens, you're not allowed to do that. You have to be straightforward and direct in developing the characters and manipulating the plot."

One Bird and *Shizuko's Daughter* are essentially the same story, seen from different points of view, according to Mori. "One is a tragic version of the story about an isolated teenager and the other is a more humorous version," the author explained. "In *One Bird*, I think there is an inherent sense of humor and resilience that Megumi doesn't take herself that seriously, not in the way that the teen in *Shizuko's Daughter* has to take herself seriously." Mori characterizes the books as "two flavors of the same thing," admitting that "maybe I needed to do that to grow up. I think that even though I didn't write those books to grow up, it became a process of that. When I first wrote *Shizuko's Daughter*, it was a way of admitting the pain in my life perhaps. And then when I wrote *One Bird*, it was a way of being able to look at that same story with more irreverence. And humor."

In 1990, with the manuscript for *Shizuko's Daughter* circulating among publishers, Mori decided to go to Japan on sabbatical "because it was the only foreign country where I speak the language," she once explained to *Authors and Artists for Young Adults*. She planned to keep a journal, out of which poems normally sprang, and then begin work on a new novel. While she was in Japan, visiting parts of the country that she had never seen as a child and spending time with beloved relatives, she thought to herself, "I'm kind of gathering material and waiting for that novel to form." Finding the time to keep a journal record of her thoughts and reflections was not difficult: "I couldn't sleep in Japan because I was jet-lagged," Mori recalled. "I kept waking up; I couldn't fall asleep, ... but in a way this was good because it gave me a lot of time to write. In the middle of the night I can't sleep; what else am I going to do? I can only read so much."

After returning to her home in Wisconsin and writing several poems based on her experiences in her native country, Mori realized that an autobiography, rather than a novel, was to be the literary outcome of her trip. "I knew in Japan that the trip was so specific to my family that I couldn't see how I could write it as a novel," the writer explained. "I would be translating these facts in an uncreative way rather than transforming them. So I decided that I would do this as a nonfiction, autobiographical narrative." Mori realized from the start of her new project that she had a wealth of literary models, including *The Woman Warrior* by Maxine Hong Kingston, that read like novels but are nonfiction. The result of her creative efforts was *The Dream of Water: A Memoir.*

In *The Dream of Water*, the reader is drawn into the narrator's reality, but that reality is as compelling as a work of fiction due to Mori's ability to imbue her relatives and her setting with qualities that transcend the mundane and everyday. Each person she meets on her trip is linked to past memories, and past and present interweave on both a physical and emotional plain. Her beloved grandfather is dead, and she is left with only memories and the journals a relative saved for Mori after his death. The house where she lived when her mother committed suicide is gone, replaced by a parking lot, and yet the memories that empty space conjures up render it almost ghostlike. Called "deeply private" by *Booklist* contributor Donna Seaman, Mori's memoir unfolds with "dignity and cathartic integrity, chronicling not only her struggle with grief, anger, and guilt" and her growing understanding of the differences between Japanese and U.S. culture, but also the author's ability to ultimately "finally feel at home in both worlds."

"I always wanted to be a writer," Mori once said. "When you're a kid, though, you have all these different aspirations, from the firefighter all the way to the great composer, all at the same time. While I had a series of these dreams, being a writer was always on the list. So every year it would be a different list, but the recurring one was that I wanted to be a writer." In grade school she did a lot of writing, but it was actually her mother and grandfather who inspired her to take her writing seriously. "My grandfather wrote journal entries every morning," Mori recalled, looking back at the visits she made to her grandparents' house as a young child. "When I would go and stay with his family, he would get up and write in his diary. And that really inspired me. Writing was a serious thing. It was something my grandfather did every morning." Mori, who now teaches creative writing at Saint Norbert College in De Pere, Wisconsin, considers herself to be a fairly disciplined writer. "I'm not disciplined all the way in my life," she admitted, "but there are three or four things I'm very disciplined about: running is one of them, and writing. Those are things that I don't have a hard time getting to."

In her first novel for adults, Mori relates the story of a Japanese-American woman who left Japan as a child to live with her mother and stepfather in the United States and reevaluates her life after learning of her Japanese father's death. (Cover photo by Jane Yeomans.)

A poet as well as a prose writer, Mori's craft follows certain stages, beginning with thoughts jotted down in journal entries, then poetry, and finally into prose. "I don't see the poems as just a process," she explained; "I see them as finished products. But once I do about ten poems, I start thinking, 'There's something I could do with this.' There's a collective thought that kind of forms in that process that leads me to do a longer prose project." Such is the process that Mori has used with each of her longer prose works. "The only time that I really think about audience is in terms of developing the plot as well as the imagery, so it has more to do with technique in the end than with the story itself," the author added.

Until Mori started teaching creative writing, she believed that anyone could write, on some level at least. "And that's still true," she once admitted. "I think that anyone can write better than he or she is doing *now*. But as I teach more I start thinking that talent really does play a valuable part in this. There are kids who, without trying, write something so much better than the kid who

is trying so hard who is a good student. It really has to do with the way they can see.

"But some of the most talented students are not the best disciplined. [While] I think I can motivate them to be disciplined because they have something to work with, they have to put something out there before I can give them direction." She maintains that the better English majors, those who "read and analyze things and write clearly in an expository manner," don't always write the best stories or poems. "They just don't seem to have the 'eye,'" she surmises. "And that, to me, is much more frustrating than working with a talented but undisciplined student whom I have to nag by saying, 'Your rewrite is due in a week,' because I can usually get that student to do it. And if it's two days late, it's okay."

In 1998, Mori published a series of twelve essays wherein she contrasts living in the Midwest and living in Japan, titled *Polite Lies: On Being a Woman Caught between Cultures.* She produced *Stone Field, True Arrow,* her first novel for adults, in 2000. The book tells the story of Maya Ishida, a Japanese-American who left Japan as a child to live with her distant, academic mother in the United States. Maya, who is married to a schoolteacher and works as a weaver, begins to reevaluate the events of her past and her present relationships after she learns of her Japanese father's death. While *Library Journal*'s Shirley N. Quan felt that the novel "appears to carry one too many story lines," a *Publishers Weekly* reviewer found Mori's text "graceful in its simplicity of language." Writing in the *New York Times Book Review,* Jeff Waggoner praised *Stone Field, True Arrow* as a "quiet, heartbreaking novel that has as much to say about art as it does about longing."

In addition to an active teaching schedule and a daily schedule given structure by her disciplined attitude towards running and writing, Mori continues to produce books, poems, and short fiction. In 1999, she contributed the autobiographical short story "Learning to Swim" to *When I Was Your Age: Original Stories about Growing Up,* a collection for young adult readers.

Biographical and Critical Sources

BOOKS

Authors and Artists for Young Adults, Volume 25, Gale, 1998.

PERIODICALS

Booklist, January 1, 1995, Donna Seaman, "Poets Remembered," p. 794; December 1, 1997, review of *Polite Lies,* pp. 590-592; June 1, 1998, Stephanie Zvirin, review of *Shizuko's Daughter,* p. 1717; July, 2000, Michelle Kaske, review of *Stone Field, True Arrow,* p. 2008.
Bulletin of the Center for Children's Books, May, 1993, p. 291; January, 1996, p. 161.
English Journal, September, 1994, p. 87.
Horn Book, May, 1993, p. 291.
Kirkus Reviews, November 1, 1997, review of *Polite Lies,* p. 1628.

Library Journal, July, 2000, Shirley N. Quan, review of *Stone Field, True Arrow,* p. 141.

Los Angeles Times Book Review, April 9, 1995, p. 6.

New York Times Book Review, August 22, 1993, Liz Rosenberg, review of *Shizuko's Daughter,* p. 19; February 5, 1995, p. 13; November 12, 1995, Francine Prose, review of *One Bird,* p. 50; March 8, 1998, p. 19; November 5, 2000, Jeff Waggoner, review of *Stone Field, True Arrow.*

Publishers Weekly, January 25, 1993, p. 87; November 7, 1994, p. 54; November 3, 1997, review of *Polite Lies,* p. 71; August 14, 2000, review of *Stone Field, True Arrow,* p. 329.

School Library Journal, September, 1997, Patricia Lothrop-Green, review of *The Dream of Water,* p. 129.

Voice of Youth Advocates, October, 1993, p. 217; February, 1996, p. 374; August, 1997, Hilary S. Crew, review of *One Bird,* pp. 173-176.

Wilson Library Bulletin, January, 1994, p. 117.*

*   *   *

MOSATCHE, Harriet (S.) 1949-

Personal

Born April 10, 1949, in New York, NY; married Ivan Lawner (an attorney), February 19, 1983; children: Robert Lawner, Elizabeth Kim Lawner. *Education:* Brooklyn College, B.A., 1970; Hunter College, M.A., 1972; Graduate Center, City University of New York, Ph.D., 1977. *Hobbies and other interests:* Reading, dancing, playing piano.

Addresses

Office—Girl Scouts of the USA, 420 Fifth Ave., New York, NY 10018. *E-mail*—hmosatche@aol.com.

Career

Psychologist. Department of Psychology, College of Mt. St. Vincent, Riverdale, NY, professor and chair of department, 1977-84; Girl Scouts of USA, New York City, director of program development, 1984-86, 1992—. *Member:* American Psychological Association, Eastern Psychological Association, Society for Research in Child Development.

Awards, Honors

National Institutes of Health grant, 1982-84; National Science Foundation grant, 1996-2000; Gold Award, National Parenting Publications, 2000, for *Too Old for This, Too Young for That! Your Survival Guide for the Middle-School Years.*

Writings

Searching: Practices and Beliefs of Religious Cults and Human Potential Movements, Stravon Educational, 1984.

(With Karen Unger) *Too Old for This, Too Young for That! Your Survival Guide for the Middle-School Years,* Free Spirit, 2000.

Girls: What's So Bad about Being Good?, Prima, 2001.

Contributor to updated editions of the *Girl Scout Handbook* and *Leaders' Guide,* Girl Scouts of the USA, 1986-2000. Author of advice column, "Ask Dr. M.," on Girl Scouts Web site, 1997-2000. Contributor to periodicals, including *Girl Scout Leader, Science and Children,* and *New Moon Network,* and to scholarly journals such as *Child Development* and *Journal of Psychology.*

Sidelights

Psychologist Harriet Mosatche told *SATA:* "My children played an enormous role in every stage of writing *Too Old for This, Too Young for That! Your Survival Guide for the Middle School Years.* They found kids for me to interview, they shared their own ideas and insights, and they were incredibly honest and helpful critics. If some bit of advice didn't ring true or the language wasn't quite right, they let me know. They have always been my inspiration."

Biographical and Critical Sources

PERIODICALS

Booklist, July, 2000, Lauren Peterson, review of *Too Old for This, Too Young for That! Your Survival Guide for the Middle School Years,* p. 2022.

School Library Journal, September, 2000, Leslie Ann Lacika, review of *Too Old for This, Too Young for That! Your Survival Guide for the Middle School Years.*

*   *   *

MULLEN, Michael 1937-

Personal

Born December 5, 1937, in Castlebar, Ireland; son of Darby (a craftsman) and Anne (Carney) Mullen; married Deirdre McLoughlin, March 31, 1973. *Education:* Attended De La Salle Teaching College, 1958; National University of Ireland, University College, Dublin, B.A., 1962; Dublin University, H.D.P., 1967. *Religion:* Roman Catholic.

Addresses

Home—Rathbawn Dr., Castlebar, County Mayo, Ireland.

Career

Writer. St. Joseph's College, Mauritius, teacher of English, 1962-66; taught English and French, 1962-85.

Writings

FOR CHILDREN

Magus the Lollipop Man, Canongate (Edinburgh, Scotland), 1981.
Sea Wolves from the North, Wolfhound Press, 1982.
Barney the Hedgehog, Children's Press (Dublin, Ireland), 1988.
The Little Drummer Boy, Poolbeg (Dublin, Ireland), 1989.
The Caravan, Poolbeg (Dublin, Ireland), 1990.
The Long March, Poolbeg (Dublin, Ireland), 1990.
The Flight of the Earls, Poolbeg (Dublin, Ireland), 1991.
Glór na Mara (in Gaelic), Coisecéim, 1991.
The Four Masters, Poolbeg (Dublin, Ireland), 1992.
Marcus the School Mouse, Poolbeg (Dublin, Ireland), 1993.
The First Christmas, Poolbeg (Dublin, Ireland), 1993.
An toileán órga (in Gaelic), Coisecéim, 1994.
To Hell or Connaught, Poolbeg (Dublin, Ireland), 1994.
Michaelangelo, Poolbeg (Dublin, Ireland), 1994.
The Darkest Years: A Famine Story, Cavendish House (Mayo, Ireland), 1996.
An Bóthar Fada (in Gaelic), Coisecéim, 2000.

Michael Mullen adds a new twist to the tale of the Nativity when his young protagonist Daniel time-travels to ancient Bethlehem and witnesses the birth of Christ. (Cover illustration by Marie Louise Fitzpatrick.)

FOR ADULTS

Kelly (novel), Wolfhound Press (Dublin, Ireland), 1981.
The Festival of Fools (novel), Wolfhound Press (Dublin, Ireland), 1984.
The Viking Princess, Wolfhound Press (Dublin, Ireland), 1985.
The Hungry Land (historical novel), Bantam (New York, NY), 1986.
Rites of Inheritance (historical novel), Bantam (New York, NY), 1990.
The House of Mirrors (historical novel), HarperCollins (London, England), 1992.
The Midnight Country, HarperCollins (London, England), 1995.

Work in Progress

"I am working on a book in Irish titled *An Ri* and a children's novel titled *Born to Be King.*"

Sidelights

"Michael Mullen," write *Twentieth-Century Children's Writers* contributors Sheila Flanagan and Rachel O'Flanagan, "has made one of the most significant contributions to children's literature in Ireland over the past dozen years." Mullen's works mostly fall in the genre of historical fiction, with an emphasis on Irish and Gaelic themes. "Mullen has mined a rich tradition of Irish history and culture," write Flanagan and O'Flanagan. "He has recognized its importance in an Ireland that is changing and developing where the deeds and events of the past can easily become submerged by the tidal wave of late twentieth century life." In novels such as *The Flight of the Earls, The Long March,* and *The Four Masters,* Mullen uses fictional characters to interpret and present "for his readers the often bleak and tragic events of Irish history," say the *Twentieth-Century Children's Writers* contributors. "These events are interpreted for the children by the creation of a knowledgeable and protective adult and this device also deepens the historical perspective for the reader. The historical character often features as largely as the fictional one and is certainly never reduced by the introduction of a fictional element."

Mullen focuses on some of the most dramatic times of Irish history, in which the island nation was struggling to maintain its political independence and unique Celtic character against various invaders. The characters and settings of *The Flight of the Earls, The Little Drummer Boy,* and *The Long March* are all based on seventeenth-century situations rooted in Catholic Ireland's attempt to maintain its identity against English invaders. *The Little Drummer Boy* culminates in the Battle of the Boyne, which made Ireland politically subservient to England for almost two and a half centuries. "Mullen's approach is uncomplex but he paints a realistic picture with an impressive attention to detail," write Flanagan and O'Flanagan. "In this as in all of Mullen's books the violence and brutality of war is not minimized." *The Four Masters, Sea Wolves from the North,* and *The Viking Princess* all draw on a more distant Irish past. They take their characters and scenes from medieval

One of Mullen's fictional works on Irish history, **Sea Wolves from the North,** *looks at the impact Viking raiders had on the Christian Irish colonies, especially the monastery on Iona island. (Cover illustrations by Angela Clarke.)*

Irish history. *The Four Masters* tells the story of the "Irish annalists and scribes who lovingly transcribed the history of Ireland," Flanagan and O'Flanagan explain. "Around this event Mullen creates a lively and dramatic narrative, people with untraditional heroes in the form of monks and scribes." *Sea Wolves from the North* looks at the impact Viking raiders had on the Christian Irish colonies, especially the monastery on the island of Iona. "*The Viking Princess* is set in Dublin," say the *Twentieth-Century Children's Writers* contributors, during the period in which Vikings established an independent kingdom on Irish soil, "and [it] draws from recent archaeological and historical findings to bring an immediacy and excitement to the complexity of subject. A strong and resourceful heroine adds another dimension to a male dominated world." Mullen also looks at the pain and trials of contemporary Irish life in novels such as *The Caravan,* in which "a fatherless family on a soulless Dublin housing estate ... are terrorised by a loan shark," state Flanagan and O'Flanagan. "Mullen paints a telling picture of the bleakness and loneliness of the family's urban surroundings.... At one level an exciting chase, Mullen's belief in the importance of home and identity is very much at the core of the book."

Mullen once commented: "To write unusual novels that lie on the edge of general experience requires dedication and confidence. Writing is lonely and bleak. A novel grows organically from key ideas and images.

"I begin a novel with a seminal idea. I let this mature in the mind over a period of six months. I write the first copy rapidly in order to set it down in total. Then I re-write at my leisure."

Biographical and Critical Sources

BOOKS

Twentieth-Century Children's Writers, 4th edition, St. James Press (Detroit, MI), 1995.*

N–P

NORTHMORE, Elizabeth Florence 1906-1974
(Elizabeth Stucley)

Personal

Born February 9, 1906, in England; died July 26, 1974; daughter of Hugh (a baronet and naval officer) and Gladys (Bankes) Stucley; married J. G. L. Northmore (a portrait painter), February 16, 1955. *Education:* Attended London School of Economics and Political Science, 1933-35. *Politics:* Conservative. *Religion:* Church of England.

Career

British author; headmistress of St. Cuthbert's Finishing School, Bathampton, England, 1960-64. Much of her adult life revolved around work with and for children—Guides' creche service, social welfare in London's poor areas, and occupational therapy in a children's hospital. During World War II, was a driver with the Mechanical Transport Corps in France and assisted in a French maternity hospital.

Awards, Honors

Mentioned in dispatches (British) for services during the retreat from France, June, 1940, as a mechanized transport driver.

Writings

FOR CHILDREN

Pollycon: A Book for the Young Economist, Basil Blackwell, 1933.
Star in the Hand, Collins, 1946.
Penfeather Family, Nicholson & Watson, 1947.
Secret Pony, Faber, 1950.
Magnolia Buildings, Bodley Head, 1960, published as *Family Walk-Up: A Story of the Berners Family,* F. Watts, 1961.

Springfield Home, Bodley Head, 1961, published as *The Contrary Orphans,* F. Watts, 1962.
Miss Georgie's Gang, Abelard, 1970.

UNDER NAME ELIZABETH STUCLEY

The Village Organizer (handbook for social workers), Methuen, 1935.
The House Will Come Down (novel), Duckworth, 1938.
Louisa (novel), Duckworth, 1939.
Trip No Further (novel), Low, 1946.
Hebridean Journey with Johnson and Boswell (travel), Christopher Johnson, 1956.
To End the Storm (novel), Hutchinson, 1957.
Teddy Boy's Picnic (autobiography), Anthony Blond, 1958.
Life Is for Living: The Erratic Life of Elizabeth Stucley, Anthony Blond, 1959.

Biographical and Critical Sources

BOOKS

Stucley, Elizabeth, *Teddy Boy's Picnic,* Anthony Blond, 1958.
Stucley, Elizabeth, *Life Is for Living: The Erratic Life of Elizabeth Stucley,* Anthony Blond, 1959.

PERIODICALS

Bulletin of the Center for Children's Books, January, 1971, p. 81.
Library Journal, January 15, 1971, p. 279.

*   *   *

PERKS, Anne-Marie 1955-

Personal

Born October 31, 1955; daughter of Michael Layne (in the telecommunications business) and Barbara Anne (a hair stylist; maiden name, McHale) Morris; divorced three times; married Michael Trezise Perks (in the publishing business), February 20, 1988; children: (previous marriages) Aaron Jon Martin, Justin Stephen Legris; (present marriage) Katherine Suzanne, Fiona

Bridgette. *Education:* College of the Desert, A.A., 1977; attended Art Center College of Design, Pasadena, CA, 1992; University of California, Riverside, certificate in graphics and design, 1998. *Hobbies and other interests:* Playing folk or traditional Irish music on the guitar, singing, herb gardening, hiking.

Addresses

Home—20 Flint Green Rd., Acocks Green, Birmingham B27 6QA, England. *Agent*—Ann Remen Willis, 2964 Colton Rd., Pebble Beach, CA 93953. *E-mail*—mtperks@appleonline.net.

Career

Illustrator and writer. Worked as graphic designer, art director, and freelance illustrator, 1980-88. Fine Arts Institute of the San Bernardino County Museum, president and exhibition curator, 1997. *Member:* Society of Children's Book Writers and Illustrators, Association of Illustrators (England).

Awards, Honors

Honorable mention in Exhibit 58, 1992, third place award in Exhibit 67, 1993, and third place award in Exhibit 78, 1997, all from Fine Arts Institute of the San Bernardino County Museum; certificate of recognition, San Bernardino Board of Supervisors, 1997.

Illustrator

Betsy Franco, adapter, *The Tortoise Who Bragged,* Stokes (Sunnyvale, CA), 1999.

Betsy Franco, *Clever Calculator Cat,* Stokes (Sunnyvale, CA), 1999.

Betsy Franco, *Clever Calculations about Cats and Other Cool Creatures* (teacher's workbook), Stokes (Sunnyvale, CA), 2000.

Work in Progress

Research on children's literature and on writing for children; *In the Language of My Ancestors,* a middle-grade novel.

Sidelights

Anne-Marie Perks told *SATA:* "There are a few phrases and concepts that have helped me the most in becoming a published children's book illustrator—phrases such as stay in the process, be willing to risk (which takes courage), practice perseverance and a daily work discipline and passion.

"When all my attention is on the final product, a published book, I lose touch with the joy and satisfaction of participating in each level of creating a satisfying book. This lack of joy comes through in the final work. Each level requires attention, the initial brainstorming, the seemingly hundreds of thumbnail and preliminary sketches, character development, and research. And this

is just the beginning, which is why passion is important. The average picture book takes the illustrator anywhere from six months to a year to create all the final, full-color art.

"The courage to risk is part of the creative process, an illusive and mysterious aspect of any creative discipline. For me, this involves a preparation that verges on a spiritual practice, by arranging my environment to best support my illustration work. I schedule in my day the time to work; putting my body in my studio for the allotted time is the most basic form of work discipline and preparation. I show up, and the rest follows—the time and opportunity to reach beyond myself by trying something new or just being open to that source from which all creativity flows.

"Perseverance comes in the form of sending out samples of your art work and continuing to send out samples to publishers despite rejections. Inside yourself there needs to be a conviction that your work will one day be in the right place at the right time, and you will get an opportunity to become a published illustrator. This process of creating sample pieces to send out and studying the craft of book illustration is also another form of preparation. You do get better and better at it, increasing your chances of eventually getting a first book to illustrate.

"The most important difference between children's book illustration and other forms of illustration has to do with consistency of character. The characters in the book need to look like the same animal or child throughout the book. There is also a consistency of style within the book, and for the illustrator each book has a different requirement about the best visual way to tell the story."

*   *   *

PHILBRICK, Rodman 1951-
(William R. Dantz, W. R. Philbrick)

Personal

Born 1951, in Boston, MA; married Lynn Harnett (a novelist and journalist). *Hobbies and other interests:* Fishing.

Addresses

Home—P.O. Box 4149, Portsmouth, NH 03802-4149. *E-mail*—Philbrick@earthlink.net.

Career

Writer, 1987—. Formerly worked as a longshoreman and boat builder.

Awards, Honors

Best Novel Award, Private Eye Writers of America, 1993, for *Brothers and Sinners;* Judy Lopez Memorial Award honor book, 1994, Nebraska Golden Sower

Award, Wyoming Soaring Eagle Award, 1997, California Young Readers award, Arizona Young Readers Award, Maryland Children's Middle School Book Award, Charlotte Award, New York State Reading Association, Best Young Adult Book of the Year and Recommended Book for the Young Adult Reluctant Reader designations, both American Library Association, all for *Freak the Mighty;* best science fiction selection, *Voice of Youth Advocates,* 2000, and Best Young Adult Book of the Year selection, American Library Association, 2001, both for *The Last Book in the Universe.*

Writings

YOUNG ADULT FICTION

Freak the Mighty, Blue Sky Press, 1993, published as *The Mighty,* Scholastic Inc. (New York, NY), 1997.
The Fire Pony, Scholastic, Inc. (New York, NY), 1996.
Max the Mighty, Scholastic, Inc. (New York, NY), 1998.
(With Lynn Harnett) *Abduction,* Scholastic, Inc. (New York, NY), 1998.
REM World, Scholastic, Inc. (New York, NY), 2000.
The Last Book in the Universe, Scholastic, Inc. (New York, NY), 2000.

"HOUSE ON CHERRY STREET" SERIES; WITH LYNN HARNETT; FOR YOUNG ADULTS

The Haunting, Scholastic, Inc. (New York, NY), 1995.
The Horror, Scholastic, Inc. (New York, NY), 1995.
The Final Nightmare, Scholastic, Inc. (New York, NY), 1995.

"VISITORS" SERIES; WITH LYNN HARNETT; FOR YOUNG ADULTS

Strange Invaders, Scholastic, Inc. (New York, NY), 1997.
Things, Scholastic, Inc. (New York, NY), 1997.
Brain Stealers, Scholastic, Inc. (New York, NY), 1997.

"WEREWOLF CHRONICLES" SERIES; FOR YOUNG ADULTS

Night Creature, Scholastic, Inc. (New York, NY), 1996.
Children of the Wolf, Scholastic, Inc. (New York, NY), 1996.
The Wereing, Scholastic, Inc. (New York, NY), 1996.

FOR ADULTS

Brothers and Sinners, Dutton (New York, NY), 1993.
Dark Matter, Xlibris, 2000.

MYSTERY NOVELS; UNDER PSEUDONYM W. R. PHILBRICK; FOR ADULTS

Shooting Star, St. Martin's Press (New York, NY), 1982.
Slow Dancer: A Connie Kale Investigation, St. Martin's Press (New York, NY), 1984.
Shadow Kills: A J. D. Hawkins Mystery, Beaufort (New York, NY), 1985.
Ice for the Eskimo: A J. D. Hawkins Mystery, Beaufort (New York, NY), 1986.
The Neon Flamingo: A T. D. Stash Crime Adventure, New American Library, 1987.
The Crystal Blue Persuasion: A T. D. Stash Crime Adventure, New American Library, 1988.

Tough Enough: A T. D. Stash Crime Adventure, New American Library, 1989.
Paint It Black: A J. D. Hawkins Mystery, St. Martin's Press (New York, NY), 1989.
The Big Chip, illustrated by Bruce Jensen, Microsoft Press, 1990.
Walk on the Water: A J. D. Hawkins Mystery, St. Martin's Press (New York, NY), 1991.

UNDER PSEUDONYM WILLIAM R. DANTZ

Pulse, Avon, 1990.
The Seventh Sleeper, Morrow, 1991.
Hunger, Tor, 1992.
Nine Levels Down, Forge, 1999.

Adaptations

The motion picture *The Mighty* was adapted from Philbrick's novel *Freak the Mighty* and produced by Miramax in 1998.

Sidelights

Rodman Philbrick, a screenwriter as well as a novelist, started his career as an author of adult thrillers before shifting his interest to young adult fiction. Gaining national accolades for his debut novel for teen readers, *Freak the Mighty,* Philbrick has gone on to lead a double life, continuing to pen adult mysteries while also adding to the body of fiction available to younger readers, sometimes in collaboration with his wife, journalist and author Lynn Harnett. Among Philbrick's novels for teens are *The Fire Pony* and *The Last Book in the Universe,* while his works for adults include such works as *Dark Matter* and *Brothers and Sinners,* which won the Private Eye Writers of America's Best Novel Award in 1993.

Born in Boston, Massachusetts, Philbrick grew up close to the New England coast, where one of his hobbies, fishing, is a prominent regional industry. Asked when he started his career as a writer, Philbrick explained in an interview with *Authors and Artists for Young Adults:* "I got the 'bug' in about sixth grade, when I started writing short stories. Later I wrote a novel-length work while in high school, although it was never published." Although he had proved he had the ability to complete an entire novel-length work without giving up, adulthood meant focusing on the day-to-day necessities of life, and Philbrick devoted much of his attention to earning a living. Drawing his livelihood from the sea in traditional New England fashion, he worked as both a longshoreman and a boatbuilder, but still found enough time to complete several novels. Unfortunately those works were not accepted for publication. In 1982, however, the author made his literary debut with *Shooting Star,* published under the name W. R. Philbrick.

Philbrick's *Slow Dancer,* the first of two novels featuring female sleuth Connie Kale, was released by St. Martin's Press two years later, and by 1987 the writer had left his other occupations behind to devote himself to novel-writing full time. Working out the twists and turns of plots to mysteries and detective novels now became his stock in trade, with some of his work published under the pseudonym William R. Dantz. The prolific Philbrick would write more than a dozen mystery novels for adults before moving into the young adult market in the early 1990s.

The move from adult whodunits to teen fiction happened, as Philbrick recalled, "more or less by accident." It was inspired by a boy from his own neighborhood, the novelist once explained. "I used to see two kids walking down the street near our apartment. One of them was a big guy and he sometimes carried the small kid on his shoulders. Later my wife and I became friends with the small boy's mother. We discovered that the small boy had Morquio Syndrome, which meant he would never grow to be more than three feet tall. He was extraordinarily bright, had a love for words and books, and an interest in sci-fi and Arthurian legends. About a year after his tragic death, I got an idea for a story inspired by his very special personality. The story is fiction, but I never would have written it if I hadn't known the boy himself."

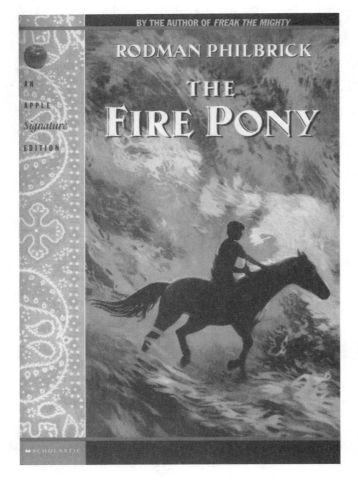

Philbrick's novel, set at a Montana horse ranch, follows eleven-year-old Roy who tries to settle in at his new home, hoping for a normal life, but fears that his half-brother's arsonist tendencies will force them to be on the run again. (Cover illustration by John Thompson.)

Inspired by the imagination and courage of his young neighbor, Philbrick was moved to write *Freak the Mighty,* which was published in 1993. An award-winning work that has been translated into numerous languages and is now read in schools throughout the world, the novel is described by *School Library Journal* contributor Libby K. White as "a wonderful story of triumph over imperfection, shame, and loss." In the book middle-school narrator Maxwell Kane feels doubly cursed. Not only is he clumsy, big boned, and condemned to an academic life of torment as a learning-disabled kid, but his dad is in prison for killing Maxwell's mom and the whole town knows about it. A loner, he spends much of his time in his room in the basement of his grandparents' house. Then something happens to change the dull despair of each passing day: a new boy moves in next door whom Max recognizes from his day-care days. The new boy, Kevin, is wheelchair-bound due to a birth defect that has prevented him from growing physically; however, he has an imagination and an energy that allow him to soar mentally. Soon Max and "Freak"—Kevin's name for himself—are the best of friends. With Kevin sitting astride Max's broad shoulders, the two dub their joint self "Freak the Mighty," channeling the one's strength and the other's intelligence to confront the taunting of other children. Caught up in the legend of King Arthur and his noble knights, the two boys search for causes to battle, one of which proves scary: "Killer" Kane returns and kidnaps Max, who escapes only with Kevin's help. Sadly, the effects of Morquio Syndrome begin to overtake Kevin, and he finally dies. Left to continue on his own, Max "is left with the memory of an extraordinary relationship," as well as a heightened sense of his own worth and a more optimistic outlook on his future, according to White.

The winner of numerous awards, *Freak the Mighty* has been lauded by reviewers for its sensitivity and ability to appeal to more reluctant readers. *Bulletin of the Center for Children's Books* reviewer Deborah Stevenson praised Philbrick's novel as "a sentimental story written with energy and goofy humor instead of sentimentality; ... kids will be drawn in by the idea and appreciate the story of an unusual relationship. In *Horn Book,* contributor Nancy Vasilakis called *Freak the Mighty* "A fascinating excursion into the lives of people whose freakishness proves to be a thin cover for their very human existence," while Stephanie Zvirin labeled it "both riveting and poignant, with solid characters, brisk pacing, and even a little humor to carry us along" in her *Booklist* review.

Freak the Mighty soon became a project that grew far beyond Philbrick's original novel. "*Freak the Mighty* was optioned by Scholastic Productions before the book was published," recalled the novelist. Philbrick was asked to adapt his novel into a screenplay, which he did; "but the producers thought it was too close to the original novel and hired another screenwriter," he explained. In 1998 *Freak the Mighty* made it into theatres, where it proved a success with young audiences as *The Mighty,* starring Sharon Stone and Gillian

Freak the Mighty *is Philbrick's tale of a loyal friendship between two disabled boys who combine one's strength with the other's intelligence to confront the taunting of other children and get out to explore the world. (Photo by Kerry Hayes from the film version of the book, titled* The Mighty.*)*

Anderson. Unlike some novelists who see their work transformed by others' hands onto the screen, Philbrick found the experience a positive one. "I'm quite pleased with the movie version—it reflects the emotional content and suspense of the novel," he once said.

Freak the Mighty also sparked a sequel, *Max the Mighty,* which was published in 1998. Reuniting with narrator Max Kane now that he is on his own, readers are introduced to Max's new friend, Rachel, a pre-teen who has escaped so far into her hobby of reading that fellow students now refer to her as the "Worm." What prompts Rachel's reading is her need to mentally escape from the abusive household in which she has found herself since her Mom's remarriage. Unfortunately, her books can't save her from her unstable stepdad, dubbed the "Undertaker" because of his creepy demeanor, and the much older Max—he's now fourteen—eventually agrees to help Rachel run away and find her biological father. On their way to Chivalry, Montana, in search of Rachel's dad, the pair encounter a colorful cast of characters ranging from wild dogs to con artists, and have numerous adventures, all the while trying to elude both the Undertaker, who follows in pursuit, and the police, who are hunting Max in response to the kidnapping charges filed by Rachel's stepfather. Noting that the novel's ending is filled with "surprises" and is "more

upbeat" than Philbrick's previous YA novel, a *Publishers Weekly* reviewer called *Max the Mighty* a "rip-roaring, heartwarming escapade." Although Nancy Vasilakis noted that several of the story's zany characters "sometimes threaten[s] to stretch the reader's sense of reality to its limits," she concluded in her *Horn Book* review that Max and Rachel "grab our attention and engage your heart."

While *Freak* and its sequel are very "issue-oriented" novels—learning disabilities, single parenting, and family violence are just a few of the subjects covered—Philbrick's more recent books for younger readers, particularly those written with his wife, are fun reads, while also containing a salting of typical teen concerns in their plots. Because of the fast-paced action and the relatively simple vocabulary in such books as *The Haunting, Abduction,* and *Children of the Wolf,* they have been praised for their ability to motivate even reluctant readers to turn the page and see what happens next.

"I don't have any 'lessons' in mind when I write about adolescent kids," Philbrick explained in response to a question regarding his opinion on the importance of inserting a "message" in books for young adult readers. "Most of what I write, and the first person 'voice' I use, comes out of my own memories of being that age. The books Lynn Harnett and I collaborate on are intended to be easy-reading mass market paperbacks. My own work might be considered slightly more 'serious', but, I hope, still entertaining enough to hold a reader's attention. For the most part I find that all young readers really want is a good story, of whatever type." However, Philbrick also expressed delight that the techniques he uses in creating his adult mysteries—"how to keep a reader turning pages to find out what happens next," for example— have been of value in his YA projects.

Philbrick's 1996 novel, *The Fire Pony,* which would be his second written for a younger readership, also uses Montana as its setting and features a young man as its narrator. In the story, half-brothers Joe and Roy Dilly are on their own, having fled from ranch to ranch after the habits of arsonist Joe put an end to job after job. Now Joe has found work at the Bar None Ranch, where the owner, Nick Jessup, raises Arabian horses. The older of the two brothers, Joe has a talent for both blacksmithing and saddle-breaking horses and soon becomes a prized employee. Meanwhile, eleven-year-old Roy, while remaining concerned that his older brother's fascination with fire will ultimately force the two to go on the run again, begins to settle in at the ranch. Trying to follow in Joe's footsteps, he attempts to break a palomino filly named Lady Luck, which Jessup has promised to Roy if he is successful. Ultimately, Roy rides Lady Luck to glory at a rodeo, despite the efforts of another man named Mullins to thwart the boy's success and get the horse for himself. Older brother Joe, angered at Mullins, first accosts the man, then goes into a hay field and sets a fire which quickly grows out of control and ultimately threatens the life of Roy and Lady Luck. Noting the complex personalities of the two brothers, *Horn Book* contributor Martha V. Parravano commented that Philbrick's portrait of "the scarred but spirited Roy is near flawless"; likewise, Joe is "loving and funny and talented even as he is scary and unpredictable and disturbed." Praising Joe's rescue effort as the high point of the novel, *School Library Journal* contributor Christina Linz noted that *The Fire Pony* "has plenty of action and suspense and is a good choice for reluctant readers."

"The idea for *The Fire Pony* came while Lynn and I were driving across the Southwest," Philbrick explained of the novel's inspiration. "I loved the landscape, and when we got to California the state was suffering from a rash of fires. The two ideas combined into a story about a boy and his older brother, who is not only a talented farrier, but a sometimes arsonist. The idea from that part may have been inspired by my love of Faulkner, in particular his story 'The Barn Burner.'"

Continuing his prolific career as an author of adult mysteries, Philbrick and his wife, Lynn Harnett, collaborate on mass-market paperbacks for school-age readers, and have begun several novel series in the horror and science fiction genres. Their novels appeal to even reluctant readers due to their fast-paced plots, with many chapters coming to a cliff-hanger conclusion that keep teens captivated—and reading. Part of their success may be credited to their ability to devise a system of working together that seems to work well. As Philbrick explained, "Lynn and I discuss story ideas. Then I write an outline and Lynn does all the heavy lifting, writing the first draft of the chapters. After more discussion we polish up a finished draft."

Philbrick returned to solo projects in 2000, with the publication of the YA novels *The Last Book in the Universe* and *REM World*. In the latter story, ten-year-old Arthur Woodbury has a weight problem that makes him the object of his classmates' jokes. He buys a weight loss device from the REM World Products company, which promises that the contraption will help him slim down while he sleeps. However, Arthur does not follow the instructions for the new gadget properly, and is instead transported to REM world, with little hope of getting back home. Arthur's arrival in REM world also disrupts the laws of the magical universe, placing its existence in jeopardy. In order to save the REM universe and return to his own world, Arthur embarks on a series of adventures involving a diverse group of fantastic creatures. With the help of these beings, Arthur is able to accomplish his twin goals, and in the process loses weight and develops courage. A *Publishers Weekly* reviewer praised the novel, noting that its "imaginative characters" make it a "fun and fast-paced read." *School Library Journal*'s Nina Lindsay found the plot to be a bit thin, but praised the book for its "action-packed, cliff-hanging chapters."

As a writer, Philbrick remains constantly busy, reserving his mornings for his craft, and rewarding himself with a chance to go fishing in the afternoon. "I've never stopped writing for adults," Philbrick explained to *Authors and Artists for Young Adults,* "although I spend more time writing YA novels these days. I've also written a number of screenplays, but none of them have been produced yet! I doubt I'll ever write much nonfiction, as I have a bad habit of making things up."

A voracious reader for many years, Philbrick counts among his favorite authors suspense novelist Elmore Leonard, as well as writers like Mark Twain and Joseph Conrad. Perhaps because of his roots in the seafaring culture of the New England shoreline, Philbrick also enjoys the seagoing fiction of Patrick O'Brien. He and his wife divide their time between their home in Maine and the Florida Keys.

Biographical and Critical Sources

PERIODICALS

ALAN Review, winter, 1999; winter, 2001, Rodman Philbrick, "Listening to Kids in America," pp. 13-16.
Booklist, December 15, 1993, Stephanie Zvirin, review of *Freak the Mighty,* p. 748; June 1, 1998, review of *Max the Mighty,* pp. 1749-1750; December 15, 1998, Ilene Cooper, review of *Freak the Mighty,* p. 751; May 1, 2000, review of *REM World,* p. 1670; November 15, 2000, Debbie Carton, review of *The Last Book in the Universe,* p. 636.

Bulletin of the Center for Children's Books, January, 1994, Deborah Stevenson, review of *Freak the Mighty,* p. 165; July-August, 1996, p. 383; April, 1998, Deborah Stevenson, review of *Max the Mighty,* p. 291.

Horn Book, January-February, 1994, Nancy Vasilakis, review of *Freak the Mighty,* p. 74; July-August, 1996, Martha V. Parravano, review of *The Fire Pony,* p. 464; July-August, 1998, Nancy Vasilakis, review of *Max the Mighty,* p. 495.

Kirkus Reviews, February 15, 1998, review of *Max the Mighty,* p. 272.

Kliatt, March, 1999, review of *Abduction,* p. 26.

New Yorker, December 13, 1993, pp. 115-116.

Publishers Weekly, January 26, 1998, review of *Max the Mighty,* p. 91; March 27, 2000, review of *REM World,* p. 81; November 27, 2000, review of *The Last Book in the Universe,* p. 77.

School Library Journal, December, 1993, Libby K. White, review of *Freak the Mighty,* p. 137; September, 1996, Christina Linz, review of *The Fire Pony,* p. 206; April, 1998, Marilyn Payne Phillips, review of *Max the Mighty,* p. 136; July, 1998, Brian E. Wilson, review of *Freak the Mighty,* p. 56; May, 2000, Nina Lindsay, review of *REM World,* p. 175; November, 2000, Susan L. Rogers, review of *The Last Book in the Universe,* p. 160.

Voice of Youth Advocates, April, 1994, p. 30; October, 1996, p. 212; June, 1998, p. 124.

ON-LINE

Rodman Philbrick Web site, http://www.rodmanphilbrick.com/

*   *   *

PHILBRICK, W. R.
See PHILBRICK, Rodman

*   *   *

PLOURDE, Lynn 1955-

Personal

Born October 1, 1955, in Dexter, ME; daughter of Leon Jr. (a store manager and chef) and Charlene (a bank teller; maiden name, Ambrose) Plourde; married James Derbyshire, 1975 (divorced, 1982); married Paul Knowles (a school administrator), December 22, 1984; children: Kylee; (stepsons) Lucas, Seth. *Education:* University of Maine, B.A. (speech communication), 1976, M.A. (speech communication), 1978. *Hobbies and other interests:* Cooking, reading, collecting teddy bears.

Addresses

Home—P.O. Box 362, Winthrop, ME 04364. *Agent*—Susan Cohen, Writers House, 21 West 26th St., New York, NY 10010.

Career

Freelance writer, 1985—. Tri-County Regional Special Education, Dover-Foxcroft, Maine, speech-language therapist, 1978-80; Redington-Fairview General Hospital, Skowhegan, Maine, part-time speech-language therapist, 1978-82; speech-language therapist at MSAD #54, 1980-83; Conley Speech and Hearing Center, University of Maine, clinical supervisor of graduate speech-language pathology practicum students, summers, 1983, 1985; classroom oral language consultant and program director for state grant project at MSAD #13, #54, #59, and #74, 1983-85; teacher at language-based summer preschool in Skowhegan, summers, 1987, 1989; part-time speech-language therapist at MSAD #54, 1989-93; part-time speech-language therapist at Winthrop Grade School, 1996-99. University of Maine, Farmington, instructor of writing for children course, 2000—. Has given lectures and presentations in classrooms and before educators throughout the United States. *Member:* Society of Children's Book Writers and Illustrators, Phi Beta Kappa, Phi Kappa Phi.

Awards, Honors

First place, *Writer's Digest* Book Club Personal Essay Contest, 1995, for "Playing with Words"; second place, Barbara Karlin Award, Society of Children's Book

Lynn Plourde

Writers and Illustrators, 1996, for *Thank You and Goodbye;* Lupine Honor Book, Maine Libraries Association, 1999, for *Wild Child.*

Writings

PICTURE BOOKS

Pigs in the Mud in the Middle of the Rud, illustrated by John Schoenherr, Scholastic (New York, NY), 1997.

Moose, of Course!, illustrated by Jim Sollers, Down East Books (Rockport, ME), 1999.

Wild Child, illustrated by Greg Couch, Simon & Schuster (New York, NY), 1999.

Winter Waits, illustrated by Greg Couch, Simon & Schuster (New York, NY), 2001.

Snow Day, illustrated by Hideko Takahashi, Simon & Schuster (New York, NY), 2001.

"CLASSROOM LISTENING AND SPEAKING" EDUCATIONAL BOOKS

Classroom Listening and Speaking K-2, Communication Skill Builders (San Antonio, TX), 1985.

Classroom Listening and Speaking 3-4, Communication Skill Builders (San Antonio, TX), 1988, revised edition, 1997.

More Classroom Listening and Speaking K-2, Communication Skill Builders (San Antonio, TX), 1989.

Classroom Listening and Speaking: Preschool, Communication Skill Builders (San Antonio, TX), 1989.

Classroom Listening and Speaking by Themes, Communication Skill Builders (San Antonio, TX), 1990.

Classroom Listening and Speaking: Early Childhood, Communication Skill Builders (San Antonio, TX), 1994.

Classroom Listening and Speaking: Kindergarten, Communication Skill Builders (San Antonio, TX), 1995.

Classroom Listening and Speaking 1-2, Communication Skill Builders (San Antonio, TX), 1995.

Classroom Listening and Speaking 5-6, Communication Skill Builders (San Antonio, TX), 1998.

OTHER

Talk t' Win, Communication Skill Builders (San Antonio, TX), 1988.

Learning Language Dramatically, Communication Skill Builders (San Antonio, TX), 1990.

(With husband Paul Knowles) *A Celebration of Maine Children's Books,* University of Maine Press (Orono, ME), 1998.

Contributor of articles and stories to periodicals, including *Humpty Dumpty, Turtle Magazine, Writer's Digest,* and *Chicken Soup for the Expectant Mother's Soul.*

Work in Progress

Children's books, including *Spring's Sprung, How Absurd, but That's What They Heard, Day Care Day,* and *Summer's Vacation,* all for Simon & Schuster; *Thank You, Grandpa* and *School Picture Day,* for Dutton; and *Grandpappy Snippy Snappies* for Harper-Collins.

In Plourde's evocative picture book, Mother Nature uses lullabies, treats, and colorful pajamas to soothe her unruly child, Autumn, to sleep so that Winter can arrive. (From Wild Child, *written by Plourde and illustrated by Greg Couch.)*

Sidelights

Picture-book author Lynn Plourde described her writing career to *SATA* as "the most *fun* work I've ever done, but also the *hardest* work I've ever done." With such popular titles as *Wild Child* and *Pigs in the Mud in the Middle of the Rud*—"Rud" being Maine-speak for "road"—to her credit, Plourde draws on her decades of experience as a speech therapist to develop rhythmic texts that appeal to young readers and listeners.

Born in Dexter, Maine, in 1955, Plourde graduated from the University of Maine in 1978 with a master's degree in speech communications. She worked for many years as a speech therapist for public school districts in her home state, while also writing about her professional work. Plourde began writing children's books in 1984, and spent thirteen years, as she described it to *SATA,* "send[ing] my manuscripts out, and they would come back rejected. Initially I received form rejection letters, then I received form letters with encouraging handwritten notes on the bottom, and then I began to receive personalized rejection letters." Although she got discouraged at times, Plourde never considered giving up her dream of publishing children's books. "I knew I was getting closer with nicer rejections (if rejections can be nice). But I also knew that even if I never had a single one of my stories published, I would still keep writing for children until the day I died. Why? Because I love the creative process. When I write a new story, I feel like I'm making something out of thin air. Where did that story come from? How did it get shaped, molded? It's creation is somehow mysterious and magical."

Plourde's first picture book, *Pigs in the Mud in the Middle of the Rud,* had its genesis in a glance out of the author's home office window one day. "I saw eight piglets running down the middle of my road," she explained. "I didn't have any farmer neighbors and to this day I have no idea where those piglets came from or went to. But they were there and my mind said 'what if?' What if pigs were blocking a road? I wanted a repetitive chant and the words 'Oh no. Won't do. Gotta shoo. But who?' popped into my head. Grandma became the central character in the book; I'm not sure why. Maybe because my favorite person in the whole world was my Grammy who had died when I was twelve. I wanted a heroine with spunk; my Grammy had spunk."

With illustrations by John Schoenherr, *Pigs in the Mud in the Middle of the Rud* was praised by critics for its engaging text and imaginative plot. In a review for *School Library Journal,* Karen James commended the text's "satisfying rhythm" and Plourde's use of "fanciful words." Equally enthusiastic, a critic for *Publishers Weekly* dubbed the book "[p]unchy and full of verve," adding that "this is one story kids will want to hear many times over."

In 1999's *Moose, of Course!* Plourde again writes about life in Maine, where the moose reigns supreme. In her story, a young boy determines to spot one of the large creatures and decides that the best way to attract a moose is with another moose—an attractive one. Putting his plan into action, he dons a moose hide, stilts, and bright red lipstick, but things backfire in a book that a *Publishers Weekly* contributor praised for its use of onomatopoeia and its "silly" rhymes. *Wild Child* also finds humor in the world of nature, as Mother Earth tries to put her young daughter down for the night. However, as with human children, the child finds all manner of excuses to avoid going to bed. Revealing clues as to the child's identity throughout the story, Plourde creates a tale that "transports readers with images of unusual clarity and depth," according to a *Kirkus Reviews* contributor, who also praised the golden palette used by illustrator Greg Couch. "Plourde's inventive rhythm and rhyme keep step with the activity in the forests and fields," added *School Library Journal* critic Wendy Lukehart.

Plourde teamed up again with Couch for her next picture book, *Winter Waits,* a story about young Winter who wants to play with his busy father, Father Time. Waiting for his father to finish his work, Winter dusts the grass with frost, cuts out snowflakes, and creates ice sculptures. When Father Time is finally finished, the two play in the sky causing snow to fall on the earth below. According to *Booklist* reviewer John Peters, Plourde's

gentle message about the importance of time spent with fathers "is delivered in a humorous, nonpreachy way, and the metaphorical nature of the cast adds an intriguing subplot." Other reviewers commended the author for her choice of words and rhyme. *School Library Journal* reviewer Kathleen Kelly MacMillan noted that "Plourde's rhyming text flows well."

Regarding her craft, Plourde has this advice for young writers: "When they write a story about something that really happens to them, it's okay to make the truth more interesting by sprinkling on some make-believe. I added a good dose of make-believe to my [first] story with hens, sheep, and bulls joining the chaos in the 'rud.' I even added some playful make-believe words—smatter, shmuffle, smarge. I don't know why. They were playful and fun and they just seemed to fit. Probably a third of *Pigs in the Mud in the Middle of the Rud* can be analyzed, and I'd discover concrete reasons why and how I wrote those parts of the story. But the remaining two-thirds is elusive. I'm not sure how those parts came to be. It's like I'm making magic with words. And I wouldn't have it any other way."

Biographical and Critical Sources

PERIODICALS

Booklist, December 15, 1999, Susan Dove Lempke, review of *Wild Child,* p. 791; December 15, 2000, John Peters, review of *Winter Waits.*

Children's Book Review Service, September, 1999, Lynn Ploof Davis, review of *Wild Child,* p. 171.

Kirkus Reviews, September 1, 1999, review of *Wild Child,* p. 1420.

Publishers Weekly, December 30, 1996, review of *Pigs in the Mud in the Middle of the Rud,* p. 66; July 5, 1999, review of *Moose, of Course!,* p. 71; August 16, 1999, review of *Wild Child,* pp. 82-83.

School Library Journal, March, 1997, Karen James, review of *Pigs in the Mud in the Middle of the Rud,* p. 163; December, 1999, Wendy Lukehart, review of *Wild Child,* p. 110; January, 2000, Jackie Hechtkopf, review of *Moose, of Course!,* p. 109; January, 2001, Kathleen Kelly MacMillan, review of *Winter Waits.*

*　　　*　　　*

PRIESTLY, Doug(las Michael) 1954-

Personal

Born January 9, 1954, in Melbourne, Victoria, Australia. *Hobbies and other interests:* Wildlife photography, keeping tropical fish, reading, gardening, films.

Addresses

Home and office—3 Downer Place, Kambah, 2902, Australian Capital Territory.

Career

Wildlife artist, 1976—; author and illustrator of books for children, 1988—. Fairhill Native Nursery, South East Queensland, Australia, native aquatic plant/watergarden consultant, 1995-97; Noosa Park Association member, 1994—. *Member:* Australian and New Guinea Fishes Association.

Writings

SELF-ILLUSTRATED

Australia's Wonderful Water Creatures, Puffin, 1995.
Curious Creatures of Australia, Puffin, 1995.
All about Whales, Dolphins, and Porpoises of the Southern Ocean, Puffin, 1998.

ILLUSTRATOR

Harry Breidahl, *Bush Secrets,* Macmillan, 1989.
Harry Breidahl, *Fantastic Facts and Figures,* Macmillan, 1989.
Reptiles (coloring book), Penguin, 1989.
Dinosaurs (coloring book), Penguin, 1989.
Space (coloring book), Penguin, 1989.

Contributed illustrations to *Macmillan's Children's Encyclopedia,* 1991.

Sidelights

Doug Priestly told *SATA:* "Ever since I was a child, the main driving force in my life, the 'core of my being,' has been a deep and abiding love of the natural world. Writing children's books about nature is my way of attempting to share and encourage that love in others, especially younger readers. I would like to awaken in them a sense of awe and wonder. A real appreciation of the beauty and endless variety of life on Earth. Something that they can nurture and take with them into adulthood. Enriching and sustaining them over the years as it has me. Even when not much else is working in your life, you can usually go for a walk and watch the birds, touch the trees, savour the sky . . . .

"It's been said many times that we can't care about things we don't know about. I hope that by reading my books, children will become aware of just how precious our wild plants and animals are. How one thing depends on another and why we need to preserve as much of nature as possible, not only for future generations, but indeed, for our own as well. Reading picture books and browsing through encyclopedias was a great influence during my childhood so now I've come full circle. With luck, some of those children who enjoy my books may be led to play an active part in conservation, possibly of their local environment or maybe even on a wider scale. A lofty aim perhaps, but I can only try.

"In writing and illustrating *Curious Creatures,* I was looking to show people, and kids in particular, some of the more unusual and unfamiliar forms of Australian wildlife. To go beyond the highly popularized 'kangaroos, kookaburras, and koalas' view and present the

Doug Priestly

lives of plants and animals most of us would consider quite extraordinary. Focusing on survival strategies such as camouflage allows me to give readers some idea of the great number of fascinating creatures that also inhabit our land, while explaining the reasons for their often bizarre appearance and habits. Many are unique to Australia and give me a great opportunity to charm and intrigue my audience to the extent that they are eager to find out more. Weird is wonderful!

"Despite many claims to the contrary, I don't think the rise of CD-ROMs and other forms of electronic publishing spell the end of the conventional book. Far from it. You can take a book with you virtually anywhere and read it almost anywhere as well. No batteries or power point needed! Books are tactile *and* visual. The best ones (especially picture books) can enthrall you with their lushness and the sense of holding something to be treasured. The act of turning the pages to reveal each new discovery is a pleasure that I hope will never be replaced by a flickering screen. Imagine cuddling up with your children to read from a computer. It's not the same, is it?

"As we venture into the twenty-first century and face all the challenges that it brings, with technological, environmental, and social change, to name a few, it's getting harder to be heard. People are inundated with information. With the book market swamped with titles and growing each year and the sheer volume of material on the Internet, authors need not only talent but also luck to be noticed. If in some small way I can influence a few children and get them to see that nature really is magical and worthwhile, my purpose in writing will have been achieved."

Priestly has written and illustrated several books for children focusing on Australian flora, fauna, and marine life. Focusing on those plants and creatures that have evolved in highly unusual ways in order to adapt to the Australian climate, Priestly offers brief descriptions of his subjects, often lightened by humorous asides, and accompanied by a watercolor illustration. A smaller, more detailed close-up of some aspect of the plant or animal or its environment may also appear. The author "lays out a surprisingly huge amount of information . . . in just thirty-two highly illustrated pages," asserted Kevin Steinberger in a *Magpies* review of *All about Whales, Dolphins, and Porpoises of the Southern Ocean.* Other reviewers made similar observations about Priestly's *Australia's Wonderful Water Creatures* and *Curious Creatures of Australia.* While some felt that the information presented might have been organized in a more clearly logical fashion, and bemoaned the lack of an index, these books also garnered praise for introducing students to the more unusual members of the Australian wildlife community. Though not overly detailed, "the range which is covered here is brief and comprehensive enough to serve as an introduction to each species," remarked Russ Merrin in *Magpies.* "Doug Priestly is a full-time wildlife painter and illustrator whose love of Australian flora and fauna is obvious," proclaimed Lynne Babbage in *Magpies.*

Biographical and Critical Sources

PERIODICALS

Magpies, September, 1995, Russ Merrin, review of *Australia's Wonderful Water Creatures* and *Curious Creatures of Australia,* p. 36; November, 1998, Kevin Steinberger, review of *All about Whales, Dolphins, and Porpoises of the Southern Ocean,* p. 42; November, 1999, Lynne Babbage, review of *Curious Creatures of Australia,* p. 43.

R

ROBERTS, M. L.
See, MATTERN, Joanne

*   *   *

RYDER, Joanne (Rose) 1946-

Personal

Born September 16, 1946, in Lake Hiawatha, NJ; daughter of Raymond (a chemist) and Dorothy (a homemaker; maiden name, McGaffney) Ryder; married Laurence Yep (an author). *Education:* Marquette University, B.A. (journalism), 1968; graduate study at University of Chicago, 1968-69. *Hobbies and other interests:* "Travel, gardening and flower arranging, reading and listening to poetry, working and playing with puppets, and hiking through woods and parks and by the sea."

Addresses

Home—Pacific Grove, CA. *Agent*—c/o William Morrow & Co., 1350 Avenue of the Americas, New York, NY 10019.

Career

Harper & Row Publishers, Inc., New York City, editor of children's books, 1970-80; full-time writer, 1980—. Lecturer at schools and conferences. Docent at the San Francisco Zoo. *Member:* Society of Children's Book Writers and Illustrators, California Academy of Sciences, San Francisco Zoological Society.

Awards, Honors

Children's Book Showcase selection, 1977, for *Simon Underground;* New Jersey Author's Award, New Jersey Institute of Technology, 1978, for *Fireflies,* and 1980, for *Fog in the Meadow* and *Snail in the Woods; Fog in the Meadow* was named Outstanding Science Trade Book of the Year, National Science Teachers Association, 1979, and a Children's Choice Book, Children's Book Council/International Reading Association, 1980; Parents Choice designation, *Parents'* magazine, and New York Academy of Sciences Children's Science Book Award, younger category, both 1982, and Golden Sower Award nomination, Nebraska Library Association, 1984, all for *The Snail's Spell;* Outstanding Book of the Year designation, National Council of Teachers of English, and Outstanding Science Trade Book of the Year designation, National Science Teachers Association, both 1985, and Outstanding Book of the Year designation, Bank Street School, all for *Inside Turtle's Shell, and Other Poems of the Field;* Outstanding Science Trade Book, National Science Teachers Association, and Children's Book Medal, Commonwealth Club of Northern California, both 1988, both for *Step into the Night;* Outstanding Science Trade Book, National Science Teachers Association, 1989, for *Where Butterflies Grow;* Favorite Book Contest winner, Aspen School (Los Alamos, NM), 1996, for *The Bear on the Moon;* Black-Eyed Susan Award nomination, Maryland Education Media Organization, 1996, for *Without Words;* Pick of the Lists designation, American Booksellers Association, 1997, for *Night Gliders;* Eva Gordon Award, American Nature Study Society; awards from National Science Teachers Association.

Writings

FOR CHILDREN

Simon Underground, illustrated by John Schoenherr, Harper (New York, NY), 1976.
A Wet and Sandy Day, illustrated by Donald Carrick, Harper (New York, NY), 1977.
Fireflies, illustrated by Don Bolognese, Harper (New York, NY), 1977.
Fog in the Meadow, illustrated by Gail Owens, Harper (New York, NY), 1979.
(With Harold S. Feinberg) *Snail in the Woods,* illustrated by Jo Polseno, Harper (New York, NY), 1979.
The Spider's Dance, illustrated by Robert Blake, Harper (New York, NY), 1981.

In Joanne Ryder's fanciful picture book **The Night Flight,** *Anna plays in the city park near her home during the day. At night, she dreams that she is flying over rooftops to the park, where she becomes friends with the animals. (Illustrated by Amy Schwartz.)*

Beach Party, illustrated by Diane Stanley, Frederick Warne (New York, NY), 1982.

The Snail's Spell, illustrated by Lynne Cherry, Frederick Warne (New York, NY), 1982.

The Incredible Space Machines, illustrated by Gerry Daly, Random House (New York, NY), 1982.

C-3PO's Book about Robots, illustrated by John Gampert, Random House (New York, NY), 1983.

The Evening Walk, illustrated by Julie Durrell, Western Publishing (Racine, WI), 1985.

Inside Turtle's Shell, and Other Poems of the Field, illustrated by Susan Bonners, Macmillan (New York, NY), 1985.

The Night Flight, illustrated by Amy Schwartz, Four Winds Press (New York, NY), 1985.

Old Friends, New Friends, illustrated by Jane Chambless-Rigie, Western Publishing (Racine, WI), 1986.

Animals in the Woods, illustrated by Lisa Bonforte, Western Publishing (Racine, WI), 1987, published as *Animals in the Wild,* 1989.

Chipmunk Song, illustrated by Lynne Cherry, Lodestar, 1987.

My Little Golden Book about Cats, illustrated by Dora Leder, Western Publishing (Racine, WI), 1988.

Puppies Are Special Friends, illustrated by James Spence, Western Publishing (Racine, WI), 1988.

Under the Moon: Just Right for 3's and 4's, illustrated by Cheryl Harness, Random House (New York, NY), 1989.

Where Butterflies Grow, illustrated by Lynne Cherry, Lodestar, 1989.

The Bear on the Moon, illustrated by Carol Lacey, Morrow (New York, NY), 1991.

Hello, Tree!, illustrated by Michael Hays, Lodestar, 1991.

When the Woods Hum, illustrated by Catherine Stock, Morrow (New York, NY), 1991.

Dancers in the Garden, illustrations by Judith Lopez, Sierra Club (San Francisco, CA), 1992.

Turtle Time, illustrated by Julie Downing, Knopf (New York, NY), 1992.

The Goodbye Walk, illustrated by Deborah Haeffele, Lodestar, 1993.

One Small Fish, illustrated by Carol Schwartz, Morrow (New York, NY), 1993.

My Father's Hands, illustrated by Mark Graham, Morrow (New York, NY), 1994.

A House by the Sea, illustrated by Melissa Sweet, Morrow (New York, NY), 1994.

Without Words (poetry), photographs by Barbara Sonneborn, Sierra Club Books for Children (San Francisco, CA), 1995.

Bears out There, illustrated by Jo Ellen McAllister-Stammen, Atheneum (New York, NY), 1995.

Night Gliders, illustrated by Melissa Bay Mathias, Bridge-Water Books (Mahwah, NJ), 1996.

Earthdance, illustrated by Norman Gorbaty, Holt (New York, NY), 1996.

Winter White, illustrated by Carol Lacey, Morrow (New York, NY), 1996.

Pondwater Faces, illustrated by Susan Ford, Chronicle Books (San Francisco, CA), 1997.

Rainbow Wings, illustrated by Victor Lee, Morrow (New York, NY), 2000.

Each Living Thing, illustrated by Ashley Wolff, Harcourt, 2000.

A Fawn in the Grass, illustrated by Keiko Narahashi, Holt (New York, NY), 2000.

The Waterfall's Gift, illustrated by Richard Jesse Watson, Sierra Club (San Francisco, CA), 2000.

Wild Birds, illustrated by Susan Kwas, HarperCollins (New York, NY), 2001.

Big Bear Ball, illustrated by Steven Kellogg, HarperCollins (New York, NY), 2001.

Mouse Tail Moon, St. Martin's Press (New York, NY), 2001.

Little Panda: The World Welcomes Hua Mei at the San Diego Zoo, Simon & Schuster (New York, NY), 2001.

"NIGHT AND MORNING" SERIES; ILLUSTRATED BY DENNIS NOLAN

Step into the Night, Four Winds Press (New York, NY), 1988.

Mockingbird Morning, Four Winds Press (New York, NY), 1989.

Under Your Feet, Four Winds Press (New York, NY), 1990.

"JUST FOR A DAY" SERIES; ILLUSTRATED BY MICHAEL ROTHMAN

White Bear, Ice Bear, Morrow (New York, NY), 1989.
Catching the Wind, Morrow (New York, NY), 1989.
Lizard in the Sun, Morrow (New York, NY), 1990.
Winter Whale, Morrow (New York, NY), 1991.
Sea Elf, Morrow (New York, NY), 1993.
Jaguar in the Rain Forest, Morrow (New York, NY), 1996.
Shark in the Sea, Morrow (New York, NY), 1997.
Tyrannosaurus Time, Morrow (New York, NY), 1999.

"FIRST GRADE IS THE BEST" SERIES; ILLUSTRATED BY BETSY LEWIN

Hello, First Grade, Troll Associates (Mahwah, NJ), 1993.
First-Grade Ladybugs, Troll Associates (Mahwah, NJ), 1993.
First-Grade Valentines, Troll Associates (Mahwah, NJ), 1993.
First-Grade Elves, Troll Associates (Mahwah, NJ), 1994.

PICTURE-BOOK ADAPTATIONS

Hardie Gramatky, *Little Toot,* illustrated by Larry Ross, Platt, 1988.
Charles Dickens, *A Christmas Carol,* illustrated by John O'Brien, Platt, 1989.
Felix Salten, *Walt Disney's Bambi,* Disney Press (New York, NY), 1993.
Felix Salten, *Walt Disney's Bambi's Forest: A Year in the Life of the Forest,* illustrated by David Pacheco and Jesse Clay, Disney Press (New York, NY), 1994.

OTHER

Contributor to periodicals. Ryder's papers are housed in a permanent collection at the Cooperative Children's Book Center, School of Education, University of Wisconsin (Madison).

Sidelights

Joanne Ryder creates picture books for readers in the primary grades that are praised for combining poetry, fantasy, and science in a particularly original and appealing manner. A prolific, popular writer, she introduces young readers to the life cycles and habits of a variety of creatures, ranging from insects and birds to dinosaurs and whales, through the context of imaginary play. Ryder invites her audience to become the creatures that she profiles by identifying with her young male and female protagonists, who imagine what it would be like to be an animal, bird, or insect. In her works, she allows her readers, to whom she often refers in the second person, to transform themselves and to take on new points of view.

Ryder describes the sensory experiences of her subjects as well as their needs for food, self-preservation, hibernation, and—discreetly—sex. She presents this factual material in lyrical, descriptive language filled with images and sounds, adjectives, and alliteration; according to John R. Pancella of *Appraisal,* these words and phrases are "much more eloquent than those usually found in children's picture books." Through this process, Ryder challenges youngsters to see the world from an unusual perspective while heightening their awareness of, and appreciation for, the natural world. Many of Ryder's works of this type are included in the "Just for a Day" series published by Morrow. Several of her books include author's notes that provide more detailed scientific information on their subjects. Ryder has also created a series of quiet, impressionistic picture books that portray young children observing the wonders of nature; the "First Grade Is the Best!" fiction series featuring a cheerful group of children and their teacher, Miss Lee, that includes some subtle lessons on nature; two pourquoi tales with polar bears as their main characters; several "Golden Books" for preschoolers; a book about robots based around C-3PO from the film *Star Wars;* and picture-book adaptations of such classic stories as *Bambi, Little Toot,* and *A Christmas Carol.* Ryder has worked with such notable illustrators as John Schoenherr, Donald Carrick, Diane Stanley, Lynne Cherry, Don Bolognese, Amy Schwartz, Betsy Lewin, Dennis Nolan, Michael Rothman, and Ashley Wolff, and her works are often noted for their union of text and illustration.

Thematically, Ryder celebrates her subjects, promoting respect for nature while representing the interconnectedness of humans and other living creatures. The author underscores her works with a message to preserve the Earth and its inhabitants. In addition, her works demonstrate that the love of nature can be passed from generation to generation. Ryder has been praised for writing informative and attractive books that prove children can be introduced to and inspired by science if it is presented in a distinctive, interesting, and compelling way. She is also acknowledged for the quality of her factual information as well as for the expressiveness and accessibility of her language. While receiving some criticism for anthropomorphicized animal characters, making some scientific omissions, including some overly abstract concepts, and for the pared-down quality of her adaptations, most observers praise Ryder for creating fascinating explorations of nature that stretch children's imaginations while providing them with solid information. Several reviewers have also noted that Ryder's works are useful complements to science classes and are good for reading aloud and for stimulating children to do further research. Writing in *St. James Guide to Children's Writers,* Christine Doyle Stott called Ryder "a leading writer of nature books for children," adding, "One of the remarkable things about all her work, and a reason for her consistent popularity, is her extraordinary use of language that is at once simple, poetic, and vividly descriptive." Stott concluded that Ryder's work "stands among the finest nature books of the last twenty years. The scientific accuracy of detail and the beauty of language for which her books are known ensures their welcome in the science and language arts sections as well as on the home bookshelf."

Born in Lake Hiawatha, New Jersey, Ryder was attracted to nature from an early age. Her birthplace was, as the author described it in an interview with *SATA,* "a small, rural town." For her parents, who were both born and bred in New York City, Lake Hiawatha was, according to Ryder, "'the country'—very different from the crowded city they knew. For me, it was a wonderful place to explore, full of treasures to discover. There were just a few houses on our street, but there were woods all around.... I loved living there and playing outdoors. There were always animals around to observe and encounter." Ryder wrote in *Sixth Book of Junior Authors and Illustrators,* "When I visit schools, children often ask me why I like to write about animals. Perhaps it's because I was an only child, and when I was young in rural New Jersey, there weren't many other children living nearby. But there were animals everywhere.... So they became my first friends." She further recalled to *SATA,* "One of my earliest memories is trying to follow a butterfly darting across the road and being scolded by a neighbor for running into the street." Growing up, Ryder had an assortment of pets, including chickens, hamsters, ducks, rabbits, and fish.

Ryder's parents were also fascinated by nature and by living in the country—"probably," their daughter surmised, "because they had spent all their lives in the city." Her mother, Dorothy, taught Joanne "to watch sunsets and to take time to stop and enjoy special moments in nature." Dorothy Ryder once stopped her chores to sit for hours and observe a hundred tiny birds, migrating spring warblers that had stopped to rest in a nearby tree. "My mother loved nature's grand displays—sunsets, ocean walks, spring trees all in bloom," Ryder recalled. In contrast, her father, Raymond, a chemist, "liked to pick things up and examine them. He was the one who introduced me to nature up close and made the discoveries we shared very personal ones." Raymond Ryder liked to tend his garden, and he would often call his daughter to come and see the interesting things in it. Ryder remembered that if her father "could catch it, he would cup the tiny creature in his hands and wait until I ran to him. Then he would open his fingers and show me whatever it was he had found—a beetle, a snail, a fuzzy caterpillar. Then gently he would let me hold it, and I could feel it move, wiggle, or crawl—even breathe—as I held it in my hand." She continued, "My father's excitement was easy to catch. As he pointed out amazing features of each animal, I could see that, even though it had a few more legs or less legs than I was used to; it was rather marvelous. So tiny, hidden animals became very much a part of my world, as real to me as the people I knew." Ryder and her father would also go for walks in the woods or to a nearby waterfall. She wrote in *Sixth Book of Junior Authors and Illustrators,* "We would always bring back armloads of treasures— rocks and leaves and, sometimes, even a wandering box turtle." Walking with her father, Ryder recalled in *SATA* that it "felt natural for me to feel comfortable and part of the world around me." She commented on the *Harper-Childrens* Web site, "My father helped me find the magic in the natural world and appreciate what it might be like to be another creature, someone wonderfully different. In my books, I try to share with my readers the experience of being 'shape changers.' We imagine together how it would feel to be someone new—a huge, furry polar bear running on an ice-covered sea, a lean

lizard changing colors in the hot sun, ... a jaguar prowling in a lush tropical rain forest, and a great white shark gliding towards its prey."

In 1991 Ryder published *When the Woods Hum,* a semi-autobiographical picture book about how a father introduces his daughter to the periodical cicadas, insects that appear once every seventeen years; at the end of the story, the protagonist, now a grown woman, introduces the cicadas to her son. In 1994 she produced *My Father's Hands,* a picture book based on her relationship with her father and on how he opened the natural world to her.

Ryder and her parents lived in the country until she was almost five years old. Then, the family moved to Brooklyn, New York, to the same apartment building where Dorothy Ryder had grown up. At first, it "was a bit of a shock for me to live where there were so many people all around. But the city seemed also to be a magical land, full of special places for me." Ryder enjoyed going to the park and to museums; in addition, the city provided lots of opportunities for her to use her imagination. She noted in *SATA:* "Every day on my way to school, I passed an old stone lion. I believed he could understand my thoughts, and I would tell him secrets. He was one of my first friends in the city. I also began to have lovely dreams at night in which I could fly over the tall trees outside my home." Ryder was later to use her childhood memories as the basis for her picture book *The Night Flight.*

When she was almost seven, Ryder moved to the city of New Hyde Park on Long Island. At about that time, she learned to read, and began to enjoy books, "especially adventures about dogs and cats," as she noted on the *HarperChildrens* Web site. Soon she was writing her own animal stories and, when she was about eight, poetry. Ryder told *SATA,* "Though I've always had trouble spelling words correctly, my parents and teachers encouraged me to keep on writing even when I made mistakes. I liked playing with words and making them up. I wrote about animals and everyday things—and also about imaginary people and creatures." Ryder became a voracious reader, borrowing multiple titles from her local library. "Reading so much," she noted, "made it easier for me to write. Since I enjoyed imagining other author's worlds, it seemed natural for me to create stories and worlds of my own."

By the age of ten, Ryder, who had first considered becoming a veterinarian, began to think seriously about being a writer. She started writing her first book, the fantasy "The Marvelous Adventures of Georgus Amaryllis the Third," when she was eleven. Although the manuscript was never finished, Ryder told *SATA,* "Maybe someday, I'll go back to it and see how it might end."

In high school, Ryder edited the school newspaper. After graduating, she enrolled at Marquette University in Wisconsin, where she studied journalism and edited the college literary magazine. She wrote on the *Harper-*

Childrens Web site that, as a journalist, "I learned to do research and discover facts. Sometimes a book idea comes from an amazing animal fact I've found." At Marquette, Ryder met Laurence Yep, an aspiring author who has become a well-respected writer of books for children and young people; the couple were later married. After receiving her bachelor's degree in journalism in 1968, Ryder studied library science at the University of Chicago for a year before moving to New York City to spend ten years working at Harper & Row as an editor of children's books. "During the day, I worked on other people's books," Ryder recalled. "Then at night, I worked on my own stories." In 1976 she produced her first picture book. *Simon Underground* describes the activities of the mole Simon from fall to spring, taking young readers into Simon's subterranean world and describing his instincts and sensations. Writing in *St. James Guide to Children's Writers,* Christine Doyle Stott stated that *Simon Underground* "exquisitely combines scientific accuracy with poetic expression. Young readers not only learn abstract facts about a mole, they are brought into such close contact with the details of its life that they must actively consider what it feels like, smells like, looks like, sounds like, to be a mole. Ryder imagines aspects of the mole's underground winter life and renders them so vividly that the reader cannot help imagining them also."

In 1985 Ryder produced her first book of verse, *Inside Turtle's Shell, and Other Poems of the Field.* She imagines a day in a field and pond from dawn to evening, and profiles the creatures that inhabit each place in short poems focusing on their essential qualities. The poems also form a picture of two turtles, one who has turned one hundred years old, and one who has recently been born, facts that the reader learns gradually. The author told *SATA,* "When I was six, I got a delightful birthday present, a big box turtle named Myrtle. She was my inspiration for the old turtle in *Inside Turtle's Shell.*" Writing in *School Library Jour-*

Hua Mei, the first giant panda cub ever to survive in captivity in the Western Hemisphere, is the focus of Ryder's book in which she recounts the panda's first year of life at the San Diego Zoo. (From Little Panda, *illustrated with photos by the Zoological Society of San Diego.)*

nal, Ruth M. McConnell noted, "With pithy delicacy touched with humor, the author of picture books and prize nature writing here distills her perceptions of nature into a series of free-verse vignettes with the punch of haiku." Noting the "quiet beauty" of the poems, Carolyn Phelan of *Booklist* concluded that Ryder "offers a collection of poetry concise, precise, and immediate." Zena Sutherland of *Bulletin of the Center for Children's Books* added that Ryder's poems "have a quiet tenderness and empathy" before concluding that most of the poems "are brief, some almost as compressed as haiku; most have delicate imagery; all are evocative." In the same year, Ryder produced her autobiographical picture book *The Night Flight.* In this work, which is based on a dream from the author's childhood, Anna plays in the city park near her home during the day. She enjoys riding Alexander, the stone lion, and hopes that the skittish goldfish in the pond will take bread from her hand. At night, Anna dreams that she is flying over the rooftops to the park. She rides Alexander, now running free, and becomes friends with the goldfish and pigeons. Anna goes to the park the next day; this time, the goldfish eat from her hands as she calls them by name. Writing in *Booklist,* Ilene Cooper stated, "Ryder's lyrical text, which paints its own word pictures, meets its match with [Amy] Schwartz' vibrant, brilliantly colored illustrations"; Cooper concluded, "A perfect pairing of author and artist in this lilting, lovely nighttime adventure." Anne E. Mulherkar of *School Library Journal* noted, "Schwartz and Ryder, each gifted artists in their own right, stretch their capabilities and children's imaginations in *The Night Flight.*"

Ryder has gone on to write several other books, such as *The Snail's Spell* and *Chipmunk's Song,* in which her child protagonists become small enough to accompany animals and observe their behavior first-hand. The first of her "Just for a Day" books, *White Bear, Ice Bear,* takes this concept a step further: in this and subsequent works in the series, the main characters actually become animals. Published in 1989, *White Bear, Ice Bear* features a boy who transforms into a polar bear in an Arctic landscape. The author defines the adaptive characteristics that allow the bear to survive in this beautiful but brutal environment: heavy fur, protective coloration, strong claws, padded soles, and an advanced sense of smell. The bear also tracks a seal for food, but it gets away before the kill. At the end of the book, the boy returns to his normal state after he smells his supper. Writing in *Booklist,* Carolyn Phelan commented, "Ryder shifts points of view so smoothly that the boy's transformations seem quite natural.... Through imaginative writing and artwork [by Michael Rothman], the book ... leads readers into deeper sympathy for their fellow creatures." Calling *White Bear, Ice Bear* "[t]he first of a projected series that one hopes will live up to the standards set here," Patricia Manning of *School Library Journal* noted that the book "is rich, empathic, and eye-pleasing," while Anne Rose of *Appraisal* concluded that *White Bear, Ice Bear* is "challenging while remaining inviting for younger readers."

In subsequent volumes of the "Just for a Day" series, Ryder continues the formula of having her young boy and girl characters shape-shift into various species of creatures; the author outlines the habits of such animals as a goose, a lizard, a whale, and a jaguar. With the publication of *A Shark in the Sea* in 1997, Ryder brought a new dimension to her series: whereas before she had only hinted at the predatory habits of her animal subjects, here she described them clearly. In this work, in which a boy dives into the ocean off the California coast and imagines himself to be a great white shark, the author includes an episode where the shark hunts and kills a young seal; it also fights off a competitor shark that tries to steal its prey. Writing in *School Library Journal,* Helen Rosenberg stated, "The part where the great white kills a young seal is rather bloody.... But is at the same time realistic." Elizabeth Bush of *Bulletin of the Center for Children's Books* commented that "the particulars of the hunt ... should sate most shark lovers' bloodlust. A good deal of information about shark physiology and hunting method is conveyed in the intense, pulsing free verse." Writing in *Booklist,* Carolyn Phelan concluded, "Ryder captures the feeling of 'otherness,' a different environment, a different kind of body for a different way of moving, and a different way of survival. Although the story may sound slightly sensational, the treatment remains matter-of-fact."

In 1999 Ryder produced *Tyrannosaurus Time,* a book in which two children uncover a fossil and, together, are turned into T-Rex. Set in a landscape that will become the western United States, the story builds in drama as the dinosaur searches for food and kills a triceratops; in the process, readers learn about the habitat of the beast and are presented with scientific information on theories about why dinosaurs became extinct. Ellen Mandel wrote in *Booklist:* "Lyrical, even mystical prose draws readers into a vivid re-creation of a day in the life of a Tyrannosaurus Rex 65 million years ago.... Melding poetic intensity with gripping visualization of the action, the book offers a memorable depiction of prehistoric life." Although a *Kirkus Reviews* critic warned that "not all children will be ready for the gory conclusion," the writer concluded, "For readers already familiar with such realistic aspects of the dinosaurs' lives, this volume is a must-have." Reviewers have generally commended Ryder's approach in the "Just for a Day" series; for example, Carolyn Phelan, reviewing *Lizard in the Sun* for *Booklist,* called the series "consciousness-expanding".

In 1995 Ryder produced a second volume of poetry, *Without Words.* With photographs by Barbara Sonneborn, the book illustrates the bonds humans share with animals. Author and photographer depict children and adults touching, holding, and playing with such animals as tigers, snakes, dolphins, chimpanzees, and elephants. A reviewer in the *Horn Book Guide* noted, "Ryder's lyrical poems convey the strength of the emotional bond between humans and beasts," while a critic in *School Library Journal* added that the author's "expressive poems are at the same time simple and thought-provoking."

As well as being respected as a writer, the author is acknowledged as a conservationist. Two of her works, *Earthdance* and *Each Living Thing*, are considered significant examples of why she has achieved this reputation. *Earthdance* is a poem that asks young readers to imagine that they are the Earth, which is personified through strong physical imagery. Ryder asks her audience to see themselves turning in space, feeling things growing and oceans shifting, and she suggests that, when taken together, the people, animals, seas, rivers, mountains, and forests of the Earth form a brightly colored quilt. A *Kirkus Reviews* contributor commented that Ryder beckons readers "to join in a cosmic appreciation of the earth and all it holds" by combining "Powerful, pulsing graphics [by Norman Gorbaty] and a valuable, almost incantatory, message." A reviewer in the *Horn Book Guide* noted that Ryder's "ecological message is clear but not heavy-handed," while Lisa Mahoney wrote in *Bulletin of the Center for Children's Books*, "Ryder's strong verbs, internal rhyme, and alliteration add force and music to her poetry."

Each Living Thing depicts a group of multicultural children who observe life in seven different habitats, including a park and the seashore, over the course of a day. In this work, which has as its theme the importance of respecting nature, Ryder asks children to be aware of animals and their needs and to take care of them—or to just let them be. She shows how animals fit into our surroundings while discouraging the notion that some animals (alligators, bats, bees, bears, snakes, and spiders, among others) are our enemies. Writing in *School Library Journal*, Susan Marie Pitard called *Each Living Thing* a "remarkable marriage of spare, poetic text and luminous, detailed paintings" by Ashley Wolff. Raising concerns about the environment in an engaging manner, Pitard deemed the book a "wonderful choice for sharing ... [and] for learning to honor each living thing."

Ryder again encouraged her audience to explore their natural surroundings with 2000's *A Fawn in the Grass*. Her text, which consists of an extended poem, focuses on a young child's solitary walk through a meadow, and recounts the animals he encounters along his way. While the little boy passes through this natural environment, he leaves its inhabitants undisturbed during his travels—thus the fawn of the title is there when he enters the meadow and, due to his respect for the surroundings, the fawn is there when the child comes back. "Though never stated explicitly," a *Publishers Weekly* reviewer summarized, "[Ryder's] book underscores the message that nature is full of beauty, grace, and unexpected pleasures." Similarly, *Booklist*'s Hazel Rochman felt that Ryder successfully presents a "child's-eye view of the amazing natural world, the things you can see when you are quiet, still, alone, and very close."

Ryder, who now lives in Pacific Grove, California, enjoys visiting schools and sharing her experiences as a writer. For preschoolers and first graders, she uses animal puppets to help illustrate her concepts of changing shape. For older students, she utilizes a personal slide show about her life as an author. She has also written and talked about her career. "[M]y language is poetic, full of images, sounds, and sensations to help readers slip into a new skin, a new shape," she added, concluding: "My father helped me discover the wonders hidden all around me, and in my books I try to share my own discoveries with children." In *SATA*, Ryder also commented that, "For a person who enjoys thinking in images and writing poems, writing picture books is a good life and a joyful way to make a living."

Ryder recalled the books she loved as a child, musing that, "When I read them again, they make me smile fondly as if I were meeting old friends. It's nice for me to think that children might have fun reading my books and using their own imaginations to enjoy the natural world. I wish that my books would turn into old and good friends for them, too."

Biographical and Critical Sources

BOOKS

Children's Literature Review, Volume 37, Gale, 1996.
St. James Guide to Children's Writers, 5th edition, edited by Tom Pendergast and Sara Pendergast, St. James Press.
Sixth Book of Junior Authors and Illustrators, edited by Sally Holmes Holtze, H.W. Wilson, 1989.
Twentieth-Century Children's Writers, 4th edition, edited by Laura Standley Berger, St. James Press, 1995.

PERIODICALS

Appraisal, autumn, 1989, Anne Rose, review of *White Bear, Ice Bear*, p. 57; summer, 1990, John R. Pancella, review of *Where Butterflies Grow*, p. 48.
Booklist, April 15, 1985, Carolyn Phelan, review of *Inside Turtle's Shell*, p. 1200; November 1, 1985, Ilene Cooper, review of *The Night Flight*, pp. 413-414; March 15, 1989, Carolyn Phelan, review of *White Bear, Ice Bear*, p. 1304; March 1, 1990, Carolyn Phelan, review of *Lizard in the Sun*, p. 1348; March 1, 1997, Carolyn Phelan, review of *Shark in the Sea*, p. 1173; September 1, 1999, Ellen Mandel, review of *Tyrannosaurus Time*, p. 142; April 15, 2000, p. 1553; May 1, 2000, Susan Dove Lempke, review of *Rainbow Wings*, p. 1679; March 1, 2001, Hazel Rochman, review of *A Fawn in the Grass*, p. 1288.
Bulletin of the Center for Children's Books, June, 1985, Zena Sutherland, review of *Inside Turtle's Shell*, p. 194; July, 1996, Lisa Mahoney, review of *Earthdance*, p. 385; April, 1997, Elizabeth Bush, review of *Shark in the Sea*, p. 295.
Horn Book Guide, fall, 1995, review of *Without Words*, p. 379; fall, 1996, review of *Earthdance*, p. 368.
Kirkus Reviews, April 1, 1996, review of *Earthdance*, p. 536; July 1, 1999, review of *Tyrannosaurus Time*, p. 1058.
Publishers Weekly, March 27, 2000, p. 79; March 19, 2001, reviews of *A Fawn in the Grass*, p. 98 and *The San Diego Panda*, p. 102.
Santa Rosa Kidnews, June, 1990.
School Library Journal, April, 1985, Ruth M. McConnell, review of *Inside Turtle's Shell*, p. 82; November, 1985, Anne E. Mulherkar, review of *The Night Flight*, p. 77;

April, 1989, Patricia Manning, review of *White Bear, Ice Bear,* p. 90; June, 1995, review of *Without Words,* p. 104; April, 1997, Helen Rosenberg, review of *Shark in the Sea,* p. 116; September, 1999, p. 203; April, 2000, Susan Marie Pitard, review of *Each Living Thing,* p. 113; May, 2000, Joy Fleischhacker, review of *Rainbow Wings,* p. 153.

ON-LINE

HarperChildrens Web site, http://www.harperchildren's. com (November 28, 2000).
Penguin/Putnam Web site, http://www.penguin/putnam. com (November 27, 2000).*

—Sketch by Gerard J. Senick

S

SCOTT, Mary
See MATTERN, Joanne

* * *

SHERRY, (Dulcie) Sylvia 1932-

Personal

Born April 20, 1932, in Newcastle upon Tyne, England; daughter of Samuel William and Evelyn (Forster) Brunt; married Norman Sherry (a professor and author), 1960. *Education:* University of Durham, B.A.

Addresses

Agent—Jonathan Clowes Ltd., 22 Prince Albert Rd., London NW1 7ST, England.

Career

Primary school teacher, 1949-51; Church High School, teacher, 1951-53; College of Education, Newcastle upon Tyne, England, teacher and lecturer, 1955-60; editor in Singapore, 1960-64; full-time writer, 1964—.

Awards, Honors

Kings College, Spence Watson Prize for literature, 1955; *Manchester Guardian* Award runner-up, 1966, for *Street of the Small Night Market;* "Honor Book" citation, Chicago *Tribune Book World* Festival, 1969, for *The Liverpool Cats;* Foyles Children's Book Club selection, 1974, for *A Snake in the Old Hut.*

Writings

FOR CHILDREN

Street of the Small Night Market, Cape, 1966, published as *Secret of the Jade Pavilion,* Lippincott, 1967.
Frog in a Coconut Shell, Lippincott, 1968.
The Liverpool Cats, Lippincott, 1969, published as *A Pair of Jesus-Boots,* Cape, 1969.
The Haven-Screamers, Lippincott, 1970, published as *The Loss of the "Night Wind,"* Cape, 1970.
A Snake in the Old Hut, Cape, 1972, Nelson, 1973.
Dark River, Dark Mountain, Cape, 1975.
Mat, the Little Monkey, Crane Russak, 1977.
A Pair of Desert-Wellies, Cape, 1985.
Rocky and the Ratman, Cape, 1988.
Rocky and the Black Eye Mystery, Cape, 1992.
Elephants Have Right of Way, illustrated by Quentin Blake, Cape, 1995.

Also author of *Man with Two Faces.*

FOR ADULTS

Girl in a Blue Shawl, Hamish Hamilton, 1978.
South of Red River, Hamish Hamilton, 1981.

Also author of *Geese-going Moon.*

OTHER

Little Pig (written for the children's television series *Stories Round the World*), British Broadcasting Corporation (BBC-TV), 1978.

Contributor to *Miscellany Five,* Oxford University Press, 1968, *In Love, Out of Love,* Macmillan, 1974, and *Eleventh Ghost Book,* Barrie & Jenkins, 1975. Reviewer for *Daily Telegraph.*

Adaptations

A Pair of Jesus-Boots was adapted as a four-part serial for BBC-TV Children's Television in 1975, and a dramatization by Alan England was published by Heinemann Educational in 1983.

Sidelights

Sylvia Sherry's children's fiction is noted for its evocation of a wide range of places and periods. Sherry is especially praised for her depiction of English inner-city life through the eyes of teenagers. Her protagonists are generally adolescent boys who overcome danger with resourcefulness, courage, recklessness, or luck, while the adult characters are unsympathetic or even hostile toward the boys. In *Twentieth-Century Children's Writers* Alasdair K. D. Campbell commented that Sherry shows "considerable skill in building up tension gradually through several short chapters while setting the scene, but her denouements are apt to be disappointing." However, *School Librarian* contributor Robert Dunbar noted that her "strength remains in the attitude—all compassion, no condescension—which she displays to her [fictional] creations."

Sherry is best known for her four Rocky O'Rourke novels, *The Liverpool Cats, A Pair of Desert-Wellies, Rocky and the Ratman,* and *Rocky and the Black Eye Mystery.* Set in Liverpool, these stories center on the lives of thirteen-year-old Rocky and his family and friends. Campbell found that the books may be challenging for young readers, explaining that in *The Liverpool Cats,* "the use of an undiluted Liverpudlian dialect by all the characters presents another possible stumbling block, yet the story has enough pace and vivacity to keep one reading." By contrast, *School Librarian* reviewer Monica Dart responded positively to Sherry's use of dialect, and noted in her review of *Rocky and the Black Eye Mystery* that the story's "vigorous pace is created by colloquial dialogue throughout." In her assessment of *A Pair of Desert-Wellies, Times Literary Supplement* contributor Penelope Farmer commented that the "lively and exciting" qualities of the novel are "due as much as anything to the vitality of the writing." While critic Carol Ann Duffy, writing in the same publication, found some of Sherry's characterizations superficial, Farmer praised the author for her portrayal of Rocky as "an endearingly tough, resilient and funny hero, in whose survival against the odds it is actually possible to believe."

Sherry once commented that she began writing at age nine and her first novel, *Street of the Small Night Market,* was inspired by the atmosphere of the Far East—particularly that of Singapore, where she lived for six years. She feels that setting is important to her novels, and when necessary, she travels to other countries to research her books. A *Times Literary Supplement* reviewer comments that Sherry writes of Singapore "with close understanding and a wealth of arresting observation.... What is memorable is the amount of everyday life in Singapore's Chinatown, its agonies and elations and its wide cast of characters."

Sherry more recently added: "I do research the environment of a novel very thoroughly so as to make it convincing and accurate, and so I was very pleased to learn the novel I wrote about a Chinese boy in the Chinatown of Singapore, *Street of the Small Night Market* (almost an historical novel now, as only a few streets of that area remain), is now used as a class reader in Singapore schools, and my Malayan novel, *Frog in a Coconut Shell,* is now a class reader in Malayan schools. Similarly, when *A Pair of Jesus-Boots* was televised, it was filmed in the eight areas of Liverpool in which the novel was set. The Liverpool novels about Rocky O'Rourke—*A Pair of Jesus-Boots* and *A Pair of Desert-Wellies*—are both ... [used as] class readers and have had an enthusiastic response in terms of children's letters and invitations to speak at schools about the books, which is very gratifying. *A Pair of Desert-Wellies* was a runner-up for the Smarties award in its year of publication."

Biographical and Critical Sources

BOOKS

Ray, Sheila G., *Children's Fiction,* Brockhampton, 1972.
Twentieth-Century Children's Writers, 4th edition, St. James Press, 1995.

PERIODICALS

Books for Keeps, March, 1987, Bill Boyle, review of *A Pair of Desert-Wellies,* p. 12.
Junior Bookshelf, December, 1992, review of *Rocky and the Black Eye Mystery,* p. 260; April, 1996, review of *Elephants Have Right of Way,* p. 71.
Observer, September 3, 1978; December, 17, 1978; December 1, 1985, Patricia Craig, "Sharp Milk Teeth," p. 20.
School Librarian, November, 1988, Robert Dunbar, review of *Rocky and the Ratman,* p. 146; August, 1992, Monica Dart, review of *Rocky and the Black Eye Mystery,* p. 115; May, 1996, review of *Elephants Have Right of Way,* p. 57.
Times Educational Supplement, May 15, 1992.
Times Literary Supplement, November 24, 1966; June 6, 1968; June 26, 1969; July 19, 1985, Penelope Farmer, review of *A Pair of Desert-Wellies,* p. 806; June 24, 1988, Carol Ann Duffy, review of *Rocky and the Ratman,* p. 716.*

*   *   *

SKURZYNSKI, Gloria 1930-

Personal

Surname pronounced "skur-zin-ski"; born July 6, 1930, in Duquesne, PA; daughter of Aylmer Kearney (a steelworker) and Serena (a telegraph operator; maiden name, Decker) Flister; married Edward Joseph Skurzynski (an aerospace engineer), December 1, 1951; children: Serena Rose, Janine, Joan, Alane, Lauren. *Education:* Attended Mount Mercy College (now Carlow College), 1948-50. *Hobbies and other interests:* Science, technology.

Addresses

Home—2559 Spring Haven Dr., Salt Lake City, UT 84109. *Agent*—Edite Kroll Literary Agency, 12 Grayhurst Pk., Portland, ME 04102. *E-mail*—skurz@ ix.netcom.com.

Career

Writer. U.S. Steel Corp., statistical clerk, 1950-52.
Member: International Women's Forum, Society of
Children's Book Writers and Illustrators, Utah Women's
Forum.

Awards, Honors

Golden Kite Honor Book Award for nonfiction, Society
of Children's Book Writers and Illustrators, 1978, for
*Bionic Parts for People: The Real Story of Artificial
Organs and Replacement Parts; Horn Book* Honor
Book, and *Booklist* Reviewer's Choice Award, both
1979, and Christopher Award, 1980, all for *What
Happened in Hamelin;* Best Books for Young Adults
Award, ALA, and Notable Children's Trade Book in the
Field of Social Studies, National Council for the Social
Studies and the Children's Book Council, both 1981,
and *Booklist* Reviewer's Choice Award, 1982, all for
Manwolf; Golden Kite Award for fiction, *School Library
Journal* Best Books of 1983 Award, and Best Books for
Young Adults Award, ALA, all 1983, all for *The
Tempering;* Utah Children's Choice Book Award, 1984,
for *Lost in the Devil's Desert;* Golden Spur Award,
Western Writers of America, 1985, for *Trapped in the
Slickrock Canyon;* Science Writing Award, American
Institute of Physics, 1992, for *Almost the Real Thing:
Simulation in Your High-Tech World; School Library
Journal* Best Books of 1992 Award, for *Good-bye, Billy
Radish; Trapped in the Slickrock Canyon* and *Bionic
Parts for People* were Junior Literary Guild selections.

Writings

The Magic Pumpkin, illustrated by Rocco Negri, Four
   Winds, 1971.
The Remarkable Journey of Gustavus Bell, illustrated by
   Tim and Greg Hildebrandt, Abingdon, 1973.
The Poltergeist of Jason Morey, Dodd, 1975.
In a Bottle with a Cork on Top, illustrated by Glo Coalson,
   Dodd, 1976.
(Adapter) *Two Fools and a Faker: Three Lebanese Folk
   Tales,* illustrated by William Papas, Lothrop, 1977.
Martin by Himself, illustrated by Lynn Munsinger, Hough-
   ton, 1979.
What Happened in Hamelin (novel; also known as *Ratten-
   fanger von Hameln*), Four Winds, 1979.
Honest Andrew, illustrated by David Wiesner, Harcourt,
   1980.
Manwolf, Clarion, 1981.
(Contributor) *Three Folktales,* Houghton, 1981.
The Tempering (novel), Clarion, 1983.
The Minstrel in the Tower, illustrated by Julek Heller,
   Random House, 1988.
Dangerous Ground, Bradbury, 1989.
Good-bye, Billy Radish (novel), Bradbury, 1992.
Here Comes the Mail, Bradbury, 1992.
Caitlin's Big Idea, illustrated by Cathy Diefendorf, Troll,
   1995.
Cyberstorm, Macmillan, 1995.
(With Alane Ferguson) *Mystery of the Spooky Shadow,*
   illustrated by Jeffrey Lindberg, Troll, 1996.

Gloria Skurzynski

Virtual War, Simon & Schuster, 1997.
Spider's Voice, Atheneum, 1999.
Rockbuster, Atheneum, 2001.

"THE MOUNTAIN WEST ADVENTURE" SERIES

Lost in the Devil's Desert, illustrated by Joseph M.
   Scrofani, Lothrop, 1982.
Trapped in the Slickrock Canyon, illustrated by Daniel San
   Souci, Lothrop, 1984.
Caught in the Moving Mountains, illustrated by Ellen
   Thompson, Lothrop, 1984,
Swept in the Wave of Terror, Lothrop, 1985.

"YOUR HIGH-TECH WORLD" SERIES

Robots: Your High-Tech World, Bradbury, 1990.
*Almost the Real Thing: Simulation in Your High-Tech
   World,* Bradbury, 1991.
*Get the Message: Telecommunications in Your High-Tech
   World,* Bradbury, 1993.
Know the Score: Video Games in Your High-Tech World,
   Bradbury, 1994.

*"NATIONAL PARKS MYSTERY" SERIES; WITH ALANE
   FERGUSON*

Wolf Stalker, National Geographic Society, 1997.
Rage of Fire, National Geographic Society, 1998.
Cliff Hanger, National Geographic Society, 1999.
Deadly Water, National Geographic Society, 1999.
The Hunted, National Geographic Society, 2000.
Ghost Horses, National Geographic Society, 2000.

NONFICTION

Bionic Parts for People: The Real Story of Artificial Organs and Replacement Parts, illustrated by Frank Schwartz, Four Winds, 1978.

Safeguarding the Land: Women at Work in Parks, Forests, and Rangelands, foreword by Cecil D. Andrus, Harcourt, 1981.

Zero Gravity, Bradbury, 1994.

Waves: The Electromagnetic Universe, National Geographic Society, 1996.

Discover Mars, National Geographic Society, 1998.

On Time: From Seasons to Split Seconds, National Geographic Society, 2000.

OTHER

Contributor of articles and short stories to periodicals, including *Teen* and *School Library Journal.*

Adaptations

What Happened in Hamelin was adapted for film and telecast by the Columbia Broadcasting System on "Storybreak" in 1987.

Sidelights

"Perhaps if I'd known how long it would take me to acquire satisfactory writing skills," wrote author Gloria Skurzynski in the *Fifth Book of Junior Authors and Illustrators,* "I would have been too intimidated to try. But with the innocence of ignorance, I began putting words on paper." Skurzynski, who had been a busy wife and mother, started writing children's books after the last of her five daughters began school, a time when she realized she would need something other than bringing up her children to fill her life. She was also encouraged by the Pulitzer Prize-winning poet Phyllis McGinley, whose verse Skurzynski had read after seeing McGinley on the cover of *Time.* When Skurzynski posted a fan letter, McGinley replied, and a correspondence began which lasted until the poet died in 1978. Reacting to Skurzynski's observation-filled letters, McGinley told her that she had talent and should consider writing professionally. Now, Skurzynski is the author of more than forty popular and acclaimed books for children and young adults.

Skurzynski was born at the beginning of the Great Depression in Duquesne, Pennsylvania, a small town built around the steel mill in which her father, Aylmer (Al) Flister, worked. Her family was fortunate because her father's job allowed them to weather the Depression with relative ease. Mr. Flister had held dreams of succeeding in Hollywood as a producer or director—he was offered a job in the production department of Metro-Goldwyn-Mayer—but finally decided that he would actually be happier staying in Duquesne and working in the mill. To pursue his interest in acting and theatre on the side, Mr. Flister staged amateur theatrical productions, a total of ninety before he died. Serena Flister, Skurzynski's mother, worked as a telegraph operator at Western Union; of her four children, only Gloria survived infancy.

As a girl, Skurzynski was a devoted library patron and often attended movies. "The books I checked out of the library and the movies I saw each week made me believe in romance," she once said. The glamorous, hero-filled world she was admitted to through movies and books was one unlike her own hometown, which was inhabited by hard-working citizens representing a rich diversity of ethnicities. Skurzynski once described the conversations she would overhear while riding around Duquesne in the daytime: "The bus would buzz with the clicking consonants and sibilant syllables of Polish, Russian, and Slovak words, underscored by liquid Italian vowels."

After graduating first in her high school class, Skurzynski received scholarships from several colleges. She decided to attend Mount Mercy, a Catholic college whose students were exclusively women, because she had been charmed by a group of nuns she had seen playing in the college's yard during her visit. Unfortunately, her delight wouldn't last; the nuns were strict and had little tolerance. This oppressive atmosphere and her own inability to choose a field to major in made Skurzynski quit after her sophomore year and get a job at U.S. Steel Corporation in Pittsburgh. She married Edward Skurzynski on December 1, 1951, as he was finishing his senior year of college. Before the end of the decade, she and her husband were the parents of five children, all daughters, who immediately became the center of their lives. As Skurzynski once wrote: "The playpen became a permanent fixture in the living room and the high chair stood rooted to the dining room floor, cemented in place by spilled baby food. All my tablecloths were plastic. By the time our oldest daughter reached six, she'd become expert at folding diapers. Had I yet thought about being a writer? Ha! I wrote nothing longer than grocery lists."

By the time her youngest daughter was about to enter school, though, Skurzynski had begun to think that she should go back to college and become a history teacher. Her plans were broken when her husband, an aerospace engineer, was transferred to Utah. Once in her new home, Skurzynski postponed her plans for college so she could have time to adjust to her new surroundings. "Then . . . pure chance, the element that controls so much of our lives, took over and changed my direction for good," she later recalled. That was when Skurzynski began to correspond with Phyllis McGinley. The housewife filled her letters with observations such as: "There's something hypnotic about a pot of boiling macaroni." She began to write stories, but for a year and a half she received nothing but rejections from magazines. Finally, on her fifty-eighth submission, Skurzynski sold a short story to *'Teen.*

The difficulties Skurzynski had in making her first sale did not disappear once she became a published writer. She struggled, but managed to have several picture books published. She enjoyed writing children's novels more, however, and her interest in history made her lean naturally toward historical fiction. Just as being a mother had absorbed all of Skurzynski's time, now writing was her passion. In the *Fifth Book of Junior Authors and*

Illustrators, Skurzynski wrote, "While I write a novel, I'm only half aware of what's happening in my family, my house, and the world." Her ability to immerse herself in her created worlds began to pay off: she received a Christopher Award for her historical novel *What Happened in Hamelin.* Skurzynski's retelling of the Pied Piper story is based on actual documents from the town of Hamelin, Germany, which indicate that, in 1284, a relative stranger led 130 children from the town into the surrounding mountains. Neither the Piper nor the children ever returned. Skurzynski's narrator, Geist, is a thirteen-year-old orphan who works in a bakery and is despondent because of the baker's harshness toward him and the drudgery of his medieval life. He becomes excited, though, when the Piper comes to town and promises to rid it of the rats that trouble the inhabitants. When he successfully does so (manipulating the children to do his work for him) and is then cheated out of his payment, he stays in Hamelin as a musician, loved by the children both for his music and the sweets he gives them. What no one suspects is that the sweets contain a drug which gives the children hallucinations, enabling the Piper to ensnare them with his piping and lead them away from their home into slavery. A *Horn Book* reviewer wrote that "the pompous councilman, the simple-minded priest, and the children are realistically and convincingly depicted," and a contributor to the *Bulletin of the Center for Children's Books* stated that the story "builds nicely toward the tense final tragedy." In the *New York Times Book Review,* Natalie Babbitt noted that "the reader is left with a strong, lingering awareness of mankind's ever-present corruptibility."

History more recent than that of thirteenth-century Europe fills Skurzynski's 1983 novel *The Tempering,* which is concerned with her father's past. As Skurzynski once wrote, "For a long while I'd wanted to write about my father's boyhood, about his decision to drop out of school to be a steelworker, his first job in the steel mill when he was only fourteen, his love of music and stage shows." Luckily, Skurzynski was able to read sections of the book to her father just before he passed away in 1982. Canaan, a fictionalized Duquesne, serves as the setting for *The Tempering,* the story of a fifteen-year-old boy living in 1912 Pennsylvania. Karl Kerner is eager to quit school so he can work in the steel mill, even though his teacher, Yulyona, encourages him to continue attending class. Because Karl is in love with Yulyona he considers taking her advice, but ultimately goes to work in the mill only to lose his job on his first day when another man pulls a stunt and gets both himself and Karl fired. The metaphor that gives the novel its title compares the process of tempering steel, during which it is melted and formed into shape, with Karl's development into a man throughout the pages of the book. Outside of Karl's struggles, Skurzynski evokes the atmosphere of an early twentieth-century mill town. According to a *Bulletin for the Center for Children's Books* contributor, Skurzynski paints "a vivid picture of the way in which poverty and life-style are shaped by the environment." In the *New York Times Book Review,* Martha Bennett Stiles praised *The Tempering* for its

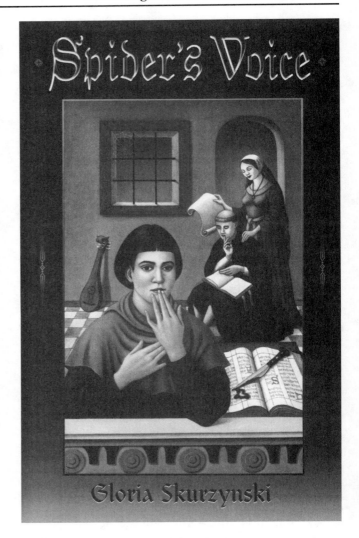

A retelling of the twelfth-century doomed romance tale of Heloise and Abelard, Skurzynski's novel is related through the narrative voice of a mute shepherd boy. (Cover illustration by Michael Nelson.)

"satisfying portrayals of love, friendship and neighborly decency."

Skurzynski's multiethnic hometown also served as an inspiration for the setting of her novel *Good-bye, Billy Radish,* which tells the story of Hank Kerner and Bazyli Radichevych, a Ukrainian boy whom Hank calls "Billy Radish." Billy, much like Karl in *The Tempering,* looks forward to his fourteenth birthday when he can go to work in the steel mill. The coming-of-age story shows how the two boys, despite their different backgrounds and languages, create a friendship that overcomes those superficial boundaries. "To me," Skurzynski once wrote, "humankind's most pervasive and deadly failing is to see the otherness of people rather than the sameness. Wistfully, I hope that in some future century, goodwill and tolerance for everyone's differences will become a universal virtue." *School Library Journal* contributor Marcia Hupp called *Good-bye, Billy Radish* a "richly textured, lovingly crafted historical novel."

Aside from crafting successful and acclaimed fiction, Skurzynski has also written several nonfiction books. *Bionic Parts for People: The Real Story of Artificial Organs and Replacement Parts,* which received a Golden Kite Honor Book Award, was inspired by family members in the same way some of her fiction has been. This time, two of Skurzynski's daughters served as her motivation: one had worked for the Division of Artificial Organs at the University of Utah, and another had studied in a building in which organ research was conducted. *Bionic Parts* examines the medical field's attempts to create machinery based on the functioning of normal, healthy body organs that can replace dysfunctional or injured organs. A reviewer for the *Bulletin of the Center for Children's Books* called *Bionic Parts* "an excellent survey of the subject."

Another of Skurzynski's nonfiction books, *Almost the Real Thing: Simulation in Your High-Tech World,* the second in a series, details some of the techniques scientists use to simulate real-world situations in order to test ideas or products and improve upon them in the early stages of development. A *School Library Journal* reviewer called *Almost the Real Thing* "an excellent and lively book on an offbeat topic," and the American Institute of Physics awarded the book its Science Writing Award in 1992.

Skurzynski's interest in the high-tech world expanded alongside developments in personal computing, virtual gaming, and the Internet. Her 1995 title, *Cyberstorm,* is set in the year 2015, when the friendship between teens Darcy and Erik comes to an abrupt halt after a betrayal. Darcy's family then moves into a restriction-filled community of new homes, and she is miserable. Only her beloved dog provides companionship, but the local authorities threaten this as well after a neighbor complains about barking. As the Animal Control workers near, Darcy takes refuge in a virtual reality machine belonging to her neighbor, Mrs. Galloway. A series of time-warp moments follow, while an actual tornado outside poses a bigger threat. Marsha Valance, writing in *Voice of Youth Advocates,* commended Skurzynski for creating "well-developed characters, breakneck pace, and believable computer world [that] combine to make this novel a real winner." Valance compared the writer to acclaimed cyberscience fiction writer William Gibson, while a *Publishers Weekly* critic likened *Cyberstorm* to a 1950 short story from a master in the genre, Ray Bradbury. The reviewer called it an "imaginative science fiction tale [that] never lets up its thrilling pace."

In her 1997 book *Virtual War,* Skurzynski delves into the world of three-dimensional gaming for her premise—a storyline that many reviewers predicted would resonate well with adolescent readers. Set in the year 2080, *Virtual War* presents the planet as a place with just two million inhabitants, due to years of environmental and biological disaster. The survivors live in domed cities awaiting news of improved ecological prospects outside. The plot focuses upon 14-year-old Corgan, a wholly bioengineered teen designed with reflexes that enable him to win at any electronic game. He is the creation of the Council of the Western Hemisphere Foundation, one of the forces that has agreed to fight a virtual war whose victor will receive a coveted archipelago that is fit for human habitation. Corgan will be the primary warrior, but in the days before the onset, he meets the other members of his team: a teen codebreaker named Sharla and a contemptuous ten-year-old strategist, Brig. For Corgan, this is first contact with actual humans, and soon he begins to question the value system with which he has been indoctrinated, one that teaches winning at all costs. "However bleak, Corgan eventually begins to realize that 'real' life is still desirable over the 'perfect' virtual world," noted *Voice of Youth Advocates* reviewer Linda Roberts, who also found *Virtual War* "a quick read" and one that "holds the reader's interest to the very last page."

Skurzynski returned to historical topics with her 1999 book, *Spider's Voice.* The work is a retelling of a classic doomed romance tale from twelfth-century Paris, the story of Heloise and Abelard. Skurzynski's heroine is renamed Eloise, and she recounts her story through the narrative voice of a mute shepherd boy. Eloise is a brilliant and spirited girl raised by her ambitious but untrustworthy uncle, while Abelard is a respected theologian. The two fall in love, and after Abelard rescues the boy Aran from a brutish circus master, he realizes that the mute Aran is the ideal servant, because the affair with Eloise must be kept secret at all costs. They begin to call him Spider, and he becomes devoted to the pair. Then Eloise becomes pregnant, and her uncle forces them into a marriage, which they then agree to keep secret in order to protect Abelard's career; the uncle becomes enraged and viciously maims Abelard in front of Spider—"but that trauma leads him to find, eventually, a voice of his own," noted a *Kirkus Reviews* critic who described it as a "spirited retelling." *Booklist*'s Ilene Cooper also praised the tale: "Throughout, Skurzynski's writing is vivid and intriguing," while Barbara Scotto, writing in *School Library Journal,* described Skurzynski as "masterful in her characterizations, showing the subtleties of each person's nature and the ways in which they are changed from the circumstances of their lives."

In the late 1990s, Skurzynski began to write a series of whodunits for teens with her daughter, Alane Ferguson. Published by the National Geographic Society, these "National Parks" mysteries are set inside various scenic nature and forest preserves belonging the U. S. National Park Service. They feature the Landon family, whose veterinarian mother and photographer father often take work assignments that bring them to one of the National Parks; twelve-year-old Jack and his younger sister, Ashley, come along, often accompanied by one of the foster children that the Landons host from time to time. The first in the series is *Wolf Stalker,* published in 1997, which introduces the Landons on their trip to the first National Park ever created, Yellowstone, whose boundaries date back to an 1872 law. Park officials have asked Dr. Landon to investigate a report that a hunting dog was killed by a pack of wolves. With the family is Troy, a troubled youth with a difficult past. The youngsters spend an unplanned night outside in the park, and a power struggle erupts between the trio. They witness the shooting of a wolf and nurse it through the night. In the end, all are rescued, and the poacher is caught. "This exciting book emphasizes the natural beauty and dangers of the wild," noted Marlene Gawron in a *School Library Journal* review.

In the third "National Parks" mystery, *Cliff Hanger,* the Landons arrive at Colorado's Mesa Verde preserve. Dr. Landon has been contacted by rangers to look into reports that a cougar in the park is attacking humans. This time, Jack and Ashley are joined by foster sibling Lucky, whose sneaky behavior makes almost all the Landons apprehensive—except for Jack, who has developed a crush on the girl. "The authors do a fine job of integrating lots of material into an exciting story," opined Cooper in a *Booklist* review. In the next book, *Deadly Water,* Skurzynski and Ferguson send the Landons to the Florida Everglades, where several manatees have inexplicably died. Jack and Ashley's foster sibling Bridger comes along as well, and learns as much about himself as he does water mammals. "An engaging read, the story features likable protagonists and plenty of action and suspense," wrote Shelle Rosenfeld in *Booklist.* The authors' 2000 book, *The Hunted,* finds the family at Montana's Glacier National Park to solve the mystery of disappearing grizzly cubs.

Skurzynski once declared: "When I work on a book like *Good-bye, Billy Radish,* I find my way back home to the smoky, sooty, western Pennsylvania town where flames from smokestacks set fire to the night. Today the smoke is gone, and so are the steel mills, but in my own memory, and through the stories my parents told me, I can recreate that time and place. It's important that I do that, because if I don't, no one will remember the rumbles and shrieks of the mills, the smell of the smoke, the blaze of the furnaces, and the enormous power of the steel mills over the townspeople.

"Then, after I've relived that past, I can flash forward. On computer screens, I can enter virtual worlds where I touch things that aren't real, and move around in them, and move them around to wherever I please. In laboratories, designers have shared with me the secrets of their work, giving me breath-stopping previews of the twenty-first century for my books *Robots, Almost the Real Thing, Get the Message,* and *Know the Score.*

"Caught up in the wonderment of the world to come, and infused with equal wonderment over the world long past, I think how lucky I am to be a writer, to be the channel through which this knowledge flows. As much as I admire the work of scientists and engineers and historians and archaeologists, I think my job is the best. I get to have it all. I only wish I could live forever, so I could see how the future turns out."

Biographical and Critical Sources

BOOKS

Fifth Book of Junior Authors and Illustrators, H. W. Wilson, 1983.

PERIODICALS

Booklist, August, 1997, Susan Dove Lempke, review of *Virtual War,* p. 1891; February 15, 1999, Ilene Cooper, review of *Spider's Voice,* p. 1060; April 15, 1999, Ilene Cooper, review of *Cliff Hanger,* p. 1532; August, 1999, Sally Estes, review of *Tomorrowland,* p. 2045; October 15, 1999, Shelle Rosenfeld, review of *Deadly Water,* p. 446; June 1, 2000, Anne O'Malley, review of *The Hunted,* p. 1898; December 15, 2000, Denise Wilms, review of *Ghost Horses,* p. 821.

Bulletin of the Center for Children's Books, October, 1975; April, 1979, review of *Bionic Parts for People: The Real Story of Artificial Organs and Replacement Parts;* February, 1980, review of *What Happened in Hamelin;* April, 1982; June, 1983, review of *The Tempering;* June, 1984; December, 1984; March, 1986.

Horn Book, December, 1971; October, 1978; February, 1980, review of *What Happened in Hamelin;* August, 1981; January-February, 1997, Margaret A. Bush, review of *The Electromagnetic Universe,* p. 80.

Junior Literary Guild, September, 1978; March, 1984.

Kirkus Reviews, January 15, 1999, review of *Spider's Voice,* p. 152.

New York Times Book Review, March 30, 1980, Natalie Babbitt, review of *What Happened in Hamelin,* p. 16; May 22, 1983, Martha Bennett Stiles, review of *The Tempering,* p. 40.

Publishers Weekly, April 1, 1983; June 26, 1995, review of *Cyberstorm,* p. 107; May 19, 1997, review of *Virtual War,* p. 76; January 18, 1999, review of *Spider's Voice,* p. 340.

School Library Journal, October, 1991, Alan Newman, review of *Almost the Real Thing: Simulation in Your High-Tech World,* p. 141; October, 1992, pp. 46-47; December, 1992, Marcia Hupp, review of *Good-bye, Billy Radish,* p. 114; January, 1998, Marlene Gawron, review of *Wolf Stalker,* p. 114; May, 1998, Bonnie Kunzel, review of *Cyberstorm,* p. 51; November, 1998, John Peters, review of *Discover Mars,* p. 143; March, 1999, Barbara Scotto, review of *Spider's Voice,* p. 215; May, 1999, Eldon Younce, review of *Cliff Hanger,* p. 130; August, 2000, Janet Gillen, review of *The Hunted,* p. 190; November, 2000, Ann Cook, review of *Ghost Horses.*

Voice of Youth Advocates, August, 1995, Marsha Valance, review of *Cyberstorm,* p. 174; August, 1997, Linda Roberts, review of *Virtual War,* p. 196; April, 1999, Vicky Burkholder, review of *Spider's Voice,* p. 42.

ON-LINE

Gloria Skurzynski Web site, http://www.gloriabooks.com (October 7, 2000).

SLATE, Joseph (Frank) 1928-

Personal

Born January 19, 1928, in Hollidays Cove, WV; son of Frank Edward (a building contractor) and Angela (Palumbo) Slate; married Patricia Griffin (a research director), September 11, 1954. *Education:* University of Washington, B.A., 1951; studied printmaking, Tokyo, Japan, 1955-56; Yale University School of Art, B.F.A., 1960; independent study, Kyoto, Japan, 1975.

Addresses

Home—15107 Interlachen Dr., Apt. 701, Silver Spring, MD 20906-5032. *Office*—Department of Art, Kenyon College, Gambier, OH 43022.

Career

Children's book author and illustrator. *Seattle Times,* Seattle, WA, member of editorial staff, 1950-53; Foreign Broadcast Information Service, editor, 1953-57. Yale University, New Haven, CT, consultant on aesthetics, 1960-66; Kenyon College, Gambier, OH, instructor, 1962-64, art professor, 1969-88, professor emeritus, 1988—, department chairman, 1963-75, 1981-82. National Endowment for the Arts, consultant and organizer of media literature program, 1977-78. *Exhibitions:* Twelfth National Print Show, Brooklyn Museum, 1960; Kenyon College, biennial group show, 1960-87, and retrospective show, 1988; Pioneer Gallery, Cooperstown, NY, 1961; Milton College and University of Wisconsin, 1963; Mt. Union College, OH, 1965; Whitney Museum, NY, 1974; Schumacher Gallery, Colum-

bus, OH, 1975; Waiting Gallery, Mt. Vernon, OH, 1976; Hopkins Gallery, Ohio State University, 1976; Mansfield Art Gallery, OH, 1978; and Ohio Expositions, Columbus, 1979. *Military service:* U.S. Marine Air Corps, 1946-48. *Member:* Society of Children's Book Writers and Illustrators, Authors' Guild.

Awards, Honors

Top-Flight Award for journalism, and Fir Tree and Oval Club Awards for service, University of Washington, both 1951; Yale University Alumni fellowship, 1960; painting award, Ohio Expositions, 1962; Kenyon College Outstanding Educators Award, 1973; Doctor of Fine Arts, Kenyon College, 1988; award for distinguished service in the field of children's literature, Ohioana Library Association, 1988; Notable Children's Books selection, American Library Association, 2000, and Sugarman Award, both for *The Secret Stars.* Several of the author's works have been included on state reading lists and have received awards from state library associations.

Writings

FOR CHILDREN

The Star Rocker, illustrated by Dirk Zimmer, HarperCollins (New York, NY), 1982.

How Little Porcupine Played Christmas, illustrated by Felicia Bond, Crowell, 1982, revised edition published as *Little Porcupine's Christmas,* Laura Geringer, 2001.

The Mean, Clean, Giant Canoe Machine, illustrated by Lynn Munsinger, Crowell, 1983.

Lonely Lula Cat, illustrated by Bruce Degan, HarperCollins (New York, NY), 1985.

Who Is Coming to Our House?, illustrated by Ashley Wolff, Putnam (New York, NY), 1988.

Miss Bindergarten Gets Ready for Kindergarten, illustrated by Ashley Wolff, Dutton (New York, NY), 1996.

Miss Bindergarten Celebrates the 100th Day of Kindergarten, illustrated by Ashley Wolff, Dutton (New York, NY), 1998.

The Secret Stars, illustrated by Felipe Davalos, Marshall Cavendish (New York, NY), 1998.

Crossing the Trestle, Marshall Cavendish (New York, NY), 1999.

Miss Bindergarten's Stays Home from Kindergarten, illustrated by Ashley Wolff, Dutton (New York, NY), 2000.

Story Time for Little Porcupine, illustrated by Jacqueline Rogers, Marshall Cavendish (New York, NY), 2000.

Miss Bindergarten Takes a Field Trip with Kindergarten, illustrated by Ashley Wolff, Dutton (New York, NY), 2001.

The Great Big Wagon That Rang, illustrated by Craig Spearing, Marshall Cavendish (New York, NY), 2002.

OTHER

(With Martin Garhart) *Poetry and Prints,* Pothanger Press, 1974.

Joseph Slate

Contributor of short stories and articles to periodicals, including the *New Yorker, Saturday Review, Art Journal, Kenyon Review,* and *Contempora.*

Sidelights

Artist and educator Joseph Slate has parlayed his creative talents into a successful second career as a children's book author. With books such as *The Secret Stars* and *Who Is Coming to Our House?* to his credit, Slate is also the creator of the popular Miss Bindergarten, a teacher of the pre-elementary set that has captured the hearts of readers and critics alike in such volumes as *Miss Bindergarten Gets Ready for Kindergarten, Miss Bindergarten Celebrates the 100th Day of Kindergarten,* and *Miss Bindergarten Stays Home from Kindergarten.*

Slate was born on January 19, 1928, in West Virginia. "I was born in Hollidays Cove, one of five children," he once recalled to *SATA.* "I suppose my greatest influence was an invalid sister. She was a wonderfully talented and witty person, and I'm sure my dual interest in art and writing was fostered by her. Rose entertained us by drawing and painting picture books on the back of discarded floral wallpaper. Then she carefully bound them with pink yarn. They were finished products—highly colored adventure stories in the style of 'Flash Gordon.'"

Slate joined the Navy in 1946, as a way to take advantage of the G.I. Bill and go on to college. The Navy transferred him to the Marine Corps. After leaving the service he majored in journalism at the University of Washington. The *Seattle Times* initially hired him as its stringer while Slate was still in college and later as a full-time reporter upon his graduation. A few years later, while on a posting to Tokyo from the Foreign Broadcast Information Service, Slate's interest turned to painting after Japanese artist Saito showed him how to cut a woodblock. "I sent a pretty shaky portfolio of [my] work to Josef Albers at Yale," Slate recalled. "I don't know why, but he admitted me to the B.F.A. program. After three years at Yale, and one year trying to make it as a painter, I came to Kenyon College and set up the art program they have now."

The death of Slate's sister Rose at age sixteen was devastating. "The first national attention my writing received was for stories inspired by her," he explained. "They were written from a child's perspective for the *New Yorker.* That child's perspective should have told me something about the future. But I had no idea I would ever write for children. The actual writing of picture books didn't come for me until the eighties. The photographer Gregory Spaid, a former student, urged me to tackle what seemed to many of my students a natural leaning."

Slate first picture book effort, 1982's *The Star Rocker,* illustrated by Dirk Zimmer, pursued a theme that was to reappear in his later books. Drawing on the myth of Cassiopeia, the author transforms her into a kindly old black woman whose tethered raft rocks the animal world to sleep. Slate told *SATA:* "I've always been fascinated at how myth functions in the human mind from cradle to grave." That same year, one of his most enduring books, *How Little Porcupine Played Christmas,* also appeared. The book reappeared with a new title, *Little Porcupine's Christmas,* and new cover art by Felicia Bond in 2001. Nearly twenty years after the publication of *How Little Porcupine Played Christmas,* Slate wrote a sequel, *Story Time for Porcupine,* featuring illustrations by Jacqueline Rogers. In a *Booklist* review, Shelley Townsend-Hudson described the work as a "terrific story-within-a-story book [that] revels in the joys of family love. From start to finish, this enchanting book is a delight."

1988's *Who Is Coming to Our House?* recounts the Nativity in quiet and simple rhymed couplets. Calling the book "A lovely addition to the Christmas canon," a contributor to *Kirkus Reviews* went on to praise the "gently cadenced couplets [which] finally reveal the arrival of Mary and Joseph." A decade later, Slate's *The Secret Stars* revisits the celebration of Jesus' birth but also continues a theme he introduced in *The Star Rocker.* Focusing on the Hispanic tradition of the Night of the Three Kings, Slate's story was given substantial praise by *School Library Journal* reviewer Mary M. Hopf, who commended the work for a text that reads like a poem and makes use of a number of poetic devices.

Miss Bindergarten Gets Ready for Kindergarten is a lively and energetic book about the first day of school. The book alternates between the teacher, Miss Bindergarten, and her pupils as they prepare for school. The characters, all young animals, are cleverly named in alphabetical sequence, the first letter of each name corresponding to the appropriate animal type—Adam is an alligator; Jessie is a jaguar. Martha V. Parravano, reviewing the book for *Horn Book,* noted that "The internal rhymes in short sentences and the recurring refrain make the book a natural for reading aloud." *Miss Bindergarten Celebrates the 100th Day of Kindergarten,* the second book in the series, concentrates on counting with Miss Bindergarten asking her pupils to collect one hundred objects to commemorate the hundredth day of school. John Peters noted in his *Booklist* review that "the short, rhymed text both comments on what's going on and provides a unifying backbeat."

Miss Bindergarten's adventures continue in *Miss Bindergarten Stays Home from Kindergarten,* the third book in the series. Like the earlier books, this one follows the days of the week and hides the alphabet as well. Writing in *School Library Journal,* Sheliah Kosco predicted "This book will alleviate the concerns of children who worry what will happen if their teacher is absent or sick." According to Slate, the next entry in the series, *Miss Bindergarten Takes a Field Trip with Kindergarten* also has some hidden lessons, but, as the author told *SATA,* "We want the books to be fun. The hidden lessons are secondary. Children want to be entertained, not preached to."

While working on the "Miss Bindergarten" series, Slate also wrote his first young adult novel, *Crossing the*

Using a poetic writing style, Slate tells a story of a family in New Mexico to familiarize readers with the way in which Mexican children celebrate the Nativity by waiting for gifts from the Three Kings. (From The Secret Stars, *written by Slate and illustrated by Felipe Davalos.*)

Trestle. Set in a fictional West Virginia town that is, according to Slate, "based somewhat on my home territory," the novel features a young boy who must overcome his fears and help his family begin a new life. Describing the book "as a warm period piece," *Bulletin of the Center for Children's Books* reviewer Elizabeth Bush claimed that the story's "happy ending is merited rather than contrived, and readers will watch them head off for new prospects westward with the utmost satisfaction." Writing in *Booklist,* Chris Sherman praised Slate's "cast of thoroughly likable, believable characters," going on to say that "it's a pleasure to see how the gentle story unfolds."

Discussing his approach to children's books, Slate explained to *SATA:* "You can't be self-indulgent when you write for children. But they do give you far more freedom than do adult readers, editors, or critics. I guess the artist in me loves the picture-book form because of that freedom."

Biographical and Critical Sources

PERIODICALS

Booklist, August, 1996, Carolyn Phelan, review of *Miss Bindergarten Gets Ready for Kindergarten,* p. 1906; September 15, 1998, Hazel Rochman, review of *The Secret Stars,* p. 240; October 15, 1998, John Peters, review of *Miss Bindergarten Celebrates the 100th Day of Kindergarten,* p. 430; January 1, 2000, Chris Sherman, review of *Crossing the Trestle,* p. 927; October 15, 2000, Shelley Townsend-Hudson, review of *Story Time for Porcupine,* p. 466.

Bulletin of the Center for Children's Books, September, 1996, Elizabeth Bush, review of *Miss Bindergarten Gets Ready for Kindergarten,* p. 31; December, 1999, Elizabeth Bush, review of *Crossing the Trestle,* p. 150.

Children's Book Review Service, March, 1985, review of *Lonely Lula Cat,* p. 80; January, 1999, Annette C. Blank, review of *The Secret Stars,* pp. 52-53; November, 1999, John E. Boyd, review of *Crossing the Trestle,* pp. 35-36.

Horn Book, September-October, 1996, Martha V. Parravano, review of *Miss Bindergarten Gets Ready for Kindergarten,* p. 587.

Kirkus Reviews, November 1, 1988, review of *Who Is Coming to Our House?,* p. 1610; June 1, 1996, review of *Miss Bindergarten Gets Ready for Kindergarten,* p. 829; October 15, 1999, review of *Crossing the Trestle,* p. 1652.

New York Times Book Review, January 5, 1997, Marigny Dupuy, review of *Miss Bindergarten Gets Ready for Kindergarten,* p. 22.

Publishers Weekly, June 28, 1985, review of *Lonely Lula Cat,* p. 74; October 28, 1988, review of *Who Is Coming to Our House?,* p. 77; July 27, 1998, review of *Miss Bindergarten Celebrates the 100th Day of Kindergarten,* p. 75.

School Library Journal, August, 1985, Joan McGrath, review of *Lonely Lula Cat,* p. 82; November, 1988, Heide Piehler, review of *Who Is Coming to Our House?,* p. 96; August, 1996, Virginia Opocensky, review of *Miss Bindergarten Gets Ready for Kindergarten,* p. 129; September, 1998, Marlene Gawron, review of *Miss Bindergarten Celebrates the 100th Day of Kindergarten,* p. 182; October, 1998, Mary M. Hopf, review of *The Secret Stars,* p. 45; October, 2000, Kate McLean, review of *Story Time for Porcupine,* p. 137; November, 2000, Sheilah Kosco, review of *Miss Bindergarten Stays Home from Kindergarten,* p. 134.

Tribune Books (Chicago), December 4, 1988, Mary Harris Veeder, review of *Who Is Coming to Our House?,* p. 13.

*   *   *

STORR, Catherine (Cole) 1913-2001 (Irene Adler, Helen Lourie)

OBITUARY NOTICE—See index for *SATA* sketch: Born July 21, 1913, in London, England; died January 6, 2001, in England. Writer and psychiatrist. Trained as a doctor, Storr developed into a prolific writer of books for children, young adults, and adults. After a fourteen-year career as a psychiatrist in the hospitals of London, Storr devoted herself full-time to storytelling and writing, and produced an extensive body of work that spans several genres, including retellings, novels, and nonfiction. Many of her works for children and teenagers are now considered classics, particularly in her native England. She is perhaps best known for her Polly stories for younger readers, which include *Clever Polly and the Stupid Wolf* (1955) and *Last Stories of Polly and the Wolf* (1992), as well as for her young adult novel *Marianne Dreams,* published in 1958. Storr wrote in many different genres, publishing ghost stories in 1994's *The Mirror Image Ghost,* and Biblical retellings in her "People of the Bible" series.

OBITUARIES AND OTHER SOURCES:

PERIODICALS

Guardian (London), January 11, 2001.
Independent (London), January 12, 2001.
Times (London), January 18, 2001.

*　　*　　*

STUCLEY, Elizabeth
See NORTHMORE, Elizabeth Florence

T

THOMSON, Pat 1939-

Personal

Born April 28, 1939, in Norwich, England; married Roy Thomson (a leather chemist), June 6, 1961; children: Susanna, Alexander. *Education:* University of Leeds, B.A. (honors), 1960, post-graduate certificate in education, 1961; University of Loughborough, M.L.S., 1982, Diploma in Librarianship, 1982. *Hobbies and other interests:* Opera and collecting baby rattles ("I make sure that the baby has finished with them, of course.")

Addresses

Home—The Long House, Behind 43 West St., Oundle PE8 4EJ, England. *Office*—University College Northampton, Boughton Green Rd., Northampton NN2 7AL, England. *Agent*—Laura Cecil, 17 Alwyne Villas, London N1 2HG, England. *E-mail*—pat.thomson@northampton.ac.uk.

Career

University College, Northampton, England, education librarian, 1975—. Has also taught French. *Member:* Federation of Children's Book Groups (honorary president), Society of Authors.

Writings

FOR CHILDREN

(Compiler) *Rhymes around the Day,* illustrated by Jan Ormerod, Lothrop, 1983.
Trouble in the Cupboard, Yearling, 1987.
Family Gathering: A Collection of Family Stories, illustrated by Toni Goffe, Dent, 1988.
Strange Exchange, Gollancz, 1991.
Beware of the Aunts!, illustrated by Emma Chichester Clark, McElderry Books, 1992.
Tales Told after Lights Out (short stories), HarperCollins, 1993.

Superpooch, illustrated by Mike Gordon, HarperCollins, 1996.
A Ghost-Light in the Attic, illustrated by Annabel Large, Black, 1996.
Superpooch and the Missing Sausages, illustrated by Mike Gordon, HarperCollins, 1996.
Superpooch and the Garden Ghosts, illustrated by Mike Gordon, HarperCollins, 1999.
The Silkworm Mystery: The Story of Louis Pasteur, illustrated by David Kearney, Macdonald Young Books, 1999.
A Cauldron of Magical Stories, Transworld, 2000.
Pirates, Gold and Custard, Oxford University Press, 2001.
Chocolate Boxes, Oxford University Press, 2001.
Ghoul School (pop-up book), Tango, 2001.

"SHARE-A-STORY" SERIES; FOR CHILDREN

The Treasure Sock, illustrated by Tony Ross, Gollancz, 1986, Delacorte, 1987.
One of Those Days, illustrated by Bob Wilson, Delacorte, 1986.
Can You Hear Me, Grandad?, illustrated by Jez Alborough, Delacorte, 1986.
My Friend Mr. Morris, illustrated by Satoshi Kitamura, Delacorte, 1987.
Thank You for the Tadpole, illustrated by Mary Rayner, Delacorte, 1987.
Good Girl Granny, illustrated by Faith Jaques, Delacorte, 1987.
Dial D for Disaster, illustrated by Paul Demeyer, Trafalgar Square, 1990.
No Trouble at All, illustrated by Jocelyn Wild, Trafalgar Square, 1990.
Best Pest, illustrated by Peter Firmin, Trafalgar Square, 1990.
The Best Thing of All, illustrated by Margaret Chamberlain, Trafalgar Square, 1990.

"JETS" SERIES; FOR CHILDREN; ILLUSTRATED BY CAROLINE CROSSLAND

Jacko, Black, 1989.
Rhyming Russell, Black, 1991.
Messages, Black, 1992.

The Man in Shades, Black, 1994.
Lost Property, Black, 1995.
Talking Pictures, Black, 1998.

EDITOR OF STORY ANTHOLOGIES FOR CHILDREN

A Basket of Stories for Seven Year Olds, illustrated by Rachel Birkett, Doubleday, 1990.

A Sackful of Stories for Eight Year Olds, illustrated by Paddy Mounter, Doubleday, 1990.

A Bucketful of Stories for Six Year Olds, illustrated by Mark Southgate, Doubleday, 1991.

A Chest of Stories for Nine Year Olds, illustrated by Peter Bailey, Doubleday, 1991.

A Pocketful of Stories for Five Year Olds, illustrated by P. Dann, Doubleday, 1992.

A Satchel of Stories, illustrated by Doffy Weir, Doubleday, 1992.

A Stocking Full of Christmas Stories, illustrated by Peter Bailey, Doubleday, 1992.

A Bus Full of Stories for Four Year Olds, illustrated by Steve Cox, Doubleday, 1995.

A Cracker Full of Christmas Stories, illustrated by J. Riley, Doubleday, 1995.

A Band of Joining-In Stories, illustrated by Steve Cox, Doubleday, 1995.

A Box of Stories for Six Year Olds, illustrated by Phillip Norman, Doubleday, 1997.

A Bed Full of Nighttime Stories, illustrated by Anthony Lewis, Corgi, 1998.

A Parcel of Stories for Five Year Olds, illustrated by Anthony Lewis, Corgi, 1999.

OTHER

Contributor to *Books for Keeps, School Librarian, Bookmark,* and *International Review of Children's Literature and Librarianship.* Thomson's short stories have also been included in several anthologies for young readers, including *Stories for 5 Year Olds, Snake on the Bus, Assemblies, Themes for Early Years: Pets, The Puffin Book of Five-Minute Stories,* and *Magical Stories for 5 Year Olds.* Nonfiction editor of *Carousel.*

Jacko has been published in Welsh, Finnish, Spanish, Gaelic, and Catalan; *Messages* has been published in Spanish and Catalan; *Dial D for Disaster* has been published in French; *The Treasure Sock* has been published in Spanish and French.

Adaptations

Rhyming Russell has been recorded for audiocassette, Collins Audio; *The Treasure Sock* has been adapted as an English language teaching CD in Japan.

Sidelights

Pat Thomson is a British writer for children whose well-received works include chapter and picture books for beginning readers. An innovator in formats that interest both parents and children, Thomson is known for such popular works in the "Share a Story" series as *Good Girl Granny, My Friend Mr. Morris,* and *Can You Hear Me, Grandad?,* books full of quirky, eccentric, loveable characters and situations that turn hilarious in a very quiet manner. "Tongue-in-cheek humor" is a phrase often touted in reviews of Thomson's work. The author has also penned non-series titles, including her popular "Superpooch" trio of books and the comical *Beware of the Aunts!,* which is about a little girl who has too many of those effusive relatives. Additionally, she has edited story collections for readers from age four to ten, books that collect fine writing in adventure, the supernatural, folktales, and humor.

Born in Norwich, England, in 1939, Thomson graduated from the University of Leeds with honors in 1960 and took a post-graduate certificate in education in 1961. She was also married in that year and soon had a busy life as a mother raising two children. It was not until her children were older that she began working as an education librarian. In 1982 she went back to school and earned a degree in librarianship. It was during this time, as she once related to *SATA,* that she first began to think about writing books herself.

"I began writing rather late," Thomson commented. "I was the typical, avid child reader; but it was not until I returned to work when my children were growing up that I decided to work with books in a teacher training college. I became particularly concerned with the quality and nature of early reading material, wondering if boring, banal 'readers' actually made children not want to read. Consequently, my first books had in mind children who were only just getting to grips with print, but who surely needed the pleasures of lively language and challenging imaginings." Thomson further noted that after having taught older children, she began to see how important it was that youngsters enjoy their early reading experiences.

As a result, Thomson created the unique "Share-a-Story" series so that young children and their parents could enjoy reading together. In the "Share-a-Story" books, the text on the right is written in a simpler style than the text on the left. The parent reads on the left side, while the child reads the simpler text on the right; the goal is for the parent to teach the child to ultimately read the more difficult text, and hence to be able to read the book on his or her own. Early installments in the series include *The Treasure Sock, Good Girl Granny, Can You Hear Me, Grandad?,* and *My Friend Mr. Morris.* In the first title, a mother is variously amused, intrigued, and disgusted by all the things her young child has collected in a sock. "The story builds to a climax which consists of a remarkably grotesque list of treasures and the offensive sock is dropped into the washing," commented M. Maran in a review for *Books for Your Children.* Maran recommended the entire series and *The Treasure Sock* "in particular," for providing books "especially designed to encourage children to read." In *Good Girl Granny* the reader learns of Granny's naughty days as a child in an "entertaining" text, according to Liz Waterland in *Books for Keeps. Good Girl Granny* was inspired by events in the life of Thomson's own grandmother.

In *Can You Hear Me, Grandad?* a grandfather and his granddaughter are going to the zoo, but the elder's supposed problem with hearing creates some humorous misunderstandings. "A leopard cannot change its spots," for example, becomes garbled as "Cannot change its socks," and "ride on llamas" is interpreted as "go in your pajamas." A reviewer for *Junior Bookshelf* felt that this was "a useful book to share, with some enjoyable word-play and lively illustrations." The same writer felt that the layout of the book enabled "beginner readers [to] gain experience of moving through a text with sufficient pace to enjoy the storyline." Misunderstandings also inform *My Friend Mr. Morris,* in which the title character interprets everything he hears literally; for example, he believes that a hat band is a band that performs on a hat.

Another series for young readers is "Jets" in which, as Thomson explained to *SATA,* "picture and extra-text reading are so entertainingly entwined." The story of Russell Fussell is told in *Rhyming Russell,* and it is a very rhyming one indeed. The young boy just cannot stop himself from speaking in rhyme, and this gets him in trouble. But his odd skill finally saves the school play from disaster. Rachel Redford, reviewing the title in *Books for Keeps,* called the audiocassette adaptation of the book a "funny story." *Talking Pictures* is a larger version of the "Jets" series that deals with the misadventures of an exceedingly rich orphan, Talitha Augusta Fortescue Fitz-Rowland. Talitha thinks she is the last Fitz-Rowland in the world until she uncovers an old letter that leads her to believe there are other relatives about. Andrew Kidd, reviewing the story in *Books for Keeps,* felt that it was an "interesting idea involving family trees," but also mentioned that "it is just too confusing for its likely audience."

Thomson's stand-alone titles are numerous and cover a wide range of genres and formats. One of her most popular titles is the picture book *Beware of the Aunts!,* which is about a young girl who describes her nine aunts' unusual habits: one wears strange clothes, one eats too much, one just might be a witch, but all are very generous as is shown one Christmas. *Children's Book Review Service* critic Emily Holchin Ferren noted that this British import has "zany, colorful illustrations" and will "tickle your funnybone." Writing about the same book in *School Librarian,* Beverley Mathias called it "a nicely written, tongue-in-cheek expose of a number of aunts, their habits and behaviour." In *Superpooch* and its sequels, Thomson presents a Superman in canine form. Mrs. May's docile little Poochie-woochie has only to duck behind a lamppost, cry out "bones and biscuits," and voila, it's Superpooch to the rescue to right the wrongs of the world. In the hero's first outing, Superpooch outwits a school bully and takes on the vile rats that have stolen a toy rabbit from a baby. "Good fun," is how a reviewer for *Magpies* characterized the initial title in the ongoing group of interrelated books.

A departure for Thomson came with 1997's *A Ghost-Light in the Attic,* a novel for older readers set in contemporary times and during the English Civil War.

Tom and Bridget, two modern youngsters, are researching material in the attic of Bridgeford Hall when they encounter Elinor, the ghost of a girl whose family was divided by the two opposing sides of the long-ago English Civil War, the Cavaliers and the Roundheads. This young girl simply steps out of the family portrait in which she is painted, and then the other two children follow her back in to find themselves in the seventeenth century. Catriona Nicholson commented in *School Librarian* that the book was a "fantasy of time-slip, between the present day and Stuart times." Nicholson also praised the book for the amount of historical information it imparts on the time, as well as for "fascinating insights into how families became divided through loyal adherence to Parliament or King."

In addition to writing her own books, Thomson has compiled many short story anthologies for children organized by age. Drawing from writers as disparate as Beverly Cleary, Catherine Storr, Astrid Lindgren, Ted Hughes, Arnold Lobel, Laura Ingalls Wilder, and Rumer Godden, among many others, Thomson presents anthologies that are both entertaining and culturally diverse. Reviewing *A Basket of Stories for Seven Year Olds,* *School Librarian* contributor David Churchill called the book "an extremely useful collection." In a review of *A Satchel of Stories,* Cathy Sutton commented in *School Librarian* on the "humour" in the collection and further noted that it was a "very entertaining collection which children will thoroughly enjoy." Writing about *A Bus Full of Stories for Four Years Olds* in *Books For Keeps,* Liz Waterland observed that Thomson "clearly believes that early years are a time for wonder and quality language," and concluded that the stories collected in the book "put to shame the impoverished and patronising language offered by Kiddy-Books and Kiddy-T.V. Buy it now and use it often." Hazel Townson, writing in *School Librarian,* found Thomson's *A Band of Joining-In Stories* "[g]reat fun, and a really useful addition to any storyteller's list," while Annabel Gibb, writing in *Books for Keeps,* felt that *A Bed Full of Nighttime Stories* was an "anthology of consistently high standard, suitable for home or school use." The every-busy Thomson has also written articles about children's books and library studies for several magazines, including *Books for Keeps, School Librarian,* and *Bookmark.*

Thomson concluded to *SATA:* "I believe I have a strong sense of the audience I am writing for, but I suppose one always ends up 'writing for oneself' to some degree, especially when the characters seize the imagination. That is the greatest pleasure—to live richly in one's head and to share that with young readers.... If I have a prime motivation for writing, it is to try to persuade children to enter the reading world and gain from it all that I did as a child. And I am aware that in writing I continue to experience those same intellectual, imaginative and emotional pleasures."

Biographical and Critical Sources

PERIODICALS

Books for Keeps, November, 1992, Rachel Redford, review of *Rhyming Russell,* p. 35; September, 1995, Liz Waterland, review of *Good Girl Granny,* p. 9; November, 1995, Liz Waterland, review of *A Bus Full of Stories for Four Year Olds,* p. 7; November, 1996, p. 8; July, 1997, pp. 21-22; November, 1997, p. 24; July, 1998, Andrew Kidd, review of *Talking Pictures,* p. 23; January, 1999, Annabel Gibb, review of *A Bed Full of Nighttime Stories,* p. 20.

Books for Your Children, autumn, 1993, p. 3; spring, 1995, M. Maran, review of *The Treasure Sock,* p. 14.

Children's Book Review Service, spring, 1992, Emily Holchin Ferren, review of *Beware of the Aunts!,* p. 138.

Junior Bookshelf, December, 1990, p. 285; February, 1992, p. 23; June, 1992, p. 115; October, 1992, p. 202; December, 1992, p. 248; February, 1995, p. 28; February, 1995, review of *Can You Hear Me, Grandad?,* p. 29.

Magpies, May, 1993, p. 30; July, 1996, review of *Superpooch,* p. 28.

Publishers Weekly, December 25, 1987, p. 73; March 9, 1992, p. 57.

School Librarian, February, 1991, David Churchill, review of *A Basket Full of Stories for Seven Year Olds,* p. 62; February, 1992, Beverley Mathias, review of *Beware of the Aunts!,* p. 58; November, 1992, Cathy Sutton, review of *A Satchel of School Stories,* p. 146; February, 1996, Hazel Townson, review of *A Band of Joining-In Stories,* p. 22; May, 1996, Catriona Nicholson, review of *A Ghost-Light in the Attic,* p. 62; August, 1997, p. 134; summer, 1999, p. 90.

School Library Journal, February, 1987, p. 35; September, 1988, p. 66; January, 1989, p. 67; February, 1991, p. 21; July, 1992, p. 65.

Times Educational Supplement, November 14, 1986, p. 40; July 11, 1988, p. 30; March 24, 1989, p. 25; September 21, 1990, p. R4.

—Sketch by J. Sydney Jones

*   *   *

TICKLE, Jack
See CHAPMAN, Jane

*   *   *

TREVOR, (Lucy) Meriol 1919-2000

OBITUARY NOTICE—See index for *SATA* sketch: Born April 15, 1919, in London, England; died January 12, 2000. Writer. Trevor authored fiction, biographies, children's books, and a volume of poetry; her books are marked by meticulous research of historical and biographical facts, as well as her strong Catholic faith. Best-known for her 1962 two-volume biography of Cardinal Newman, *Newman: The Pillar of Cloud* and *Newman: Light in Winter,* this work brought Trevor the 1963 James Tait Black Memorial Prize for Biography. Her first book was the 1949 children's novel *Forest and the Kingdom,* which introduced young readers to the World Dionysus, a fantasy realm Trevor and friend Margaret Priestley created as children. Her last works included *The Shadow of a Crown: The Life Story of James II of England and VII of Scotland,* published in 1988, and the four novels comprising the "Letzenstein" series for children, released in the years between 1997 and 1999. Following World War II, she served as a relief worker with the United Nations Relief and Rehabilitation Administration in Italy.

OBITUARIES AND OTHER SOURCES:

PERIODICALS

Times (London), January 14, 2000.

V

VAN DRAANEN, Wendelin

Personal

Married; children: two sons. *Hobbies and other interests:* Reading, running, and playing in a rock band.

Addresses

Home—California.

Wendelin Van Draanen

Career

Writer. Has taught high school math and computer science.

Awards, Honors

Edgar Award for Best Children's Mystery, and Best Book for Young Adults selection, American Library Association, both 1999, both for *Sammy Keyes and the Hotel Thief.*

Writings

How I Survived Being a Girl, HarperCollins, 1997.
Flipped, Knopf, 2001.

"SAMMY KEYES" SERIES

Sammy Keyes and the Hotel Thief, illustrated by Dan Yaccarino, Knopf, 1998.
Sammy Keyes and the Skeleton Man, illustrated by Dan Yaccarino, Knopf, 1998.
Sammy Keyes and the Sisters of Mercy, illustrated by Dan Yaccarino, Knopf, 1999.
Sammy Keyes and the Runaway Elf, illustrated by Dan Yaccarino, Knopf, 1999.
Sammy Keyes and the Curse of Moustache Mary, illustrated by Dan Yaccarino, Knopf, 2000.
Sammy Keyes and the Hollywood Mummy, illustrated by Dan Yaccarino, Knopf, 2001.

Work in Progress

Another Sammy Keyes novel.

Sidelights

Wendelin Van Draanen is the author of the popular "Sammy Keyes" mystery series for young readers, featuring an indomitable tomboy with a penchant for landing herself in trouble. The misunderstood heroine, whose formal name is Samantha, often starts out as the primary suspect in some sort of minor crime and finds the real culprit through efforts to clear her own name.

The junior-high schooler also combats some tough family and social situations with the same sense of humor and adventure. Van Draanen's first book in the series—only her second ever published—won the Edgar Award for Best Children's Mystery in 1999. "The audience I have in mind is the kid who's coming to a place where they have to make decisions on their own," the writer once told *Authors and Artists for Young Adults.* "I try to shed a little light on the merits of being good, heroic, and honest. I hope that kids come away from reading my work with a little more strength and belief in themselves and the sense that they *can* shape their own destiny."

Until she was in the fourth grade when her sister was born, Van Draanen grew up the sole daughter in a family with three children, having an older and a younger brother. The situation provided the inspiration for her intrepid, tomboy protagonists of her books, though the future author described her own juvenile persona as tentative and shy. "My parents immigrated to the United States, so there was always something 'foreign' about our family," Van Draanen once said. "I never really felt like I fit in unless I was with my family." Still, she admitted to a daring streak when backed up by her siblings. "I did a lot of 'boy stuff,'" she recalled. "We spied on the neighbors, played in the school yard across the street—roller-skating, kickball, dodgeball, hide 'n' seek—we also loved to go swimming at the Plunge (community pool) and ride bikes. Indoor activities included reading (loved mysteries) and endless hours of chess. We also had chores, chores, chores!"

Like other shy children, Van Draanen found comfort in the world of books. She particularly enjoyed popular teen sleuth series, including *Nancy Drew,* the *Hardy Boys,* and *Encyclopedia Brown.* "My father would read to us at bedtime," she once noted. "He'd gather my brothers and me up in a bed and read from a collection of stories for children. We relished storytime and the way he read. My mother did this, too, but I remember the times with my father the best." Van Draanen remembered learning to read at an early age, thanks to one of her siblings. "I began to read by watching my older brother learn to read. I'd hang over his shoulder while he got help from my mother, and that's how I picked it up. My mother worked with all of us, teaching us reading and mathematics at a very early age. One of my favorite pictures of me as a young girl was taken at the age of about eighteen months—I'm sitting on the toilet, feet dangling, engrossed in a book that's in my lap."

Entering adolescence was a time of added uncertainty for Van Draanen, however. Her coming-of-age adventures would form the basis for the comical problems she later forces Sammy Keyes to suffer. "I liked elementary school, but beginning in junior high I felt terribly awkward and on the outskirts of social circles," she remembered in an interview with *Authors and Artists for Young Adults.* "I guess you'd call me a straight-A student. Academics were important in our family. I liked learning." She remained rather shy throughout her teens,

and did not even have her first date until the night of her senior prom.

Van Draanen looked forward to an impressive career. "My parents were both chemists, so I was sure I'd become something scientific," she once said. "I really wanted to be a singer, but was much too shy to put that forward, so I stuck to science and math. I certainly did not want to be a writer! It seemed so dull!" But when she was in college, a catastrophe in her family would inadvertently open up a new door for her: their family business was destroyed by arson, and she took time off from school to help out. For a time, they were financially ruined, and Van Draanen was troubled by feelings of anger and helplessness. She began to have problems sleeping, and to help alleviate some of the stress, she decided to write about the incident, with the hope of turning it into a screenplay.

Van Draanen discovered that writing was not only cathartic but enjoyable. What she found most rewarding, she would later note, was the ability to create a happy ending, to have her characters make positive gains through personal difficulties. Van Draanen would eventually find her vocation as a teacher of computer science to high schoolers, but she also had ten finished novels, each around four hundred pages long, by the mid-1990s. By then she had married and had begun a family of her own in California.

Van Draanen was inspired to try her hand at writing for children as a result of a chance gift. "My husband gave me *Dandelion Wine* (by Ray Bradbury) and told me it was one of his favorite books. I read it and it reminded me of all the wonderful mischief my brothers and I got into when we were young, and decided it would be fun to write a book like *Dandelion Wine* about my experiences growing up." The result was *How I Survived Being a Girl,* published in 1997. It is Van Draanen's first work for young readers outside of her "Sammy Keyes" series, and the works share a heroine with pointed similarities. Carolyn, the narrator of *How I Survived Being a Girl,* is a tomboy who feels herself somewhat alienated from the girls in her neighborhood and at school. She much prefers tagging along with her brothers and their friends, especially a neighbor boy named Charlie. During the summer of her twelfth year, Carolyn spies on neighbors, digs foxholes with Charlie, steals a book, and helps her brother with his paper route.

The setting of *How I Survived Being a Girl* is vague, but reviewers seemed to agree that Van Draanen placed her story at some point in the relatively recent past. Girls must still wear dresses to school, for instance, and are strongly discouraged from becoming newspaper carriers—official and unofficial biases that had vanished by the end of the 1970s. Carolyn manages to skirt the skirt issue by wearing shorts under hers; meanwhile, she derides her peers who play with dolls and wear frilly, impractical clothes. Yet as she begins a new school year in September, Carolyn finds that some of her attitudes are beginning to change. She sees Charlie in a new way, and starts to speak out and become more politically active. She even starts a petition drive to force some changes at her school. When a baby sister arrives in her family, this softens her attitude, too. "I tell her ... how being a girl is actually all right once you figure out that you should break some of the rules instead of just living with them," says Carolyn at the end.

A *Publishers Weekly* reviewer called *How I Survived Being a Girl* an "energetic first novel" and "a sunny, funny look at a girl with a smart mouth and scabby knees." Writing in *School Library Journal,* Kathleen Odean found some fault with the premise that a new sibling can bring out an adolescent girl's feminine instincts. "Perhaps the unspecified time setting ... makes it inevitable that she will be 'tamed a bit,' as she puts it," remarked Odean. Yet a *Kirkus Reviews* critic praised Van Draanen's style and the narrative voice of her alter ego, Carolyn. "Her irreverent narration is engaging," stated the reviewer about the book's heroine, "and she's refreshingly astute about family and neighborhood dynamics."

Twelve-year-old Sammy must determine whether she has witnessed a crime when she uses her binoculars to peek into the windows of the nearby Heavenly Hotel in Van Draanen's award-winning humorous mystery novel. (Cover illustration by Dan Yaccarino.)

Van Draanen found that "I loved writing in the voice of a twelve-year-old so much that I haven't gone back, and have no desire to go back, to writing for adults," she once stated. She began writing a teen-detective story that would evolve into a popular and much-praised series. The first of these arrived in 1998 with *Sammy Keyes and the Hotel Thief.* Here, readers are introduced to the feisty, intelligent title character who lives with her grandmother in a seniors-only apartment building. Because of this, Sammy is forced to sneak around just to get to school; naturally, her social life is severely curtailed as well. Sammy lives with her grandmother, readers learn, because her mother, to whom she refers as "Lady Lana," has moved to Hollywood.

Sammy has some formidable enemies. One is the nosy Mrs. Graybill, who lives down the hall; another is a girl, Heather, who torments her daily at school. To keep herself amused at home, Sammy often observes the goings-on of the outside world with a pair of binoculars from her fifth-floor window. "Usually you just see people looking out their windows, pointing to stuff on the street or talking on the phone," Sammy states, "but sometimes you can see people yelling at each other, which is really strange because you can't *hear* anything."

Sammy is particularly fascinated by the shady Heavenly Hotel across the street, and one afternoon spots a fourth-floor resident moving about a room rather quickly. She then sees the man rifling through a purse while wearing gloves. As Sammy tells it: "And I'm trying to get a better look at his face through all his bushy brown hair and beard, when he stuffs a wad of money from the purse into his jacket pocket and then looks up. Right at me. For a second there I don't think he believed his eyes. He kind of leaned into the window and stared, and I stared right back through the binoculars. Then I did something really, really stupid. I waved."

The man flees the room, and she wonders whether she has just witnessed a crime and if she ought to tell someone about it. But her grandmother is making dinner, and she can't call 911 from the kitchen; getting to a police station is also problematic. Then, her grandmother calls her into the kitchen and reminds her to feed the cat. When the doorbell rings, Sammy is so agitated that she does not quietly make for the closet, as is her usual drill when an unexpected visitor arrives. "This time, though, I jumped. I jumped and yelped like a puppy. And all of a sudden my heart's pounding because I know who it is," Sammy panics. "It's the guy I saw at the Heavenly Hotel, come to shut me up for good."

Eventually, Sammy manages to tell the police, who fail to take her seriously at first. Meanwhile, Heather is plotting against her at school, but Sammy's cleverness uncovers the plot in time. She also learns that a burglar has indeed been stealing from purses in the neighborhood. Other characters in the book include a pair of comical detectives, her friend Marissa, a local DJ, and an eccentric astrologer who is also a robbery victim. They all help Sammy bring the thief to justice. "The solution will likely come as a surprise, and the sleuth delights from start to finish," asserted a *Publishers Weekly* critic in a review of *Sammy Keyes and the Hotel Thief.* A *Horn Book* review by Martha V. Parravano described Van Draanen's protagonist as "one tough, smart, resourceful seventh grader," and compared the heroine and structure of the lighthearted detective novel to popular adult mystery writers such as Sue Grafton, who are adept at "making the investigator's character and private life at least as interesting and complex as the plot," noted Parravano.

Van Draanen followed the success of the first Sammy Keyes book with a second that same year, *Sammy Keyes and the Skeleton Man.* As it opens around Halloween time, Sammy still lives with her grandmother and is eagerly outfitting herself as the Marsh Monster for the holiday. While trick-or-treating, she and her friends bravely approach the "Bush House," a scary manse with wildly overgrown shrubbery. But then Sammy is nearly knocked down by a man wearing a skeleton costume and carrying a pillowcase. She and her friends advance and discover a fire in the house, and Sammy puts it out. They also find that a burglary has just taken place, and several valuable books are missing from the house.

Sammy, naturally, finds herself drawn into the drama and wants to solve the whodunit. She learns that the Bush House is neglected because its owners, the LeBard brothers, are feuding with one another. Once again, her cleverness helps her find a solution, and also helps her keep one step ahead of Heather, who continues to plot against her. Sammy, for instance, sneaks into Heather's Halloween party and plants a baby monitor in her room—which provides Sammy with evidence that Heather has been making prank phone calls in Sammy's name. Yet Sammy's natural talent for making friends also helps her forge an unusual bond with Chauncy LeBard, and she even gets the two warring brothers to agree to talk. In the end, she unmasks the skeleton man and recovers the missing rarities. Parravano, reviewing the story for *Horn Book,* praised it as a "highly readable mystery [that] hits the ground running." Critic Lynda Short also offered positive words in *School Library Journal:* "Readers will enjoy the mystery, hijinks, plotting, and adult comeuppance."

Van Draanen's third entry in the series, *Sammy Keyes and the Sisters of Mercy,* was published in 1999. Still walking that fine line between intellectual brilliance and juvenile delinquency, Sammy finds herself sentenced to twenty hours of detention, which she must fulfill by helping out at the local Roman Catholic church. One day, cleaning the windows of St. Mary's, she sees a girl she does not know and approaches her, but the girl vanishes and Sammy is suddenly alerted to the distress of Father Mayhew, who has just discovered his valuable ivory cross missing. Sammy, of course, is the first suspect in the theft. Yet other possible culprits surface as well, and in order to clear her own name, she resolves to catch the thief herself. On another day, she again sees the mysterious girl at the church's soup kitchen and eventually learns that she is homeless.

The third title of Van Draanen's 'Sammy Keyes' mystery series features the quirky characters and the indefatigable Sammy who must prove her innocence when she is accused of stealing a valuable ivory cross. (Cover illustration by Yaccarino.)

Again, Van Draanen tries to make Sammy a typical adolescent. There is more enmity with Heather, and she is determined to beat her foe in the local softball league championships. In the end, it is Sammy's offer to help a group of musical nuns who do missionary work out of an old school bus that helps solve the mystery of Father Mayhew's missing cross. "As always, quirky characters are Van Draanen's strength," remarked Kay Weisman in a *Booklist* review. An assessment from Jennifer Ralston in *School Library Journal* praised the main plot of *Sammy Keyes and the Sisters of Mercy* as well as the other story lines, both recurring and new. Ralston noted the story lines provide "depth and interest to an already engrossing mystery while capturing the angst of junior high school." Beth E. Anderson, reviewing it for *Voice of Youth Advocates,* commended Van Draanen's heroine. "Sammy is genuine, funny, devoted to her friends and blessed with a strength of character that lets her reach for a peaceful solution," Anderson wrote.

Van Draanen wrote another entry in the series that also appeared in 1999, *Sammy Keyes and the Runaway Elf.* Set during the Christmas season, Sammy is still in seventh grade and becomes involved in her community's holiday parade. She is assigned to the "Canine Calendar Float" and is charged with babysitting a famous Pomeranian, the calendar cover dog, Marique. Parade chaos ensues, however, when a trio of culprits dressed as the Three Kings throw cats onto the hound-laden float. The prized Marique vanishes, and its owner, wealthy Mrs. Landvogt, blackmails Sammy into finding Marique in order to avoid paying the fifty thousand dollar ransom demanded. An elfin girl, Elyssa, turns out to be a runaway, and Van Draanen weaves her plight and the dognapping together and ties it up with another, according to critics, satisfying conclusion. Once again, however, several suspects must first be eliminated and comical plot twists steered through. This time, Sammy manages to befriend the formidable Mrs. Graybill, too. Remarking upon Sammy's penchant for making friends both younger and much older than herself, *School Library Journal* reviewer Linda Bindner noted that "Van Draanen handles the relationships with style and sensitivity."

A fifth book in the series, *Sammy Keyes and the Curse of Moustache Mary,* was published in 2000, followed by *Sammy Keyes and the Hollywood Mummy* in 2001. Reviewing the latter title in *School Library Journal,* critic Wanda Meyers-Hines noted that it is "clever and fast-paced, and ... filled with cliff-hanger chapter endings and characters with secrets." As with all of her books, Van Draanen finds that the complex plots seem to come to her slowly. "I get an idea and just let it stew and stew in my brain until it's boiling over," she once said. "Then I start writing and can't stop until the story's out." She conducts all of her research herself and then sits down to writing in her inimitable character's voice. "I need to be able to get into the 'Sammy-zone,' where I feel like I'm channeling her. I work best when the computer can just suck me in and trap me. That's when things start cookin'!"

The success of her career as an author led Van Draanen to give up her teaching job. "This is my first year as a full-time writer," she said in the summer of 2000. "All those years before I'd get up when my husband got ready for work (5:00 AM) and just stumble over to the computer to get in an hour or two before I had to get the kids up (I have a six year old and a nine year old) and go off to teach school. I still get up early with my husband and find that early morning is still my most productive time." She plans to continue writing for adolescents. "They're growing, they're changing, and they're receptive to making the world a better place," Van Draanen

enthused. "They have big dreams that they want to reach for. I try to give them the strength to believe that—with determination, thought, and persistence—they can attain them. Growing up's not easy. Everyone feels awkward through adolescence, but when you're a kid it seems that you're the only one who's not fitting in. Everyone else seems to have it together, or be comfortable with themselves. It's not true, but that's how we feel when we're kids.

"It's my goal to get kids through those awkward years and onto adulthood safely. The choices they make in the areas of honesty, convictions, friendships, and compassion now will effect them their entire lives."

Biographical and Critical Sources

BOOKS

Authors and Artists for Young Adults, Volume 36, Gale, 2000.

PERIODICALS

Booklist, September 1, 1998, p. 131; April 1, 1999, Kay Weisman, review of *Sammy Keyes and the Sisters of Mercy,* p. 1415; September 1, 1999, p. 146; March 1, 2001, Gillian Engberg, review of *Sammy Keyes and the Hollywood Mummy,* p. 1272.

Horn Book, July-August, 1998, Martha V. Parravano, review of *Sammy Keyes and the Hotel Thief,* pp. 498-499; November-December, 1998, Martha V. Parravano, review of *Sammy Keyes and the Skeleton Man,* p. 743.

Kirkus Reviews, December 1, 1996, review of *How I Survived Being a Girl.*

Publishers Weekly, January 6, 1997, review of *How I Survived Being a Girl,* p. 73; April 27, 1998, review of *Sammy Keyes and the Hotel Thief,* p. 67.

San Luis Obispo Tribune, September 27, 1999.

School Library Journal, February, 1997, Kathleen Odean, review of *How I Survived Being a Girl,* p. 106; July, 1998, p. 100; September, 1998, Lynda Short, review of *Sammy Keyes and the Skeleton Man,* p. 211; July, 1999, Jennifer Ralston, review of *Sammy Keyes and the Sisters of Mercy,* p. 101; September, 1999, Linda Bindner, review of *Sammy Keyes and the Runaway Elf,* p. 229; August, 2000, p. 190; February, 2001, Wanda Meyers-Hines, review of *Sammy Keyes and the Hollywood Mummy,* p. 122; March, 2001, Sarah Flowers, review of *Sammy Keyes and the Hotel Thief,* p. 87.

Voice of Youth Advocates, April, 2000, Beth E. Anderson, review of *Sammy Keyes and the Sisters of Mercy,* pp. 40-41.

W

WADEMAN, Peter John 1946-
(Spike Wademan)

Personal

Born December 25, 1946, in Nottingham, England; son of Robert Wademan (an electrical engineer) and Eveyn Shar Hutton; married Sue Simmons (a textile artist), July 12, 1974; children: Holly, Rowan, Brecon. *Education:* South Essex College of Technology and Art, Diploma in technical illustration, 1965. *Hobbies and other interests:* Model ship building.

Addresses

Home—117-B Wynyard Cr., Queenstown, Otago, New Zealand. *E-mail*—wademan@xtra.co.nz.

Career

Illustrator. The Design Group, London, England, commercial illustrator, 1966-69; Combined Graphics, London, advertising illustrator, 1969-74; freelance illustrator, Sydney, Australia, and Queenstown, New Zealand, 1974—; Wademan Artworks P/L, founder, 1979—. Randwick Tafe and University of Western Sydney, guest tutor of illustration, 1982-95; Extended (an afterschool learning center for gifted and talented children), teacher, 1982-95. Australian Air League, education officer, 1994-98. *Exhibitions:* Work exhibited at galleries in Sydney, Australia, and Queenstown, New Zealand. *Military service:* 44th Parachute Battalion, Airborne Forces of England, driver; 4 Royal New South Wales Regiment, Infantry Battalion, Australia.

Illustrator

"INVESTIGATE" SERIES

(With Mark Vesey) *Racing Cars,* Random House (Milsons Point, New South Wales), 1999.

Paul Payne, *Space Consultant,* Random House (Milsons Point, New South Wales), 2000.

Peter John Wademan

Margaret McPhee and Judith Simpson, *Planes,* Random House (Milsons Point, New South Wales), 2000.

(With Kevin Stead and Jenny Black) Judith Simpson, *Dinosaurs,* Random House (Milsons Point, New South Wales), 2000.

OTHER

Anitomica, Global, 2000.

Also contributor of illustrations to magazines, including *Aviation History.*

Work in Progress

Illustrations for a book about boats and ships for the "Investigate" series.

Sidelights

Growing up amid the bombed buildings in Nottingham, England, Peter John "Spike" Wademan learned about aircrafts as his father, who flew a Spitfire aircraft, shared stories about his experiences in World War II. Wademan told *SATA* that "from a young age, my father took me to every air display in and around London, which initiated a great love for these war-time aircrafts." A member of the Air Cadets until he was eighteen, Wademan enjoyed drawing and making models of airplanes. Eventually, he attended South Essex College for Technical Art, graduating in 1965, and began working as an illustrator at commercial and advertising companies in London.

In 1974 Wademan decided to ply his craft in Australia where he worked as a freelance illustrator for advertising agencies as well as an instructor at schools and universities in Sydney. While in Australia, he also met the woman who would become his wife, Sue Simmons, a textile artist. After another move, this time to New Zealand, Wademan began to develop what he called his "own style of oil painting, specializing in original aviation artworks." Branching out into new areas, the artist also lent his hand to a series of "Investigate" books for Random House, providing the artwork for *Racing Cars, Space Consultant, Planes,* and *Dinosaurs.*

"It has been thirty years of drawing experience and meeting deadlines in the advertizing industry, combined with a growing knowledge of aircraft as an avid reader of aviation books and magazines, that has brought me to this point in my career," Wademan explained: "The chance to follow my passion and paint what I love ... aircraft."*

* * *

WADEMAN, Spike
See WADEMAN, Peter John

* * *

WEDD, Kate
See GREGORY, Philippa

WEISGARD, Leonard (Joseph) 1916-2000

OBITUARY NOTICE—See index for *SATA* sketch: Born December 13, 1916, in New Haven, CT; died January 14, 2000, in Glumso, Denmark. Artist, writer. Weisgard was the author and illustrator of several books for children who won the 1947 Caldecott Medal for his drawings in Margaret Wise Brown's *Little Island.* His first book, *Suki, the Siamese Pussy,* was published in 1937, and his 1939 retelling of *Cinderella* followed; his final writing emerged in 1968 with *The Beginnings of Cities.* Thereafter, Weisgard focused on drawings for juvenile books, including his work for Rudyard Kipling's 1971 *Elephant's Child.* From 1959 to 1963 he served as chairman of the Roxbury, Connecticut School Board. In 1953 he joined the United Nations Children's Emergency Fund art committee.

OBITUARIES AND OTHER SOURCES:

BOOKS

Benet's Reader's Encyclopedia of American Literature, Harper, 1991, p. 1114.

PERIODICALS

New York Times, January 27, 2000, p. A22.

* * *

WEITZMAN, David L. 1936-

Personal

Born November 24, 1936, in Chicago, IL; son of Louis (a pharmacist) and Louise (Ottenheimer) Weitzman; children: Arin, Brooks, Peter. *Education:* Attended Art Institute of Chicago; Purdue University, B.S. (English), 1958; Northwestern University, M.A. (history), 1959. *Politics:* Liberal. *Religion:* Jewish.

Addresses

Home—P.O. Box 456, Covelo, CA 95428. *Office*—Nancy Ellis Literary Services, P.O. Box 1564, Willits, CA 95490. *E-mail*—weitzman@mcn.org.

Career

Freelance writer and illustrator. Former school teacher in the San Francisco Bay Area and in Round Valley, CA; instructor at University of California, Berkeley, Merritt College, and University of California Education Extension. Member of curriculum delegation to People's Republic of China, 1978; participant in museum education programs, film documentaries, and workshops. *Exhibitions:* Bedford Gallery, Walnut Creek, CA; Gallery 10, Sutter Creek, CA; Elizabeth Stone Gallery, Birmingham, MI; Janice Charach Epstein Museum, West Bloomfield, MI; Columbus Public Library, Columbus, OH; American Institute of Graphic Arts, New York City; Art Center of Battle Creek, Battle Creek, MI; College of Dupage, Glenn Ellen, IL; Slater Mill Historic

David L. Weitzman

Site, Pawtucket, RI; and Allen County Museum, Lima, OH. *Military service:* U.S. Air Force, 1959-63; became first lieutenant. *Member:* Society for Industrial Archeology.

Awards, Honors

Distinguished Book designation, Association of Children's Librarians, and PEN Book Award, both 1982, both for *Windmills, Bridges, and Old Machines;* Bronze Medal, Leipzig International Book Design Exhibition, 1989, for *Superpower;* Books for the Teen Age designations, New York Public Library, 1994, for *Great Lives: Human Culture,* and 1996, for *Great Lives: Theatre;* Notable Social Studies Trade Books for Young People designation, Children's Book Council/National Council for the Social Studies, 1999, for *Locomotive.*

Writings

NONFICTION

Chinese Studies in Paperback (bibliography), McCutchan (Berkeley, CA), 1967.

(Coauthor) *Asia* (textbook), Addison-Wesley, 1969.

Asian Studies Curriculum Project, Field/Addison-Wesley, 1969.

(With Richard E. Gross) *The Human Experience* (textbook), Houghton, 1974.

Eggs and Peanut Butter: A Teacher's Scrapbook, Word Wheel (Menlo Park, CA), 1975.

The Brown Paper School Presents My Backyard History Book, illustrated by James Robertson, Little, Brown, 1975.

Underfoot: An Everyday Guide to Exploring the American Past, Scribner's, 1976.

Traces of the Past: A Field Guide to Industrial Archaeology, Scribner's, 1980.

A Day in Peking (textbook), Houghton, 1981.

Windmills, Bridges, and Old Machines: Discovering Our Industrial Past, Scribner's, 1982.

(With David King and Mariah Marvin) *United States History* (textbook), Addison-Wesley, 1984.

Industrial Eye, photographs by Jet Lowe, J. Wiley, 1987.

The Mountain Man and the President, illustrated by Charles Shaw, Raintree/Steck-Vaughn, 1992.

Great Lives: Theatre, Scribner's, 1994.

Great Lives: Human Culture, Scribner's, 1994.

(And illustrator) *Locomotive: Building an Eight-Wheeler,* Houghton, 1999.

FICTION; SELF-ILLUSTRATED

Superpower: The Making of a Steam Locomotive, Godine, 1987.

Thrashin' Time: Harvest Days in the Dakotas, Godine, 1991.

Old Ironsides: Americans Build a Fighting Ship, Houghton, 1997.

Pouring Iron: An Old Foundry Ghost Story, Houghton, 1998.

Rama and Sita: A Tale from Ancient Java, Godine, 2001.

OTHER

Working Shadows (fiction), Atheneum, 1996.

(Illustrator) Catherine Salton, *Rafael and the Noble Task* (fiction), HarperCollins, 2000.

Writer for video documentaries, with Terry Moyemont, *USS Constitution: Living the Legend* and, with Andy Fahrenwald, *Pouring Iron.*

Work in Progress

Text and illustrations for *Model T* (working title), for Random House, 2002; *Rider in the Sky* (working title), with John Hulls, for Random House, 2002.

Sidelights

A creative and inspiring educator, David L. Weitzman has found an outlet for his curiosity about early American technology through writing and illustrating a number of highly praised books for children. Within the pages of such works as *Windmills, Bridges, and Old Machines: Discovering Our Industrial Past* and *Pouring Iron,* readers can learn about the development of crafts and their role in the development of modern industry. In addition to his writing, Weitzman is also an illustrator; his highly detailed drawings have appeared in exhibitions around the United States, and he has been involved in several film documentaries.

Born in 1936 in Chicago, Weitzman attended Purdue University, where he earned a degree in English before moving on to Northwestern for an advanced history degree. Fortunately for many young people in Weitzman's adopted state of California, after a three-year stint with the United States Air Force, he turned to teaching, spending over two decades moving between elementary, secondary, and college classrooms. His first books for a general audience, 1975's *The Brown Paper School Presents My Backyard History Book* and 1976's *Underfoot: An Everyday Guide to Exploring the American Past,* were the result of his work with young people in the classroom, where a project on discovering one's roots taught students to collect oral histories, search cemeteries and historic archives, and chart their lineage. As he explained to Herbert Mitgang in the *New York Times,* his interest in uncovering personal history began at home: "I began getting involved in my own family and then applied the techniques in the classroom. When I taught in the Bay area, many of my students were Blacks and Asians. Searching for their own pasts, the youngsters discovered much about themselves—and restored pride and understanding at home." *My Backyard History Book* contains directions for collecting and preserving family history, as well as indulging in such creative projects as making gravestone rubbings and learning to identify historic architecture. Calling the underlying concept "fresh," *Booklist* contributor Denise M. Wilms maintained that *My Backyard History Book* would inspire readers to "take interest in their own and their community's roots." *Underfoot* takes a more personal approach, as Weitzman walks readers through a search for local history, traveling from attics to cemeteries to the library stacks. "Although Weitzman appears to be self-taught, his amateur approach ... has an engaging quality that might well keep many readers reading," noted a contributor to *Wilson Library Bulletin*.

Weitzman indulged in his love affair with industrial technology in 1982's *Windmills, Bridges, and Old Machines*. Dubbed "a kind of ode to the old machine, a sonnet to the sawmill or steam locomotive" by *New York Times Book Review* contributor Holcomb B. Noble, Weitzman's book follows the growth of technology from the paddle wheel to the wind mill to the saw mill to building the Erie Canal. Praising *Windmills, Bridges, and Old Machines* for its inclusion of photographs, easy-to-read diagrams, and numerous interesting facts, *Booklist* contributor Barbara Elleman cited the author's "chatty style and personal, enthusiastic approach" in increasing the book's readability. *School Library Journal* reviewer Jeffrey A. French commented that the volume's "description of old industries and machinery is notable for its breadth."

Weitzman has mixed a pinch of fiction with several handfuls of fact in such books as *Thrashin' Time: Harvest Days in the Dakotas* and *Pouring Iron: An Old Foundry Ghost Story*. In *Pouring Iron* readers are introduced to young Howard as he takes a tour of a nineteenth-century foundry near Sacramento, California. Through the people—and ghosts of former foundry workers—Howard meets, readers learn everything from the area's history to the building of the foundry to the manner in which iron was shaped. While *School Library Journal* contributor Shirley Wilton found confusing Weitzman's effort to mix "fact and fiction, past and present" in *Pouring Iron,* she deemed the mix a success in a similar work, the 1997 novel *Old Ironsides*.

In *Old Ironsides* Weitzman returns readers to the late eighteenth century, as the fledgling United States looks for a way to remove the threat to its merchant ships from pirates. John Aylwin, the son of a Boston shipbuilder, is at the center of the effort to construct a ship that would be able to withstand the effects of both piracy and warfare. That ship—a 1,500 ton frigate named the *USS Constitution* but dubbed "Old Ironsides"—became the first United States man-of-war. The story's text is "buoyed by precise pen-and-ink drawings that help

readers grasp the scope of the project and understand how a ship is constructed," Elizabeth S. Watson noted in *Horn Book*. A *Kirkus Reviews* contributor also praised Weitzman's "captivating black-and-white" renderings, adding that the author/illustrator "has a draftsman's eye for detail." In *School Library Journal,* contributor Shirley Wilton commented favorably on the inclusion of an epilogue describing the *USS Constitution*'s decisive role in the War of 1812, adding that *Old Ironsides* "should find readers among young people interested in ships, in how things are made, or in American history."

Other books by Weitzman that focus on technology through a fictional lens include *Superpower: The Making of a Steam Locomotive,* first published in 1987, and 1999's *Locomotive: Building an Eight-Wheeler.* In both books Weitzman creates highly detailed drawings of the locomotive's construction and development, setting them within a historical framework. In *Superpower,* eighteen-year-old Ben starts work at the Lima, Ohio, locomotive works in the mid-1920s and becomes involved in the production of the new "Berkshire" steam locomotive. Along with Ben, readers learn every step of the manufacturing process, from drawings to foundry work to machine shop to assembly. *Locomotive* draws young train buffs further back in time, as its author reveals the development of an 1870s wood-burning locomotive, this time without the fictional framework that some critics have argued detracts from the author's purpose. Praising Weitzman's discussion of the process in constructing the passenger locomotive, as well as his inclusion of sophisticated technical details, *School Library Journal* contributor Margaret Bush concluded

Son of a shipbuilder, John Aylwin is eyewitness to the construction of the **U.S.S. Constitution** *from the felling of the oak trees to the launching of the man-of-war. (From* Old Ironsides, *written and illustrated by Weitzman.)*

that *Locomotive* "will be enjoyed most by readers with a strong mechanical bent." Bush's praise was echoed by a *Kirkus Reviews* writer who proclaimed *Locomotive* to be "a bull's-eye for meeting the desires of both railroad buffs and the mechanically inclined."

Biographical and Critical Sources

PERIODICALS

Booklist, October 15, 1975, Denise M. Wilms, review of *The Brown Paper School Presents My Backyard History Book,* pp. 306-307; February 1, 1983, Barbara Elleman, *Windmills, Bridges, and Old Machines,* p. 728; April 15, 1991, Ann D. Carlson, review of *Windmills, Bridges, and Old Machines,* p. 1635; March 1, 1992, Deborah Abbott, review of *Thrashin' Time,* p. 1279; May 1, 1997, Susan Dove Lempke, review of *Old Ironsides,* p. 1498; December 15, 1998, John Peters, review of *Pouring Iron,* p. 752.

Bulletin of the Center for Children's Books, March, 1983, Zena Sutherland, review of *Windmills, Bridges, and Old Machines,* p. 139; June, 1997, Elizabeth Bush, review of *Old Ironsides,* pp. 377-378.

Choice, October, 1975, review of *Eggs and Peanut Butter,* p. 1052.

Five Owls, September-October, 1994, review of *Thrashin' Time,* p. 5.

Horn Book, May, 1997, Elizabeth S. Watson, review of *Old Ironsides,* p. 312.

Kirkus Reviews, February 15, 1997, review of *Old Ironsides,* p. 307; September, 1999, review of *Locomotive,* p. 1423.

New York Times, February 11, 1977, Herbert Mitgang, review of *Underfoot,* p. C25.

New York Times Book Review, November 16, 1975, Barbara Karlin, review of *The Brown Paper School Presents My Backyard History Book,* p. 31; February 6, 1983, Holcomb B. Noble, review of *Windmills, Bridges, and Old Machines,* p. 33; July 26, 1992, Verlyn Klinkenborg, review of *Thrashin' Time,* p. 19.

Publishers Weekly, November 30, 1998, review of *Pouring Iron,* p. 73; September 6, 1999, review of *Locomotive,* p. 103.

School Library Journal, January, 1976, Sandra Weir, review of *The Brown Paper School Presents My Backyard History Book,* pp. 42-43; August, 1983, Jeffrey A. French, review of *Windmills, Bridges, and Old Machines,* p. 72; January, 1988, French, review of *Superpower: The Making of a Steam Locomotive,* pp. 94-95; April, 1992, Lee Bock, review of *Thrashin' Time,* p. 144; April, 1995, Kristin Lott, review of *Human Culture,* p. 148; April, 1997, Shirley Wilton, review of *Old Ironsides,* p. 142; January, 1999, Wilton, review of *Pouring Iron,* p. 132; November, 1999, Margaret Bush, review of *Locomotive,* p. 178.

Wilson Library Bulletin, January, 1978, review of *Underfoot,* p. 371.

WELLMAN, Sam(uel) 1939-

Personal

Born 1939, in Kansas; son of Leonard (a rail-worker) and Iris (a retail buyer; maiden name, Reinhold) Wellman; married Ruth Austin (a travel agent), 1972; children: Amy, Keith. *Education:* University of Nebraska, B.S., 1962; Princeton University, Ph.D., 1968. *Politics:* "American." *Religion:* Christian.

Addresses

Home—Kansas. *E-mail*—xnwriter7@hotmail.com.

Sam Wellman

Career

Writer.

Writings

BIOGRAPHIES; FOR YOUNG ADULTS

Michelle Kwan ("Female Sports Stars" series), Chelsea House (Philadelphia, PA), 1997.

Kristi Yamaguchi ("Female Figure Skating Legends" series), Chelsea House (Philadelphia, PA), 1999.

Mariah Carey ("Galaxy of Superstars" series), Chelsea House (Philadelphia, PA), 1999.

T. D. Jakes: Religious Leader ("Black Americans of Achievement" series), Chelsea House (Philadelphia, PA), 1999.

Ben Affleck ("Galaxy of Superstars" series), Chelsea House (Philadelphia, PA), 2000.

BIOGRAPHIES; "HEROES OF THE FAITH" SERIES

David Livingstone: Missionary and Explorer, Barbour (Uhrickville, OH), 1995.

Corrie ten Boom, Barbour (Uhrickville, OH), 1995.

Billy Graham: The Great Evangelist, Barbour (Uhrickville, OH), 1996.

John Bunyan: Author of the Pilgrim's Progress, Barbour (Uhrickville, OH), 1996.

C. S. Lewis: Author of Mere Christianity, Barbour (Uhrickville, OH), 1997.

John Wesley: Founder of the Methodist Church, Barbour (Uhrickville, OH), 1997.

Mother Teresa: Missionary of Charity, Barbour (Uhrickville, OH), 1997.

William Carey: Father of Missions, Barbour (Uhrickville, OH), 1997.

Amy Carmichael: A Life Abandoned to God, Barbour (Uhrickville, OH), 1998.

George Washington Carver: Inventor and Naturalist, Barbour (Uhrickville, OH), 1998.

Mary Slessor: Queen of Calabar, Barbour (Uhrickville, OH), 1998.

Gladys Aylward: Missionary in China, Barbour (Uhrickville, OH), 1998.

Florence Nightingale: Lady with the Lamp, Barbour (Uhrickville, OH), 1999.

Brother Andrew: God's Undercover Agent, Barbour (Uhrickville, OH), 1999.

Francis and Edith Schaeffer: Defenders of the Faith, Barbour (Uhrickville, OH), 2000.

BIOGRAPHIES; "YOUNG READERS CHRISTIAN LIBRARY" SERIES

Abraham Lincoln, illustrated by Ken Save, Barbour (Uhrickville, OH), 1995.

Christopher Columbus, illustrated by Ken Save, Barbour (Uhrickville, OH), 1995.

Billy Graham, illustrated by Ken Save, Barbour (Uhrickville, OH), 1997.

David, illustrated by Ken Landgraf, Barbour (Uhrickville, OH), 1999.

John Wesley: The Horseback Preacher, illustrated by Ken Landgraf, Barbour (Uhrickville, OH), 2000.

OTHER

Bible Promise Book for Fathers, Barbour (Uhrickville, OH), 1997.

Bible Promise Book for Kids, Barbour (Uhrickville, OH), 1997.

The Cabinet (textbook; "Your Government—How It Works" series), Chelsea House (Philadelphia, PA), 2000.

Work in Progress

Secretary of State, a book in the "Your Government—How It Works" series for Chelsea House; biographical research on Abraham Lincoln, Aleksandr Solzhenitsyn, and Black Elk.

Sidelights

A prolific author of nonfiction books for young adults, Sam Wellman told *SATA:* "Writing improved my life. Is there any self-contained activity that hones the thoughts like writing? Writing prose is like a debate with inner truths you didn't know you possessed. It was not until I attempted to become a writer that these inner truths surfaced and defeated many years of accumulated, very muddled values. The act of writing overhauled my thinking and values. But writing can be more than a self-improvement exercise. Writing can also be an effective method for communicating with others. And then there is writing for publication . . . ."

Biographical and Critical Sources

PERIODICALS

Booklist, Hazel Rochman, review of *David Livingstone,* p. 338.

Children's Book Watch, July, 1996, review of *Christopher Columbus,* p. 2; November, 1998, review of *Billy Graham,* p. 5; December, 1998, review of *Michelle Kwan,* p. 2.

School Library Journal, January, 1999, Ann W. Moore, review of *C. S. Lewis* and *John Bunyan,* and Cindy Darling Codell, review of *Mother Teresa,* p. 157; February, 1999, Shirley Wilton, review of *John Wesley,* p. 113.

*   *   *

WILLIAMSON, Joanne S. 1926-

Personal

Born May 13, 1926, in Arlington, MA; daughter of Floyd (in public relations) and Gertrude (Small) Williamson. *Education:* Attended Barnard College, 1942-44; Diller Quaile School of Music, 1944-46. *Politics:* Independent. *Religion:* Congregationalist.

Addresses

Home—P.O. Box 491, Kennebunkport, ME 04046.

Joanne S. Williamson

Career

Powers Charm School of the Air, Kaye-Martin Productions, New York City, 1946-47; *Bridgeport Herald,* Bridgeport, CT, feature writer, 1948-50; *Retail Apparel Outlook,* New York City, editor, 1950-55; Fairfield County Publications, Fairfield, CT, production manager, 1955-56; piano teacher, Kennebunkport, ME, 1956-90.

Awards, Honors

Honors citation, *New York Herald Tribune,* 1956, for *Jacobin's Daughter.*

Writings

YOUNG ADULT HISTORICAL NOVELS

Jacobin's Daughter, Knopf (New York, NY), 1956.
The Eagles Have Flown, Knopf (New York, NY), 1957.
Hittite Warrior, Knopf (New York, NY), 1960, Bethlehem Books, 1999.
The Glorious Conspiracy, Knopf (New York, NY), 1961.
The Iron Charm, Knopf (New York, NY), 1964.
And Forever Free, illustrated by Jim McMullan, Knopf (New York, NY), 1966.
To Dream upon a Crown, illustrated by Jacob Landau, Knopf (New York, NY), 1967.
God King, Bethlehem Books, 2002.

An excerpt from *The Glorious Conspiracy* appeared in *Wide Horizons Reader,* Book 6, Scott-Foresman, and in *History of the United States,* Vol. 1, Houghton Mifflin.

Sidelights

Calling writing and music her "two great loves," journalist and historical novelist Joanne S. Williamson went on to explain to *SATA* that her third love is history. "I'm a member of a family of writers," Williamson added by way of background. "My father was a newspaperman. My brother, Bill Williamson, is an award-winning columnist for Maine newspapers. A nephew, Josh Williamson, is a staff writer on a York County, Maine, daily.

"What originally steered me into historical writing for young people was the fact that, too often, historical figures come across as names to be memorized in textbook date lists, lifeless and incomprehensible. They weren't, and I hope my books make them come alive as recognizable human beings with the same desires, hopes, fears, and problems as the young people who read about them.

"This sometimes results in a rather different slant on historical events and characters. The Robespierre I present in my novel *Jacobin's Daughter* is very different from [nineteenth-century British historian] Thomas Carlyle's Robespierre. In *The Glorious Conspiracy,* eighteenth-century American statesmen [Alexander] Hamilton and [Aaron] Burr exchange the roles of villain and hero. King Arthur, at least, in *The Iron Charm,* remains a hero.

"After all, Shakespeare himself managed to make Brutus 'the noblest Roman of them all,' and as such he appears in *The Eagles Have Flown.*"

Extending her comments to music, which Williamson teaches, the novelist added that she was "happy to say that several of my pupils have gone on to major in music in college. Another works in music publishing. A niece was a pianist in a local rock band during her high school years, and a nephew works in a New Orleans music bar and handles bookings for bands. I like to think I had something to do with kindling their interest."

Biographical and Critical Sources

PERIODICALS

Bulletin of the Center for Children's Books, November, 1966, review of *And Forever Free,* p. 51; December 1, 1967, review of *To Dream upon a Crown,* p. 68.
Kirkus Reviews, November 15, 1967, review of *To Dream upon a Crown,* p. 1370.
New York Times Book Review, February 11, 1968, review of *To Dream upon a Crown,* p. 26.
Teacher's College Record, November, 1966, review of *And Forever Free,* p. 185.

WITTLINGER, Ellen 1948-

Personal

Born October 21, 1948, in Belleville, IL; daughter of Karl (a grocer) and Doris (a grocer and secretary; maiden name, Malzahn) Wittlinger; married David Pritchard (a reference editor), June 23, 1978; children: Kate, Morgan. *Education:* Millikin University, B.A., 1970; University of Iowa, M.F.A., 1973. *Politics:* Democrat. *Hobbies and other interests:* Photography, theater, folk music, gardening.

Addresses

Home—47 Beach Ave., Swampscott, MA 01907.

Career

Writer, 1970—; children's librarian, Swampscott Public Library, Swampscott, MA, 1989-92; writing instructor, Emerson College, Boston, MA. *Member:* Society of Children's Book Writers and Illustrators, Swampscott Cultural Council (member, 1983-86, 1994-98), Friends of the Swampscott Library (second vice president, 1992—).

Awards, Honors

Finalist, Massachusetts Artists Fellowship, 1980 and 1983, for poetry, and 1989, for playwriting; Best Book for Young Adults selection and Recommended Book for the Reluctant Reader selection, both American Library Association (ALA), both 1994, both for *Lombardo's Law;* Michael R. Printz honor book, Lambda Literary Book Award, Best Books for Young Adults selection and Quick Picks for Reluctant Readers selection, both ALA, all for *Hard Love;* Best Books for Young Adults selection, ALA, 2001, for *What's in a Name; What's in a Name* and *Gracie's Girl* are both Junior Library Guild selections.

Writings

YOUNG ADULT NOVELS

Lombardo's Law, Houghton, 1993.
Noticing Paradise, Houghton, 1995.
Hard Love, Simon & Schuster, 1999.
What's in a Name, Simon & Schuster, 2000.
Gracie's Girl, Simon & Schuster, 2000.
Razzle, Simon & Schuster, 2001.

OTHER

Breakers (poetry), Sheep Meadow Press, 1979.
One Civilized Person (play), first produced by Playwright's Platform, Boston, MA, 1982.
Coffee (play), produced by Egg Rock Players, Swampscott, MA, 1985.

Contributor of short story "Stevie in the Mirror" to *On the Edge,* edited by Lois Duncan, Simon & Schuster, 2000; numerous short stories and poems published in

Ellen Wittlinger

periodicals, including *Ploughshares, Antioch Review,* and *Iowa Review.*

Work in Progress

The Long Night of Leo and Bree, for Simon & Schuster, 2002.

Sidelights

"I get a little aggravated when people label my books 'romances,'" remarked young adult novelist Ellen Wittlinger in an essay for *Something about the Author Autobiography Series* (*SAAS*). "I prefer to think of my books as coming-of-age stories, books that remember what it feels like to be thirteen or fifteen or seventeen and to feel for the first time the tumult of adult emotions." In novels such as *Lombardo's Law, Noticing Paradise, Hard Love,* and *What's in a Name,* Wittlinger explores this adolescent landscape through the eyes of outsiders and loners. "I find I'm most interested in those kids who are on the fringes," Wittlinger once noted, "the slight oddballs and lovable misfits who aren't quite comfortable in their own skins, or if they are, their differentness makes those around them uncomfortable. I want to celebrate their differences because they are likely to be the most fascinating people the rest of us will ever know." Often Wittlinger's protagonists are artists in the making—writers, photographers, filmmakers. "I'm most interested in the kids with their ears to the ground, the ones who can tell us secrets, and in my experience, that kind of person is often an artist of one kind or another."

Wittlinger herself was the sort of kid she now writes about. Born on October 21, 1948, in Belleville, Illinois, she grew up an only child. Her parents first managed and then later operated their own mom-and-pop grocery in Belleville. Much of the time as a young child she was under the eye of a watchful grandparent while both her parents worked, and this increased the sense of isolation that Wittlinger felt. "I felt always under surveillance—safe but too safe," the author noted in *SAAS*. "Early on I longed for more freedom, for adventure, although the fear of it was instilled in my heart too by the succession of well-meaning old ladies who guarded my early life." Her Uncle Walt, a roving jazz musician, gave her a glimpse of a bigger world on his occasional visits to town. But more importantly, books filled her world.

"For children who find themselves alone a good deal and thrown back onto their own resources, reading often becomes their escape, their friend, their adventure, their imaginary life," Wittlinger once commented. She became a regular at the local library, graduating from the children's section to the young reader section, and finally to adult works. The library became for Wittlinger a "beloved refuge." She also found refuge in a pet, a Welsh corgi named Penny. "I think having the dog helped me move from loneliness to an enjoyment of being alone," Wittlinger recalled.

She gained much of her identity as the kid from the local grocery, and when her parents operated their own market, the family lived on the premises. No other parents in town could offer the variety of after-school snacks Wittlinger's parents could. She took to working in the store for her allowance, and about this time also found a group of kids who became her friends at school. Mostly outsiders like herself, these kids provided another refuge for the young Wittlinger. One group from junior high school called itself the Horse and Pony Club, though none of them were riders. They traded horse figurines, read classic horse books together, and sketched equine portraits. Wittlinger was soon convinced that she would become a painter when she grew up, and turned the small living room of her home into an artist's studio in pursuit of this dream.

By high school she had become certain that painting was her destiny; at the same time, however, she had graduated from reading mushy romances to experiencing plays. "I became particularly interested in the bizarre world of Eugene O'Neill's characters, ravaged by drink or drugs and tied to each other by the bandages of love and need," Wittlinger remembered. From O'Neill she went on to Tennessee Williams as well as poetry. Her friends were still "an eclectic bunch who didn't really fit in." Wittlinger was also particularly attracted to the Air Force "brats" from nearby Scott Field. They, like her jazz-playing uncle, would bring a glimpse of the larger world to her small town environment. Together with these friends she shared the usual amusements of a teenager in the 1960s: going to the drive-in movie and then to a drive-in hamburger stand afterward. Or

sneaking off to nearby St. Louis, across the Mississippi from her hometown, to sit under the newly constructed Arch, "an enormous silver croquet hoop over the Mississippi River, reflecting in the moonlight," as Wittlinger described it in *SAAS*.

Wittlinger attended Millikin University in Decatur, Illinois, second choice to the Kansas City Art Institute, which did not offer her any scholarship money. She majored in art and sociology—the latter so as to satisfy her mother who felt a sociology degree would provide some employment possibilities. Actually, neither of Wittlinger's majors made her very employable. A young teacher and his wife became important in Wittlinger's college life when they encouraged her propensity for poetry, giving her books to read and reading her own writing efforts. Upon graduation, she moved west to Ashland, Oregon, influenced in her decision by a college friend who lived there. She loved the small town in southern Oregon and found work putting ads together for the local newspaper. By this time, however, Wittlinger was writing more poetry; she no longer thought of

Wittlinger unfolds the story of sixteen-year-old John, who falls in love with fellow editor Marisol, despite his realization that the relationship is futile because Marisol is a lesbian. (Cover illustration by Heather Wood.)

herself as an artist in the making. Accepted to the graduate program at the University of Iowa's Writers' Workshop, she reluctantly left Oregon to pursue this new goal.

Work at Iowa was intense and very competitive. Wittlinger stuck with it, learning fictional techniques of plot, setting, and characterization, as well as verse models. "This was ... the first time in my life I had been *identified* as a writer," Wittlinger remarked. "Just the fact of being in the program at Iowa empowered me to be able to say to people, 'I'm a writer.'" Another benefit of the program was the people she met there, including a young short story writer, David Pritchard, who would later become her husband.

From Iowa, Wittlinger moved to Cambridge, Massachusetts, and worked at a variety of part-time jobs while pursuing a writing career. Fellowships at the Fine Arts Work Center in Provincetown, Massachusetts, from 1974 to 1976 gave her the time she needed to find her voice, both in poetry and in playwriting. Married in 1978, Wittlinger and her husband moved to Boston, where they could more easily find work. Her first publication, *Breakers,* a book of poetry, was published in 1979, not long before her first child, Kate, was born. "It was a surprise to me (who believed herself a feminist, and still do[es]) that of the two events, it was the birth of my child—not holding the hardcover book in my hands—which filled me with the most complete joy," Wittlinger noted.

With husband David working as a reference editor for Houghton Mifflin, the couple moved to the oceanside suburban town of Swampscott, and Wittlinger became a full-time mom with the birth of her second child, son Morgan. "I wanted to be with my children when they were young, but also ... I could sometimes sneak in a few hours of writing now and then." This writing consisted of poetry, as well as plays, which had increasingly captured her creative attention. Two of these plays for adults, *One Civilized Person* and *Coffee,* were produced by local theatrical groups, and Wittlinger had hopes of larger productions. But the more she became involved with theater, the more she began to understand that such a career would mean traveling with the play and helping to develop it, something that would take her away from home and from her family too much.

When her son started school, Wittlinger took a job as children's librarian in the local Swampscott library. Soon she became self-educated in the world of children's literature, more specifically in YA novels. Influenced by the work of people such as Brock Cole, M. E. Kerr, Katherine Paterson, Gary Paulson, Avi, and Lois Lowry, Wittlinger began to see that here was a field she could happily take part in. "It seemed to me they took the YA genre and pulled it in new directions," Wittlinger once recalled. "And I wanted to try it too."

Engaged with her first young adult novel, Wittlinger soon realized that writing such novels was a lot like writing plays. Characterization is all-important, and the characters in YA books must be established just as

quickly as the central problem. Keep the plot simple, and the theme as well, and move the action forward at a rapid pace with dialogue-driven scenes. The ending needs resolution, but it need not always be a happy one. Such craft lore was a part of the bag of tools that Wittlinger had already developed in writing for the theater. "So you see, my transition from writing plays to writing young adult novels was not a difficult one," she once wrote. "I loved them immediately."

Wittlinger's first young adult novel, *Lombardo's Law,* is about Justine Trainor, a shy, intelligent, fifteen-year-old loner whose mother would like her to have more friends. As a result, her mother introduces her to Heather and her brother, Mike, who are new to the neighborhood. Justine is quickly snubbed by Heather, a beautiful, boy-crazy teen who easily adjusts to their high school. However, Mike, a thirteen-year-old junior high student, develops a close friendship with Justine due to their common interests and a shared desire to make a movie. As time goes by and they continue writing and then filming a screenplay together, Justine and Mike begin to secretly feel romantic interests toward one another. These two adolescents have a difficult time concealing their fondness from each other, as well as from people at school. At times, such an attachment proves awkward, as when her friends see the two together and wonder if Justine is not babysitting the younger boy.

Reviewing this debut novel in *Horn Book,* Nancy Vasilakis remarked that Justine's "qualms over this social transgression will seem much more compelling and real to young teens than other more serious problems that are currently topical. Wittlinger has hit the bull's-eye with her first try." Lucinda Snyder Whitehurst, a critic for *School Library Journal,* stated: "Beyond entertainment, the story's value lies in its message of reassurance to young teens who feel out of step with their peers." *Lombardo's Law* also fared well with *Bulletin of the Center for Children's Books* contributor Kathryn Jennings, who wrote, "This first young adult novel by Wittlinger not only strikes at a real dating issue for teenagers, but also has a plot that is satisfying and not too crowded." Wittlinger's first novel earned not only positive reviews, but also spots on the 1994 ALA Best Books for Young Adults list, as well as on the ALA Recommended Books for the Reluctant Reader list for the same year. Its success prompted Wittlinger to give up her day job as a children's librarian and work on YA fiction full time.

Wittlinger's next novel, *Noticing Paradise,* utilizes a trip the author and her family had taken to Ecuador and the Galapagos Islands as a setting. The story takes place on a boat in the Galapagos, involving the mysterious disappearance of endangered tortoises. Two lonely sixteen year olds, Cat and Noah, alternately narrate the action in first person, accounts that sometimes differ. The two are caught up in dramatic events in one of the most exotic if not romantic spots in the world and ultimately fall in love with each other. Noah, from Brookline, begins to question all that he was taught and all that he believes when his parent's divorce unhinges his reality. Cat, another passenger on this international summer excursion, is from Oregon, a reclusive and sheltered child who has never had a date. Noah, too involved in his own pain, does not even notice the paradise all around, until Cat "wakes him up and makes him see," according to *Booklist*'s Hazel Rochman. Their romance is powered by the plot involving stolen endangered tortoises and a near drowning. "Wittlinger breaks new ground in YA romance," Rochman further noted, and her dialogue "is lively and immediate." Sharon Neff, reviewing the novel in *Voice of Youth Advocates,* felt that there was a "flatness" to the characters, but that Wittlinger's novel found its real strength in "its naturalist's view of a world of scientific and cultural significance."

Hard Love, published in 1999, features another sixteen-year-old boy torn apart by his parents' divorce. John is having trouble coping, until he begins publishing a zine called *Bananafish.* Here he puts down all his feelings about the divorce and his changed role vis-à-vis both his parents. Marisol, another zine writer, then makes her entrance, and these two troubled teens feel an attraction for each other, but on Marisol's part this can go only so far. She lets John know that she is a lesbian. But John cannot help himself; he finds himself falling in love with Marisol despite his conviction to feel no emotions. "John's simmering passions for Marisol, which come to a full boil at the prom, predictably lead to disaster," remarked a reviewer for *Publishers Weekly.* In a *School Library Journal* review of the book, Dina Sherman observed, "Teen angst is always a popular route for young adult literature, and Wittlinger has successfully created an intense example here." Sherman concluded, "This is a smart addition to YA collections."

A cast of ten teenagers fill the pages of *What's in a Name,* a book that explores personal identity. All residents of the small town of Scrub Harbor, Massachusetts, these teenagers start a search for their own identities when the residents of the town are contemplating whether or not to change the name of Scrub Harbor. Inspired by this naming quest, various teenagers share their own thoughts on personal meaning and identity, from the gorgeous country-club type Gretchen, to bookish and gay O'Neill. These glimpses of each character intertwine into a larger story. While Mary Ann Capan, writing in *Voice of Youth Advocates,* felt that the characters in Wittlinger's book "lack the depth that could make them memorable," they still display emotions that "ring true."

Wittlinger has also penned a novel dealing with homelessness. *Gracie's Girl* features middle-schooler Bess, who volunteers to work on the school musical. Another of Wittlinger's outsiders, Bess hopes that such involvement will lead to her fitting in. But when she and a friend get to know Gracie, an elderly homeless woman, Bess begins to wonder what really is important in life. A *Publishers Weekly* reviewer called the novel "bittersweet" and "convincing" in its portrayal of Bess's friendship with Gracie. While *Booklist*'s Hazel Rochman noted that the story can be somewhat "didactic," she

praised Wittlinger for conveying "a strong message" that is ultimately "neither simplistic nor sweet." Catherine T. Quattlebaum, writing in *School Library Journal,* found the characterization of Bess "engaging and believable," noting that the protagonist's interests in fashion, romance, and her commitment to the school play "round out this perceptive, realistic novel."

For Wittlinger, the growing pains of adolescence are all too real and present. "I sometimes tell people I never got over being thirteen," she once wrote. "I got kind of stuck back there. But I don't only mean stuck with that feeling of being an oddball kid, with not quite the right looks or interests to fit in ... but also I never quite got over what's so good about being thirteen. At that age ... we're still optimistic, the world is right in front of us waiting to be embraced, and we have unlimited hope that it will open its arms to us as well.... This is why I love writing young adult novels. Who lives a more exciting life than a teenager just moving from the safety of home and family into the wide world of emotional possibilities? It's the equivalent of boarding one of the first manned spacecrafts. And yet teenagers rush enthusiastically into this rare atmosphere, as they have always done and will always do. I hope only to show them there have been others there before them and they have survived."

Biographical and Critical Sources

BOOKS

Something about the Author Autobiography Series, Volume 25, Gale, 1998.

PERIODICALS

ALAN Review, fall, 1999, p. 40.
Booklist, September 15, 1993, p. 144; November 1, 1995, Hazel Rochman, review of *Noticing Paradise,* p. 464; September 15, 1998, p. 220; October 1, 1999, p. 355; March 15, 2000, p. 1370; September 15, 2000, Hazel Rochman, review of *Gracie's Girl,* p. 244.
Bulletin of the Center for Children's Books, October, 1993, Kathryn Jennings, review of *Lombardo's Law,* p. 63.
Choice, December, 1979, p. 1311.
Horn Book, November, 1993, Nancy Vasilakis, review of *Lombardo's Law,* p. 748; July-August, 1999, p. 474.
Horn Book Guide, spring, 1994, p. 92.
Library Journal, December 15, 1979, p. 2626; March 15, 1980, p. 728.
Publishers Weekly, October 11, 1993, p. 89; June 21, 1999, review of *Hard Love,* p. 69; November 13, 2000, review of *Gracie's Girl,* p. 104.
School Library Journal, September, 1993, Lucinda Snyder Whitehurst, review of *Lombardo's Law,* pp. 253-54; June, 1999, Dina Sherman, review of *Hard Love,* p. 102; November, 2000, Catherine T. Quattlebaum, review of *Gracie's Girl,* p. 165.
Voice of Youth Advocates, December, 1993, p. 304; February, 1996, Sharon Neff, review of *Noticing Paradise,* p. 380; April, 2000, Mary Ann Capan, review of *What's in a Name,* pp. 41-42.

—*Sketch by J. Sydney Jones*

Y

YOUNG, Ed (Tse-chun) 1931-

Personal

Born November 28, 1931, in Tientsin, China; immigrated to the United States, 1951; naturalized U.S. citizen; son of Qua-Ling (an engineer) and Yuen Teng Young; married first wife, 1962 (divorced, 1969); married Natasha Gorky, June 1, 1971; children: one daughter. *Education:* Attended City College of San Francisco, 1952, and University of Illinois at Urbana-Champaign, 1952-54; Art Center College of Design, Los Angeles, B.P.A., 1957; graduate study at Pratt Institute, 1958-59.

Addresses

Home—Hastings-on-Hudson, NY.

Career

Children's book illustrator and author, 1962—. Mel Richman Studio, New York City, illustrator and designer, 1957-62; Pratt Institute, Brooklyn, NY, instructor in visual communications, 1960-66; Shr Jung Tai Chi Chuan School, New York City, secretary and instructor, 1964-73, director, 1973; Sarah Lawrence College, Bronxville, NY, instructor, 1975—. Has also taught at the Pratt Institute, Naropa Institute, Yale University, and the University of California at Santa Cruz.

Awards, Honors

Award from American Institute of Graphic Arts, 1962, for *The Mean Mouse and Other Mean Stories;* Caldecott Medal runner-up, 1968, for *The Emperor and the Kite; Horn Book* Honor List and Child Study Association Book Award, both 1969, both for *Chinese Mother Goose Rhymes; The Girl Who Loved the Wind* was named a Children's Book Showcase Title, 1973; *New York Times* Best Illustrated Children's Book Award, 1984, for *Up a Tree; Horn Book* Honor List, 1986, for *Foolish Rabbit's Big Mistake; New York Times* Best Illustrated Children's Book Award, 1988, for *Cats Are Cats;* Caldecott Medal

YOUNG FU OF THE UPPER YANGTZE
Elizabeth Foreman Lewis

LAUREL-LEAF ❧ NEWBERY

Set in the Chinese city of Chungking in the 1920s, Elizabeth Foreman Lewis's novel follows the adventures of Young Fu, whose seven-year apprenticeship to Tang, a coppersmith, offers him the opportunity to savor the dangers and pleasures of the big city. (Cover illustration by Ed Young.)

and *Boston Globe/Horn Book* Award, both 1990, both for *Lon Po Po; Boston Globe/Horn Book* Award, 1992, and Caldecott Honor Book, 1993, for *Seven Blind Mice;* U.S. nominee for Hans Christian Andersen Award, 1992.

Writings

SELF-ILLUSTRATED; FOR CHILDREN

(With Hilary Beckett) *The Rooster's Horns: A Chinese Puppet Play to Make and Perform,* Collins, 1978.

(Reteller) *The Terrible Nung Gwama: A Chinese Folktale,* Collins, 1978.

(Adaptor) *The Lion and the Mouse: An Aesop Fable,* Doubleday, 1979.

High on a Hill: A Book of Chinese Riddles, Collins, 1980.

Up a Tree, Harper, 1983.

The Other Bone, Harper, 1984.

(Translator) *Lon Po Po: A Red-Riding Hood Story from China,* Philomel, 1989.

(Reteller) *Seven Blind Mice,* Philomel, 1992.

(Reteller) *Moon Mother: A Narrative American Creation Tale,* HarperCollins, 1993.

(Reteller) *Red Thread,* Philomel, 1993.

(Reteller) *Little Plum,* Philomel, 1994.

(Reteller) *Donkey Trouble,* Atheneum Books for Young Readers, 1995.

(Adaptor) *Pinocchio,* Philomel, 1995.

(Reteller) *Night Visitors,* Philomel, 1995.

Cat and Rat: The Legend of the Chinese Zodiac, Holt, 1995.

(Reteller) *Mouse Match: A Chinese Folktale,* Silver Whistle, 1997.

(Adaptor) *Genesis,* Laura Geringer, 1997.

Voices of the Heart, Scholastic, 1997.

(Reteller) *The Lost Horse: A Chinese Folktale,* Silver Whistle, 1998.

Monkey King, HarperCollins, 2001.

ILLUSTRATOR

Janice M. Udry, *The Mean Mouse and Other Mean Stories,* Harper, 1962.

Leland B. Jacobs and Sally Nohelty, editors, *Poetry for Young Scientists,* Holt, 1964.

Margaret Hillert, *The Yellow Boat,* Follett, 1966.

Jane Yolen, editor, *The Emperor and the Kite,* World Publishing, 1968, Penguin Putnam, 1998.

Robert Wyndam, editor, *Chinese Mother Goose Rhymes,* World Publishing, 1968, Penguin Putnam, 1998.

Kermit Krueger, *The Golden Swans: A Picture Story from Thailand,* World Publishing, 1969.

Mel Evans, *The Tiniest Sound,* Doubleday, 1969.

Jane Yolen, *The Seventh Mandarin,* Seabury, 1970.

Renee K. Weiss, *The Bird from the Sea,* Crowell, 1970.

Diane Wolkstein, *Eight Thousand Stones: A Chinese Folktale,* Doubleday, 1972.

Jane Yolen, *The Girl Who Loved the Wind,* Crowell, 1972.

L. C. Hunt, editor, *The Horse from Nowhere,* Holt, 1973.

Elizabeth F. Lewis, *Young Fu of the Upper Yangtze,* new edition, Holt, 1973.

Diane Wolkstein, *The Red Lion: A Tale of Ancient Persia,* Crowell, 1977.

Fourteen-year-old Albanian Adem endures brutality against his family at the hands of Serbian soldiers who are trying to reclaim the land of Kosovo in Alice Mead's book. (Cover illustration by Young.)

Feenie Ziner, *Cricket Boy: A Chinese Tale,* Doubleday, 1977.

N. J. Dawood, *Tales from the Arabian Nights,* Doubleday, 1978.

Diane Wolkstein, *White Wave: A Chinese Tale,* Crowell, 1979.

Priscilla Jaquith, *Bo Rabbit Smart for True: Folktales from the Gullah,* Philomel, 1981.

Al-Ling Louie, *Yeh-Shen: A Cinderella Story from China,* Putnam, 1982.

Mary Scioscia, *Bicycle Rider,* Harper, 1983.

Rafe Martin, *Foolish Rabbit's Big Mistake,* Putnam, 1985.

Jean Fritz, *The Double Life of Pocahontas,* Putnam, 1985.

Margaret Leaf, *Eyes of the Dragon,* Lothrop, 1987.

James Howe, *I Wish I Were a Butterfly,* Harcourt, 1987.

Tony Johnston, *Whale Song,* Harcourt, 1987.

Richard Lewis, *In the Night, Still Dark,* Atheneum, 1988.

Nancy Larrick, editor, *Cats Are Cats,* Philomel, 1988.

Robert Frost, *Birches,* Holt, 1988.

Oscar Wilde, *The Happy Prince,* Simon & Schuster, 1989.

Lafcadio Hearn, *The Voice of the Great Bell,* retold by Margaret Hodges, Little, Brown, 1989.

Ruth Y. Radin, *High in the Mountains,* Macmillan, 1989.

Nancy Larrick, editor, *Mice Are Nice,* Philomel, 1990.

Richard Lewis, *All of You Was Singing,* Atheneum, 1991.

Nancy White Carlstrom, *Goodbye, Geese,* Philomel, 1991.

Barabara Savage Horton, *What Comes in Spring?,* Knopf, 1992.

Mary Calhoun, *While I Sleep,* Morrow, 1992.

Audrey Osofsky, *Dreamcatcher,* Orchard Books, 1992.

Laura Krauss Melmed, *The First Song Ever Sung,* Lothrop, 1993.

Eleanor Coerr, *Sadako,* Putnam, 1993.

Isaac Olaleye, *Bitter Bananas,* Boyds Mills, 1994.

Shulamith Levey Oppenheim, reteller, *Iblis,* Harcourt, 1994.

Penny Pollock, reteller, *The Turkey Girl: A Zuni Cinderella Story,* Little, Brown, 1996.

Lisa Westberg Peters, *October Smiled Back,* Holt, 1996.

Jack London, *White Fang,* Viking, 1999.

Mary Casanova, *The Hunter: A Chinese Folktale,* Simon & Schuster, 2000.

Dorothea P. Seeber, *A Pup Just for Me—A Boy Just for Me,* Philomel, 2000.

Tony Johnston, *Desert Song,* Sierra Club Books for Children, 2000.

Also illustrator of *The Child's First Books* by Donnarae MacCann and Olga Richard, 1973, and of film *Sadako and the Thousand Paper Cranes,* based on the story by Eleanor Coerr.

Sidelights

A critically acclaimed illustrator of children's books since the early 1960s, Ed Young often uses the folklore and folktales of his native China for inspiration. Illustrating the work of other writers as well as his own tales and adaptations, Young has put a visual face to historical China, from the days of the Han dynasty onward. His awards include Caldecott honors for Jane Yolen's *The Emperor and the Kite* and his own retelling of *Seven Blind Mice* and a Caldecott Medal for his translation of *Lon Po Po: A Red-Riding Hood Story from China.* Often working with charcoals and pastels on rice paper, Young literally captures the feel of Chinese art in his illustrations, citing the philosophy of Chinese painting as his inspiration. "A Chinese painting is often accompanied by words," Young explained for *Authors Online.* "They are complementary. There are things that words do that pictures never can, and likewise, there are images that words can never describe." "Mr. Young is one of those illustrators not to be missed," wrote M. P. Dunleavey in the *New York Times Book Review,* "especially if you share his fondness for legends from far-off lands, retold to appeal to young Americans." In addition to such exotic tales, Young has also moved closer to his adopted home with retellings of Native American myths and of adaptations from European fairy and folktales as well as from the Old Testament.

But when January froze all her fingers and toes.
We played jungle inside in our tropical clothes.

Young's vibrant paper-collage illustrations depict the unique personalities that Lisa Westberg Peter's poem assigns to each month of the year. (From *October Smiled Back.)*

Born in a Chinese coal-mining town and raised in Shanghai and Hong Kong, Young exhibited a talent for drawing early in life. After he emigrated to the United States at the age of nineteen, he studied architecture but soon turned to art. Following graduation from the Los Angeles Art Center College of Design, he moved to New York City, where he embarked on a career in advertising design. He spent his lunch breaks sketching animals at the zoo, and when the studio for which he worked went out of business, a friend suggested that Young try his hand at illustrating children's books. Although he was reluctant—he did not want to draw cartoons, as he mistakenly thought all children's books were—Young agreed to illustrate *The Mean House and Other Mean Stories* for Harper & Row. When it was published in 1962, *The Mean House* won an award from the American Institute of Graphic Artists. Since then Young has written or retold many children's books and done the illustrations for books by other authors, including the *Horn Book* honor listees *Chinese Mother Goose Rhymes* and *Foolish Rabbit's Big Mistake,* and *Up a Tree,* which the *New York Times* called the Best Illustrated Children's Book of 1984.

"I feel the story has to be an exciting and moving experience for a child," Young told *Authors Online.* "Before I am involved with a project, I must be moved, and as I grow, I try to create something exciting. It is my purpose to stimulate growth in the reader as an active participant." Much of Young's early work was in collaboration with writers. For his 1968 illustrations of Yolen's *The Emperor and the Kite,* he won a Caldecott honor; the Caldecott Medal came to him in 1990 for the self-illustrated title *Lon Po Po: A Red-Riding Hood Story from China.* The story of three sisters who outwit an evil wolf who sneaks into their home, *Lon Po Po* was translated from the Chinese by Young. Reviewing the title in *School Library Journal,* John Philbrook commented that this "gripping variation of Red Riding Hood . . . possesses that matter-of-fact veracity that characterizes the best fairy tales," and further noted that Young's "outstanding achievement . . . will be pored over again and again." Writing in the *Los Angeles Times Book Review,* George Shannon observed, "Rather than illustrating only the words of his tale . . . Young has given new life to its metaphoric essence and created a book to savor." A "must for folklore and storytelling collections" was Carolyn Phelan's verdict in a *Booklist* review.

Further efforts in retelling Chinese myth and folklore have led to similarly attractive results. A *Kirkus Reviews* writer called Young's *Red Thread* "another spellbinding Chinese tale" with "an imaginative, innovative use of traditional elements of Chinese art." In recounting this story of matchmaking and destiny, "Young dapples his pages with delectable clouds of pastels and watercolors," according to the same writer. Phelan noted the "ethereal" look of the artwork. *Little Plum,* another Chinese fable, has the tiny defeating the powerful when a boy the size of a plum seed outsmarts an evil lord and beats his soldiers. "The narration moves as nimbly as Little Plum himself," commented Elizabeth Bush in *Bulletin of the Center for Children's Books.* Bush further noted that

"Young has a field day playing with perspectives in his ruggedly textured pastels."

Young introduces the Chinese zodiac in *Cat and Rat,* a story that explains how the enmity between the two animals began five thousand years ago in a race in which the first dozen finishers would have a year named after them. In a starred *Booklist* review, Phelan observed, "Young captures the emotional content of the scenes with quick, sure strokes of charcoal and pastels on rice paper." Margaret A. Chang, writing in *School Library Journal,* felt that "Young tells his story in lively, spare prose." With *Voices of the Heart* Young delves more deeply into explicating the Chinese world. He examines twenty-six Chinese characters that highlight personal traits such as virtue, shame, and mercy. "Ed Young pushes the envelope of picture-book illustration once again with this unusual combination of image and language," wrote Janice M. Del Negro in the *Bulletin of the Center for Children's Books.* "This is a powerful combination of words and imagery," Del Negro further commented. Philbrook, writing in *School Library Journal,* called *Voices of the Heart* "perhaps [Young's] most conceptually brilliant work to date." Philbrook concluded, "Though certainly an interesting introduction to Chinese characters, this highly original tour de force will awaken children to the relation between language and thought, providing many hours of fascination and discussion."

Young returns to more traditional Chinese tales with *Night Visitors* and *Mouse Match,* the latter being one of the author-illustrator's personal favorites. In the former title, an animal lover believes that all living things are worthy. When ants plague his father's storehouse, the young man must find a way to get rid of them without killing the ants. Julie Cummins, writing in a *School Library Journal* review, noted that the "deftly crafted story concludes with a message of respect for all forms of life," while *Booklist* reviewer Hazel Rochman called attention to Young's "exquisite illustrations," which "express the changing point of view that is the heart of the story." In *Mouse Match* a father mouse travels to the four corners of the earth to find the perfect husband for his daughter. Rejected in turn by the sun, the moon, and others, the father finally discovers that the best choice is also the most obvious one of all. A reviewer for *Booklist* noted that this Chinese folktale "is inventively illustrated with collages and innovatively designed with pages that fold out to tell the story." A contributor for *Kirkus Reviews* called the artwork a "polished, effective presentation that . . . redefines [Young's] role as a picture-book creator."

A further Chinese tale is presented in *The Lost Horse,* in which a man who loves his fantastic horse comes to discover that things are not as good or bad as they appear on the surface. "This story is an excellent springboard for a discussion of the changing nature of life," noted Marianne Saccardi in a *School Library Journal* review of the book. Young chose to illustrate his tale with collage artwork in pastel and watercolor; a contributor for *Kirkus Reviews* commented that Young's "sensitive illustrations portray both the panoramic sweeps of life in ancient China, and the individual characters in the story." A writer for *Publishers Weekly* felt *The Lost Horse* "may be among the Caldecott Medalist's finest works."

Young has also retold a number of tales from the European tradition as well as from Native America. His 1992 Caldecott Honor Book, *Seven Blind Mice*, is a retelling of "The Blind Men and the Elephant." "The story unfolds in a series of striking paper collages ingeniously arranged on a background of black bordered in white," according to Mandy Cheetham in a *Magpies* review. Cheetham thought that "the sheer artistry and delight of both text and illustrations will ensure that it becomes a classic for pre-school storytime programmes." A reviewer for *School Library Journal* felt this "perfect picture book" was "[b]rilliantly elegant in design and artwork."

Young has also borrowed from La Fontaine and Aesop, as in his retelling of *Donkey Trouble*, in which a simple man and his grandson go off to market to sell their donkey. On the way, however, they are mocked for the manner in which they are traveling and finally, after trying to please everyone, end up without a donkey. Young transplanted this tale to a Mideastern desert, creating a "striking picture book" and "an elegant retelling," according to Judith Constantinides in *School Library Journal*. A writer for *Kirkus Reviews* called the same book a "timeless interpretation of an ancient fable." Additionally, Young has adapted more modern tales, such as Carlo Collodi's *Pinocchio*, as well as Oscar Wilde's fairy tale, *The Happy Prince*. In *Moon Mother*, he introduces a Native American creation myth. "Images within images add visual layers of meaning to the complex creation myth, which Young tells with deceptive simplicity" noted Janice Del Negro in a *Booklist* review. "The landscapes are as large as the story," commented Ruth K. MacDonald in *School Library Journal*, "as timeless as history."

In addition to a busy writing schedule, Young also reserves time to work with children in schools around the country, reading stories to them and then seeing what illustration they might come up with. He encourages youngsters to take up the pen themselves. "If they love to draw pictures, and love to tell stories by drawing pictures, then they can become children's book artists as well," Young speculated in an interview for *Authors Online*. "The rest is an interest in everything—music, nature, art. And to be open to everything that comes their way. Do not rely on training from school, because training for an artist is a lifetime endeavor."

Biographical and Critical Sources

BOOKS

Major Authors and Illustrators for Children and Young Adults, Gale, 1993.
Silvey, Anita, editor, *Children's Books and Their Creators*, Houghton, 1995.

St. James Guide to Children's Writers, 5th edition, St. James, 1999.

PERIODICALS

Booklist, November 15, 1989, Carolyn Phelan, review of *Lon Po Po*, p. 672; March 1, 1993, Carolyn Phelan, review of *Red Thread*, p. 1233; March 15, 1993, p. 1329; October 15, 1993, Janice Del Negro, review of *Moon Mother*, pp. 439-440; September 15, 1995, Hazel Rochman, review of *Night Visitor*, p. 174; November 1, 1995, Carolyn Phelan, review of *Cat and Rat*, p. 1995; January 1, 1996, p. 744; June 12, 1996, p. 1727; October 15, 1997, p. 403; January 1, 1998, review of *Mouse Match*, p. 736; March 15, 1998, p. 1246.

Bulletin of the Center for Children's Books, November, 1989, p. 74; May, 1993, p. 299; October, 1994, Elizabeth Bush, review of *Little Plum*, p. 71; November, 1995, p. 111; December, 1995, p. 146; April, 1997, Janice M. Del Negro, review of *Voices of the Heart*, p. 301; December, 1997, p. 144.

Children's Book Review Service, September, 1995, p. 5; January, 1996, p. 54; February, 1997, p. 80; April, 1998, p. 101.

Five Owls, May-June, 1999, pp. 96, 97.

Horn Book, May-June, 1997, p. 347; November-December, 1997, pp. 674-675.

Kirkus Reviews, January 1, 1993, review of *Red Thread*, p. 70; September 15, 1995, review of *Donkey Trouble*, p. 1360; January 15, 1997, p. 148; October 1, 1997, review of *Mouse Match*, p. 1540; April 1, 1998, review of *The Lost Horse*, p. 504.

Los Angeles Times Book Review, December 10, 1989, George Shannon, "Of Metaphors and a Boy Flat as a Page," p. 9.

Magpies, November, 1994, Mandy Cheetham, review of *Seven Blind Mice*, p. 24.

New York Times Book Review, May 5, 1996, M. P. Dunleavey, review of *Cat and Rat* and *Night Visitors*, p. 27.

Publishers Weekly, February 24, 1989, pp. 208-209; September 5, 1994, p. 109; August 26, 1996, p. 98; April 27, 1998, review of *The Lost Horse*, p. 66; November 23, 1998, p. 70.

School Library Journal, December, 1989, John Philbrook, review of *Lon Po Po*, p. 97; December, 1992, p. 24; November, 1993, Ruth K. MacDonald, review of *Moon Mother*, p. 103; April, 1994, p. 43; October, 1995, Julie Cummins, review of *Night Visitors*, p. 130; December, 1995, Margaret A. Chang, review of *Cat and Rat*, p. 101; December, 1995, Judith Constantinides, review of *Donkey Trouble*, p. 101; June, 1997, John Philbrook, review of *Voices of the Heart*, p. 150; April, 1998, Marianne Saccardi, review of *The Lost Horse*, p. 127; November, 1998, p. 43; January, 2000, review of *Seven Blind Mice*, p. 58.

Voice of Youth Advocates, August, 1998, p. 186.

ON-LINE

Authors Online, http://teacher.scholastic.com/ (October 29, 2000).*

—Sketch by J. Sydney Jones

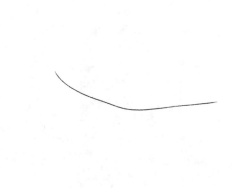